THE *unofficial* GUIDE®

TO Disneyland*

2025

SETH KUBERSKY *with* BOB SEHLINGER,
LEN TESTA, *and* GUY SELGA JR.

*Disneyland® is officially known as the Disneyland Resort®.

Please note that prices fluctuate in the course of time and that travel information changes under the impact of many factors that influence the travel industry. We therefore suggest that you write or call ahead for confirmation when making your travel plans. Every effort has been made to ensure the accuracy of information throughout this book, and the contents of this publication are believed to be correct at the time of printing. Nevertheless, the publishers cannot accept responsibility for errors or omissions, for changes in details given in this guide, or for the consequences of any reliance on the information provided by the same. Assessments of attractions and so forth are based upon the authors' own experiences; therefore, descriptions given in this guide necessarily contain an element of subjective opinion, which may not reflect the publisher's opinion or dictate a reader's own experience on another occasion. Readers are invited to write the publisher with ideas, comments, and suggestions for future editions.

The Unofficial Guides
An imprint of AdventureKEEN
2204 First Ave. S., Ste. 102
Birmingham. AL 35233

Cover design by Scott McGrew with updates by Jonathan Norberg

Text design by Vertigo Design with updates by Annie Long

For information on our other products and services or to obtain technical support, please contact us from within the United States at 800-678-7006 or by fax at 877-374-9016.

AdventureKEEN also publishes its books in a variety of electronic formats. Some content that appears in print may not be available in electronic formats.

ISBN 978-1-62809-155-7 (pbk); ISBN 978-1-62809-156-4 (ebook)

Manufactured in the United States of America

5 4 3 2 1

CONTENTS

▋ LIST *of* MAPS

ACKNOWLEDGMENTS

A BIG SALUTE to our whole Unofficial Guides team, who rendered a Herculean effort in what must have seemed like a fantasy version of Jean-Paul Sartre's *No Exit* to the tune of "It's a Small World." We hope you all recover to tour another day.

Special thanks to cartoonist Tami Knight; child psychologist Karen Turnbow, PhD; Unofficial Guide statistician Fred Hazleton; Touring Plans data analyst David Davies; "Unheralded Treasures" writer Lani Teshima; our Hollywood informer Eric Oh; and Unofficial research assistant Genevieve Bernard.

Holly Cross, Monica Ahlman, Annie Long, Andrew Mollenkof, Emily Beaumont, and Jenna Barron all contributed energetically to shaping this latest edition. Much appreciation also goes to publisher Molly Merkle, cartographer Steve Jones, and indexer Rich Carlson.

—*Bob Sehlinger*

INTRODUCTION

◼ WHY "UNOFFICIAL"?

DECLARATION OF INDEPENDENCE

THE AUTHORS AND RESEARCHERS OF THIS GUIDE specifically and categorically declare that they are and always have been totally independent of the Walt Disney Company, Inc.; of Disneyland, Inc.; of Walt Disney World Company, Inc.; and of any and all other members of the Disney corporate family.

The material in this guide originated with the authors and researchers and has not been reviewed, edited, or in any way approved by Walt Disney Company, Inc.; Disneyland, Inc.; or Walt Disney World Company, Inc.

With no obligation to toe the Disney line, we represent and serve you, the reader. The contents were researched and compiled by a team of evaluators who are completely independent of the Walt Disney Company, Inc. If a restaurant serves bad food, if a gift item is overpriced, or if a ride isn't worth the wait, we say so. And in the process, we hope to make your visit more fun, efficient, and economical.

DANCE TO THE MUSIC

A DANCE HAS A BEGINNING AND AN END. But when you're dancing, you're not concerned about getting to the end or where on the dance floor you might wind up. You're totally in the moment. That's the way you should be on your Disneyland vacation.

You may feel a bit of pressure concerning your vacation. Vacations, after all, are very special events—and expensive ones to boot. So you work hard to make your vacation the best that it can be. Planning and organizing are essential to a successful Disneyland vacation, but if they become your focus, you won't be able to hear the music and enjoy the dance.

So think of us as your dancing coaches. We'll teach you the steps to the dance in advance, so when you're on vacation and the music plays, you will move with effortless grace and ease.

THE DEATH OF SPONTANEITY

ONE OF OUR ALL-TIME favorite letters is from a man in Chapel Hill, North Carolina. He writes:

> *Your book reads like the operations plan for an amphibious landing: Go here, do this, proceed to Step 15. You must think that everyone is a hyperactive, type-A theme park commando. What happened to the satisfaction of self-discovery or the joy of spontaneity? Next you will be telling us when to empty our bladders.*

More recently, a reader from Seattle wrote online:

> *We skipped the touring plans and instead took our time to smell the flowers and truly take in the entire experience of Disney—isn't that what it is all about?! Our friends decided to strictly follow the touring plans. Their whole family was quite exhausted at the end.*
>
> *Maximizing the number of rides/events one does is NOT the same as maximizing one's true enjoyment of Disney.*

As it happens, we at The Unofficial Guides are a pretty existential crew. We are big on self-discovery when walking in the woods or watching birds. Some of us are able to improvise jazz without reading music, while others can whip up a mean pot of chili without a recipe. When it comes to Disneyland, however, we all agree that you either need a good plan or a frontal lobotomy. The operational definition of self-discovery and spontaneity at Disneyland is the "pleasure" of heat prostration and the "joy" of standing in line.

It's easy to spot the free spirits at Disneyland Park and Disney California Adventure, especially at opening time. While everyone else is stampeding to Rise of the Resistance or Radiator Springs Racers, they're standing in a cloud of dust puzzling over the park map. Later, they're running around like chickens in a thunderstorm, trying to find an attraction with less than a 40-minute wait. Face it: Disneyland Resort is not a very existential place. In many ways it's the ultimate in mass-produced entertainment, the most planned and programmed environment imaginable. Self-discovery and spontaneity work about as well at Disneyland as they do on your tax return. One mother of two young boys had this to say about our book:

> *Your book was invaluable in giving us the tools to plan a great day. We had a magical day thanks to being able to prioritize our goals. Thank you for the full descriptions of rides—with only one day, you really need to pick your battles.*

We're not saying that you can't have a great time at Disneyland. Bowling isn't very spontaneous either, but lots of people love it. What we *are* saying is that you need a plan. You don't have to be inflexible. Just think about what you want to do—before you go. Don't delude yourself by rationalizing that the information in this book is only for the pathological and superorganized. For those who truly want to stop and smell the roses at Disneyland, we recommend our Anti-Touring Plan (see pages 245–248), which guarantees a day without stress, waiting in queues, or bouncing around the park. You won't actually get on many (if any) rides, but you can enjoy a full day of live entertainment and people-watching without sticking to a strict schedule. Just step out of the way when guests sprinting toward their next headliner rush by.

HOW *This* GUIDE WAS RESEARCHED *and* WRITTEN

WHILE MUCH HAS BEEN WRITTEN concerning Disneyland Resort, very little has been comparative or evaluative. In preparing this guide, nothing was taken for granted. The theme parks were visited at different times throughout the year by a team of trained observers who conducted detailed evaluations, rating the theme parks along with all of their component rides, shows, exhibits, services, and concessions according to formal, pretested rating criteria. Interviews with attraction patrons were conducted to determine what tourists of all age groups enjoyed most and least during their Disneyland visit.

Though our observers are independent and impartial, we do not claim special expertise or scientific backgrounds relative to the types of exhibits, performances, or attractions viewed. Like you, we visit the Disneyland parks as tourists, noting our satisfaction or dissatisfaction. Disneyland offerings are marketed to the touring public, and it is as the public that we have experienced them.

The primary difference between the average tourist and the trained evaluator is that the latter approaches attractions equipped with professional skills in organization, preparation, and observation. The trained evaluator is responsible for much more than simply observing and cataloging. While the tourist is being entertained and delighted by the *Enchanted Tiki Room*, the professional evaluator seated nearby is rating the performance in terms of theme, pace, continuity, and originality. The evaluator also checks out the physical arrangements: Is the sound system clear and audible without being overpowering; is the audience shielded from the sun or rain; is seating adequate; can everyone in the audience clearly see the stage? Similarly, detailed and relevant checklists are prepared by observer teams and applied to rides, exhibits, and concessions, as well as to the theme park in general. Finally, observations and evaluator ratings are integrated with audience reactions and the opinions of patrons to compile a comprehensive profile of each feature and service.

In compiling this guide, we recognize the fact that tourists' age, gender, background, and interests will strongly influence their taste in

Disneyland offerings and will account for their preference of one ride or feature over another. Given this fact, we make no attempt at comparing apples with oranges. How, indeed, could a meaningful comparison be made between the serenity and beauty of the Storybook Land Canal Boats and the wild roller-coaster ride of the Incredicoaster? Instead, our objective is to provide the reader with a critical evaluation and enough pertinent data to make knowledgeable decisions according to individual tastes.

The essence of this guide, then, consists of individual critiques and descriptions of each feature of the Disneyland parks, supplemented with maps to help you get around and detailed touring plans to help you avoid bottlenecks and crowds. Because so many Disneyland guests also visit Universal Studios Hollywood to see The Wizarding World of Harry Potter and Super Nintendo World, we have included comprehensive coverage and a touring plan for that park as well.

A WORD TO OUR READERS ABOUT ANNUAL REVISIONS

SOME OF YOU WHO PURCHASE EACH NEW EDITION of *The Unofficial Guide to Disneyland* have chastised us for retaining examples, comments, and descriptions from previous years' editions. This letter from a Grand Rapids, Michigan, reader is typical:

> *Your guidebook still has the same example stories. I expected a true update and new stuff, not the same old, same old!*

First, *The Unofficial Guide to Disneyland* is a reference work. Though we are flattered that some readers read the guide from cover to cover, and that some of you find it entertaining, our objective is fairly straightforward: to provide information that enables you to have the best possible Disneyland vacation.

Each year during our revision research, we check every attraction, restaurant, hotel, shop, and entertainment offering. Though there are many changes, much remains the same from year to year. When we profile and critique an attraction, we try to provide the reader with the most insightful, relevant, and useful information, written in the clearest possible language. It is our opinion that if an attraction does not change, then it makes little sense to risk clarity and content for the sake of freshening up the prose. Disneyland guests who try the Mad Tea Party or Pinocchio's Daring Journey today, for example, experience the same presentation as guests who visited Disneyland in 2020, 2008, or 1995. Moreover, according to our extensive patron surveys, today's guests still respond to these attractions in the same way as prior-year patrons.

The bottom line: We believe that our readers are better served if we devote our time to that which is changing and new as opposed to that which remains the same. The success or failure of this *Unofficial Guide* is determined not by the style of the writing but by the accuracy of the information and, ultimately, whether you have a positive experience at Disneyland. Every change to the guide we make (or don't make) is evaluated in this context.

WE'VE GOT ATTITUDE

SOME READERS DISAGREE with our attitude toward Disney. A 30-something woman from Golden, Colorado, lambasts us, writing:

> You were way too hard on Disney. It's disappointing, when you're all enthused about going, to be slammed with all these criticisms and possible pitfalls.

A reader from Little Rock, Arkansas, also takes us to task:

> Your book was quite complimentary of Disney, perhaps too complimentary. Maybe the free trips you travel writers get at Disneyland are chipping away at your objectivity.

For the record, we've always paid our own way at Disneyland Resort: hotels, admissions, meals, the works. We don't dislike Disney, and we most definitely don't have an ax to grind. We're positive by nature and much prefer to praise than to criticize. We have enjoyed the Disney parks immensely over the years, both experiencing them and writing about them. Disney, however, as with all corporations, is better at some things than others. Because our readers shell out big bucks to go to Disneyland, we believe that they have the right to know in advance what's good and what's not. For those who think we're overly positive, please understand that *The Unofficial Guide to Disneyland* is a guidebook, not an exposé. Our overriding objective is for you to enjoy your visit. To that end we try to report fairly and objectively. When readers disagree with our opinions, we, in the interest of fairness and balance, publish their point of view right alongside ours. To the best of our knowledge, The Unofficial Guides are the only travel guides in print that do this.

THE UNOFFICIAL GUIDE PUBLISHING YEAR

WE RECEIVE MANY QUERIES each year asking when the next edition of *The Unofficial Guide to Disneyland* will be available. Usually our new editions are published and available in stores by late August or early September. Thus, the 2026 edition will be on the shelves in fall 2025.

LETTERS, COMMENTS, AND
QUESTIONS FROM READERS

MANY OF THOSE WHO USE *The Unofficial Guide to Disneyland* write to us, asking questions, making comments, or sharing their own strategies for visiting Disneyland. We appreciate all such input, both positive and critical, and encourage our readers to continue writing. Readers' comments and observations are frequently used in revised editions of *The Unofficial Guide to Disneyland* and have contributed immeasurably to its improvement.

Reader Survey

Please fill out our reader survey online by visiting touringplans.com /disneyland-resort/survey. You can rest assured that we won't release your name and address to any mailing-list companies, direct mail advertisers, or other third parties. Unless you instruct us otherwise, we will assume that you do not object to being quoted in a future edition.

How to Contact the Author

Write to Seth Kubersky at this address:

> *The Unofficial Guide to Disneyland*
> 2204 First Ave. S., Ste. 102
> Birmingham, AL 35233
> info@theunofficialguides.com

When you write, put your address on both your letter and envelope; sometimes the two get separated. It is also a good idea to include your phone number and email address. If you email us, please tell us where you're from. Remember, as travel writers, we're often out of the office for long periods of time, so forgive us if our response is slow. Unofficial Guide email is not forwarded to us when we're traveling, but we will respond as soon as possible when we return.

Questions from Readers

Questions frequently asked by readers are answered in an appendix at the back of this *Unofficial Guide*.

DISNEYLAND RESORT: *An* OVERVIEW

IF YOU HAVEN'T BEEN TO DISNEYLAND in a while, you'll hardly know the place. First, of course, there is **Disneyland Park,** which celebrates its 70th year as the original Disney theme park in 2025; it's also the only park that Walt Disney saw completed in his lifetime. Much more than the Magic Kingdom at Walt Disney World, Disneyland Park embodies the quiet, charming spirit of nostalgia that so characterized Walt himself. The park is vast yet intimate, steeped in the tradition of its creator yet continually changing.

Disneyland opened in 1955 on a 107-acre tract surrounded almost exclusively by orange groves, just west of the sleepy and little-known Southern California community of Anaheim. Constrained by finances and ultimately enveloped by the city it helped create, Disneyland operated on that same modest parcel of land until 2001.

Disneyland Park is a collection of adventures, rides, and shows symbolized by the Disney characters and Sleeping Beauty Castle. It's divided into nine subareas, or "lands," arranged around a central hub. First encountered is **Main Street, U.S.A.,** which connects the Disneyland entrance with the central hub. Moving clockwise around the hub, the other lands are **Adventureland, Frontierland, Fantasyland,** and **Tomorrowland.** Two major lands, **Critter Country** and **New Orleans Square,** are accessible via Adventureland and Frontierland but do not connect directly with the central hub. Another land, **Mickey's Toontown,** is accessed from Fantasyland. Finally, the huge **Star Wars: Galaxy's Edge** opened in 2019 on 14 acres of former backstage areas behind Critter Country and Frontierland, making it the biggest expansion in Disneyland Park's history. All nine lands will be described in detail later.

Growth and change at Disneyland (until 1996) had been internal, in marked contrast to the ever-enlarging development of Walt Disney World near Orlando, Florida. When something new was added at Disneyland, something old had to go. The Disney engineers, to their credit, however, have never been shy about disturbing the status quo. Patrons of the park's earlier, modest years are amazed by the transformation. Gone are the days of the "magical little park" with the Monsanto House of the Future, donkey rides, and Captain Hook's Pirate Ship. Substituted in a process of continuous evolution and modernization are state-of-the-art fourth-, fifth-, and sixth-generation attractions and entertainment. To paraphrase Walt Disney, Disneyland will never stop changing as long as there are new ideas to explore.

Disneyland's success spawned a wave of development that rapidly surrounded the theme park with mom-and-pop motels, souvenir stands, and fast-food restaurants. The steady decline of the area encircling Disneyland continued to rankle Walt. After tolerating the blight for 30 years, the Walt Disney Company (finally flush with funds and ready for a good fight) set about putting Disneyland Park right. Quietly at first, then aggressively, Disney began buying up the mom-and-pop motels, as well as the few remaining orange and vegetable groves near the park.

By the end of 2000, Disneyland had developed into a complete destination resort, including a Disney-owned hotel district and two new parking facilities. All of the changes, modifications, and additions were finished, and Disneyland began the new century as a complete multi–theme park resort destination. **Disney California Adventure** (or DCA to the initiated), a second theme park situated in what was once the Disneyland parking lot, celebrated its grand opening on February 8, 2001.

DCA is an oddly shaped park built around a lagoon on one side and the Grand Californian Hotel on the other, with one of Disney's trademark mountains, **Grizzly Peak,** plopped down in the middle. **Buena Vista Street,** an entranceway evoking 1920s Los Angeles, leads to seven "lands." Inside the front gate and to the left is **Hollywood Land** (formerly Hollywood Pictures Backlot), a diminutive version of the Disney's Hollywood Studios theme park at Walt Disney World. Then there are **Grizzly Peak** (which absorbed the former Condor Flats area), celebrating California's natural resources, and **San Fransokyo Square** (previously called Pacific Wharf), celebrating the superhero cartoon *Big Hero 6*. **Cars Land** is dedicated to the desert town of

Radiator Springs from Disney-Pixar's *Cars*. **Avengers Campus,** the West Coast home for Marvel superheroes like Spider-Man, occupies the space between Cars Land and Hollywood Land that formerly featured attractions based on the Disney-Pixar film *A Bug's Life*. Finally, **Pixar Pier** incongruously integrates the grand old seaside amusement parks of the early 20th century with computer-animated characters from *Toy Story* and *The Incredibles*, while **Paradise Gardens Park** incorporates the viewing areas for the nighttime lagoon show, along with assorted non-Pixar attractions from the former Paradise Pier.

The entrances to Disneyland Park and DCA face each other across a palm-studded pedestrian plaza called the **Esplanade,** which begins at Harbor Boulevard and runs west, between the parks, passing into **Downtown Disney,** a dining, shopping, entertainment, and nightlife venue. From Downtown Disney, the Esplanade continues via an overpass across Downtown Drive and past the monorail station to the **Disneyland** and **Pixar Place Hotels.**

Sandwiched between the Esplanade and Downtown Disney on the north and DCA on the south is the **Grand Californian Hotel,** designed in the image of rustic national park lodges, which includes the **Grand Californian Villas.**

North of the hotels and across West Street from Disneyland Park are two huge multistory parking garages—named Mickey & Friends and Pixar Pals—that can be accessed directly from I-5. With a combined total of over 15,000 parking spaces, this is where most Disneyland guests park. Tram transport is provided from the garages to the Esplanade, and buses ferry guests in from the outlying lots. Wheelchair and stroller rentals are to the right of the Disneyland Park main entrance. Ticket booths are situated along the Esplanade.

In 2024, Disney announced their intention to "turbocharge" investment in their worldwide resorts to the tune of $30 billion over the next decade. The "DisneylandForward" proposal approved by the local government will invest $1.9 to $2.5 billion into the Anaheim resort. An environmental impact report for the proposed project suggests that theme park expansions wrapping around the Pixar Place and Disneyland Hotels could potentially add two major outdoor thrill rides, several outdoor family rides, and more than half a dozen indoor attractions, along with shows and other amenities. Disney CEO Bob Iger already has promised an area based on James Cameron's resurgent *Avatar* franchise; other potential themed lands in the expansion may include Arendale from *Frozen,* Wakanda from *Black Panther,* and Peter Pan's Neverland. The Toy Story parking lot at Harbor and Katella could be filled in with multiple new hotels; restaurants, retail, and entertainment establishments; and even indoor theme park–style experiences, all connected to the main Disneyland campus with a monorail, PeopleMover, or Skyliner cable cars. To compensate for the lost parking spots, Disney will finally develop their lot along Disney Way east of the parks with a terraced structure holding more than 17,000 cars, and pedestrian bridges will be added over Harbor Boulevard to access the Esplanade.

SHOULD I GO TO DISNEYLAND PARK IF I'VE SEEN WALT DISNEY WORLD?

DISNEYLAND PARK IS ROUGHLY COMPARABLE to the Magic Kingdom theme park at Walt Disney World near Orlando, Florida. Both are arranged by "lands" accessible from a central hub and connected to the entrance by a main street. Both parks feature many rides and attractions of the same name: Space Mountain, Jungle Cruise, Pirates of the Caribbean, It's a Small World, and Dumbo the Flying Elephant, to name a few. Interestingly, however, the same name does not necessarily connote the same experience. Pirates of the Caribbean at Disneyland Park is much longer and more elaborate than its Walt Disney World counterpart. Haunted Mansion is more elaborate in Florida, and the *Enchanted Tiki Room* is about the same in both places.

Disneyland Park is more intimate than the Magic Kingdom, not having the room for expansion enjoyed by the Florida park. Pedestrian thoroughfares are narrower, and everything from Big Thunder Mountain to the castle is scaled down somewhat. Large crowds are more taxing at Disneyland Park because there is less room for them to disperse. At Disneyland Park, however, there are dozens of little surprises, small unheralded attractions tucked away in crooks and corners of the park, which give Disneyland Park a special charm and variety that the Magic Kingdom lacks. Subtle differences in the resorts' line-skipping services make Genie+ and Lightning Lane far easier to take advantage of in Disneyland than in the Magic Kingdom, even on busy days. And, of course, Disneyland Park has the stamp of Walt Disney's personal touch.

A Minnesota couple who have sampled Disney both east and west offered this observation:

> For parents with children 10 years of age and younger, I highly recommend Disneyland instead of WDW. Its size is much more manageable. You can stay within walking distance of the front gate. That makes it practical and easy to get to the gates early in the morning (imperative) and get away in the afternoon for a break (always helpful). The size and scale of WDW make this impractical.

A Salem, Massachusetts, family, who had visited WDW three years prior to their Disneyland trip, agreed:

> We heard from many that Disneyland was small and that the castle was underwhelming. But the Disney magic was there, and we had a great time exploring what was unique about each park. We spent three days at the parks and wished that we had planned to be there longer. The parks may be smaller, but there is still plenty to see and do.

ATTRACTIONS FOUND ONLY AT DISNEYLAND PARK

ADVENTURELAND

- Indiana Jones Adventure

CRITTER COUNTRY

- Davy Crockett's Explorer Canoes

FANTASYLAND

- Alice in Wonderland   • Casey Jr. Circus Train   • Fantasyland Theatre
- Matterhorn Bobsleds   • Mr. Toad's Wild Ride   • Pinocchio's Daring Journey
- Royal Theatre at Fantasy Faire   • Sleeping Beauty Castle Walk-Through
- Snow White's Enchanted Wish   • Storybook Land Canal Boats

FRONTIERLAND

- *Fantasmic!* (in WDW at Disney's Hollywood Studios)   • The Golden Horseshoe
- Sailing Ship *Columbia*

MAIN STREET, U.S.A.

- *The Disneyland Story,* presenting *Great Moments with Mr. Lincoln*

MICKEY'S TOONTOWN

- Chip 'n' Dale's GADGETcoaster   • Donald's Duck Pond
- Goofy's How-to-Play Yard   • Mickey's House   • Minnie's House
- Mickey and Minnie's Runaway Railway (in WDW at Disney's Hollywood Studios)
- Roger Rabbit's Car Toon Spin

STAR WARS: GALAXY'S EDGE

- *Millennium Falcon:* Smugglers Run (in WDW at Disney's Hollywood Studios)
- Star Wars: Rise of the Resistance (in WDW at Disney's Hollywood Studios)

TOMORROWLAND

- Disneyland Monorail System   • Finding Nemo Submarine Voyage
- Star Tours—The Adventures Continue (in WDW at Disney's Hollywood Studios)

This WDW veteran from Goose Creek also appreciated Disneyland's compact design:

> *Overall, the trip was more expensive coming from the east coast . . . But what made it one of my best Disney trips was the ease—walkable resort property, lower crowds, and simply fewer parks. It made it easy to do everything you wanted and in a lot less time.*

Another experienced WDW visitor who now lives in Oakland, California, wrote:

> *We were amazed at how easy Disneyland is to navigate compared to WDW. I appreciated how Disneyland felt like Disney Lite. No one was pushy about the vacation club, Visa card, or even the annual pass. It was great to experience the parks this way.*

From an Orlando veteran in Highlands Ranch, Colorado:

> *Disneyland is the supreme resort! So easy to navigate and park hop. Great walkability—we clocked 30,000 steps/day and never needed to take a 30-minute bus ride. With early entry and Genie+ (which actually enhances your trip, unlike at WDW), we were able to do everything we wanted to do multiple times—all while taking 3–5–hour breaks midday to lounge by the pool and nap before heading back to the park.*

CRITICAL COMPARISON OF ATTRACTIONS FOUND AT BOTH PARKS

ADVENTURELAND

- **Adventureland Treehouse/Swiss Family Treehouse** Disneyland's tree is slightly taller and has newer animatronic scenery.
- *Enchanted Tiki Room* Similar at both parks; slightly longer show at Disneyland but more advanced rainstorm effects at Walt Disney World.
- **Jungle Cruise** Funnier narrators at Disneyland but longer ride at Walt Disney World.

CRITTER COUNTRY

- **The Many Adventures of Winnie the Pooh** Longer and with more motion at the Magic Kingdom.
- **Tiana's Bayou Adventure** Longer ride and bigger logs at the Magic Kingdom; story and effects are about the same.

FANTASYLAND

- **Carrousels** About the same at both parks.
- **Castles** Far larger and more beautiful at Magic Kingdom; Disneyland has walk-through display.
- **Dumbo the Flying Elephant** About the same, but WDW version has double the capacity and an interactive circus-themed queue.
- **It's a Small World** Disneyland version is longer with hidden Disney characters, and it gets a holiday overlay.
- **Mad Tea Party** Disneyland's is open-air; otherwise the same at both parks.
- **Peter Pan's Flight** Shorter but with upgraded special effects at Disneyland.
- **Royal Hall at Fantasy Faire/Princess Fairytale Hall** About the same.

FRONTIERLAND

- **Big Thunder Mountain Railroad** More monumental mountain and an interactive queue at Magic Kingdom; smoother track and explosive special effects at Disneyland.
- **Tom Sawyer Island** Comparable; pirate theme with more elaborate effects at Disneyland but more caves and play structures to explore at Magic Kingdom.
- **Various river cruises (canoes, boats, and such)** More interesting sights at Disneyland, and only Disneyland offers canoes.

MAIN STREET, U.S.A.

- **Railroads** The Disneyland Railroad is far more entertaining by virtue of the Grand Canyon Diorama and the Primeval World components not found at the Magic Kingdom.

NEW ORLEANS SQUARE

- **Haunted Mansion** Longer ride and interactive queue give Magic Kingdom the edge. Holiday version is offered only at Disneyland.
- **Pirates of the Caribbean** Far superior at Disneyland.

TOMORROWLAND

- **Astro Orbitor** About the same at both parks but much higher in the air at the Magic Kingdom.
- **Autopia/Tomorrowland Speedway** Disneyland version is superior.
- **Buzz Lightyear** More mobile guns and better game play at Disneyland.
- **Space Mountain** Much better effects and smoother track at Disneyland but a wilder ride with sharper drops at Magic Kingdom.

*Note that some of the attractions at Disney California Adventure, such as Toy Story Midway Mania!, Mickey's PhilharMagic, and Turtle Talk with Crush, appeared first at one of the Walt Disney World theme parks. Versions of Ariel's Undersea Adventure and Soarin' Around the World have been exported to Walt Disney World. None of the remaining DCA attractions are found at Disney World.

And these die-hard Disney veterans from Pleasantville, New York, praised the Anaheim resort's employees:

> *Disneyland is such a wonderful alternative to the traditional trip to Walt Disney World. We particularly were impressed with the cast members. The Disneyland cast members consistently went above and beyond for us, even compared to Orlando's cast members.*

To allow for a meaningful comparison, we have provided a summary of those features found at Disneyland Park and not WDW's Magic Kingdom (listed alphabetically on page 10), accompanied by a critical look at the attractions found at both parks on page 11, and a guide to key differences between the two resorts below.

DIFFERENCES BETWEEN DISNEYLAND RESORT & WALT DISNEY WORLD

DISNEYLAND	WALT DISNEY WORLD
Guests can walk to both parks from all on-site and many off-site hotels.	Guests can only walk to some theme parks from select on-site hotels; all others require transportation.
On-site resort guests get 30 minutes daily early entry at one park.	On-site resort guests get 30 minutes daily early entry at all four parks.
No extended evening hours for resort guests.	Extended park hours on select nights for Deluxe Resort guests.
MagicBand+ or smartphone app can be used for admission.	MagicBand or MagicBand+; app, mobile pass, or smart watch can be used for admission.
Theme park reservations still required for all ticket types.	Theme park reservations no longer required for date-based tickets.
Magic Key passholders must make reservations before all park visits.	Annual Passholders may enter without reservations after 2 p.m. (except Magic Kingdom on weekends).
No sales tax is charged on park admission.	Taxes apply to park tickets.
Park hopping is allowed after 11 a.m.	Visitors can park hop immediately after opening.
Genie+ can be purchased with tickets or after entering the park.	Genie+ can be purchased after midnight on the morning of your visit.
Make first Genie+ and individual Lightning Lane reservations after entering the park.	Make first Genie+ reservation at 7 a.m. from outside the park. On-site guests can buy individual Lightning Lane at 7 a.m., off-site at park opening.
Virtual Queue is only used for Tiana's Bayou Adventure and *World of Color* viewing.	Virtual Queue is required for Tiana's, TRON, and Guardians of the Galaxy rides.
Prepaid dining plans are not offered.	Prepaid dining plans (sometime free) are available with vacation packages.
Characters often roam "free range" around the parks.	Characters are usually confined to controlled meet and greets.

PART 1

PLANNING *Before* YOU LEAVE HOME

▌█ GATHERING INFORMATION

IN ADDITION TO THIS GUIDE, we recommend that you first visit our website, theunofficialguides.com, which is dedicated to news about our guidebooks, as well as a blog with posts from Unofficial Guide authors. You can also sign up for the Unofficial Guides Newsletter, containing even more travel tips and special offers.

Our sister website, touringplans.com, offers essential tools for planning your trip and saving you time and money. At blog.touringplans .com, you'll find breaking news for the Disneyland Resort and Disney theme parks worldwide. Touringplans.com also offers computer-optimized touring plans for Disneyland and Disney California Adventure (DCA), as well as searchable dining menus, including wine lists, for every food cart, stand, kiosk, counter-service restaurant, and sit-down restaurant in the Disneyland Resort.

Another popular part of touringplans.com is its Crowd Calendar, which shows crowd projections for Disneyland and DCA for every day of the year. Look up the dates of your visit, and the calendar will not only show daily projected wait times, but it will also indicate for each day which theme park will be the least crowded. Historical wait times are also available, so you can see how crowded the parks were last year for your upcoming trip dates.

Much of the content on touringplans.com—including the menus, resort photos and videos, and errata for this book—is completely free for anyone to use. Access to parts of the site, most notably the Crowd Calendar, premium touring plans, and in-park wait times, requires a small annual subscription fee (current-book owners get a substantial discount). This nominal charge helps keep touringplans.com online and costs less than a souvenir bucket of popcorn at Disneyland. Plus touringplans.com offers a 45-day money-back guarantee.

A subscriber from Arvada, Colorado, wrote in to say:

I purchased a membership to your website approximately one month before we went to Disneyland in the summer. I would never go without it again. I knew what kind of crowds to expect in advance, and not having to ask nine people what they wanted to do or go on next was great. Lunch and dinner were planned at certain times, and we even made adjustments to your recommended plan, so my 4½-year-old niece got to ride a couple of the kids' rides right away.

Disneyland Main Information Phone and Website

The following website and phone numbers provide general information. Inquiries may be expedited by using phone numbers specific to the nature of the inquiry (other phone numbers are listed elsewhere in this chapter, under their relevant topics, and in the table below).

DISNEYLAND GUEST RELATIONS
☎ 714-781-4565 or ☎ 714-781-4636; disneyland.com

The Phone from Hell

Sometimes it is virtually impossible to get through on the Disneyland information numbers listed above. When you get through, you will hear a recording that offers various information options. If none of the recorded options answer your question, you will have to hold for a live person. Eat before you call—you may have a long wait. If, after repeated attempts, you get tired of a busy signal in your ear or, worse, 20 minutes' worth of singing mice warbling "Cinderelly" in alto falsettos while you are on hold, call the Disneyland Hotel at ☎ 714-778-6600. You can also

IMPORTANT DISNEYLAND RESORT PHONE NUMBERS	
Anaheim Travel Information	☎ 714-765-2800
Annual Passholder (Magic Key) Member Services	☎ 714-781-7277
Dining Reservations & Viewing Packages	☎ 714-781-3463
Disability Services	☎ 407-560-2547
Disney Cruise Line	☎ 800-951-3532
Disney Guided Tours	☎ 714-300-7710
Disney Website Technical Support	☎ 714-520-6222
Disneyland Hotel	☎ 714-778-6600
Disneyland Resort Room Reservations	☎ 714-956-6425
Disneyland Vacation Packages	☎ 714-520-5060
General Information	☎ 714-781-4636, Option 3
Grand Californian Hotel	☎ 714-635-2300
Lost & Found	☎ 714-817-2166
Merchandise	☎ 877-560-6477
Pixar Place Hotel	☎ 714-999-0990
PhotoPass Guest Support	☎ 714-520-7106
Theme Park Tickets	☎ 714-781-4636, Option 1

try using the "Chat with Us" feature in the main menu of the Disneyland smartphone app.

RECOMMENDED WEBSITES, SOCIAL MEDIA, AND APPS

BEST OFFICIAL THEME PARK SITES At the official Disneyland website, disneyland.com, you must create an account before booking, or log in with an existing my.disney.com account (which is shared between all the Disney resorts, and online services like Disney+ and Hulu). You'll have to do this in order to make mandatory daily reservations prior to your park visit, so get yourself set up on this site as soon as you begin planning your trip. There's a ton of information, but it usually takes a lot of clicks to find what you're looking for. Disney's official PlanDisney website, plandisney .disney.go.com, and its companion podcast share answers to common guest questions from a diverse team of dedicated park fans.

The Universal Studios website is universalstudioshollywood.com. Like the Disneyland site, it has a lot of information, and you'll want to register an account for ticket purchases. Both sites are filled with photos and videos that can be slow to load, so as far as your internet connection is concerned, be high-speed or be gone.

BEST OFFICIAL AREA WEBSITE Visitanaheim.org is the official website of the Anaheim–Orange County Visitor & Convention Bureau. You'll find everything from hotels and restaurants to weather and driving directions on this site.

BEST GENERAL UNOFFICIAL WEBSITES We recommend the following websites for general information related to the Disneyland Resort.

Mouseplanet.com is a comprehensive resource for Disneyland data, offering features and reviews by guest writers, information on the Disney theme parks, discussion groups, and news. The site includes an interactive Disney restaurant and hotel review page, where users can voice opinions on their Disney dining and lodging experiences. We particularly enjoy the weekly Disneyland update column.

Disneytouristblog.com, run by park photographer extraordinaire and Touring Plans contributor Tom Bricker, hosts a comprehensive introduction to planning a Disneyland vacation, along with reporting on more exotic Disney destinations in France, China, and Japan.

Deb Wills, the founder of allears.net, has now retired, but the website still includes extensive information about the Disney resorts and attractions (including reader reviews), Disney restaurant menus, ticketing information, maps, and more.

True to its name, disneylanddaily.com features near-daily updates from Casey Starnes, a mom of three and frequent visitor to the resort.

BEST DISNEYLAND HISTORY WEBSITES At yesterland.com you can visit the Disneyland of the past, where retired Disneyland attractions are brought back to life through vivid descriptions and historical photos. Yesterland attraction descriptions relate what it was once like to experience the Flying Saucers, the Mine Train through Nature's Wonderland, the *Tahitian Terrace,* and dozens of other rides, shows, and restaurants.

For statistics fans, thrill-data.com tracks and graphs historical wait times and Lightning Lane availability at Disneyland and other resorts.

BEST WEBSITE FOR RUMORS AND THE INSIDE SCOOP Jimhillmedia .com is perfectly attuned to what's going on behind the scenes—Jim Hill always has good gossip.

BEST DISNEYLAND NEWS SITES Micechat.com, with a dedicated group of local editors, gives definitive on-the-ground coverage of the Disneyland Resort. Check out Dusty Sage's regular update columns that stay on the pulse of the parks, complete with photos. Robert Niles's themeparkinsider. com is another great source for breaking Southern California theme park news, as is Brady McDonald at *The Orange County Register* (ocregister. com/things-to-do/amusement-parks). For official news, the Disney Parks Blog (disneyparks.com/blog) covers news from all Disney resorts. For Universal Studios Hollywood updates, visit insideuniversal.net.

BEST MONEY-SAVING SITE Mousesavers.com specializes in finding you the deepest discounts on hotels, park admissions, and rental cars. MouseSavers does not actually sell travel but rather unearths and publishes special discounts that you can use. It's the first place we look for deals when we go to Disneyland Resort.

BEST DISNEY DISCUSSION BOARDS The best online discussion of all things Disney can be found at discuss.micechat.com and disboards.com. With tens of thousands of members and millions of posts, they are the most active and popular discussion boards online. There is also a rousing chat room inside the touringplans.com mobile application, Lines, where folks can ask questions and give travel tips. Hundreds of "Liners" interact every day in discussions that stay remarkably on-topic for an internet forum, and the group organizes regular in-park meets (learn more at touringplans.com/lines).

BEST DISNEY PODCASTS *Mousetalgia,* found at mousetalgia.com, covers Disneyland, DCA, and everything else Disney. The hosts appreciate the history of the resort while maintaining balanced coverage of new Disneyland developments. *The Sweep Spot* (thesweepspot.com) features Disney news from the irreverent perspective of two former Disneyland custodians. Seasonpasspodcast.com has breaking news and in-depth interviews with theme park designers and executives from Disneyland and parks around the world. Hosted by industry veterans (and fans!), the show provides detailed discussions about how and why theme parks work. And if you want warts-and-all tales from behind the scenes of Mickey's kingdoms, don't miss *The Unofficial Guide Disney Dish Podcast with Jim Hill* (disneydish.bandcamp.com), hosted by coauthor Len Testa.

BEST DISNEY SOCIAL MEDIA FEEDS If you want your Disney news and rumors in 140 character bites or 30-second reels, follow us @TheUGseries on X and @TheUnofficialGuides on Instagram and Threads, along with these prolific park posters:

@thedisneyblog @disneyland @disneylandcats @disneyparks
@micechat @ocregister @touringplans @guyselga @skubersky

BEST DISNEYLAND YOUTUBE CHANNELS We don't necessarily advocate spoiling attractions you haven't yet experienced in person, but YouTube videos can be very useful for assuaging anxious children (see page 161) or reliving the magic once you return home. You can visit theugseries.com/youtube to subscribe to our YouTube channel and get automatically notified of all our new videos. The TouringPlans You Tube channel (youtube.com/touringplans) hosts a wealth of clips from every Disney park. Other good sources for Disney park videos are the official Disney Parks channel (youtube.com/disneyparks), *Attractions* Magazine (youtube.com/attractionsmagazine), LMG Vids (youtube .com/@LMGVids), and SoCal Attractions 360 (youtube.com/socal attractions360), which uploads 4K ultra-low-light footage of dark rides that look sharper and brighter than actually being there. Provost Park Pass (youtube.com/provostparkpass) and FreshBaked! (youtube .com/@FreshBakedDisney) both provide timely updates from inside the parks, packed with helpful pointers and positivity.

BEST DISNEYLAND MOBILE APPS Smartphone apps are a great way to stay up-to-date on Disneyland info inside and outside the parks. First and foremost, we suggest installing Disneyland's free app for Apple (iOS 15 and up) or Android (ver. 8 and up) devices, which features park hours, wait times, show schedules, menus, and maps. You will need it to store and redeem digital admission tickets, secure spots in Lightning Lanes and Virtual Queues for select shows and attractions, review your park and dining reservations, compliment exceptional cast members, and link to all your PhotoPass pictures. Guests staying at Disney's on-site resorts can use the app to check in, charge purchases to their hotel bill, and even unlock their room.

In 2021, Disneyland added **Genie** to its smartphone app, a free service that integrates many of the aforementioned features to make customized daily itineraries based on your interests. Originally, Genie sounded a lot like our computer-optimized touring plans: you tell Genie what rides you want to ride, and Genie tells you the order in which you should ride those rides to minimize your waits in line, based on Disney's wait-time forecasts. In practice, Genie's suggestions are almost entirely useless, often directing users to attractions they have no interest in instead of the rides they prioritized. And unlike our touring plans, Genie arbitrarily limits the number of attractions on your daily itinerary.

unofficial **TIP**
Pick an easy-to-remember password for your Disney account because the app has a habit of unexpectedly logging users out.

The basic version of Genie is complimentary. For an additional fee, **Genie+** gives guests the ability to make same-day reservations and skip the regular queues at participating Lightning Lane attractions; a few other rides sell expedited entry à la carte (see page 97).

You'll need to register for a free Disney online account to use most of these features. Create a unique log-in for each member of your traveling party old enough to carry a smartphone, and be sure to link all of your tickets inside everybody's apps so everyone can try for the Virtual Queue boarding passes (see pages 107–110) and see each other's plans.

It's best to download this app in advance via Wi-Fi, so you don't waste time and bandwidth inside the park. You'll need to keep your mobile device powered up and connected to the internet to take advantage of the service, which can be an issue for international visitors. Disneyland's Wi-Fi network is free to use but frustratingly flaky outside of the hot spots designated on the park map. We recommend using your cell provider's data connection instead, especially during the daily Virtual Queue distributions, when Disney's network is often overloaded.

You may also want to install and log in to the official **Play Disney Parks** app ahead of time, particularly if you want to explore the interactive experiences inside Star Wars: Galaxy's Edge. By playing the app's simple time-killing games, you can unlock Apple Music playlists of theme park soundtracks or get free readings from the fortune-telling machines found at Disneyland. Be sure to enable Bluetooth, Push Notifications, and background Location services; and beware that this app is a battery hog, so turn Low Power Mode back on when you're finished playing. For free audio tours and trivia tied to different locations around the Disneyland Resort, try the unofficial MouseTour app.

We also recommend **Lines,** the mobile application of touringplans .com, available for the Apple iPhone and iPad at the iTunes Store (search for "TouringPlans") and for Android devices at the Google Play Store. Owners of other phones can use the web-based version at m.touringplans .com. The app is free to download, but you'll need to log in with a paid TouringPlans subscription to access most of its features.

Touringplans.com website's touring plans, menus, Crowd Calendar, and more are available in Lines, which provides continuous real-time updates on wait times at Disneyland. Using in-park staff and updates sent in by readers, Lines shows you the current wait and Lightning Lane distribution times at every attraction in every park, as well as the estimated actual waits for these attractions for the rest of the day. For example, Lines will tell you that the posted wait time for Space Mountain is 60 minutes, and that based on what we know about how Disney manages Space Mountain's queue, the actual time you'll probably wait in line is 48 minutes. Lines is the only Disney app that shows you both posted and actual wait times.

As long as you have that smartphone handy while visiting the parks, we and your fellow *Unofficial Guide* readers would love it if you could report on the actual wait times you get while you're there. Run Lines, log in to your user account, and click +TIME in the upper right corner to help everyone out. We'll use that information to update the wait times for everyone in the park, and make everyone's lives just a little bit better.

A couple from Easton, Pennsylvania, found Lines especially useful:

> I don't know what we would have done without The Unofficial Guide to Disneyland *and the Lines app. This was our first and possibly only trip to Disneyland. We were able to do everything we wanted and ride many big attractions like the Matterhorn several times. We also enjoyed using the menu feature on the site and app. I was able*

to plan all our meals before arriving at a restaurant instead of realizing later that there were no good vegetarian options.

As did this family from Folsom, California:

The Lines app proved to be invaluable on our trip. Without Lines, we could not have accomplished nearly as much as we did. We used Lines to find out what was off-line and what had a reasonable wait time. For instance, we were going to give up on Radiator Springs Racers until we noticed that the single-rider line had a reasonable wait.

And this reader from New York:

The Lines app is the best thing you can use to maximize your time in the parks. My traveling companion was very skeptical about using the app (she's an [annual pass] holder and [Disney Vacation Club member], so she thinks she has it all down pat), and within the first hour, she was asking, "What does it say to do next? We should trust it."

RIDES AND SHOWS CLOSED
FOR REPAIRS OR MAINTENANCE

RIDES AND SHOWS at Disneyland parks are sometimes closed for maintenance or repairs. In addition, some attractions may be closed or modified due to health concerns. If a certain attraction is important to you, call ☎ 714-781-4636 or visit disneyland.disney.go.com/calendars before you go to make sure it will be operating. You'll also find an unofficial schedule of current and upcoming closures at touringplans.com/disney land-resort-resort/closures. A mother from Dover, Massachusetts, lamented:

We were disappointed to find Space Mountain and the riverboat closed for repairs. We felt that a large chunk [of the park] was not working, yet the tickets were still full price and expensive!

Even if an attraction isn't on the disabled list, unplanned outages may prevent you from riding, as a woman from Antioch, Illinois, discovered:

The biggest drawback of the whole trip was the numerous breakdowns of the rides. We were aware of Big Thunder Mountain and a few other rides closed for long-term scheduled maintenance, but a lot of the rides broke down as soon as we headed to them! The only things that didn't have any breakdowns were the cash registers!

This mom from Las Vegas, Nevada, had some terrible luck during a busy Christmas holiday visit:

We had five—yes, count them, five—rides break down after being in line for over an hour. That was 5 hours spent standing in lines and not getting to ride a ride. Fortunately, the rides we went on were top-notch Disney quality and worth every ticket and time spent at the parks. And all but two of those rides were fixed, and we were able to ride them on a different day.

Disney's attractions are technically complex, so it's almost inevitable that you will experience some unscheduled downtime during your visit. If a ride is temporarily closed, ask the attendants outside if there is an estimated reopening time (usually they can't tell you) and continue with your touring, returning later if possible. If a ride stops running while you're already in the queue, decide whether to stay based on how long the posted wait was when you entered and how much time you've already invested. Most "brief operational delays" are resolved in about 15 minutes, but there are no guarantees.

If a ride halts unexpectedly while you're on it, remain calm and rest assured that Disney has extremely safe evacuation procedures for every contingency. Stay seated and listen for announcements, and be patient because employees may need to evacuate ride vehicles one at a time in a specific order. On the plus side, you may get an exclusive backstage view of how the ride operates, and you should be offered either an immediate re-ride (if the attraction resumes operating) or a return pass to let you skip the standby line later on.

On the upside, broken-down rides can be great opportunities for Genie+ users to harvest valuable Multiple Experiences Lightning Lane passes; see page 104 for details.

ADMISSION OPTIONS

THEME PARK ADMISSION options are now more complicated than ever at Disneyland Resort. For starters, you have three things to decide:

1. How many days admission you'll need.
2. The exact dates you wish to attend.
3. Whether you want to go to both Disneyland Park and DCA on the same day. This is known as park hopping.

ADMISSION OPTIONS	ADULT (age 10 and UP)	CHILD (ages 3–9)
One-Day, One Park *(depending on season)*	$104–$194	$98–$183
One-Day Park Hopper *(depending on season)*	$169–$259	$163–$248
Two-Day, One Park Per Day	$310	$290
Two-Day Park Hopper	$375	$365
Three-Day, One Park Per Day	$390	$365
Three-Day Park Hopper	$460	$435
Four-Day, One Park Per Day	$445	$420
Four-Day Park Hopper	$515	$490
Five-Day, One Park Per Day	$480	$450
Five-Day Park Hopper	$555	$525
Imagine Key annual pass *(many blockout dates, 2 reservations at a time, only available to residents of certain zip codes)*	$499	$499
Enchant Key annual pass *(some blockout dates, 4 reservations at a time)*	$849	$849
Believe Key annual pass *(a few blockout dates, 6 reservations at a time, 50% off parking)*	$1,249	$1,249
Inspire Key annual pass *(no blockout dates, 6 reservations at a time, parking included)*	$1,649	$1,649

All admission tickets currently sold for the Disneyland Resort are date-specific, and you must choose your attendance dates at time of purchase. Multiday tickets expire 13 days after the first use (unless otherwise specified as part of a special offer), so you don't want to buy more days than you'll need. Needless to say, tickets expire after you've used the number of days purchased even if 13 days haven't passed yet. Finally, all one-day passes expire at the end of the year after they were purchased; passes purchased in 2024 expire December 30, 2025, while multiday passes must be used up by January 12, 2026. This means you can't stockpile current tickets as a hedge against future inflation, but Guest Services will let you pay the difference and apply the full amount paid for a wholly unused expired ticket toward a new one at current prices, as long as it costs the same or more than you originally paid.

All admissions can be purchased at the park entrance, at Disneyland Resort hotels, on the Disneyland website and app, by calling ☎ 714-781-4636 or 800-854-3104. All 1- and 2-year-olds are exempt from admission fees. There are no taxes levied on any Disneyland Resort tickets or **Magic Key** passes (see pages 25–26).

THEME PARK RESERVATIONS

IN ADDITION TO PURCHASING a park ticket, every Disneyland guest—including those with single-day and multiday tickets—must also make a park reservation for each day of their visit, up to 180 days in advance. Be sure to check the calendar of park reservation availability at disneyland.disney.go.com/availability-calendar *before* purchasing tickets. Online buyers of single and multiday tickets can make their park reservations during the checkout process, while guests holding pre-purchased tickets or Magic Keys must book reservations at disneyland.disney.go.com/entry-reservation.

ADMISSION COSTS AND AVAILABLE DISCOUNTS

YOU CAN LEARN ABOUT any special seasonal discounts offered directly from Disney at disneyland.disney.go.com/offers-discounts; some offers may only be available for purchase through the website and not on the app.

unofficial **TIP**
The money you can save makes researching Disney's dizzying array of ticket options worthwhile.

If you purchase tickets on the Disneyland website, you will be emailed e-tickets, which can be downloaded as PDF files and printed at home or scanned from your mobile device. E-tickets normally arrive in your email inbox within minutes of purchase (and automatically attach to your app account if you're signed in while buying) but can take up to 24 hours for delivery. An e-ticket printed from your home computer will show two bar codes. A cast member will scan these at the turnstiles. Once the bar codes are read, the cast member will hand you a physical ticket to use during the rest of your visit.

It's possible to obtain discounts on all multiday tickets, but only in the 4%–8% range. The deepest discounts we've found are from **ARES**

Travel (arestravel.com). ARES usually beats the Disney advance purchase price by $4–$7 per day or up to $36 per ticket. Guests may take their digital tickets straight to the park gates; a $2-per-ticket convenience fee applies. You can order online or call ☎ 800-434-7894. You must provide the dates you intend to visit when purchasing the ticket. Another option is **Discount Tickets & Tours** (discountticketsandtours .com), which also sells legitimate, modestly discounted tickets online for Disney and other area attractions. Whatever you do, never buy cheap Disney tickets on eBay, Craigslist, or off the street. The passes are probably partially used and not authorized for resale, and Mickey will not give you your money back if you are turned away at the turnstiles.

If you plan to visit other Southern California attractions in addition to Disneyland, you might want to consider a **CityPass**. CityPass includes between two and five days of admission to Disneyland Park and DCA (one park per day or park hopper, with or without Genie+), combined with your pick of tickets to Universal Studios Hollywood, SeaWorld San Diego, Legoland California, and/or the San Diego Zoo. By making full use of all the admissions you select for your personalized CityPass, you can save $3–$7 per day on the Disneyland portion and $10 or more per day on the other attractions. If you don't use all of the admissions, however, you will save little or nothing by purchasing the CityPass. The pass does not include dining or shopping discounts. Details concerning other CityPass destinations are available at citypass.com/southern-california.

Military discounts are available for all Disney theme parks, usually in the 25%–50% range. Check with your base Morale, Welfare, & Recreation office for info. Be aware that one member of your party must show military ID at the park turnstiles to use the tickets, so you can't purchase them for friends or relatives you won't be traveling with. Learn about current military discount offers at disneyland.disney .go.com/offers-discounts.

Disneyland Resort and other area attractions sometimes offer discounted afternoon and evening tickets for conventioneers. See disney meetingsandevents.com.

Admission prices increase from time to time. For planning your budget, however, the table on page 20 provides a fair estimate. Note that Walt Disney World tickets are *not* valid for admission to Disneyland.

LINKING ADMISSION IN THE DISNEYLAND APP

NO MATTER HOW YOU OBTAIN YOUR TICKETS, you'll want to link them to your Disneyland mobile app (see page 17) before arriving at the parks by following these steps:

1. In the Disneyland app, press the Main Menu icon (three bars) in the bottom right corner of the screen.
2. Press "Tickets and Passes."
3. You should already see your own ticket if you're logged in to the same account that you used to purchase the ticket. If not, contact Disney.
4. Press the blue button with the "+" sign in the top right corner of the screen.

5. Press "Link Tickets & Passes."

6. Use your camera to scan the barcode (or manually input the number) on your friend's/family member's ticket, and it will be added to the app.

7. Repeat these steps for the remaining members of your party.

You may choose to pick one member of your party to handle everyone's tickets, Lighting Lane selections, and Virtual Queues on their phone. Better, each person with a smartphone can create a personal account and attach everyone's ticket to it so that you will all be able to try for Virtual Queue show passes or boarding groups. This also gives your group the option of splitting up but still retaining access to each other's plans; however, each person must still use their own ticket to enter the park or redeem Virtual Queues and Lightning Lane reservations.

SINGLE-DAY TICKETS WITH VARIABLE PRICING

DISNEY HAS FOLLOWED the lead of airline and ski resort industries by instituting seven seasonal tiers for all single-day tickets, charging more money for tickets on the busiest days and offering a modest discount during periods of lower attendance.

The price difference between a Tier 0 (cheapest) and Tier 6 (most expensive) single day is currently $90 for one-park tickets and Park Hoppers. That may not be enough of a premium to dictate plans for many out-of-state visitors, whose vacation dates are mandated by school and work schedules, but it has definitely encouraged locals to shift their visits toward cheaper days, perversely pumping up crowds when the parks would otherwise be empty, while somewhat shrinking attendance on peak days.

Because of the tiered pricing structure and park reservation system, you must be certain of which date you will visit Disneyland when buying your ticket, or risk buying a more expensive ticket than you need. A Tier 6 ticket can be used to secure an available park reservation any day of the year, while a Tier 3 ticket can be used to make a park reservation on Tier 1 and 2 days but not 4 through 6. Tier 0 tickets are only accepted on those select days, but they (or any other admission) can be upgraded to any more expensive pass, presuming reservations for your preferred day aren't already sold out.

With a one-day ticket, you may exit and return to the park on the same day as many times as you like. Disneyland photographs every guest upon first entry for identification purposes; be prepared to have your pass (and face) scanned shortly before passing the turnstiles, with your picture replacing the old exit handstamps for readmission.

MULTIDAY TICKETS

THESE ARE GOOD FOR two, three, four, or five days, respectively. Multiday tickets are not affected by the single-day pricing tiers and can be used with a park reservation on any day of the year. These multiday tickets do not have to be used on consecutive days, but they do expire 13 days after their first use, which must happen on or before December 30th of the year after purchase (currently December 30, 2025, for tickets bought in 2024). If you mistakenly bought multiday tickets because you were not aware of the 13-day expiration, call ☎ 714-781-4636 or ☎ 714-781-4565 and ask to be connected to Guest Communications, which has the authority to issue you a voucher for the unused days on your ticket.

Any time before a pass expires, you can apply the full original amount you paid for the ticket toward the cost of a higher-priced ticket. If you buy a Four-Day, One-Park-Per-Day ticket, for example, and then decide you'd rather have a Five-Day Park Hopper or a Magic Key pass, you can apply the full original cost of the former toward the purchase of the latter. (If your original tickets were discounted, you'll have to make up the difference when upgrading; tickets can only be applied toward a new Magic Key, not a renewal, and designated promotional tickets cannot be upgraded.) The maximum number of days you can purchase on a standard Disneyland ticket is five. After that you have to upgrade to a Magic Key pass or buy another ticket, which makes a six- or seven-day visit extremely cost-ineffective. Upgraded passes expire on the same 13-day deadline date as the original ticket; annual passes expire one year from the first usage of the original ticket. Remember, you must perform any upgrades before midnight on your current ticket's last valid day; passes can be upgraded to Magic Keys on the tickets screen inside the Disneyland app.

PARK HOPPER TICKETS

BY DEFAULT, TICKETS WITHOUT Park Hopper require you to choose one park or the other to visit each day. All single and multiday tickets may be purchased with the Park Hopper option, which allows you to visit both Disneyland Park and DCA during the same day. The Park Hopper premium on a single-day admission is quite pricey (currently $65), but on a five-day pass it drops to only $15 per day.

Guests purchasing Park Hoppers must still use Disney's park reservation system to select where to start their day, and they must first enter the park they picked before visiting the other. Park hopping is prohibited until 11 a.m., and you may see guests parked outside designated park entry turnstiles up to an hour prior, but the lines usually dissipate within 30 minutes. After that, you may go back and forth as often as you like until closing time (or 15 minutes after at DCA on nights when a *World of Color* performance begins after park closing). Park hoppers who arrive after 11 a.m. may enter either gate first, regardless of which park they reserved, but a reservation at one of them is still required.

If you are spending more than two days at Disneyland Resort, we strongly encourage you to spring for the park-to-park access. The ease of walking from one park to the other makes the Park Hopper premium more than worth it. Park hopping is especially handy when one park closes early for a special event, or when multiple major rides in one park break down simultaneously. If you buy a multiday one-park-per-day pass, you can upgrade it to a Park Hopper before it expires, but you'll pay the premium based on the pass's original length, even if you are on its final day of admission.

MAGIC KEY *(previously Annual Passports)*

AFTER DECADES OF CULTIVATING a passionate fan base of annual passholders over 1 million strong, Disneyland Resort seized on its pandemic shutdown as an opportunity to retire and reboot the increasingly unwieldy program under a new name.

Magic Key, the replacement program for Disneyland annual passes, resembles the previous system—with several significant changes. Most important, the mandatory advance reservation system first introduced in 2019 with the lower-cost Flex Passport has now been imposed on all levels of passholders, with strict limits on how many park visits can be booked. Before arriving at the parks, Magic Key holders must use the Disneyland app or visit disneyland.disney .go.com/entry-reservation, up to 90 days in advance, to select the date and initial park for their visit. (Park hopping is permitted after 11 a.m., but until then you may only enter your reserved park.)

unofficial **TIP**
If you are a local who visits Disneyland five or more days each year, or a tourist making at least two five-day trips, a Magic Key pass is a potential money saver.

The pool of park pass reservations for Magic Key holders is separate from those for guests with single-day or multiday tickets, and availability is limited, so you aren't guaranteed to be able to make a reservation for any particular day. Once you've reached your pass's reservation limit, you can't book another day until you use or cancel one. Unwanted reservations must be canceled (or rescheduled for a later available date) before midnight on the day prior because being a no-show for three park reservations within a rolling 90-day window will result in being banned from making new reservations for 30 days. As a result, the days of local residents making spur-of-the-moment visits to Disneyland are probably done.

Note: Sales of all new Magic Key annual passes were suspended at press time. New sales are usually announced a day or two ahead of time on Disney's social media. When Magic Keys or other limited availability tickets are released online, you can avoid hovering over your computer all day by registering for the "notify me" option. When your turn in the purchasing queue arrives, you'll receive a link via email and have 10 minutes to log in and make your transaction, lest you lose your virtual place in line. While Magic Key sales are suspended, guests who already have Magic Keys are still able to renew their current passes within 30 days before expiration, at which time they may select a different tier of pass.

The **Inspire Key** pass, which replaced the Dream Key Pass, is the top-tier annual pass with the fewest blockout dates, although it is invalid during the two weeks around Christmas and New Year's. (Disneyland no longer offers any annual pass valid 365 days a year). The Inspire Key includes admission to both parks during normal operating hours, free self-parking in the theme park garages and lots, and unlimited PhotoPass downloads. The pass also provides up to 15% discounts at most resort dining locations, as well as 20% off the daily Genie+ fee and most merchandise. Inspire Key passholders may hold up to six theme park reservations at one time.

Believe Key passes are valid 317 days of the year, with 48 blockout dates around Easter, Fourth of July, Thanksgiving, Christmas, and many Saturdays. Believe Key passholders can hold up to six theme park reservations at a time; they also get a 10% discount on most food and merchandise, 20% off the daily Genie+ fee, and a 50% discount on parking, along with unlimited PhotoPass downloads.

Enchant Key passes are valid 216 days of the year, with 150 blockout dates, including all holidays, all of early June through mid-August, and most Saturdays and Sundays in the fall and spring. Enchant Key passholders get the same 10% discount on food and merchandise as Believe Key holders, as well as 20% off the daily Genie+ fee, but they can only hold four theme park reservations at a time and receive 25% off self-parking at the Toy Story lot only.

Finally, **Imagine Key** passes are only available to Southern California residents living in certain zip codes (90000–93599). The pass has only 147 valid dates, with blockouts on 218 days, including all of summer and nearly every Friday, Saturday, and Sunday. Imagine Key holders are limited to two theme park reservations at a time, but they do get 10% off select dining and merchandise, 20% off the daily Genie+ fee, and 25% off self-parking at the Toy Story lot.

Californians living in zip codes 90000–96199 can purchase any of the Magic Keys on an interest-free monthly installment plan, after an initial down payment equal to a one-day park hopper ticket. Everyone living outside those areas must pay for their Magic Key in full at time of purchase. Prices for children are the same as those for adults on all Magic Key passes, but DVC Members save $20 off the top 3 pass tiers when purchasing a new Magic Key at the parks' ticket booths (membership card required).

If you first use your Magic Key pass in July of 2025 and schedule your next visit for June of 2026, you'll cover two years' vacations with a single pass. Magic Keys are good for one full year after being activated by using them for the first time at a park turnstile (or receiving free parking), and they must be activated within one year of purchase or they expire. You can, however, make park reservations using an unactivated Magic Key. Expired unactivated Magic Keys will have any associated park reservations canceled, and their original value can only be applied toward the purchase of a new Magic Key of equal or greater price. The easiest way to purchase or upgrade to a Magic Key is online through the Disneyland app. You must visit the ticket booths outside the parks in person if you wish to upgrade from one Magic Key tier to another or to purchase a Magic Key using cash, Disney Chase Visa rewards, Disney gift cards worth over $1,000, or by upgrading a wholly unused admission ticket. Visit disneyland.disney.go.com/magic -key for more details and updates about the passes.

TICKETS AND MAGICBAND+

WE'VE USED THE WORD *ticket* to describe that thing you carry around as proof of your admission to the park. In fact, Disney admission media come in three forms: paper tickets, e-tickets, and MagicBand+.

The latest admission option is a rubber wristband called a MagicBand+. MagicBands have been available for several years at Walt Disney World and were introduced at Disneyland Resort in late 2022. About the size and shape of a small wristwatch, it contains a tiny radio frequency identification (RFID) chip, on which is stored a link to the record of your admission purchase in Disney's computers. Your MagicBand+ gives you access to the park turnstiles and Lightning Lanes you've reserved, tracks PhotoPass images you've collected, and in the future may also function as your Disney hotel-room key. MagicBand+ also includes motion sensors, haptic vibrations, and multicolored lights that synchronize with select nighttime spectaculars and allow you to play interactive games like Batuu Bounty Hunters using the PlayDisney app.

MagicBand+s are available for purchase in a variety of styles for about $35–$55, with modest discounts for Magic Key holders. Each member of your family gets their own MagicBand+, each with a unique serial number. The wristbands are removable, resizable, and waterproof, and they have ventilation holes for cooling. Their built-in batteries will need to be charged before first use, then recharged every couple of days; a USB charging cable is included in the box, but not a wall plug. When it's drained of power, you'll still be able to use the band to enter the park or Lightning Lanes, but interactive features won't work.

A MagicBand+ from Walt Disney World may also be linked to a Disneyland account (or vice versa) without first being deactivated, but you may need to reset your Bluetooth connection by holding down the button on the band's back for 8 seconds. (Only MagicBand+s will work at Disneyland, not original MagicBands or MagicBand 2s.)

Some guests, particularly those with hand- or wrist-mobility issues, find using the MagicBand physically challenging. To help with this, the center portion of the band (essentially a puck the size of a quarter) is removable. The puck can then be placed on a lanyard or clipped on a bag, making it easier to maneuver.

We don't think MagicBand+ is essential (or even especially useful) at Disneyland, particularly if you keep your admission on your smartphone. If you do want one, purchase and set it up in advance to avoid wasting time in the park. You'll need to charge it, connect it to the Disneyland app, and update the software before first use. Increase the motion sensitivity settings if you are having trouble triggering interactive features.

If you don't want a MagicBand+, your second option is a credit card–size piece of paper with a barcode, which will be handed to you for free the first time you enter the park using a single-day or multiday ticket. Your third option is to use the Disneyland app to display your ticket as a barcode. This option allows guests with single-day tickets, multiday tickets, or Magic Keys to scan their smartphone for admission at park entrances. If using this option, it's a smart idea to store a screenshot of your ticket's barcode, in case you ever have trouble opening the app.

HOW MUCH DOES IT COST TO GO TO DISNEYLAND FOR A DAY?

LET'S SAY THAT we have a family of four—Mom, Dad, Tim (age 12), and Tami (age 8)—driving their own car. Because they plan to be in the area for a few days, they intend to buy the Three-Day Park Hopper tickets, but are not adding on Genie+ or Individual Lightning Lanes. A typical day would cost $991, excluding lodging and transportation. See the table below for a breakdown of expenses.

HOW MUCH DOES A DAY COST?	
Breakfast for 4 at Denny's with tax and tip	$78
Disneyland parking fee	$35
1 day's admission for 4 on a Three-Day Park Hopper Pass	$605
Dad: *Adult 3-day is $460 divided by 3 days* = $153	
Mom: *Adult 3-day is $460 divided by 3 days* = $153	
Tim: *Adult 3-day is $460 divided by 3 days* = $153	
Tami: *Child 3-day is $435 divided by 3 days* = $145	
Morning break (soda or coffee)	$23
Fast-food lunch (burger, fries, and soda), no tip	$69
Afternoon break (soda and popcorn)	$48
Dinner in park at counter-service restaurant with tax	$79
Souvenirs (Mickey T-shirts for Tim and Tami) with tax*	$54
One-day total (without lodging or transportation)	**$991**

* *Cheer up—you won't have to buy souvenirs every day.*

▌ TIMING *Your* VISIT

SELECTING THE TIME OF YEAR FOR YOUR VISIT

CROWDS TRADITIONALLY ARE LARGEST at Disneyland when schools are out of session during the summer and specific holiday periods. The busiest time of all is spring break and Easter (late March–mid-April), followed closely by December 25–January 1. Attendance during the Halloween season has begun to rival Christmas, making October one of the busiest months of the year. Thanksgiving week, the week of Presidents' Day, and the first two weeks of summer are also extremely

TOP 10 AMERICAN THEME PARKS		
THEME PARK	ANNUAL ATTENDANCE	AVERAGE DAILY ATTENDANCE
Walt Disney World's Magic Kingdom	17.1 million	46,940
Disneyland Park	16.9 million	46,247
Universal Orlando's Islands of Adventure	11.0 million	30,205
Disney's Hollywood Studios	10.9 million	29,863
Universal Studios Florida	10.8 million	29,452
Walt Disney World's EPCOT	10.0 million	27,397
Disney's Animal Kingdom	9.0 million	24,732
Disney California Adventure	9.0 million	24,658
Universal Studios Hollywood	8.4 million	23,014
SeaWorld Orlando	4.5 million	12,203

Source: Themed Entertainment Association (2022)

busy. Historically, Disneyland saw large crowds from Memorial Day through Labor Day, but recently attendance has been moderate during the hottest weeks of late June and July. To give you some idea of what *busy* means at Disneyland, more than 88,000 people have toured Disneyland Park in one day! While this level of attendance is far from typical, the possibility of its occurrence should prevent all but the ignorant and the foolish from challenging this mega-attraction at its busiest periods.

unofficial **TIP**
You can't pick a less crowded time to visit Disneyland Resort than late August through September.

The slowest period of the year is from early August through late September (especially late August and the first two weeks in September), as a family from Vancouver, Canada, found:

> With many California schools starting in late August, we found a sweet spot to visit during the second-to-last week of August when our kids are still on vacation. The parks were still open late, and all entertainment was still running, but crowds were down from the summer peak.

The next slowest times are early January through mid-February (excepting Martin Luther King Jr. Day and Presidents' Day weekends), early March, the week following Easter to Memorial Day weekend, and after Thanksgiving weekend until the week before Christmas. At the risk of being blasphemous, our research team was so impressed with the relative ease of touring in the fall and other off-season periods that we would rather take our children out of school for a few days than do battle with the peak season crowds. Though we strongly recommend going to Disneyland in the fall or in the spring, it should be noted that there are certain trade-offs. The parks often close earlier on fall, winter, and spring days, sometimes early enough to eliminate evening parades, fireworks, and other

unofficial **TIP**
In our opinion, the risk of encountering colder weather and closed attractions during an off-season visit to Disneyland is worth it.

live-entertainment offerings such as *Fantasmic!* Also, because these are slow times of the year at Disneyland, you can anticipate that some rides and attractions may be closed for maintenance or renovation. Finally, if the parks open late and close early, it's tough to see everything, even if the crowds are light.

Most readers who have tried Disney parks at varying times of the year concur. A wintertime visitor from Sacramento, California, agrees:

> *Though there was a torrential storm on two days of our four-day visit, I can safely say that I will never visit in high season again. Yes, we were wet. Yes, attractions and rides were closed for refurb. BUT the longest line we waited in was 25 minutes to see the princesses. Characters were EVERYWHERE, and access to them was easy as pie. There were no issues with heat or sunburn. And we saved a boatload of money.*

Not to overstate the case: We want to emphasize that you can have a great time at the Disneyland parks regardless of the time of year or crowd level. In fact, a primary objective of this guide is to make the parks fun and manageable for those readers who visit during the busier times of year.

unofficial **TIP**
If it's not your first trip to Disneyland and you must join the holiday-weekend crowds, you may have just as much fun enjoying Disney's fantastic array of shows, parades, and fireworks as you would riding the rides.

The rule of thumb is that Disneyland is more crowded when school is out and less crowded when kids are in school. However, Disney has become increasingly adept at loading slow periods of the year with special events (conventions, food festivals, and the like) while using crowd management schemes such as tiered pricing and park reservations to smooth out the peaks and valleys of park attendance. And we've observed that Disney's crowd management schemes (like Lightning Lane and park reservations) make walkways feel a little less overcrowded at the busiest times, but increase standby wait times during off-season days. Discounts on rooms, variable pricing for single-day tickets, and blockouts on Magic Key passes and discounted tickets for local residents also figure in. Other factors affecting crowding and long lines include a combination of closed rides and the state of the global economy. As a result, we've added more data about ride closures and economic indicators to our crowd level forecasts.

The bottom line is that Disneyland can be packed at any time, and you need to dig a little deeper than merely the time of year to pinpoint the least-crowded periods. For a calendar of scheduled Disney events, see touringplans.com/disneyland-resort/events.

Of course, crowds are not the only consideration when deciding what time of year to visit Disneyland. Holidays are celebrated at Disneyland like nowhere else, and the festive decor is almost worth the price of admission. The parks are decked out for Halloween from late August through October. Be aware that after-hours extra-cost Halloween parties may cause one of the parks to close early three evenings each week through the fall, as a Tucson, Arizona, family found:

The Halloween event changes the low season to a zoo. Every local with an annual pass showed up in the afternoon. The park closed early for this event, and [the other park] backed up because of the early closure.

Christmas trappings transform the Disneyland Resort from mid-November until after New Year's Day. There's also a Christmas parade, and several attractions such as Haunted Mansion and It's a Small World offer a special holiday version. Disneyland's holiday entertainment and seasonal fireworks are included in regular admission. A reader from Union City, California, who visited during the second week of December, wrote:

The park was extremely crowded, but we knew what we were getting into and were ready to handle it. The holiday offerings are wonderful, but if you are not mentally prepared to deal with the massive crowds and congested walkways that plague the park throughout the entire month of December, it can be a very stressful vacation.

A mom from McLean, Virginia, chimed in:

We were there over New Year's Eve, and Disneyland Park was crushingly crowded. We dared not leave for DCA or to go back to the hotel for a break for fear of not getting back in, and the younger ones really wanted to be in Disneyland Park for the fireworks. The weather was so horrible (COLD AND WINDY), they canceled the show anyway.

In spring, the parks hold Disneyland After Dark late-night events that require special tickets to attend, and daytime seasonal events like Lunar New Year and the Disney California Adventure (DCA) Food & Wine Festival draw crowds during what would otherwise be a slow period. Finally, beware of Grad Nite late-night parties for high school seniors on select days each May and June. The kids have after-hours access to DCA, but they also get admission to both parks during the daytime and make their presence known starting midafternoon, as this reader from Hamilton, New Jersey, was unlucky to learn:

If we were planning a solo Disneyland trip, we would definitely not choose a Grad Nite. The grads were obnoxious, often talking and yelling loudly during the rides about unrelated things. Additionally, they often jumped the lines.

THE SPOILER

SO YOU CHOOSE YOUR OFF-SEASON DATES and then find it almost impossible to find a hotel room. What gives? In all probability you've been foiled by a mammoth convention or trade show at the Anaheim Convention Center. One of the largest and busiest convention venues in the country, the convention center hosts meetings with as many as 100,000 attendees and was expanded in a $190-million project that added 200,000 square feet to the center. The sheer numbers alone guarantee that hotel rooms will be hard to find. Compounding the problem is the fact that most business travelers don't have roommates. Thus a trade show with 8,000 people registered might suck up 13,000 rooms (including people who registered late)! The final straw, as you might expect, is that room rates climb into the stratosphere based on the high demand and scarcity of supply.

In regard to increased crowds at the theme parks, it's estimated that less than 10% of convention attendees will find time to enjoy the parks. It's also true, however, that business travelers are more likely to bring their spouse and even kids to a convention held in Anaheim, as this reader learned the hard way.

> *A music festival, with about 115,000 attendees, is held at the end of January every year at the Anaheim Convention Center. I am certain all of them extended their vacation and went to [Disneyland Resort] the week of January 28–February 2. It was unbelievably crowded! Previously, we went to Disneyland at the beginning of December and experienced about ¼ of the crowds.*

The bottom line is that you don't want to schedule your vacation while a major event is going on at the convention center. Visit anaheim.net /calendar.aspx?CID=26 to see what conventions are scheduled during your visit. Pay particular attention to dates for the bi-annual D23 Expo, last held August 9-11 2024, which draws tens of thousands of Disney super-fans to town. In addition, the Disney parks can sometimes be overrun by events not associated with the convention center, such as unofficial fan gatherings like Dapper Day (April and November, dapperday .com); Bats Day (May, batsday.net); or RunDisney footraces, which resumed in 2024 (January and September, rundisney.com). Schedules vary each year, so check the respective websites when planning your trip. For a calendar of scheduled Disney events, see touringplans.com/ disneyland-resort/events.

SELECTING THE DAY OF THE WEEK FOR YOUR VISIT

THE CROWDS AT WALT DISNEY WORLD in Florida are comprised mostly of out-of-state visitors. This is not necessarily so at Disneyland Resort, which, along with Six Flags Magic Mountain, serves as an often-frequented recreational resource for the greater Los Angeles and San Diego communities. To many Southern Californians, Disneyland Park and DCA are their private theme parks. Historically, this meant that weekends were usually packed with local annual passholders. However, the majority of the busiest days now fall on weekdays rather than weekends, likely due to blockout restrictions on Magic Key holders.

During summer, Monday and Friday are very busy, Tuesday and Wednesday are usually less so, and Thursday is normally the slowest day. In off-season (September–May, holiday periods excepted), Thursday is usually the least crowded day, followed by Friday and Wednesday.

Disneyland Park usually hosts crowds 50% larger than those at DCA, but because DCA is smaller, crowd conditions are comparable. Expressed differently, the most crowded and least crowded days are essentially the same for both Disneyland parks, except during special events or after the opening of a major new attraction.

EARLY ENTRY ATTRACTIONS	
DISNEYLAND PARK	
• Alice in Wonderland	• Mr. Toad's Wild Ride
• Astro Orbitor	• Peter Pan's Flight
• Buzz Lightyear Astro Blasters	• Pinocchio's Daring Journey
• Disneyland Monorail	• Snow White's Scary Adventures
• Dumbo the Flying Elephant	• Space Mountain
• King Arthur Carrousel	• Star Tours—The Adventures Continue
• Mad Tea Party	
DISNEY CALIFORNIA ADVENTURE	
• Guardians of the Galaxy—Mission: Breakout!	• Monsters, Inc. Mike & Sulley to the Rescue!
• Incredicoaster	• Soarin' Around the World
• The Little Mermaid: Ariel's Undersea Adventure	• WEB SLINGERS: A Spider-Man Adventure
• Mater's Junkyard Jamboree	

EARLY ENTRY (formerly EXTRA MAGIC HOUR)

EARLY ENTRY FOR ON-SITE HOTEL GUESTS allows guests of the Pixar Place, Grand Californian, and Disneyland Hotels holding a valid park ticket to enjoy select Disneyland or Disney California Adventure attractions 30 minutes before the general public on most mornings. Early entry is offered at Disneyland every Tuesday, Thursday, and Saturday; it's offered at DCA on Sunday, Monday, Wednesday, and Friday. The participating park will open its gates to all guests when early entry begins. Once inside, hotel guests must show their reservation in the app for access to the rides, while everyone else awaits the regular rope drop from the central hub. During the early-entry period at Disneyland, most of the Fantasyland attractions and select rides in Tomorrowland will usually be open. The rest of the park's attractions—including all of Star Wars: Galaxy's Edge—remain off-limits until the official opening time. DCA's early entry offers access to all of Avengers Campus, along with select attractions in Cars Land, Paradise Gardens Park, Pixar Pier, and Grizzly Peak. Both parks also open a small selection of shops and quick-service restaurants for early arrivals. Eligible dates and participating venues are subject to change, so double-check Disneyland's calendar before arrival.

Note that several of the parks' top draws don't open during early entry, including Matterhorn Bobsleds, Radiator Springs Racers, and Toy Story Midway Mania! Thirty minutes is only enough time to enjoy one or two rides, but early entry does give participants an edge over day guests in queuing for certain nonparticipating attractions.

Security checkpoints don't open until 30 minutes before early entry and can be painfully understaffed during early entry, especially at the Grand Californian's direct entrance to DCA, so on-site guests should plan on departing their hotel room up to 60 minutes before early entry begins to take full advantage of it.

If you are ineligible for early admission, try to begin your day at the park that is not offering early entry. Barring that, you should still try to start your morning at an attraction that does not offer early entry, since queues for rides that do participate may already be busy by the time ordinary guests enter.

OPERATING HOURS

DISNEYLAND RESORT RUNS a dozen or more different operating schedules during the year, making it advisable to consult the Disneyland smartphone app, visit disneyland.disney.go.com/calendar, or call ☎ 714-781-4565 the day before you arrive for exact hours of operation.

PACKED-PARK COMPENSATION PLAN

THE THOUGHT OF TEEMING, jostling throngs jockeying for position in endless lines under the baking Fourth of July sun is enough to wilt the will and ears of the most ardent Mouseketeer. Why would anyone go to Disneyland Park or DCA on a summer Saturday or during a major holiday period? The Disney folks, however, feel kind of bad about those interminably long lines and the basically impossible touring conditions on packed days, so they compensate patrons with an incredible array of first-rate live entertainment and happenings throughout the park.

Throughout the day, the party goes on with shows, cavalcades, concerts, and pageantry. In the evening, there is so much going on that you have to make some tough choices. Musical acts sometimes perform on the Tomorrowland Terrace stage in Disneyland and in Hollywood Land at DCA. There are always fireworks, and the Disney characters make frequent appearances. No question about it—you can go to the Disneyland parks on the Fourth of July (or any other crowded extended-hours day), never get on a ride, and still get your money's worth. Even on the busiest days, there are attractions at each park that rarely require more than a 15-minute wait: *Great Moments with Mr. Lincoln,* the *Enchanted Tiki Room,* the railroad, and monorail at Disneyland Park, as well as *Mickey's PhilharMagic,* Disney Animation, and the Bakery Tour at DCA.

If you decide to go on one of the parks' big days, we suggest that you arrive at least 1 hour and 20 minutes before the stated opening time. Use the touring plan of your choice until about 1 p.m., and then take the monorail or walk to Downtown Disney for lunch and relaxation. Southern Californian visitors often chip in and rent a room for the group (make reservations well in advance) at one of the Disneyland Resort hotels, thus affording a place to meet, relax, have a drink, or change clothes before enjoying the pools at the hotel. A comparable arrangement can be made at other nearby hotels, as long as they are within walking distance or furnish a shuttle service to and from the park. After an early dinner, return to the park for the evening's festivities, which really crank up at about 8 p.m.

GETTING THERE

WHILE MANY DISNEYLAND VISITORS hail from California and drive to the resort area, if you are flying in from across the country (or globe), you have three options for your arrival airport. With domestic and international service from nearly every airline known to man, **Los Angeles Airport** (LAX) is one of the largest and busiest in the world—and one of the more frustrating to navigate. LAX is also located 34 miles west of Anaheim, a 45-minute drive along the busy I-105 and I-55 freeways at the best of times, or an hour and a half or more in typical terrible traffic. Unless you are starting or ending your Disneyland vacation with a visit to Hollywood, we recommend looking at flights into **John Wayne Airport** (SNA) or **Long Beach Airport** (LGB), both of which are significantly calmer and closer to Disneyland. John Wayne (also known as Orange County Airport) is only 14 miles southeast of Disneyland on CA 55 and I-5 and is serviced by Air Canada, Alaska, Allegiant, American, Breeze, Delta, Frontier, Southwest, Spirit, United, and WestJet airlines. Capacity caps have caused some airlines to reduce their service at SNA, especially towards the end of the year. Long Beach (our personal favorite airport) is 24 miles west of Disneyland but can be reached using surface streets, making it the shortest drive when the highways are halted. Long Beach is only serviced by Delta, Hawaiian, and Southwest, but it boasts the most painless on-site rental car return and security screening we've ever experienced; going from the airport parking lot to sitting at your departure gate usually takes about 15 minutes.

There is no official Disney-authorized shuttle service from the airports to Disneyland, free or otherwise. Your best third-party airport shuttle options are **PrimeTime** (primetimeshuttle.com) or **Karmel Shuttle** (karmel.com). PrimeTime charges $79 one-way to take up to three people from LAX to the Anaheim resort area or $170 for a luxury SUV that seats six. Karmel charges $135 one-way for a van holding two to five passengers or $206 for up to nine riders; single riders can share a van for $75 per person. Rates vary for Long Beach and John Wayne. None of the shuttle prices include tip (18% of the total or $5 per person each way is suggested). California law prohibits infants and toddlers from riding on laps, and shuttle vans do not supply child seats, so you'll need to provide your own.

Rental cars are also available at all local airports, as are taxis, but the price of a cab can become extremely expensive after sitting in Los Angeles traffic on the way to Disneyland Resort. We've heard reports from people who have paid almost $180 to get from LAX to their Anaheim hotel; for that price, you could book a chauffeured limousine that seats up to five from **Lansky** (golansky.com). Less expensive rideshare services (such as Uber and Lyft) are also readily available to and from Los Angeles International, John Wayne, and Long Beach Airports. At LAX, take a free shuttle from the downstairs arrivals area to LAXit, the designated rideshare pickup area. At SNA, follow signs to the pickup

Southern California at a Glance

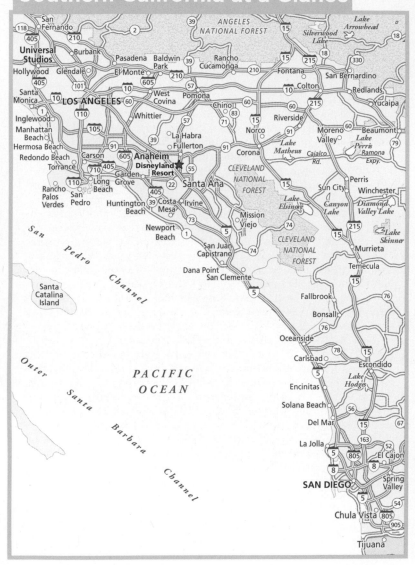

Around Disneyland

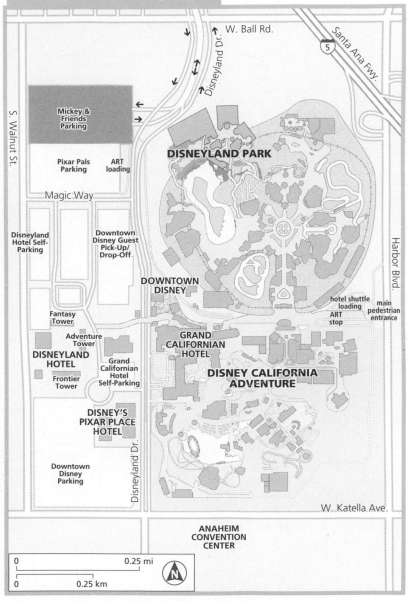

W. Ball Rd.

Santa Ana Fwy.

5

Disneyland Dr.

S. Walnut St.

Mickey & Friends Parking

Pixar Pals Parking

ART loading

DISNEYLAND PARK

Magic Way

Disneyland Hotel Self-Parking

Downtown Disney Guest Pick-Up/ Drop-Off

Harbor Blvd.

DOWNTOWN DISNEY

hotel shuttle loading
ART stop

main pedestrian entrance

Fantasy Tower

Adventure Tower

GRAND CALIFORNIAN HOTEL

DISNEYLAND HOTEL

Grand Californian Hotel Self-Parking

DISNEY CALIFORNIA ADVENTURE

Frontier Tower

DISNEY'S PIXAR PLACE HOTEL

Disneyland Dr.

Downtown Disney Parking

W. Katella Ave.

ANAHEIM CONVENTION CENTER

| 0 | | 0.25 mi |
| 0 | 0.25 km | |

N

areas on level 3 of each parking garage. We've had great results using Lyft and Uber from the airports and Disney hotels.

Once in Anaheim, Disney patrons can drive directly into and out of parking facilities without becoming enmeshed in surface-street traffic. To avoid traffic problems, we recommend the following:

1. Stay as close to Disneyland as possible. If you are within walking distance, leave your car at the hotel and walk to the park using the pedestrian entrance on the east side of the resort, along Harbor Boulevard between Disney Way and Manchester Avenue, or through the security checkpoint between Downtown Disney and the Pixar Place Hotel if walking from the west side along Disneyland Drive. If your hotel provides efficient shuttle service (that is, it will get you to the parks at least 30 minutes before opening), use the shuttle.

2. If your hotel is more than 5 miles from Disneyland and you intend to drive your car, leave for the park extra early, say 1 hour or more.

3. If you must use the Santa Ana Freeway (I-5), give yourself lots of extra time.

4. Any time you leave the park just before, at, or just after closing time, you can expect considerable congestion in the parking lots and in the loading area for hotel shuttles. The easiest way to return to your hotel (if you do not have a car in the Disneyland Resort parking lot) is to take the monorail to the Disneyland Hotel or walk to the Grand Californian Hotel, and then take a cab to your own hotel. While cabs in Anaheim are a little pricey, they are usually available in ample numbers at the Disneyland hotels and at the taxi stand in Downtown Disney. When you consider the alternatives of fighting your way onto a hotel shuttle or trudging back to your hotel on worn-out feet, spending $10–$15 for a cab often sounds pretty reasonable. Rideshare services (such as **Uber** and **Lyft**) are an even cheaper option, costing about half the price of an equivalent taxi ride. The easiest places for rideshare drivers to access are the drop-off points on the west side behind Downtown Disney and off Harbor Boulevard to the east, as well as the driveways outside the main lobbies of the Disneyland Hotel and Grand Californian.

5. The Orange County Transit District provides very efficient bus service to Disneyland with several different long-distance lines. Running about every 30 minutes during the day and evening, service runs 10 a.m.–midnight, depending on the season and your location. Buses drop off and pick up passengers at the east shuttle loop off Harbor Boulevard. From there, guests can walk to the park entrance. Bus fare costs $2, and up to three kids (age 5 and under) can ride free with each fare-paying adult; you can pay in cash (exact change required) or through the free OC Bus mobile app. A bus day pass is available for $5 ($4.50 if prepurchased); 30-day passes are $69 for adults and $22.25 for seniors 60+ and persons with disabilities. For additional information, call ☎ 714-636-7433 or visit octa.net. For public transportation in the immediate area surrounding Disneyland, see our discussion of the Anaheim Resort Transit (ART) system on page 41.

DISNEYLAND PARKING

DISNEYLAND HAS SEVERAL PARKING AREAS. The main parking facility, the Mickey & Friends and Pixar Pals parking garages, can be accessed directly from I-5, Disneyland Drive, or Ball Road. One of the largest parking structures in the world, the garages are connected to Downtown Disney and the theme parks by Disney trams. Noncollapsible strollers are permitted on trams only in the first or last car, where there are extra-large sections for strollers and wheelchairs. If you'd rather hoof it, the walking distance to the park gates is about a mile, cutting south to Downtown Disney; use the pedestrian bridge on the Pixar Pals garage's south side to cross over Magic Way and access the sidewalk past the parking lot. You'll have to pass through Disney's metal detectors and baggage screening on the ground floor of the garage before walking or tramming to the parks.

The secondary parking area is the Toy Story lot south of the corner of Katella Avenue and Harbor Boulevard, a favorite of local pass-holders and our top pick for the most convenient place to park. Toy Story, which is the only lot that accommodates oversize vehicles like buses and RVs, offers shuttles to and from the bus loop east of the Esplanade, or you can walk (about 0.9 mile). A security checkpoint here before boarding the bus allows you to bypass the screening at the Esplanade during the peak morning arrival period, but if entering later in the day, you may get screened after being bussed to the Esplanade. The Toy Story buses can accommodate collapsible strollers, but larger models can be challenging to wrangle on board. If you are coming from I-5 southbound and want to park in the Toy Story Lot, the shortest route is to exit at Katella Avenue and make a left on Clementine Street. However, this entrance is not open to vehicles all the time, unlike the lot's main entrance on Harbor Boulevard. The Pumbaa lot off Disney Way across from the Anaheim GardenWalk is usually used as cast member or special event parking.

Parking fees for these lots are $35 for cars and motorcycles, $40 for RVs and oversize vehicles without trailers, and $45 for buses and tractors with extended trailers. For $55 you can get Preferred Parking, which puts you in the first three rows of each level closest to the elevators and escalators; we'd rather spend the money on churros and use the extra yards to walk off the calories. After parking your car, save yourself a frantic search at the end of your day by taking a digital photo of the lot name and section number.

Guests who drive a Tesla or another electric vehicle will be happy to know that the Mickey & Friends, Pixar Pals, and Toy Story parking structures have dozens of spots where you can recharge your EV while enjoying the resort. Inform the toll booth attendant that you need an EV charging spot, and navigate to the designated section. You'll need to install the ChargePoint app (chargepoint.com) on your smartphone ahead of time to power up, which costs $0.35 per KWh. Tesla owners will need their j1772 adapter to attach the plug.

If you plan on driving to Disneyland, be advised that the Mickey & Friends and Pixar Pals parking structures and Toy Story parking lots officially open only 60 minutes before the standard park opening time, by which time there will already be a line of cars waiting for the tollbooth. Due to this, we recommend arriving at the parking facilities at least an hour (75 minutes during holidays) before park opening. You'll spend a bit of time waiting in your car for the parking structures to open, but it's necessary to get to Disneyland in time for rope drop.

While the trams and buses to the parks operate fairly efficiently in the morning, at closing time they can become completely overwhelmed by exiting guests, as an unfortunate reader from Quincy, Massachusetts, found out:

The worst part of our vacation by far was taking the tram back to the parking garage at the end of the day. It is a complete free-for-all once the tram shows up. We waited through three trams boarding and leaving before we got to the front of the pack, and when the tram came, we still got split up into three different rows as a group of five adults. People were pushing and shoving their way on; it was completely chaotic.

If you find yourself in a similar situation, it's possible to walk back to any of the parking facilities from the park.

The first hour of parking costs $10 at Downtown Disney's Simba lot, located between West Katella Avenue and the Pixar Place Hotel. After that, you can park for free for up to 3 additional hours in the Downtown Disney parking lot with a $20 purchase at any Downtown Disney location, or up to 5 free additional hours with validation from select table-service dining restaurants. Additional half hours cost $7 each up to a $66 daily maximum. There's a free 15-minute grace period for quick drop-offs using the parking area along Downtown Drive south of Magic Way. A section of the Simba lot is also available to guests with disability license plates and placards. From Simba you can walk through Downtown Disney to the parks or alternatively walk to the Downtown Disney monorail stop and take the monorail into Disneyland Park (not Disney California Adventure [DCA]). Valet parking is not offered at Downtown Disney but is available on a space-available basis at the resort hotels ($70 for the first hour plus $10 per additional hour, up to $140 daily for nonguests). If you have money to burn, valet parking at the Grand Californian puts you closest to the parks, but it may not be available during busy times for guests without reservations at the hotel or its facilities. There are no Magic Key or other discounts on parking at the hotels (though you can get 3–5 hours of complimentary parking by patronizing select restaurants or the spa), and overnight parking is not permitted in the theme park or Downtown Disney lots.

TAKING A TRAM OR SHUTTLE BUS FROM YOUR HOTEL

unofficial **TIP**
Warning: Most shuttles don't add vehicles at park-opening or park-closing times. In the mornings, you may not get a seat.

TRAMS AND SHUTTLE BUSES service many of the hotels and motels in the vicinity of Disneyland. Some are without charge, while others are operated by Anaheim Resort Transit (ART) and charge a nominal fee (see page 41). Either way, they represent a fairly carefree means of getting to and from the theme parks, letting you off near the entrances and saving you the cost of parking. The rub is that they might not get you there as early as you desire (a critical point if you take our touring advice) or be available at the time you wish to return to your lodging. Also, while a few hotels have grandfathered-in shuttles driving directly to Disneyland, all newer hotels must use the shared ART buses, which make stops at other motels and hotels in the vicinity. Each shuttle service is a little bit different, so check out the particulars before you book your hotel. If the shuttle provided by your hotel runs regularly throughout the day to and from Disneyland and if you have the flexibility to tour the parks over two or three days, the shuttle provides a wonderful opportunity to tour in the morning and return to your lodging for lunch, a swim, or perhaps a nap; then you can head back to Disneyland refreshed in the early evening for a little more fun.

Be forewarned that most hotel shuttle services do not add more vehicles at the parks' opening or closing times. In the mornings, your biggest problem is that you might not get a seat on the first shuttle. This occurs most frequently if your hotel is the last stop for a shuttle that serves several hotels. Because hotels that share a shuttle service are usually located close together, you can improve your chances of getting a seat by walking to the hotel preceding yours on the pickup route. At closing time, and sometimes following a hard rain, expect a mass exodus from the parks. The worst-case scenario in this event is that more people will be waiting for the shuttle to your hotel than the bus will hold and that some will be left. While most (but not all) hotel shuttles return for stranded guests, you may wait 15 minutes–1 hour. Our suggestion, if you are depending on hotel shuttles, is to exit the park at least 45 minutes before closing. If you stay in a park until closing and lack the energy to deal with the shuttle or hike back to your hotel, go to the Disneyland Hotel and catch a cab or rideshare from there. A cab stand is also behind the monorail station in Downtown Disney, and another is at the Grand Californian Hotel.

The shuttle-loading area is located on the Harbor Boulevard side of Disneyland Park's main entrances. The loading area connects to a pedestrian corridor that leads to the park entrances. Each hotel's shuttle bus has a designated numbered stop where the shuttles load and unload. You'll also find a passenger drop-off loop (parking strictly prohibited) off Harbor; taxis and rideshares may also pick up and drop off here. If you are staying south of the corner of Harbor and Katella, you can walk into the Toy Story parking lot and use its park shuttle for free; just be aware that the bus stop is located at the eastern edge of the parking lot, near the pedestrian gate at Clementine Street and Katella Avenue, which is over a quarter-mile walk from the Harbor Boulevard entrance.

Anaheim Resort Transit

Anaheim Resort Transit (ART) provides shuttle service to the Disneyland Resort, Anaheim GardenWalk, and the convention center. The service operates over a dozen routes, each with its own designated number and color. There are just three to nine well-marked stops on each route, so a complete circuit on any given route usually takes about 20 minutes, but some take up to 1 hour. All of the routes originate and terminate at

Disneyland's bus loop east of the Esplanade near Harbor Boulevard, where each stop sports a digital sign displaying destination and time until next departure. There is also service from Disneyland to Knott's Berry Farm, downtown Anaheim's Packing House district, and Angel Stadium (in case you want to catch an afternoon ballgame).

The colorful buses are wheelchair accessible. They ideally run every 20 minutes but can take up to 30 minutes when it's really busy. Service begins 90 minutes before park opening and ends 30 minutes after park closing (may vary seasonally). If you commute to Disneyland on ART and then head to Downtown Disney after the parks close, you'll have to find your own way home. All shuttle vehicles and respective stops are clearly marked with the route designation. ART's service is usually pretty dependable.

One-way fares are $4 for adults, $1.50 for children. ART also sells one-, three-, and five-day passes for $6 ($2.50 for kids), $16 ($3.50 for kids), and $25 ($5.50 for kids), respectively. Children age 2 years and under ride free with a paying adult, but they must be taken out of strollers to ride. The most convenient way to buy bus passes is through the free smartphone app, which can be found by searching for "A-Way WeGo" on the Apple or Google Play app stores.

Passes cannot be purchased from the driver using cash, but you can tap your contactless credit card or mobile wallet to pay the one-way fare. For more information, call ☎ 888-364-ARTS (2787) or check rideart.org.

PART 2

ACCOMMODATIONS

▌█ WHERE *to* STAY

TRAFFIC AROUND DISNEYLAND, and in the Anaheim–Los Angeles area in general, is so terrible that we advocate staying in accommodations within 2–3 miles of the park. Included in this radius are many expensive hotels, as well as a considerable number of moderately priced establishments and a small number of bargain motels.

READERS' DISNEYLAND RESORT REPORT CARD

EACH YEAR OUR READERS grade their hotel in several categories (see table on page 44). Room quality indicates cleanliness, bed comfort, and room size. Check-in efficiency rates how quickly and accurately the hotel staff get you into your room. Quietness of room considers sound-proofing from neighbors and exterior noise. The pool rating includes the size of the pool, how crowded it gets, and how clean the pool and pool area are. The staff category assesses how friendly and effective the hotel staff are at handling problems and special requests. Our hotel dining rating applies to any on-site counter-service dining, and the overall rating is the summary for every category.

Readers rate Disneyland hotels better than neighboring hotels, continuing a years-long trend. Much of the lodging around Disneyland consists of motels with aging rooms, many in need of refurbishment, content to trade on their proximity to the park rather than the quality of their rooms.

Readers indicate that Disneyland's top two hotels are substantially better than nearby hotels; however, the Anaheim Desert Inn & Suites (the off-site hotel that appears most often on our reader surveys) scores higher than Pixar Place (formerly Paradise Pier) in key categories. In this year's reader report card, Disney's highest grades are in room quality and staff friendliness—two things you'd expect to see, given the premium Disney charges for its lodging.

The Disneyland hotels fare poorly in the dining category, but some context is necessary. Each of the hotels offers decent choices for breakfast, from quick grab-and-go options to table-service meals. And the hotels' short walk to Downtown Disney and surrounding neighborhoods provides plenty of options for good lunches and dinners.

READERS' DISNEYLAND RESORT REPORT CARD							
HOTEL	ROOM QUALITY	CHECK-IN EFFICIENCY	QUIETNESS OF ROOM	POOL	STAFF	HOTEL DINING	OVERALL RATING
Disneyland Hotel	A-	B+	B	B-	A-	C	B
Grand Californian	A-	B	B	B-	A-	C	B
Pixar Place	B+	A-	C+	C	A	D-	B-

WALKING TO DISNEYLAND FROM NEARBY HOTELS

WHILE IT IS TRUE that most Disneyland-area hotels provide shuttle service, or are on the ART routes, it is equally true that an ever-increasing number of guests walk to the parks from their hotels. Shuttles are not always available when needed, and parking in the Disneyland lot has become expensive. A pedestrian walkway from Harbor Boulevard provides safe access to Disneyland for guests on foot. This pedestrian corridor extends from Harbor Boulevard west to the Disneyland Hotel, connecting Disneyland Park, Disney California Adventure, and Downtown Disney.

Close proximity to the theme parks figures prominently in the choice of a hotel. Harbor Boulevard borders Disneyland Resort on the east, and Katella Avenue runs along the resort's southern boundary. The closest non-Disney hotels, and the only ones really within walking distance, are on Harbor Boulevard from just south of I-5 to the north to just south of the intersection with Katella Avenue, and along Katella Avenue near Harbor. The eastern gateway, which leads between the guest drop-off and bus loops off Harbor Boulevard to a security checkpoint at the edge of the Esplanade, is the most popular entry point for pedestrians. It's hard to overemphasize how beneficial it can be to stay at one of the hotels in close proximity to this entryway, as a reader from Pflugerville, Texas, happily reported:

Staying at a hotel across the street from Disneyland was the best decision I made. It was easy to come and go whenever we wanted to.

Farther south on Harbor are some of the best hotels in the area. They are a little far removed for commuting to the parks on foot, but you can walk into the Toy Story parking lot and take a free bus to the parks. Additionally, these hotels are close to the Anaheim Convention Center and tend to cater, though certainly not exclusively, to business travelers.

While the hotels near Disneyland Drive appear close to Disney property on a map, pedestrian access to the parks from the west is a bit more circuitous. If staying along Katella Avenue to the west of the convention center, you can walk north on Disneyland Drive past the Pixar Place Hotel and through the security checkpoint on Downtown Disney's western end, which is usually less crowded than the eastern entrance. A keycard-operated pedestrian gate on the Grand

Californian's Disneyland Drive entrance prevents anyone not registered there from entering, and the neighboring entrance into DCA is
exclusively for guests at the Pixar Place hotel. From West Ball Road,
you can't enter the Mickey & Friends garage from its north side;
instead, you must take a long walk south along Walnut Street or Disneyland Drive to the parking structures' tram stop, which isn't particularly convenient with children in tow.

It's worth noting that we've observed a marked increase in the
homeless population on the streets surrounding the Disneyland Resort
since the pandemic. Although incidents of serious conflicts with visitors
remain rare, when walking to and from your hotel it's wise to remain
aware of your surroundings and stick to the well-lit sidewalks.

For families, a second important consideration is the quality of
the hotel swimming pool. We mention this because, unfortunately,
many of the non-Disney hotels closest to the theme parks have really
crummy pools, sometimes just a tiny rectangle on a stark slab of concrete surrounded on four sides by a parking lot.

Our lodging reviews include the walking time from each hotel to
the theme park entrances. The times provided are averages—a couple
of fit adults might cover the distance in less time, while a family with
small children will likely take longer. The walk times do not include
the wait to pass through security screenings, which can be substantial.
Note that several non-Disney hotels are closer than the Disneyland
Resort hotels, except for the Grand Californian. Also in the reviews,
we rate the swimming areas of the hotels listed on a scale of 1–5 stars,
with 5 being best. As a rule of thumb, any pool with a rating less than
3 stars is not a place where most folks would want to spend much time.

The above discussion might lead you to wonder whether there's
any real advantage to staying in a Disney-owned hotel. The Disney
hotels, of course, are very expensive, but if you can handle the tariff,
here are the primary benefits of staying in one:

1. You are eligible for early entry 30 minutes before official opening every day
   at either Disneyland Park or DCA.
2. Preferred access to dining reservations at select hotel table-service restaurants
   (availability is limited).
3. The Disney hotels (especially the Grand Californian) offer some of the nicest
   rooms of any of the hotels within walking distance.
4. The Disney hotels offer the nicest swimming pools of any of the hotels within
   walking distance.
5. Numerous dining and shopping options are within walking distance, with
   hotel lobby delivery service from select Downtown Disney restaurants.
6. It's easy to retreat to your hotel for a meal, a nap, or a swim.
7. You don't need a car.
8. You can charge purchases at most Disney-owned shops and restaurants to
   your hotel account and have packages delivered to your hotel.
9. You can use the Disneyland mobile app to check in and unlock your room.
10. The "Hey Disney!" digital assistant in the Amazon Alexa devices inside all
    on-site hotel rooms allow you to communicate with Disney characters and
    get information about your vacation.

DISNEYLAND RESORT HOTELS

DISNEY OFFERS THREE ON-SITE HOTELS: Grand Californian Hotel & Spa, Disneyland Hotel, and Pixar Place Hotel. The **Grand Californian Hotel & Spa,** built in the rustic stone-and-timber style of the grand national park lodges, is the flagship property. Newer, more elaborately themed, and closer to the theme parks and Downtown Disney than the other two on-property hotels, the Grand Californian is without a doubt the best place to stay . . . if you can afford it.

The next most convenient is the sprawling **Disneyland Hotel,** the oldest of the three, though repeatedly renovated. Comprising three guest-room towers, the hotel is lushly landscaped with a new vintage Disneyana theme and offers large, luxurious guest rooms. **The Villas at Disneyland Hotel,** an expansion tower of luxurious Disney Vacation Club (DVC) rooms, was added in 2023. Walking time to the monorail station, with transportation to Disneyland Park, is about 3–6 minutes.

The east side of the third Disney hotel overlooks the Paradise Gardens Park and Pixar Pier sections of Disney California Adventure (DCA); it has been known over the decades as the Paradise Pier, Pan Pacific, and Emerald Hotel. In 2024, it was renamed and rethemed once again to **Pixar Place Hotel,** inspired by the CGI film studio's favorite films. Guest rooms here are large. Walking to the monorail station and Downtown Disney takes about 7–10 minutes.

All the on-site hotels offer club-level rooms with luxury amenities, such as nightly turndown service and access to a private club. One reader from Ontario, Canada, didn't feel that it was worth the extra money:

> The club lounge was open 6:30 a.m.–8:30 p.m. each day. The early-morning park hours began at 7 a.m., and one needs to be at the park at least 45 minutes before park opening, so breakfast in the lounge was not possible. The lounge also closed too early in the evening for us to stop and pick up a water or soda on our way back from the parks.

But another visitor from Oakland, California, managed to make good use of the club:

> We stayed at [Pixar Place] club level, and it was SO NICE to have access to the club. We were able to get there when it opened at 6:30 a.m., divide and conquer between coffee and food, and make it to the 7 a.m. park opening. While I doubt I would ever pay rack rate for a club-level room, this perk was greatly appreciated and worthwhile.

Guests at all Disney-owned hotels can use their keys to charge dining and shopping within the resort to their room. Third-party vendors (including most Downtown Disney restaurants) are excluded, and you'll need to show photo ID along with your room key. Ask for a "pool key" when you check out if you want to use the amenities until closing on your departure day. Parking for registered resort guests at any of the Disney-owned hotels is $40 per night for self-parking ($45 for oversize vehicles; free for DVC members) or $70 per night for valet. On the plus side, none of the hotels charge a resort fee, and all provide safes, mini-fridges, coffee makers, and free Wi-Fi (capable of over 100Mbps, fast enough to stream HD video or upload your vacation photos) in rooms and public areas.

Disney's Grand Californian Hotel & Spa
★★★★½

Rate per night $745–$948. **Maximum occupants per room** 5. **Pool** ★★★★★. **Fridge in room** Yes. **Breakfast** Paid. **Wi-Fi** Free. **Parking** $40 self/$70 valet. **Walk to Esplanade** 5 minutes (0.2 mile).

1600 S. Disneyland Dr.
Anaheim
☎ 714-635-2300
disneyland.com

STRENGTHS	WEAKNESSES
• Beautiful Pacific Northwest theming	• Very expensive
• Direct access to DCA and Downtown Disney	• Some rooms are snug.
• Excellent on-site spa and restaurants	• Some rooms have sound issues.

THE GRAND CALIFORNIAN HOTEL is the crown jewel of Disneyland Resort's hotels. With its shingle siding, rock foundations, cavernous hewn-beam lobby, polished hardwood floors, and cozy hearths, the hotel is a stately combination of elements from Western national park lodges. Designed by architect Peter Dominick (who also designed the Wilderness Lodge at Walt Disney World), the Grand Californian is rendered in the Arts and Crafts style of the early 20th century, with such classic features as fly roofs, projecting beams, massive buttresses, and an earth-toned color palette. We strongly encourage visitors with an interest in architecture to take the fascinating (and free) 45-minute Art of the Craft walking tour of the resort, offered several times each week through the Guest Services desk. Most reminiscent of The Majestic Yosemite Hotel (formerly The Ahwahnee) at Yosemite National Park, the Grand Californian combines rugged craftsmanship and grand scale with functional design and intimate spaces. Pull up a vintage rocker in front of a blazing fire, and the bustling lobby instantly becomes a snug cabin.

The hotel's main entrance off Downtown Drive is meant for vehicular traffic. Two pedestrian-only entrances open into Downtown Disney and DCA; this last makes it easy to return to the hotel from DCA for a nap, a swim, or lunch.

The features we like in the 948 guest rooms include excellent light for reading in bed, more than adequate storage space, a two-sink vanity outside the toilet and bath, and, in some rooms, a balcony. All guest rooms have hardwood flooring, bright-toned carpets, white soft goods, orange tree–inspired wall art, and oak furnishings featuring headboards inlaid with Chip 'n' Dale (not Chippendale) designs. Lighting is adequate, USB charging outlets are plentiful, and storage space is abundant. Views from the guest rooms overlook the swimming pool, Downtown Disney, or DCA theme park. Guest rooms are the most expensive at Disneyland Resort. A Houston, Texas, mother of two wrote to tell us:

> The Grand Californian's proximity to the parks is AMAZING! Still, it's not worth the exorbitant cost. I'm glad we did it, but I'd almost be embarrassed to recommend it to someone else because it's so expensive.

Unfortunately, this La Center, Washington, family found themselves assigned to one of the Grand Californian's handful of undersize rooms:

I requested that we have a sixth-floor room; however, they put us in the small-est room on the entire floor (#6416). The bathroom was so tiny that when you opened the shower door it would smack into the toilet, and you had to turn sideways to get in. Please understand, we are not big people. I am 5'2" and even I had difficulties. This room is crammed into the corner of the hotel, so our balcony was only big enough to hold one adult and one child. It had a great view, but that was the only good thing about it. . . . On the positive side, the staff are friendly, and the hotel is beautiful, but those are the only nice things I can recommend about our stay. You can get those two things for free by just walking through the hotel.

The Villas at Disney's Grand Californian, part of Disney's time-share condo enterprise, the Disney Vacation Club, consist of 48 two-bedroom equivalent vil-las and two Grand Villas. *Equivalent* is the term used to describe single units that can be sold (or rented) as studio suites or combined to make two- and three-bedroom villas. All villas (except studio suites) include kitchens, living rooms, and dining areas, as well as washers and dryers. Master bedrooms offer a king bed, while other bedrooms provide two queen beds. Studio suites have a single queen bed. All bedrooms have a flat-panel TV, private bath, and private balcony. Though studio suites don't have full kitchens, they do include a small fridge, a microwave, and a coffee maker. Two-bedroom villas consist of a one-bedroom villa joined to a studio suite. Three-bedroom Grand Villas are two-story affairs with the living area, kitchen, and master bedroom on the lower level and two bedrooms on the upper level. Rooms here are spacious but have not received the same upgrades in recent years as the rest of the resort.

The resort's beautiful High Sierra–themed pool complex, with an expan-sive outdoor bar, features three pools surrounded by handlaid stone, private cabanas that can be rented by the day or half-day, and a 90-foot waterslide that wraps around a redwood stump. The Grand Californian's full-service Tenaya Stone Spa offers massages and salon treatments in a soothing Crafts-man-inspired setting. Services range from manicures and pedicures to a vari-ety of massages; the foot treatments might be especially tempting after a few days tromping around the theme parks. If you spend $125 or more at the spa, you receive 5 hours of complimentary parking. Rounding out the Grand Cali-fornian's amenity mix are two clubby lounges and the well-equipped Eureka Fitness Center, featuring Life Fitness and Cybex equipment. Tenaya Stone Spa and Eureka Fitness Center offer early-morning yoga sessions, power walks, and boot camps, held inside DCA or Disneyland before the park opens to guests. Sessions cost $25–$40 for 45 minutes and are open to registered guests staying at all three on-site Disneyland Resort hotels. Space is limited; visit na.spatime.com/dlr92802 for class times and reservations.

GOOD (AND NOT-SO-GOOD) ROOMS AT GRAND CALIFORNIAN HOTEL
Grand Californian's rooms are large and attractive, but unless you're willing to pay extra, you'll be stuck looking at a parking lot or the backs of buildings. Standard rooms that don't have a great view but are close to the hotel's exclusive entrance into DCA are 2336, 2338–2346, 3334, 3336, and 3338.

Avoid even-numbered rooms X240–X260, as these are next to a loud roller coaster. Also avoid even-numbered rooms 3240–3252, as these are expensive, premium, theme-park-view rooms but don't offer a great view of the park.

For the best views of DCA, we like even-numbered rooms 5424–5448 (which overlook the Grizzly Peak area of the park) or the ultra-expensive concierge-level rooms, which are even-numbered rooms 6402–6412. Odd-numbered rooms 4419–4447 and 5419–5447 are the expensive Downtown Disney or deluxe view room types, but these offer views of Disneyland's fireworks show.

Disneyland Hotel ★★★★ (★★★★½ for Villas)

Rate per night $579–$660. **Maximum occupants per room** 5. **Pool** ★★★★½. **Fridge in room** Yes. **Breakfast** Paid. **Wi-Fi** Free. **Parking** $40 self/$70 valet. **Walk to Esplanade** 9 minutes (0.5 mile).

1150 W. Magic Way
Anaheim
☎ 714-778-6600
disneyland.com

STRENGTHS	WEAKNESSES
• Nostalgic retro theming	• Expensive
• Access to Disneyland via monorail	• Connecting rooms are poorly soundproofed.
• Best on-site recreation and dining for families	• Longer walk to DCA than from off-site hotels

WALT DISNEY BARELY managed to finance the construction of Disneyland Park. He certainly didn't have the funds to purchase adjacent property or build hotels, though on-site hotels were central to his overall concept. So he cut a deal with petroleum engineer and TV producer Jack Wrather to build and operate Disneyland Hotel. The deal not only gave Wrather the rights to Disneyland Hotel but also allowed him to build other Disneyland Hotels within the state of California until 2054. It always irked Walt that he didn't own the hotel that bore his name, but Wrather steadfastly refused to renegotiate the rights. After Jack Wrather died in 1984, the Walt Disney Company bought the entire Wrather Corporation, which among other things held the rights to the *Lone Ranger* and *Lassie* TV series and, improbably, the RMS *Queen Mary,* docked at Long Beach. By acquiring the whole corporation, the Walt Disney Company brought Disneyland Hotel under Disney ownership in 1988.

Disneyland Hotel consists of three towers facing each other across a verdant landscaped plaza, as well as a swimming complex, restaurants, and shops. Guest registration for all three towers is situated in the Fantasy Tower (previously called the Magic Tower, and the Marina Tower before that), which is connected to the Disneyland Convention Center and Disneyland Hotel's self-parking garage. Though all three towers share restaurants, shopping, and recreational amenities, the Fantasy Tower is most conveniently located. It and the Adventure Tower (formerly Dreams, née Sierra) are closest to Downtown Disney and the theme parks. The Frontier Tower (formerly Wonder, formerly Bonita) is the farthest from the action.

The Villas at Disneyland Hotel opened in late 2023 on a 2-acre plot between the Disneyland Hotel's Frontier Tower and Walnut Street. The 12-story, 280,000-square-foot, L-shaped Discovery Tower features over 340 Disney Vacation Club (DVC) time-share units, including 38 two-person studios (similar to the small rooms at Walt Disney World's Riviera Resort), 271 larger studios, 20 two-bedroom suites, 19 one-bedroom suites, and two multilevel Grand Villas that sleep 12 and come outfitted with full-size kitchens and indoor-outdoor fireplaces. All rooms feature colorful modernist furniture with artwork referencing animated classics like *The Jungle Book, Princess and the Frog,* and *Fantasia.* The expansion also features the paint-themed Palette Pool with an interactive *Steamboat Willie*–themed splash pad that changes from monochrome to color under nighttime lighting. The modernist aesthetic was subtly inspired by the hand-drawn animation process; multicolored panels stretch up one end of the building, while a crackled cream pattern decorates the other side, with balconies on either end and a wall of glass in between. Rooms in this new DVC property are currently available for rental by the general public or for sale to DVC members.

Disneyland Hotel embraces the retro-nostalgia of baby boomer Disneyland devotees with decorative elements evoking the park's early years; look for 1950s-style signage outside each tower and a tribute to Frontierland's long-gone Old Unfaithful geysers. The main lobby evokes Mary Blair's It's a Small World designs and features an enlarged fun map of the original park. The check-in area sports early attraction concept artwork and seating styled after the spinning teacups, whimsical touches that stand in stark contrast with the ultramodern sculpted steel behind the front desk. Peek inside the Frontier Tower lobby to see an amazingly detailed model of Big Thunder Mountain. Large windows, specially designed to filter outside noise, give the facade a glistening sky-blue tint. Free hour-long guided walking tours of Disneyland Hotel are available weekly by reservation, departing from Guest Services in the Fantasy Tower's lobby. A family from Fort Collins, Colorado, wrote us in praise of the hotel's theme:

> We loved the ambience of the Disneyland Hotel. I was impressed with how the piped-in music changed from tropical around Adventure tower and Tangaroa Terrace to the Davy Crockett theme as you approached the Frontier tower.

This reader from Shelby Charter Township, Michigan, praised the hotel's staff but had a more cynical take on the decor:

> My wife loves it because it is themed to classic Disneyland and Walt, but I feel the theming is lazy: mice shapes and nostalgia prints on a plain straight-out-of-the-70s hotel building. Also, everyone always says, "Well, it's the original!" No, the original was torn down and replaced with a boring trio of business towers and a convention center.

The standard rooms sport exploding fireworks in the royal blue carpeting. Each room has one king or two queen platform beds with voluminous storage space underneath, along with a pullout couch; one-bedroom suites with a wet bar and living room are also available. Features include a headboard with a carving of Sleeping Beauty Castle; fiber optics in the headboard create a skyline with fireworks (accompanied by a tinny rendition of "When You Wish Upon a Star") at the flick of a switch. There are USB ports at each nightstand, but standard electrical outlets are difficult to access. Other decorative touches include black-and-white photography depicting the history of Disneyland and hidden Mickey designs in the shower tile, though the overall feel is more business modern than Disney whimsy. Each room has a flat-panel HDTV, perfect for connecting a laptop or video game console. Other room amenities include mini-fridges, Keurig coffee makers, safes large enough for laptops, and wireless internet connections.

The bathrooms are small for an upscale hotel, but a sink and vanity are outside the bathrooms. As in most family hotels built in the 1950s and '60s, a connecting door, situated by the closet and the aforementioned single sink, leads to an adjoining room. Soundproofing around the connecting doors is nonexistent, so be prepared to revel in the sounds of your neighbors brushing their teeth, coping with indigestion, and arguing over what to wear. Fortunately, these sounds don't carry into the sleeping area.

A mother of four from Denver, Colorado, wrote us in defense of the rooms' oft-maligned pull-out beds:

> Our family of six stayed in a two-bedroom suite in the Disneyland Hotel. The bedroom has two queen beds, and there is a queen sleeper sofa in the sitting room. My husband and I wanted to be able to put the kids to bed and then be able to review plans for the next day, but we were nervous about taking the sleeper sofa for ourselves. Not to worry! It must be Disney Magic. That sleeper sofa offered better support and was much more comfortable than most regular hotel mattresses. Parents should not be afraid to book this room out of anxiety over the sleeper sofa.

Over in the Villas, the tight-but-efficient Duo Studio rooms feature pull-down queen beds that are easy to convert and comfortable. Bathrooms feature illuminated mirrors and ample counter space; larger Villa studios and suites have split setups with separate toilet and shower areas. All Villa rooms have great functionality, with all the standard amenities, plus additional USB-C charging ports. Select rooms have gigantic balconies with nearly as much floor space as the Duo Studios themselves. We like these villas even better than the somewhat dated rooms in the Grand Californian's DVC wing.

If the Villas aren't pixie-dusted (or pricey) enough for you, five different elaborately themed Signature Suites allow big spenders to sleep in a pirate's lair, the Big Thunder mine, or Mickey's penthouse. Rates and availability for Disneyland Hotel Signature Suites can now be searched online at disneyland .disney.go.com/hotels/disneyland-hotel/rates-rooms.

The main swimming complex's centerpiece is a pair of waterslides (187 feet and 112 feet long, respectively) themed to resemble vintage monorail trains, topped by the classic Disneyland block letter logo. There's also a 19-foot kiddie slide and bubble jets for the little ones. Family films are screened here in the evenings, and guests of the other on-site hotels may attend. A 4-foot-deep pool separates the 4,800-square-foot E-Ticket Pool and the waterslides, with a footbridge allowing easy passage from one side of the water to the other. On sunny days, expect long, inefficient lines for the slides, as well as a severe shortage of lounge chairs and elbow room.

Tangaroa Terrace and Trader Sam's, a casual restaurant and bar, bank on fond memories of Adventureland's 1960s-era *Tahitian Terrace* dinner show. Disneyland Hotel's other restaurant is Goofy's Kitchen, the hotel's character-meal headquarters. The former Steakhouse 55 in the Disneyland Hotel has been converted into a seasonal bar called The Lounge at Disneyland Hotel, which serves upscale cocktails and small bites amid Eyvind Earle-esque enchanted-forest murals. The Villas at Disneyland Hotel has its own Palm Breeze pool bar serving cocktails and Southwestern fare. (All Disneyland Hotel restaurants are profiled in full in Part Eight.)

As concerns practical matters, parking is a royal pain at the Disneyland Hotel. The self-parking garage is convenient only to the Fantasy Tower, and even there you'll probably have a long walk. To reach the other two towers, you must pass through the Fantasy Tower and navigate across the hotel's inner plaza and pool area. The Frontier Tower on the southern end of the property has a small parking lot to the rear, accessible via Downtown Drive and Paradise Way. Unfortunately, many of the already limited spaces are reserved for the adjacent DVC time-share sales office. Even so, if you're staying at the Frontier Tower, it's your best bet. If there's no room in the Frontier lot, you're better off parking in the Pixar Place Hotel's lot than in the Disneyland Hotel parking garage. The only valet parking is at the Fantasy Tower, so even if you valet park, you'll still have to hoof it to the other towers.

While the monorail station in Downtown Disney is convenient when the train is operational, you can't always count on it for transportation into Disneyland Park, as this Buffalo, New York, woman discovered:

I found it annoying that the monorail closed with the rest of the park (or before!) and could not be used for transportation back to the hotel in the evening. It also shuts down if it's too hot in the afternoon because there is no AC.

GOOD (AND NOT-SO-GOOD) ROOMS AT DISNEYLAND HOTEL There are three guest-room buildings at Disneyland Hotel: Fantasy, Adventure, and Frontier Towers. Each tower has three room view types: standard (of trees or parking lots), deluxe (of the resort's pool complex), and premium (facing Disneyland Park and Downtown Disney, or the pool). The best views can be had from the east-west-facing Adventure Tower, which overlooks the hotel's inner plaza and pool area on the west and Downtown Disney and the theme parks to the east. The most lackluster views are the north-facing vistas of the Fantasy Tower.

The Fantasy Tower's north side looks out onto several massive parking lots, but you can catch a glimpse of Disneyland Park if you crane your neck to the right. Rooms facing south in Fantasy Tower look out onto the pool and are categorized as deluxe view rooms. If you opt for standard view and want a slightly better view of Disneyland, go for odd-numbered rooms XX25–XX35 on floors 7–11. If you want to avoid views of parking lots but don't want to drop the extra cash on a room upgrade, even-numbered rooms XX00–XX34 on floors 2–3 on the tower's south side are categorized as standard.

Adventure Tower faces Disneyland and Downtown Disney on the east and the pool complex on the west. On Adventure Tower's east side, standard view rooms (odd-numbered rooms XX37–XX67 on floors 2–6) are better than the equivalently priced rooms in the other towers—instead of parking lots you'll mostly see trees. Almost all of the other rooms in Adventure are categorized as deluxe or premium and carry a hefty price tag. If you're willing to pay the extra money, go for odd-numbered rooms XX37–XX51 on floors 7–10 for the best views of Disneyland.

Rooms on Frontier Tower's north side face the hotel's pool, and most above the fourth floor are categorized as deluxe or premium views. Avoid any standard rooms facing south (odd-numbered rooms XX69–XX99, floors 2–14) in Frontier, as these are the worst views of any of the Disneyland Hotel's rooms.

Disney's Pixar Place Hotel ★★★★

Rate per night $446–$546. **Maximum occupants per room** 5. **Pool** ★★★½. **Fridge in room** Yes. **Breakfast** No. **Wi-Fi** Free. **Parking** $40 self/$70 valet. **Walk to Esplanade** 12 minutes (0.6 mile).

1717 S. Disneyland Dr. Anaheim
☎ 714-999-0990
disneyland.com

STRENGTHS	WEAKNESSES
• Cheapest on-site hotel (but still pricey)	• Minimal theming compared to other Disney hotels
• Exclusive entrance to DCA	• Limited on-site dining
• Larger-than-average guest rooms	• Longer walk to Disneyland than from off-site hotels

DISNEY ACQUIRED THE INDEPENDENT Pan Pacific Hotel just south of the Disneyland Hotel in 1995 and changed its name to the Disneyland Pacific Hotel. Just before DCA opened in 2001, the hotel was rechristened as the Paradise Pier Hotel in recognition of the Paradise Pier district (now known as Pixar Pier and Paradise Gardens Park) of DCA the hotel overlooks. In 2024, Disney completed yet another renaming and retheming, this time featuring favorite Pixar characters.

The 481-room property now known as Pixar Place sports eye-catching stripes of bold primary colors on its stark white exterior and original artwork celebrating the studio's stories throughout its common areas and guest rooms. The sunny lobby sports a stunning glass-enclosed exterior elevator with confounding high-tech touch screen controls; if it induces vertigo, interior elevators are available, but all are frustratingly slow and require inputting your floor before boarding. A statue of Luxo Jr. (the lamp from Pixar's logo) balanced atop its iconic tricolored ball also adorns the lobby, across from the equally vibrant STOR-E sundry shop.

The modernist rooms feature Luxo Jr. table lamps and carpet patterns, Pixar logo ball bolsters and duvets, and Pixar character murals above the headboards. Some room configurations offer a king-size bed and a sofa with pull-out queen bed; others have two queen beds and a twin-size sofa. Lighting has been dramatically improved with adjustable dimmer switches, and each side of the firm bed has power outlets, USB-C, and USB-A plugs to charge your devices. A desk with a comfortable chair provides ample space to work, and the closet has plenty of storage space. Bathrooms are also highly functional with excellent illumination, a walk-in shower, and lots of counter space.

Pixar Place's limited dining options are led by the Great Maple restaurant, a local chain specializing in upscale fried chicken and waffles. The lobby's Sketch Pad Cafe supplies coffee and pastries to go, and Small Bytes on the pool deck serves specialty sodas and snacks. Amenities include a fitness center, conference rooms, a kids' game room, and an often breezy rooftop pool complex complete with fire pits and shuffleboard courts, a *Finding Nemo*–themed splash pad, and a 186-foot-long waterslide (the view from the top of the slide is killer). Self-parking in Pixar Place's on-site garage is fast and convenient, and an Alamo rental car agency is located on the property. Bing Bong from *Inside Out* greets guests on the pool deck, and Joe from *Soul* plays piano near the ground-floor staircase.

Somewhat isolated on the Disneyland Resort property, the hotel is a 12-minute hike to the theme park entrances, farther away than most non-Disney hotels lining Harbor Boulevard on the east side of the resort. However, Pixar Place guests can cut through the Grand Californian Hotel to reach the Esplanade, and a direct private entrance into DCA is available directly across the street from the hotel lobby; it opens in time for early entry, and it leads to Paradise Gardens Park near the Corn Dog Castle.

Pixar Place's greatest assets—aside from the perks that come with staying on-site—are its roomy guest rooms, which offer more space to stretch out than the standard rooms at its sister properties. Many guests overlook Pixar Place, but this Superior, Colorado, family had a positive experience:

> It was great with one exception: the tiny pool (especially compared to the other two Disney hotels). Staff was awesome, and the room was nice. We would definitely stay again.

However, this reader from Kirkland, Washington, felt exactly the opposite:

> The quality of the hotel for the cost is NOT worth it . . . PP had terrible beds, terrible walls, and was an incredibly long walk to the park. No thank you.

GOOD (AND NOT-SO-GOOD) ROOMS AT PIXAR PLACE HOTEL There are two guest-room buildings at Pixar Place Hotel. Rooms facing east have excellent views of the Pixar Pier area of DCA. Rooms facing west look out onto parking lots and a nearby residential neighborhood. There are two room-view categories at Pixar Place, standard and premium. All rooms facing west are tagged as standard, while all rooms facing east on the sixth floor and above are premium. Request rooms 300–318 and 326–345 if you want to be on the same floor as the pool. If you want to catch a small glimpse of DCA but don't want to pay the extra cost for a premium room, even-numbered rooms 502–518 are standard view rooms facing the park. Even-numbered rooms 1200–1218, 1300–1318, 1400–1418, 1500, and 1510 are premium rooms that offer the best views of DCA. Rooms with views of the park can occasionally be a curse for light sleepers, as this Edmonton, Alberta, family found out:

> Our room had a view of Pixar Pier, which was beautiful at night. It was less wonderful when Disney tested out a new show at full volume late at night and early on our one sleep-in morning.

HOW TO GET DISCOUNTS ON LODGING AT DISNEYLAND RESORT HOTELS

unofficial **TIP**
For the best rates and least-crowded conditions, try to avoid visiting Disneyland Resort when a major convention or trade show is in progress.

SO MANY GUEST ROOMS are in and around Disneyland Resort that competition is brisk, and everyone, including Disney, wheels and deals to keep them filled. Here are tips for getting price breaks:

1. DISNEYLAND RESORT WEBSITE Disney has become more aggressive about offering deals on its website. Go to disneyland.com and check the page for "Special Offers." When booking rooms on Disney's or any other site, be sure to click on "Terms and Conditions" and read the fine print *before* making reservations.

DISNEY LODGING FOR LESS

The people at mousesavers.com (see page 59) know more about Disney hotel packages than anyone on the planet. Here are their money-saving suggestions.

• **BOOK ROOM-ONLY.** It's frequently a better deal to book a room-only reservation instead of buying a vacation package. When you buy a package, you're typically paying a premium for convenience. You can often save money by putting together your own package—just book room-only at a resort and buy passes, meals, and extras separately.

Disney prices its standard packages at the same rates as if you had purchased individual components separately, plus a few dollars a day extra. However, what Disney doesn't tell you is that components can usually be purchased separately at a discount. (Sometimes you can get special-offer packages that have exclusive discounts; see below.)

Disney's packages often include extras you are unlikely to use. Also, packages require a $200 deposit and full payment 30 days in advance and have stringent change and cancellation policies. Generally, booking room-only requires a deposit of one night's room rate with the remainder due at check-in. Your reservation can be changed or canceled for any reason until five days before check-in.

Whether you decide to book a Disney vacation package or create your own, there are a number of ways to save:

• **BE FLEXIBLE.** Buying a room or package with a discount is a little like shopping for clothes at a discount store: if you wear size XX-small or XXX-large, or you like green when everyone else is wearing pink, you're a lot more likely to score a bargain. Likewise, resort discounts are available only when Disney has excess rooms. You're more likely to get a discount during less-popular times and at larger or less-popular resorts.

• **BE PERSISTENT.** This is the most important tip. Disney allots a certain number of rooms to each discount. Once the discounted rooms are gone, you won't get that rate unless someone cancels. Fortunately, people change and cancel reservations all the time. If you can't get your preferred dates or hotel with one discount, try another one (if available) or keep calling back first thing in the morning to check for cancellations; the system resets overnight, and any reservations with unpaid deposits are automatically released for resale.

2. SEASONAL SAVINGS You can save $15 to more than $200 per night on a Disneyland Resort hotel room by visiting during the slower times of the year. Disney uses so many adjectives (regular, holiday, peak, value, and such) to describe its seasonal calendar, however, that it's hard to keep up without a scorecard. To confuse matters more, the dates for each season vary from hotel to hotel. Understand that Disney seasonal dates are not sequential like spring, summer, fall, and winter. For any specific resort, there are sometimes several seasonal changes in a month. This is important because your room rate per night is determined by the season prevailing when you check in. Let's say that you checked in to the Disneyland Hotel on April 20 for a five-night stay. April 20 is in the more expensive holiday season that ends April 21, followed by the less-pricey regular season beginning April 23. Because you arrived during a holiday season, the holiday season rate will be applied for your entire stay, even though almost half of your stay will be in regular season. Your strategy, therefore, is to shift your dates (if possible) to arrive during a less expensive season.

3. ASK ABOUT SPECIALS When you talk to Disney reservationists, inquire specifically about special deals. Ask, for example, "What special rates or discounts are available at Disney hotels during the time of our visit?" Being specific and assertive paid off for an Illinois reader:

> *I called Disney's reservations number and asked for availability and rates. [Because] of The Unofficial Guide warning about Disney reservationists answering only the questions posed, I specifically asked, "Are there any special rates or discounts for that room during the month of October?" She replied, "Yes, we have that room available at a special price." [For] the price of one phone call, I saved $440.*

Along similar lines, a Warren Township, New Jersey, dad chimed in with this:

> *Your tip about asking Disney employees about discounts was invaluable. They will not volunteer this information, but, by asking, we saved almost $500 on our hotel room.*

4. LEARN ABOUT DEALS OFFERED TO SPECIFIC MARKETS The folks at mousesavers.com keep an updated list of discounts for use at Disney resorts. The discounts are separated into categories such as "for anyone," "for residents of certain states," "for Magic Key passholders," and so on. For example, the site once listed a deal targeted to residents of the San Diego area published in an ad in a San Diego newspaper. Dozens of discounts are usually listed on the site, covering almost all Disneyland Resort hotels. Usually anyone calling the Disneyland Resort Reservations Office (call ☎ 714-956-6425 and press 1 on the menu) can cite the referenced ad and get the discounted rate.

Disney also targets potential customers with PIN codes (officially known as "Unique Offer Codes" or UOCs) in emails and direct mailings. PIN-code discounts are offered to specific individuals and are correlated with that person's name and address. PIN-code offers are nontransferable. When you try to make a reservation using the code, Disney will verify that the street or email address to which the PIN code was sent is yours.

To enhance your chances of receiving a PIN-code offer, you need to get your name and street or email address into the Disney system. One way is to call the Disneyland Resort Travel Sales Center at ☎ 714-520-5060 and request that info be sent to you. If you've been to Disneyland previously, your name and address will already be on record, but you won't be as likely to receive a PIN-code offer as you would by calling and requesting to be sent information. The latter is regarded as new business. Or, expressed differently, if Disney smells blood, they're more likely to come after you.

Mousesavers.com also features a great links page with short descriptions and URLs of the best Disney-related websites and a current-year seasonal rates calendar.

5. MAGIC KEY PASSHOLDER DISCOUNTS Magic Key passholders are eligible for discounts on dining, shopping, and lodging. If you visit Disneyland Resort once a year or more, or if you plan on a visit of five or more days, you might save money overall by purchasing a Magic Key pass. We've seen resort discounts as deep as 30% offered to passholders. It doesn't take long to recoup the extra bucks you spent on a Magic Key pass when you're saving that kind of money on lodging. Discounts in the 10%–15% range are more the norm.

6. TRAVEL AGENTS Travel agents are active players in the market and are particularly good sources of information on time-limited special programs and discounts. In our opinion, a good travel agent is the best friend a traveler can have. And though we at The Unofficial Guides know a thing or two about the travel industry, we always give our agent a chance to beat any deal we find. If our agent can't beat the deal, we let her book it if she can receive commission from it. In other words, we create a relationship that gives her plenty of incentive to really roll up her sleeves and work on our behalf.

As you might expect, some travel agents and agencies specialize, sometimes exclusively, in selling Disneyland and Walt Disney World. These agents have spent an incredible amount of time at both resorts and have completed extensive Disney education programs. They are usually the most Disney-knowledgeable agents in the travel industry. Most of these specialists and their agencies display the Earmarked logo indicating that they are Authorized Disney Vacation Planners. These Disney specialists are so good that we use them ourselves. They save us time and money, sometimes lots of both. The best of the best include **Sue Pisaturo,** whom we've used many times and who is a contributor to this guide (sue@smallworldvacations.com, smallworldvacations.com); **Magical Vacations Travel** (magicalvacationstravel.com); **Mouse Fan Travel** (mousefantravel.com); **The Magic for Less** (themagicforless.com); and **TouringAndCruises.com** (formerly TouringPlans Travel).

7. ROOM UPGRADES Sometimes a room upgrade is as good as a discount. If you're visiting Disneyland Resort during a slower time, book the least expensive room your discounts will allow. Checking in, ask very politely about being upgraded to a pool view room. A fair percentage of the time, you will get one at no additional charge.

▌NON-DISNEY HOTELS

MANY OF THE HOTELS AND MOTELS near Disneyland were built in the early 1960s, and they are small and sometimes unattractive by today's standards. Quite a few motels adopted adventure or fantasy themes in emulation of Disneyland. As you might imagine, these themes from five decades ago seem hokey and irrelevant today. Although several upscale lodging options are available off-site, there are also still a number of seedy hotels near Disneyland, and even some of the chain properties fail to live up to their national standards.

If you consider a non-Disney-owned hotel in Anaheim, check its quality as reported by a reliable independent rating system such as those offered by The Unofficial Guides, AAA Directories, Forbes Guides, or Frommer's guides. Also, before you book, ask how old the hotel is and when the guest rooms were last refurbished. Be aware that almost any hotel can be made to look good on a website, so don't depend on websites alone. Locate the hotel on our street map (see page 66) to verify its proximity to Disneyland. If you will not have a car, make sure that the hotel has a shuttle service that will satisfy your needs.

GOOD NEIGHBOR HOTELS

A GOOD NEIGHBOR HOTEL is a hotel that has paid Disney a marketing fee to display that designation. Usually a ticket shop in the lobby will sell full-price Disney tickets. Other than that, the Good Neighbor designation means little to nothing for the consumer. It does not guarantee quality or proximity to Disneyland. Unlike at Walt Disney World, Disneyland does not require Good Neighbor hotels to provide free shuttle service to the park, though many do. You can book Good Neighbor hotels in a package with park tickets through the Walt Disney Travel Co.; prices are the same as if booked à la carte, though they toss in a card for 10% discounts at select Downtown Disney locations and a free collectible pin lanyard. (Travel package collectible lanyards can be picked up inside Disneyland at 20th Century Music on Main Street or Little Green Men Store Command in Tomorrowland; in Disney California Adventure Park at Julius Katz & Sons on Buena Vista Street; or in Downtown Disney at World of Disney or Disney's Pin Traders near the monorail station.) In our opinion, you shouldn't let the presence or absence of the Good Neighbor designation influence your hotel choice.

GETTING A GOOD DEAL AT NON-DISNEY HOTELS

FOLLOWING ARE SOME TIPS and strategies for getting a good deal on a hotel room near Disneyland. Though the following list may seem a bit intimidating and may refer to players in the travel market that are unfamiliar to you, acquainting yourself with the strategies will serve you well in the long run. Simply put, the tips we provide for getting a good deal near Disneyland will work equally well at just about any other place where you need a hotel. Once you have invested a little time and have experimented with these strategies, you will be able to routinely obtain rooms at the best hotels and at the lowest possible rates.

Remember that Disneyland Resort is right across the street from the Anaheim Convention Center, one of the largest and busiest convention centers in the country. Room availability and rates are affected significantly by trade shows and other events at the convention center. To determine whether such an event will be going on during your projected dates, visit anaheim.net/calendar.aspx?CID=26 to view the convention calendar.

1. MOUSESAVERS.COM is a site dedicated to finding great deals on hotels, admissions, and more at Disneyland Resort and Walt Disney World. The site covers discounts on both Disney and non-Disney hotels and is especially effective at keeping track of time-limited deals and discounts offered in a select market—San Diego, for example. However, the site does not sell travel products.

2. KAYAK.COM is a travel search engine that searches the better hotel-discount sites, as well as chain and individual hotel websites. Kayak used to be purely a search engine but now sells travel products, raising the issue of whether products not sold by Kayak are equally likely to come up in a search.

3. EXPEDIA.COM, PRICELINE.COM, AND TRAVELOCITY.COM sometimes offer good discounts on area hotels. We find that Expedia offers the best deals if you're booking within two weeks of your visit. In fact, some of Expedia's last-minute deals are amazing, really rock-bottom rates. Travelocity frequently beats Expedia, however, if you reserve two weeks to three months out. Another good website to check is Priceline's Express Deals; see tinyurl.com/ugpricelinetips for the latest on these deals. None of these sites offer anything to get excited about if you book more than three months from the time of your visit. If you use one of these sites, be sure to take into consideration the demand for rooms during the season of your visit, and check to see if any big conventions or trade shows are scheduled for the convention center.

4. SPECIAL WEEKEND RATES If you are not averse to about an hour's drive to Disneyland, you can get a great weekend rate on rooms in downtown Los Angeles. Most hotels that cater to business, government, and convention travelers offer special weekend discounts that range 15%–40% below normal weekday rates. You can find out about weekend specials by calling the hotel or by consulting your travel agent.

5. WHOLESALERS, CONSOLIDATORS, AND RESERVATION SERVICES Wholesalers and consolidators buy rooms, or options on rooms (room blocks), from hotels at a low negotiated rate. They then resell the rooms at a profit through travel agents, tour packagers, or directly to the public. Most wholesalers and consolidators have a provision for returning unsold rooms to participating hotels, but they are disinclined to do so. The wholesaler's or consolidator's relationship with any hotel is predicated on volume. If they return rooms unsold, the hotel might not make as many rooms available to them the next time around. Thus, wholesalers and consolidators often offer rooms at bargain rates, anywhere from 15%–50% off rack, occasionally sacrificing their profit margin to avoid returning the rooms to the hotel unsold.

When wholesalers and consolidators deal directly with the public, they frequently represent themselves as reservation services. When you call, you can ask for a rate quote for a particular hotel or, alternatively, ask for their best available deal in the area where you prefer to stay. If there is a maximum amount you are willing to pay, say so. Chances are that the service will find something that will work for you, even if they have to shave a dollar or two off their own profit. Sometimes you will have to prepay for your room with your credit card when you make your reservation. Most often, you will pay when you check out. Listed below are some services that frequently offer substantial discounts in the Anaheim area.

ANAHEIM AREA WHOLESALERS AND CONSOLIDATORS

HOTEL RENTAL GROUP ☎ 800-780-5733   hotelrentalgroup.com

HOTELS.COM ☎ 800-246-8357   hotels.com

HOTEL TONIGHT hoteltonight.com (for last-minute deals)

6. CLUBS AND ORGANIZATIONS If you belong to AAA, AARP, or a number of other organizations, you can obtain lodging discounts. Usually the discounts are modest, 5%–15%, but occasionally higher.

7. IF YOU MAKE YOUR OWN RESERVATION As you poke around trying to find a good deal, there are several things you should know. First, always call the hotel in question as opposed to the hotel chain's national toll-free number. Quite often, the reservationists at the national numbers are unaware of local specials. Always ask about specials before you inquire about corporate rates. Do not be reluctant to bargain. If you are buying a hotel's weekend package, for example, and want to extend your stay into the following week, you can often obtain at least the corporate rate for the extra days. Do your bargaining before you check in, however, preferably when you make your reservations. Work far enough in advance to receive a confirmation.

▮▮ TRAVEL PACKAGES

PACKAGE TOURS THAT INCLUDE LODGING, park admission, and other features are routinely available. Some packages are very good deals if you make use of the features you are paying for.

HOW TO EVALUATE
A DISNEYLAND TRAVEL PACKAGE

HUNDREDS OF DISNEYLAND package vacations are offered to the public each year. Some are created by the Disneyland Resort Travel Sales Center, others by airline touring companies, and some by independent travel agents and wholesalers. Almost all Disneyland packages include lodging at or near Disneyland and theme park admission. Packages offered by the airlines include air transportation.

Package prices vary seasonally, with school break and holiday periods being the most expensive. During the off-season, forget packages;

there are plenty of empty rooms, and you can negotiate great discounts (at non-Disney properties) yourself. Similarly, airfares and rental cars are cheaper at off-peak times.

When considering a package, choose one that includes features that you are sure to use. Whether you use all the features or not, you will most certainly pay for them. If cost is of greater concern than convenience, make a few phone calls and see what the package would cost if you booked its individual components (such as airfare, rental car, and lodging) on your own. If the package price is less than the à la carte cost, the package is a good deal. If the costs are about the same, the package is probably worth it for the convenience.

If you buy a package from Disney, do not expect Disney reservationists to offer suggestions or help you sort out your options. As a rule they will not volunteer information but will only respond to specific questions you pose, adroitly ducking any query that calls for an opinion. A reader from North Riverside, Illinois, wrote to *The Unofficial Guide,* complaining:

> *I have received various pieces of literature from Disney, and it is very confusing to try and figure everything out. My wife made two phone calls, and the [Disney] representatives were very courteous. However, they answered only the questions posed and were not very eager to give advice on what might be most cost-effective. The reps would not say if we would be better off doing one thing over the other. I feel that a person could spend 8 hours on the phone with [Disney] reps and not have any more input than you get from reading the literature.*

If you cannot get the information you need from the Disney people, try a good travel agent. Chances are that the agent will be more forthcoming in helping you sort out your options.

Information Needed for Evaluation

For quick reference, visit disneyplanning.com to view vacation package offers for all of Disney's travel destinations. In addition, you can call the Disneyland Resort Travel Sales Center at ☎ 714-520-5060 and ask for a rate sheet listing admission options and prices for the theme parks. With this in hand, you are ready to evaluate any package that appeals to you. Remember that all packages are quoted on a per-person basis, two to a room (double occupancy). Good luck.

VISITING OTHER LOS ANGELES-AREA ATTRACTIONS

If your travel plans include a stay in the area of more than two or three days, lodge near Disneyland Resort only just before and on the days you visit the parks. The same traffic you avoid by staying close to the park will eat you alive when you begin branching out to other Los Angeles–area attractions. Also, the area immediately around Disneyland is uninspiring, and there is a marked scarcity of decent restaurants. (See page 369 at the end of Part 9 for recommendations on Disney-adjacent attractions around Southern California.)

VACATION HOMES

SOME OF THE BEST LODGING DEALS in the Disneyland Resort area are vacation homes. Prices range from about $195 a night for two-bedroom condos and town homes to $200–$600 a night for three- to five-bedroom vacation homes.

Let's compare renting a vacation home with staying at a three-star hotel near Disneyland. A family of two parents, two teens, and two grandparents would need three hotel rooms at the Fairfield Inn Anaheim Resort. At the lowest rate obtainable, they'd be spending about $200 per night per room, or more than $600 total per night with tax and parking. Rooms are 228 square feet each, so they'd have a total of 684 square feet. Each room has a private bath, TV, and mini-fridge. The hotel has a pool and hot tub, but parking costs extra.

At the same time of year, they can rent a 1,400-square-foot, three-bedroom, two-bath vacation home with a private pool within easy walking distance of Disneyland for about $300 per night—a savings of about $300 per night over Fairfield Inn (a total savings of around $1,500 on a five-night stay). But that's not all: the home comes with a washer and dryer; an outdoor hot tub; a grill; an air hockey table; a family room with a 52-inch TV and surround sound; a dining room with seating for eight; and off-street parking. The only trade-off for our hypothetical family would be having two bathrooms instead of three.

You can find homes similar to the one described above at **Vacation Rental by Owner** (vrbo.com) and **Airbnb** (airbnb.com), listing services for owners of vacation properties worldwide. Both websites offer detailed information, including a good number of photos of each specific home. When you book, the home you've been looking at is the actual one you're reserving. On the other hand, some vacation-home rental companies, like rental car agencies, don't assign you a specific home until the day you arrive—these companies provide photos of a "typical" home instead of making information available on each of the individual homes in their inventory. In this case, you have to take the company's word that the typical home pictured is representative and that the property you'll be assigned will be just as nice.

Location is everything, especially in Southern California with its legendary traffic. Before renting a home, get the address. Then, using maps.google.com, obtain exact directions from the home to Disneyland. This will tell you how long and how complicated your commute will be. Avoid homes for which it's necessary to drive on a freeway for more than a couple of miles. Don't worry if the home isn't in Anaheim per se; it's the distance to Disneyland that counts.

The only practical way to shop for a rental home is online. Going online makes it relatively easy to compare different properties and rental companies. The best sites are easy to navigate, let you see what you're interested in without having to log in or divulge any personal information, and list memberships in such organizations as the Better Business Bureau. Before you book, ask about minimum stays, damage deposits, cleaning charges, and pets, as well as how any problems will be addressed once you're in the home.

The Anaheim City Council imposed a moratorium on new short-term rentals (including services like VRBO and Airbnb), but their proposal to phase out existing rentals was overturned, leaving 277 permitted properties operating within the city limits. Short-term rentals are also plentiful in neighboring towns like Buena Park, where we found a room near Knott's Berry Farm through Airbnb for about $100 a night.

THE BEST HOTELS *and* MOTELS NEAR DISNEYLAND

WHAT'S IN A ROOM?

EXCEPT FOR CLEANLINESS, state of repair, and decor, most travelers do not pay much attention to hotel rooms. There is, of course, a discernible standard of quality and luxury that differentiates Motel 6 from Holiday Inn, Holiday Inn from Marriott, and so on. In general, however, hotel guests fail to appreciate that some rooms are better engineered than others.

Contrary to what you might suppose, designing a hotel room is (or should be) a lot more complex than picking a bedspread to match the carpet and drapes. Making the room usable to its occupants is an art, a planning discipline that combines both form and function.

Decor and taste are important, certainly. No one wants to spend several days in a room where the decor is dated, garish, or even ugly. But beyond the decor, there are variables that determine how livable a hotel room is. In Anaheim, for example, we have seen some beautifully appointed rooms that are simply not well designed for human habitation. The next time you stay in a hotel, pay attention to the details and design elements of your room. Even more than decor, these are the things that will make you feel comfortable and at home.

HOW TO GET THE ROOM YOU WANT

MOST HOTELS, INCLUDING DISNEY'S, won't guarantee a specific room when you book but will post your request on your reservations record and try to accommodate you. Our experience indicates that if you give them your first, second, and third choices, you'll probably get one of the three.

When speaking to the reservationist or your travel agent, be specific. If you want a room overlooking the pool, say so. Similarly, be sure to clearly state preferences such as a particular floor, a corner room, a room close to restaurants, a room away from elevators and ice machines, a nonsmoking room, a room with a balcony, or any other preference. If you have a list of preferences, type it up in order of importance, and email or fax it to the hotel or to your travel agent.

HOW THE HOTELS COMPARE

HOTEL	OVERALL QUALITY RATING	WALKING DISTANCE TO PARKS	COST
DISNEYLAND AREA			
Disney's Grand Californian Hotel & Spa	★★★★½	0.2 mi.	$745–$948
Hyatt House at Anaheim Resort/Convention Center	★★★★½	0.6 mi.	$279–$329
JW Marriott Anaheim Resort	★★★★½	0.9 mi.	$283–$329
Westin Anaheim Resort	★★★★½	1.0 mi.	$356–$369
Villas at the Disneyland Hotel	★★★★½	0.5 mi.	$1304–$1441
Courtyard Anaheim Theme Park Entrance	★★★★	0.5 mi.	$445–$596
Disneyland Hotel	★★★★	0.5 mi.	$579–$660
Disney's Pixar Place Hotel	★★★★	0.6 mi.	$446–$546
Four Points by Sheraton Anaheim	★★★★	0.8 mi.	$170–$335
Home2 Suites by Hilton Anaheim Resort	★★★★	0.6 mi.	$276–$299
Homewood Suites by Hilton Anaheim Resort–Convention Center	★★★★	1.0 mi.	$186–$274
Hotel Indigo Anaheim	★★★★	0.7 mi.	$188–$242
Residence Inn at Anaheim Resort Convention Center	★★★★	1.0 mi.	$269–$543
Sheraton Park Hotel at the Anaheim Resort	★★★★	0.8 mi.	$188–$719
Springhill Suites at Anaheim Resort Area/Convention Center	★★★★	0.7 mi.	$269–$484
The Viv Hotel Anaheim	★★★★	1.1 mi.	$221–$273
Wyndham Anaheim	★★★★	0.7 mi.	$174–$269
The Anaheim Hotel	★★★½	0.4 mi.	$235–$308
Anaheim Majestic Garden	★★★½	1.2 mi.	$182–$236
Best Western Plus Anaheim Inn	★★★½	0.3 mi.	$299–$324
Best Western Plus Park Place Inn	★★★½	0.2 mi.	$334–$369
Candy Cane Inn	★★★½	0.6 mi.	$326

Keep in mind that Disney's reservations computer is limited to storing a short block of text, so keep your request as brief and specific as possible. Be sure to include your own contact information and, if you've already booked, your reservation confirmation number. If it makes you feel better, call back in a few days to make sure that your preferences were posted to your reservations record.

About Hotel Renovations

*un*official **TIP**
Request a renovated room at your hotel—these can be much nicer than the older rooms.

Most hotels more than five years old refurbish 10%–20% of their guest rooms each year. This incremental approach minimizes disruption of business but makes your room assignment a crapshoot. You might luck into a newly renovated room or be assigned a threadbare room. Disney resorts will not guarantee a recently renovated room but will note your request and try to accommodate you. Non-Disney hotels will often guarantee an updated room when you book. Before you begin to shop

HOW THE HOTELS COMPARE			
HOTEL	**OVERALL QUALITY RATING**	**WALKING DISTANCE TO PARKS**	**COST**
DISNEYLAND AREA *(continued)*			
Desert Palms Hotel & Suites	★★★½	0.7 mi.	$168–$270
Element Anaheim Resort Convention Center	★★★½	0.8 mi.	$224–$439
Howard Johnson Anaheim	★★★½	0.6 mi.	$289–$294
Park Vue Inn	★★★½	0.3 mi.	$264–$289
Anaheim Camelot Inn & Suites	★★★	0.3 mi.	$274–$341
Anaheim Desert Inn & Suites	★★★	0.3 mi.	$154–$207
Best Western Plus Stovall's Inn	★★★	0.9 mi.	$174–$334
Fairfield Inn Anaheim Resort	★★★	0.5 mi.	$195–$360
Hotel Lulu	★★★	0.8 mi.	$212–$268
Solara Inn and Suites	★★★	1.0 mi.	$124–$199
Tropicana Inn & Suites	★★★	0.3 mi.	$261–$324
Alpine Inn	★★½	0.8 mi.	$206–$939
Castle Inn & Suites	★★½	0.5 mi.	$199–$209
Eden Roc Inn & Suites	★★½	1.0 mi.	$152–$180
Grand Legacy at the Park	★★½	0.3 mi.	$247–$341
Kings Inn Anaheim	★★½	0.8 mi.	$130–$200
Del Sol Inn	★★	0.3 mi.	$222–$327
Riviera Motel	★★	0.8 mi.	$90–$100
UNIVERSAL AREA			
The Garland	★★★★	1.3 mi.	$245–$351
Hilton Universal City	★★★★	0.3 mi.	$289–$345
Sheraton Universal Hotel	★★★★	0.3 mi.	$306–$364
Tilt Hotel	★★★½	0.9 mi.	$221–$323
BLVD Hotel & Spa	★★★	0.7 mi.	$179–$219

for a hotel, take a hard look at this letter we received from a couple in Hot Springs, Arkansas:

> *We canceled our room reservations to follow the advice in your book [and reserved a hotel highly rated by The Unofficial Guide]. We wanted inexpensive but clean and cheerful. We got inexpensive but dirty, grim, and depressing. I really felt disappointed in your advice and the room. It was the pits. That was the one real piece of information I needed from your book!*

Needless to say, this letter was as unsettling to us as the bad room was to our reader. Our integrity as travel journalists, after all, is based on the quality of the information we provide to our readers. When we rechecked the hotel that our reader disliked so intensely, we discovered that our review was correctly representative but that he and his wife had unfortunately been assigned to one of a small number of threadbare rooms scheduled for renovation.

The key to avoiding disappointment is to do some snooping around in advance. We recommend that you check out the hotel's website to

Disneyland-Area Hotels

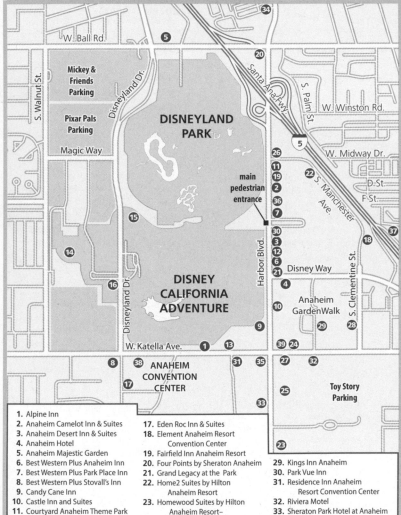

1. Alpine Inn
2. Anaheim Camelot Inn & Suites
3. Anaheim Desert Inn & Suites
4. Anaheim Hotel
5. Anaheim Majestic Garden
6. Best Western Plus Anaheim Inn
7. Best Western Plus Park Place Inn
8. Best Western Plus Stovall's Inn
9. Candy Cane Inn
10. Castle Inn and Suites
11. Courtyard Anaheim Theme Park Entrance
12. Del Sol Inn
13. Desert Palms Hotel & Suites
14. Disneyland Hotel
15. Disney's Grand Californian Hotel & Spa
16. Disney's Pixar Place Hotel

17. Eden Roc Inn & Suites
18. Element Anaheim Resort Convention Center
19. Fairfield Inn Anaheim Resort
20. Four Points by Sheraton Anaheim
21. Grand Legacy at the Park
22. Home2 Suites by Hilton Anaheim Resort
23. Homewood Suites by Hilton Anaheim Resort– Convention Center
24. Hotel Indigo Anaheim
25. Hotel Lulu
26. Howard Johnson Anaheim
27. Hyatt House at Anaheim Resort/Convention Center
28. JW Marriott Anaheim Resort

29. Kings Inn Anaheim
30. Park Vue Inn
31. Residence Inn Anaheim Resort Convention Center
32. Riviera Motel
33. Sheraton Park Hotel at Anaheim
34. Solara Inn and Suites
35. SpringHill Suites Anaheim Resort/Convention Center
36. Tropicana Inn & Suites
37. The Viv Hotel Anaheim
38. Westin Anaheim Resort
39. Wyndham Anaheim

see a standard guest room photo before you book. Be forewarned, however, that some hotel chains use the same guest room photo for all hotels in the chain, and that the guest room in a specific property may not resemble the photo on the website. When you or your travel agent call, ask how old the property is and when the guest room you are being assigned was last renovated. If you arrive and are assigned a room inferior to that which you had been led to expect, demand to be moved to another room.

ROOM RATINGS

OVERALL STAR RATINGS		
★★★★★	Superior rooms	Tasteful and luxurious by any standard
★★★★	Extremely nice rooms	What you'd expect at a Hyatt Regency or Marriott
★★★	Nice rooms	Holiday Inn or comparable quality
★★	Adequate rooms	Clean, comfortable, and functional without frills—like a Motel 6

ON PAGES 64–65, we provide a selective list of our preferred lodgings near Disneyland Resort. If you used an earlier edition of this guide, you will notice that we've revamped the way we review hotels. In the years since we began publishing, the internet has utterly upended the art of researching hotel rooms, with websites such as TripAdvisor now providing crowd-sourced ratings of hundreds more properties than our team could possibly properly investigate. Instead of attempting to appear comprehensive by filling pages with superficial statistics, we've focused on crafting a curated collection of properties across a range of price points, and supplied succinct details on what sets each one apart from its competition. Our recommendations take into consideration not only room quality but also location, services, recreation, and amenities.

Just because a hotel isn't listed here doesn't necessarily mean it's a bad bet for bedding down, but these properties are all places that we can personally vouch for. However, below is a short list of places near Disneyland where we do not recommend you stay, regardless of how tempting their room rates:

• Americas Best Value Inn & Suites	• Anaheim Maingate Inn

Special thanks to Tom Bricker of disneytouristblog.com for contributing to this section; hop over to his website for more in-depth vacation recommendations.

To separate properties according to the relative quality, tastefulness, state of repair, cleanliness, and size of their standard rooms, we have grouped the hotels and motels into classifications denoted by stars. Star ratings in this guide apply to Anaheim properties only and do not necessarily correspond to ratings awarded by Forbes, AAA, or other travel critics. Because stars have little relevance when awarded in the absence of commonly recognized standards of comparison, we have tied our ratings to expected levels of quality established by specific American hotel corporations.

DISNEYLAND AREA

Alpine Inn ★★½

715 W. Katella Ave.
Anaheim
☎ 714-535-2186
alpineinnanaheim.com

Rate per night $206–$939. **Maximum occupants per room** 4. **Pool** ★½. **Fridge in room** Yes. **Breakfast** Free (cold). **Wi-Fi** Free. **Parking** Free. **Walk to Esplanade** 15 minutes (0.8 mile).

ALPINE INN HAS MORE CURB APPEAL than the average cheap motel, with its cute chalet-style check-in building; however, none of this look is present anywhere else in the property. You can walk to the parks without having to cross busy Harbor Boulevard (a consideration if you have kids), but it's slightly farther from the parks and slightly more expensive than its closest competition. Rooms are clean and well kept but on the small side, with dated TVs. It's not a resort—just a place for sleeping and showering—and better bang-for-your-buck value accommodations are usually available, but there's absolutely nothing wrong with it for a budget motel.

Anaheim Camelot Inn & Suites ★★★

1520 S. Harbor Blvd.
Anaheim
☎ 714-635-7275
camelotinn-anaheim.com

Rate per night $274–$341. **Maximum occupants per room** 4. **Pool** ★★½. **Fridge in room** Yes. **Breakfast** No. **Wi-Fi** Free. **Parking** $22/day. **Walk to Esplanade** 6 minutes (0.3 mile).

YOU CAN'T SPEND THE NIGHT inside the castle on Disney property, but you can sleep in one mere steps across the street. The medieval theming at Camelot Inn & Suites is mostly skin deep; the rooms themselves sport castle-themed artwork and overstuffed headboards fit for royalty but are otherwise outfitted with standard-issue motel decor that was refreshed post-pandemic. A limited number of two-room family suites are available that sleep up to 6. The top reasons to stay here are location, the 4th-floor terrace pool with a view of the fireworks, location, on-site ECV scooter rental, and location. There's no free breakfast or on-site restaurant, but there's a McDonald's next door. Before booking, be sure to compare prices with its Harbor Boulevard neighbors such as Best Western Plus and Park Vue Inn, which are often somewhat better bargains.

Anaheim Desert Inn & Suites ★★★

1600 S. Harbor Blvd.
Anaheim
☎ 714-772-5050
anaheimdesert
inn.com

Rate per night $154–$207. **Maximum occupants per room** 4. **Pool** ★★½. **Fridge in room** Yes. **Breakfast** Free (cold). **Wi-Fi** Free. **Parking** $23/day. **Walk to Esplanade** 6 minutes (0.3 mile). **Comments** $7/night resort fee.

DESERT INN IS THE ULTIMATE no-frills hotel. Suites sport small sitting rooms with charm-free furnishings, and your room view includes a parking lot and the back side of another hotel. The decor, while functional, isn't especially attractive, but the availability of parlor layouts that sleep up to 10 guests makes this an economical choice for large families who want to sleep within steps of the magic. A small number of standard-size rooms are available in the rear of the property. The indoor pool is basic and too small to swim laps, but there is a convenient changing area with lockers. Right next door is a breakfast room serving cold pastries, hard-boiled eggs, coffee, and not much else. With that out of the way, we recommend Desert Inn because the rooms are good enough, and it only takes a few minutes to walk to Disneyland. The hotel is directly across the street from the parks, and that more than makes up for its shortcomings. We've received more positive reader surveys about the Desert Inn than any other area motel, with 90% saying they'd stay again.

The Anaheim Hotel ★★★½

Rate per night $235–308. **Maximum occupants per room** 4 (up to 6 in suites). **Pool** ★★★½. **Fridge in room** Yes. **Breakfast** Paid. **Wi-Fi** Free. **Parking** $22/day. **Walk to Esplanade** 9 minutes (0.4 mile). **Comments** $7.50/night resort fee. Pets under 40 lbs. allowed for non-refundable fee of $50 per night, per pet.

1700 S. Harbor Blvd.
Anaheim
☎ 714-772-5900
theanaheimhotel.com

A LONGSTANDING BUDGET MOTEL that was given a retro-modern makeover by the same owners as the upscale Westin, The Anaheim Hotel is a favorite of Magic Key holders for its reasonable rates, exceptionally friendly service, and proximity to the parks. The sprawling complex of freestanding low-rise buildings covers nearly half a city block, with some rooms only steps from the GardenWalk. Guest rooms are spacious, with charming throwback touches like rotary-style telephones and 1960s-style art prints (as well as modern charging ports). There's great hot-water pressure in the roomy bathrooms, but the poly-blend towels are only adequate. Rooms come in a variety of configurations, including family suites; some have big balconies with partial views of the park. The Pizza Press restaurant attached to the lobby is one of our favorite spots on the street for a post-park nosh, and there's a swinging full-service bar and well-stocked marketplace inside as well. A pristine pool is large enough to practice for the Olympics, plus they have a fitness room and golf simulator. The entire property is lovingly landscaped, with flourishing succulents and live trees in the outdoor corridors. Join their free Anabella Club for discounts and loyalty rewards.

Anaheim Majestic Garden ★★★½

Rate per night $182–$236. **Maximum occupants per room** 4. **Pool** ★★★. **Fridge in room** Yes. **Breakfast** Paid. **Wi-Fi** Free. **Parking** $30/day. **Walk to Esplanade** 25 minutes (1.2 miles). **Comments** Pets allowed with $150 nonrefundable deposit; must notify the hotel in advance. Free shuttle to Disneyland.

900 S. Disneyland Dr.
Anaheim
☎ 714-778-1700
majesticgarden
hotel.com

ANAHEIM MAJESTIC GARDEN HOTEL'S Tudor facade is a touch tacky, but the medieval theming inside is subtly executed. We enjoyed the peaceful and beautifully landscaped hotel grounds. For those with children, the Legend of the Lair is told throughout the hotel on the carpet and walls, and Princess Corinne makes appearances during breakfast at the unexpectedly upscale on-site bistro. Guest rooms are modern and among the most spacious standard rooms in the area, with comfortable bedding. We usually see affordable prices at Majestic when comparing it to other local hotels, likely due to its slightly inconvenient location. We clocked the walk to the Mickey & Friends parking structure (where you can catch a tram to Disneyland Resort) at a little over 15 minutes. That, plus the time it takes to go through security and get on the tram, means it'll take over a half hour to be anywhere near the entrance of Disneyland. Luckily, a free shuttle is available, which takes about

5 minutes to drive to and from Disneyland, but we observed it filling up with guests quickly in the mornings and evenings.

Best Western Plus Anaheim Inn   ★★★½

1630 S. Harbor Blvd.
Anaheim
☎ 714-774-1050
anaheiminn.com

Rate per night $299–$324. **Maximum occupants per room** 4 (6 in suites). **Pool** ★★½. **Fridge in room** Yes. **Breakfast** Free (hot). **Wi-Fi** Free. **Parking** $20/day. **Walk to Esplanade** 6 minutes (0.3 mile).

BEST WESTERN PLUS ANAHEIM INN is the sister property to the popular Best Western Plus Park Place Inn, located just four doors up the street (see below). The decor isn't quite as nice, and the walk to the parks is a minute longer, but it has a more pleasant pool and breakfast area, plus a laundry facility. Otherwise, the properties are nearly identical, and the Anaheim Inn is usually a little cheaper.

Best Western Plus Park Place Inn & Mini Suites   ★★★½

1554 S. Harbor Blvd.
Anaheim
☎ 714-776-4800
parkplaceinnand
minisuites.com

Rate per night $334–$369. **Maximum occupants per room** 4 (6 in suites). **Pool** ★★. **Fridge in room** Yes. **Breakfast** Free (hot). **Wi-Fi** Free. **Parking** $20/day. **Walk to Esplanade** 5 minutes (0.2 mile).

BEST WESTERN PLUS PARK PLACE INN boasts that it is the closest hotel to Disneyland (even closer than Disney's own hotels). This is not hyperbole; it takes barely 5 minutes to walk from your room to the front gate, and if that's too far you can rent an ECV in the lobby from Select Scooters (anaheimscooters.com). Besides the location, Park Place Inn has very nice and stylish rooms (including mini-suites that sleep six) that feature comfortable beds, a desk and office chair, HDTV, a microwave, a mini-fridge, and a safe. Coffee makers and tea are provided in the rooms. Also, a decent grab-and-go breakfast is included in the price of the room. This is Tom Bricker's #1 pick for a Disneyland-adjacent motel. The only downsides are the unappealing, undersize pool and the hefty parking fee for leaving your car in the lot after checkout.

Best Western Plus Stovall's Inn   ★★★

1110 W. Katella Ave.
Anaheim
☎ 714-778-1880
stovallsinn.com

Rate per night $174–$334. **Maximum occupants per room** 4. **Pool** ★★★½. **Fridge in room** Yes. **Breakfast** Free (hot). **Wi-Fi** Free. **Parking** $20/day. **Walk to Esplanade** 18 minutes (0.9 mile). **Comments** Free EV charging stations available for registered guests.

AS A FAMILY-OWNED MOTEL that has been across the street from Disneyland's southwest corner since the 1960s, Stovall's Inn (originally known as The Inn of Tomorrow) is showing its age, but it's still rather comfortable thanks to repeated refurbishments that have honored its space-age origins. The glittering lobby offers a small business center, filtered water to refill your bottles, a self-service shop for snacks and sundries, and a better-than-average free breakfast buffet with hot items such as eggs and sausage. The motel's centerpiece is an expansive pool complex, with hot tubs and a fitness room surrounded by painstakingly pruned animal topiaries. Rooms are of average size for the era, and between the in-room air-conditioning units, thin walls, and exterior hallways, they can be noisy. Though it's a longer walk to the Esplanade than comparable properties on Harbor Boulevard, the west side's security checkpoint is often swifter, and Stovall's Inn is convenient if you're stopping by the Disneyland Resort hotels for an après-park cocktail.

Candy Cane Inn ★★★½

Rate per night $326. **Maximum occupants per room** 4. **Pool** ★★★½. **Fridge in room** Yes. **Breakfast** Free (hot). **Wi-Fi** Free. **Parking** Free. **Walk to Esplanade** 11 minutes (0.6 mile). **Comments** Free shuttle to Disneyland.

1747 S. Harbor Blvd.
Anaheim
☎ 714-774-5284
candycaneinn.net

THIS FRIENDLY, FAMILY-RUN HOTEL has a charming homespun style, with grounds that are always lined with beautiful, flowering plants. The service here always has given the place some seriously loyal customers, and an extensive pandemic-era renovation has bumped it up even higher on our list of favorite motels. Guest rooms are clean and cozy with big bathtubs and fast Wi-Fi, but the HDTVs only receive streaming services, not broadcast or cable networks. Candy Cane's pair of pools and hot tub are wonderfully warm, as are the waffles at the free breakfast. This has long been a top pick for parties wanting California boutique hotel charm. It's a little longer walk from here than from other hotels across Harbor Boulevard, but you can reach the parks without having to cross the road, and a free hourly shuttle is available for anyone wanting to save their feet.

Castle Inn and Suites ★★½

Rate per night $199–$209. **Maximum occupants per room** 4. **Pool** ★½. **Fridge in room** Yes. **Breakfast** No. **Wi-Fi** Free. **Parking** Free. **Walk to Esplanade** 11 minutes (0.5 mile).

1734 S. Harbor Blvd.
Anaheim
☎ 714-774-8111
castleinn.com

CASTLE INN, the other medieval fortress on Harbor Boulevard (not to be confused with the Camelot), goes even further with the kitschy facade, extending the theme into the lobby and guest rooms with heavy wooden furniture and artwork of European chateaus. Tackiness aside, this is a surprisingly pleasant place to stay, offering clean rooms with the essential amenities, if not many frills such as free breakfast. The biggest black mark is the bare-bones pool. Castle Inn is neither the cheapest, nor the closest, property near the parks, but it's an acceptable compromise when your first choices are all booked.

Courtyard Anaheim Theme Park Entrance ★★★★

Rate per night $445–$596. **Maximum occupants per room** 6. **Pool** ★★★★½. **Fridge in room** Yes. **Breakfast** Paid. **Wi-Fi** Free. **Parking** $35 valet only; no self-parking. **Walk to Esplanade** 10 minutes (0.5 mile).

1420 S. Harbor Blvd.
Anaheim
☎ 714-254-1442
marriott.com

IN TERMS OF QUALITY, the Courtyard Anaheim Theme Park Entrance sets a high bar for off-site Disneyland hotels, particularly for families with kids. The overall quality and the reasonably short walk to the park are the strong selling points here, with 530-square-foot standard rooms that are far larger than the area's average. Rooms feature two queen-size beds plus twin bunk beds, which are perfect for kids and serviceable for not-too-tall adults. The Surfside water park is significantly better than your average hotel pool, with a large splash playground and two short slides. Price is unquestionably the biggest negative, with rates around $100/night more expensive than some off-site alternatives; even comparable hotels can be significantly less expensive depending upon when you're traveling. This is our top pick for families wanting a short walk but who are not on a tight budget.

Del Sol Inn   ★★

1604 S. Harbor Blvd.
Anaheim
☎ 714-234-3411
delsolinn.com

Rate per night $222–$327. **Maximum occupants per room** 4–6. **Pool** ★½. **Fridge in room** Yes. **Breakfast** No. **Wi-Fi** Free. **Parking** $28/day. **Walk to Esplanade** 7 minutes (0.3 mile).

THIS MOTEL IS FINE for sleeping, showering, and spending all day in the parks. Rooms have blandly contemporary furnishings and ugly carpets, but at least they're spacious, with decent beds and pillows. It's a fine option from a cleanliness and basic functionality perspective. Family rooms with bunk beds are available. The real reason to stay here is because it's often the cheapest hotel directly across the street from Disneyland. Request an upper floor near the front of the complex to avoid hearing stomping above you and to save a couple of minutes on your walk to the parks, as this is a fairly long hotel.

Desert Palms Hotel & Suites   ★★★½

631 W. Katella Ave.
Anaheim
☎ 888-521-6420
desertpalms
hotel.com

Rate per night $168–$270. **Maximum occupants per room** 4. **Pool** ★★. **Fridge in room** Yes. **Breakfast** Free (hot). **Wi-Fi** Free. **Parking** $28/day. **Walk to Esplanade** 14 minutes (0.7 mile).

DESERT PALMS HOTEL & SUITES is a solid hotel overall, with some nice advantages like indoor hallways and an inviting lobby that make it seem superior to the hotels directly on Harbor Boulevard. The free hot breakfast buffet is another plus. The location (right by 7-11 and the CVS Pharmacy) is convenient, and the rooms are fairly nice, but the high prices relative to other hotels in its class give us some pause with this one.

Disneyland Hotel *(see pages 49–52)*

Disney's Grand Californian Hotel & Spa *(see pages 47–49)*

Disney's Pixar Place Hotel *(see pages 53–54)*

Eden Roc Inn & Suites   ★★½

1830 S. West St.
Anaheim
☎ 714-663-8700
edenrocanaheim.com

Rate per night $152–$180. **Maximum occupants per room** 4. **Pool** ★½. **Fridge in room** Yes. **Breakfast** No. **Wi-Fi** Free. **Parking** $15/day. **Walk to Esplanade** 20 minutes (1 mile).

A TOP-TO-BOTTOM RENOVATION late last decade gave the Eden Roc rooms a fresh, modern feel. In-room amenities include a microwave, a mini-fridge, a desk with chair, a laptop-size safe, and a K-Cup coffee maker. Deluxe single king and double queen rooms are on the small side, but superior rooms provide significantly more square footage. Unfortunately, some of these L-shaped rooms wrap around the stairwells, making them noisier than the standard rooms. Family suites that sleep six with a sofa bed are also available, usually for less than the cost of regular rooms at neighboring properties. Mattresses are acceptable if not luxurious, but the pillows are poor quality and the walls are thin. Bathrooms have plenty of hot water and steady pressure, but their toilets are uncomfortably low. Eden Roc's grounds include a tiny pool that doesn't open until midmorning, a parking lot, and not much else. Walking from your room to Disneyland (via the entrance at the western end of Downtown Disney, past Pixar Place Hotel) can take over 20 minutes; ask for a room at the north end of the property to save some steps. You can make the short drive up Disneyland Drive and be at the park's parking structures in no time. Eden Roc is a basic budget motel dressed up like a hipster hotel, but it often offers some of the least expensive rooms within a mile of the Disneyland Resort.

Element Anaheim Resort Convention Center
★★★½

1600 Clementine St.
Anaheim
☎ 714-326-7800
marriott.com

Rate per night $224–$439. **Maximum occupants per room** 6. **Pool** ★★½. **Fridge in room** Yes. **Breakfast** Free (hot). **Wi-Fi** Free. **Parking** $22/day. **Walk to Esplanade** 16 minutes (0.8 mile).

THIS MARRIOTT-ASSOCIATED HOTEL is less than a mile's walk from Disneyland's front gates and has rooms that fit families and large groups—a winning combination. Element Anaheim Resort Convention Center's lobby features wooden design elements, large windows that let in a ton of natural light, and plenty of seating to relax, as well as a couple of computers for guest use and a small selection of snacks. Studio and one-bedroom suites are available in a few different configurations, some with bunk beds or sleeper sofas. Mattresses and sheets are comfortable (but pillows are a bit too soft), and between the beds you'll find electrical outlets with USB charging ports. Rooms lack enough luggage storage but do feature surprisingly fully-equipped kitchenettes that include a two-burner stove, a microwave, a dishwasher, and all the utensils you could need. Bathrooms have great lighting, decent counter space, and glorious showers with excellent heat and pressure. Rooms facing west point near Disneyland Resort, and the hotel charges a bit extra for theme park view rooms looking at the back side of Cars Land. The pool is very small, but there's a large outdoor seating area with grills, plus a modest fitness center with weights, ellipticals, and treadmills. The included hot buffet breakfast (6:30–9:30 a.m. daily) with eggs and turkey bacon is another huge plus.

Fairfield Inn Anaheim Resort ★★★

1460 S. Harbor Blvd.
Anaheim
☎ 714-772-6777
marriott.com

Rate per night $195–$360. **Maximum occupants per room** 5. **Pool** ★★★. **Fridge in room** Yes. **Breakfast** No. **Wi-Fi** Free. **Parking** $27/day. **Walk to Esplanade** 9 minutes (0.5 mile). **Comments** Small on-site food court.

FAIRFIELD INN ANAHEIM RESORT is a nice midtier name-brand hotel that offers close proximity to Disneyland, solid rooms, and a decent slate of amenities. It's not the nicest hotel near Disneyland, but it offers excellent balance. The rates are slightly higher than the hotels to which it's adjacent, and the parking is pricey, but it is arguably worth the slightly higher rates. Guests staying here can always recoup those higher prices by eating breakfast at McDonald's or Panera Bread (right in front of the hotel) instead of in the parks.

Four Points by Sheraton Anaheim ★★★★

1221 S. Harbor Blvd.
Anaheim
☎ 714-758-0900
marriott.com

Rate per night $170–$335. **Maximum occupants per room** 4. **Pool** ★★★½. **Fridge in room** Yes. **Breakfast** Paid. **Wi-Fi** Free. **Parking** $29/day. **Walk to Esplanade** 16 minutes (0.8 mile).

THIS PROPERTY FILLS A NICHE at Disneyland occupied by few other hotels—let's call it adult fun spots. The only other hotels nearby that somewhat appeal to this same demographic are Disneyland Hotel and the major brand-name hotels near the convention center, all of which are considerably more expensive. All guest rooms have a contemporary sensibility and some of the most comfortable beds in all of Anaheim. Amenities and common areas are great, making this an excellent place to unwind after (or pregame before) a night in the parks. It's not for everyone, but for honeymooners and adult gatherings, it should not be overlooked. It's a top pick for adult fun on a budget thanks to its Asian-American fusion restaurant and poolside tiki bar with a focus on craft cocktails. The only catch is that it's located right next to the interstate, and you must cross busy on and off ramps while walking to the parks.

Grand Legacy at the Park ★★½

1650 S. Harbor Blvd.
Anaheim
☎ 714-772-0440
grandlegacyhotel.com

Rate per night $247–$341. **Maximum occupants per room** 4. **Pool** ★★★½. **Fridge in room** Yes. **Breakfast** Yes (cold). **Wi-Fi** Free. **Parking** $20/day. **Walk to Esplanade** 7 minutes (0.3 mile).

THE LOFTILY NAMED GRAND LEGACY AT THE PARK used to be a Ramada, and aside from a spiffed-up lobby and an expansion tower, it still feels like a budget motel. As long as you know what you're getting into, the rooms are comfortable enough for the price, if not particularly roomy. The heated pool is impressively large and includes a small splash pad for the kids, and adults can enjoy the chic bar on the rooftop. There are also a few convenient shops and restaurants on the ground floor, including a Hawaiian barbecue takeout and a boba tea shop, which is good because the grab-and-go breakfast is pretty paltry. The best reason to book the Grand Legacy is because it's almost as close to Disneyland as the Park Vue Inn but usually costs less. Be aware that parking your car past checkout is not permitted.

Home2 Suites by Hilton Anaheim Resort ★★★★

1441 S. Manchester Ave.
Anaheim
☎ 714-844-2811
hilton.com

Rate per night $276–$299. **Maximum occupants per room** 6. **Pool** ★★★. **Fridge in room** Yes. **Breakfast** Free (hot). **Wi-Fi** Free. **Parking** $32/day (valet only). **Walk to Esplanade** 13 minutes (0.6 mile).

FUNCTIONAL BUT NOT FLASHY, Home2 Suites has huge rooms, decent prices, and close proximity to Disneyland Resort, making it a great option for families. The lobby is clean and modern, with room to relax, and has a small shop with snacks and drinks. The pool is heated and has a splash pad for the kids. Studio rooms with two queen beds and a sleeper sofa can fit six with room to spare; one- and two-bedroom suites are also available. Mattresses are on the firm side, but pillows are extremely soft. There are power outlets and USB charging ports all over the place, including at the laptop-friendly work desk. The kitchenette has everything you need to heat up food and brew coffee, with ample fridge space for all that uneaten park food you swear you'll eat before you go back to the airport, but then never do. The bathroom is solid, with plenty of counter space and good water pressure, but the barn-style sliding door offers very little sound dampening. There's a huge exercise room on the second floor with treadmills and exercise bikes. The only real negatives are road noise from I-5 for rooms on the east end of the building and mandatory valet parking.

Homewood Suites by Hilton Anaheim Resort–Convention Center ★★★★

2010 S. Harbor Blvd.
Anaheim
☎ 714-750-2010
hilton.com

Rate per night $186–$274. **Maximum occupants per room** 6. **Pool** ★★★½. **Fridge in room** Yes. **Breakfast** Free (hot). **Wi-Fi** Free. **Parking** $30/day. **Walk to Esplanade** 20 minutes (1 mile).

ALTHOUGH THE WALK from Homewood Suites to Disneyland can take 20 minutes, you can skip that thanks to its location next door to Disneyland Resort's Toy Story parking lot. From there, you can take a bus to the eastern entrance of the Esplanade between Disneyland and Disney California Adventure. Homewood Suites' large rooms and full kitchens (with full-size fridge, dishwasher, microwave, stove top, and dishes) are great for families or large groups. We really enjoyed relaxing at the large pool area, which also includes a hot tub.

Hotel Indigo Anaheim ★★★★

435 W. Katella Ave.
Anaheim
☎ 714-772-7755
hotelindigo.com

Rate per night $188–$242. **Maximum occupants per room** 4. **Pool** ★★½. **Fridge in room** Yes. **Breakfast** Paid. **Wi-Fi** Free. **Parking** Free. **Walk to Esplanade** 14 minutes (0.7 mile). **Comments** Pets up to 40 pounds welcome with $100 nonrefundable fee; limit 2 pets.

INDIGO IS A BIT MORE EXPENSIVE than its immediate neighbors, but the rooms are very nice and modern. The entire hotel has a chic and trendy vibe. Luckily, Indigo has more than just its looks going for it. Beds are comfortable, and on-site amenities include a pool, laundry room, fitness center, and café. A drawback for some families is there are no bathtubs, only walk-in showers. A huge benefit is the hotel's location—Disneyland is about a 10-minute walk north on Harbor Boulevard, while the Anaheim Convention Center is about the same distance to the south. Hotel Indigo is one of our favorite hotels in the Disneyland Resort area. Check out the dancing fountain show out front; it's like a pint-size World of Color.

Hotel Lulu ★★★

1850 S. Harbor Blvd.
Anaheim
☎ 657-688-5858
hotellulu.com

Rate per night $212–$268. **Maximum occupants per room** 4. **Pool** ★★★. **Fridge in room** Yes. **Breakfast** Paid. **Wi-Fi** Free. **Parking** $29. **Walk to Esplanade** 16 Minutes (0.8 mile).

THIS ATTRACTIVE BOUTIQUE PROPERTY under Best Western's "Premier Collection" makes a great first impression, but beneath the colorful lobby mural and curly-haired cartoon mascot, Hotel Lulu is really the old Red Lion with a fresh face. Good points include larger-than-average rooms with comfortable bedding, large flat-screen TVs, fancy electric tea kettles, and decent toiletries in the roomy bathroom. Other positives are the pool, which is longer and deeper than most and features a couple of fire pits, and the small fitness room stuffed with late-model exercise machines. However, some of the room furniture is visibly worn, wallpaper peels around the fanless bathtubs, and the window-mounted air-conditioning units are annoyingly loud. We've also experienced M.I.A. amenities and inconsistent housekeeping. The entrance to the Toy Story parking lot is right next door, but the path back to the shuttle bus stop is nearly as long as walking straight to the Esplanade.

Howard Johnson Anaheim ★★★½

1380 S. Harbor Blvd.
Anaheim
☎ 714-776-6120
hojoanaheim.com

Rate per night $289–$294. **Maximum occupants per room** 5. **Pool** ★★★★. **Fridge in room** Yes. **Breakfast** No. **Wi-Fi** Free. **Parking** $25/day. **Walk to Esplanade** 11 minutes (0.6 mile). **Comments** Rollaway beds available for $15+tax/night.

THIS HOJO HAS BEEN AROUND for a long time, and it's leaning into mid-century modern nostalgia with its terrazzo-tiled lobby and retro-mod Shag artwork on the walls. The two main selling points of Howard Johnson Anaheim are its close location to Disneyland Resort (just over a 10-minute walk) and the hotel's elaborate water playground and pool area, which is slightly smaller than the one at Courtyard across the street. A laundry room and convenience store are also available on-site, and the sprawling grounds are well kept. We like the spacious rooms and bathrooms, and the renovated rooms sport smart TVs and Amazon Alexa digital assistants alongside throwback blue-and-orange coffee cups. Vintage Tomorrowland fans may want to book the House of the Retro Future suite, inspired by the extinct Monsanto-sponsored attraction. One negative is the lack of a free breakfast, or any on-site restaurant, although Mimi's Cafe is a short walk away. Be sure to check the hotel's website, as it frequently offers discounts.

Hyatt House at Anaheim Resort/Convention Center ★★★★½

1800 S. Harbor Blvd.
Anaheim
☎ 714-971-1800
anaheimresort.house
.hyatt.com

Rate per night $279–$329. **Maximum occupants per room** 4. **Pool** ★★★½. **Fridge in room** Yes. **Breakfast** Free (hot). **Wi-Fi** Free. **Parking** $38/day. **Walk to Esplanade** 13 minutes (0.6 mile).

SIMPLY ONE OF THE BEST hotels near Disneyland, Hyatt House's rooms and public areas have a fresh, modern feel, with wonderfully comfortable beds and plenty of room for you and your family to relax. Rooms contain a king bed and a sofa bed, or two queens; family suites are available with a king bed and twin bunk beds. Guest rooms also have a couch, desk with chair, microwave, coffee maker, HDTV, and safe. The pool features plenty of lounge chairs to relax in. Hyatt House's fitness center is especially large when compared to other Anaheim hotels. We recommend Hyatt House over many other hotels in the area, when you can find a competitive nightly rate.

JW Marriott Anaheim Resort ★★★★½

1775 S. Clementine St.
Anaheim
☎ 714-294-7800
marriott.com

Rate per night $283–$329. **Maximum occupants per room** 3–4. **Pool** ★★★½. **Fridge in room** Yes. **Breakfast** Paid. **Wi-Fi** $9.95–$17.95; free for Bonvoy members and in public areas. **Parking** $65 (valet only). **Walk to Esplanade** 18 minutes (0.9 mile). **Comments** Pets welcome with $150 nonrefundable fee; limit 2 per room.

BILLED UPON ITS 2021 OPENING as the Anaheim Resort area's first luxury hotel outside of Disney property, Orange County's only JW Marriott has a private entrance into the adjoining Anaheim GardenWalk. Rooms start at a relatively spacious 385 square feet for a double queen or single king with pull-out bed, and there are 19 suites up to 1,554 square feet should you need to really spread out. All rooms include 400-thread-count bedsheets, both a walk-in shower and soaking tub, and tastefully understated decor inspired by natural materials. The beds are gloriously comfortable, and Guy says the toilet paper is the softest he's ever used in a hotel. Other upscale amenities include a fitness center with Peloton bikes, a Zen room for yoga and meditation, a lovely garden to lounge in, and a heated outdoor pool. Along with offering room service, the hotel has an on-site Italian restaurant that serves breakfast through dinner, a market open only until early afternoon, and a rooftop lounge featuring views of Disney's fireworks shows. There are activities for kids and lush landscaping, but beware the bite of steep parking and internet fees.

Kings Inn Anaheim ★★½

Rate per night $130–$200. **Maximum occupants per room** 4. **Pool** ★★. **Fridge in room** Yes. **Breakfast** No. **Wi-Fi** Free. **Parking** $20/day. **Walk to Esplanade** 15 minutes (0.8 mile).

415 W. Katella Ave. Anaheim
☎ 714-778-6900
kingsinn anaheim.com

KINGS INN, which used to be a Super 8, is a bargain-basement motel with virtually no exceptional amenities to boast about. The refurbished furnishings still aren't fancy, with queen beds in single rooms instead of kings, and the internet can be unreliable, but you can see fireworks from the second-story deck. A small self-service shop offers 24/7 access to grab-and-go grub, but there's no free breakfast. The main reason we include it here is because it is often the cheapest room available within a 15-minute walk from Disneyland that we're comfortable staying in overnight. As long as you don't plan on spending much time lounging around your smaller-than-average room, or doing laps in the kidney-shaped pool, this is a safe spot for travelers on a tight budget to crash for a few hours between park visits.

Park Vue Inn ★★★½

Rate per night $264–$289. **Maximum occupants per room** 4. **Pool** ★★★. **Fridge in room** Yes. **Breakfast** No. **Wi-Fi** Free. **Parking** Free. **Walk to Esplanade** 5 minutes (0.3 mile). **Comments** Good fireworks viewing from rooftop terrace.

1570 S. Harbor Blvd. Anaheim
☎ 714-722-3691
parkvueinn.com

PARK VUE INN IS CLOSER to Disneyland than any of Disney's pricey hotels. It'll take you less than 10 minutes to walk from your room to the front gate of the park. That's hard to accomplish even at Disney's Grand Californian hotel. Park Vue's rooms are very modern with excellent bedding and contain the usual amenities you would expect—an HDTV, a desk, free Wi-Fi, a mini-fridge, a coffee maker, and a microwave. A small but well-maintained pool with a spa and an exercise room are also available, as well as a Coldstone Creamery next to the lobby and an IHOP right next door. Free parking is another big plus.

Residence Inn Anaheim Resort
Convention Center   ★★★★

640 W. Katella Ave.
Anaheim
☎ 714-782-7500
marriott.com

Rate per night $269–$543. **Maximum occupants per room** 6. **Pool** ★★★½. **Fridge in room** Yes. **Breakfast** Free (hot). **Wi-Fi** Free. **Parking** $30/day. **Walk to Esplanade** 21 minutes (1 mile). **Comments** Pets up to 50 pounds welcome with $150 nonrefundable fee.

IF YOU'RE LOOKING for more spacious accommodations than a standard hotel room, this property offers exceptional bang for your buck. Technically an extended stay hotel brand, this Residence Inn was built with families visiting Disneyland in mind. High-quality, family suite–size rooms with fully equipped kitchens make it ideal for couples looking to spread out a bit and families with small children wanting to save money by cooking their own meals. The decor is sort of "meh," but that's a very minor quibble considering all you get for a relatively reasonable price point. This is a top pick for families on a budget or anyone needing more space but not wanting to get two separate rooms. The only drawback is the walk to Disneyland is significantly longer than some of our other favorites.

Riviera Motel   ★★

410 W. Katella Ave.
Anaheim
☎ 714-776-9100

Rate per night $90–$100. **Maximum occupants per room** 4. **Pool** ★½. **Fridge in room** Yes. **Breakfast** Free (cold). **Wi-Fi** Free. **Parking** Free. **Walk to Esplanade** 16 minutes (0.8 mile). **Comments** Bring your own soap and shampoo.

RIVIERA DOESN'T LOOK LIKE MUCH, but it's hard to not recommend it to budget-conscious visitors due to its cheap price and location to the parks (just over a 15-minute walk). Rooms are extremely dated but clean and well maintained, plus they have mini-fridges, microwaves, and great air-conditioners. Riviera even has a tiny pool tucked away in the corner of the parking lot.

Sheraton Park Hotel at Anaheim Resort   ★★★★

1855 S. Harbor Blvd.
Anaheim
☎ 714-750-1811
marriott.com

Rate per night $188–$719. **Maximum occupants per room** 4. **Pool** ★★★½. **Fridge in room** Yes. **Breakfast** Paid. **Wi-Fi** $10–$15/day; free for Bonvoy members. **Parking** $37 self/$45 valet. **Walk to Esplanade** 16 minutes (0.8 mile). **Comments** Pets up to 40 pounds welcome with $100 nonrefundable fee; limit 1 pet.

THE SHERATON PARK HOTEL received a major refurbishment in 2022, adding two additional rooms (for an even 500) and modernizing the property inside and out with a classy lobby and on-site wine bar. Guest rooms here are huge, and most have balconies that either overlook Disney California Adventure or the Anaheim Convention Center. The beds are comfortable, and we especially liked the fluffy pillows. We also enjoyed the relaxing pool area, which is surrounded by trees and other vegetation. Overall, this is a fantastic hotel, especially if you're attending Disney's D23 Expo at the convention center. The walk to Disneyland from the hotel is over 15 minutes, but there is an ART bus stop out front, or you can catch a free shuttle from the Toy Story lot across the street. Big downsides are the hefty nightly fees for Wi-Fi and parking.

Solara Inn and Suites ★★★

Rate per night $124–$199. **Maximum occupants per room** 4. **Pool** ★★★. **Fridge in room** Yes (upgraded rooms only). **Breakfast** Free (cold). **Wi-Fi** Free. **Parking** Free. **Walk to Esplanade** 21 minutes (1 mile).

921 S. Harbor Blvd.
Anaheim
☎ 714-999-0684
solarainnsuites.com

THIS BUDGET HOTEL is a rebranded Ramada that's worth considering for travelers who can't afford the hotels closer to Disneyland. Walking to the parks will take over 20 minutes, and no shuttle is provided. Uber and Lyft are decent options, with rides available for $5–$9. Solara's recently renovated rooms are clean and well maintained, and one good perk is the free parking, which is rare for hotels located near Disneyland.

SpringHill Suites Anaheim Resort Area/ Convention Center ★★★★

Rate per night $269–$484. **Maximum occupants per room** 6. **Pool** ★★★. **Fridge in room** Yes. **Breakfast** Free (hot). **Wi-Fi** Free. **Parking** $30/day. **Walk to Esplanade** 15 minutes (0.7 mile). **Comments** Pets up to 40 pounds welcome with $75 nonrefundable fee; limit 2 pets.

1801 S. Harbor Blvd.
Anaheim
☎ 714-533-2101
marriott.com

THE SPACIOUS SUITES HERE contain either a king or two queen beds plus a bunk bed or sofa sleeper. Mattresses were a bit firm, but that was one of the only negatives. A CVS located at the bottom level of the hotel allows you to easily stock up on groceries. Free hot breakfast, a gym, a rooftop pool with a view of Disneyland's fireworks, and close proximity to the parks make this one of the best hotel options in the area.

Tropicana Inn & Suites ★★★

Rate per night $261–$324. **Maximum occupants per room** 5. **Pool** ★★½. **Fridge in room** Yes. **Breakfast** Paid. **Wi-Fi** Free. **Parking** $22/day. **Walk to Esplanade** 6 minutes (0.3 mile).

1540 S. Harbor Blvd.
Anaheim
☎ 714-635-4082
tropicanainn-
anaheim.com

TROPICANA INN IS another solid budget option for travelers who want to pay the least amount of money and stay as close as possible to Disneyland. Standard rooms aren't huge, but the park-view suites (which look toward Tomorrowland) are spacious, as are the adjoining kitchen suites. All rooms offer colorful palm tree artwork and plenty of space to sleep or relax thanks to each having one king or two queen beds, two cushioned chairs, and a desk with another chair. The usual HDTV, safe, microwave, coffee maker, and mini-fridge are included as well. Bathrooms are basic, but they do have plenty of counter space. Mediocre mattresses are the biggest minus. The courtyard pool with spa isn't fancy, but it is a little nicer than several of its neighbors. The Cove on Harbor, a small market and coffee bar, is open 6 a.m.–1 a.m.

The Viv Hotel Anaheim ★★★★

Rate per night $221–$273. **Maximum occupants per room** 4. **Pool** ★★★★. **Fridge in room** Yes. **Breakfast** Paid. **Wi-Fi** Free. **Parking** $38/day. **Walk to Esplanade** 23 Minutes (1.1 mile).

1601 S. Anaheim Blvd.
Anaheim
☎ 714-408-2787
thevivhotelanaheim
.com

A TRENDY PROPERTY with both style and substance, this Tribute Portfolio hotel (which originally opened as the Radisson Blu Anaheim) offers a lot of attractive amenities at a competitive price, but the 1.1-mile walk from the far side of I-5 may be a deal-breaker for some. The stylish, open lobby has a fully stocked shop and snack bar, and whimsical artworks—such as an oversize ViewMaster reel of local landmarks and a wall of Disney LEGO minifigs—enliven the public areas. Standard rooms have a decent amount of space, and we appreciate the effective light-blocking curtains. Beds are comfortable with a padded headboard and medium-firm pillows, twin bunk beds are available in some rooms, and the bathrooms are very functional with large showers and excellent lighting. There is plenty of desktop space, but the backless chairs are uncomfortable for extended work sessions. The hotel's signature is the rooftop saltwater pool and hot tub, which are restricted to guests 21 and up; an all-ages pool with ample seating is located on the ground level. The roof is also home to the pricey Top of the V restaurant and an outdoor lounge, both with views of Disneyland's fireworks.

Westin Anaheim Resort ★★★★½

1030 W. Katella Ave.
Anaheim
☎ 657-279-9786
marriott.com

Rate per night $356–$369. **Maximum occupants per room** 5. **Pool** ★★★★. **Fridge in room** Yes. **Breakfast** Paid. **Wi-Fi** Free **Parking** $39 self/$49 valet. **Walk to Esplanade** 20 minutes (1.0 mile).

WESTIN ANAHEIM RESORT is a gorgeous ground-up replacement for the old Anabella Hotel that gives the JW Marriott a run for its money as the area's most luxurious off-site hotel. From the dramatic driveway with Vegas-style marquee and the opulent lobby staffed with ever-attentive concierges, it's instantly clear the Westin is a cut above the motels that share its corner. Rooms are a moderate size but immaculate, with Heavenly beds and double-nozzle showers that live up to their names. High-quality details abound: the Keurig coffee makers are supplied with bottled water and Starbucks pods, there are USB charging ports in both the alarm clock and nightstand, high-tech touchpads handle environmental controls, and the huge televisions with streaming services are neatly recessed in the wall. Our only complaints about the accommodations are that the desk chairs aren't great for long laptop sessions, and that a mini-fridge is provided (plus wineglasses and corkscrew) but no microwave. Park-view rooms overlook Pixar Pier for a premium price, while standard rooms see the back side of the convention center. The Westin's amenities are just as expertly executed and feature an Olympic-size fitness room, with everything from free weights to an automated recovery massager, and an organic-shaped heated pool and hot tub with massaging waterfalls and private cabanas. Multiple dining options are available on-site, including a high-end Fleming's steakhouse, RISE rooftop tapas lounge, and the lobby's Tangerine Room, a terrific choice for a leisurely breakfast or special dinner. Its pleasures may be wasted on theme park commandos who only want a cot to crash on, but the Westin is so relaxing that you may decide to ditch rope drop, stay wrapped up in your robe, and order room service.

Wyndham Anaheim ★★★★

515 W. Katella Ave.
Anaheim
☎ 714-783-2793
wyndhamhotels.com

Rate per night $174–$269. **Maximum occupants per room** 5. **Pool** ★★★. **Fridge in room** Yes. **Breakfast** Paid. **Wi-Fi** Free. **Parking** Free. **Walk to Esplanade** 13 minutes (0.7 mile).

WYNDHAM ANAHEIM is a smart compromise when you want to step up from the open-corridor motels around the corner, without paying the prices of the luxury properties down the block. Guest rooms are generically contemporary, with faux-hardwood tile and herringbone carpeting on the floors and functional earth-tone furniture featuring ample drawers and cubby holes. We like the padded pleather headboard on the comfy bed, the excellent work desk and chair with Ethernet and USB ports, and the Bumble & Bumble soap products in the oversize bathroom. Rooms include a small microwave, fridge, and K-cup coffee maker, but you can get Starbucks coffee and hot breakfast sandwiches at the lobby bar every morning; drinks and dinner are also served here on select nights, although the adjoining restaurant is only open until midday. A small but well-maintained heated pool and spa overlook the entrance to the free underground parking garage, another big perk. Wyndham Anaheim isn't as hip as the Hotel Indigo next door, but it's a few steps closer to the theme parks—and often a few bucks cheaper.

UNIVERSAL STUDIOS HOLLYWOOD AREA

BLVD Hotel & Spa ★★★

10730 Ventura Blvd.
Studio City
☎ 818-623-9100
blvdstudiocity.com

Rate per night $179–$219. **Maximum occupants per room** 4. **Pool** ★★. **Fridge in room** Yes. **Breakfast** Paid. **Wi-Fi** Free. **Parking** $34/day. **Walk to Universal** 17 minutes (0.7 mile). **Comments** Viya Spa is open daily; treatments are by appointment only. $21/night resort fee.

ONE OF THE CLOSEST affordable hotels to Universal Studios, BLVD's full-service bar and 24-hour grab-and-go café give it the appealing vibe of a hipster hangout. The guest rooms received refreshed furnishings in 2024 but exhibit some odd form-over-function design decisions. Rooms have lots of electrical outlets but no USB plugs, and the Wi-Fi is painfully slow. You can walk across the street to catch a free shuttle bus up to Universal, or spring for a rideshare. There's nothing wrong with BLVD for a night or two, but for a little more money we'd much rather stay at The Garland or Tilt.

The Garland ★★★★

4222 Vineland Ave.,
North Hollywood
☎ 818-980-8000
thegarland.com

Rate per night $245–$351. **Maximum occupants per room** 4. **Pool** ★★★★. **Fridge in room** Yes. **Breakfast** Paid. **Wi-Fi** Free. **Parking** $36 self/$39 valet. **Walk to Universal** 35 minutes (1.3 miles). **Comments** Pets up to 40 pounds welcome with $75/week nonrefundable fee; limit 1 pet.

THE GARLAND, WHICH CELEBRATED its golden anniversary in 2022, is a favorite of Universal Orlando executives visiting the West Coast—and *The Unofficial Guide*—for its classic mid-century style, friendly service, and convenient trolley providing free hourly rides to the Studios' doorstep. Rooms are large for the era and fully updated with retro-future furnishings. We especially like the comfy mattresses; ample charging outlets; and roomy, well-lit restrooms. The immaculately landscaped Craftsman campus is brimming with outdoor sculptures and boasts a beautifully maintained pool complex, a charming shop stocked with local goods, a full-service restaurant, and a cozy lobby bar. The hotel hosts a jam-packed daily schedule of happy hours, art walks, and dive-in movies, making The Garland ideal if one member of your party would rather recreate while the rest wrangle with theme park crowds.

Hilton Universal City ★★★★

555 Universal Hollywood Dr.
Universal City
☎ 818-506-2500
hilton.com

Rate per night $289–$345. **Maximum occupants per room** 4.
Pool ★★★★. **Fridge in room** Yes. **Breakfast** Paid. **Wi-Fi** $7.95
(free with Hilton Honors). **Parking** $45 self/$55 valet. **Walk to
Universal** 5 minutes (0.2 mile). **Comments** Pets up to 75 pounds
welcome with $100/week nonrefundable fee.

UNTIL UNIVERSAL OPENS its planned on-site resorts, this Hilton is the
closest hotel to the theme park gates, which are just a brief (but very steep) walk
or shuttle bus ride away. If you've ever stayed in a Hilton, you know what to
expect from this by-the-numbers corporate chain hotel. Public areas were
originally opulent but are showing their age, and the rooms are large but
awkwardly designed, with worn furnishings and inadequate lighting. The
luxurious bedding and stunning views of the valley are the best things about the
dated guest rooms, which also suffer from noisy plumbing and a lack of USB
ports. The lobby restaurant and room service are extremely pricey; head to
CityWalk instead for an affordable meal. Like the similarly priced Sheraton that's
a few steps farther down the hill, you get no benefits in the park for staying here.

Sheraton Universal Hotel ★★★★

333 Universal Hollywood Dr.
Universal City
☎ 818-980-1212
sheratonuniversal.com

Rate per night $306–$364. **Maximum occupants per room** 4.
Pool ★★★½. **Fridge in room** Yes. **Breakfast** Paid. **Wi-Fi** Free.
Parking $46 self/$55 valet. **Walk to Universal** 8 minutes (0.3
mile). **Comments** Pets up to 40 pounds welcome with $75 non-
refundable fee; limit 1 pet.

A PERFECTLY ADEQUATE BUSINESS-CLASS HOTEL, Sheraton Universal
has slightly small rooms with stylishly modern furnishings. The property got a
major overhaul around the time the Wizarding World of Harry Potter opened,
and aside from a few confounding trendy touches, such as a lack of drawer
space, we find the facilities satisfactory. The problem is that, considering the
steep price, we'd expect amenities equal to those afforded guests at the
exceptional Loews-operated hotels at Universal Orlando. Sadly, however,
there are practically zero in-park perks for guests staying here; you don't even
get free early park entry.

Tilt Hotel ★★★½

3241 Cahuenga Blvd. W.
Los Angeles
☎ 213-319-7318
tilthoteluniversal.com

Rate per night $221–$323. **Maximum occupants per room** 4. **Pool**
★★½. **Fridge in room** Yes. **Breakfast** Free (cold). **Wi-Fi** Free. **Parking** $25/day. **Walk to Universal** 19 minutes (0.9 mile).

INSPIRED BY THE ECLECTIC movie-star haunts of
Hollywood's golden age, the Tilt Hotel is a charmingly chic
property on the periphery of Universal and our favorite spot to stay when
visiting the Studios. The high-end boutique furnishings—complete with quirky
touches such as film-strip headboards and bordello-red curtains—belie a very
reasonable rack rate. Standard rooms are adequate in size (if not enormous),
and king suites with in-room hot tubs are available. A tiny indoor pool rounds
out the amenities. It's a longer walk to Universal's front gates from here than
the BLVD, but you'll pass through CityWalk on the way, which is convenient
for grabbing a bite before or after your adventures.

PART 3

MAKING *the* MOST *of* YOUR TIME

▌ ALLOCATING TIME

THE DISNEY PEOPLE RECOMMEND spending two to four full days at Disneyland Resort. While this may seem a little self-serving, it is not without basis. Disneyland Resort is *huge*, with something to see or do crammed into every conceivable space. In addition, there are two parks, and touring requires a lot of walking and often a lot of waiting in line. Moving in and among large crowds all day is exhausting, and often the unrelenting Southern California sun zaps even the most hardy, making tempers short.

During our many visits to Disneyland, we observed, particularly on hot summer days, a dramatic transition from happy, enthusiastic touring on arrival to almost zombielike plodding along later in the day. Visitors who began their day enjoying the wonders of Disney imagination ultimately lapsed into an exhausted production mentality ("We have two more rides in Fantasyland; then we can go to the hotel").

If your schedule and budget permit, try building in a day of rest to break up your park visits, as a mom from Folsom, California, suggests:

> You are SPOT ON *when you emphasize how exhausting a Disneyland Resort trip is. If I could go back and do the trip again, I would spend one day at Disneyland, have a day of rest at the motel (with the kids swimming and me being in the shade and off my feet), and then go to California Adventure on our third day in Anaheim.*

A family from Vancouver, Canada, concurs:

> *With a four- or five-day pass, I strongly recommend a day's break in between where you can sleep in, swim, read a book, and have a day off from theme parks. In hindsight, I think this would have made the back end of our holiday that much more enjoyable.*

Alternately, plan to spread your touring over additional days so that you can spend afternoons outside the park, as this Fort Collins, Colorado, family did:

We had a four-day park hopper ticket, which allowed for a much more leisurely pace compared to our previous visits. We were present each day at rope drop, which enabled us to complete our desired attractions and lunch by noon or 1 p.m., then head back to the hotel to rest or visit the pool, and then return to the parks later for parades, shows, or other events (DCA Food and Wine Festival). For the first time on a Disney vacation, I felt somewhat relaxed.

OPTIMUM TOURING SITUATION

WE DON'T BELIEVE THAT THERE IS ONE IDEAL ITINERARY. Tastes, energy levels, and perspectives on what constitutes entertainment and relaxation vary. This understood, here are some considerations for developing your own ideal itinerary.

Optimum touring at Disneyland requires a good game plan, a minimum of three to five days on-site (excluding travel time), and a fair amount of money. It also requires a fairly prodigious appetite for Disney entertainment. The essence of optimum touring is to see the attractions in a series of shorter, less-exhausting visits during the cooler, less-crowded times of day, with plenty of rest and relaxation between excursions.

Because optimum touring calls for leaving and returning to the theme parks, it makes sense to stay in one of the Disney hotels or in one of the non-Disney hotels within walking distance. If you visit Disneyland during busy times, you need to get up early to beat the crowds. Short lines and stress-free touring are incompatible with sleeping in. If you want to sleep in *and* enjoy your touring, visit Disneyland when attendance is lighter.

The **CARDINAL RULES** *for* SUCCESSFUL TOURING

MANY VISITORS DON'T HAVE three days to devote to Disneyland Resort. For these visitors, efficient touring is a must. Even the most time-effective plan, however, won't allow you to cover both Disney theme parks in one day. Plan to allocate at least one day to each park. We provide "best of" one-day park hopper plans for those who insist on seeing the resort's highlights, but it's an expensive and exhausting option. Instead, if your schedule permits only one day of touring, we recommend that you concentrate on one theme park and save the other for another visit.

ONE-DAY TOURING

A COMPREHENSIVE ONE-DAY TOUR of Disneyland Park or Disney California Adventure (DCA) is possible, but it requires knowledge of the parks, good planning, and plenty of energy and endurance. One-day touring doesn't leave much time for full-service meals, prolonged shopping, or lengthy breaks. One-day touring can be fun and rewarding, but allocating two days per park, especially for Disneyland Park, is always preferable, if possible.

Successful touring of Disneyland Resort hinges on three rules:

1. DETERMINE IN ADVANCE WHAT YOU REALLY WANT TO SEE What rides and attractions most appeal to you? Which additional rides and attractions would you like to experience if you have any time left? What are you willing to forgo?

To help you establish your touring priorities, we describe every attraction in detail. We include the author's critical evaluation of the attraction as well as the opinions of Disneyland Resort guests expressed as star ratings. Five stars is the highest (best) rating possible.

Finally, because Disneyland Resort attractions range in scope from midway-type rides and horse-drawn trolleys to colossal, high-tech extravaganzas spanning the equivalent of whole city blocks, we have developed a hierarchy of categories for attractions to give you some sense of their order of magnitude:

SUPER-HEADLINERS The best attractions that the theme park has to offer. They are mind-boggling in size, scope, and imagination and represent the cutting edge of modern attraction technology and design.

HEADLINERS Full-blown, full-scale, multimillion-dollar, themed adventure experiences and theater presentations. They are modern in their technology and design and employ a full range of special effects.

MAJOR ATTRACTIONS Themed adventure experiences on a more modest scale but incorporating state-of-the-art technologies, or larger-scale attractions of older design.

MINOR ATTRACTIONS Small-scale dark rides (spook house–type rides), midway-type rides, minor theater presentations, transportation rides, and elaborate walk-through attractions.

DIVERSIONS Exhibits, both passive and interactive. Also include playgrounds, video arcades, and street theater.

Though not every attraction fits neatly into the above descriptions, the categories provide a relative comparison of attraction size and scope. Remember, however, that bigger and more elaborate does not always mean better. Peter Pan's Flight, a minor attraction, continues to be one of the park's most beloved rides. Likewise, for many small children, there is no attraction, regardless of size, that can surpass Dumbo the Flying Elephant.

2. ARRIVE EARLY! ARRIVE EARLY! ARRIVE EARLY! This is the single most important key to touring efficiently and avoiding long lines. With your admission pass in hand, be at the gate ready to go at least 30–45 minutes before the theme park's stated opening time. There are shorter lines and relatively fewer people first thing in the morning. Early risers receive even more of an advantage at Disneyland than at Walt Disney World because local Californians rarely rope drop. The same four rides

you can experience in 1 hour in the early morning will take more than 3 hours to see after 11 a.m. Have breakfast before you arrive, so you will not have to waste prime touring time sitting in a restaurant.

A mother of two from Houston wrote:

I always rope drop parks but was shocked at how drastically different the crowds were just 3 hours apart. We went from 5 rides per hour to all rides being over an hour wait (including D-list attractions).

From a Cincinnati mom:

Arriving early made a tremendous difference. I'll admit that at 6:15 in the morning when I was dragging our children out of bed, I thought that we'd lost our minds. But we had so much fun that morning riding rides with no waiting in line. It was worth the early arrival.

A couple from Austin, Texas, waxed enthusiastic:

I tell everyone about your book. It saved my girlfriend and me hours and hours of waiting in line (during spring break no less!). We were first in line for the parks every morning, and boy was it worth it.

Be aware that all park guests must pass through a security checkpoint to enter Disneyland Resort. In addition to having their bags opened and manually inspected, guests must also empty their pockets and step through a metal detector or be scanned with a handheld wand. Security is set up to the east of the Esplanade between the two parks for guests entering from Harbor Boulevard and on the west end of Downtown Disney; additional checkpoints screen guests exiting the Mickey & Friends and Pixar Pals parking garages and Grand Californian Hotel. When entering the resort from the east, the far-left security line is often the shortest; feel free to "excuse me" your way through the long queue of folks snaking toward a central checkpoint while you beeline for the briefer wait. The checkpoint for guests from the Disneyland and Pixar Place Hotels is usually far less crowded than the Harbor Boulevard entrance, except during early-entry hour. Queues at the east entrance can look intimidating, but there are usually enough open screening lanes in the early morning to keep the line moving; arrive around midday after the checkpoints have been consolidated and you'll face longer waits. Security checkpoints don't open until 60 minutes before park opening. If you arrive before security is set up, wait outside the screening area for the security folks to arrive.

3. AVOID BOTTLENECKS Helping you avoid bottlenecks is what this guide is all about. Bottlenecks occur as a result of crowd concentrations and/or less-than-optimal traffic engineering. Concentrations of hungry people create bottlenecks at restaurants during the lunch and dinner hours; concentrations of people moving toward the exit near closing time create bottlenecks in the gift shops en route to the gate; concentrations of visitors at new and unusually popular rides create bottlenecks and long waiting lines; rides slow to load and unload passengers create bottlenecks and long waiting lines. Avoiding bottlenecks involves being able to predict where, when, and why they occur. To this end, we provide field-tested touring plans to keep you ahead of the crowd or out of its way (see discussion following). In addition, we provide critical data on all rides and shows that helps you estimate how long you may have to wait in line, compares rides in terms of their capacity to accommodate large crowds, and rates the rides according to our opinions and the opinions of other Disneyland visitors.

WHAT'S A QUEUE?

THOUGH IT'S NOT COMMONLY used in the United States, *queue* (pronounced "cue") is the universal English word for a line, such as one in which you wait to cash a check at the bank or to board a ride at a theme park. There's a mathematical area of specialization within the field of operations research called queuing theory, which studies and models how lines work. Because The Unofficial Guides draw heavily on this discipline, we use some of its terminology. In addition to the noun, the verb *to queue* means "to get in line," and a queuing area is a waiting area that accommodates a line.

TOURING PLANS

OF UTMOST IMPORTANCE: READ THIS!

IN ANALYZING READER SURVEYS, we were astonished by the percentage of readers who do not use our touring plans. Scientifically tested and proven, these plans can save you 4 entire hours or more of waiting in line. Four hours! Four fewer hours of standing, 4 hours freed up to do something fun. Our groundbreaking research that created the touring plans has been the subject of front-page articles in the *Dallas Morning News* and *The New York Times* and has been cited in numerous scholarly journals. So the question is, why would you not use them?

We get a ton of email from both our Disneyland and Walt Disney World readers—98% of it positive—commenting on our touring plans. First, from a family from Stockton, California, who descended on Disneyland Park over the Easter holiday:

> *We're not much for plans and regimentation, so we winged it the first day. It was so awful that the next day we gave one of your itineraries a shot. It worked so well that I was telling strangers about it that night like [I was] some kind of Bible thumper.*

From a Palo Alto, California, mother of three boys:

My husband viewed my extensive planning with a great deal of amusement and humorously vowed to sabotage my plans by tempting the kids to go on an unplanned ride at the very start. I countered by involving the kids in crafting our touring plan, so they were as excited and committed to it as I was.

My favorite part was when we rode the monorail in the late morning. By that time, we had already gone on a bunch of rides and never waited in a single line longer than 5–10 minutes. The monorail passed over the park entrance, which was mobbed with people. My 10-year-old exclaimed, "Wow! Look at the lines now!" My previously doubtful husband looked at me with a smile and said, "Thank you."

From a Chicago mom:

I feel strongly that you have to go into a Disney trip with a firm plan or else all you will remember of your vacation will be the squabbles and the long lines! The daily touring plans not only allowed me to see everything that I wanted but also allowed me time to revisit my favorite attractions multiple times! Those who complain that the touring plans are too rigid need a serious reality check. Yes, they are structured, but they save you mountains of time! RELAX and use the touring plans if you are going during a busy part of the year. Not only will it save you the time that you are spending complaining about the plans in the first place, but it will also save you the complaining you will be doing when you are in line for Space Mountain for 90 minutes!

From a Missoula, Montana, family:

My wife and I hadn't been to Disneyland in 40 years. I was a little cynical about the costs and the hassle of getting there, the crowds, etc. When we started reading your book, I really got excited. I thought, "Hey, we can do this and we have a friend with us telling us what to do the whole way!" We did 61 things in three days. Your book made it all come together for us.

An Akron, Ohio, reader reports:

We rode 36 rides at Disneyland in ONE DAY using your touring plan/Lines app combined with the skills I have developed based on reading your books over the years. You are amazing. We rode EVERY ride and saw EVERY show in Disneyland that was open . . . and we rode the three major roller coasters twice each.

A multigenerational matriarch in Olympia, Washington, writes:

With children ranging from 4 to 14 years old, we needed a plan that would meet everyone's expectations. We weren't able to see or do everything, but we knew that when we arrived, and everyone was able to do a few of the things they wanted to. We all had realistic expectations, and everyone was very, very happy with the trip.

And finally, from a reader in Mililani, Hawaii:

With the personalized plans, we were able to hit every ride, show, and parade we wanted to see on the first day at both Disneyland and DCA without EVER waiting in a real line. As I passed people standing in 70- to 120-minute lines, I felt so relieved that we used your process. It was an incredible, stress-free, and enjoyable experience, all thanks to you.

TOURING PLANS: WHAT THEY ARE AND HOW THEY WORK

WHEN WE INTERVIEWED DISNEYLAND VISITORS who toured the theme park(s) on slow days, they invariably waxed eloquent about the sheer delight of their experience. When we questioned visitors who toured on moderate or busy days, however, they talked at length about the jostling crowds and how much time they stood in line. What a shame, they said, that so much time and energy are spent fighting crowds in a place as special as Disneyland.

Given this complaint, our researchers descended on Disneyland to determine whether a touring plan could be devised that would liberate visitors from the traffic flow and allow them to see any theme park in one day with minimal waiting in line. On some of the busiest days of the year, our team monitored traffic into and through Disneyland Park, noting how it filled and how patrons were distributed among the attractions. We also observed which rides and attractions were most popular and where bottlenecks were most likely to occur.

After many years of collecting data, we devised preliminary touring plans, which we tested during one of the busiest weeks of the year. Each day, our researchers would tour the park using one of the preliminary plans, noting how long it took to walk from place to place and how long the wait in line was for each attraction. Combining the information gained on trial runs, we devised a master plan that we retested and fine-tuned. This plan, with very little variance from day to day, allowed us to experience all major rides and attractions and most lesser ones in one day, with an average wait in line of less than 10 minutes at each.

From this master plan, we developed alternative plans that took into account the varying tastes and personal requirements of different Disneyland patrons. Each plan operated with the same logic as the master plan but addressed the special needs and preferences of its intended users.

Finally, after all of the plans were tested by our staff, we selected (using convenience sampling) Disneyland visitors to test the plans. The only prerequisite for being chosen to test the plans was that the guests must have been visiting a Disney park for the first time. A second group of patrons was chosen for a control group. These were first-time visitors who would tour the park according to their own plans but who would make notes about what they did and how much time they spent in lines.

When the two groups were compared, the results were amazing. On days when major theme park attendance exceeded 42,000, visitors touring without our plans *averaged* 2 hours and 36 minutes more waiting in line per day than the patrons touring with our plans, and they experienced 33% fewer attractions. In 2004 the application of a cutting-edge algorithm to our touring plan software increased the waiting time saved to an average of 4 hours. Our latest advancements give subscribers to TouringPlans.com the ability to build personalized plans online, and then use the Lines smartphone app while inside the parks to optimize their itineraries with real-time wait-time data.

General Overview of the Touring Plans

Our touring plans are step-by-step guides for seeing as much as possible with a minimum of standing in line. They're designed to help you avoid crowds and bottlenecks on days of moderate to heavy attendance. On days of lighter attendance (see "Selecting the Time of Year for Your Visit," page 28), the plans still save time but aren't as critical to successful touring.

What You Can Realistically Expect from the Touring Plans

Though we present one-day touring plans for both parks, you should understand that Disneyland Park has more attractions than you can see in one day, even if you never wait in line. If you must cram your visit to Disneyland Park into a single day, the one-day touring plans will allow you to see as much as is humanly possible. Under certain circumstances you may not complete the plan, and you definitely won't be able to see everything. For Disneyland Park, the most comprehensive, efficient, and relaxing touring plans are the two-day plans. Though Disney California Adventure (DCA) has grown, you should be able to see everything in one day by following our touring plans.

Variables That Will Affect the Success of the Touring Plans

How quickly you move from one ride to another; when and how many refreshment and restroom breaks you take; when, where, and how you eat meals; and your ability (or lack thereof) to find your way around will all have an impact on the success of the plans. Smaller groups almost always move faster than larger groups, and parties of adults generally can cover more ground than families with young children. Switching off (see page 165), among other things, prohibits families with little ones from moving expeditiously among attractions. Plus, some children simply cannot conform to the "early to rise" conditions of the touring plans. A mom from Nutley, New Jersey, writes:

> [Though] the touring plans all advise getting to parks at opening, we just couldn't burn the candle at both ends. Our kids (10, 7, and 4) would not go to sleep early and couldn't be up at dawn and still stay relatively sane. It worked well for us to let them sleep a little later, go out and bring breakfast back to the room while they slept, and still get a relatively early start by not spending time on eating breakfast out. We managed to avoid long lines with an early morning and by hitting popular attractions during parades, mealtimes, and late evenings.

And a family from Centerville, Ohio, says:

The toughest thing about your touring plans was getting the rest of the family to stay with them, at least to some degree. Getting them to pass by attractions to hit something across the park was no easy task (sometimes impossible).

A multigenerational family wonders how to know if you are on track or not, writing:

It seems like the touring plans were very time dependent, yet there were no specific times attached to the plan outside of the early morning. On more than one day, I often had to guess as to whether we were on track.

There is no objective measurement for being on track. Each group's experience will differ to some degree. Regardless of whether your group is large or small, fast or slow, the sequence of attractions in the touring plans will allow you to enjoy the greatest number of attractions in the least possible time. Two quickly moving adults will probably take in more attractions in a specific time period than will a large group comprised of children, parents, and grandparents. However, given the characteristics of the respective groups, each will maximize their touring time and experience as many attractions as possible. That said, if you really want specific times for each step of your touring plan, use the online versions and customize them for your specific day of travel.

Finally, if you have young children in your party, be prepared for character encounters. The appearance of a Disney character is usually sufficient to stop a touring plan dead in its tracks. What's more, while some characters continue to stroll the parks, it is becoming more the rule to assemble characters in a specific venue, where families must queue for photos and autographs. Meeting characters, posing for photos, and collecting autographs can burn hours of touring time. If your kids are into character-autograph collecting, you will need to anticipate these interruptions to the touring plan and negotiate some understanding with your children about when you will follow the plan and when you will collect autographs. Our advice is to either go with the flow or alternatively set aside a certain morning or afternoon for photos and autographs. Be aware, however, that queues for autographs, especially in Fantasy Faire and Mickey's Toontown at Disneyland Park, are as long as the queues for major attractions. The only time-efficient way to collect autographs is to line up at the character-greeting areas first thing in the morning. Because this is also the best time to experience the more popular attractions, you may have some tough decisions to make.

While we realize that following the touring plans is not always easy, we nevertheless recommend continuous, expeditious touring until around noon. After that hour, breaks and diversions won't affect the plans significantly.

Some variables that can profoundly affect the touring plans are beyond your control. Chief among these are the manner and timing of bringing a particular ride to capacity. For example, Big Thunder Mountain Railroad, a roller coaster in Disneyland Park, has five trains. On a given morning it may begin operation with two of the five, and then add the other three if and when they are needed. If the waiting line builds rapidly before operators decide to go to full capacity, you could have a long wait, even in the early morning.

Another variable relates to the time you arrive for a show. Usually your wait will be the length of time from your arrival to the end of the presentation in progress. Thus, if the *Enchanted Tiki Room* show is 15 minutes long and you arrive 1 minute after a show has begun, your wait for the next show will be 14 minutes. Conversely, if you arrive as the show is wrapping up, your wait will be only 1 or 2 minutes.

What to Do If You Lose the Thread

Anything from a blister to a broken attraction can throw off a touring plan. If unforeseen events interrupt a plan:

1. If you're following a printed touring plan, skip one step on the plan for every 20 minutes' delay. If, for example, you lose your billfold and spend an hour hunting for it, skip three steps and pick up from there, or

2. Forget the plan; organize the remainder of your day using the standby wait times listed in the app or the recommended attraction visitation times in each attraction profile.

3. If you're following a touring plan in the **Lines** app (TouringPlans.com/lines), just press the OPTIMIZE button when you're ready to start touring again. Lines will figure out the best possible plan for the remainder of your day.

Flexibility

The attractions included in the touring plans are the most popular attractions as determined by our reader surveys. Even so, your favorite attractions might be different. Fortunately, the touring plans are flexible. If the touring plan calls for an attraction that you don't wish to experience, simply skip it and move on to the next attraction on the plan. Additionally, you can substitute similar attractions in the same area of the park. If the plan calls for riding Dumbo, for example, and you're not interested but would enjoy the Mad Tea Party (which is not on the plan), then substitute the Mad Tea Party for Dumbo. As long as the substitution is a similar attraction (it won't work to substitute a show for a ride) and located pretty close to the attraction called for in the plan, you won't compromise the overall effectiveness of the touring plan.

For the ultimate in flexibility and efficiency, use the Lines smartphone app to check off steps on your plan as you complete them (or delete ones you decide to skip), and then let the optimizer get you back on track after any detours. For example, let's say that your touring plan calls for riding Haunted Mansion next, but your family really needs an ice-cream break and 30 minutes out of the sun. Get the ice cream and take the break. When you're done, click the OPTIMIZE button on your plan, and it will be updated with what to do next. The ability to redo your plan allows you to recover from any situation while still minimizing your waits for the rest of the day.

A family of four from South Slocan, British Columbia, found that they could easily tailor the touring plans to meet their needs:

> We amended your touring plans by taking out the attractions we didn't want to do and just doing the remainder in order. It worked great, and by arriving before the parks opened, we saw everything we wanted, with virtually no waits! The best advice by far was to get there early!

A multigenerational family from South Jordan, Utah, found it helpful to use this book in conjunction with TouringPlans.com:

> We didn't follow an exact touring plan, but I used the tips in your book and touring plans to make our own. We decided to do all the major attractions first before the crowds came. We arrived at about 8:05 a.m., and by 11 we were walking to our eighth attraction. We saw all we wanted and then took a more relaxed pace the rest of the day. A downside was that after getting on so many rides so quickly, we didn't want to wait in line for even 20 minutes the rest of the day.

Clip-Out Pocket Outlines of Touring Plans

Select the plan appropriate for your party, and then clip the pocket version from the back of this guide and carry it with you as a quick reference at the theme park. If you're feeling crafty, upgrade your clip-out plans like this lady from London, England:

> I cut out the touring plan; wrote parade times, dining reservations, showtimes, etc., around the side; and then laminated it for our day.

Will the Plans Continue to Work Once the Secret Is Out?

Yes! First, all of the plans require that a patron be there when the theme parks open. Many Disneyland patrons simply refuse to get up early while on vacation. Second, less than 1% of any day's attendance has been exposed to the plans, too little to affect results. Last, most groups tailor the plans, skipping rides or shows according to personal taste.

How Frequently Are the Touring Plans Revised?

Because Disney is always adding new attractions and changing operations, we revise the touring plans every year. Most complaints we receive about them come from readers who are using out-of-date editions of *The Unofficial Guide*. Be prepared, however, for surprises. Opening procedures and showtimes, for example, may change, and you never know when an attraction might break down. Touring plans inside our Lines app are updated even more often and can instantly adapt to any refurbishments or breakdowns during your visit.

Tour Groups from Hell

Tour groups of up to 200 people sometimes use our plans. Unless your party is as large as that tour group, this development shouldn't alarm you. Because tour groups are big, they move slowly and have to stop periodically to collect stragglers. The tour guide also has to accommodate the unpredictability of five dozen or so bladders. In short, you should have no problem passing a group after the initial encounter.

Bouncing Around

Many readers object to crisscrossing a theme park, as our touring plans sometimes require. A woman from Decatur, Georgia, said she "got dizzy from all the bouncing around" and that the "running back and forth reminded [her] of a scavenger hunt." We empathize, but here's the rub.

In Disneyland Park, the most popular attractions are positioned across the park from one another. This is no accident. It's good planning, a method of more equally distributing guests throughout the park. If you want to experience the most popular attractions in one day without long waits, you can arrive before the park fills and see those attractions first thing (which requires crisscrossing the park), or you can enjoy the main attractions on one side of the park first thing in the morning, and then use Lightning Lane for the popular attractions on the other side. All other approaches will subject you to incredible waits at some attractions if you tour during busy times of the year.

The best way to minimize bouncing around at Disneyland Park is to use one of our two-day touring plans, which spread the more popular attractions over two mornings and work beautifully even when the park closes at 8 p.m. or earlier.

DCA is configured in a way that precludes an orderly approach to touring, or to a clockwise or counterclockwise rotation. Orderly touring is further frustrated by the limited guest capacity of the midway rides in the Paradise Gardens Park and Pixar Pier districts of the park. At DCA, therefore, you're stuck with bouncing around, whether you use the touring plan or not, if you want to avoid horrendous waits.

We suggest you follow the touring plans religiously, especially in the mornings, if you're visiting Disneyland during busy, more crowded times. The consequence of touring spontaneity in peak season is hours of otherwise avoidable standing in line. During quieter times of year, there's no need to be compulsive about following the plans.

Touring Plan Rejection

We've discovered that you can't implant a touring plan in certain personalities without vehement rejection. Some folks just do not respond well to regimentation. If you bump into this problem with someone in your party, it's best to roll with the punches, as did this couple:

> *The rest of the group was not receptive to the use of the touring plans. They all thought I was being a little too regimented about*

planning this vacation. Rather than argue, I left the touring plans behind as we ventured off for the parks. You can guess the outcome. When we returned home, we watched the videos we took during our vacation. About every 5 minutes there is a shot of us all gathered around a park map trying to decide what to do next.

If possible, try to convince your family to compromise and follow the plan for at least a few hours each morning, as this mom from Shawnee, Kansas, suggests:

I told my family that we were following "Mom's Checklist" for the first 3 hours and then after that we could waste time wherever they wanted. Arriving at park opening and following your touring plans pretty much guarantees you'll hit all major attractions and many others with short lines within half a day.

Finally, as a Connecticut woman alleges, the touring plans are incompatible with some readers' bladders as well as their personalities:

When you write those day schedules next year, can you schedule bathroom breaks in there too? You expect us to be at a certain ride at a certain time and with no stops in between. The schedules are a problem if you are a laid-back, slow-moving, careful detail noticer. What were you thinking when you made these schedules?

Before you injure your urinary tract, feel free to deviate from the touring plan as necessary to heed the call of nature. If you are using a customized plan in Lines, you can build in as many breaks (bathroom or otherwise) as you like, and the optimizer will plan around them.

A Clamor for Customized Touring Plans

We're inundated by letters urging us to create additional touring plans. These include a plan for rainy days, a seniors' plan, a plan for folks who sleep late, a plan omitting rides that "bump, jerk, and clonk," a plan for gardening enthusiasts, and a plan for single women.

The touring plans in this book are intended to be flexible. Adapt them to your preferences. If you don't like rides that bump and jerk, skip them when they come up in a touring plan. If you want to sleep in and go to the park at noon, use the afternoon part of a plan. If you're a ninth-grader and want to ride Space Mountain three times in a row, do it. Will it decrease the touring plan's effectiveness? Sure, but the plan was created only to help you have fun. It's your day.

If you really want to tailor your itinerary, we suggest subscribing to TouringPlans.com, where you can customize your day's to-do list down to the last snack. Choose the date of your visit and the attractions you want to experience, including character greetings, parades, fireworks, meals, and midday breaks; the computer will generate an optimized step-by-step itinerary, showing you how to see everything with minimal waits in line. The touring plans can incorporate any Lightning Lane reservations you retrieve and accommodate options like child swap. From a father of two teens from Superior, Colorado:

We used a custom touring plan for our day at Disneyland and found it super useful. As always, arriving early was the key to success.

For a truly personalized experience, some of our team members (including this book's coauthor) offer professional tour-planning services; visit tinyurl.com/PersonalTouringPlan or sethkubersky.com for details.

WHAT *to* EXPECT WHEN YOU ARRIVE *at the* PARKS

BECAUSE EACH TOURING PLAN is based on being present when the theme park opens, you need to know a little about opening procedures. Disney security checkpoints and the theme park parking lots open up to 60 minutes before official opening time.

An entrance plaza is just outside the turnstiles of the parks. Usually all guests are held outside the turnstiles until about 30 minutes prior to official park opening. Use this time to pull up your tickets on your smartphone (turn the screen brightness to maximum for easier scanning) or make sure each person is holding their own pass if using paper tickets. All guests are admitted during the early-entry period, but those without hotel credentials will be confined to a small section of the park until the official opening time. At Disneyland Park you will be admitted to Main Street, U.S.A.; at DCA to Buena Vista Street. If you proceed farther into a park, you will encounter Disney cast members who will keep you from entering the remainder of the park. You will remain here until the proverbial "rope drop," when the park and all (or most) of its attractions are opened at the official opening time.

A WORD ABOUT THE ROPE DROP

DISNEY HAS A NUMBER OF cast members supervising the rope drop in order to suppress the mayhem of anxiously waiting guests. A pleasantly parental prerecorded "Please walk; don't run" announcement attempts to have a somewhat subduing effect on the straining crowds, but upbeat music at the opening moment revs them right back up again. After removing the rope barrier, Disney cast members may lead you at a fast walk toward the attraction you're straining to reach, forcing you (and everyone else) to maintain their pace. Not until they come within close proximity of the attraction do the cast members step aside.

So here's the scoop. If cast members persist in walking the crowd back, the only way you can gain an advantage over the rest of the crowd is to arrive early enough to be one of those close to the front. Be alert, though; sometimes the Disney folks will step out of the way after about 50 yards or so. If this happens, you can fire up the afterburners and speed the remaining distance to your destination.

Early entry–eligible guests must show their hotel reservation in the Disneyland app to a cast member after entering the park, and then they may immediately proceed to select attractions. When the official opening time arrives, early-entry guests have an advantage reaching certain E-Ticket rides, especially Rise of the Resistance and Radiator Springs Racers.

LIGHTNING LANE
and DISNEY GENIE+

NOTE: AS OF JULY 2024, Genie+ was renamed to **Lightning Lane Multi Pass,** and Individual Lightning Lane is now **Lightning Lane Single Pass.**

FastPass was a free system for moderating the waiting times for popular attractions. This program was retired in 2021 and replaced with Lightning Lane, an option that allows guests to skip the regular line for an extra fee. Here's how it works:

Select attractions at Disneyland and Disney California Adventure (DCA) offer a special entrance called a "Lightning Lane," in addition to their traditional standby queue. Guests using the Lightning Lane get expedited access, typically boarding the ride in 15–20 minutes or less.

To gain access to the Lightning Lanes, guests must use the Disneyland smartphone app. Each participating attraction will display its current standby wait time in the app, along with the next available Lightning Lane entry window. To get started, go to the "Tip Board" from the app's main menu, scroll until you find an attraction displaying Lightning Lane availability, and tap "Book Experience" to purchase access. You can also purchase Genie+ by tapping "My Genie Day" on the main menu, followed by "Get Genie+ for Today."

LIGHTNING LANE ATTRACTIONS	
DISNEYLAND PARK	**DISNEY CALIFORNIA ADVENTURE**
Autopia	Goofy's Sky School
Big Thunder Mountain Railroad	Grizzly River Run
Buzz Lightyear Astro Blasters	Guardians of the Galaxy—Mission: Breakout!
Haunted Mansion	Incredicoaster
Indiana Jones Adventure	The Little Mermaid: Ariel's Undersea Adventure
It's a Small World	Monsters, Inc. Mike & Sulley to the Rescue!
Matterhorn Bobsleds	Radiator Springs Racers*
Mickey & Minnie's Runaway Railway	Soarin' Around the World
Millennium Falcon: Smugglers Run	Toy Story Midway Mania!
Roger Rabbit's Car Toon Spin	WEB SLINGERS: A Spider-Man Adventure
Space Mountain	
Star Tours—The Adventures Continue	
Star Wars: Rise of the Resistance*	
Tiana's Bayou Adventure	

Denotes rides that sell individual attraction access (not included in Genie+).

Guests can pay $30 per person per day (when purchased in advance with park admission) or $30–$35 depending on demand (if purchased on the day of your visit) for Genie+, which lets them claim Lightning Lane return times for about 20 of the attractions across both parks. Genie+ users can only claim one return window at a time (unless they're using the **2-hour** or **Multiple Experiences** loopholes described below) and must redeem it at the selected ride, cancel or modify it, or let it expire before picking another. Unlike FastPass, guests may only use each participating Lightning Lane once per day, so you'll be back in standby if you want to re-ride your favorites. Purchase of Genie+ also includes unlimited PhotoPass digital image downloads for the day (see page 124), which may be as valuable as the queuing time you'll save with the service. Finally, Genie+ includes access to Snapchat-style photo filters and "Audio Tales," which are brief sound clips with trivia about a particular park location, inside the Disneyland app. Be sure to bring headphones if you want to be able to hear these over the ambient noise.

Genie+ closely resembles MaxPass, the old extra-cost app-based version of FastPass. Occasional cell service snafus aside, we've found the experience of using both MaxPass and its successor Genie+ to be eerily blissful; on a busy weekend, we used it to knock off a dozen headliners without ever queuing for more than 15 minutes. To be frank, it usually works so well (especially in comparison to Walt Disney World's version) that we're surprised Disneyland isn't charging even more for Genie+.

Lightning Lane access is not bundled into Genie+ for one or two selected rides in each park—currently Star Wars: Rise of the Resistance at Disneyland and Radiator Springs Racers at DCA—but instead must be purchased individually through the app. Pricing for these rides varies daily between $15 and $28 based on demand, and you may only purchase individual Lightning Lane access for a maximum of two attractions per day (and only once per attraction). You don't have to purchase Genie+ to buy Lightning Lane for individual attraction access, and you also do not have to purchase either service on every day of your trip, or for every member of your party. Lightning Lane and Genie+ are not included in Magic Key passes, although all key-holders get 20% off the daily Genie+ fee, and there are currently no DVC discounts available for the services.

To use Genie+ and Lightning Lanes, first download the Disneyland mobile app and sign in with your existing disney.com credentials, or create a new account with an email and password. Next, purchase your admission tickets through the app, or scan the barcodes of any tickets you've already purchased to link them to your account. Genie+ can be added on at the time of ticket purchase, or after you enter the park on the day of your visit. Prepurchasing Genie+ is the easier and potentially cheaper option, but paying day by day allows you to test the service without committing for the full length of your ticket. Once you are registered, you must scan your admission and enter the park turnstiles (or

Downtown Disney monorail terminal) before making your first Genie+ or individual attraction Lightning Lane selections of the day.

Lightning Lane works remarkably well, primarily because Lightning Lane users get amazingly preferential treatment. As a telling indication of their status, Disney (borrowing a term from the airlines) refers to those in the regular line as standby guests. Clearly Disney is sending a message here, to wit: Lightning Lane is heaven; anything else is limbo at best and probably purgatory. In either event, you'll think you've been in purgatory if you get stuck in the regular line during the hot, crowded part of the day like this family that owns timeshares in nearby Oceanside:

> We felt like second-class citizens since we did not order Lightning Lane passes. We stood in line for hours and rode two rides, at which point we were so frustrated and tired we left.

Lightning Lane, however, doesn't eliminate the need to arrive at the theme park early. Because each park offers a dozen Lightning Lane attractions at most, you still need to get an early start if you want to see as much as possible in a single day. Plus, there's a limited supply of Lightning Lane return windows sold for each individual attraction on a given day. So if you don't show up on a busy day until the middle of the afternoon, you might discover that all of the Lightning Lanes for the top rides have been claimed by other guests. Lightning Lane does, happily, make it possible to see more with less waiting. A Touring-Plans.com data analysis showed Genie+ saves users an average of 20 minutes per ride at DCA and over 30 minutes per ride at Disneyland. That adds up to spending 1½–3 hours less in line (depending on the crowd levels) during a full day at DCA, while Genie+ users at Disneyland wait a total of 2½–4½ hours less than guests going standby.

UNDERSTANDING THE LIGHTNING LANE SYSTEM

THE PURPOSE of the Lightning Lane system is to reduce the waiting time at designated attractions for guests who are willing to pay extra for the privilege. The system also, in effect, imposes a penalty—that is, being relegated to standby status—to those who opt not to pay for Lightning Lane.

When you use the Disneyland app to secure a Lightning Lane reservation, it will assign you the next available return time, such as "1 p.m. to 2 p.m.," "1:15 p.m. to 2:15 p.m.," and so on; you can return to enjoy the ride anytime within your selected return window. Disneyland Resort strictly enforces the 1-hour Lightning Lane windows; however, Lightning Lane allows an unpublicized 15-minute grace period and exceptions for ride breakdowns. Pay close attention to the time when you receive your Lightning Lane reservation and plan your return accordingly.

When you report back to the attraction later, you'll enter a line marked LIGHTNING LANE that will route you more or less directly to the boarding area or preshow area. Everyone in your party must have their own Lightning Lane reservation and be ready to scan their admission pass, MagicBand+, or mobile device at the entrance of the Lightning Lane.

You may show up at any time within your Lightning Lane return window, and from our observation, no specific time is better or worse. This holds true because cast members are instructed to minimize waits for Lightning Lane users. Thus, if the Lightning Lane is suddenly inundated (something that occurs more or less by chance), cast members rapidly intervene to reduce the Lightning Lane.

Disney will normally allocate 80%–90% of a ride's hourly capacity to Lightning Lane riders. In practice, that means that Disney puts between 4 and 10 people from the Lightning Lane on the ride for every 1 person it takes from the standby line; if Lightning Lane becomes backed up, that ratio can temporarily spike as high as 100:1. Because Genie+ costs real money, we believe Disney sets an upper limit on how long people will wait in the Lightning Lane. In practice, we've rarely experienced a Lightning Lane wait longer than 15 minutes (notwithstanding technical difficulties), and usually the wait is under 5 minutes; the biggest backup is usually found just outside the Lightning Lane entrance, where guests fumble to scan their phones. The exceptions are attractions that merge their Standby and Lightning Lanes before a preshow, and then have another queue before boarding, such as Rise of the Resistance, Indiana Jones Adventure, or Guardians of the Galaxy. In these instances, Lightning Lane guests usually get near-instant access to the first preshow, but they may still wait 15 minutes or more before boarding the ride vehicle.

However, Lightning Lane's efficiency falls apart when multiple Genie+ attractions break down simultaneously, as this couple from San Antonio, Texas, encountered:

> We had Lightning Lane passes for three rides that were canceled due to ride closures. This dumped a lot of people with open Lightning Lane passes (with no set arrival window) into the remaining open ride lines. At one point the Lightning Lane line for Haunted Mansion wrapped all the way in front of the Mansion and down the street.

Whatever time you obtain a Lightning Lane reservation, you can usually be assured that there will be a period of time between when you receive your time and the beginning of your return window. The interval can be as short as 30 minutes or as long as 7 hours depending on park attendance, the popularity of the attraction, and the attraction's hourly capacity. However, at certain times select attractions—including Haunted Mansion, Buzz Lightyear Astro Blasters, Roger Rabbit's Cartoon Spin, and It's a Small World—may offer immediate Lightning Lane return times or return times that are significantly quicker than waiting standby.

As a general rule, the earlier in the day you secure a Lightning Lane reservation, the shorter the interval between time of issue and the beginning of your return window. The exact time is determined by how many other guests obtained Lightning Lane reservations before you.

If an attraction is exceptionally popular and/or its hourly capacity is relatively small, the return window might be pushed back to park closing time. When this happens, the app will stop issuing return times. It would not be unusual, for example, for Rise of the Resistance at Disneyland to sell an entire day's allocation of Lightning Lane reservations by late morning during peak season and by midafternoon on an average day. When this happens, the Disneyland app will indicate that Lightning Lane return times are all gone for the day. Genie+ itself has sold out entirely on a handful of days during holiday weeks, but it will usually be available for purchase even after Lightning Lane return times for some (or many) attractions are already gone.

Lightning Lane Guidelines

- Park tickets must be activated at the park turnstiles (or Downtown Disney monorail station) before being used to purchase Genie+ or obtain Lightning Lane return times, so you can't send one family member into the park while the others snooze.

- Use Lightning Lane when it can save you 20 minutes or more at an attraction or if the Lightning Lane return time is shorter than the standby wait.

- Lightning Lane reservations can be obtained as soon as a park's gates open for early entry, but return windows won't begin until the park officially opens.

- Always check the Lightning Lane return period before obtaining your reservation, and be careful of conflicts with your dining reservations.

- If using Genie+, obtain Lightning Lane return times for Indiana Jones Adventure, Matterhorn Bobsleds, and Space Mountain at Disneyland Park and for Soarin' Around the World, Guardians of the Galaxy—Mission: Breakout!, and Toy Story Midway Mania! at DCA as early in the day as practical.

- Don't depend on Lightning Lane being available for individual attractions (especially Rise of the Resistance) after noon during busier times of the year.

- Make sure everyone in your party has their own Lightning Lane return time. Reservations are tied to each individual admission pass and may not be transferred.

- You can obtain your next Genie+ Lightning Lane return time as soon as you redeem your current pass at the attraction's entrance or when the return window expires. Maximize efficiency by always obtaining a new Lightning Lane return time for the next attraction while waiting to board the previous one.

- If your Genie+ return time is more than 2 hours away, you may retrieve an additional reservation for a different Genie+ attraction 120 minutes after scheduling your first. This trick, known as the **2-hour loophole,** can be used to stack multiple overlapping Lightning Lane reservations in the evening; see the tips below for details.

- If you change your mind about a Genie+ Lightning Lane you selected, Disney's app allows you to modify an existing Lightning Lane reservation by picking a different time or attraction (if available) instead of having to cancel and rebook. Try reserving your desired ride even if the return window isn't ideal, then refresh the app repeatedly until a preferable return time appears. Modifying a Lightning Lane return time (instead of canceling and rebooking) doesn't reset the 2-hour time before another return time can be retrieved, which facilitates stacking reservations for later. Be aware that if you change your mind back, your initial reservation may no longer be available.

- Once you've entered the park for the day, you can use Genie+ to continue to retrieve Lightning Lane return times after you've exited, so you can reserve another ride while lunching in Downtown Disney or napping at your hotel.

- Be mindful of your Lightning Lane return time, and plan intervening activities accordingly. You may use your Lightning Lane entry **5 minutes before** its start time and up to **15 minutes after** it expires. This unadvertised grace period (subject to change) is typically the only exception allowed to your assigned return window. If you are within your 15-minute grace period but the Lightning Lane pass has already vanished from your app, simply scan your park ticket at the attraction entrance instead. These windows are strictly enforced at Genie+ attractions, but cast members at Individual Lightning Lane rides may show leniency toward late arrivals.

- Guests with park hopper tickets may only secure morning Lightning Lane return times at the park they have a reservation for. However, you may retrieve Lightning Lane return times for the opposite park before 11 a.m. (when park hopping is permitted) as long as the requested ride is already distributing return times later than 11 a.m. If the current return times are still before 11 a.m., you'll be told to try that reservation again later.

- Attractions will not dispense Lightning Lane reservations while they are closed for extended refurbishments or special events, but they may continue to dispense return times through Genie+ when temporarily unavailable, with a time buffer added to accommodate the anticipated downtime.

- If an attraction is temporarily unavailable due to technical difficulties during your Lightning Lane return window, your Lightning Lane automatically converts to a Multiple Experiences Lightning Lane replacement pass. Multiple Experiences passes remain valid for use until closing time at that attraction (if it reopens) or at selected other Lightning Lane attractions in both parks. If the original return window was near closing time, the Multiple Experiences pass may be valid on the following day. Individual Lightning Lane purchases may be automatically refunded if you are unable to ride because the attraction never reopens that day, but no refunds are issued for Genie+ due to attraction closures. Multiple Experiences replacement passes are also accepted at many attractions inside Disney California Adventure that do not offer Lightning Lane; tap "find out where you can go" in the app to see exactly where your pass may be redeemed. The most valuable tier of Genie+ attractions for Multiple Experiences Lightning Lane passes come from Tiana's Bayou Adventure, Space Mountain, Indiana Jones Adventure, Haunted Mansion Holiday, Mickey & Minnie's Runaway Railway, and Matterhorn Bobsleds in Disneyland, and Guardians of the Galaxy, WEB SLINGERS, and Toy Story Midway Mania in DCA. They are valid virtually anywhere except Individual Lightning Lane rides and Fantasyland attractions. See advanced tips for taking advantage of Multiple Experiences passes on page 104.

- You may hold only one Genie+ Lightning Lane reservation at a time and/or up to two reservations for individual Lightning Lane attractions. The only exceptions to this rule are the 2-hour loophole, described above, and Multiple Experiences Lightning Lane replacement passes; there is no limit to the number of those you can simultaneously hold.

- You may want to pick one member of your party to handle everyone's tickets and Lightning Lane reservations on their phone. Alternatively, each person can create a personal account and attach everyone's ticket to it so that you will be able to see each other's Lightning Lane selections within the app (similar to the "Friends and Family" feature found in Walt Disney World's app). This gives your group the option of splitting up but still retaining access to each other's plans. Note that each person must still use their own ticket to enter the park or redeem Lightning Lane reservations.

10 STEPS TO MASTERING GENIE+

GENIE+ AND LIGHTNING LANE don't negate the need for a good touring plan, particularly for families focused on the slow-loading childrens' rides that don't offer the service. However, expert Genie+ users can adopt a carpe diem attitude that will allow you to hit most—if not all—of the headliners with minimal preplanning.

1. Before your visit, make two lists: one of all the attractions you want to experience that offer Genie+ Lightning Lane, and another of those you want to see that don't participate in the service.

2. Make sure your Disneyland smartphone app is properly set up with your admission tickets attached before arriving at the park, and be sure to bring a phone charger or backup battery.

3. Arrive early and try to enter the park 30 minutes before the official opening.

4. Purchase Genie+ and make a Lightning Lane reservation for an eligible attraction on your list as soon as you enter the park. Pick an available attraction with the earliest return time, and set an alarm on your phone to remind you when your next return time arrives.

5. As soon as you're permitted, head to the most popular non-Genie+ ride on your list and get in the standby queue.

6. While waiting for your first ride, review available Lightning Lane return times to plan your next selection, and modify your current reservation if you see something better.

7. If your first Lightning Lane's expiration is still more than 30 minutes away, go ahead and ride the next closest non-Genie+ attraction on your list first. Otherwise, go straight to use your first Lightning Lane.

8. You can claim another reservation in Genie+ after scanning in for your first Lightning Lane. (A few attractions may require a second scan farther inside the queue before you can make another reservation.)

9. Repeat this cycle until the soonest available Lightning Lane return time is more than 120 minutes away. At that point, begin selecting the latest available return times, keeping an eye out for evening return times on outdoor rides that look better after sunset (like Incredicoaster and Big Thunder Mountain).

10. Remember to take advantage of the 2-hour loophole and keep retrieving another Lightning Lane return time at least every 120 minutes, stockpiling them for later in the day, even if you leave the park for a break. You can only hold one Lightning Lane reservation per attraction, but if a ride breaks down you'll get a Multiple Experiences replacement pass valid on selected rides for the rest of the day (and possibly the next).

ADVANCED GENIE+ HACKS: HOLD & MODIFY AND MULTIPLE EXPERIENCES FARMING

AFTER YOU'VE MASTERED THOSE 10 BASIC STEPS, here are two advanced techniques for maximizing your investment in Genie+. Play your cards right, and you may literally end the night with more Lightning Lane passes than you know what to do with. Be warned that these methods will compel you to spend even more time staring and swiping at your smartphone, which may (or may not) outweigh the extra time you'll avoid in standby queues. (Search Github.com for an unofficial tool designed for securing virtual queue Boarding Group 1, which also helps makes executing these tricks less taxing.)

HOLD & MODIFY Our basic method prioritizes using all of your available Lightning Lanes but doesn't necessarily maximize your total time savings because it has you using Genie+ early in the day before the standby lines have grown. To shift your return times later in the day when waits are longer, follow the first 5 steps above. Then on step 6, always modify your existing return time to be later, and modify again every time your return window approaches, until standby waits in the park are no longer bearable. Keep pushing back your reservation for 2 hours, and you'll be able to pick up an additional return time. Repeat this cycle every 2 hours, and by midafternoon you can stack up to five Lightning Lane return times for the late afternoon and evening—ideal after returning from the hotel for a midday nap—even on days when return times aren't being distributed hours in advance.

MULTIPLE EXPERIENCES FARMING Nobody likes it when theme park rides break down, but you can turn downtime to your advantage by farming Multiple Experiences passes from temporarily closed attractions. Monitor the app for Genie+ rides whose standby lines say "Not Currently Offered" but are still distributing Lightning Lanes for the near future. Grab one, and if the ride remains closed when your return time arrives, it will instantly convert to a coveted Multiple Experiences pass valid all day at designated attractions in both parks. You'll also instantly be able to select another Genie+ attraction—even if its been less than 2 hours since your last—including the ride you just had. If the ride keeps distributing return times while offline—as often happens in early morning—you can accumulate multitudes of Multiple Experiences passes in a matter of hours. During one visit, when Haunted Mansion and Matterhorn Bobsleds were both having issues, we collected eight Multiple Experiences passes before 11 a.m.!

GENIE+ AND LIGHTNING LANE AT DISNEYLAND VERSUS WALT DISNEY WORLD

ALTHOUGH THE LINE-SKIPPING SERVICES at Disneyland and Walt Disney World share the same name, there are some subtle operational differences that we feel make Genie+ a far superior experience in Anaheim than in Orlando. The only advantages the Floridian version has over its Californian counterpart is that it sometimes costs $5 less per day (but may be up to $5 more), and it gives Walt Disney World on-site resort guests a head start in purchasing Individual Lightning Lanes. But those positives are offset by several differences that make Disneyland's system much more pleasant to use:

- Walt Disney World guests can purchase Genie+ starting at midnight before their visit and make their first Lightning Lane selection from their beds at 7 a.m. Disneyland guests can't activate or use the service until after they enter the park, so there's no early-morning fumbling for the smartphone.

- Walt Disney World on-site resort guests can also purchase Individual Lightning Lanes starting at 7 a.m., and they are often all claimed before off-site guests get their chance at park opening. At Disneyland, Individual Lightning Lanes can't be purchased until entering the park, and all guests are on equal footing. WDW guests get to choose their Individual Lightning Lane return window (if any are available), but Disneyland's times are assigned on a first-come, first-served basis, the same as Genie+.

- PhotoPass photographers are included in Disneyland's Genie+, whereas Walt Disney World charges an additional $75 per day (or $210 for 30 days; $25 off if purchased online at least 3 days in advance) for its similar Memory Maker service. PhotoPass on-ride snapshots and attraction video downloads are included in Genie+ at Walt Disney World, but they're complimentary for everyone at Disneyland.

- All Lightning Lane return times for popular rides at Walt Disney World may be claimed before park opening or shortly after, and Disney admits Genie+ buyers may only be able to use the service on 2–3 attractions per day. Disneyland's return times are available until afternoon or later, even on busy days, and it's possible to take advantage of Genie+ at every participating ride in both parks during a single (very long) day.

- It only takes minutes to park hop back and forth between Disneyland and DCA as your Lightning Lane return times dictate. Commuting between Walt Disney World's parks can take a half hour or longer, making it inefficient to repeatedly leave and return.

- Most Lightning Lane queues at Disneyland tend to have little or no wait (usually 15 minutes or less), whereas at Walt Disney World we've frequently faced Lighting Lane waits of 15–30 minutes or more.

- Multiple Experiences passes, issued when a Lightning Lane is temporarily unavailable, are only valid at other Lightning Lane attractions within the same park in Walt Disney World, but they're accepted at several non-Lightning Lane rides in Disney California Adventure.

In other words, if you've tried using Lightning Lanes at Walt Disney World and hated it, give the service another shot at Disneyland. A well-traveled couple from Australia who visited both resorts back-to-back confirmed our assessment:

The performance and usefulness of Genie+ was substantially better in Disneyland. We were happy to pay $5 more than WDW per day per person to have PhotoPass included in our Genie+ purchase [and] we appreciated that we were not able to purchase Genie+ and make our first attraction selection until we entered the park. This avoided the stressful 7 a.m. scramble online to secure our preferred first attraction for the day, and it seemed to be a fairer process that allowed on-site and off-site guests equal access. In Disneyland we were able to manage the system to ensure that there was a consistent flow of attraction reservations, but there were often large (sometimes very large) gaps between available return times in WDW.

USING LIGHTNING LANE WITH LINES

THE LINES APP can automatically recommend the best Genie+ selections for your touring plan. To enable this feature, select the "I plan to buy Genie+" option when you create your plan, and before you click the "Optimize" button. If you prefer, you can choose your own Lightning Lane reservations and estimate their return times manually when following a personalized plan. Inside the Disneyland Lines app, you must have a custom plan (or a copy of a premium plan) for the current day, and select it as active. Click "edit plan," then click "add reservation" under Lightning Lane. A drop-down box will appear; select the attraction and return time, then click "submit" at the bottom. Repeat as you make more reservations. Now, the optimizer will accommodate your Lightning Lane reservation(s), as long as it predicts doing so will save time over waiting standby. (If Lines ignores your reservation after optimizing your plan, return to "edit plan" and select "force Optimize to use Lightning Lane" to compare the results.)

THE BOTTOM LINE: ARE GENIE+ AND LIGHTNING LANE WORTH THE MONEY?

IF YOU'VE ALREADY DROPPED a dump truck of dough on Disneyland admission, you may be feeling resentful about being asked to shell out even more money for Genie+ and Lightning Lane, especially if you remember when such services were free. As much as we also hate Disney's nickle-and-dime-ing, our honest advice is to bite the bullet and buy Genie+ anyway, especially if you plan on park hopping. If you are only visiting DCA during a slow time of year, or are spreading out your resort visit over four or more days, you can probably get away without Genie+, but at Disneyland Park the service is a huge boon even during moderately busy seasons. In short, we agree with the reader from Denver, Colorado, who said:

On busy days, Genie+ should be considered part of your ticket price.

Likewise, a family from Short Hills, New Jersey, agrees:

Genie+ is an essential add-on if you want any chance of getting on all preferred rides when the park is crowded.

Perhaps the biggest downside of using Genie+ is the increased dependence on your smartphone, as you recheck the app through the day for available return times. This observation from a North Wales, Pennsylvania, woman was typical:

Vacation was less than magical this time. I'm not entirely sure why, but I think it had something to do with working my phone so much. I am not high tech, but I was able to do Mobile Ordering, Genie+, and ILL with few problems. But my phone became the focus too many times during the day instead of the park.

In terms of dollars and cents, using Genie+ at DCA averages out to $10–$16 per hour saved waiting standby, depending on crowd levels;

at Disneyland, the cost drops to $7–$10 per hour, and the value gets even better if you park hop. That compares very favorably to the average hourly rates for Genie+ at Walt Disney World, which range from around $7–$12 at Magic Kingdom up to over $20 at EPCOT.

Individual Lightning Lanes, on the other hand, are more available but far less valuable at Disneyland, and are therefore relatively overpriced. In particular, Rise of the Resistance's Lightning Lane costs $20–$28 at Disneyland, versus $15–$25 at Disney's Hollywood Studios, even though Anaheim's standby wait is usually shorter than Orlando's. Also, the ride at DCA selling Individual Lightning Lane access also offers a single-rider line, providing a free alternative to waiting standby. While we wholeheartedly endorse buying Genie+, we don't advocate investing in Individual Lightning Lanes unless you are visiting on a busy day and anxious to ride Rise of the Resistance.

If you do choose to buy Individual Lightning Lanes, don't rush to make your purchase right at rope drop. Instead, monitor the return times and grab one when they reach the busier part of the day, for maximum time savings. Don't worry too much about them being sold out before breakfast like in Florida. Individual Lightning Lane reservations for Rise of the Resistance remain available on busy days until around 11 a.m., or until 4–6 p.m. on an average day; Radiator Springs Racers rarely runs out before closing time.

VIRTUAL QUEUES

ALONG WITH THE OPENING OF Star Wars: Galaxy's Edge came the arrival at Disneyland Resort of Virtual Queues (also referred to as Virtual Boarding Passes), which Disney devised to help manage the overwhelming demand for popular attractions like Rise of the Resistance. The system was also used for Mickey & Minnie's Runaway Railway in Toontown and WEB SLINGERS: A Spider-Man Adventure at Disney California Adventure (DCA) when they first opened. At press time, those rides all offer standby queues; Virtual Queues are currently only employed at Tiana's Bayou Adventure and for controlling access to World of Color viewing areas. Virtual Queues may also be reintroduced during peak attendance periods or on popular new attractions. Check Disneyland's app or website ahead of your visit to see if they are offered.

When in use, Virtual Queue boarding passes, which are free for all guests, become available for nighttime spectaculars at noon daily; when offered for rides, they are released each morning exactly at 7 a.m., with a second batch made available daily at noon. Guests must use their smartphone's Disneyland app to secure their place in the Virtual Queue; fast fingers are required because passes are all snapped up within a matter of minutes or even seconds.

If you're lucky enough to successfully join a Virtual Queue for a show, you'll be assigned a performance time (on days when there are multiple showings) along with a time to enter the designated viewing area; see the show descriptions (pages 223 and 277) for details on where to go. For rides using Virtual Queues, you won't receive a set time at which you schedule your return; rather, you'll be assigned a group number and receive a push notification on your phone when your turn has arrived. At that point you will then have a 1-hour window in which to arrive at the attraction and show your boarding code. (Those without a phone can periodically check their Virtual Queue status at a designated kiosk.) Cast members have some discretion in enforcing the boarding end time, so plead your case if you are late because you were stuck on another attraction or had a dining reservation.

In theory, you should then be able to experience the attraction with a minimal wait. In practice, between the line to scan the pass and the queue to board, we waited up to 30 minutes for Rise of the Resistance, and up to 60 for WEB SLINGERS, on top of the Virtual Queue. Guests with Disability Access Service (DAS) should tell a cast member about their status when redeeming their boarding pass so they can bypass most of the subsequent wait.

Guests can try for the 7 a.m. Virtual Queue ride boarding group distribution from anywhere inside or outside the Disneyland Resort area, but you must already have tickets and a theme park reservation booked for that day, and park hoppers can only join the queue for a ride that is in the reserved park. For the noon distribution of both rides and shows, all members of your party must have scanned their admission at the entrance of the reserved park before joining a Virtual Queue, but guests with park hopper tickets can try for attractions while inside either park, or from outside the resort entirely, if you want to take a midday break back at your hotel.

You may only join one ride's Virtual Queue at a time, and you can only use the Virtual Queue for a particular attraction once per day. It is possible to experience two different Virtual Queue attractions in the same day (assuming more than one is operating), but you must get a low boarding group number for the first ride at 7 a.m., and then redeem it at the attraction's entrance before joining your second Virtual Queue at noon. Virtual Queue reservations for *World of Color* should not interfere with any Lightning Lane reservations you might hold for other attractions. If you want to see both fountain shows on the same night, your best bet is to join the Virtual Queue for the first *World of Color* showing, enjoy it, and then cross into Disneyland in time to watch the second *Fantasmic!* from a standby section. Alternatively, get a dining package with reserved viewing for the first *Fantasmic!*, watch it (and the fireworks), then hop to DCA to watch the second *World of Color* (when offered) from a standing-room area.

Your virtual place in line can't be traded or transferred, and a boarding group number doesn't guarantee you'll ride if there are unexpected problems with the attraction.

A Step-by-Step Guide to Joining Virtual Queues at Disneyland Resort

1. Download and install the official Disneyland Resort smartphone app in advance, and make sure all of your party's admission tickets are properly linked (see page 22) and that you have park reservations for the day you plan to attend (see page 21).

2. You can try for the 7 a.m. ride distribution from your hotel room or anywhere else. For the noon distribution of rides and nighttime spectaculars, ensure that all members of your party who want to join the Virtual Queue have scanned in at the turnstiles.

3. If you are inside the park, stake out a spot in a less-congested area away from Main Street, U.S.A. and the central hub (head toward Critter Country if possible) and disable Wi-Fi if you have cellular data.

4. Close all open apps, then reopen the Disneyland app starting around 6:45 a.m. or 11:45 a.m.

5. Tap the main menu button (three bars icon) in the lower right corner, then tap "Virtual Queues."

6. On the "My Queues" screen, press "Join Virtual Queue."

7. On the next screen you'll see tabs for Disneyland Park and Disney California Adventure. Click on the DCA tab for the *World of Color* Virtual Queue or Disneyland for any participating attractions there. In the morning you may only pick a ride in the park you have a reservation for; park hoppers can pick either at midday.

8. Tap "Confirm Your Party" and select all the people in your group who want to participate. You can do this up to 15 minutes before the distribution time. If for some reason a member of your group is missing off this screen, talk to guest services after you finish joining, and they can usually help.

9. Exactly on the hour (7:00:00 a.m. or 12:00:00 p.m.), tap "Refresh" or pull down the screen to refresh, then immediately click the "Join" button. If possible, monitor time.gov on another device for a more accurate clock. Every second counts if you want to ride these attractions!

10. Remember that multiple members of your party can try to join a Virtual Queue at the same time, thereby improving everyone's odds. The first person to successfully join will select everyone else, while the others will get an "already in a queue" message once the group number is confirmed.

11. If the Virtual Queue gods smile upon you, you'll be blessed with a performance time or boarding group number and a rough estimated wait time (barring breakdowns). Otherwise, you'll receive a disappointing message saying that all Virtual Queue reservations are full.

12. Once the app notifies you that your boarding group has been called, be sure to arrive at the attraction entrance before the stated end time. If you are running late because of a dining reservation or similar scheduling snafu, ride attendants will usually allow you to enter anyway.

13. If an attraction using Virtual Queue has temporary technical difficulties, it will pause calling new boarding groups until operating again. Guests who have already redeemed their boarding pass and are waiting in the physical queue (or mid-ride) during a shutdown may receive a line-skipping pass valid when it reopens.

14. If a Virtual Queue attraction experiences extended downtime, guests still in the Virtual Queue may have their boarding passes automatically exchanged for expedited access to an alternate attraction; guests with high boarding numbers (designated as "backup groups") will not be compensated in case of closure. There is also no compensation for show cancellations.

SINGLE-RIDER LINES

AN OFTEN-OVERLOOKED TIME-SAVER is the single-rider line, a separate line for individuals who are visiting the park alone or don't mind being separated from their party. The objective is to fill odd spaces left by groups that don't quite fill the entire ride vehicle. Because there aren't many singles and most groups are unwilling to split up, single-rider lines are usually much shorter than regular lines. The only downside—aside from being briefly separated from your traveling companions—is that single riders skip most of the scene-setting queues, which first-time riders may want to experience.

Single riders are usually welcomed in Disneyland Park at Matterhorn Bobsleds, *Millennium Falcon:* Smugglers Run, Space Mountain, and Tiana's Bayou Adventure; and in Disney California Adventure (DCA) at Goofy's Sky School, Grizzly River Run, Incredicoaster, Radiator Springs Racers, Soarin' Around the World, and WEB SLINGERS. Star Tours in Disneyland accommodates single riders intermittently, and Toy Story Midway Mania! and Monsters Inc. Mike & Sulley to the Rescue! sometimes offer a similar "buddy pass" shortcut.

Note that single-rider lines are not always available and may be closed if there is too much (or too little) demand. Most participating attractions have a dedicated single-rider lane that is clearly marked, but at a few you may need to ask a cast member at the entrance for a paper pass, which will permit you to walk up the exit pathway.

SAVING TIME *in* LINE *by* UNDERSTANDING *the* RIDES

THERE ARE MANY TYPES OF RIDES IN DISNEYLAND. Some rides, such as It's a Small World, are engineered to carry several thousand people every hour. At the other extreme, rides such as Dumbo can accommodate only around 500 people an hour. Most rides fall somewhere in between, so we provide for each attraction an estimate (based on published information and our own observations) of its typical guest throughput, assuming normal operating conditions. Lots of factors figure into how long you will have to wait to experience a particular ride: the popularity of the ride, how it loads and unloads, how many people can ride at one time, how many units (cars, rockets, boats, flying elephants, or whatever) of those available are in service at a given time, and how many staff are available to operate the ride. Let's take them one by one:

1. HOW POPULAR IS THE RIDE? Newer rides such as WEB SLINGERS: A Spider-Man Adventure or Star Wars: Rise of the Resistance attract a lot of people, as do longtime favorites such as Space Mountain. If you know a ride is popular, you need to learn a little more about how it operates to determine when might be the best time to ride.

2. HOW DOES THE RIDE LOAD AND UNLOAD? A ride need not be especially popular to form long lines. The lines can be the result of less-than-desirable traffic engineering; that is, it takes so long to load and unload that a line builds up. This is the situation at the Mad Tea Party and Dumbo. Only a small percentage of the visitors to Disneyland Park (mostly kids) ride Dumbo, for instance, but because it takes so long to load and unload, this ride can form long waiting lines.

Some rides never stop. They are like a circular conveyor belt that goes around and around. We call these continuous loaders. Haunted Mansion is a continuous loader. The more cars or ships or whatever on the conveyor, the more people can be moved through in an hour. Haunted Mansion has lots of cars on the conveyor belt and consequently can move more than 2,400 people an hour.

Other rides are interval loaders. This means that cars are unloaded, loaded, and dispatched at certain set intervals (sometimes controlled manually and sometimes by a computer). Matterhorn Bobsleds is an interval loader. It has two separate tracks (in other words, the ride has been duplicated in the same facility). Each track can run up to 10 sleds, released at 23-second or greater intervals (the bigger the crowd, the shorter the interval). In another kind of interval loader, such as the Jungle Cruise, empty boats return to the starting point, where they line up waiting to be reloaded. In a third type of interval loader, one group of riders enters the vehicle while the last group of riders departs. We call these in-and-out interval loaders. Indiana Jones Adventure is a good example of an in-and-out interval loader. As a troop transport pulls up to the loading station, those who have just completed their ride exit to the left. At almost the same time, those waiting to ride enter the troop transport from the right. The troop transport is released to the dispatch point a few yards down the line where it is launched according to whatever time interval is being used. Interval loaders of all three types can

CYCLE RIDES		
AT DISNEYLAND PARK		
FANTASYLAND • Casey Jr. Circus Train • Dumbo the Flying Elephant • King Arthur Carrousel • Mad Tea Party		
MICKEY'S TOONTOWN • Chip 'n' Dale's GADGETcoaster		
TOMORROWLAND • Astro Orbitor		
AT DISNEY CALIFORNIA ADVENTURE		
PARADISE GARDENS PARK • Golden Zephyr • Jumpin' Jellyfish • Silly Symphony Swings		
PIXAR PIER • Inside Out Emotional Whirlwind • Jessie's Critter Carousel • Pixar Pal-A-Round		
CARS LAND • Luigi's Rollickin' Roadsters • Mater's Junkyard Jamboree		

be very efficient at moving people if (1) the release (launch) interval is relatively short and (2) the ride can accommodate a large number of vehicles in the system at one time. Because many boats can be floating through Pirates of the Caribbean at a given time and the release interval is short, almost 3,400 people an hour can see this attraction.

A third group of rides are cycle rides. Another name for these same rides is stop-and-go rides; those waiting to ride exchange places with those who have just ridden. The main difference between in-and-out interval rides and cycle rides is that with a cycle ride, the whole system shuts down when loading and unloading is in progress. While one boat is loading and unloading in It's a Small World, many other boats are proceeding through the ride. But when Dumbo touches down, the whole ride is at a standstill until the next flight is launched.

In discussing a cycle ride, the amount of time the ride is in motion is called ride time. The amount of time that the ride is idle while loading and unloading is called load time. Load time plus ride time equals cycle time, or the time expended from the start of one run of the ride until the start of the succeeding run. Cycle rides are the least efficient of all the Disneyland rides in terms of traffic engineering. Disneyland Park has six cycle rides, while DCA has eight, an astonishing number for a modern park.

3. HOW MANY PEOPLE CAN RIDE AT ONE TIME? This figure is defined in terms of per-ride capacity or system capacity. Either way, the figures refer to the number of people who can ride at the same time. Our discussion above illustrates that the greater a ride's carrying capacity (all other things being equal), the more visitors it can accommodate in an hour.

4. HOW MANY UNITS ARE IN SERVICE AT A GIVEN TIME? A unit is simply a term for the vehicle you sit in during your ride. At the Mad Tea Party the unit is a teacup, and at Alice in Wonderland it's a caterpillar. On some rides (mostly cycle rides), the number of units in operation at a given time is fixed. Thus, there are always 16 elephant units operating on the Dumbo ride, 72 horses on King Arthur Carrousel, and so on. What this fixed number of units means to you is that there is no way to increase the carrying capacity of the ride by adding more units. On a busy day, therefore, the only way to carry more people each hour on a fixed-unit cycle ride is to shorten the loading time (which, as we will see in number 5, is sometimes impossible) or by decreasing the riding time, the actual time the ride is in motion. The bottom line on a busy day for a cycle ride is that you will wait longer and be rewarded for your wait with a shorter ride. This is why we try to steer you clear of the cycle rides unless you are willing to ride them early in the morning or late at night.

Other rides at Disneyland can increase their carrying capacity by adding units to the system as the crowds build. Big Thunder Mountain Railroad is a good example. If attendance is very light, Big Thunder can start the day by running one of five available mine trains. When lines start to build, more mine trains can be placed into operation. At full capacity, a total of five trains can carry about 2,400 people an hour. Sometimes a long line will disappear almost instantly when new units are brought online. On the other hand, the queue may stop altogether for a few minutes while new units are added, extending the wait for guests who were about to board. When an interval-loading ride places more units into operation, it usually shortens the dispatch interval, so more units are being dispatched more often.

5. HOW MANY CAST MEMBERS ARE AVAILABLE TO OPERATE THE RIDE? Allocation of additional staff to a ride can allow extra units to be placed in operation, or additional loading areas or holding areas to be opened. Pirates of the Caribbean and It's a Small World can run two separate waiting lines and loading zones. Haunted Mansion has a short preshow, which is staged in a "stretch room." On busy days a second stretch room can be activated, thus permitting a more continuous flow of visitors to the actual loading area. Additional staff make a world of difference on some cycle rides. Often, if not usually, one attendant will operate the Golden Zephyr. This single person must clear the visitors from the ride just completed, admit and seat visitors for the upcoming ride, check that all zephyrs are properly secured (which entails an inspection of each zephyr), return to the control panel, issue instructions to the riders, and finally, activate the ride (whew!). A second attendant allows for the division of these responsibilities and has the effect of cutting loading time by 25%–50%.

BEWARE OF THE DARK, WET, ROUGH, AND SCARY

OOPS, ALMOST FORGOT: There's a member of our team you need to meet. Called a Wuffo, she's our very own character. She'll warn you when rides are too scary, too dark, or too wet. You'll bump into her throughout the book doing, well, what characters do. Pay attention to her—she knows what she's talking about.

SAVING TIME *in* LINE *by* UNDERSTANDING *the* SHOWS

MANY OF THE FEATURED ATTRACTIONS at Disneyland are theater presentations. While they're not as complex as rides from a traffic-engineering viewpoint, a little enlightenment concerning their operation may save some touring time.

Most Disneyland theater attractions operate in three distinct phases:

1. First, there are visitors who are in the theater viewing the presentation.

2. Next, there are visitors who have passed through the turnstile into a holding area or waiting lobby. These people will be admitted to the theater as soon as the current presentation has concluded. Several attractions offer a preshow in the waiting lobby to entertain members of the crowd until they are admitted to the main show.

3. Finally, there is the outside line. Visitors waiting here will enter the waiting lobby when there is room and then move into the theater when the audience turns over (is exchanged) between shows.

The theater capacity and popularity of the presentation, along with the level of attendance in the park, determine how long the lines will be at a given theater attraction. Except for holidays and other days of especially heavy attendance, the longest wait for a show usually does not exceed the length of one complete performance.

Because almost all Disneyland theater attractions run continually, only stopping long enough for the previous audience to leave and the

waiting audience to enter, a performance will already be in progress when you arrive. If the *Enchanted Tiki Room* show lasts 15 minutes, the wait under normal circumstances should be 15 minutes if you were to arrive just after the show began.

All Disneyland theaters (except the Main Street Cinema and some amphitheater productions) are very strict when it comes to controlling access. Unlike at a regular movie theater, you can't just walk in during the middle of a performance; you will always have at least a short wait.

GUIDED TOURS *at* DISNEY-LAND PARK *and* DCA

SEVERAL GROUP TOURS are offered year-round, in addition to ultra-expensive private VIP tours. All require a valid park admission and park reservation, in addition to the price of the tour. Disneyland Resort tours can be booked up to 60 days in advance online at disneyland.disney .go.com/events-tours or by calling ☎ 714-781-8687 for the standard tours or ☎ 714-300-7710 for the VIP treatment. Tours are subject to change without notice, and some tours are offered only on certain days, so call ahead. During the Halloween and Christmas seasons, tours highlighting holiday decorations may also be available. Disneyland Park tours begin at the Tour Gardens kiosk to the left of City Hall on Main Street, U.S.A. Disney Visa cardholders and DVC members get a 15% discount on guided tours.

WALT'S MAIN STREET STORY TOUR This 90-minute walking tour, which replaced the 3½-hour Walk in Walt's Footsteps tour, still offers a historical perspective on both Disneyland Park and the man who created it, but it now focuses only on Main Street, U.S.A., and it doesn't include rides on any attractions. The tour's highlight is a visit to Walt's private apartment above the Main Street firehouse—including a photo op, as well as a snack on the second-story patio overlooking Town Square—which is a bucket-list experience for any die-hard Disney devotee. Cost is $160 for all ages, and the tour is offered multiple times in the morning and early afternoon. (The tour is considered inappropriate for younger children, who will likely be bored; guests under age 14 must be accompanied by an adult.) Walt's Main Street Story tours depart hourly, 9 a.m.–2 p.m., daily. We think the tour is a good introduction to Disney lore for fans of midcentury American culture but a poor use of time for casual tourists. A reader from Superior, Colorado, gave its predecessor a mixed review:

> *The tour was good, but I wouldn't do it more than once. Our guide was a little too rehearsed (read: memorization), and several people on the tour (including my husband and I) knew things she didn't know.*

CULTIVATING THE MAGIC TOUR This 2-hour introduction to the resort's horticultural treasures features an insider's peek at the park's remarkable landscaping efforts. You'll also get express entry onto the Jungle Cruise, with exclusive narration pointing out its often-overlooked agricultural elements. The tour is a photographer's paradise, and even if you don't have a green thumb, we think this is one of the most entertaining and educational ways to experience a unique aspect of Disneyland Park. The tour is offered daily, with six hourly departures from 8:45 a.m. to 1:45 p.m.; cost is $110 per guest and includes a souvenir pin and seed packet.

DISNEYLAND RAILROAD GUIDED TOUR If you love steam trains as much as Walt did, this 2-hour tour is made for you. It begins with a brief breakfast snack and walking tour of Disneyland Park, followed by a look inside the maintenance roundhouse, before the main event: a round-trip journey on the Disneyland Railroad inside the Lilly Belle, a private parlor car named for Mrs. Disney that isn't ordinarily open to the public. The $135 fee includes a collectible railroad map, and the tour is offered six times each day, between 8:30 a.m. and 1 p.m.

HOLIDAY TIME AT DISNEYLAND RESORT This 2½-hour guided walking tour highlights seasonal traditions in both theme parks, from It's a Small World's holiday overlay to the Christmas Fantasy Parade. The tour costs $110 for all guests ages 3 and up; guests under 14 must be accompanied by an adult. Tours run from mid-November through early January and depart daily around 1 p.m. and 4 p.m.

VIP TOURS Exclusive VIP tours are available for an eye-popping $500–$800 per hour (rates vary depending on the specific date) for up to 10 guests with a 7-hour minimum. VIP guides will arrange special parade and show seating, make dining reservations, dispense Disneyland trivia, and (most crucially) take you through the "back door" past the queues for unlimited expedited boarding at most attractions. You must make reservations 72 hours in advance and cancel at least 48 hours in advance or face a 2-hour cancellation fee.

PART 4

ESSENTIALS

⏹ *The* BARE NECESSITIES

CREDIT CARDS

AMERICAN EXPRESS, MASTERCARD, VISA, Discover, and Japan Credit Bureau credit cards are accepted for theme park admission. Disneyland shops, fast-food and counter-service restaurants, sit-down restaurants, and the Disneyland Resort hotels also accept all the cards listed above. Most vendor carts accept credit cards, but a handful do not—ask before you order.

Disney Visa cardholders can get a private character meet and greet in Disney California Adventure's Hollywood Land 10:30 a.m.–1:30 p.m. and an exclusive face-to-face with a *Star Wars* villain outside Disneyland's Star Wars Launch Bay 2–6 p.m. or 4–8 p.m., depending on the season. Cardholders also get a code to download all their private poses from disneyland.com/photopass or the Disneyland smartphone app. Disney Visa cardholders save 10% on merchandise ($50 minimum purchase) and dining at select resort locations and 15% on guided tours. Instant application kiosks can be found in Downtown Disney, with $100 or more in statement credits sometimes offered as an incentive to approved applicants. Visit disneyrewards.com for current offer details.

Disney gift cards can be used for payment at the same locations as credit cards and can also be used in the Disneyland app account; hold onto your original card in case of any problems. Mobile payment or tap-to-pay, a wireless payment method on newer iPhones, Apple Watches, and NFC-equipped Android smartphones, is supported at most Disneyland Resort ticket booths, stores, quick-service restaurants, and outdoor vending carts. Locations that support tap-to-pay have a small black pad with a Contactless Indicator symbol (also known as an EMVCo symbol, which looks like a Wi-Fi symbol turned sideways). When it works, mobile payment is the swiftest way to pay, even quicker than scanning a hotel charge barcode.

SALES TAX

A COMBINED STATE AND LOCAL sales tax of 7.75% applies to all purchases made at Disneyland Resort, except for admission tickets, which are untaxed. Hotels in Anaheim charge a 15% room occupancy tax. All prices listed in this book are before tax, unless otherwise noted.

FACE MASKS AND SANITIZING

FACE COVERINGS ARE OPTIONAL indoors and outdoors for all guests, including while riding Disney-operated or public transportation, and no proof of vaccination is required at any Southern Californian attraction. However, even in the absence of coronavirus, wearing a face mask in the parks is a great way to reduce your odds of coming down with a post-vacation common cold. If you wear them, we recommend bringing at least two disposable masks per person, per day (preferably N95 or KN95 with elastic ear loops and a wire for fitting along the nose) from home.

Likewise, complimentary hand sanitizer dispensers are available near the entrances or exits of most attractions, but their use is not mandatory, and they frequently need refilling. Pack a travel-size squeeze bottle of sanitizer for each member of your group, and remember to visit the restrooms regularly for thorough handwashing.

WHAT SHOULD I BRING?

IN ADDITION TO THE BASICS that you would bring along on any vacation—casual clothing, comfortable footwear, bathing attire, necessary medications and toiletries—you'll want to stock up on the following before your Disneyland visit:

- Small bottles of hand sanitizer and sunscreen
- Cell phone backup battery or charger with cord and plug (see page 122)
- Zip-top plastic bags, to protect electronics and masks on water rides
- A hat with brim and sunglasses (even during the winter)
- Pocket-size umbrella and/or poncho
- Refillable water bottle

By the same token, there are some items you'll definitely want to leave behind:

- Alcohol, controlled substances (including medical cannabis), and illegal drugs
- Weapons, including knives, firearms, and explosives
- Glass containers or glassware (except baby food, medicine, or perfume containers under 4 oz.)
- Loose ice cubes or dry ice (reusable ice packs are allowed)
- Large or hard-sided coolers
- Food that requires refrigerating or reheating (bottled water and small snacks are OK)
- Pets (excluding service animals)
- Selfie sticks (small folding tripods or monopods are allowed)

- Drones, hoverboards, skateboards, scooters, or Segways
- Wagons, stroller-wagons, or strollers over 31" (79 cm.) x 52" (132 cm.)

RAIN

IF IT RAINS, GO ANYWAY; the bad weather will diminish the crowds. Additionally, most of the rides and attractions at the parks are under cover. Likewise, all but a few of the waiting areas are protected from inclement weather. Some outdoor attractions—such as Tom Sawyer's Island, Mad Tea Party, Alice in Wonderland, Adventureland's Treehouse, and Chip 'n' Dale's Gagetcoaster at Disneyland Park, and Radiator Springs Racers, Redwood Creek Challenge Trail, and Golden Zephyr at Disney California Adventure (DCA)—may close for safety reasons in inclement weather. Radiator Springs Racers may require hours of downtime after a storm before safely reopening. Roller coasters such as Big Thunder Mountain Railroad and the Incredicoaster can operate in a drizzle but will close if lightning is nearby. Fireworks are rarely canceled solely due to rain but may be scuttled by strong winds, and parades may be shortened or modified for safety. A father from Petaluma, California, recommends some supplemental supplies for wet weather, writing:

> Ride operators make a token effort to use a shop vac or towels, but it's good to have your own towel even on sunny days for the water ride seats. For multiday park touring in the rain, have a second pair of shoes to switch off every night at the hotel, allowing 24 hours to dry. We used a small fan overnight in the hotel room to dry shoes and jackets that got wet on rides.

If you get caught in an unexpected downpour, raingear can be purchased at a number of shops. Whatever you do, don't flee for the parking trams during a sudden thunderstorm, or you may find yourself in an unpleasant scene, like this mother of two from Los Angeles:

> It was pouring rain, and the park rapidly emptied out. There was complete chaos by the tram loading area [with] hundreds of people pushing and shoving—desperate to get on a tram and get out of there. The trams were arriving very sporadically and tempers were rising.

Instead, wait out the storm inside a self-paced indoor attraction, such as *Great Moments with Mr. Lincoln*, Main Street Cinema, or the Sleeping Beauty Castle walkthrough at Disneyland Park, and Boudin Bakery Tour or Disney Animation at DCA. A mother of two teens from Edmonton, Canada, wrote:

> This recent trip, we had continual rain and cold our first two days at Disney, and this was when all your extra advice really came together for our family. We went to the parks with umbrellas and raincoats and were amazed at how many of the experiences really are indoors. You don't think about it when it's nice out! When the rain got too heavy and others were standing shivering in doorways to wait out the rain, I had ideas from *Unofficial Guide* up my sleeve, and those quieter moments ended up being some of my best memories from our

time at Disney. They wouldn't even have made the list for my roller coaster–loving family otherwise!

EXCUSE ME, *but*
WHERE CAN I FIND . . .

FOREIGN-LANGUAGE ASSISTANCE? Translation services are available to guests who do not speak English. Inquire by calling ☎ 714-781-4636 or visiting City Hall at Disneyland Park or Guest Relations at DCA.

LOST ADULTS? Have a plan for regrouping with those in your party should you become separated. Failing this, you can leave a message at City Hall or Guest Relations for your missing person. For information concerning lost children, see pages 168–170.

MESSAGES? Messages for your fellow group members can be left at City Hall in Disneyland Park or at Guest Relations in DCA.

CAR TROUBLE ASSISTANCE? If you elected to decrease the chance of losing your keys by locking them in your car, or decided that your car might be easier to find if you left your lights on, you may have a problem to deal with when you return to the parking lot. Fortunately, the security patrols that continually cruise the parking lots are equipped to handle these types of situations and can quickly put you back in business.

LOST AND FOUND? The lost-and-found office, which services both theme parks and Downtown Disney, is located in the Guest Services building in the Esplanade to the west of the park entrances. If you don't discover your loss until after you have left the parks, fill out an online claim form at chargerback.com/disneyland or call ☎ 714-817-2166 from 8 a.m. to 8 p.m. daily. If you lose your park ticket, Guest Services may be able to retrieve it using the credit card with which it was purchased, but it's far easier for them to reprint if you take a digital photo of the bar code when you first get your pass.

SOME PLACE TO PUT ALL THESE PACKAGES? Lockers are available both outside the entrance of each park, for $7–$15 per day, and inside each park, for $7–$10. Pricing depends on size and includes unlimited in-and-out access throughout the day. Disneyland Resort will deliver purchases to on-site hotels but has discontinued free package pickup at the front of the parks; however, you can check your souvenirs at most major stores and retrieve them later in the day.

GROCERIES? Several convenience stores are on Harbor Boulevard near Disneyland, but no supermarkets are within easy walking distance. The closest stores with a good selection are **Food 4 Less** at 1616 W. Katella Ave. and the **Walmart Neighborhood Market** at 1120 S. Anaheim Blvd., both about a mile from Disneyland Resort. **Target** is about a 5-minute drive south of Disneyland on Harbor. The adjacent **Viva Bargain Center** is a good place for cheap supplies. If you don't have a car, **Pavilions** (pavilions.com) will bring food directly to your hotel for $10 with a $30 minimum order. You must be present to receive the delivery but can select a 1- to 4-hour time window when placing your order.

A MIXED DRINK OR BEER? At Disneyland Park, you will have to exit the park and try one of the hotels or Downtown Disney unless you have a reservation at Galaxy's Edge's cantina or a table service restaurant, or an ultraexpensive membership to the exclusive Club 33 hidden in New Orleans Square. At DCA alcoholic beverages are readily available.

A DRINK OF WATER? Drinking fountains are found across the resort, and a growing number feature spouts for refilling reusable water bottles. Cups of ice water are also available free upon request at all quick-service restaurants. Bottled water is sold throughout the parks at over $4 per bottle; consider bringing your own bottles instead.

SOME RAINGEAR? At Disneyland, raingear is available at most shops but is not always displayed. You have to ask for it. Ponchos are $12 for adults and $10 for kids, and umbrellas are $20 and up.

A CURE FOR THIS HEADACHE? Aspirin and various sundries can be purchased on Main Street at the Emporium in Disneyland Park and at Elias and Company at the DCA entrance plaza (they're behind the counter, so you have to ask). Basic medical supplies are in each hotel's gift shop.

A PHARMACY? Unfortunately, there is no place in Disneyland Resort to have a prescription filled. The nearest full-service pharmacies are the **Walgreens** and **CVS** on the corner of Harbor Boulevard at Katella Avenue, about a block south of Disneyland.

A DOCTOR? If you're feeling under the weather or have another non–life-threatening medical issue, **Exer Urgent Care** (exerurgentcare.com) has two walk-in locations near Disneyland Resort, at 2100 Euclid Street, Suite 102 (☎ 714-644-9100) and 831 S. State College Boulevard (☎ 714 533-2273); both are open daily, 8 a.m.–8 p.m. The closest hospital to Disneyland is the **University of California Irvine Medical Center,** which is about 2 miles distant at Chapman Avenue and City Drive. For dental emergencies, there is **7 Day Dental** at 637 N. Euclid St. in Anaheim (☎ 714-772-2893; 7daydental.com).

If you are staying at a Disneyland on-site hotel, dial 911 on the in-house phone to connect with the resort's medical services, who can send a registered nurse to your room free of charge.

SUNTAN LOTION? Suntan lotion and various sundries can be purchased in Disneyland Park on Main Street at the Emporium and at Elias and Company at the DCA entrance plaza (they're behind the counter, so you have to ask).

A SMOKE? You won't find cigarettes for sale at Disneyland parks, and smoking and vaping are prohibited inside the Disney parks and Downtown Disney. There are designated locations at the resort hotels where you may still inhale, but if you need a puff while inside the parks, you'll have to exit the Esplanade and pass through security again after you're done. And even though recreational and medical marijuana are now legal in California, it's explicitly prohibited on Disney property.

FEMININE-HYGIENE PRODUCTS? Tampons and sanitary pads are available for free in most women's restrooms and gender-neutral bathrooms at Disneyland Resort.

CASH? Basic banking services and foreign currency exchange are provided at City Hall in Disneyland Park, Guest Relations at DCA, and the front desks of Disneyland hotels. ATMs can be found in the following places:

AT DISNEYLAND PARK

- Outside the main entrance   • At the entrance to Frontierland on the left
- On Main Street, next to the *Disneyland Story* at the Town Square end

AT DOWNTOWN DISNEY

- Next to Salt & Straw

AT DISNEY CALIFORNIA ADVENTURE

- Near the restrooms across from The Little Mermaid: Ariel's Undersea Adventure entrance

A PLACE TO LEAVE MY PET? Pets (except for service dogs) are not allowed in the parks, and none of the on-site Disneyland hotels accept pets, although some nearby Good Neighbor properties do. Disneyland's pet care facilities never reopened following the pandemic; look into **Camp Bow Wow** (1431 N. Daly St; ☎ 714-533-2267; campbowwow .com/anaheim) or **Animal Friends Pet Hotel** (13220 S. Euclid St.; ☎ 714-537-4500; animalfriendspethotel.com) for off-site alternatives.

A PLACE TO CHARGE MY CELL PHONE? A few free accessible power outlets can be found around the parks (our favorites are along the stage in *Great Moments with Mr. Lincoln,* inside the Main Street train station, at Royal Street Veranda, and in the balcony in the Golden Horseshoe). Be sure not to block traffic or remove any installed plugs or covers, and even then you may still be ushered away by an employee. We prefer to charge on the go, so we carry Jackery and Anker external batteries for our devices; a 10,000 mAh unit smaller than a deck of playing cards can recharge your phone multiple times during a day.

Another energy option is the FuelRod, a precharged battery pack sold from a dozen-odd automated kiosks around the parks and inside each on-site hotel. You can find higher-capacity batteries online for less than the $30 FuelRod, but FuelRod's advantage is that, whenever it's drained, you can simply stop at any kiosk on Disney property and swap it for a full one free of charge. (Search "portable phone charging systems kiosks" inside the Disneyland app for a map of Fuel-Rod locations.) FuelRods can also be found in airports and malls for about $20, or two for $35 on Amazon, and all are compatible with Disneyland's kiosks, so save yourself some money by buying them outside the resort. You'll also find FuelRods at Walt Disney World, so bicoastal Mouse fans may get double mileage out of them. Google for a discount code to get $3 off your initial purchase, and sign into the FuelRod smartphone app for five free swaps at kiosks outside Disney. If you experience issues using a FuelRod kiosk, call the toll-free number on the box for swift remote service.

This father from Marlborough, Connecticut, is a FuelRod fan:

> Between using the app, taking pictures, and everything else we used our phones for, batteries drained fast. FuelRod was our best find ever. Yes, we all had portable chargers, but they never seem to be with you and charged when you really need them. For our family of 4 (2 adults, 2 teens) it was super convenient. We would charge our phone while on a ride or in a show, then swap it out for a freshly charged one, and hand it off to the next person in need of power. I don't know how we would have made it through each day without it.

Incidentally, cell phone coverage inside Disneyland can be a crapshoot at best, especially on crowded days. We've watched our AT&T 5G service drop down to an antiquated 4G data stream when transmission towers become overloaded by Instagramming guests.

Disneyland offers free Wi-Fi access inside its parks. No password is required to join the "Disney Guest" Wi-Fi network, but you will need to agree to the terms and conditions before accessing the internet (open Disneywifi.com in a browser if the login doesn't appear automatically). Connections can be inconsistent, especially inside attraction queues; find one of the hot spot locations marked on the park map and in the official app for your best shot at a stable signal.

Disney's spotty Wi-Fi coverage ensures that your phone will constantly be seeking a signal, thereby draining the battery, which quickly becomes a Catch-22 for users of the internet-dependent smartphone app. This can be especially aggravating for international guests without data plans who use the Disneyland app to store their tickets, since the parks' turnstile plazas have patchy Wi-Fi coverage. Here are a few hints for helping your smartphone survive a Disney day:

- Take a screenshot of your admission bar code as a backup; you can even make it your phone's lock screen for easy access.
- Only turn on your Wi-Fi when you know you're near a hot spot.
- Switch your cell phone into low power mode as soon as you arrive. (Disable it when using the Star Wars Datapad in the Disney Play app.)
- Turn your screen brightness up to full whenever approaching a turnstile or Lightning Lane scanner, so that your code can be read, then lower it to save power.

CELEBRATION PINS? Disneyland first-timers (along with honeymooners and birthday or anniversary celebrants) are rewarded with a special pin, as this Oregon mom relates:

> City Hall on Main Street had pins to proudly announce it was a first visit to DL. I didn't know about this during my older son's first visit. Fortunately, there is no date on it, so I got one for each son.

Another reader, who celebrated her 50th birthday there, reports:

I recommend getting birthday buttons. Not a single cast member failed to see them and make a big deal about it! And you don't have to show proof or anything; just go ask for one.

You can pick up free celebration buttons and character stickers from Guest Services inside either park or at any on-site hotel. They're also kept behind the counter at most park shops, so don't waste time in a long Guest Services line just to get one.

CAMERAS AND PHOTO SERVICES? You can buy a disposable camera, with or without a flash, as well as digital memory cards and batteries, throughout the parks. If you'd rather let professionals take the pictures, Disney PhotoPass photographers are stationed at scenic spots around the parks. You'll find them located at key landmarks, such as Sleeping Beauty Castle and Carthay Circle, as well as accompanying most character meet and greets; some even offer Magic Shots that superimpose an animated character into your family's pose; ask a photographer outside Star Wars: Rise of the Resistance for a priceless picture with Grogu (aka, "Baby Yoda") or a Porg. They'll take your snapshot with their camera for free, and then either scan your smartphone or hand you a PhotoPass identification card, which you can continue using during your vacation. Later, log onto the Disneyland app or disneyland.com/photopass within 45 days of your visit to preview and purchase all your pictures. You can download photos individually for $17 each or get a glossy print for $19 and up each. Alternatively, purchase a one-week PhotoPass+ package from disneyland .com/memories for $78 and get unlimited digital downloads of an entire week's worth of photos. Better yet, have at least one member of your party purchase Genie+ (see pages 97–106) for $30–$35, and they can download unlimited PhotoPass images from the day.

All PhotoPass packages also include your pictures taken at character meals in the parks and hotels, as well as on-ride snapshots from select attractions, including Space Mountain and Tiana's Bayou Adventure at Disneyland, and Radiator Springs Racers, the Incredicoaster, and Guardians of the Galaxy—Mission: Breakout! at DCA. Find a complete list of locations at disneyland.disney.go.com/guest-services/photopass-service or inside the official Disneyland app under the "PhotoPass" tab. Currently, all guests using the Disneyland app can get on-ride photos at select attractions for free, but not character or scenic photos; Genie+ still includes all PhotoPass locations. For assistance with PhotoPass, visit the photo concierge booth in the Esplanade to the left of Disneyland's entrance.

Be sure to use the Disneyland app to secure your Genie+ one-day photo package and attach it to your admission ticket before the park closes, as a mom from St. Louis learned the hard way:

We couldn't figure out how to purchase the [photo] upgrade on the day of our visit to download the park photos for our one-day visit. I decided to wait until I had more time to figure it out, but by that time customer service was closed. I called the next morning but was told that it had to be purchased on the day of the visit and was not available after the fact. The only option at that point was the one-week photo package, so it ended up costing much more than it should have.

All PhotoPass photos expire 45 days after the photo was taken, so remember to download and archive your purchases; a one-time 15-day extension on the expiration date can be purchased for $20.

DISNEYLAND RESORT *for* VISITORS *with* SPECIAL NEEDS

IF MEMBERS OF YOUR PARTY are disabled or have special needs, you'll want to visit disneyland.disney.go.com/guest-services/guests-with-disabilities as soon as you begin planning your trip. Visitors who are sight- or hearing-impaired, or partially or wholly nonambulatory, will find the downloadable Park Guides for Guests with Disabilities very helpful. Downloadable guides are also available for guests with cognitive disabilities, including autism spectrum disorders, which provide sensory information about all the attractions. Disney does not mail these guides, but copies are readily available at the parks.

For guests with visual or auditory impairments, digital audio and Braille guides, assistive listening devices, captioning, and sign language services are available through City Hall and Guest Relations. Trained service animals are welcome but must be kept on a leash at all times. Note the special symbol on park maps designating service animal relief areas in both parks.

VISITORS WITH MOBILITY ISSUES Rental wheelchairs are available outside Disneyland Park, just east of the main gates. Daily wheelchair rentals are $15 (manual) or $60 (electric ECV); a $20 refundable deposit is required. Note that wheelchairs and electric convenience vehicles rented inside the resort are not permitted beyond the security checkpoints. A limited supply of manual wheelchairs, which may be taken through Downtown Disney, are available to rent at the Disneyland Resort hotels. Manual wheelchairs and a limited number of ECVs are available to rent inside the bottom level of the Pixar Pals parking structure.

Close-in parking is available for the disabled; inquire when you pay your parking fee. Parking trams can accommodate guests who bring their own wheelchairs, and a special transportation van is also available (ask a parking lot cast member). Curbside drop-off is only available at the Harbor Boulevard entrance, near the stops for hotel shuttles and local buses. It may be challenging for disabled guests who don't bring their own wheelchairs to walk from there into the parks. If you don't think that you can travel the necessary distance, consider renting a chair or scooter for the length of your vacation from a third-party vendor like Apple Scooter (applescooter.com, ☎ 714-747-6177) who can deliver it to your hotel for a five-day rental for about $155.

If you can afford the room rate, this North Wales, Pennsylvania, reader raved about the convenience of staying at the Grand Californian:

This was a once-in-a-lifetime trip, and I have some mobility issues. So staying at the Grand Californian for its location and renting an ECV from an off-site company were worth the cost. The Grand Californian is just gorgeous, and I was constantly finding new things to amaze me.

Even with all of Disneyland's accommodations for disabled guests, one Claremont, California, woman says the resort still has a ways to go:

For disabled guests, restrooms are terrible. Usually there is only one handicapped stall, and it is OFTEN used by teens and even cast members, as well as moms taking strollers or multiple kids into the stall.

There are only two companion restrooms in each park (outside of first aid). Other theme parks in Southern California have staff who assist and tell guests not to use these stalls, and other parks have added many more family and companion restroom facilities.

There still are not enough handicapped parking spaces on more crowded days, nor adequate seating at many restaurants to accommodate the various types of need.

Most rides, shows, attractions, restrooms, and restaurants are engineered to accommodate the disabled. Some attraction ride vehicles can accommodate manual wheelchairs, but the majority require guests to transfer from their chair on their own power or with the help of their party; Disney employees provide portable benches but are not permitted to physically assist. Many shows and walk-through attractions can accommodate ECVs, but most rides cannot; manual wheelchairs are provided for transfers where required. For specific inquiries, download the park-specific "Guides for Guests With Disabilities" from disneyland.disney.go.com/guest-services/guests-with-disabilities or call ☎ 714-560-2547.

VISITORS WITH COGNITIVE AND DEVELOPMENTAL ISSUES If anyone in your party has a developmental or cognitive impairment like autism that makes it difficult to wait in a traditional queue for an extended period, register for **Disability Access Service (DAS),** at disneyland.disney.go.com/guest-services/disability-access-service/register. You can register for DAS online via video-chat between 9 a.m. and 8 p.m. PT daily, up to 30 days before your visit; you can also register in person at the Accessibility Services booths in the Esplanade between the theme parks, but we strongly recommended that you do it in advance of your arrival.

This program is free and available for the disabled visitor and up to three additional guests. You should not have to show a doctor's note or proof of disability, but you will need to discuss your (or your family member's) limitations and requested accommodations with a cast member or a health professional from Inspire Health Alliance. While it may feel uncomfortable to ask for assistance, we advise all eligible guests to inquire about the service because DAS can make the difference between having a miserable visit or a magical one. However, be warned that trying to defraud the DAS system by making untrue statements to a cast member can result in being permanently banned from the parks without a refund. As a woman from Bellingham, Washington, whose brother benefited from DAS wrote us:

> I never want to see people abuse the DAS card, but when used for its intended purpose, it is an excellent tool that really helped us keep things as smooth as possible.

With DAS, if the posted wait time is 15 minutes or less, guests are given on-demand access to an expedited ride. If the wait is over 15 minutes, instead of being immediately admitted to an attraction's entrance, users can claim return times based on the current standby wait (minus 10 minutes) through the Disneyland smartphone app by tapping "Request DAS Return Time" on an attraction's information screen. Alternatively, DAS users can get human assistance requesting return times at designated kiosks strategically scattered around the parks. At Disneyland Park, Guest Experience kiosks (which are marked by green or blue umbrellas) can be found at City Hall on Main Street U.S.A., in the central hub, between Dumbo and Casey Jr. in Fantasyland, outside Star Wars Launch Bay in Tomorrowland, near the Fantasyland tunnel into Star Wars Galaxy's Edge, and near Harbour Galley in Critter Country. DCA has fewer kiosks, all located along the park's central spine on Buena Vista Street, outside Carthay Circle, near the entrance to Cars Land, and on Pixar Pier at Jessie's Critter Carousel. These remote guest relations locations can do almost anything that the main locations at the front of the parks can do (except Magic Key upgrades), so find one instead of waiting in a long line at City Hall.

When your DAS return time arrives—or at any time after until park closing—you'll be granted expedited admission to the attraction using either the Lightning Lane (for rides that offer it) or an alternate entrance (for those that don't). In effect, DAS is a special Genie+ for disabled guests, and it can be used in conjunction with Genie+, individual Lightning Lane attractions, and/or Virtual Queue. DAS users must join a boarding group (or purchase a Lightning Lane time) to ride select attractions when the use of Virtual Queue is required, but they can request priority access once their number is redeemed. You can also view or cancel DAS reservations inside the Disneyland app. A DAS enrollment is valid for 120 days, after which it must be renewed in person or online. Like Genie+, users can hold one DAS reservation at a time, but unlike Genie+, the Disneyland app can only be used to request DAS return times at the park users are currently in. However, kiosks in one park can issue return times for rides in the other to guests eligible for park hopping.

Like Genie+, DAS passes can be redeemed up to 5 minutes before the stated return time, and DAS users cannot get a return time for an attraction that is temporarily closed through the app, but they can by visiting a Guest Experience kiosk. If a ride is closed when your DAS redemption time arrives, your pass should automatically convert to a Multiple Experiences pass. If the ride breaks down after your DAS becomes valid (but before you use it), the pass will still be good for that attraction until closing, but you'll need to cancel and rebook if you'd rather ride something different.

The other main differences between DAS and Genie+ are: DAS is available at essentially every attraction with a standby queue, including those selling Individual Lightning Lane access; DAS may be used to re-ride the same attraction multiple times in a day; DAS return times are tied to the posted standby wait and can be requested even after all Genie+ reservations are gone; once valid, DAS return times don't expire until park closing; and there is no charge for DAS.

In June 2024, Disney made the qualification guidelines for DAS more stringent in order to curb rampant demand for the service, whose usage had more than tripled since the pandemic. DAS is now largely reserved for those with autism spectrum disorders, leaving out guests with other nonvisible disabilities who previously were accommodated. Be aware that DAS will not be issued to guests with mobility issues that can be accommodated by renting a wheelchair, and guests requiring frequent restroom breaks will be asked to exit and then rejoin the queue (ask a cast member at the attraction for assistance). Additional services, such as rider switch and break areas, are available for all guests. If you feel you may need the DAS program or other accommodations, be sure to read up on your options in advance at disneyland.disney.go.com/guest-services/guests-with-disabilities.

Guests in wheelchairs (or strollers with wheelchair tags) who do not have additional cognitive or sensory issues do not need to sign up for DAS because all attraction standby queues in DCA, and most in Disneyland, are fully wheelchair accessible. At those in Disneyland that are not fully accessible, guests in wheelchairs will go to the ride's main entrance and be issued a return time based on the current wait time (minus 10 minutes), at which point they can report to an alternate accessible entrance. Though similar to DAS, this program is independent of it and does not require preregistration.

VISITORS WITH DIETARY RESTRICTIONS Guests on special or restricted diets, including those requiring kosher meals, can arrange for assistance at City Hall at Disneyland Park or at Guest Relations at DCA. These locations can also provide information on vegan or gluten-free menu options at restaurants in the resort. For special service at Disneyland Resort restaurants, call the restaurant at least one day in advance for assistance. See pages 292–293 for more details on allergies and dietary restrictions at Disneyland Resort.

PART 5

DISNEYLAND *with* KIDS

I am very grateful for the help your book gave me. The best part was that there were no surprises that spoiled the fun. I was ready for rain, wind, cold, expensive food, small-child meltdowns, and 40-minute potty stops for the grandparents (well, maybe not quite ready for the 40-minute potty stops). I did need an hour alone in the Grand Californian bar after the third day.

—Mom from Lompoc, California

The BRUTAL TRUTH *About* FAMILY VACATIONS

IT HAS BEEN SUGGESTED that the phrase *family vacation* is a bit of an oxymoron because you can never take a vacation from the responsibilities of parenting if your children are traveling with you. Though you leave work and normal routine far behind, your children require as much attention, if not more, when traveling as they do at home.

Parenting on the road requires imagination and organization. You have to do all the usual stuff (feed, dress, bathe, supervise, comfort, discipline, and so on) in an atmosphere where your children are hyperstimulated, without the familiarity of place and the resources available at home. Though not impossible—and possibly even fun—parenting on the road is not something you want to learn on the fly.

The point is that preparation, or the lack thereof, can make or break your Disneyland vacation. Believe us: you don't want to leave the success of your expensive Disney vacation to chance. Your preparation can be organized into several categories: mental, emotional, physical, organizational, and logistical. You also need a basic understanding of the two theme parks and a well-considered plan for how to go about seeing them.

MENTAL *and* EMOTIONAL PREPARATION

MENTAL PREPARATION BEGINS with realistic expectations about your Disney vacation and consideration of what each adult and child in your party most wants and needs from their Disneyland experience. Getting in touch with this aspect of planning requires a lot of introspection and good, open family communication.

DIVISION OF LABOR

TALK ABOUT WHAT you and your partner need and what you expect to happen on the vacation. This discussion alone can preempt some unpleasant surprises mid-trip. If you are a two-parent family, do you have a clear understanding of how the parenting workload will be distributed? We've seen some disruptive misunderstandings in two-parent households in which one parent is (pardon the legalese) the primary caregiver. Often, the other parent expects the primary caregiver to function on vacation as they do at home. The primary caregiver, on the other hand, is ready for a break. They expect their partner to either shoulder the load equally or perhaps even assume the lion's share, so they can have a real vacation. However you divide the responsibility is up to you. Just make sure that you negotiate a clear understanding before you leave home.

TOGETHERNESS

ANOTHER DIMENSION TO CONSIDER is how much togetherness seems appropriate to you. For some parents, a vacation represents a rare opportunity to really connect with their children, to talk, exchange ideas, and get reacquainted. For others, a vacation affords the time to get a little distance, to enjoy a round of golf while the kids are enjoying the theme park. The point here is to think about your and your children's preferences and needs concerning your time together. A typical day at a Disney theme park provides the structure of experiencing attractions together, punctuated by periods of waiting in line, eating, and so on, which facilitate conversation and sharing. Most attractions can be enjoyed together by the whole family, regardless of age ranges. This allows for more consensus and less dissent when it comes to deciding what to see and do. For many parents and children, however, the rhythms of a Disneyland day seem to consist of passive entertainment experiences alternated with endless discussions of where to go and what to do next.

Two observations: First, fighting the crowds and keeping the family moving along can easily escalate into a pressure-driven outing. Having a plan or itinerary eliminates moment-to-moment guesswork and decision-making, thus creating more time for savoring and connecting. Second, external variables such as crowd size, noise, and weather, among others, can be so distracting as to preclude any meaningful togetherness. These negative impacts can be moderated, as previously discussed in

Part One, by being selective concerning the time of year, day of the week, and the time of day you visit the theme parks, as well as the number of days of your visit. The bottom line is that you can achieve the degree of connection and togetherness you desire with a little advance planning and a realistic awareness of the distractions you will encounter.

LIGHTEN UP

PREPARE YOURSELF MENTALLY to be a little less compulsive on vacation about correcting small behavioral deviations and pounding home the lessons of life. So what if Matt eats hamburgers for breakfast, lunch, and dinner every day? You can make him eat peas and broccoli when you get home. Roll with the little stuff, and remember when your children act out that they are wired to the max. At least some of that adrenaline is bound to spill out in undesirable ways. Coming down hard will send an already frayed little nervous system into orbit. Especially if you're traveling with children, you'll need a sense of humor, more than a modicum of patience, and the ability to roll with the punches.

SOMETHING FOR EVERYONE

IF YOU TRAVEL WITH AN INFANT, toddler, or any child who requires a lot of special attention, make sure that you have some energy and time remaining for the rest of your brood. While planning, invite each child to name something special to do or see at Disneyland with Mom or Dad alone. Work these special activities into your trip itinerary. Whatever else, if you commit, write it down so that you don't forget. Remember that a casually expressed willingness to do this or that may be perceived as a promise.

unofficial **TIP**
Try to schedule some time alone with each of your children—if not each day, then at least a couple of times during the trip.

WHOSE IDEA WAS THIS, ANYWAY?

THE DISCORD THAT many vacationing families experience arises from the kids being on a completely different wavelength from Mom and Dad. Parents and grandparents are often worse than children when it comes to conjuring fantasy scenarios of what a Disneyland vacation will be like. It can be many things, but believe us when we tell you that there's a lot more to it than just riding Dumbo and seeing Mickey.

In our experience, most parents and nearly all grandparents expect children to enter a state of rapture at Disneyland, bouncing from attraction to attraction in wide-eyed wonder, appreciative beyond words to their adult benefactors. What they get, more often than not, is not even in the same ballpark. Preschoolers will, without a doubt, be wide-eyed, often with delight but also with a general sense of being overwhelmed by noise, crowds, and Disney characters as big as toolsheds. We've substantiated through thousands of interviews and surveys that the best part of a Disney vacation for a preschooler is the hotel swimming pool. With some grade-schoolers and pre-driving-age teens, you get near-manic hyperactivity coupled with periods of studied nonchalance. This last phenomenon, which relates to the importance of being cool at all costs, translates into a maddening display of boredom and a "been there, done that" attitude. Older teens are frequently the exponential version of younger teens and grade-schoolers, but without the manic behavior.

unofficial **TIP**
The more information your kids have before arriving at Disneyland, the less likely they'll be to act out.

For preschoolers, you can keep things light and happy by limiting the time you spend in the theme parks. Most critical is that the overstimulation of the parks must be balanced by adequate rest and more-mellow activities. For grade-schoolers and early teens, you can moderate the hyperactivity and false ennui by enlisting their help in planning the vacation, especially by allowing them to take a leading role in determining the itinerary for days at the theme parks. Putting them in charge of specific responsibilities that focus on the happiness of other family members also works well. For example, one reader turned a 12-year-old liability into an asset by asking him to help guard against attractions that might frighten his 5-year-old sister. Knowledge enhances anticipation and at the same time affords a level of comfort and control that helps kids understand the big picture. The more they feel in control, the less they will act out of control.

KNOW THYSELF AND NOTHING TO EXCESS

FIRST, CONCERNING THE "know thyself" part, do some serious thinking about what you want in a vacation. Entertain the notion that having fun and deriving pleasure from your vacation may be very different from doing and seeing as much as possible.

Because Disneyland Resort is expensive, many families confuse seeing everything to get your money's worth with having a great time. Sometimes the two are compatible, but more often they're not. So if sleeping in, relaxing with a cup of coffee, sunbathing by the pool, or taking a nap rank high on your vacation hit parade, you need to give them due emphasis on your Disney visit, even if it means that you see less of the theme parks.

unofficial **TIP**
Get a grip on your needs and preferences before you leave home, and develop an itinerary that incorporates all the things that make you happiest.

Which brings us to the "nothing to excess" part. At the Disneyland parks, especially if you're touring with children, less is definitely more. Trust us: it's tough to go full tilt from dawn to dusk in the theme parks. First you'll get tired, then you'll get cranky, and then you'll adopt a production mentality ("We have three more rides, and then we can go back to the hotel"). Finally, you'll hit the wall because you just can't maintain the pace.

This mom had a great vacation, but not exactly the vacation she had been expecting:

I was unprepared for traveling with a 2-year-old. All the indoor rides were deemed too dark and scary, and all she wanted to do was see the characters (which I thought she'd be petrified of!). We had a great trip once I threw all my plans out the window and just went with the flow! We all would have appreciated more pool time. Think twice before bringing a 2-year-old. It is one exhausting trip!

Plan on seeing the Disneyland parks in bite-size chunks with plenty of swimming, napping, and relaxing in between. Most Disneyland vacations are short. Even if you have to stay an extra day to build in some relaxation, you'll be happier while you're there and more rested when you get home, as this Palo Alto, California, parent found:

I recommend that families—especially those with young children— put regular buffers in their plans. Having open buffer time made it easier to slow down periodically during the day and smell the roses. While we loved doing all the rides, we also enjoyed soaking up the atmosphere, having an ice-cream cone, and so on.

Ask yourself over and over in both the planning stage and while you are at Disneyland: what will contribute the greatest contentedness, satisfaction, and harmony? Trust your instincts. If stopping for ice cream or returning to the hotel for a dip feels like more fun than seeing another attraction, do it—even if it means wasting the remaining hours of an expensive admission pass.

The AGE THING

THERE'S A LOT OF SERIOUS COGITATION among parents and grandparents regarding how old a child should be before embarking on a trip to Disneyland. The answer, not always obvious, stems from the personalities and maturity of the children, and the personalities and parenting style of the adults.

Disneyland for Infants and Toddlers

We believe that traveling with infants and toddlers is a great idea. Developmentally, travel is a stimulating learning experience for even the youngest of children. Infants, of course, won't know Mickey Mouse from a draft horse but will respond to sun

unofficial **TIP**
Traveling with infants and toddlers sharpens parenting skills and makes the entire family more mobile and flexible, resulting in a richer, fuller life for all.

and shade, music, bright colors, and the extra attention they receive from you. From first steps to full mobility, toddlers respond to the excitement and spectacle of the Disneyland parks, though, of course, in a much different way than you do. Your toddler will prefer splashing in fountains and clambering over curbs and benches to experiencing most attractions, but no matter: they will still have a great time.

An Iowa City, Iowa, mother of three says, "Get over it!":

Get over it! In my opinion, people think too much about the age thing. If taking your 3-year-old would make you happy, that's all that counts. It doesn't matter if the trip is really for you or your child. You shouldn't have to jump through hoops to give yourself permission to go.

Somewhere between 4 and 6 years of age, your child will experience the first vacation that they will remember as an adult. Though more likely to remember the coziness of the hotel room than the theme parks, the child will be able to experience and comprehend many attractions. Even so, their favorite activity is likely to be swimming in the hotel pool.

As concerns infants and toddlers, there are good reasons and bad reasons for vacationing at Disneyland. A good reason for taking your little one to Disneyland Resort is that you want to go and there's no one available to care for your child during your absence. Philosophically, we are very much against putting your life (including your vacation) on hold until your children are older. Especially if you have children of varying ages, it's better to take the show on the road than to wait until the youngest reaches the perceived ideal age.

An illogical reason, however, for taking an infant or toddler to Disneyland Resort is that you think Disneyland is the perfect vacation destination for babies. It's not, so think again if you are contemplating Disneyland Resort primarily for your child's enjoyment. For starters, attractions are geared more toward older children and adults. Even designer play areas such as the Pirate's Lair on Tom Sawyer Island in Disneyland Park are developed with older children in mind.

That said, let us stress that, for the well prepared, taking a toddler to Disneyland Resort can be a totally glorious experience. There's truly nothing like watching your child respond to the color, the sound, the festivity, and, most of all, the characters. You'll return home with photos that you will treasure forever. Your little one won't remember much, but your memories will be unforgettable.

If you elect to take your infant or toddler to Disneyland Resort, rest assured that their needs have been anticipated. The theme parks have centralized facilities for infant and toddler care. Everything necessary for changing diapers, preparing formula, and warming bottles and food is available. At the Disneyland Park, the Baby Care Center is next to the Plaza Inn at the end of Main Street and to the right. At Disney California Adventure (DCA) the Baby Care Center is tucked out of the way next to the Ghirardelli Chocolate Shop in the San Fransokyo Square area of the park. Dads in charge of little ones are welcome at the centers and can use most services offered. In addition, both men's and women's restrooms in the parks have changing tables.

unofficial **TIP**
Baby supplies—including disposable diapers, formula, and baby food—are for sale, and rockers and special chairs are available for nursing mothers at each park's Baby Care Center.

Infants and toddlers are allowed to experience any attraction that doesn't have minimum height or age restrictions. A mother of three from Utah wrote to us, saying:

> We traveled with my 9-month-old, so we did the switching-off option a lot. However, I would appreciate it if you provided a complete list of all the rides that babies can be carried on. I was there alone with all three kids, and it would've been really nice to just look at a list of all the rides that we could've gone on with a baby.

It's actually far easier to list the attractions that you *can't* take a baby on at Disneyland. Unless a minimum height or age requirement is explicitly posted, children of any size—even handheld infants—are welcome on any ride. That includes all the family dark rides, kiddie carnival attractions, and slow-moving boats. On page 162 is a table of all the rides that impose a height restriction; if a ride isn't listed, you can bring the young 'uns along. But as a Minneapolis mother reports, some attractions are better for babies than others:

> *Shows and boat rides are easier for babies (ours was almost 1 year old, not yet walking). Rides where a bar comes down are doable but harder. Peter Pan's Flight was our first encounter with this type, and we had barely gotten situated when I realized that he might fall out of my grasp. The 3-D films are too intense; the noise level is deafening and the images inescapable.*
>
> *I thought you might want to know what a baby thought (based on his reactions). At Disneyland Park: Jungle Cruise: didn't get into it. Pirates of the Caribbean: slept through it. Mark Twain Riverboat: the horn made him cry. It's a Small World: wide-eyed, took it all in. Peter Pan's Flight: couldn't really sit on the seat. A bit dangerous. He didn't get into it. Disneyland Railroad: liked the motion and scenery. Enchanted Tiki Room: loved it. Danced, clapped, sang along.*

The same mom also advises:

> *We used a baby sling on our trip and thought it was great when standing in the lines—much better than a stroller, which you have to park before getting in line and navigate through crowds. It is impractical to go to the Baby Care Center every time your baby needs to nurse, so moms should be comfortable nursing in public situations.*

The rental strollers at the parks are designed for toddlers and children up to 4 and 5 years old but definitely not for infants. Still, if you bring pillows and padding, the strollers can be made to work. You can alternatively bring your own stroller, but only a limited number of non-collapsible strollers fit on each parking tram, and only collapsible strollers are allowed on Toy Story lot's shuttle buses.

unofficial **TIP** In addition to providing an alternative to carrying your child, a stroller serves as a handy cart for diaper bags, water bottles, and other necessary items.

Even if you opt for a stroller (your own or a rental), we recommend that you bring a baby sling or baby/child backpack. Simply put, there will be many times in the theme parks when you will have to park the stroller and carry your child.

Many nursing moms recommend breastfeeding during a dark Disney theater presentation. This only works, however, if the presentation is long enough for the baby to finish nursing. Shows at the Hyperion Theater at DCA are usually long enough, but the theater is not as dark as those that show films. Tomorrowland Theater (currently closed) at Disneyland Park is way too loud, as is the 3-D movie in Hollywood Land at DCA.

Many Disney shows run back-to-back with only 1 or 2 minutes in between to change the audience. If you want to breastfeed and require more time than the length of the show, tell the cast member on entering that you want to breastfeed and ask if you can remain in the theater while your baby finishes.

If you feel comfortable nursing in more public places with your breast and the baby's head covered with a shawl or some such, nursing will not be a problem at all. Even on the most crowded days, you can always find a back corner of a restaurant or a comparatively secluded park bench or garden spot to nurse.

Disneyland for 4-, 5-, and 6-Year-Olds

Kids in this age group vary immensely in their capacity to comprehend and enjoy Disneyland Resort. With this age group, the go-no-go decision is a judgment call. If your child is sturdy, easygoing, and fairly adventuresome and demonstrates a high degree of independence, the trip will probably work. On the other hand, if your child tires easily, is temperamental, or is a bit timid or reticent in embracing new experiences, you're much better off waiting a few years. Whereas the travel and sensory-overload problems of infants and toddlers can be addressed and (usually) remedied on the go, discontented 4- to 6-year-olds have the ability to stop a family dead in its tracks, as this mother of three from Cape May, New Jersey, attests:

My 5-year-old was scared pretty badly on [a dark ride] our first day. For the rest of the trip, we had to coax and reassure her before each and every ride before she would go.

A grandfather from San Antonio, Texas, told us:

We had one issue when our 6-year-old granddaughter REALLY disliked Space Mountain (but loved the Matterhorn and Big Thunder Mountain). An emergency Dole Whip and Tiki Room performance put us back on track!

If you have a retiring, clinging, and/or difficult 4- to 6-year-old who, for whatever circumstances, will be part of your group, you can sidestep or diminish potential problems with a bit of preparation. Even if your preschooler is plucky and game, the same prep measures (described later in this section) will enhance their experience and make life easier for the rest of the family.

Parents who understand that a visit with 4- to 6-year-old children is going to be more about the cumulative experience than about seeing it all will have wonderful memories of their children's amazement.

Tweens: The Ideal Age

Though our readers report successful trips as well as disasters with children of all ages, the consensus is that children's ages ideal for family compatibility and togetherness at Disneyland are 8–12 years. This "tweenage" group is old enough, tall enough, and sufficiently stalwart to experience, understand, and appreciate practically all Disney attractions. Moreover, they are developed to the extent that they can get around the parks on their own steam without being carried or collapsing. Best of all, they are still young enough to enjoy being with Mom and Dad. From our experience, ages 10–12 are better than 8–9, though what you gain in maturity is at the cost of that irrepressible, wide-eyed wonder so prevalent in the 8- and 9-year-olds. A reader from Folsom, California, strongly agrees:

> I recommend other families consider waiting until your kids are past the preschooler stage to go. My kids were 12, 10, and 6 (almost 7). These were the perfect ages for them to appreciate most of the attractions and also, generally, have the patience to wait in line and the stamina to tour the parks. They were also tall enough to go on anything.

Disneyland for Teens

Teens love Disneyland, and for parents of teens, Disneyland Resort is a nearly perfect, albeit expensive, vacation choice. Though your teens might not be as wide-eyed and impressionable as their younger sibs, they are at an age where they can sample, understand, and enjoy practically everything Disneyland Resort has to offer.

For parents, Disneyland Resort is a vacation destination where you can permit your teens an extraordinary amount of freedom. The entertainment is wholesome, the venues are safe, and the entire complex of hotels, theme parks, restaurants, and shopping is easily accessible on foot. Because most adolescents relish freedom, you may have difficulty keeping your teens with the rest of the family. Thus, if one of your objectives is to spend time with your teenage children during your Disneyland vacation, you will need to establish some clear-cut guidelines regarding togetherness and separateness before you leave home. Make your teens part of the discussion and try to meet them halfway in crafting a decision with which everyone can live. For your teens, touring on their own at Disneyland is tantamount to being independent in an exotic city. In any event, we're not suggesting that you just turn them loose. Rather, we are just attempting to sensitize you to the fact that, for your teens, some transcendent issues are involved. (Children must be at least 14 years old to enter a Disneyland Resort park without an accompanying parent or guardian.)

Most teens crave the company of other teens. If you have a solitary teen in your family, do not be surprised if they want to invite a friend on your vacation. If you are invested in sharing quality time with your solitary teen, the presence of a friend will make this more difficult, if not impossible. However, if you turn down the request to bring a friend, be prepared to go the extra mile to be a companion to your teen at Disneyland. If you're a teen, it's not much fun to ride Space Mountain by yourself.

Some parents have asked if there are unsafe places at Disneyland Resort or places where teens simply should not be allowed to go. Though the answer depends more on your family values and the relative maturity of your teens than on Disneyland Resort, the basic answer is no. Though it's true that teens who are looking for trouble can find it anywhere, there is absolutely nothing at Disneyland Resort that could be construed as a precipitant or a catalyst. Be advised, however, that adults consume alcohol at most Disneyland Resort restaurants, including table-service locations inside Disneyland Park.

About **INVITING** Your
CHILDREN'S FRIENDS

IF YOUR CHILDREN WANT TO INVITE FRIENDS on your Disneyland vacation, give your decision careful thought. First, consider the logistics. Is there room in the car? Will you have to leave something at home that you had planned on taking to make room in the trunk for the friend's luggage? Will additional hotel rooms or a larger suite be required? Will the increased number of people in your group make it hard to get a table at a restaurant?

If you determine that you can logistically accommodate one or more friends, the next step is to consider how the inclusion of the friend will affect your group's dynamics. Generally speaking, the presence of a friend will make it harder to really connect with your own children. So if one of your vacation goals is an intimate bonding experience with your children, the addition of friends will possibly frustrate your attempts to realize that objective.

If family relationship building is not necessarily a primary objective of your vacation, it's quite possible that the inclusion of a friend will make life easier for you. This is especially true in the case of only children, who may otherwise depend exclusively on you to keep them happy and occupied. Having a friend along can take the pressure off and give you some much-needed breathing room.

If you allow a friend to accompany you, limit the selection to children you know really well and whose parents you also know. Your children's friends who have spent time in your home will have a sense of your parenting style, and you will have a sense of their personality, behavior, and compatibility with your family. Assess the prospective child's potential to fit in well on a long trip. Are they polite, personable, fun to be with, and reasonably mature? Do they relate well to you and to the other members of your family?

Inviting the friend to share dinner with the family in a sit-down restaurant and then spend the night will provide a lot of relevant

unofficial TIP
We suggest that you arrange for the friend's parents to reimburse you after the trip for things such as restaurant meals and admissions. This is much easier than trying to balance the books after every expenditure.

information. Ideally this type of evaluation should take place early on in the normal course of family events, before you discuss the possibility of a friend joining you on your vacation. This will allow you to size things up without your child (or the friend) realizing that an evaluation is taking place. By seizing the initiative, you can guide the outcome.

We recommend that you do the inviting, instead of your child, and that the invitation be extended parent to parent (to avoid disappointment, you might want to sound out the friend's parent before broaching the issue with your child). Observing this recommendation will allow you to query the friend's parents concerning food preferences, any medical conditions, how discipline is administered in the friend's family, and how the friend's parents feel about the way you administer discipline.

Before you extend the invitation, give some serious thought to who pays for what. Make a specific proposal for financing the trip a part of your invitation; for example: "There's room for Marty in the hotel room, and transportation's no problem because we're driving. So we'll just need you to pick up Marty's meals, theme park admissions, and spending money."

"He Who Hesitates Is Launched!"
TIPS AND WARNINGS
for GRANDPARENTS

SENIORS OFTEN GET INTO PREDICAMENTS caused by touring with grandchildren. Run ragged and pressured to endure a blistering pace, many seniors just concentrate on surviving Disneyland rather than enjoying it. The theme parks have as much to offer older visitors as they do children, and seniors must either set the pace or dispatch the young folks to tour on their own. An older reader writes:

> Being a senior is not for wusses. At Disney [parks] particularly, it requires courage and pluck.... Half the time, your grandchildren treat you like a crumbling ruin, and then turn around and trick you into getting on a roller coaster in the dark. Seniors have to be alert and not trust anyone. Not their children or even the Disney people, and especially not their grandchildren. When your grandchildren want you to go on a ride, don't follow along blindly like a lamb to the slaughter. Make sure you know what the ride is all about. Stand your ground and do not waffle. He who hesitates is launched!

If you have a good relationship with your grandchildren and have had positive one-on-one experiences taking care of them, you might consider a trip to Disneyland. If you do, we recommend visiting Disneyland without them to get an idea of what you're getting into. A scouting trip will also allow you to enjoy some of the attractions that won't be on the itinerary when you return with the grandkids.

Tips for Grandparents

1. It's best to take one grandchild at a time, two at the most. Cousins can be better than siblings because they don't fight as much. To preclude sibling jealousy, try connecting the trip to a child's milestone, such as finishing the sixth grade.

2. Let your grandchildren help plan the vacation, and keep the first visit short. Be flexible, and don't overplan.

3. Discuss mealtimes and bedtime. Fortunately, many grandparents are on an early dinner schedule, which works nicely with younger children.

4. Gear plans to your grandchildren's age levels because if they're not happy, you won't be happy.

5. Create an itinerary that offers some supervised activities for children in case you need a rest.

6. If you're traveling by car, this is the one time we highly recommend earbuds. It's simply more enjoyable when everyone can listen to their own preferred style of music, at least for some portion of the trip.

7. Take along a night-light.

8. Carry a notarized statement from parents for permission for medical care in case of an emergency. Also be sure that you have insurance information and copies of any prescriptions for medicines the kids may take. Ditto for eyeglass prescriptions.

9. Tell your grandchildren about any medical problems you may have, so they can be prepared if there's an emergency.

10. Many attractions and hotels offer discounts for seniors, so be sure to check ahead of time for bargains.

11. Plan your evening meal early to avoid long waits. And make reservations if you're dining in a popular spot, even if it's early. Take some crayons and paper to keep kids occupied. If planning a family-friendly trip seems overwhelming, try a tour operator–travel agent aimed at kids and their grandparents.

A **FEW WORDS** *for* **SINGLE PARENTS**

BECAUSE SINGLE PARENTS are generally also working parents, planning a special getaway with your children can be the best way to spend some quality time together. But remember, the vacation is not just for your child—it's for you too. You might invite a grandparent or a favorite aunt or uncle along; the other adult provides nice company for you, and your child will benefit from the time with family members. You might likewise consider inviting an adult friend.

Though bringing along another adult is the best option, many single parents don't have someone who can make the trip. And while spending time with your child is wonderful, it is difficult to match the energy level of your child if you are the sole focus of their world.

One alternative: Try to meet other single parents at Disneyland. It may seem odd, but most of them are in the same boat as you; besides, all you have to do is ask. The easiest way to meet other single parents is to hang out at the hotel pool. Another option, albeit expensive, is to take along a trustworthy babysitter (18 or up) to travel with you.

If you visit Disneyland Resort with another single parent, get adjoining rooms; take turns watching all the kids; and, if possible, get a sitter and enjoy an evening out.

Throughout this book we mention the importance of good planning and touring. For a single parent, this is an absolute must. In addition, make sure that you set aside downtime each day back at the hotel.

Finally, don't try to spend every moment with your children on vacation. Instead, plan some activities for your children with other children. Then take advantage of your free time to do what you want to do: Read a book, have a massage, take a long walk, or enjoy a catnap.

PHYSICAL PREPARATION

YOU'LL FIND THAT some physical conditioning, coupled with a realistic sense of the toll that Disneyland takes on your body, will preclude falling apart in the middle of your vacation. As one of our readers put it, "If you pay attention to eat, heat, feet, and sleep, you'll be OK."

As you contemplate the stamina of your family, it's important to understand that somebody is going to run out of steam first, and when they do, the whole family will be affected. Sometimes a cold drink or a snack will revive the flagging member. Sometimes, however, no amount of cajoling or treats will work. In this situation it's crucial that you recognize that the child, grandparent, or spouse is at the end of their rope. The correct decision is to get them back to the hotel. Pushing the exhausted beyond their capacity will spoil the day for them—and you. Accept that stamina and energy levels vary, and be prepared to administer to members of your family who poop out. One more thing: no guilt trips. "We've driven 300 miles to take you to Disneyland, and now you're going to ruin everything!" is not an appropriate response.

THE AGONY OF THE FEET

IF YOU SPEND A DAY at Disneyland Park, you will walk 3–6 miles! If you walk to the park from your hotel, you can add 1–2 miles, and another couple of miles if you park hop to DCA. The walking, however, will be nothing like a 5-mile hike in the woods. At Disneyland Park and DCA, you will be in direct sunlight most of the time, navigate through huge jostling crowds, walk on hot pavement, and endure waits in line between bursts of walking. The bottom line, if you haven't figured it out, is that Disney theme parks (especially in the summer) are not for wimps, as this step-tracking reader from Phoenix, Arizona, was surprised to discover:

> We walked more than the equivalent of two marathons in four days. When I consider that people train for marathons for months in advance, I feel a little bit better about needing a few days post-vacation to recover!

Prevent Blisters In Five Easy Steps

1. PREPARE As mentioned above, you can easily cover 5–10 miles a day at the parks, so get your feet and legs into shape before you leave home. Though most children are active, their normal play usually doesn't condition them for the exertion of touring a Disney theme park. We recommend starting a program of family walks 6 weeks or more before your trip. A Pennsylvania mom who did just that offers the following:

> *We had our 6-year-old begin walking with us a bit every day one month before leaving—when we arrived [at Disneyland], her little legs could carry her and she had a lot of stamina.*

Start with short walks around the neighborhood. Increase your distance gradually until you can do 6 miles without needing CPR. As you begin, remember that little people have little strides, and though your 6-year-old may create the appearance of running circles around you, consider that (1) they won't have the stamina to go at that pace very long, and (2) they probably have to take two strides or so to every one of yours to keep up when you walk together.

2. PAY ATTENTION During your training program, your feet will tell you if you're wearing the right shoes. Choose well-constructed, broken-in running or hiking shoes. If you feel a hot spot coming on, chances are a blister isn't far behind. The most common sites for blisters are heels, toes, and balls of feet. If you develop a hot spot in the same place every time you walk, cover it with a blister bandage or cushion before you set out.

Don't wear sandals, flip-flops, or slip-ons in the theme parks. Even if your feet don't blister, they'll get stepped on by other guests or run over by strollers.

3. SOCK IT UP Good socks are as important as good shoes. When you walk, your feet sweat like a mule in a peat bog, and the moisture only increases friction. To counteract friction, wear socks made from material such as Smartwool or CoolMax, which wicks perspiration away from your feet (Smartwool socks come in varying thicknesses). To further combat moisture, dust your feet with antifungal powder.

4. DON'T BE A HERO Take care of foot problems the minute you notice them. Carry a small foot-emergency kit with gauze, antibiotic ointment, disinfectant, and moleskin or blister bandages. KT tape, beloved by athletes and dancers, is useful for supporting strained ankles and arches. Extra socks and foot powder are optional.

If carrying all of that sounds like too much, stop by a park First Aid Center as soon as you notice a hot spot forming on your foot.

5. CHECK THE KIDS Young children might not say anything about blisters forming until it's too late. Stop several times a day and check their feet. If you find a blister, either treat it using the kit you're carrying, or stop by a First Aid Center.

Finally, a stroller will provide your child the option of walking or riding, and if they poop out, you won't have to carry them. Even if your child hardly uses the stroller, it serves as a convenient place for water bottles and other stuff you may not feel like carrying. Strollers at Disneyland are covered in detail beginning on page 153.

REST AND RELAXATION

PHYSICAL CONDITIONING is important but is not a substitute for rest. Even marathon runners need recovery time. If you push too hard and try to do too much, you'll either crash or, at a minimum, turn what should be fun into an ordeal. Rest means plenty of sleep at night and, if possible, naps during the afternoon and planned breaks in your vacation itinerary. Don't forget that the brain, as well as the body, needs rest and relaxation. The stimulation inherent in touring a Disney theme park is enough to put many children and some adults into system overload. It is imperative that you remove your family from this unremitting assault on the senses and do something relaxing and quiet such as swimming or reading.

The theme parks are pretty big, so don't try to see everything in one day. Even during the off-season, when the crowds are smaller and the temperatures more pleasant, the size of the theme parks will exhaust most children under age 8 by lunchtime, as this mom from Pflugerville, Texas, discovered:

> There is no way we would have had the stamina to fit both parks in with three-day tickets if it was hot. Both of my kids are in good shape, and they were exhausted, even taking the break you recommended.

Another Texas family underscores the importance of naps and rest:

> Despite not following any of your touring plans, we did follow the theme of visiting a specific park in the morning, leaving midafternoon for either a nap back at the room or a trip to the pool, and then returning to one of the parks in the evening. On the few occasions we skipped your advice, I was muttering to myself by dinner. I can't tell you what I was muttering.

When it comes to naps, this mom does not mince words:

> One last thing for parents of small kids—take the book's advice and get out of the park and take the nap, take the nap, TAKE THE NAP! Never in my life have I seen so many parents screaming at, ridiculing, or slapping their kids. (What a vacation!) Disney [parks are] overwhelming for kids and adults.

If you plan to return to your hotel at midday and would like your room made up, let housekeeping know before you leave in the morning. If the location of your hotel room makes returning to the room impractical, you should still find alternative ways to take an afternoon break, as this California family advises:

We found it to be less tiring to just get off our feet within a park, have a cool drink, and sit in some shade than to add in an extra trip to and from the hotel.

The Main Street Opera House and old motorboat landing at Disneyland, Disney Animation and the Boudin Bakery Tour at DCA, and the lobby of the Grand Californian Hotel are all great places to pause and recharge without leaving the resort.

Routines That Travel

If when at home you observe certain routines—for example, reading a book before bed or having a bath first thing in the morning—try to incorporate these familiar activities into your vacation schedule. They will provide your children with a sense of security and normalcy.

Maintaining a normal routine is especially important with toddlers, as a mother of two from Lawrenceville, Georgia, relates:

The first day, we tried an early start, so we woke the children (ages 2 and 4) and hurried them to get going. BAD IDEA with toddlers. This put them off schedule for naps and meals the rest of the day. It is best to let young ones stay on their regular schedule and see Disney at their own pace, and you'll have much more fun.

∎ DEVELOPING *a* GOOD PLAN

ALLOW YOUR CHILDREN to participate in the planning of your time at Disneyland. Guide them diplomatically through the options, establishing advance decisions about what to do each day. Begin with your trip to Disneyland, deciding what time to depart, who sits by the window, whether to stop for meals or eat in the car, and so on. For the Disneyland part of your vacation, build consensus for wake-up call, bedtime, and naps into the itinerary, and establish ground rules for eating, buying refreshments, and shopping. Determine the order for visiting the two theme parks and make a list of must-see attractions. To help you fill in the blanks of your days, and especially to prevent you from spending most of your time standing in line, we offer a number of field-tested touring plans. The plans are designed to minimize your waiting time at each park by providing step-by-step itineraries that route you counter to the flow of traffic. The plans are explained in greater detail starting on page 87.

Generally, it's better to just sketch in the broad strokes on the master plan. The detail of what to do when you actually arrive at the park can be decided the night before you go, or with the help of one of our touring plans once

unofficial **TIP**
To keep your thinking fresh and to adequately cover all bases, develop your plan in two or three family meetings no longer than 40 minutes each. You'll discover that all members of the family will devote a lot of thought to the plan both in and between meetings. Don't try to anticipate every conceivable contingency, or you'll end up with something as detailed and unworkable as the tax code.

you get there. Above all, be flexible. One important caveat: Make sure that you keep any promises or agreements that you make when planning. They may not seem important to you, but they will to your children, who will remember for a long, long time if you let them down.

The more you can agree to and nail down in advance, the less potential you'll have for disagreement and confrontation once you arrive. Because children are more comfortable with the tangible than the conceptual, and also because they sometimes have short memories, we recommend typing up all of your decisions and agreements and providing a copy to each child. Create a fun document, not a legalistic one. You'll find that your children will review it in anticipation of all the things they will see and do, will consult it often, and will even read it to their younger siblings.

Your itinerary should provide minimum structure and maximum flexibility, specifying which park the family will tour each day without attempting to nail down exactly what the family will do there. No matter how detailed your itinerary is, be prepared for surprises at Disneyland, both good and bad. If an unforeseen event renders part of the plan useless or impractical, just roll with it. And always remember that it's your itinerary; you created it, and you can change it. Just try to make any changes the result of family discussion and be especially careful not to scrap an element of the plan that your children perceive as something you promised them.

LOGISTIC PREPARATION

WHEN WE WERE DISCUSSING good logistic preparation for a Disneyland vacation, a friend from Phoenix said, "Wait, what's the big deal? You pack clothes, a few games for the car, and go!" So OK, we confess, that will work, but life can be sweeter and the vacation smoother (as well as less expensive) with the right gear.

CLOTHING

LET'S START WITH CLOTHES. We recommend springing for vacation uniforms. Buy for each child several sets of jeans (or shorts) and T-shirts, all matching, and all the same. For a one-week trip, for example, get each child three pairs of khaki shorts, three light-yellow T-shirts, and three pairs of Smartwool or Coolmax hiking socks. What's the point? First, you don't have to play fashion designer, coordinating a week's worth of stylish combos. It's simple, it saves time, and there are no decisions to make or arguments about what to wear. Second, uniforms make your children easier to spot and keep together in the theme parks. Third, the uniforms give your family, as well as the vacation itself, some added identity. If you're like an ever-increasing number of families we see in the parks, you might go so far as to create a logo for the trip to be printed on the shirts.

unofficial **TIP**
Give your teens the job of coming up with the logo for your shirts. They will love being the family designers.

Buy short-sleeved shirts in light colors for warm weather, or long-sleeved, darker-colored T-shirts for cooler weather. All-cotton shirts are a little cooler and more comfortable in hot, humid weather. Polyester-cotton blend shirts are more wrinkle-resistant and dry a bit faster if they get wet.

LABELS A great idea, especially for younger children, is to attach labels with your family name, hometown, the name of your hotel, the dates of your stay, and your cell phone number inside the shirt—for example:

HODDER FAMILY OF DENVER, CO.;
CAMELOT INN; MAY 5-12; 303-555-2108

Instruct your smaller children to show the label to an adult if they get separated from you. Elimination of the child's first name (which most children of talking age can articulate in any event) allows you to order labels that are all the same; that can be used by anyone in the family; and that can also be affixed to such easily lost items as hats, jackets, hip packs, ponchos, and umbrellas. If fooling with labels sounds like too much of a hassle, check out "Lost Children" (pages 168–170) for some alternatives.

> *unofficial* **TIP**
> Equip each child with a big bandanna. These come in handy for wiping noses, scouring ice cream from chins and mouths, and dabbing sweat from the forehead and can also be tied around the neck to protect from sunburn.

DRESSING FOR COOLER WEATHER Southern California experiences temperatures all over the scale November–March, so it could be a bit chilly if you visit during those months. Our suggestion is to layer: for example, a breathable, waterproof or water-resistant windbreaker over a light, long-sleeved polypropylene shirt over a long-sleeved T-shirt. As with the baffles of a sleeping bag or down coat, the air trapped between the layers is what keeps you warm. If all the layers are thin, you won't be left with something bulky to cart around if you want to pull off one or more. Later in this section, we'll advocate wearing a hip pack. Each layer should be sufficiently compactible to fit easily in that hip pack along with whatever else is in it.

ACCESSORIES

SUNGLASSES Smog notwithstanding, the California sun is so bright and the glare so blinding that we recommend sunglasses for each family member. For children and adults of all ages, a good accessory item is an eyeglass strap for spectacles or sunglasses. The best models have a little device for adjusting the amount of slack in the strap. This allows your child to comfortably hang sunglasses from their neck when indoors or, alternately, to secure them fast to their head while experiencing a fast ride outdoors.

HIP PACKS AND WALLETS Unless you are touring with an infant or toddler, the largest thing anyone in your family should carry is a hip pack or fanny pack. Each person should have one. The pack should be large enough to carry at least a half-day's worth of snacks and other items deemed necessary (lip balm, bandanna, alcohol-based hand-sanitizing gel, disposable face mask, and so on) and still have enough room left to stash a hat, poncho, or light windbreaker. We recommend buying full-size hip packs at outdoor retailers as opposed to small, child-size hip packs. They are light; can be made to fit any child large enough to tote a hip pack; have slip-resistant, comfortable, wide belting; and will last for years.

Do not carry billfolds or wallets, car keys, Disney Resort IDs, or room keys in your hip packs because children tend to inadvertently drop their wallet in the process of rummaging around in their hip packs for snacks and other items.

You should weed through your billfold and remove to a safe place anything that you will not need on your vacation (photos, library card, department store credit cards, business cards, and so on). In addition to having a lighter wallet to lug around, you will decrease your exposure in the event that your wallet is lost or stolen. When we are working at Disneyland, we carry a small-profile billfold with a driver's license, a credit card, our room key, and a small amount of cash. You don't need anything else.

DAY PACKS We see a lot of folks at Disneyland carrying day packs (that is, small, frameless backpacks) and/or water bottle belts that strap around your waist. Day packs might be a good choice if you plan to carry a lot of camera equipment or if you need to carry baby supplies on your person. Otherwise, try to travel as light as possible. Packs are hot, cumbersome, and not very secure, and they must be removed every time you get on a ride or sit down for a show. Hip packs, by way of contrast, can simply be rotated around the waist from your back to your abdomen if you need to sit down. Additionally, our observation has been that the contents of one day pack can usually be redistributed to two or so hip packs (except in the case of camera equipment).

CAPS Kids pull caps on and off as they enter and exit attractions, restrooms, and restaurants, and—big surprise—they lose them. If your children are partial to caps, purchase a short, light cord with little alligator clips on both ends, sold at ski and camping supply stores. Hook one clip to the shirt collar and the other to the hat.

RAINGEAR Rain is a fact of life, though persistent rain day after day is unusual. Check out the Weather Channel or weather forecasts online for three or so days before you leave home to see if any major storm systems are heading for Southern California. Weather predictions concerning systems and fronts four to seven days out are pretty reliable. If it appears that you might see some rough weather during your visit, you're better off bringing raingear from home. If, however, nothing big is on the horizon weather wise, you can take your chances.

Ponchos sell for about $12 for adults, $10 for children, and are available in seemingly every retail shop; they're even cheaper at local discount stores (such as Target). If you do find yourself in a big storm, you'll want to have both a poncho and an umbrella. As one Unofficial reader puts it, "Umbrellas make the rain much more bearable. When rain isn't beating down on your ponchoed head, it's easier to ignore."

And consider this tip from a Memphis, Tennessee, mom:

Scotchgard your shoes. The difference is unbelievable.

MISCELLANEOUS ITEMS

MEDICATION Some parents of hyperactive children on medication discontinue or decrease the child's normal dosage at the end of the school year. Be aware that the Disneyland parks might overly stimulate such a child. Consult your physician before altering your child's medication regimen. Also, if your child has attention deficit disorder, remember that especially loud sounds can drive him or her right up the wall. Unfortunately, some Disney theater attractions are almost unbearably loud, so consider bringing foam earplugs or noise-canceling headphones.

unofficial **TIP**
Several companies, such as Neutrogena and California Baby, make sunscreens that won't burn your eyes. Look for a product *without* the active ingredient avobenzone, which is usually the culprit when it comes to stinging and burning.

SUNSCREEN Overheating and sunburn are among the most common problems of younger children at Disneyland. Carry and use sunscreen of SPF 30 or higher. Be sure to put some on kids in strollers, even if the stroller has a canopy. To avoid overheating, rest regularly in the shade or in an air-conditioned restaurant or show.

WATER BOTTLES Don't count on keeping young children hydrated with soft drinks and water fountains. Long lines may impede buying refreshments, and fountains may not be handy. Furthermore, excited children may not realize or tell you that they're thirsty or hot. We recommend carrying bottles of water and sports drinks. Bottled water is about $4 in all major parks, or bring your own water bottle and strap from home.

ENERGY BOOSTERS Kids get cranky when they're hungry, and when that happens, your entire group has a problem. Like many parents you might, for nutritional reasons, keep a tight rein on snacks available to your children at home. At Disneyland, however, maintaining energy and equanimity trumps snack discipline. For maximum zip and contentedness, give your kids snacks containing complex carbohydrates (fruits, crackers, nonfat energy bars, and the like) before they get hungry or show signs of exhaustion. You should avoid snacks that are high in fats and proteins because these foods take a long time to digest and will tend to unsettle your stomach if it's a hot day.

ELECTRONICS Regardless of your kid's ages, always bring a night-light. Flashlights are handy for finding stuff in a room after the kids are asleep.

Tablets, iPods, and handheld video games are often controversial gear for a family outing. We recommend compromise. Earbuds allow kids to create their own space even when they're with others, and that can be a safety valve. That said, try to agree before the trip on some parameters, so you don't begin to feel as if they're being used to keep other family members and the trip itself at a distance. If you're traveling by car, take turns choosing the radio station or playlist for part of the trip.

Likewise, cell phones are a mixed blessing. On the one hand, they can be invaluable in an emergency or if your party wants to split up, and if you have a smartphone, you can use Disneyland's app to see current wait times in the parks. Unfortunately, they also lead to guests missing out on what's around them and bumping into each other because they're glued to a tiny screen. Disneyland's free Wi-Fi is still somewhat unreliable, and local cell towers become overloaded on busy days, so posting social media from the parks may drain your phone in a matter of hours. Put your device in airplane mode when you aren't using it, and see page 122 for more power-saving tips.

Be especially cautious about taking expensive iPads or other tablets into the parks, and for Mickey's sake, beware while using them as cameras during shows and parades, lest you blind or block everyone behind you. Also, extendable selfie sticks are not allowed in Disney parks, though handheld stabilizers, collapsible monopods, and tripods are OK.

DON'T FORGET THE TENT When Bob's daughter was preschool age, he almost went crazy trying to get her to sleep in a shared hotel room. She was accustomed to having her own room at home and was hyperstimulated whenever she traveled. Bob tried makeshift curtains and room dividers and even rearranged the furniture in a few hotel rooms to create the illusion of a more private, separate space for her. It was all for naught. It wasn't until she was around 4 years old and Bob took her camping that he seized on an idea that had some promise. She liked the cozy, secure, womblike feel of a backpacking tent and quieted down much more readily than she ever had in hotel rooms. So the next time the family stayed in a hotel, he pitched his backpacking tent in the corner of the room. In she went, nested for a bit, and fell asleep.

Modern tents are self-contained with floors and an entrance that can be zipped up for privacy but cannot be locked. Affordable and sturdy, many are as simple to put up as opening an umbrella. Some tents are even specifically made to turn a bed into a fort. Kids appreciate having their own space and enjoy the adventure of being in a tent, even one set up in the corner of a hotel room. Sizes range from children's play tents with a 2- to 3-foot base to models large enough to sleep two or three husky teens. Light and compact when stored, a two-adult-size tent in its own storage bag (called a stuff sack) will take up about one-tenth or less of a standard overhead bin on a commercial airliner. Another option for infants and toddlers is to drape a sheet over a portable crib or playpen to make a tent.

THE BOX Bob here: On one memorable Disneyland excursion when my children were younger, we began each morning with an immensely annoying, involuntary scavenger hunt. Invariably, seconds before our scheduled departure to the theme park, we discovered that some combination of shoes, billfolds, sunglasses, hip packs, or other necessities was missing.

For the next 15 minutes we would root through the room like pigs hunting truffles in an attempt to locate the absent items. I finally swung by a local store and mooched a big empty box. From then on, every time we returned to the room, I had the kids deposit shoes, hip packs, and other potentially wayward items in the box. After that, the box was off-limits until the next morning, when I doled out the contents.

PLASTIC GARBAGE BAGS At the Grizzly River Run raft ride at DCA and at Tiana's Bayou Adventure in Disneyland Park, you are certain to get wet and possibly soaked. If it's really hot and you don't care, then fine. But if it's cool or you're just not up for a soaking, bring a large plastic trash bag or a cheap poncho to the park. By cutting holes in the top and on the sides of a trash bag, you can fashion a sack poncho that will keep your clothes from getting wet. On the raft ride, you will also get your feet wet. If you're not up for walking around in squishing, soaked shoes, bring a second, smaller plastic bag to wear over your feet while riding. Even if you don't mind getting wet yourself, a small zip-top bag (or free plastic bag from a gift shop) is handy for saving your cell phone and wallet from a fatal soaking.

SUPPLIES FOR INFANTS AND TODDLERS

BASED ON RECOMMENDATIONS from hundreds of Unofficial Guide readers, here's what we suggest that you carry with you when touring with infants and toddlers:

- A disposable diaper for every hour you plan to be away from your hotel
- A cloth diaper or kitchen towel to put over your shoulder for burping
- Two receiving blankets: one to wrap the baby and one to lay the baby on or to drape over you when you nurse
- Ointment for diaper rash
- A package of wipes
- Prepared formula in bottles if you are not breastfeeding
- A washable bib, baby spoon, and baby food if your infant is eating solids
- For toddlers, a small toy for comfort and to keep them occupied during attractions

Baby Care Centers at the theme parks will sell you just about anything that you forget or run out of. Like all things Disney, prices will be higher than elsewhere, but at least you won't need to detour to a drugstore in the middle of your touring day.

▌◖ REMEMBERING *Your* TRIP

1. Purchase a notebook for each child and spend time each evening recording the day's events. If your children have trouble getting motivated or don't know what to write about, start a discussion; otherwise, let them write or draw whatever they want to remember from the day.

2. Collect mementos along the way and create a treasure box in a small tin or cigar box. Months or years later, it's fun to look at postcards, pins, or ticket stubs to jump-start a memory.

3. Add inexpensive postcards to your photographs to create an album; then write a few words on each page to accompany the images.

4. Give each child a disposable camera to record their version of the trip. One 5-year-old snapped an entire series of photos that never showed anyone above the waist—his view of Disneyland (and the photos were priceless).

5. Most families travel with a digital camera or camera phone, though we recommend using one sparingly—parents end up viewing the trip through the lens rather than being in the moment. If you must, take it along, but only record a few moments of major sights (too much is boring anyway). And let the kids record and narrate. On the topic of narration, speak loudly so as to be heard over the not-insignificant background noise of the parks. Make use of lockers at the parks when the equipment becomes a burden or when you're going to experience an attraction that might damage it or get it wet. Unless you have a camera designed for underwater shots or a waterproof carrying case, leave it behind on Tiana's Bayou Adventure, Grizzly River Run, and any other ride where water is involved. Don't forget extra batteries or external battery chargers.

6. Consider using Disney's PhotoPass service for some professional-quality pictures; you can take photos for free and only pay for the images you want to keep, or buy Genie+ and get all of your day's pictures (see page 124 for more details).

Finally, when it comes to taking photos and collecting mementos, don't let the tail wag the dog. You are not going to Disneyland to build the biggest scrapbook in history. Or as this Houston mom put it:

Tell your readers to get a grip on the photography thing. We were so busy shooting pictures that we kind of lost the thread. We had to look at our pictures when we got home to see what all we did [while on vacation].

TRIAL RUN

IF YOU GIVE THOUGHTFUL CONSIDERATION to all areas of mental, physical, organizational, and logistical preparation discussed in this chapter, what remains is to familiarize yourself with the Disneyland parks and, of course, to conduct your field test. Yep, that's right, we want you to take the whole platoon on the road for a day to see if you are combat ready. No joke—this is important. You'll learn who tuckers out first, who's prone to developing blisters, who has to pee every 11 seconds, who keeps losing their cap, and, given the proper forum, how compatible your family is in terms of what you like to see and do.

For the most informative trial run, choose a local venue that requires lots of walking, dealing with crowds, and making decisions on how to spend your time. Regional theme parks and state fairs are your best bets, followed by large zoos and museums. Devote the whole day. Kick off the morning with an early start, just like you will at Disneyland, paying attention to who's organized and ready to go and who's dragging their butt and holding up the group. If you have to drive 1 or 2 hours to get to your test venue, no big deal. You may have to do some commuting at Disneyland too. Spend the whole day, eat a couple of meals, and stay late.

Don't mess with the outcome by telling everyone that you are practicing for Disneyland. Everyone behaves differently when they know that they are being tested or evaluated. Your objective is to find out as much as you can about how the individuals in your family, as well as the family as a group, respond to and deal with everything they experience during the day. Pay attention to who moves quickly and who is slow; who is adventuresome and who is reticent; who keeps going and who needs frequent rest breaks; who sets the agenda and who is content to follow; who is easily agitated and who stays cool; who tends to dawdle or wander off; who is curious and who is bored; who is demanding and who is accepting. You get the idea.

Discuss the findings of the test run with your spouse or partner the next day. Don't be discouraged if your test day wasn't perfect; few (if any) are. Distinguish between problems that are remediable and problems that are intrinsic to your family's emotional or physical makeup (no amount of hiking, for example, will toughen up some people's feet).

Establish a plan for addressing remediable problems (further conditioning, setting limits before you go, trying harder to achieve family consensus) and develop strategies for minimizing or working around problems that are a fact of life (waking sleepyheads 15 minutes early, placing moleskin on likely blister sites before setting out, or packing familiar food for the toddler who balks at restaurant fare). If you are an attentive observer, a fair diagnostician, and a creative problem solver, you'll be able to work out many of the problems you're likely to encounter at Disneyland before you leave home.

ABOUT *the* **UNOFFICIAL GUIDE TOURING PLANS**

PARENTS WHO EMBARK on one of our touring plans are often frustrated by the various interruptions and delays occasioned by their young children. Here's what to expect:

1. Many small children will stop dead in their tracks whenever they see a Disney character. Our advice: Live with it. An attempt to haul your children away before they have satisfied their curiosity is likely to precipitate anything from whining to a full-scale revolt.

2. The touring plans call for visiting attractions in a specified sequence, often skipping certain attractions along the way. Children do not like skipping anything! If they see something that attracts them, they want to experience it now. Some children can be persuaded to skip attractions if parents explain things in advance. Other kids severely flip out at the threat of skipping something, particularly something in Fantasyland. A mom from Charleston, South Carolina, had this to say:

   Following the touring plans turned out to be a train wreck. The main problem is that the plan starts in Fantasyland. When we were on Dumbo, my 5-year-old saw eight dozen other things in Fantasyland she wanted to see. After Dumbo, there was no getting her out of there.

3. Children seem to have a genetic instinct when it comes to finding restrooms. We have seen perfectly functional adults equipped with all manner of maps search interminably for a restroom. Small children, on the other hand, including those who cannot read, will head for the nearest restroom with the certainty of a homing pigeon. While you may skip certain attractions, you can be sure that your children will ferret out (and want to use) every restroom in the park.

STROLLERS

unofficial **TIP**
Strollers are also great for older kids who tire easily.

STROLLERS MAY BE RENTED for $18 per day for a single, $36 per day for a double; the rental covers the entire day and is good at both parks. If you rent a stroller and later decide to go back to your hotel for lunch, a swim, or a nap, turn in your stroller but keep your rental receipt. When you return to either park later in the day, present your receipt. You will be issued another stroller at no additional charge. The rental procedure is fast and efficient, and a central stroller rental facility is in the Esplanade between Disneyland and DCA, to the right of the Disneyland Park entrance. Likewise, returning the stroller is a breeze. Even in the evening, when several hundred strollers are turned in following the fireworks or water show, there is no wait or hassle. *Note:* Rented strollers are permitted in Downtown Disney but cannot exit the security checkpoints.

The strollers come with sun canopies and small cargo compartments under the seat. For infants and toddlers, strollers are a must, and we recommend a small pillow or blanket to help make the stroller more comfortable for your child during what may be long periods in the seat. We have also observed many sharp parents renting strollers for somewhat older children. Strollers prevent parents from having to carry children when they run out of steam and provide an easy, convenient way to carry water, snacks, diaper bags, and the like.

When you enter a show or board a ride, you will have to park your stroller, usually in an open, unprotected area. If it rains before you return, you'll need a cloth, towel, or spare diaper to dry off the stroller.

Bringing Your Own Stroller

You are allowed to bring your own stroller to the theme parks, provided it is no larger than 31 inches wide by 52 inches long, and is not a wagon or stroller wagon (such as a Keenz 7s). However, only collapsible strollers are allowed on the monorail and Toy Story parking lot buses. Your stroller is unlikely to be stolen, but mark it with your name. We strongly recommend bringing your own stroller. In addition to the parks, there is the walk from and to your hotel, the parking lot bus, or the bus/hotel-shuttle boarding area, not to mention many other occasions at your hotel or during shopping when you will be happy to have a stroller handy.

*un*official **TIP**
Often little ones fall asleep in their strollers (hallelujah!). Bring a large lightweight cloth to drape over the stroller to cover your child from the sun. A few clothespins will keep it in place.

If you do not want to bring your own stroller, you may consider buying one of the umbrella-style collapsible strollers. The on-site hotel gift shops sell them for less than $50. You may consider renting a stroller from a third party, or even buying one online and shipping it right to your hotel. Make sure you leave enough time between your order and arrival dates.

Having her own stroller was indispensable to this mother of two toddlers:

How I was going to manage to get the kids from the parking lot to the park was a big worry for me before I made the trip. I found that, for me personally, since I have two kids ages 1 and 2, it was easier to walk to the entrance of the park from the parking lot with the kids in my own stroller than to take the kids out of the stroller, fold the stroller (while trying to control the two kids and associated gear), load the stroller and the kids onto the bus, etc. No matter where I was parked, I could always just walk to the entrance. It sometimes took a while, but it was easier for me.

An Oklahoma mom, however, reports a bad experience with bringing her own stroller:

The first time we took our kids we had a large stroller (big mistake). It is so much easier to rent one in the park. The large [personally owned] strollers are nearly impossible to get on [airport shuttle] buses and are a hassle at the airport. I remember feeling dread when a bus pulled up that was even semifull of people. People look at you like you have a cage full of live chickens when you drag heavy strollers onto the bus.

Stroller Wars

Sometimes rental strollers disappear while you are enjoying a ride or a show. Do not be alarmed. You won't have to buy the missing stroller, and you will be issued a new stroller for your continued use. Lost strollers can be replaced at the main rental facility outside Disneyland's entrance.

While replacing a ripped-off stroller is not a big deal, it is an inconvenience. One family complained that their stroller had been taken six times in one day. Even with free replacements, larceny on this scale represents a lot of wasted time. Through our own experiments and suggestions from readers, we have developed several techniques for hanging on to your rented stroller:

1. Write your name in permanent marker on a 6-by-9-inch card, put the card in a transparent freezer bag, and secure the bag to the handle of the stroller with masking or duct tape.

2. Affix something personal (but expendable) to the handle of the stroller. Evidently most strollers are pirated by mistake (because they all look the same) or because it's easier to swipe someone else's stroller (when yours disappears) than to troop off to the replacement center. Because most stroller theft is a function of confusion, laziness, or revenge, the average pram-pincher will balk at hauling off a stroller bearing another person's property. After trying several items, we concluded that a bright, inexpensive scarf or bandanna tied to the handle works well, and a sock partially stuffed with rags or paper works even better (the weirder and more personal the object, the greater the deterrent).

A multigenerational family tried this:

We decorated our stroller with electrical tape to make it stand out. We also zip-tied an unused, small, insulated diaper bag to the handle to make carrying things easier. One of your readers mentioned using a bike chain or cable lock to ensure their stroller was not stolen but said the Disney cast members were a little disturbed. So I took an extra firearm lock (looks like a mini-bike lock) to lock a wheel to the frame while parked. My son added a small cowbell to make it clang if moved. The stroller could then be moved easily for short distances by lifting the back, but trying to go farther would be uncomfortable and noisy.

We receive quite a few letters from readers debating the pros and cons of bringing your own stroller versus renting one of Disney's. A mother with two small children opted for her own pram:

I took my own stroller because the rented strollers aren't appropriate for infants (we had a 5-year-old and a 5-month-old). No one said anything about me using a bike lock to secure our brand-new Aprica stroller. However, an attendant came over and told us not to lock it anywhere because it's a fire hazard! (Outside?) When I politely asked the attendant if she wanted to be responsible for my $300 stroller, she told me to go ahead and lock it but not tell anyone! I observed the attendants constantly moving the strollers. This seems very confusing— no wonder people think their strollers are getting ripped off!

As the reader mentioned, Disney cast members often rearrange strollers parked outside an attraction. Sometimes this is done simply to tidy up. At other times the strollers are moved to make additional room along a walkway. In any event, do not assume that your stroller is stolen because it is missing from the exact place you left it. Check around. Chances are that it will be neatly arranged just a few feet away.

▐ BABYSITTING

CHILDCARE SERVICES are unavailable in the Disney parks and hotels. Ask your hotel concierge to recommend a third-party babysitting service if you need one.

DISNEY, KIDS, *and* SCARY STUFF

DISNEYLAND PARK and Disney California Adventure (DCA) are family theme parks. Yet some of the Disney adventure rides can be intimidating for small children. On certain rides, such as Tiana's Bayou Adventure and the roller coasters (Incredicoaster, Space Mountain, Matterhorn Bobsleds, and Big Thunder Mountain Railroad), the ride itself may be frightening. On other rides, such as Haunted Mansion and Pinocchio's Daring Journey, it is the special effects. We recommend a little parent-child dialogue coupled with a "testing the water" approach. A child who is frightened by Peter Pan's Flight should not have to sit through Haunted Mansion. Likewise, if Big Thunder Mountain Railroad is too much, don't try Space Mountain or the Incredicoaster. Just because a child in your party isn't ready for a ride doesn't mean that the grown-ups have to miss out; learn about Disney's Rider Switch system on page 165.

Disney rides and shows are adventures. They focus on the substance and themes of all adventure, and indeed of life itself: good and evil, beauty and the grotesque, fellowship and enmity, quest, and death. Though the endings are all happy, the impact of the adventures, with Disney's gift for special effects, is often intimidating and occasionally frightening for small children.

There are rides with menacing witches, rides with burning towns, and rides with ghouls popping out of their graves, all done tongue in cheek and with a sense of humor, provided you are old enough to understand the joke. And there are bones, lots of bones—human bones, cattle bones, and whole skeletons are everywhere you look. There have to be more bones at Disneyland Park than at the Smithsonian and the School of Medicine at UCLA combined. Skeletal corpses lunge at riders on the Indiana Jones Adventure; a veritable platoon of skeletons sails ghost ships in Pirates of the Caribbean; a macabre assemblage of skulls and skeletons are in Haunted Mansion; and more skulls, skeletons, and bones punctuate Peter Pan's Flight and Big Thunder Mountain Railroad.

One reader wrote us after taking his preschoolers on Star Tours:

We took a 4- and 5-year-old, and they had the *#%! scared out of them at Star Tours. We did it in the morning, and it took hours of Tom Sawyer Island and It's a Small World to get back to normal.

Preschoolers should start with Dumbo and work up to the Jungle Cruise in the late morning, after being revved up and before getting hungry, thirsty, or tired. Pirates of the Caribbean is out for preschoolers. You get the idea.

The reaction of young children to the inevitable system overload of Disney parks should be anticipated. Be sensitive, alert, and prepared for almost anything, even behavior that is out of character for your child at home. Most small children take Disney's variety of macabre trappings in stride, and others are quickly comforted by an arm around the shoulder or a little squeeze of the hand. For parents who have observed a tendency in their kids to become upset, we recommend taking it slowly and easily by sampling more benign adventures such as the Jungle Cruise, gauging reactions, and discussing with children how they felt about the things they saw. A mother of two reported this:

> We pressured our kids into going on Pirates of the Caribbean because my husband and I wanted us all to ride as a family. Big mistake! I had not read enough about what the ride would be like. My 12-year-old (who is very sensitive) balked when we were in the queue, but still we pressured her to go on. Well, both she and her 6-year-old sister ended up sobbing through the whole ride.

Sometimes, small children will rise above their anxiety in an effort to please their parents or siblings. This behavior, however, does not necessarily indicate a mastery of fear, much less enjoyment. If children come off a ride in ostensibly good shape, we recommend asking if they would like to go on the ride again (not necessarily right now, but sometime). The response to this question will usually give you a clue as to how much they actually enjoyed the experience. There is a big difference between having a good time and mustering the courage to get through something.

Evaluating a child's capacity to handle the visual and tactile effects of the Disney parks requires patience, understanding, and experimentation. Each of us, after all, has our own demons. If a child balks at or is frightened by a ride, respond constructively. Let your children know that lots of people, adults as well as children, are scared by what they see and feel. Help them understand that it is OK if they get frightened. Take pains not to compound the discomfort by making a child feel inadequate; try not to undermine self-esteem, impugn courage, or subject a child to ridicule. Most of all, do not induce guilt, as if your child's trepidation is ruining the family's fun. When older siblings are present, it is sometimes necessary to restrain their taunting and teasing.

A visit to a Disney park is more than an outing or an adventure for a small child. It is a testing experience, a sort of controlled rite of passage. If you help your little one work through the challenges, the time can be immeasurably rewarding and a bonding experience for both of you.

The Fright Factor

While each youngster is different, there are essentially seven attraction elements that alone or combined can push a child's buttons:

1. THE NAME OF THE ATTRACTION Small children will naturally be apprehensive about something called Haunted Mansion.

2. THE VISUAL IMPACT OF THE ATTRACTION FROM OUTSIDE Tiana's Bayou Adventure, Guardians of the Galaxy—Mission: Breakout!, and Big Thunder Mountain Railroad look scary enough to give even adults second thoughts. To many small kids, the rides are visually terrifying.

continued on page 161

SMALL-CHILD FRIGHT-POTENTIAL TABLE

As a quick reference, we provide this table to warn you which attractions to be wary of and why. The table represents a generalization, and all kids are different. It relates specifically to kids 3–7 years of age. On average, as you would expect, children at the younger end of the age range are more likely to be frightened than children in their 6th or 7th year.

Disneyland Park

MAIN STREET, U.S.A.

- **Disneyland Railroad** Tunnel with dinosaur display frightens some small children.
- *The Disneyland Story,* presenting *Great Moments with Mr. Lincoln* Brief battle sound effects may surprise small children.
- **Main Street Cinema** Not frightening in any respect.

ADVENTURELAND

- **Adventureland Treehouse** Not frightening in any respect.
- *Enchanted Tiki Room* A small thunderstorm momentarily surprises very young children.
- **Indiana Jones Adventure** Visually intimidating, with intense effects and a jerky ride. Switching-off option (see p. 165).
- **Jungle Cruise** Moderately intense, with some macabre sights; a good test attraction for little ones.

NEW ORLEANS SQUARE

- **Haunted Mansion** Name of attraction raises anxiety, as do sights and sounds of waiting area. An intense attraction with humorously presented macabre sights. The ride itself is gentle.
- **Pirates of the Caribbean** Slightly intimidating queuing area; an intense boat ride with gruesome (though humorously presented) sights and two short, unexpected slides down flumes.

CRITTER COUNTRY

- **Davy Crockett's Explorer Canoes** Not frightening in any respect.
- **The Many Adventures of Winnie the Pooh** Not frightening in any respect.
- **Tiana's Bayou Adventure** Less visually intimidating than its predecessor Splash Mountain, but the ride still culminates in a 52-foot plunge down a steep chute, which is somewhat hair-raising for all ages. Switching-off option (see p. 165).

STAR WARS: GALAXY'S EDGE

- *Millennium Falcon:* **Smugglers Run** Simulated space flight with intense visual effects may discombobulate droids (and guests) of all ages. Switching-off option (see p. 165).
- **Rise of the Resistance** Intense visual effects, close encounters with sci-fi villains, and one brief drop that can scare kids and sensitive adults. Switching-off option (see p. 165).

FRONTIERLAND

- **Big Thunder Mountain Railroad** Visually intimidating from the outside; moderately intense visual effects. The roller coaster may frighten many adults, particularly seniors. Switching-off option (see p. 165).
- *Fantasmic!* Loud and intense with fireworks and some scary villains, but most young children like it.
- **Frontierland Shootin' Exposition** Frightening to children scared of guns.
- *Mark Twain* **Riverboat** Not frightening in any respect.
- **Pirate's Lair on Tom Sawyer Island** Some very small children are intimidated by dark walk-through tunnels that can be easily avoided.
- **Sailing Ship** *Columbia* Not frightening in any respect, aside from a single loud cannon blast that is announced well in advance.

SMALL-CHILD FRIGHT-POTENTIAL TABLE *(continued)*

FANTASYLAND

- **Alice in Wonderland** Pretty benign but frightens a small percentage of preschoolers.
- **Casey Jr. Circus Train** Not frightening in any respect.
- **Dumbo the Flying Elephant** A tame midway ride; a great favorite of most small children.
- **Fantasyland Theatre** Not frightening in any respect.
- **It's a Small World** Not frightening in any respect.
- **King Arthur Carrousel** Not frightening in any respect.
- **Mad Tea Party** Midway-type ride can induce motion sickness in all ages.
- **Matterhorn Bobsleds** The ride itself is wilder than Big Thunder Mountain Railroad but not as wild as Space Mountain. Switching-off option (see p. 165).
- **Mr. Toad's Wild Ride** Name of ride intimidates some. Moderately intense spook house–genre attraction with jerky ride. Frightens only a small percentage of preschoolers.
- **Peter Pan's Flight** Not frightening in any respect.
- **Pinocchio's Daring Journey** The imagery is more intense than Mr. Toad, and Monstro's appearance scares a few very young preschoolers.
- **Pixie Hollow** Not frightening in any respect.
- **Royal Hall at Fantasy Faire** Not frightening in any respect.
- **Royal Theatre at Fantasy Faire** Not frightening in any respect.
- **Sleeping Beauty Castle** Not frightening in any respect.
- **Snow White's Enchanted Wish** Another spook house dark ride; not quite as intense as Mr. Toad. Much less terrifying than it used to be, but the witch still rattles some preschoolers.
- **Storybook Land Canal Boats** Not frightening in any respect.

MICKEY'S TOONTOWN

- **Chip 'n' Dale's GADGETcoaster** A tame coaster, but may frighten some small children.
- **Donald's Duck Pond** Not frightening in any respect.
- **Goofy's How-to-Play Yard** Not frightening in any respect.
- **Mickey & Minnie's Runaway Railway** Dark ride with intense cartoon visuals and some mild twists and turns. May scare kids 6 and under.
- **Mickey's House and Meet Mickey** Not frightening in any respect.
- **Minnie's House** Not frightening in any respect.
- **Roger Rabbit's Car Toon Spin** Intense special effects, coupled with a dark environment and wild ride; frightens many preschoolers.

TOMORROWLAND

- **Astro Orbitor** Waiting area is visually intimidating to preschoolers. The ride is a lot higher, but just a bit wilder, than Dumbo.
- **Autopia** The noise in the waiting area slightly intimidates preschoolers; otherwise, not frightening.
- **Buzz Lightyear Astro Blasters** Intense special effects plus a dark environment frighten some preschoolers.
- **Disneyland Monorail System** Not frightening in any respect.
- **Finding Nemo Submarine Voyage** Being enclosed, as well as certain ride effects, may frighten preschoolers.
- **Space Mountain** Very intense roller coaster in the dark; Disneyland's wildest ride and a scary roller coaster by anyone's standards. Switching-off option (see p. 165).
- **Star Tours—The Adventures Continue** Extremely intense visually for all ages; one of the wildest in Disney's repertoire. Switching-off option (see p. 165).

SMALL-CHILD FRIGHT-POTENTIAL TABLE (continued)
Disney California Adventure

BUENA VISTA STREET

- **Red Car Trolley** Not frightening in any respect.

GRIZZLY PEAK

- **Grizzly River Run** Frightening to guests of all ages. Wet too! Switching-off option (see p. 165).
- **Redwood Creek Challenge Trail and Wilderness Explorer Camp** Trail is a bit overwhelming to preschoolers but not frightening.
- **Soarin' Around the World** Frightens some children 7 years and under, especially anyone afraid of heights. Really a very sweet ride. Switching-off option (see p. 165).

HOLLYWOOD LAND

- **Anna & Elsa's Royal Welcome** Not frightening in any respect.
- **Disney Animation** Not frightening in any respect.
- *Disney Junior Dance Party* Not frightening in any respect.
- *Mickey's PhilharMagic* Loud with intense 3-D effects. Frightens some preschoolers.
- **Monsters, Inc. Mike & Sulley to the Rescue** May frighten children under 7 years of age.
- *Turtle Talk With Crush* Not frightening in any respect.

AVENGERS CAMPUS

- **Guardians of the Galaxy—Mission: Breakout!** Frightening to guests of all ages. Switching-off option (see p. 165).
- **WEB SLINGERS: A Spider-Man Adventure** A loud, colorful video game infested with robotic spiders, which may disturb sensitive children and cyber-anachrophobes.

SAN FRANSOKYO SQUARE

- **Bakery Tour** Not frightening in any respect.

PARADISE GARDENS PARK

- **Golden Zephyr** Frightening to a small percentage of preschoolers.
- **Goofy's Sky School** Frightening to the under-8 crowd. Switching-off option (see p. 165).
- **Jumpin' Jellyfish** The ride's appearance frightens some younger children. The ride itself is exceedingly tame.
- **The Little Mermaid: Ariel's Undersea Adventure** Moderately intense effects; Ursula may frighten children under 7 years of age.
- **Silly Symphony Swings** Height requirement keeps preschoolers from riding. Moderately intimidating to younger grade-schoolers.
- *World of Color Nighttime Spectacular* Not frightening for most children, but it is very loud with bursts of flame and a chance of getting wet.

PIXAR PIER

- **Incredicoaster** A launched looping roller coaster that's potentially terrifying for guests of all ages. Switching-off option (see p. 165).
- **Inside Out Emotional Whirlwind** Not frightening in any respect.
- **Jessie's Critter Carousel** Not frightening in any respect.
- **Pixar Pal-A-Round** The ride in the stationary cars is exceedingly tame. The ride in the swinging cars is frightening to guests of all ages.
- **Toy Story Midway Mania!** Loud and intense but not frightening.

CARS LAND

- **Luigi's Rollickin' Roadsters** Not frightening, aside from some brief moderate spinning at the end.
- **Mater's Junkyard Jamboree** Can induce motion sickness in all ages.
- **Radiator Springs Racers** Moderately intense effects, with high-speed sections that may frighten younger children. Switching-off option (see p. 165).

continued from page 157

3. THE VISUAL IMPACT OF THE INDOOR QUEUING AREA Pirates of the Caribbean with its dark bayou scene and Haunted Mansion with its "stretch rooms" are capable of frightening small children before they even board the ride.

4. THE INTENSITY OF THE ATTRACTION Some attractions are so intense as to be overwhelming; they inundate the senses with sights, sounds, movement, and even smell. *Mickey's PhilharMagic* in DCA, for instance, combines loud music, tactile effects, lights, and 3-D cinematography to create a total sensory experience. For some preschoolers, this is two or three senses too many.

5. THE VISUAL IMPACT OF THE ATTRACTION ITSELF As previously discussed, the sights in various attractions range from falling boulders to lurking buzzards, from underwater volcanoes to attacking hippos. What one child calmly absorbs may scare the owl poop out of another child the same age.

6. DARK Many Disneyland attractions are dark rides—that is, they operate indoors in a dark environment. For some children, this fact alone is sufficient to trigger significant apprehension. A child who is frightened on one dark ride, for example Pinocchio's Daring Journey, may be unwilling to try other indoor rides.

7. THE RIDE ITSELF; THE PHYSICAL EXPERIENCE Some Disney rides are downright wild—wild enough to induce motion sickness, wrench backs, and generally discombobulate patrons of any age.

A Bit of Preparation

We receive many tips from parents relating how they prepared their children for the Disneyland experience. A common strategy is to acquaint kids with the characters and the stories behind the attractions by reading Disney books and watching Disney movies at home.

You can view a clip of every attraction and show on youtube .com. Videos of dark rides aren't stellar but are good enough to get a sense of what you're in for. The mom of a 7-year-old found YouTube quite effective:

> *We watched every ride and show on YouTube before going, so my timid 7-year-old daughter would be prepared, and we cut out all the ones that looked too scary to her.*

A mother from Gloucester, Massachusetts, handled her son's preparation a bit more extemporaneously:

> *The 3½-year-old was afraid of Haunted Mansion. We pulled his hat over his face and quietly talked to him while we enjoyed the ride.*

A Word About Height Requirements

Many attractions require children to meet minimum height requirements, ranging from 32 inches tall (to ride Autopia with an adult) up to at least 48 inches (for the Incredicoaster or Silly Symphony single swings). If you have children who are too little to ride, you have several options, including switching off (described on page 165). Though the alternatives may resolve some practical and logistical issues, be forewarned that your smaller children might nonetheless be resentful of their older (or taller) siblings who qualify to ride. A mom from Virginia bumped into this situation, writing:

> You mention height requirements for rides but not the intense sibling jealousy this can generate. Frontierland was a real problem in that respect. Our very petite 5-year-old, to her outrage, was stuck hanging around while our 8-year-old went on [Tiana's Bayou Adventure] and Big Thunder Mountain with Grandma and Granddad, and the nearby alternatives weren't helpful [too long a line for rafts to Tom Sawyer Island, and so on]. If we had thought ahead, we would have left the younger kid back in Mickey's Toontown with one of the grown-ups for another roller coaster or two and then met up later at a designated point. The best areas had a playground or other quick attractions for short people near the rides with height requirements.

ATTRACTION MINIMUM HEIGHT REQUIREMENTS

DISNEYLAND PARK

Autopia 32" *(54" to drive unassisted)*

Big Thunder Mountain Railroad 40"

Chip 'n' Dale's GADGETcoaster 35"

Indiana Jones Adventure 46"

Matterhorn Bobsleds 42"

***Millennium Falcon:* Smugglers Run** 38"

Space Mountain 40"

Star Tours—The Adventures Continue 40"

Star Wars: Rise of the Resistance 40"

Tiana's Bayou Adventure 40"

DISNEY CALIFORNIA ADVENTURE

Goofy's Sky School 42"

Grizzly River Run 42"

Guardians of the Galaxy—Mission: Breakout! 40"

Incredicoaster 48"

Jumpin' Jellyfish 40"

Luigi's Rollickin' Roadsters 32"

Mater's Junkyard Jamboree 32"

Radiator Springs Racers 40"

Redwood Creek Challenge Trail 42" *(rock wall and zip line only)*

Silly Symphony Swings 40" *(tandem swing)* 48" *(single swing)*

Soarin' Around the World 40"

The reader makes a valid point, though splitting the group and then meeting later can be more complicated in practical terms than she might imagine. If you choose to split up, ask the Disney greeter at the entrance to the height-restricted attraction(s) how long the wait is. If you tack 5 minutes for riding onto the anticipated wait, and then add 5 or so minutes to exit and reach the meeting point, you'll have an approximate sense of how long the younger kids (and their supervising adult) will have to do other stuff. Our guess is that even with a long line for the rafts, the reader would have had more than sufficient time to take her daughter to Tom Sawyer Island while the sib rode Tiana's Bayou Adventure and Big Thunder Mountain with the grandparents. For sure she had time to tour the Treehouse in adjacent Adventureland.

Additionally, children under age 7 must be accompanied on all attractions by another guest age 14 or older, who must sit in the same ride vehicle in the same row or an adjacent one. While this shouldn't pose a problem on most attractions, some with small vehicles (such as Chip 'n' Dale's GADGETcoaster) may require use of a Rider Switch (see page 165) if your party has more little members than big ones; ask a cast member at the ride entrance for assistance if you have questions.

Attractions that Eat Adults

You may spend so much energy worrying about Junior's welfare that you forget to take care of yourself. Several attractions likely to cause motion sickness or other problems for older children and adults are listed in the table below. Fast, jerky rides are also noted with icons in the attraction profiles.

POTENTIALLY PROBLEMATIC ATTRACTIONS FOR ADULTS
DISNEYLAND PARK
• **ADVENTURELAND**   Indiana Jones Adventure
• **CRITTER COUNTRY**   Tiana's Bayou Adventure
• **FANTASYLAND**   Mad Tea Party | Matterhorn Bobsleds
• **FRONTIERLAND**   Big Thunder Mountain Railroad
• **STAR WARS: GALAXY'S EDGE**   *Millennium Falcon:* Smugglers Run | Star Wars: Rise of the Resistance
• **TOMORROWLAND**   Space Mountain | Star Tours—The Adventures Continue
DISNEY CALIFORNIA ADVENTURE
• **CARS LAND**   Mater's Junkyard Jamboree | Radiator Springs Racers
• **GRIZZLY PEAK**   Grizzly River Run
• **AVENGERS CAMPUS**   Guardians of the Galaxy—Mission: Breakout!
• **PARADISE GARDENS PARK**   Goofy's Sky School
• **PIXAR PIER**   Incredicoaster | Pixar Pal-A-Round (swinging)

WAITING-LINE STRATEGIES *for* FAMILIES *with* SMALL CHILDREN

CHILDREN HOLD UP BETTER through the day if you minimize the time they spend in lines. Arriving early and using the touring plans in this guide will reduce waiting time immensely. There are, however, additional measures that you can employ to reduce stress on little ones.

1. LINE GAMES Smart parents know that a little structured activity can relieve the stress and boredom of waiting in line. In the morning, kids handle the inactivity of waiting in line by discussing what they want to see and do during the course of the day. Later, however, as events wear on, they need a little help. Watching for, and counting, Disney characters is a good diversion. Simple guessing games such as 20 Questions also work well. Lines for rides move so continuously that games requiring pen and paper are cumbersome and impractical. Waiting in the holding area of a theater attraction, however, is a different story. Here, tic-tac-toe, hangman, drawing, and coloring can really make the time go by.

For Apple and Android smartphone users, our favorite queue distraction is Ellen DeGeneres's Heads Up, a Taboo-style game where one player holds a phone against their forehead, and the others help guess the phrase displayed before the timer counts down. The app costs $1.99 and includes several starter "decks" of clues to play. If you're inside Disneyland Resort, you can unlock a deck featuring Disney characters and attractions for free. Don't be surprised if you see several shouting families playing Heads Up in any given line. There's also a free official Play Disney Parks app with simple games that unlock inside select attraction queues and all around the Star Wars area; beware that this power-hungry program doesn't drain your battery before you board.

2. LAST-MINUTE ENTRY If a ride or show can accommodate an unusually large number of people at one time, it is often unnecessary to stand in line. The *Mark Twain* Riverboat in Frontierland is a good example. The boat holds about 450 people, usually more than are waiting in line to ride. Instead of standing uncomfortably in a crowd with dozens of other guests, grab a snack and sit in the shade until the boat arrives and loading is underway. After the line has all but disappeared, go ahead and board.

In large-capacity theaters, ask the entrance greeter how long it will be until guests are admitted to the theater for the next show. If the answer is 15 minutes or more, use the time for a restroom break or to get a snack; you can return to the attraction just a few minutes before the show starts. You will not be permitted to carry any food or drink into the attraction, so make sure you have time to finish your snack before entering.

To help you determine which attractions to target for last-minute entry, we provide the following table.

ATTRACTIONS YOU CAN USUALLY ENTER AT THE LAST MINUTE
DISNEYLAND PARK
• **ADVENTURELAND** *Enchanted Tiki Room*
• **FANTASYLAND** Fantasyland Theatre
• **FRONTIERLAND** *Mark Twain* Riverboat | Sailing Ship *Columbia*
• **MAIN STREET, U.S.A.** *Disneyland Story,* presenting *Great Moments with Mr. Lincoln*
DISNEY CALIFORNIA ADVENTURE
• **HOLLYWOOD LAND**   Disney Animation | *Mickey's PhilharMagic*

3. THE HAIL MARY PASS Certain waiting lines are configured in such a way that you and your smaller children can pass under the rail to join your partner just before boarding or entry. This technique allows the kids and one adult to rest, snack, cool off, or tinkle, while another adult or older sibling does the waiting. Other guests are understanding when it comes to using this strategy to keep small children content. You are likely to meet hostile opposition, however, if you try to pass older children or more than one adult under the rail. Attractions where it is usually possible to complete a Hail Mary pass are listed in the table below.

ATTRACTIONS WHERE YOU CAN USUALLY COMPLETE A HAIL MARY PASS
DISNEYLAND PARK
• **FANTASYLAND** Casey Jr. Circus Train | Dumbo the Flying Elephant | King Arthur Carrousel | Mad Tea Party | Mr. Toad's Wild Ride | Peter Pan's Flight | Snow White's Enchanted Wish | Storybook Land Canal Boats
DISNEY CALIFORNIA ADVENTURE
• **PARADISE GARDENS PARK** Golden Zephyr | Jumpin' Jellyfish
• **PIXAR PIER** Jessie's Critter Carousel
• **CARS LAND**   Luigi's Rollickin' Roadsters | Mater's Junkyard Jamboree

4. SWITCHING OFF (ALSO KNOWN AS RIDER SWITCH, BABY SWAP, OR CHILD SWAP) Several attractions have minimum height requirements (see the table on page 162) or are too intense for sensitive youngsters. Some couples with children too short or too young forgo these attractions, while others take turns riding. Missing some of Disneyland's best rides is an unnecessary sacrifice, and waiting in line twice for the same ride is a tremendous waste of time.

Instead, take advantage of switching off. To switch off, there must be at least two adults. When you approach the queue, tell the first ride attendant you see (known as a greeter) that you want to switch off.

The cast member will ask your party to split into two groups, with up to three people selected to stay outside the attraction and supervise the kids while the rest ride first. Those remaining behind will have their admission passes (or apps) scanned to receive a Rider Switch

ATTRACTIONS WHERE SWITCHING OFF IS COMMON
DISNEYLAND PARK
• **ADVENTURELAND** Indiana Jones Adventure
• **CRITTER COUNTRY** Tiana's Bayou Adventure
• **FANTASYLAND** Matterhorn Bobsleds
• **FRONTIERLAND** Big Thunder Mountain Railroad
• **STAR WARS: GALAXY'S EDGE** *Millennium Falcon:* Smugglers Run | Star Wars: Rise of the Resistance
• **TOMORROWLAND** Space Mountain | Star Tours—The Adventures Continue
DISNEY CALIFORNIA ADVENTURE
• **CARS LAND** Radiator Springs Racers
• **GRIZZLY PEAK** Grizzly River Run | Soarin' Around the World
• **AVENGERS CAMPUS** Guardians of the Galaxy—Mission: Breakout!
• **PARADISE GARDENS PARK** Goofy's Sky School
• **PIXAR PIER** Incredicoaster

entitlement on their account, which functions just like an immediate Lightning Lane return time. Once the first group exits the ride, the second set of guests has up to an hour to redeem its Rider Switch passes by entering through the ride's Lightning Lane queue. You can only hold one Rider Switch pass at a time, but it will not interfere with any other Lightning Lane reservations. This system eliminates confusion and congestion at the boarding area while sparing the nonriding adult and child the tedium and physical exertion of waiting in line. While this system usually works fairly well, using Rider Switch can become frustrating when Lightning Lane return lines grow long, especially if, like this La Center, Washington, mom, you've previously experienced the child swap waiting rooms at Universal's park.

> *Disney does a terrible job with rider swaps. The process is ridiculous and confusing. Why would I want to wait in the [Lightning Lane] line twice just to do a rider swap? Universal Studios does it right by letting you swap when you are getting ready to load. They also give you a nice place to sit and rest while you wait for your party to disembark. Disney makes you wait at the back of the line!*

There is no cost to use the switching-off option. The attractions where switching off is routinely practiced, often oriented to more mature guests, are listed below. Sometimes children suddenly fear abandonment when one parent leaves to ride. Prepare your children for switching off, or you might have an emotional crisis on your hands. A mom from Edison, New Jersey, writes:

> *Once my son understood that the switch-off would not leave him abandoned, he did not seem to mind. I would recommend practicing the switch off at home, so your child is not concerned that he will be left behind. At the very least, explain the procedure in advance, so little ones know what to expect.*

5. HOW TO RIDE TWICE IN A ROW WITHOUT WAITING Many small children like to ride a favorite attraction two or more times in succession. Riding the second time often gives the child a feeling of mastery and accomplishment. Unfortunately, repeat rides can be time-consuming, even in the early morning. If you ride Dumbo as soon as Disneyland Park opens, for instance, you will only have a 1- or 2-minute wait for your first ride. When you come back for your second ride, your wait will be about 12 minutes. If you want to ride a third time, count on a 20-minute or longer wait. The best way for getting your child on the ride twice (or more) without blowing your whole morning is by using the Chuck-Bubba Relay (named in honor of a reader from Kentucky):

1. Mom and little Bubba enter the waiting line.
2. Dad lets a certain number of people go in front of him (32 in the case of Dumbo) and then gets in line.
3. As soon as the ride stops, Mom exits with little Bubba and passes him to Dad to ride the second time.
4. If everybody is really getting into this, Mom can hop in line again, no less than 32 people behind Dad.

The Chuck-Bubba Relay will not work on every ride because of differences in the way the waiting areas are configured (that is, it is impossible in some cases to exit the ride and make the pass). The rides where the Chuck-Bubba Relay does work, along with the number of people to count off, appear in the table below.

When practicing the Chuck-Bubba Relay, if you are the second adult in line, you will reach a point in the waiting area that is obviously the easiest place to make the handoff. Sometimes this point is where those exiting the ride pass closest to those waiting to board. In any event, you will know it when you see it. Once there, if the first parent has not arrived with little Bubba, just let those behind you slip past until Bubba shows up.

ATTRACTIONS WHERE THE CHUCK-BUBBA RELAY USUALLY WORKS
DISNEYLAND PARK *Number of people between adults*
• **Alice in Wonderland** (tough, but possible) 38
• **Casey Jr. Circus Train** 34, if 2 trains are operating
• **Davy Crockett's Explorer Canoes** 94, if 6 canoes are operating
• **Dumbo the Flying Elephant** 32 • **King Arthur Carrousel** 70
• **Mad Tea Party** 53 • **Mr. Toad's Wild Ride** 32
• **Peter Pan's Flight** 25 • **Snow White's Enchanted Wish** 30
DISNEY CALIFORNIA ADVENTURE *Number of people between adults*
• **Golden Zephyr** 64 • **Jessie's Critter Carousel** 64
• **Jumpin' Jellyfish** 16 • **Luigi's Rollickin' Roadsters** 40

6. LAST-MINUTE COLD FEET If your small child gets cold feet at the last minute after waiting for a ride (where there is no age or height requirement), you can usually arrange with the loading attendant for a switch-off;

see the table on page 166. This situation arises frequently at Pirates of the Caribbean—small children lose their courage en route to the loading area.

There is no law that says you have to ride. If you get to the boarding area and someone is unhappy, just tell a Disney attendant that you have changed your mind, and one will show you the way out. Older children and adults who are unable or unwilling to ride an attraction may also experience the queue with their party and exit before boarding without embarrassment.

LOST CHILDREN

LOST CHILDREN NORMALLY do not present much of a problem at Disneyland Resort. All Disney employees are schooled in handling such situations. If you lose a child while touring, report the situation to a Disney employee; then check in at City Hall (Disneyland Park) or Guest Relations (DCA) where lost-children logs are maintained. In an emergency, an alert can be issued throughout the park through internal communications. If a Disney cast member encounters a lost child, the cast member will escort the child to the Baby Care Center located at the central-hub end of Main Street in Disneyland Park and at the entrance plaza in DCA. Guests age 11 or under are taken to the Baby Care Center in the San Fransokyo Square area at DCA. Guests age 12 and older may leave a written message at City Hall or the Guest Relations lobby or wait there.

unofficial **TIP**
We suggest that children younger than 8 years old be color-coded by dressing them in purple T-shirts or equally distinctive clothes.

It is amazingly easy to lose a child (or two) at a Disney park. It is a good idea to sew a label into each child's shirt that states their name, your name, and the name of your hotel. The same task can be accomplished by writing the information on a strip of masking tape; hotel security professionals suggest that the information be printed in small letters, and that the tape be affixed to the outside of the child's shirt 5 inches or so below the armpit.

HOW KIDS GET LOST

CHILDREN GET SEPARATED from parents every day at the Disney parks under remarkably similar (and predictable) circumstances.

1. PREOCCUPIED SOLO PARENT In this scenario, the only adult in the party is preoccupied with something such as buying refreshments or using the restroom. Junior is there one moment and gone the next.

2. THE HIDDEN EXIT Sometimes parents wait on the sidelines while allowing two or more young children to experience a ride together. As it usually happens, the parents expect the kids to exit the attraction in one place, and lo and behold, the young ones pop out somewhere else. The exits of some Disney attractions are considerably distant from the entrances. Make sure that you know exactly where your children will emerge before letting them ride by themselves.

TIPS FOR KEEPING TRACK OF YOUR BROOD
• Same-colored T-shirts for the whole family will help you gather your troops in an easy and fun way. Opt for just a uniform color or have the T-shirts printed with a logo, such as The Brown Family's Assault on the Mouse. You might also include the date or the year of your visit. Light-colored T-shirts can even be autographed by the Disney characters.
• Clothing labels are great. If you don't sew, buy labels that you can iron on the garment. Include your cell phone number or the number of the hotel where you'll be staying on the label.
• An easier option is a temporary tattoo with your child's name and your phone number. Unlike other methods, the tattoos cannot fall off or be lost. Temporary tattoos last about two weeks, won't wash or sweat off, and are not irritating to the skin. They can be purchased online at safetytat.com. Special tattoos are available for children with food allergies or cognitive impairment such as autism.
• In pet stores you can have name tags printed for a very reasonable price. These are great to add to necklaces and bracelets, or attach them to your child's shoelaces or a belt loop.
• When you check into the hotel, take a business card of the hotel for each member in your party, especially those old enough to carry wallets and purses.
• Always agree on a meeting point before you see a parade, fireworks, or nighttime spectacles. Make sure the meeting place is in the park (as opposed to the car or some place outside the front gate).
• If you have a digital camera or camera phone, take a picture of your kids every morning. If they get lost, the picture will show what they look like and what they are wearing.
• If all members of your party have cell phones, it's easy to locate each other. However, the noise in the parks is so loud that you probably won't hear your cell phone ring. Carry your phone in a front pants pocket and program the phone to vibrate. Or communicate via text message. If any of your younger kids carry cell phones, secure the phones with a strap.
• Save key tags and luggage tags for use on items you bring to the parks, including your stroller, diaper bag, and backpack or hip pack.
• Don't underestimate permanent markers. They are great for labeling pretty much anything. Mini-Sharpies are useful for collecting character autographs.

3. AFTER THE SHOW At the completion of many shows and rides, a Disney staffer will announce, "Check for personal belongings and take small children by the hand." When dozens, if not hundreds, of people leave an attraction at the same time, it is easy for parents to temporarily lose contact with their children unless they have them directly in tow.

4. RESTROOM PROBLEMS Mom tells 6-year-old Tommy, "I'll be sitting on this bench when you come out of the restroom." Three situations: One, Tommy exits through a different door and becomes disoriented (Mom may not know there is another door). Two, Mom belatedly decides that she will also use the restroom, and Tommy emerges to find her absent. Three, Mom pokes around in a shop while keeping an eye on the bench but misses Tommy when he comes out. A restroom adjacent to Rancho del Zocalo Restaurante in Frontierland accounts for many lost children. Because it's located in a passageway connecting Frontierland and Fantasy Faire, children can wander into a totally different area of the park from where they came by simply making a wrong turn out of the restroom.

If you can't be with your child in the restroom, make sure that there is only one exit. Designate a meeting spot more distinctive than a bench, and be specific in your instructions: "I'll meet you by this flagpole. If you get out first, stay right here." Have your child repeat the directions back to you.

5. PARADES There are many special parades and shows at the theme park during which the audience stands. Children, because they are small, tend to jockey around for a better view. By moving a little this way and a little that way, it is amazing how much distance kids can put between themselves and you before anyone notices.

6. MASS MOVEMENTS Another situation to guard against is when huge crowds disperse after shows, fireworks, or parades, or at park closing. With 5,000–12,000 people suddenly moving at once, it is very easy to get separated from a small child or others in your party. Extra caution is recommended following the evening parades, fireworks, and night-time spectaculars. Families should develop specific plans for what to do and where to meet in the event they are separated.

7. CHARACTER GREETINGS A fair amount of activity and confusion is commonplace when the Disney characters are on the scene. See the next section on meeting the Disney characters.

The DISNEY CHARACTERS

FOR YEARS THE COSTUMED, walking versions of Mickey, Minnie, Donald, Goofy, and others have been a colorful supporting cast at Disneyland and Walt Disney World. Known unpretentiously as the Disney characters, these large and friendly figures help provide a link between Disney animated films and the Disney theme parks.

About 250 of the Disney animated-film characters have been brought to life in costume. Of these, a relatively small number (about 50) are greeters (the Disney term for characters who mix with the patrons). The remaining characters are relegated exclusively to performing in shows or participating in parades. Some appear only once or twice a year, usually in holiday parades.

Up-close character meet and greets with autographs, parades, and similar experiences were temporarily suspended during the coronavirus pandemic in favor of socially distanced appearances, but guests can once again hug and high-five their Disney friends.

CHARACTER ENCOUNTERS

CHARACTER WATCHING has developed into a pastime. Where families were once content to stumble across a character occasionally, they

now pursue them armed with autograph books and cameras. For those who pay attention, some characters are more frequently encountered than others. Mickey, Minnie, and Goofy, for example, are seemingly everywhere, while Thumper rarely appears. Other characters are seen regularly but limit themselves to a specific location.

The fact that some characters are seldom seen has turned character watching into character collecting. Mickey Mouse may be the best-known and most-loved character, but from a collector's perspective, he is also the most common. To get an autograph from Mickey is no big deal, but Daisy Duck's signature is a real coup. Commercially tapping into the character-collecting movement, Disney sells autograph books throughout the parks. One *Unofficial Guide* reader offers this suggestion regarding character autographs:

> *Young children learn very quickly! If they see another child get an autograph, they will want an autograph book as well. I recommend buying an autograph book right away. My 4-year-old daughter saw a child get Goofy's autograph, and right away she wanted to join the fun.*

PREPARING YOUR CHILDREN TO MEET THE CHARACTERS Because most small children are not expecting Minnie Mouse to be the size of a forklift, it's best to discuss the characters with your kids before you go. Almost all of the characters are quite large, and several, such as Goofy and Chewbacca, are huge! All of them can be extremely intimidating to a preschooler.

unofficial **TIP**
Don't underestimate your child's excitement at meeting the Disney characters—but also be aware that very small kids may find the large, costumed characters a little frightening.

On first encounter, it is important not to thrust your child upon the character. Allow the little one to come to terms with this big thing from whatever distance the child feels safe. If two adults are present, one should stay close to the youngster while the other approaches the character and demonstrates that the character is safe and friendly. Some kids warm to the characters immediately, while some never do. Most take a little time and often require several different encounters.

There are two kinds of characters: those whose costume includes a face-covering headpiece (animal characters plus some human characters such as Captain Hook), and face characters, or actors who resemble the cartoon characters to such an extent that no mask or headpiece is necessary. Face characters include Mary Poppins, Ariel, Jasmine, Aladdin, Cinderella, Mulan, Tarzan, Moana, Belle, Snow White, and Prince Charming, to name a few.

Only the face characters are allowed to speak. Headpiece characters, called furs in Disney-speak, do not talk or make noises of any kind.

unofficial **TIP**
Explain to your children that the headpiece characters do not talk. Keep in mind, too, that the characters are clumsy and have a limited field of vision.

Because the cast members could not possibly imitate the distinctive voice of the characters, the Disney folks have determined that it is more effective to keep them silent. Lack of speech notwithstanding, the headpiece characters are extremely warm and responsive, and they communicate very effectively with gestures. As with the characters' size, children need to be forewarned that the characters do not talk. The only exceptions are the costumed stars of some newer shows and parades, who boast articulated facial features that blink and flap in sync with the soundtracks, and select *Star Wars* characters (like Darth Vader and Kylo Ren) who use prerecorded dialogue clips to converse with guests.

Parents need to understand that some of the character costumes are very cumbersome and that cast members often suffer from very poor visibility. You have to look closely, but the eyeholes are frequently in the mouth of the costume or even down on the neck. What this means in practical terms is that the characters are sort of clumsy and have a limited field of vision. Children who approach the character from the back or the side may not be noticed, even if the child is touching the character. It is perfectly possible in this situation for the character to accidentally step on the child or knock him or her down. The best way for a child to approach a character is from the front, and occasionally not even this works. For example, the various duck characters (Donald, Daisy, Uncle Scrooge, and so on) have to peer around their bills. If it appears that the character is ignoring your child, pick your child up and hold her in front of the character until the character responds.

It is OK to touch, pat, or hug the character if your child is so inclined. Understanding the unpredictability of children, the characters will keep their feet very still, particularly refraining from moving backward or to the side. Most of the characters will sign autographs (except for *Star Wars* characters) or pose for pictures. Once again, be sure to approach from the front so that the character will understand your intentions. If your child collects autographs, it is a good idea to carry a big, fat pen about the size of a Magic Marker. The costumes make it exceedingly difficult for the characters to wield a smaller pen, so the bigger the better.

THE BIG HURT Many children expect to bump into Mickey the minute they enter a park and are disappointed when he is not around. If your children are unable to settle down and enjoy things until they see Mickey, simply ask a Disney cast member where to find him. If the cast member does not know Mickey's whereabouts, they can find out for you in short order.

"THEN SOME CONFUSION HAPPENED" Be forewarned that character encounters can give rise to a situation during which small children sometimes get lost. There is usually a lot of activity around a character, with both adults and children touching the character or posing for pictures. In the most common scenario, the parents stay in the crowd while their child marches up to get acquainted. With the excitement of the encounter, all the milling people, and the character moving around, a child may get turned around and head off in the wrong direction. In the words of a Salt Lake City mom:

> Milo was shaking hands with Dopey one moment, then some confusion happened, and he [Milo] was gone.

Families with several small children, and parents who are busy fooling around with cameras, can lose track of a youngster in a heartbeat. Our recommendation for parents of preschoolers is to stay with the kids when they meet the characters, stepping back only long enough to take a picture, if necessary.

*un*official **TIP**
Characters make appearances in all the "lands" but are especially thick in Fantasyland, Mickey's Toontown, and Town Square on Main Street.

MEETING CHARACTERS You can *see* the Disney characters in live shows and in parades. For times, consult your app. If you have the time and money, you can share a meal with the characters (more about this later). But if you want to *meet* the characters, get autographs, and take photos, it's helpful to know where the characters hang out.

Disneyland Resort includes information about characters in its mobile app and handout park maps. The app specifies where and when certain characters will be available and also provides information on character dining. On the maps of the parks themselves, Mickey's gloved hand is used to denote locations where characters can be found.

At Disneyland Park, Mickey and Minnie have all-day tours of duty in their Toontown homes (see pages 215–216), where Mickey's old nemesis Pete also makes appearances. All of the "fab five" (including Goofy, Pluto, and Donald), along with Chip 'n' Dale and Cruella De Vil, also make morning appearances in Main Street, U.S.A.'s Town Square. Likewise, Pooh, Tigger, and Eeyore can usually be found in Critter Country. The Fantasy Faire plaza adjacent to Sleeping Beauty Castle is the prime place to meet Ariel, Asha, Aurora, Cinderella, Belle, Princess Elena of Avalor, Merida, and Rapunzel with Flynn Rider. Tinker Bell and her fairy friends draw long lines at their **Pixie Hollow** area off the central hub between Tomorrowland and the Matterhorn. The meet and greets in Star Wars Launch Bay remain closed, but a Dark Side character (often Darth Vader) can be spotted just outside the entrance. (This photo op is reserved for Disney Visa card holders in the afternoon.) Miguel from *Coco* and Mirabel from *Encanto* take turns greeting guests in El Zocalo Park.

At DCA, the fab five—plus Daisy Duck and throwback characters such as Horace Horsecollar, Oswald the Lucky Rabbit, and Clarabelle Cow—can be found on Buena Vista Street and around Carthay Circle (the central hub) dressed in Depression-era duds. Also look for characters in Hollywood Land near the Animation Building, in parades, and in shows at the Hyperion Theater. San Fransokyo Square hosts a permanent meet and greet with Baymax and Hiro from *Big Hero 6*. In Cars Land, you'll find interactive incarnations of the series' automotive stars. Anna and Elsa from *Frozen* hold court inside the Disney Animation attraction, sometimes accompanied by Olaf the Snowman, while current Disney Junior stars greet guests right outside the building. A veritable who's-who of Marvel superheroes hang out around Avengers Campus, ranging from old-guard icons like Iron Man, Thor, and Captain America, to later-day legends such as Black Panther, the Guardians of the Galaxy, and The Wasp. Nick and Judy from *Zootopia* stake out the San Francisco street near Ariel's ride, Chip 'n' Dale camp out at Redwood Creek Challenge Trail, as does Raya from *Raya and the Last Dragon*, and The Incredibles stand guard outside their coaster as their plastic *Toy Story* pals play on Pixar Pier.

While making the characters routinely available has taken the guesswork out of finding them, it has likewise robbed character encounters of much of their surprise and spontaneity. Instead of chancing on a character as you turn a corner, it is much more common now to wait in a queue to meet the character. However, you are still far more likely to encounter free-range characters in Disneyland than at Walt Disney World, especially in the slower morning hours when they are given a longer leash to roam. Be aware that lines for face characters move much more slowly than lines for nonspeaking characters do, as you might surmise. Because face characters are allowed to talk, they do, often engaging children in lengthy conversations, much to the consternation of the families stuck in the queue.

If you believe that Disneyland Park already has quite enough lines, and furthermore, if you prefer to bump into your characters on the fly, here's a quick rundown of where the free-range characters roam. In the morning, there is almost always a princess or two posing in front of the Mickey flower bed just inside the park entrance. There will almost always be a character in Town Square on Main Street and often at the central hub; for example, Mary Poppins and Bert are frequently found near Coke Corner. Snow White's Wicked Queen hangs out near the wishing well in the courtyard of the castle, occasionally accompanied by Aladdin and Jasmine. Alice and her Wonderland friends, as well as Peter Pan and Captain Hook, wander around Fantasyland. *Star Wars* celebrities, including Chewbacca, Ahsoka Tano, and the Mandalorian (with Grogu), stalk the alleyways of Batuu's Black Spire Outpost in Galaxy's Edge. Redd, the female rumrunner from Pirates of the Caribbean, and Jack Sparrow sometimes roam around New Orleans Square, as do Tiana and friends from *The Princess and the Frog*. Any characters whom we haven't specifically mentioned generally continue to turn up randomly throughout the park. Character selection can vary seasonally, with some (such as Jack Skellington) appearing only around Halloween or Christmas.

Characters are also featured in the afternoon and evening parades, *Fantasmic!*, and Fantasy Faire. Performance times for all of the shows and parades are listed in the app. After the shows, characters will sometimes stick around to greet the audience.

Be aware that the characters bug out for parades and certain other special performances. Check the app for performance times and plan your visit to Toontown accordingly.

CHARACTER DINING

FRATERNIZING WITH DISNEY CHARACTERS has become so popular that Disney offers character breakfasts, brunches, and dinners where families can dine in the presence of Minnie, Goofy,

*un*official **TIP**
Arrange dining reservations as far in advance as possible. Your wait for a table will usually be less than 15 minutes.

and other costumed versions of animated celebrities. Character meals provide a familiar, controlled setting in which young children can warm gradually to the characters. All meals are attended by several characters. Adult prices apply to persons age 10 or older, children's prices to ages 3–9. Little ones under age 3 eat free. Because character dining is very popular, we recommend that you arrange reservations as far in advance (up to 60 days) as possible.

CHARACTER DINING: WHAT TO EXPECT Character meals are bustling affairs, held in hotels' or theme parks' largest table-service or "buffeteria" restaurants. Character breakfasts offer a fixed menu served family-style or as a buffet. The typical family-style breakfast includes scrambled eggs; bacon, sausage, and ham; hash browns; waffles, pancakes, or French toast; biscuits, rolls, or pastries; and fruit. The meal is served in large skillets or platters at your table. If you run out of something, you can order seconds (or thirds) at no additional charge. Buffets offer much the same fare, but you have to fetch it yourself.

Whatever the meal, characters circulate around the room while you eat. During your meal, each of the three to five characters present will visit your table, arriving one at a time to cuddle the kids (and sometimes the adults), pose for photos, and sign autographs. Keep autograph books (with pens) and cameras handy. For the best photos, adults should sit across the table from their children. Always seat the children where characters can reach them most easily. If a table is against a wall, for example, adults should sit with their backs to the wall and children should sit nearest the aisle.

Usually, there's also a character with a PhotoPass photographer stationed at the entrance, but prints are not included in the price of your meal, so you'll want to use a Genie+ or PhotoPass+ package rather than paying à la carte for your poses.

You will not be rushed to leave after you've eaten. Remember, however, lots of eager children and adults might be waiting not so patiently to be admitted.

You can dine with Disney characters at the restaurants listed below. For information about character meals and to make dining reservations up to 60 days in advance, call ☎ 714-781-DINE (3463) or use the Disneyland app. *Note:* The following prices don't include tax or gratuities.

GOOFY'S KITCHEN Located at the Disneyland Hotel, Goofy's Kitchen serves a daily character breakfast buffet 7 a.m.–1:30 p.m. and a character dinner buffet 4–9 p.m. Breakfast costs $52 for adults ($31 kids), while dinner costs $59 ($34 kids), although around holidays like Easter it can be as much as $75 ($37 kids). Goofy, of course, is the head character, but he's usually joined by Minnie, Pluto, and others.

NAPA ROSE Disneyland Resort's most luxurious character meal is the Disney Princess Breakfast Adventure, held Thursday–Monday, 8–11 a.m., at the Grand Californian Hotel's toniest table, Napa Rose. The three-course meal includes a three-tier tower of upscale starters, plus an array of brunch standards and desserts. Before eating, Belle, Mulan, Rapunzel, and friends invite guests onto the outdoor patio for interactive storytelling. A photo session and souvenirs are included in the $135 price (adults and kids cost the same).

PLAZA INN Located in Disneyland Park at the end of Main Street and to the right, the Plaza Inn character buffet is usually packed. Served from park opening until 11 a.m., the buffet costs $46 for adults ($27 kids). Characters present at this meal usually include Minnie, Goofy, Pluto, and Chip 'n' Dale.

STORYTELLERS CAFÉ Storytellers Café, at the Grand Californian Hotel, is the setting for the only meal featuring both Mickey and Minnie. A breakfast buffet is served daily, 7–10:45 a.m., and brunch is available 11 a.m.–1:30 p.m. The buffets cost $52 for adults ($31 kids). The meal is periodically punctuated by interactive parades around the dining room, led by the Mouse power couple and a few of their closest friends.

PART 6

DISNEYLAND PARK

ARRIVING *and* GETTING ORIENTED

AFTER PARKING AT OR WALKING into the resort, guests pass through security screenings before entering the Esplanade to approach Disneyland's front turnstiles. Two entrance gates, 14 and 19, are blocked by trees situated in the entrance plaza about 10 feet from the security checkpoint. The trees sometimes inhibit the formation of a line in front of both of the obstructed gates. Gates 14 and 19 are staffed nonetheless and draw guests from adjacent lines 13 or 15 and 18 or 20. When this happens, it significantly speeds up the entry process for guests waiting in lines 13 and 20. Our advice on arriving, therefore, is to inspect the lines leading to gates 14 and 19 and join whichever looks to be shortest. Later in the day, the outside gates (1 and 32) tend to be fastest for reentry. Stroller and wheelchair rentals are available at the Esplanade's east end, to the right of Disneyland's front gates.

In 2024, the parks deployed new self-service turnstiles with automated gates that can accommodate strollers, similar to those used at Disneyland Paris. Have your ticket ready for scanning or tapping before you approach the turnstiles. To prevent resale of unexpired passes, all guests are photographed upon their first park entry; if your mug isn't yet in Mickey's mainframe, you'll be asked to pose before proceeding.

As you enter Main Street, City Hall is to your left, serving as the center for general information, lost and found, and entertainment information. Maps are available in the passages connecting the park entrance to Main Street, U.S.A.; at City Hall; and at a number of shops throughout the park. Detailed daily entertainment schedules for live shows, parades, fireworks, and character greetings can be found in the Disneyland smartphone app. If you are attending a special

Continued on page 180

Disneyland Park

Tomorrowland

Mickey's
Toontown

Fantasyland

Star Wars:
Galaxy's Edge

Frontierland

Critter Country

Disneyland Dr.

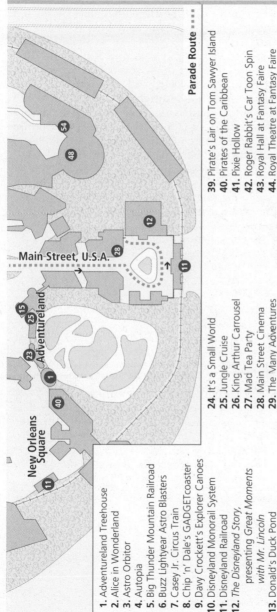

New Orleans Square

Main Street, U.S.A.

Adventureland

Parade Route ▪▪▪▪

1. Adventureland Treehouse
2. Alice in Wonderland
3. Astro Orbitor
4. Autopia
5. Big Thunder Mountain Railroad
6. Buzz Lightyear Astro Blasters
7. Casey Jr. Circus Train
8. Chip 'n' Dale's GADGETcoaster
9. Davy Crockett's Explorer Canoes
10. Disneyland Monorail System
11. Disneyland Railroad
12. *The Disneyland Story,*
    presenting *Great Moments*
    with *Mr. Lincoln*
13. Donald's Duck Pond
14. Dumbo the Flying Elephant
15. *Enchanted Tiki Room*
16. *Fantasmic!*
17. Fantasyland Theatre
18. Finding Nemo Submarine Voyage
19. Frontierland Shootin' Exposition
20. The Golden Horseshoe
21. Goofy's How-To-Play Yard
22. Haunted Mansion
23. Indiana Jones Adventure

24. It's a Small World
25. Jungle Cruise
26. King Arthur Carrousel
27. Mad Tea Party
28. Main Street Cinema
29. The Many Adventures
    of Winnie the Pooh
30. *Mark Twain Riverboat*
31. Matterhorn Bobsleds
32. Mickey & Minnie's Runaway Railway
33. Mickey's House and Meet Mickey
34. *Millennium Falcon: Smugglers Run*
35. Minnie's House
36. Mr. Toad's Wild Ride
37. Peter Pan's Flight
38. Pinocchio's Daring Journey

39. Pirate's Lair on Tom Sawyer Island
40. Pirates of the Caribbean
41. Pixie Hollow
42. Roger Rabbit's Car Toon Spin
43. Royal Hall at Fantasy Faire
44. Royal Theatre at Fantasy Faire
45. *Sailing Ship Columbia*
46. Sleeping Beauty Castle
47. Snow White's Enchanted Wish
48. Space Mountain
49. Star Tours—The Adventures Continue
50. Star Wars Launch Bay
51. Star Wars: Rise of the Resistance
52. Storybook Land Canal Boats
53. Tiana's Bayou Adventure
54. Tomorrowland Theater

continued from page 177

hard-ticket event, the daily entertainment schedule may be included in the park map. The park map lists all the attractions and eateries and provides helpful information about first aid, baby care, assistance for the disabled, and more.

Notice on your map that Main Street ends at a central hub from which branch the entrances to four other sections of Disneyland: **Adventureland, Frontierland, Fantasyland,** and **Tomorrowland.** Two other "lands," **New Orleans Square** and **Critter Country,** can be reached through Adventureland and Frontierland, and **Star Wars: Galaxy's Edge** connects to Critter Country and Frontierland. **Mickey's Toontown** is located on the far side of the railroad tracks from It's a Small World in Fantasyland. **Sleeping Beauty Castle,** the entrance to Fantasyland, is a focal landmark and the visual center of the park. The castle is a great place to meet if your group decides to split up during the day, and it can serve as an emergency meeting place if you are accidentally separated. Keep in mind, however, that the castle covers a lot of territory, so be specific about *where* to meet at the castle. Also be forewarned that parades and live shows sometimes make it difficult to access the entrance of the castle fronting the central hub. Another good meeting spot is the *Partners* statue of Mickey and Walt in the central hub.

STARTING THE TOUR

EVERYONE WILL SOON FIND their own favorite and not-so-favorite attractions in Disneyland Park. Be open-minded and adventuresome. Don't dismiss a ride or show as not being for you until *after* you have tried it. Our personal experience and our research indicate that each visitor is different in terms of which Disney offerings they most enjoy. So don't miss seeing an attraction because a friend from home didn't like it; that attraction may turn out to be your favorite.

We do recommend that you take advantage of what Disney does best—the fantasy experiences such as Indiana Jones Adventure and Haunted Mansion and the Audio-Animatronics (talking robots, that is) attractions such as Pirates of the Caribbean. Unless you have almost unlimited time, don't burn a lot of daylight browsing through the

NOT TO BE MISSED AT DISNEYLAND PARK
ADVENTURELAND Indiana Jones Adventure
CRITTER COUNTRY Tiana's Bayou Adventure
FRONTIERLAND Big Thunder Mountain Railroad
NEW ORLEANS SQUARE Haunted Mansion | Pirates of the Caribbean
STAR WARS: GALAXY'S EDGE *Millennium Falcon:* Smugglers Run | Star Wars: Rise of the Resistance
TOMORROWLAND Space Mountain | Star Tours—The Adventures Continue
TOONTOWN Mickey & Minnie's Runaway Railway
LIVE ENTERTAINMENT *Fantasmic!* | *Wondrous Journeys*

DISNEYLAND PARK SERVICES	
BABY CARE CENTER At the central-hub end of Main Street	
BANKING SERVICES/CURRENCY EXCHANGE At City Hall at the railroad station end of Main Street	
DISNEYLAND AND LOCAL ATTRACTION INFORMATION At City Hall	
FIRST AID Two doors down from Plaza Inn at the central-hub end of Main Street	
LIVE ENTERTAINMENT AND PARADE INFORMATION At City Hall	
LOST ADULTS AND MESSAGES At City Hall	
LOST AND FOUND Lost and Found for the entire resort is located west of the entrance to Disneyland Park.	
LOST CHILDREN At the central-hub end of Main Street	
STORAGE LOCKERS Down Main Street one block (as you walk toward the castle) and to the right	
GUEST RELATIONS AND DISABILITY ASSISTANCE At City Hall; central hub near Plaza Inn; Fantasyland at Dumbo; Tomorrowland near Star Trader; New Orleans Square at Haunted Mansion exit; Frontierland outside Galaxy's Edge	

shops. Except for some special Disney souvenirs, you can find much of the same merchandise elsewhere. Try to minimize the time you spend on midway-type rides, as you probably have an amusement park, carnival, or state fair close to your hometown. Don't, however, mistake rides such as Tiana's Bayou Adventure and Big Thunder Mountain Railroad for amusement park rides. They may be of the flume ride or roller-coaster genre, but they represent pure Disney genius. Similarly, do not devote a lot of time to waiting in line for meals. Eat a good early breakfast before you come, snack on vendor-sold foods during the touring day, or follow the suggestions for meals incorporated into the various touring plans presented.

SINGLE-RIDER LINES

YOU CAN OFTEN SAVE TIME waiting in line by taking advantage of single-rider lines, separate lines for people who don't mind riding alone or with a stranger (see page 110). In Disneyland Park, Matterhorn Bobsleds, *Millennium Falcon:* Smugglers Run, Space Mountain, Tiana's Bayou Adventure, and (sometimes) Star Tours have single-rider lines. A single-rider line was previously available at Indiana Jones Adventure, but it's currently closed. Be aware that single riders miss seeing some interesting preshow entertainment in the queues for *Millennium Falcon* and Star Tours. Ask an attraction employee how to enter the single-rider queue; you may be given a paper pass and directed up the exit.

PARK-OPENING PROCEDURES

YOUR PROGRESS AND SUCCESS during your first hour of touring will be affected by your decisions during the minutes leading up to opening. The standard park opening procedure is for all guests to be admitted through the turnstile onto Main Street about 30 minutes before the official park opening. On early-entry days, eligible hotel guests should stay to the right side of Main Street and show their room reservation inside the Disneyland app to a cast member near Plaza Inn for immediate access into Tomorrowland and Fantasyland. Otherwise, guests are allowed to proceed to the end of Main Street but are held short of the castle in the central hub. At the official opening time, everyone is released into every land at the same time, with all attractions open (unless otherwise noted).

If you've got early-entry privileges, make the most of them by arriving at the gates as quickly as possible after security screenings start, so you can be one of the first guests to enter your preferred land. Ride a few attractions, then get ready to rope-drop from Fantasyland toward Galaxy's Edge or Toontown (depending on your touring plan). All other visitors should also enter the park as early as possible, and then stake out one of these three spots in the hub to await the opening:

A. If you are going to **Star Wars Galaxy's Edge** or **Frontierland** first, proceed as far forward in the central hub as allowed and line up to the left of Walt and Mickey's central statue. To rope-drop Rise of the Resistance, use the Frontierland entrance instead of going through Adventureland; guests may make it to the attraction entrance slightly faster by sprinting through Critter Country, but they will be forced to join the queue behind folks coming from Frontierland. Note that early-entry guests coming from Fantasyland along Big Thunder Trail have a slight edge over everyone coming from the hub.

B. If you are going to **Indiana Jones Adventure, Tiana's Bayou Adventure,** or **Haunted Mansion** first, stand in front of Jolly Holiday Bakery on the left side of the central hub and wait next to the walkway to Adventureland. When the rest of the park opens, proceed to Adventureland for Indiana Jones, or continue past the Treehouse for New Orleans Square and Critter Country. Off-site guests have the advantage over early-entry users at these attractions.

C. If you are going to **Tomorrowland, Fantasyland,** or **Toontown** first, wait on the right side of the central hub. For Finding Nemo Submarine Voyage, Star Tours, or Space Mountain, bear right at opening and zip into Tomorrowland. Guests going to Fantasyland tend to bottleneck on the left side of the hub, so you can beat most of the crowd by starting on the right side and cutting straight toward the castle. If you are going first to Matterhorn Bobsleds or Mickey & Minnie's Runaway Railway, head between the castle and the left side of the mountain. Early-entry guests will always have a large lead on these rides.

▌■ MAIN STREET, U.S.A.

THIS SECTION OF DISNEYLAND PARK is where you'll begin and end your visit. The Disneyland Railroad stops at the Main Street Station, and you can board here for a grand circle tour of the park, or you can get off the train in New Orleans Square, Mickey's Toontown/Fantasyland, or Tomorrowland.

Main Street is an idealized version of a turn-of-the-20th-century American small-town street. Many visitors are surprised to discover that all the buildings are real, not elaborate props. Attention to detail is exceptional—interiors, furnishings, and fixtures conform to the period. As with any real Main Street, the Disney version is essentially a collection of shops and eating places, with a city hall, a fire station, and an old-time cinema. A mixed-media attraction combines static exhibits recalling the life of Walt Disney with a patriotic remembrance of Abraham Lincoln. Horse-drawn trolleys, fire engines, and horseless carriages give rides along Main Street and transport visitors to the central hub.

Disneyland Railroad ★★★½

APPEAL BY AGE	PRESCHOOL ★★★★½	GRADE SCHOOL ★★★★	TEENS ★★★½
YOUNG ADULTS ★★★½	OVER 30 ★★★★		SENIORS ★★★★½

What it is Scenic railroad ride around the park's perimeter; also transportation to New Orleans Square, Mickey's Toontown, Fantasyland, and Tomorrowland. **Scope and scale** Major attraction. **When to go** After 11 a.m. or when you need transportation. **Duration of ride** About 22 minutes for a full circuit. **Average wait in line per 100 people ahead of you** 7 minutes; assumes 3 trains operating. **Loading speed** Fast.

DESCRIPTION AND COMMENTS This transportation ride blends an eclectic variety of sights and experiences with an energy-saving way of getting around the park. In addition to providing a glimpse of all the lands except Adventureland and Galaxy's Edge, the train passes through the Grand Canyon Diorama (between Tomor-

Thumbs Up for the Whole Family

rowland and Main Street), a three-dimensional replica of the canyon, complete with wildlife, as it appears from the southern rim. Another sight on the train circuit is Primeval World, a depiction of a prehistoric peat bog and rainforest populated by Audio-Animatronic (robotic) dinosaurs. Opened in 1966, Primeval World uses animatronics recycled from the Disney-designed Ford's Magic Skyway pavilion for the 1964 World's Fair, and it was a precursor to a similar presentation at EPCOT's former Universe of Energy.

The train's path was shifted south over what was once a portion of the Rivers of America to accommodate Galaxy's Edge. Passengers' views of the new land are blocked by a mountain range, complete with elevated train trestles and waterfalls that recall the park's original Nature's Wonderland.

TOURING TIPS Save the train ride until after you've seen the featured attractions, or use it when you need transportation. It can also be a way to relax during the peak times of the day when the crowds are swelling. You can get a good estimate of how long you'll wait for the next train by using the posted wait time sign outside each station. It will either list 5 minutes (three trains operating), 10 minutes (two trains), or 20 minutes (only one train). If you have small children who are hell-bent on seeing Mickey first thing in the morning, you might consider taking the train to Mickey's Toontown (a half circuit) and visiting Mickey in his dressing room as soon as you enter the park. Many families find that this tactic puts the kids in a more receptive frame of mind for the other attractions. On busy days, lines form at the New Orleans Square and Mickey's Toontown/Fantasyland Stations but rarely at the Main Street or Tomorrowland Stations.

The Disneyland Story, presenting Great Moments with Mr. Lincoln ★★★½

APPEAL BY AGE	PRESCHOOL ★★	GRADE SCHOOL ★★★	TEENS ★★★
YOUNG ADULTS ★★★½	OVER 30 ★★★★		SENIORS ★★★★½

What it is Nostalgic exhibits documenting the Disney success story, followed by an Audio-Animatronics patriotic presentation. **Scope and scale** Minor attraction. **When to go** During the hot, crowded period of day. **Duration of show** 15 minutes, plus pre-shows of Disney exhibits. **Probable waiting time** Usually none.

DESCRIPTION AND COMMENTS A warm and well-presented remembrance of the man who started it all. Well worth seeing. The attraction lobby consists of a museum of Disney and patriotic memorabilia. Especially interesting are rotating Disney Gallery displays of concept art and historical artifacts, most recently honoring the company's 100th anniversary with over 100 items documenting the connections between Disney's films and theme park attractions, including a multiplane animation camera and the long-lost Old Hag figure from Main Street's Jewelry Shop. A screen in the gallery shows the *Once Upon a Studio* animated short created to celebrate Disney's centennial. Before guests are admitted to a large theater where *Great Moments with Mr. Lincoln* is presented, a 9-minute video preshow produced by *National Geographic* and narrated by ABC News's Robin Roberts shares the story of the president's friendship with Black abolitionist Frederick Douglass, whose bust is displayed alongside images of the Great Emancipator. The patriotic main performance stars an extremely lifelike and sophisticated Audio-Animatronic Abraham Lincoln delivering an amalgamation of his notable speeches (though the overfamiliar "Gettysburg Address" is not recited in full) as originally recorded by actor Royal Dano for the 1964 World's Fair. Lincoln's head is stunningly emotive, capable of wrinkling his brow and pursing his lips with uncanny realism. Surround sound effects and songs borrowed from EPCOT's *American Adventure* add to this brief-but-inspiring biography of America's 16th president. The show is periodically preempted for previews of Disney's upcoming feature films.

Thumbs Up for the Whole Family

Note: This show was closed at press time for a $5 million refurbishment, which will update the stage with a new turntable and upgrades to the lighting and audio effects.

TOURING TIPS *Great Moments with Mr. Lincoln* starts a new show every 20 minutes, with the Fredrick Douglass preshow film beginning 15 minutes prior. You usually do not have to wait long for this show, so see it during the busy times of day when lines are long elsewhere or as you are leaving the park. Sit up close to best see the detail on the Lincoln figure, or sit a few rows back for a more comfortable view of the screen. For crowd-control reasons, *The Disneyland Story* shuts down during evening parades, a fact often not noted in the entertainment schedule.

Main Street Cinema   ★★

APPEAL BY AGE	PRESCHOOL ★★★½	GRADE SCHOOL ★★★½	TEENS ★★★½
YOUNG ADULTS ★★½	OVER 30 ★★★½		SENIORS ★★★★

What it is Vintage Disney cartoons. **Scope and scale** Diversion. **When to go** Whenever you want. **Duration of show** Runs continuously. **Probable waiting time** None.

DESCRIPTION AND COMMENTS An opening-day attraction, this small theater shows six classic Disney cartoons simultaneously. Early black-and-white Mickey Mouse shorts such as *Steamboat Willie* and *Plane Crazy* are screened, along with the celebrity caricature–stocked oddity *Mickey's Polo Team*. The films are played at a low enough volume that the theater remains a quiet respite from the rest of the park.

TOURING TIPS Good place to get out of the sun or rain or to kill time while others in your group shop on Main Street. Fun, but not something you can't afford to miss. No seating is provided.

Transportation Rides

DESCRIPTION AND COMMENTS Trolleys, buses, and the like add color to Main Street. One-way only.

TOURING TIPS The rides will save you a walk to the central hub. Not worth waiting in line. If you catch the first trolley of the morning, you may be serenaded onboard by the Dapper Dans.

▊ ADVENTURELAND

ADVENTURELAND IS THE FIRST "LAND" to the left of Main Street and somehow manages to seamlessly combine South Pacific island, Middle Eastern bazaar, and African safari themes. Transitions from one part of Adventureland to another feel quite natural, and the identity crisis inherent in the mixed-theme cocktail never registers in the minds of most guests. Before Galaxy's Edge opened, Adventureland's stroller parking and seating areas were rearranged to relieve what was among the worst pedestrian bottlenecks in any Disney theme park, but space is still tight. If you're just passing through Adventureland, say on your way to Tiana's Bayou Adventure, you can avoid the congestion by transiting Frontierland instead.

Adventureland Treehouse ★★★½

APPEAL BY AGE	PRESCHOOL ★★★★	GRADE SCHOOL ★★★½	TEENS ★★
YOUNG ADULTS ★★★	OVER 30 ★★★½		SENIORS ★★★

What it is Walk-through tree house exhibit. **Scope and scale** Minor attraction. **When to go** Anytime. **Duration of tour** 8–12 minutes. **Average wait in line per 100 people ahead of you** 7½ minutes.

DESCRIPTION AND COMMENTS Originally inspired by the 1960 live-action feature *Swiss Family Robinson,* this venerable Adventureland icon spent a couple of decades being decorated after Disney's 1999 animated film *Tarzan,* before closing in late 2021 for a return to its roots. The rustic entry staircase has been relocated and

Thumbs Up for the Whole Family

its suspension bridge removed, widening pedestrian pathways between Adventureland and New Orleans Square, and restoring the giant working waterwheel. Among the bogus boughs, new *Swiss Family*–inspired scenes depict the mother's music room (complete with bamboo organ), the teen daughter's astronomy loft, and her little brothers' nature study. Sharp-eyed fans will also find references to Disney's Society of Explorers and Adventurers, an Easter egg connecting various attractions around the globe. Fortunately for those unable or unwilling to climb stairs, the kitchen and art studio on the ground floor—home to an animatronic ostrich named Jane, in honor of the tree's previous occupants—are fully accessible.

TOURING TIPS This self-guided, walk-through tour involves a lot of climbing up and down stairs but with no ropes or ladders or anything fancy. People who stop to look extra-long or go against the one-way crowd flow sometimes create bottlenecks. We recommend visiting this attraction in the late afternoon or early evening if you are on a one-day touring schedule.

Enchanted Tiki Room ★★★½

APPEAL BY AGE **PRESCHOOL** ★★★★ **GRADE SCHOOL** ★★★★ **TEENS** ★★★½
YOUNG ADULTS ★★★★ **OVER 30** ★★★★ **SENIORS** ★★★★½

What it is Audio-Animatronic Pacific island musical show. **Scope and scale** Minor attraction. **When to go** Anytime. **Duration of show** 14½ minutes plus preshow of talking totem poles. **Probable waiting time** 11 minutes.

  DESCRIPTION AND COMMENTS An unusual sit-down theater performance in which more than 200 birds, flowers, and tiki-god statues sing and whistle through a Polynesian-style musical program. One of Walt's first large-scale uses of Audio-Animatronics, *Tiki Room* might be more impressive for the technology it took to get the show (ahem) flying in 1963. Beloved by Disneyland fans for its detail and immersive setting, the current version of the show is only slightly altered from the original.

TOURING TIPS One of the most bizarre (yet endearing) of the Disneyland Park entertainments and rarely crowded. We like it in the late afternoon, when we can especially appreciate sitting for a bit in an air-conditioned theater. Back-row seats provide the broadest view with the least neck strain.

The Tiki Juice Bar that straddles the *Tiki Room* entrance dispenses Dole Whip, a delectable blend of pineapple slush and vanilla soft-serve ice cream, one of the park's most popular snacks. Dole sponsors the attraction and provides the propagandistic preshow video, so you can enjoy your Tiki Juice Bar treats while watching the show. Using mobile ordering is mandatory here; if you need a cashier, go around the corner to Tropical Hideaway.

Indiana Jones Adventure *(Lightning Lane)* ★★★★★

APPEAL BY AGE **PRESCHOOL** ★★½ **GRADE SCHOOL** ★★★★ **TEENS** ★★★★½
YOUNG ADULTS ★★★★½ **OVER 30** ★★★★½ **SENIORS** ★★★★

What it is Motion-simulator dark ride. **Scope and scale** Super-headliner. **When to go** Before 9:30 a.m. or just before closing. **Comments** Not to be missed. Must be 46" tall to ride; switching-off option (see page 165). **Duration of ride** A little over 3 minutes. **Average wait in line per 100 people ahead of you** 3 minutes. **Loading speed** Fast.

      DESCRIPTION AND COMMENTS The adventure begins in the queue, where you find yourself at the site of an archaeology expedition with the Temple of the Forbidden Eye entrance beckoning only 50 feet away. After crossing a wooden bridge, you step into the temple and enter Indiana Jones's indoor queuing area, a system of tunnels and passageways extending to within 50 yards of the Santa Monica Pier. You wind through caves, down the interior corridors of the temple, and into subterranean rotundas where the archaeologists have been hard at work. Along the way there are various surprises (be sure to disregard any DO NOT TOUCH signs you see on safety ropes), as well as a succession of homilies etched in an "ancient" language on the temple walls; play the "Gifts of Mara" game in the Disney Play app to translate the glyphs. You will eventually stumble into a chamber where a short movie will explain the safety instructions. From there, it's finally on to the loading area.

This is a combination tracked dark ride and motion simulator. In addition to moving along its path through a themed building (the dark ride part), the military troop transport vehicle bucks and pitches (the simulator part) in sync with the visuals and special effects.

Though the plot is complicated and not altogether clear, the bottom line is that if you look into the Forbidden Eye, you're in big trouble. The Forbidden Eye, of course, stands out like Kim Kardashian in a bikini, and *everybody* stares at it. The rest of the ride consists of a mad race to escape the temple as it collapses around you. In the process, you encounter snakes, spiders, lava pits, rats, swinging bridges, and the house-size granite bowling ball that everyone remembers from *Raiders of the Lost Ark*.

The Indiana Jones ride is a Disney masterpiece—nonstop action from beginning to end with brilliant visual effects. Elaborate even by Disney standards, the attraction provides a level of detail and variety of action that make use of the entire Imagineering arsenal of high-tech gimmickry. Over the years, the ride has been upgraded with dazzling digital projections that bring the Chamber of Destiny doors and idol to life, and a major refurbishment ahead of the fifth Indy film's release in 2023 repaired several long-broken effects while adding some exciting new surprises.

TOURING TIPS Indiana Jones stays fairly mobbed all day and is prone to frequent breakdowns. Try to ride during the first hour the park is open. If you miss Indiana Jones in the early morning and the line is long, try again during a parade or *Fantasmic!*, or during the hour before the park closes. Regarding the latter, the Disney folks often inflate the posted wait late in the day; we hopped in the line when it said 45 minutes and boarded in 10.

Note that the standby and Lightning Lane queues merge outside the interior queue, so Lightning Lane guests will still usually wait 15 minutes or more before boarding.

Though the Indiana Jones ride is wild and jerky, it is primarily distinguished by its visual impact and realistic special effects. Thus, we encourage the over-50 crowd to give it a chance; we think you'll like it. As for children, most find the ride extremely intense and action-packed but not particularly frightening. We encountered very few children who met the 46-inch minimum-height requirement who were in any way intimidated.

Jungle Cruise ★★★½

APPEAL BY AGE	PRESCHOOL ★★★★	GRADE SCHOOL ★★★★	TEENS ★★★★
YOUNG ADULTS ★★★★	OVER 30 ★★★★		SENIORS ★★★★

What it is A Disney outdoor-adventure boat ride. **Scope and scale** Major attraction. **When to go** Before 10 a.m. or after 6 p.m. **Duration of ride** 7½ minutes. **Average wait in line per 100 people ahead of you** 3½ minutes; assumes 10 boats operating. **Loading speed** Moderate–slow.

DESCRIPTION AND COMMENTS On this boat ride through jungle waterways, passengers encounter elephants, lions, piranhas, and menacing hippos. It's a long-enduring Disney favorite, with the boat skipper's spiel adding measurably to the fun.

Thumbs Up for the Whole Family

As more technologically advanced attractions have been added to the park over the years, the Jungle Cruise had, by comparison, lost some of its luster. However, a long-overdue overhaul in 2021 finally removed several racially insensitive tableaus, replacing them with comical new scenes involving an expedition of lost skippers. The updated figures are sculpted in the classic Marc Davis style, and their amusing animations are enhanced by boosted sound effects and some unexpected spritzes of water.

Though the updated script is corny as ever, the Jungle Cruise can still draw long waits, as this Anacortes, Washington, family found out:

Jungle Cruise's line can be insanity-inducing long. If the line goes upstairs, expect a very long wait through the grandfather of switchback queues. Nearly every time you expect the queue to turn around back to the ride, it continues into another room.

TOURING TIPS This ride loads slowly, and long lines form as the park fills. To compound problems, guests exiting Indiana Jones tend to head for the Jungle Cruise. Go early, or during a parade or *Fantasmic!* Be forewarned that the Jungle Cruise has an especially deceptive line: just when you think that you are about to board, you are shunted into yet another queuing maze (not visible outside the ride). Regardless of how short the line *looks* when you approach the Jungle Cruise, inquire about the length of the wait—at least you will know what you are getting into. If the second floor of the queue building is in use, you're in for at least a 20-minute wait. If you are sent upstairs, peek in the office above the entrance to see Dwayne "The Rock" Johnson's and Emily Blunt's costumes from the 2021 film. When the queue splits before the loading dock, the left lane (which is slightly quicker) leads to seats in the rear and left side of the boat; the right lane is seated starboard. Finally, many readers consider the Jungle Cruise much better at night.

NEW ORLEANS SQUARE

ACCESSIBLE VIA ADVENTURELAND AND FRONTIERLAND, New Orleans Square is one of the four "lands" that don't emanate from the central hub. The architecture and setting are Caribbean Colonial, like New Orleans itself, with exceptional attention to detail.

Disneyland Railroad

DESCRIPTION AND COMMENTS The Disneyland Railroad stops in New Orleans Square on its circle tour around the park. See the description beginning on page 183 for additional details regarding the sights en route. This is a pleasant, feet-saving way to commute to Mickey's Toontown/Fantasyland, Tomorrowland, or Main Street. Be advised, however, that the New Orleans Square Station is usually the most congested.

Haunted Mansion *(Lightning Lane)* ★★★★

| **APPEAL BY AGE** | **PRESCHOOL** ★★★ | **GRADE SCHOOL** ★★★★ | **TEENS** ★★★★½ |
| **YOUNG ADULTS** ★★★★½ | | **OVER 30** ★★★★½ | **SENIORS** ★★★★½ |

What it is Indoor haunted-house ride. **Scope and scale** Major attraction. **When to go** Before 11:30 a.m. or after 6:30 p.m. **Comments** Not to be missed. Frightens some small children. **Duration of ride** 5½-minute ride plus a 2-minute preshow. **Average wait in line per 100 people ahead of you** 2½ minutes; assumes both "stretch rooms" operating. **Loading speed** Fast.

DESCRIPTION AND COMMENTS Haunted Mansion is a fun attraction more than it is a scary one. An ingenious preshow serves as a vehicle to deliver guests to the ride's boarding area, where they board "doom buggies" for a ride through the mansion's parlor, dining room, library, halls, and attic before descending to an uncommonly active graveyard. Disney employs almost every special effect in its repertoire in Haunted Mansion, making it one of the most inventive and different of all Disney attractions. Be warned that some youngsters build a lot of anxiety concerning what they think they will see. The actual attraction scares almost nobody. Though this mansion is the original, the ride is somewhat shorter and lacks the M. C. Escher–esque stairway scene that the Walt Disney World version has. In 2024, the Mansion's grounds were renovated with an extended outdoor queue (inspired by Master Gracey and the one-eyed cat), along with a new carriage-house gift shop themed to Madame Leota at the exit.

Haunted Mansion is one of veteran Unofficial Guide writer Eve Zibart's favorite attractions. She warns:

Don't let the childishness of the old-fashioned Haunted Mansion put you off: this is one of the best attractions in the park. It's jam-packed with visual puns, special effects, hidden Mickeys, and really lovely Victorian-spooky sets. It's not scary, except in the sweetest of ways.

Each Halloween season, Haunted Mansion substitutes a special holiday version of the attraction that runs through early January. Inspired by Tim Burton's 1993 stop-motion musical *The Nightmare Before Christmas,* the overlay features characters such as Jack Skellington and Oogie Boogie cavorting among the familiar mansion haunts to songs from Danny Elfman's classic score. *Note:* The attraction closes for several weeks before and after the holiday season to install and remove the overlay.

TOURING TIPS This attraction would be more at home in Fantasyland, but no matter—it's Disney at its best: another not-to-be-missed attraction. Because Haunted Mansion is in an especially high traffic corridor (located between Pirates of the Caribbean and Tiana's Bayou Adventure), it stays busy all day. Try to see Haunted Mansion before 11:30 a.m., after 6:30 p.m., or during a parade. In the evening, crowds for *Fantasmic!* gather in front of Haunted Mansion, making it very difficult to access. The holiday version of this attraction is so popular that Virtual Queue (see page 107) may be mandated to manage the crowds.

Pirates of the Caribbean ★★★★★

APPEAL BY AGE   PRESCHOOL ★★★★   GRADE SCHOOL ★★★★½   TEENS ★★★★½
YOUNG ADULTS   ★★★★½   OVER 30   ★★★★½   SENIORS   ★★★★½

What it is A Disney indoor-adventure boat ride. **Scope and scale** Major attraction. **When to go** Before 11:30 a.m. or after 4:30 p.m. **Comments** Not to be missed. Frightens some small children. **Duration of ride** Approximately 14 minutes. **Average wait in line per 100 people ahead of you** 2 minutes; assumes 42 boats operating. **Loading speed** Fast.

Dark   Loud   Scary

DESCRIPTION AND COMMENTS Another boat ride, this time indoors, Pirates of the Caribbean takes you through a series of sets depicting a pirate raid on an island settlement, from the bombardment of the fortress to the debauchery that follows the victory. The attraction includes characters Jack Sparrow and Barbossa from the *Pirates of the Caribbean* movies in animatronic form. In 2018 the infamous "take a wench for a bride" scene was reworked, transforming the auction of women into a sale of looted goods and upgrading the fan-favorite Redhead into Redd, a rum-rustling pirate queen.

TOURING TIPS Undoubtedly one of the most elaborate and imaginative attractions in Disneyland Park. Though engineered to move large crowds, this ride sometimes gets overwhelmingly busy in the early and midafternoon. Try to ride before noon or while a parade or *Fantasmic!* is in progress. A Genie+ Lightning Lane was temporarily added in 2024, but it should be removed once Tiana's Bayou Adventure and Haunted Mansion are both operating. If you have only experienced the Walt Disney World version of Pirates, don't bypass Disneyland's version thinking that it's more of the same: the original ride is far longer, more detailed, and better maintained than its Floridian cousin. Fans of Redd can sometimes find the sassy swashbuckler interacting with guests around New Orleans Square. A reader from Sacramento, California, shares this important tip:

You CAN get wet on Pirates of the Caribbean! That had never happened to me before, but we sat in the very front one time, and we got absolutely drenched and had to walk around with wet butts for a few hours.

CRITTER COUNTRY

SITUATED BETWEEN New Orleans Square and a meandering pathway to Galaxy's Edge, Critter Country sports a pioneer appearance not unlike that of Frontierland. Originally christened for the Country Bears and Br'er Rabbit, the critters in question now hail from both Tiana's bayou and Pooh's Hundred Acre Wood.

Davy Crockett's Explorer Canoes *(seasonal)* ★★★

APPEAL BY AGE	PRESCHOOL ★★★★	GRADE SCHOOL ★★★½	TEENS ★★★½
YOUNG ADULTS ★★★½	OVER 30 ★★★½		SENIORS ★★★★

What it is Scenic canoe ride. **Scope and scale** Minor attraction. **When to go** As soon as it opens, usually 11 a.m. **Duration of ride** 8–10 minutes, depending on how fast you paddle. **Average wait in line per 100 people ahead of you** 12½ minutes; assumes 6 canoes operating. **Loading speed** Slow.

DESCRIPTION AND COMMENTS This paddle-powered ride around Tom Sawyer Island and Fort Wilderness runs the same route with the same sights as the steamboat and sailing ship. The canoes operate only on busier days and close at sunset. The sights are fun, and the ride is a little different in that patrons paddle the canoe. Those with tender rotator cuffs be warned: the trip can give your shoulders quite a workout, unless you slack off and let your fellow passengers handle the hard rowing.

TOURING TIPS The canoes are the most interactive (and exhausting) of three ways to see the same waterways. Because the canoes are slower in loading, we usually opt for the larger steamboat or sailing ship. If you're not up for a boat ride, a different view of the same sights can be had by hoofing around Tom Sawyer Island. Try to ride at 11 a.m. or shortly thereafter. The canoes operate on selected days during seasonal periods only, and they close by 5 p.m. If the canoes are a big deal to you, check online to make sure that they are operating.

The Many Adventures of Winnie the Pooh   ★★★½

APPEAL BY AGE   PRESCHOOL ★★★★½   **GRADE SCHOOL** ★★★★   **TEENS** ★★★
YOUNG ADULTS ★★★½   **OVER 30** ★★★½   **SENIORS** ★★★★

What it is Indoor track ride. **Scope and scale** Minor attraction. **When to go** Before 11 a.m. or late afternoon or evening. **Duration of ride** About 3 minutes. **Average wait in line per 100 people ahead of you** 5 minutes. **Loading speed** Moderate.

DESCRIPTION AND COMMENTS Pooh is the rare "dark ride" that's simply sunny, upbeat, and fun. You ride inside an oversize beehive dripping with "hunny" through the Hundred Acre Wood, where you encounter Pooh, Eeyore, Owl, Rabbit, Tigger, Kanga, Roo, and Piglet, too, as they

Thumbs Up for the Whole Family

contend with a blustery day. There's even a dream sequence with Heffalumps and Woozles, a favorite of this 30-something couple from Lexington, Massachusetts, who think Pooh has plenty to offer adults:

The attention to detail and special effects make this ride worth seeing even if you don't have children in your party. The Pooh dream sequence was great!

TOURING TIPS Though well done, The Many Adventures of Winnie the Pooh is not wildly popular. The wait is rarely more than 15 minutes and is typically less than 5. The only exceptions are on supercrowded days or when Tiana's Bayou Adventure is temporarily closed, which then causes crowds to swarm Winnie the Pooh.

Tiana's Bayou Adventure   *(Lightning Lane)*   ★★★★½

APPEAL BY AGE   PRESCHOOL ★★★★†   **GRADE SCHOOL** ★★★★½   **TEENS** ★★★★½
YOUNG ADULTS ★★★★½   **OVER 30** ★★★★½   **SENIORS** ★★★★

†*Many preschoolers are too short to meet the height requirement, while others are intimidated by watching the ride while standing in line. Of those preschoolers who actually ride, most give the attraction high marks.*

What it is Water-flume adventure boat ride. **Scope and scale** Headliner. **When to go** Before 11 a.m. or use the single-rider line. **Comments** Not to be missed. Must be 40" tall to ride; those age 7 or younger must ride with an adult; switching-off option (**see page 165**). Virtual Queue (see page 107) or Genie+ Lightning Lane (see page 97) may be required. **Duration of ride** About 10 minutes. **Average wait in line per 100 people ahead of you** 3½ minutes. **Loading speed** Moderate.

Scary

Lose Things

Queasy

Muss Your 'Do

DESCRIPTION AND COMMENTS Tiana's Bayou Adventure is a Disney-style amusement park flume ride that combines steep chutes with a variety of Disney's best special effects. Covering more than 0.5 mile, the ride splashes through swamps, caves, and backwoodsy bayous before climaxing in a 52-foot plunge. Originally known as Splash Mountain, that ride's *Song of the South* storyline was scrapped, and the attraction reopened in late 2024 as Tiana's Bayou Adventure, a sequel to the 2009 film *The Princess and the Frog*. Set in 1927, the reimagined attraction sees guests queuing inside the old salt mine that Tiana has turned into an employee-owned food co-op (look for her beignets recipe in the kitchen), then boarding log-shaped boats to help her find the missing ingredients for a special recipe. Along the journey, you'll recruit a band of musical critters to play at Tiana's party, then get shrunk down to the size of a frog before making a big splash at the Mardi Gras celebration. The ride path and drops remain unchanged, but the revamped ride includes advanced animatronic figures of Princess Tiana and her bayou buddies, elaborate nighttime effects, and songs and dialogue recorded by the original voice actors, including Anika Noni Rose. While the new additions are adorable, there are fewer animatronics overall, with video projections papering over some of the gaps. The Dr. Facilier–free plot lacks the dramatic tension of the old Briar Patch climax, making the attraction slightly more kid-friendly, but the big drop still packs a punch.

TOURING TIPS Splash Mountain was among the most popular rides in Disneyland Park for patrons of all ages, so Disney is dealing with pent-up demand by mandating use of either the free Virtual Queue service (see page 107) or paid Genie+ Lightning Lane (see page 97). Once opening crowds subside and a standby queue becomes available, lines will persist throughout the day, from early morning until a few minutes before closing. This will be particularly true on hotter days, as weather affects the wait times significantly. This ride is most popular during daylight hours, but its exterior scenes look especially lovely after dark. Single riders can save time by entering through the attraction's exit.

A Suffolk, Virginia, mom contends that there are more important considerations than beating crowds:

Definitely wait to do [Tiana's Bayou Adventure] at the end of the day. We were seated in the front of the ride, and we were drenched to the bone. If we had ridden first thing in the morning, I personally would have been miserable for the rest of the day. Parents, beware! It says you will get wet, not drowned.

It is almost a certainty that you will get wet, though probably not drenched, on this ride. Be warned: no matter how dry everyone exiting the ride looks, a rogue wave may swamp your log unexpectedly. If you visit on a cool day, you may want to carry a plastic garbage bag. By tearing holes in the bottom and sides, you can fashion a sort of raincoat. Be sure to tuck the bag under your bottom. Though you can get splashed regardless of where you sit, riders in the front seat generally get the worst of it. If you have a camera, either leave it with a nonriding member of your party or wrap it in a plastic bag.

One final word: This is not just a fancy flume ride—it is a full-blown Disney adventure. The scariest part by far is the big drop into the pool (visible from the sidewalk in front of the attraction), and even this plunge looks worse than it really is. Despite reassurances, however, many children wig out after watching it from the sidewalk. A Grand Rapids, Michigan, mother recalls her kids' rather unique reaction:

We discovered after the fact that our children thought they would go underwater after the five-story drop and tried to hold their breath throughout the ride in preparation. They were really too preoccupied to enjoy the clever story.

STAR WARS: *Galaxy's Edge*

CAREFULLY CONCEALED from the rest of the park by a mountainous berm, the 14-acre Galaxy's Edge is accessed either via two rocky tunnels branching off from Frontierland's Big Thunder Trail or along a forested path winding north from Critter Country. All three routes lead

to Black Spire Outpost on the planet Batuu, an exotic Outer Rim spaceport on the fringe of the Galactic Empire frontier that was once a hub
of commerce, before being bypassed by the hyperspace highways and
becoming a haven for outcasts. (Sounds suspiciously like the backstory
of Cars Land's Radiator Springs to us.)

This location—which hasn't yet been seen on the big screen but is
referenced in *Solo: A Star Wars Story,* the Star Tours attraction, and
various tie-in media—incorporates design elements similar to iconic
Star Wars locales such as Naboo, Yavin 4, Mos Eisley, and Maz Kanata's hideaway, without re-creating any single familiar setting.

Chronologically speaking, Galaxy's Edge is set during the *Star
Wars* sequel trilogy in the gap between *The Last Jedi* and *The Rise
of Skywalker,* and characters from outside that timeframe were initially forbidden to appear. Canonical restrictions have been relaxed
to allow popular characters from the Disney+ series *The Mandalorian*
to appear around Black Spire Outpost's bazaar, including Boba Fett,
Fennec Shand, Ahsoka Tano, Din Djarin, and Grogu (aka Baby Yoda).
However, these characters will not interact with those from the sequel
trilogy, like Rey or Kylo Ren.

Visitor reaction to Galaxy's Edge has been unexpectedly mixed,
with many finding the authenticity overwhelming, as this family from
Petaluma, California, opined:

> *We were definitely immersed in the world of Galaxy's Edge. It was
> almost too immersive—it didn't feel like we were even in Disneyland
> anymore. There aren't any obvious signs or directional arrows for the
> attractions, so you have to take your time and explore it to find all
> the hidden features.*

On the other hand, this reader from Ellicott City, Maryland, didn't
find Batuu immersive enough:

> *Batuu is cool and beautiful, but the cast members seemed lost, some-
> what uncertain of their roles, and not at all up to the standard of the
> immersive experience we had at the Wizarding World of Harry Pot-
> ter at Universal.*

Finally, this reader from Princeton, Indiana, just found the whole
Black Spire Outpost experience frustrating:

> *I was so excited to go there, as I'm a Star Wars fan, but in their aim
> to be authentic, I couldn't figure out where anything was! Was this
> a store, or just a facade? Was this the entry to a restaurant? Bath-
> rooms? Who knew! Maybe I just missed the signs that were in En-
> glish, or maybe it was the heat getting to me after standing in the sun
> for too long, but I walked away from Galaxy's Edge without going
> inside a single shop.*

GALAXY'S EDGE IN DETAIL

OUTSIDE OF THE AREA'S TWO HEADLINER RIDES (detailed on
pages 196–198), Batuu boasts a Marrakech-esque marketplace of shops

selling unique in-universe merchandise, some of which are practically attractions in themselves. Note how none of the packaging being sold bears the standard *Star Wars* or Disney parks logos, in order to maintain the illusion that all the souvenirs for sale were actually crafted by and for the Black Spire villagers themselves.

At **Savi's Workshop (★★★★½),** 14 guests at a time are led by "Gatherers" through the ritual-like process of building their own lightsabers, from picking a colorful kyber crystal, to selecting customizable handles from a range of eras and alignments. Lightsabers come with a price tag of $220. It's ludicrously expensive and time-consuming, but the experience at Savi's Workshop is pure Disney magic, and holding our lightsaber as it turned on for the first time was an emotional moment. It's fun picking out the components and building the lightsaber you've always wanted, and the custom hilts with removable light-up blades don't feel like cheap theme park toys; they feel solid in the hand, thanks to high-quality metal parts with great paint jobs. Sound emits from the bottom of each lightsaber, so every time you wave it around or clash against another one you'll hear the satisfying noises as heard in the *Star Wars* films. Advance reservations are required (see below), and you must arrive 20–60 minutes prior to your appointment, or you forfeit your turn.

You can proudly pair your lightsaber with a screen-accurate Jedi tunic ensemble from **Black Spire Outfitters,** but only wear it outside the park (costumes are still forbidden for guests 14 and older except during specially ticketed events).

Dok-Ondar's Den of Antiquities is overseen by a surly hammerheaded Ithorian who's the local godfather of black market goods; if you want to buy a historical character's lightsaber or Sith holocron, you may need to barter with the animatronic bi-mouthed bigwig, who haggles with guests through his human helpers. Sharp-eyed fans will spot Easter eggs from practically every *Star Wars* film and television show, including a 12-foot-tall taxidermy Wampa from *The Empire Strikes Back*.

Two shops allow guests to take an interactive pal back to their home planet. At Mubo's **Droid Depot (★★★★),** you can pick robot parts off of conveyor belts to build your own pint-size R-series or BB-series droid for $100 (and up), which will then communicate with its full-scale counterparts around the land. We didn't expect much going in to the Droid Depot building experience, but it ended up being a lot of fun to sift through the parts, really making the droid our own. You're then taken to a station where you can assemble the droid with actual tools. The experience wraps up with a delightful little moment where you activate the droid and it begins beeping and booping. The droids themselves are sturdy and made of good-quality components, and each includes a remote control. Preassembled droids, such as a chatty C-3PO, a DJ Rex bluetooth speaker, and even a $25,000 life-size R2-D2 (who occasionally roams the land), are also available.

Bina's Creature Stall allows guests to adopt a plush Porg puppet, an adorably disgusting writhing baby Rathtar, or a shoulder-sitting

Kowakian monkey-lizard like Salacious Crumb. All of the animals react to your touch with sound and movement, and the stall is stuffed with additional animatronic aliens that unfortunately can't be taken home. Kids should ask the shopkeeper for a free creature guide; complete all the scavenger hunt questions in the booklet and return it for a gift.

For kids young and old, Zabaka the **Toydarian Toymaker** has plush dolls of legendary characters that look handcrafted from upcycled scraps of fabric, alien musical instruments, and other unconventional playthings. For more typical T-shirts, hats, pins, and the like, you can either report to **First Order Cargo,** a spaceport hangar selling Dark Side propaganda, or sign up at the makeshift **Resistance Supply** stall and show your support for the freedom fighters. Finally, **Jewels of Bith** has pins, patches, and trinkets from across the Outer Rim.

When you get hungry, you'll find that just as much attention has gone into the food and drink of Galaxy's Edge as everything else; even the Coca-Cola sodas come in unique spherical bottles emblazoned in Aurebesh, the *Star Wars* alphabet. There is no sit-down table service inside the land, but you can rustle up galactic food-truck grub from **Docking Bay 7** or grab a sausage that's been grilled under a podracer engine at **Ronto Roasters.** More importantly, **Oga's Cantina** introduced publicly available alcohol to Disneyland Park, pouring exclusive drinks from Black Squadron beer to Jedi Mind Trick cocktails. See Part Eight for more dining details.

Note: Since Savi's Workshop can only handle around 42 builders per hour, and Oga's Cantina is always elbow-to-elbow, if you want a customized lightsaber or alien cocktail, you must make a reservation at 12 a.m. PST 60 days before the morning of your visit, either through the Disneyland app or at disneyland.com/savisworkshop or disneyland.com/cantina. Be aware that Oga's charges $10 a head for cancellations, and Savi's bills no-shows a staggering $220.

INTERACTIVITY IN GALAXY'S EDGE

GUESTS WHO INSTALL the Play Disney Parks app will find their smartphones turning into *Star Wars* datapads upon entering Galaxy's Edge. Embark on your personalized adventure by aligning yourself with either the Resistance heroes, First Order evildoers, or a shady gang of Scoundrels. Then you can check the app's jobs board to select a mission, such as recovering a missing shipment or recruiting new forces. The quests are completed through four touchscreen puzzle games, disguised as "tools": the **hack** tool lets slicers interact with droids, the **scan** tool uses your camera to decode cargo shipping labels, **translate** helps interpret alien languages, and **tune** intercepts coded radio communications. It all ties together with a land-wide outpost control meta-game, where opposing teams compete to claim the First Order's surveillance system control panels secreted in doorways around the outpost. The game continues until one side secures a majority of stations, and then resets for further play, with the winners receiving Galactic Credits good for digital collectibles that upgrade their avatars. There's also a **Batuu Bounty**

Hunters hide-and-seek game, exclusively for guests with MagicBand+. Look for the digital message board outside Droid Depot to get started by claiming a target, then follow the vibrations on your band until you can scan the doorway your quarry is hidden behind.

In addition, visitors can complete two different challenges inside the Rise of the Resistance ride queue and can play a third while waiting to fly the *Millennium Falcon.* Your experiences on those attractions were initially advertised as having a lasting impact, but after earning thousands of credits and dozens of virtual badges, we've yet to be hailed as a hero of the Resistance by any cast members.

Millennium Falcon: Smugglers Run *(Lightning Lane)* ★★★★

APPEAL BY AGE   PRESCHOOL ★★★½ **GRADE SCHOOL** ★★★★½ **TEENS** ★★★★½
YOUNG ADULTS ★★★★½   **OVER 30** ★★★★½   **SENIORS** ★★★★

What it is Interactive simulator ride. **Scope and scale** Headliner. **When to go** In the first or the last 2 hours of the day, or use the single-rider line. **Comments** Not to be missed. Must be 38″ tall to ride; switching-off option (see page 165). **Duration of ride** 4½ minutes. **Average wait in line per 100 people ahead of you** 3½ minutes. **Loading speed** Moderate–fast.

Queasy

DESCRIPTION AND COMMENTS This next-generation flight simulator lets guests fulfill their childhood fantasy of flying at the helm of Han Solo's *Millennium Falcon,* the "fastest hunk of junk in the galaxy." Guests approaching the attraction will see all 110 feet of the *Falcon* parked outside the spaceport but can't walk under or touch it.

Hondo Ohnaka, a pirate familiar to viewers of the *Clone Wars* and *Rebels* cartoons, has cut a deal with Chewbacca for use of the *Falcon* in his sketchy Ohnaka Transport Solutions company. Before boarding the bird, visitors enter Ohnaka's command center, where Hondo and his astromech assistant R5-P8 explain the setup, while the *Falcon* can be seen through the video screen "windows" behind them preparing for launch. Ohnaka is one of Disney's most advanced A-1000 animatronics, with electric motors capable of 50 functions. Riders then enter the *Falcon* through an umbilical bridge and are assigned to a six-person flight crew. While awaiting your turn, you can relax in the ship's instantly recognizable main hold, complete with a holographic chess board to pose behind (though not play) and a plethora of familiar props.

When the time arrives, your group of six guests appears to enter the *Falcon*'s one and only cockpit, thanks to a patented carousel system that keeps the small simulator cabins hidden from each other. Each rider is assigned an individual station—a pilot and copilot up front to steer around obstacles and activate the hyperdrive; two gunners in the middle to shoot down enemy fighters; and a pair of engineers in the rear to repair the ship when the pilots and gunners mess up—and computer-generated scenery is projected on an ultra-high-definition dome outside the windshield. Your mission sees you hijacking a trainload of Coaxium on Corellia, Han Solo's homeworld.

What separates this ride from other simulators (like Star Tours) is that its graphics are generated in real time by an array of Nvidia processors, creating cinema-quality images that react instantly to guests' actions. Watch for indicator rings to illuminate around certain controls, clueing you in to the correct moment to punch them.

Smugglers Run's queue and preshow represent some of Disney's best work, but members of our team were let down by the ride itself, reckoning it a marginal improvement over older simulators. Everyone loves being one of the pilots, who have the most say over how successful—or motion sick—their team ends up (Pro Tip: Go easy on the oversensitive steering). Gunners can pick "automatic targeting" to make it easier on themselves, while engineers just bash blinking buttons and get blasted with air. The latter two positions must use controls mounted 90 degrees to their side, making it awkward to focus on the screen, and although the ship will never destruct due to your incompetence, there's no way to opt out entirely from the interactivity.

If your team members can communicate and coordinate, flying the *Falcon* can truly feel like the Force is with you; if not, it often ends in fighting and frustration. Even though the attraction as a whole is ultimately entertaining, the simulator finale is somewhat of a D-Ticket disappointment in an E-Ticket wrapper.

TOURING TIPS Most guests who rope-drop Galaxy's Edge sprint to Rise of the Resistance, making the *Falcon* a less-stressful first stop. The full queue and preshow are worth experiencing your first time through, but the single-rider queue (which skips straight to the holochess room) can save you significant time on follow-up flights, as long as you don't mind being assigned to engineer. Guests who go standby or use Lightning Lane may request their preferred position. There are two simulators that allow disabled guests to experience the attraction without interrupting operations for other guests.

If you participate in the Datapad game, make sure your Bluetooth is on and your low power mode is off in order to receive credit for your mission.

Star Wars: Rise of the Resistance *(Lightning Lane)* ★★★★★

APPEAL BY AGE	PRESCHOOL ★★★★	GRADE SCHOOL ★★★★★	TEENS ★★★★★
YOUNG ADULTS ★★★★★		OVER 30 ★★★★★	SENIORS ★★★★½

What it is Next-generation dark ride. **Scope and scale** Super-headliner. **When to go** At rope drop, about 60–90 minutes after park opening, just before it closes, or whenever using Lightning Lane. **Comments** Not to be missed. Must be 40" tall to ride; switching-off option (see page 165). Individual Lightning Lane available (see page 97). **Duration of ride** About 20 minutes with all preshows; about 5 minutes for ride. **Average wait in line per 100 people ahead of you** 4 minutes. **Loading speed** Moderate–fast.

Dark   Queasy   Loud   Scary

DESCRIPTION AND COMMENTS The most epic indoor dark ride in Disneyland, Rise of the Resistance innovatively integrates at least four different ride experiences—including trackless vehicles, a motion simulator, walk-through environments, and even an elevator drop—into Disney's longest attraction ever.

The adventure begins as you are exploring the Resistance military outpost that has been laser-carved out of ancient stone. An animatronic BB-8 rolls in, accompanied by a hologram of Rey (Daisy Ridley), who recruits you to strike a blow against the First Order. Several dozen guests at a time exit the briefing room to board a standing-room-only shuttlecraft piloted by Nien Nunb from *Return of the Jedi;* you can feel the rumble as the ship breaks orbit and see Poe Dameron (Oscar Issac) accompanying you in his X-wing, until a Star Destroyer snags you in its tractor beam and sucks you into its belly.

When the doors to your shuttlecraft reopen, you've been convincingly transported into an enormous hangar, complete with 50 Stormtroopers, TIE Fighters, and a 100-foot-wide bay window looking into outer space. Cast members clad as First Order officers brusquely herd captive guests into holding rooms to await their interrogation by helmet-headed baddie Kylo Ren (Adam Driver) and General Hux (Domhnall Gleeson).

Before long, you're making a break for it in an eight-passenger (two four-seat rows) troop transport with an animatronic astromech droid as your driver; the car is capable of traveling without a fixed track, like EPCOT's Ratatouille ride. The ride blends robotic characters and enormous sets with video projections to create some of the most overwhelming environments ever seen in an indoor ride. One sequence sends you in between the legs of two towering AT-ATs while dodging laser fire from legions of Stormtroopers, while another puts you face-to-face with the Solo-slaying Ren. In the epic finale (spoiler alert), you'll survive an escape pod's dramatic crash back to Batuu, a brief-but-exhilarating plunge enhanced by digital projections.

TOURING TIPS We think Rise of the Resistance is the best ride Disney has produced in decades. It is the most popular attraction in the park, and the most complex ride in the resort, which means it experiences delays on an almost daily basis that cut into its already meager hourly carry capacity, so always check Disneyland's app to make sure it's operating before hiking to Batuu. Note that Disney's posted wait for Rise of the Resistance only represents your time until arriving at the first briefing room; there are 15-plus minutes of preshows until you reach the final ride vehicle.

At rope drop, Batuu-bound guests exit the hub into Frontierland and go through the tunnel behind Big Thunder Mountain. Early entry–eligible guests should wait near Red Rose Taverne for the passage to Big Thunder Trail to open, then take the second right into Galaxy's Edge. Don't try to beat the Rise of the Resistance rope-drop crowd by going through Critter Country; you will be forced to queue behind the crowd coming from Frontierland. Rise of the Resistance has become reasonably reliable in the mornings, but a delayed opening is still not uncommon, making your morning workout wasted. Even if everything goes according to plan and you're among the first few hundred guests inside the queue, it will take you 25–40 minutes to emerge from the attraction, so lines at the rest of the park's E-Tickets will be growing by the time you return to Planet Earth. Wait times for those lagging just a few minutes behind the leaders are often worse than at midday, so don't bother rope-dropping Rise if you aren't at the head of the pack. Better options for riding with a reasonable wait are to go about 60–90 minutes after park opening or late in the day, or spring for Individual Lightning Lane reservations. Be aware that Rise of the Resistance stops new guests from entering its queue one hour before park closing, or at 10 p.m. at the latest. Your wait should be modest if you get in the standby line during the last half hour of operation, after most Lightning Lane guests have redeemed their return times. Be sure to check Disneyland's app for the exact closing time, and be aware that you'll likely miss the evening fireworks if you join the queue less than an hour before showtime.

As far as physical thrills go, the ride is much less rough than Indiana Jones, and the drop at the end isn't nearly as intense as Mission: Breakout! at DCA, but it may still unsettle sensitive stomachs.

 FRONTIERLAND

FRONTIERLAND ADJOINS New Orleans Square as you move clockwise around the park. The focus here is on the Old West, with log stockades and pioneer trappings. Along the Big Thunder Trail to Fantasyland, where a petting zoo and barbecue restaurant once stood, you'll now find two tunnels leading to Star Wars: Galaxy's Edge. Be warned that, since the advent of Lightning Lane and Galaxy's Edge, Big Thunder Trail has become one of the most congested pinch-points in Disneyland Park.

Big Thunder Mountain Railroad *(Lightning Lane)* ★★★★

APPEAL BY AGE PRESCHOOL ★★★½ **GRADE SCHOOL** ★★★★½ **TEENS** ★★★★★
YOUNG ADULTS ★★★★★ **OVER 30** ★★★★½ **SENIORS** ★★★★½

What it is Tame roller coaster with exciting special effects. **Scope and scale** Headliner. **When to go** Before 10:30 a.m. or after 6:30 p.m. **Comments** Not to be missed. Must be 40″ tall to ride; switching-off option (see page 165). **Duration of ride** 3½ minutes. **Average wait in line per 100 people ahead of you** 3 minutes; assumes 5 trains operating. **Loading speed** Moderate–fast.

Scary Lose Things Queasy Rough Muss Your 'Do

DESCRIPTION AND COMMENTS On this coaster through and around a Disney "mountain," the idea is that you're on a runaway mine train during gold rush days. Along with the usual thrills of a roller coaster (about a 5 on a scary scale of 10), the ride showcases some first-rate examples of Disney creativity: lifelike scenes depicting a mining town, colorful caverns, and a dynamite-chewing goat, all humorously animated.

The ride's ramshackle exterior (featuring reconstructions of the Rainbow Ridge storefronts from 1956) belies a remarkably smooth track and impressive special effects, including a fog-fueled explosion inside the final lift hill.

TOURING TIPS A superb Disney experience but not too wild a roller coaster. The emphasis here is much more on the sights than on the thrill of the ride itself. Regardless, it's a not-to-be-missed attraction. Finally, give Big Thunder a try after dark. The lighting gives the attraction a whole new feel.

As an example of how differently guests experience Disney attractions, consider this letter from a reader in Brookline, Massachusetts:

As senior citizens with limited time, my friend and I confined our activities to those attractions rated as 4 or 5 stars for seniors. Because you listed it as not to be missed, we waited an hour to board Big Thunder Mountain Railroad, which you rated a 5 on a scary scale of 10. After living through 3½ minutes of pure terror, I rate that attraction a 15 on a scary scale of 10. We were so busy holding on and screaming and even praying for our safety that we did not see any falling rocks or a mining town. In our opinion, it should not be recommended for seniors or preschool children.

A woman from New England discovered that there's more to consider about Big Thunder than being scared:

I won't say it warranted a higher scare rating, but it was much higher on the lose-your-lunch meter.

Frontierland Shootin' Exposition ★★

What it is Electronic shooting gallery. **Scope and scale** Diversion. **When to go** Whenever convenient. **Comments** Costs extra.

DESCRIPTION AND COMMENTS A very elaborate electronic shooting gallery that costs a couple of quarters to play. One of the few attractions in Disneyland Park not included in the admission pass.

TOURING TIPS Good fun for those who like to shoot, but definitely not a place to blow time if you are on a tight schedule. You get 25 infrared bullets for your 50 cents. Try it on your second day if time allows.

Thumbs Up for the Whole Family

Mark Twain Riverboat ★★★

What it is Scenic boat ride. **Scope and scale** Minor attraction. **When to go** 11 a.m.–5 p.m. **Duration of ride** About 14 minutes. **Average wait to board** 10 minutes. **Loading speed** Fast—en masse.

DESCRIPTION AND COMMENTS This large-capacity paddle wheel riverboat navigates the waters around Tom Sawyer Island and Fort Wilderness. A beautiful craft, the riverboat provides a lofty perch from which to see Frontierland and New Orleans Square, as well as the impressive mountain range built to shield views of Galaxy's Edge. The *Mark Twain*, Sailing Ship *Columbia,* and Davy Crockett's Explorer Canoes travel through the Rivers of America. The show scenes include a home for Mike Fink (and one of his keelboats, a former Disneyland attraction) and 26 Audio-Animatronic animals; the audio spiel includes a musical nod to the New Orleans–set *The Princess and the Frog.*

TOURING TIPS One of three boat rides that survey the same real estate. Because the Explorer Canoes are slower in loading and the *Columbia* operates seasonally, we think the riverboat makes more efficient use of touring time. If you're not in the mood for a boat ride, many of the same sights can be seen by hiking around Tom Sawyer Island. The riverboat typically operates until 75 minutes before the park closes, except on *Fantasmic!* performance nights, when the voyages end at 5:45 p.m. If you're looking for a new experience aboard the *Mark Twain,* try asking a cast member if you can enjoy the trip from the pilothouse.

Pirate's Lair on Tom Sawyer Island ★★★

What it is Walk-through exhibit and rustic playground. **Scope and scale** Minor attraction. **When to go** Midmorning–late afternoon. **Duration of experience** For the raft, a little more than 1 minute one-way. As long as you want on the island. **Average wait in line per 100 people ahead of you** For raft, 4½ minutes; assumes 3 rafts operating. **Loading speed** For raft, moderate.

DESCRIPTION AND COMMENTS Pirate's Lair on Tom Sawyer Island manages to impart a sense of isolation from the rest of the park. It has hills to climb, tipsy bridges to cross, paths to follow, and a "rock climbing" play area. It's a delight for adults but a godsend for children who have been in tow all day. The realignment of Rivers of America removed a sliver of the island's northern tip, and the tree house and fort are permanently off-limits, but for the most part, this is the same oasis that's been entertaining kids for more than 60 years.

As an aside, a mother of four from Duncan, South Carolina, found Tom Sawyer Island as much a refuge as an attraction, writing:

In the afternoon, when the crowds were at their peak, the weather was hottest, and the kids started lagging behind, our organization began to suffer. We then retreated over to Tom Sawyer Island, which proved to be a true haven. My husband and I found a secluded bench and regrouped. Meanwhile, the kids were able to run freely in the shade. Afterward, we were ready to tackle the park again, refreshed and with direction once more.

The island has sets from the *Pirates of the Caribbean* films, such as William Turner's blacksmith shop, tucked into every nook and cranny. Kids exploring the caverns of Dead Man's Grotto will encounter spooky voices, ghostly apparitions, and buried treasure. Elsewhere, a sunken chest can be discovered by operating a hoist.

Evidently, you can't have a pirate's lair without a bunch of gore. A pop-up head and moving skeletal arm are just the beginning. There's also a "bone cage" and, our favorite, a treasure chest containing Davy Jones's beating heart. The Bootstrappers pirate band occasionally rides the rafts over to administer pirate oaths and lead sing-alongs, and Captain Jack Sparrow can sometimes be spotted stumbling along the island's shoreline.

TOURING TIPS Pirate's Lair is not one of Disneyland Park's more celebrated attractions, but it's certainly one of the most well-done. Attention to detail is excellent, and kids particularly revel in its adventuresome atmosphere. We think it's a must for families with children ages 5–15. If your party has only adults, visit the island on your second day, or stop by on your first day if you have seen the attractions you most wanted to see. We like the island from about noon until it closes at sunset. Access is by raft from Frontierland, and you may have to stand in line to board both coming and going. Two or three rafts operate simultaneously, however, and the round-trip is usually pretty time efficient. Tom Sawyer Island takes about 30 minutes or so to see, but many children could spend a whole day there.

Sailing Ship *Columbia (seasonal)* ★★★½

APPEAL BY AGE	PRESCHOOL ★★★★	GRADE SCHOOL ★★★★	TEENS ★★★
YOUNG ADULTS ★★★	OVER 30 ★★★★		SENIORS ★★★★½

What it is Scenic boat ride. **Scope and scale** Minor attraction. **When to go** 11 a.m.–5 p.m. **Duration of ride** About 14 minutes. **Average wait to board** 10 minutes. **Loading speed** Fast—en masse.

DESCRIPTION AND COMMENTS The *Columbia* is a stunning replica of a three-masted 18th-century merchant ship. Both its above- and belowdecks are open to visitors, with belowdecks outfitted to depict the life and work

Thumbs Up for the Whole Family

environment of the ship's crew in 1787. The *Columbia* operates only on busier days and runs the same route as the canoes and the riverboat.

TOURING TIPS The *Columbia,* along with the *Mark Twain* Riverboat, provides a short-wait, high-carrying-capacity alternative for cruising the Rivers of America. We found the beautifully crafted *Columbia* by far the most aesthetically pleasing and historically interesting of any of the three choices of boat rides on the Rivers of America. If you have time to be choosy, ride aboard the *Columbia.* After boarding, while waiting for the cruise to begin, tour below. Once the ride begins, come topside and stroll the deck, taking in the beauty and complexity of the rigging.

The *Columbia* does not usually require a long wait, which makes it a good bet during the crowded afternoon hours. Like the other attractions on the river, the *Columbia* closes early on *Fantasmic!* performance evenings.

FANTASYLAND

TRULY AN ENCHANTING PLACE, spread gracefully like a miniature alpine village beneath the towers of Sleeping Beauty Castle, Fantasyland is the heart of the park. A few Fantasyland attractions (namely Peter Pan's Flight and Snow White's Enchanted Wish) may close for fireworks during certain wind conditions but should reopen once the fire marshal gives the all clear.

Alice in Wonderland ★★★½

APPEAL BY AGE	PRESCHOOL ★★★★	GRADE SCHOOL ★★★★	TEENS ★★★½
YOUNG ADULTS ★★★½		OVER 30 ★★★½	SENIORS ★★★★

What it is Track ride in the dark. **Scope and scale** Minor attraction. **When to go** Before 11 a.m. or after 5 p.m. **Duration of ride** Almost 4 minutes. **Average wait in line per 100 people ahead of you** 12 minutes; assumes 16 cars operating. **Loading speed** Slow.

Dark   Muss Your 'Do

DESCRIPTION AND COMMENTS This attraction recalls the story of *Alice in Wonderland* with some nice surprises and colorful effects. Guests ride nifty caterpillar cars in this Disney spook-house adaptation. Though not a spring chicken, Alice is a third-generation Disney dark ride with more vibrant, evocative, and three-dimensional sets and characters than Pinocchio's Daring Journey or Mr. Toad's Wild Ride. This is also the only two-story Disney dark ride with an outdoor section. The ride turned 60 in 2018, but its classic charms still remain relevant with the aid of advanced projection effects, which utilize original hand-drawn animation to bring the static sets to life.

TOURING TIPS This is a well-done ride in the best Disney tradition, with familiar characters, good effects, and a theme you can follow—too bad it loads very slowly. Do not confuse it with the Mad Tea Party ride. This very popular attraction can build a lengthy line as the morning progresses, so we like to ride as early in the day as possible, usually right after Peter Pan's Flight.

Bibbidi Bobbidi Boutique ★★★½

This pricey beauty salon for little ones is located next to Sleeping Beauty Castle. Here, Fairy Godmothers–in–training make would-be princesses look like prom queens (or vice versa). A range of packages is offered, including everything from hair styling and makeup to princess gowns and accessories. The top-of-the-line package includes skip-the-line VIP access to the nearby Royal Hall princess meet and greet, which may be worth its *wait* in gold. If you have the bucks, the girls love it. For reservations, call ☎ 714-781-7895 up to 60 days in advance. A Winston, Oregon, mom thinks highly of Bibbidi Bobbidi:

> *Bibbidi Bobbidi Boutique is a must if traveling with little girls. Our party had three girls ages 4, 4, and 6, and this was their favorite and most memorable event of the trip. Even though we traveled during the off-season, it was hectic and a little unorganized. We made reservations and still had to wait 30 minutes, but once the girls were matched with their Fairy Godmother–in-training, we were absolutely pleased with the service. It is a little spendy, but it was completely worth it. The hair survived the rest of the day and looked perfect when they put their princess gowns on at night for the fireworks.*

Casey Jr. Circus Train   ★★½

APPEAL BY AGE	PRESCHOOL ★★★★½	GRADE SCHOOL ★★★½	TEENS ★★★
YOUNG ADULTS ★★★	OVER 30 ★★★½		SENIORS ★★★½

What it is Miniature train ride. **Scope and scale** Minor attraction. **When to go** Before 11 a.m. or after 5 p.m. **Duration of ride** A little under 4 minutes. **Average wait in line per 100 people ahead of you** 12 minutes; assumes 2 trains operating. **Loading speed** Slow.

DESCRIPTION AND COMMENTS A long-standing attraction and a pet project of Walt Disney, Casey Jr. circulates through a landscape of miniature towns, farms, and lakes. Visible from this ride are some stunning bonsai specimens, as well as some of the most manicured landscaping you are ever likely to see.

TOURING TIPS This ride covers the same sights as the Storybook Land Canal Boats but does it faster and with less of a wait. Accommodations for adults, however, are less than optimal on this ride, with some passengers having to squeeze into diminutive caged cars (after all, it is a circus train). If you do not have children in your party, you can enjoy the same sights more comfortably by riding the Storybook Land Canal Boats, which also benefit from live narration instead of Casey Jr.'s canned soundtrack.

A father of two toddlers from Menlo Park, California, explains that issues of redundancy were not uppermost in his children's minds.

> *Contrary to your advice, the Casey Jr. Circus Train and Storybook Land Canal Boats are totally different experiences—if you are 4 or younger. Hey, one is a boat, and one is a train! Seems obvious to the mind of a 4-year-old. We did both, and the kids loved both.*

Disneyland Railroad

DESCRIPTION AND COMMENTS Fantasyland and Mickey's Toontown share a station on Disneyland Railroad's route around the perimeter of the park. The station is located to the left of It's a Small World, next to Fantasyland Theatre. From this often-crowded boarding point, transportation is available to Tomorrowland, Main Street, and New Orleans Square. See the description beginning on page 183 for additional details regarding the sights en route.

Dumbo the Flying Elephant ★★½

**APPEAL BY AGE PRESCHOOL ★★★★½ GRADE SCHOOL ★★★★½ TEENS ★★★
YOUNG ADULTS ★★★ OVER 30 ★★★½ SENIORS ★★★½**

What it is Disneyfied midway ride. **Scope and scale** Minor attraction. **When to go** Before 10 a.m. or during parades, fireworks, or *Fantasmic!* performances. **Duration of ride** 1⅔ minutes. **Average wait in line per 100 people ahead of you** 12 minutes. **Loading speed** Slow.

DESCRIPTION AND COMMENTS A nice, tame, happy children's ride based on the lovable Disney flying elephant, this is an upgraded rendition of a ride that can be found at state fairs and amusement parks across the country. Shortcomings notwithstanding, Dumbo is the favorite Disneyland Park attraction of most preschoolers. A lot of readers take us to task for lumping Dumbo in with state-fair midway rides. These comments from a reader in Armdale, Nova Scotia, are representative:

I think you have acquired a jaded attitude. I know Dumbo is not for everybody, but when we took our oldest child (then just 4), the sign at the end of the line said there would be a 90-minute wait. He knew and he didn't care, and he and I stood for 90 blissful minutes waiting for his 90-second flight. Anything that a 4-year-old would wait for that long and that patiently must be pretty special.

TOURING TIPS This is a slow-loading ride that we recommend you bypass unless you are on a very relaxed touring schedule. If your kids are excited about Dumbo, try to get them on the ride before 10 a.m., during the parades or *Fantasmic!,* or just before the park closes. Also, consider this advice from an Arlington, Virginia, mom:

Grown-ups, beware! Dumbo is really a tight fit with one adult and two kids. My kids threw me out of their Dumbo, and I had to sit in a Dumbo all by myself. Pretty embarrassing, and my husband got lots of pictures.

Fantasyland Theatre ★★★★

**APPEAL BY AGE PRESCHOOL ★★★★ GRADE SCHOOL ★★★★½ TEENS ★★★
YOUNG ADULTS ★★★★ OVER 30 ★★★★½ SENIORS ★★★★**

What it is Musical stage show. **Scope and scale** Major attraction. **When to go** Check the app for schedule; arrive at least 15 minutes before showtime for the best seats. **Duration of show** Varies.

DESCRIPTION AND COMMENTS This venue is a sophisticated amphitheater where concerts and elaborate stage shows are performed according to the daily entertainment schedule. Better productions that have played here include *Beauty and the Beast Live, Snow White,* and *The Spirit of Pocahontas,* all musical stage adaptations of the respective Disney-animated features.

The latest production to take up residency here was *Tale of the Lion King,* a first-rate live retelling of the film featuring energetic African-inspired dance, percussive music, and traditional storytelling. No new long-term production for the Fantasyland Theatre has been announced since its closure in early 2024. During February, gospel music tribute concerts starring headliners with local choirs may be performed inside the Fantasyland Theatre. During Pixar Fest, the theatre hosts a temporary "Pixar Pals Playtime Party," where kids can play games, take photos, and watch Pixar shorts on the big screen. If a fresh production is running in this venue during your visit, it's probably well worth fitting it into your schedule during a multiday visit.

TOURING TIPS Performance times are listed in the app. Arrive at least 15 minutes early for optimal seating. The best seats are the ones farther back and slightly raised, in the center of the theater.

It's a Small World *(Lightning Lane)* ★★★★

APPEAL BY AGE   PRESCHOOL ★★★★½ **GRADE SCHOOL** ★★★★ **TEENS** ★★★½
YOUNG ADULTS ★★★½   **OVER 30** ★★★★   **SENIORS** ★★★★½

What it is World brotherhood–themed indoor boat ride. **Scope and scale** Major attraction. **When to go** Anytime except after a parade. **Duration of ride** 14 minutes. **Average wait in line per 100 people ahead of you** 2½ minutes; assumes busy conditions with 56 boats operating. **Loading speed** Fast.

DESCRIPTION AND COMMENTS A happy and upbeat attraction with a world-brotherhood theme and a catchy tune that will stick in your head for weeks. Small boats convey visitors on a tour around the world, with singing and dancing dolls showcasing the dress and culture of each nation. Almost everyone enjoys It's a Small World

Thumbs Up for the Whole Family

(well, there are those jaded folks who are put off by the dolls' homogeneous appearance, especially in light of the diversity theme) but it stands, along with the *Enchanted Tiki Room,* as an attraction that some could take or leave but that others consider one of the real masterpieces of Disneyland Park. More than 20 Disney and Pixar characters have been integrated into the classic attraction; tastefully crafted in the style of original artist Mary Blair, the additions don't detract from the ride, except in the tacky U.S.A. tribute added to the end. A mom from Castleton, Vermont, commented:

It's a Small World was like a pit stop in The Twilight Zone. *They were very slow unloading the boats, and we were stuck in a line of about six boats waiting to get out while the endless chanting of that song grated on my nerves. I told my husband that I was going to swim for it just to escape one more chorus.*

From November through New Year's, the attraction receives an annual holiday overlay inside the attraction as well as outside, featuring "Jingle Bells" and "Deck the Halls" instead of the usual earworm soundtrack. We particularly enjoy the nighttime light show and projection effects outside the attraction that happen every 15 minutes. At other times, a projection show featuring "We Don't Talk About Bruno" from *Encanto* is shown intermittently after sunset (see page 230).

A dad from New Brunswick, Canada, gives this advice for surviving the Happiest Cruise That Ever Sailed:

Ask to sit at the back of the boat. Pull out your earbuds once you're in the building, and blast some heavy metal. You'd be amazed how different and deceptively funny the ride becomes!

TOURING TIPS This fast-loading ride is usually a good bet during the busier times of the day. The boats are moved along by water pressure, which increases as boats are added. Thus, the more boats in service when you ride (up to a maximum total of 60), the shorter the duration of the ride (and wait). Small World is taken off-line in mid-October and reopened in November with a special Christmas holiday theme. Removal of the overlay also keeps the ride closed for several weeks after the holiday season. Note that while the loading can be very quick when many boats are running, the unloading can be very slow.

King Arthur Carrousel ★★★

**APPEAL BY AGE   PRESCHOOL ★★★★½   GRADE SCHOOL ★★★★   TEENS ★★★½
YOUNG ADULTS   ★★★½   OVER 30   ★★★½   SENIORS   ★★★½**

What it is Merry-go-round. **Scope and scale** Minor attraction. **When to go** Before 11:30 a.m. or after 5 p.m. **Duration of ride** A little more than 2 minutes. **Average wait in line per 100 people ahead of you** 7½ minutes. **Loading speed** Slow.

DESCRIPTION AND COMMENTS A merry-go-round to be sure, but certainly one of the most elaborate and beautiful you will ever see, especially when lit at night. Even adults enjoy the nostalgia of this showpiece carousel. A white horse named Jingles (with bells all over) pays tribute to Julie Andrews and her iconic role in *Mary Poppins*. She's the horse closest to the handicapped ramp.

TOURING TIPS Unless you have small children in your party, we suggest that you appreciate this ride from the sidelines. If your children want to ride, try to get them on before 11:30 a.m. or after 5 p.m. While nice to look at, the carousel loads and unloads very slowly.

Mad Tea Party ★★

**APPEAL BY AGE   PRESCHOOL ★★★★½   GRADE SCHOOL ★★★★½   TEENS ★★★★
YOUNG ADULTS   ★★★★   OVER 30   ★★★★   SENIORS   ★★★½**

What it is Midway-type spinning ride. **Scope and scale** Minor attraction. **When to go** Before 11 a.m. or after 5 p.m. **Duration of ride** 1½ minutes. **Average wait in line per 100 people ahead of you** 5½ minutes. **Loading speed** Slow.

Quasy   Muss Your 'Do

DESCRIPTION AND COMMENTS Well done in the Disney style, but still just an amusement park ride. *Alice in Wonderland's* Mad Hatter provides the theme, and patrons whirl around feverishly in big teacups. A rendition of this ride, sans

Disney characters, can be found at every local carnival and fair. Colorful overhead lanterns make the ride especially attractive after dark.

TOURING TIPS This ride, besides not being particularly special, loads notoriously slowly. Skip it on a busy schedule if the kids will let you. Ride in the morning of your second day if your schedule is more relaxed. A warning for parents: Teenagers like to lure adults onto the teacups and then turn the wheel in the middle (which makes the cup spin faster) until the adults are plastered against the side of the cup and on the verge of throwing up.

Matterhorn Bobsleds *(Lightning Lane)* ★★★½

APPEAL BY AGE	PRESCHOOL ★★★†	GRADE SCHOOL ★★★★	TEENS ★★★★½
YOUNG ADULTS ★★★★½		OVER 30 ★★★★	SENIORS ★★★½

†*Some preschoolers love Matterhorn Bobsleds; others are frightened.*

What it is Roller coaster. **Scope and scale** Major attraction. **When to go** During the first 90 minutes the park is open, during the hour before it closes, or anytime using the single-rider line. **Comments** Must be 42″ tall to ride; switching-off option (see page 165). **Duration of ride** 2½ minutes. **Average wait in line per 100 people ahead of you** 3½ minutes; assumes both tracks operating with 10 sleds per track with 23-second dispatch intervals. **Loading speed** Moderate.

Scary   Lose Things   Queasy   Rough   Muss Your 'Do

DESCRIPTION AND COMMENTS The Matterhorn is the most distinctive landmark on the Disneyland scene, visible from almost anywhere in the park. Open since 1959, the Matterhorn maintains its popularity and long lines year in and year out. Matterhorn Bobsleds is a roller coaster with an alpine motif. On the scary scale, the ride ranks about 6 on a scale of 10. The special effects don't compare to Space Mountain's, but they do afford a few surprises. Riders first glimpse the mysterious yeti during the initial uphill climb as a menacing silhouette distorted by ice, then they cruise past an ominous collection of old ride vehicles (including vintage bobsleds and an antique Skyway bucket) that the beast has hoarded. Finally, you'll come face-to-face with the furry legend not once but twice; the encounters are brief, but he moves with a fluid ferocity that his frozen cousin in Disney World's Expedition Everest can only dream of. Added padding has made the ride marginally less murderous on tailbones, but the three-passenger cars with individual seats are unfriendly to the long-legged. Tall riders are advised to ask for the middle or back rows, which have slightly more room, and slide their feet forward into the snug footwells on either side of the seat ahead. For the short-limbed, the front seat is usually the smoothest. But be warned that, wherever you sit, this is the bumpiest coaster in Disneyland's inventory. As a visitor from San Francisco, California, puts it:

The Matterhorn is really just a fast, jarring roller coaster. The [bobsleds] don't have much legroom, and my husband was very uncomfortable the whole ride!

A Richboro, Pennsylvania, dad disagrees with our scary rating of the Matterhorn:

My biggest disappointment was the Matterhorn. I understand it's iconic, but the notion that it could rate a 6 out of 10 on the scare factor is pure insanity. I'd rate it a 1! After the steep climb in the dark, you basically just go down in circles until you are left baffled that the "roller-coaster" ride is over.

TOURING TIPS Lines for the Matterhorn form as soon as the gates open and persist throughout the day. If you are a roller-coaster person, ride Space Mountain and then hurry over and hop on the Matterhorn. If roller coasters are not the end-all for you, we recommend choosing one of the other coasters or saving this one for a second day. The Matterhorn Bobsleds' single-rider queue is located to the right of the entrance at the ride's exit near Alice in Wonderland.

The Matterhorn is actually made up of two separate coasters. Though the two sides are similar, they are not identical; veterans say the left-hand Tomorrowland track is faster with steeper drops, while the Fantasyland side on the right is slightly longer with sharper turns.

Mr. Toad's Wild Ride   ★★★

APPEAL BY AGE   PRESCHOOL ★★★½   GRADE SCHOOL ★★★½   TEENS ★★★½
YOUNG ADULTS   ★★★½   OVER 30   ★★★½   SENIORS   ★★★★

What it is Track ride in the dark. **Scope and scale** Minor attraction. **When to go** Before 11 a.m. **Duration of ride** Almost 2 minutes. **Average wait in line per 100 people ahead of you** 9 minutes; assumes 12 cars operating. **Loading speed** Slow.

Dark

DESCRIPTION AND COMMENTS Mr. Toad's Wild Ride is a twisting, curving ride in the dark that passes two-dimensional sets and props. There are a couple of clever effects, but basically it's at the technological basement of the Disney attraction mix. Though Mr. Toad doesn't compare well with newer high-tech attractions, many Disneyland veterans appreciate it because it's one of a handful of attractions remaining from the park's beginning, and Len considers it his favorite Fantasyland dark ride. Hannah, an official Touring Plans Stunt Kid™, summed the ride's appeal up perfectly:

Mr. Toad's Wild Ride is awesome, and everyone should go on it because it's about a toad who goes to hell. I feel like that's a neglected topic in theme parks these days.

TOURING TIPS Not a great but certainly a popular attraction. Lines build early in the day and never let up. Catch Mr. Toad before 11 a.m. Parents beware: There are some loud sound effects as well as a spooky "hell" scene at the end of the attraction.

Peter Pan's Flight   ★★★★

APPEAL BY AGE   PRESCHOOL ★★★★½   GRADE SCHOOL ★★★★½   TEENS ★★★★
YOUNG ADULTS   ★★★★   OVER 30   ★★★★½   SENIORS   ★★★★½

Thumbs Up for the Whole Family

What it is Indoor fantasy-adventure ride. **Scope and scale** Minor attraction. **When to go** Immediately at park opening or after 6 p.m. **Duration of ride** Just over 2 minutes. **Average wait in line per 100 people ahead of you** 10 minutes; assumes 13 ships operating. **Loading speed** Slow.

DESCRIPTION AND COMMENTS Though it is not considered one of Disneyland Park's major attractions, Peter Pan's Flight is superbly designed and absolutely delightful, with a happy theme, a reunion with some unforgettable Disney characters, beautiful effects, and charming music. Tiny pirate ships suspended from an overhead track launch you from Wendy's window to fly over nighttime London and on to Never Land and an encounter with Captain Hook, Mr. Smee, and the ubiquitous crocodile. Over the years, updated special effects have been added, including digital pixie dust projections and floating figures of Wendy and the Darling boys in the nursery scene. The colorful London flyover and rippling water effects are especially lovely. We think Peter Pan's Flight is the best attraction in Fantasyland.

TOURING TIPS This attraction has a consistent wait of at least 20 minutes within the first few minutes of park operation. On the busiest of days, we've seen the wait go up to more than 60 minutes at the extreme. Try to ride right at rope drop or after 6 p.m., during the afternoon or evening parade(s), or during a performance of *Fantasmic!*

Pinocchio's Daring Journey ★★½

APPEAL BY AGE	PRESCHOOL ★★★½	GRADE SCHOOL ★★★½	TEENS ★★★
YOUNG ADULTS ★★★		OVER 30 ★★★½	SENIORS ★★★½

What it is Track ride in the dark. **Scope and scale** Minor attraction. **When to go** Before noon or after 3:30 p.m. **Duration of ride** Almost 3 minutes. **Average wait in line per 100 people ahead of you** 8 minutes; assumes 15 cars operating. **Loading speed** Slow.

DESCRIPTION AND COMMENTS This is another twisting, curving track ride in the dark, this time tracing the adventures of Pinocchio as he tries to find his way home. The action is hard to follow, and it lacks continuity. Though the sets are three-dimensional and more visually compelling than, say, Mr. Toad, the story line is dull and fails to engage the guest. In the ride's defense, it features some deliciously trippy Pleasure Island imagery, a clever vanishing Blue Fairy effect, and almost always an empty queue.

TOURING TIPS The word must be out about Pinocchio because the lines are seldom very long. Still, the longest waits occur 11:30 a.m.–4:30 p.m. While most small children seem to handle this ride well, a Manhattan mom warns:

Pinocchio is quite scary; it seems to feature one nightmare after another, particularly if a child is not familiar with the story/movie. Our son refused to ride any other rides for an hour or two after it, and it was our first one!

Royal Hall at Fantasy Faire ★★★

APPEAL BY AGE	PRESCHOOL ★★★★★	GRADE SCHOOL ★★★★½	TEENS ★★★½
YOUNG ADULTS ★★★★★		OVER 30 ★★★★	SENIORS ★★★★★

What it is Princess meet and greet. **Scope and scale** Major attraction. **When to go** If meeting the princesses is important to your little ones, try to arrive 15 minutes before it opens at 10 a.m. **Duration of experience** 5 minutes. **Probable waiting time** 35–60 minutes.

DESCRIPTION AND COMMENTS This indoor meet and greet just off the central hub features three princesses always on duty (often Ariel, Cinderella, and Snow White). The usual Disneyland queue (mercifully mostly shaded) must be endured to meet and be photographed, but the Royal Hall's intimate wood-paneled interior actually houses two identical meeting areas with duplicate trios of princesses (perhaps the product of an EPCOT cloning experiment?) for double the greeting capacity.

TOURING TIPS Little girls love the Royal Hall, as do boys age 6 and younger. Look around the courtyard for the snoozing animatronic Figaro kitty, crank-operated Clopin's music box, and twinkling hair on the *Tangled*-inspired tower. On busy days, you may be barred from bringing your stroller into Fantasy Faire, unless your child is asleep in it, so teach your kid to play possum on command if you don't want to park.

Royal Theatre at Fantasy Faire ★★★★

APPEAL BY AGE PRESCHOOL ★★★★½ GRADE SCHOOL ★★★★ TEENS ★★½
YOUNG ADULTS ★★★★½   OVER 30 ★★★★   SENIORS ★★★★½

What it is Interactive storytelling show. **Scope and scale** Minor attraction. **When to go** Check the app for showtimes. **Duration of show** 20 minutes. **Probable waiting time** 30 minutes.

DESCRIPTION AND COMMENTS Royal Theatre, which once hosted jazz greats such as Dizzy Gillespie, now houses a rotating repertory of 20-minute stage shows dramatizing the tales of popular Disney royalty. *Tangled* and *Beauty and the Beast* are the featured fables, with Rapunzel and Flynn Rider or Belle joining in their respective reenactments, accompanied by narrators Mr. Smythe and Mr. Jones, milkmaid stagehands, and a live pianist. Rather than straightforward retellings, these fast-paced comic condensations capture the anarchic slapstick of a Renaissance fair trunk show. Witty enough to keep adults far outside the target demographic awake, the Royal Theatre's shows are the sleeper hits of Fantasy Faire. Stick around after the curtain falls for an autograph session with the stars.

The Royal Theatre usually presents three shows of *Tangled* and three of *Beauty and the Beast,* swapping daily which one goes in the morning and which in the afternoon. If you must pick between those two, *Tangled* has the better script.

TOURING TIPS The theater only seats a little more than 200 people (with room for 50 kids on the floor up front), so you may want to line up 30 or more minutes before showtime or simply settle for standing right outside the theater.

Sleeping Beauty Castle ★★★

APPEAL BY AGE PRESCHOOL ★★★★ GRADE SCHOOL ★★★½ TEENS ★★★
YOUNG ADULTS ★★★½   OVER 30 ★★★½   SENIORS ★★★½

What it is Walk-through exhibit. **Scope and scale** Minor attraction. **When to go** Anytime. **Duration of exhibit** Varies; about 10 minutes. **Probable waiting time** Usually none.

DESCRIPTION AND COMMENTS Disneyland Park's most famous icon, Sleeping Beauty Castle is at the heart of Disneyland and serves as a stage for shows and special events. For the non-claustrophobic, the Sleeping Beauty Castle walk-through exhibit is a miniature 3-D series, arranged along a narrow passage inside the castle, that tells the story of Sleeping Beauty. Originally opened on April 29, 1957, to preview the upcoming 1959 movie *Sleeping Beauty,* and then closed for most of a decade after 9/11, the attraction reopened in 2008 with new dioramas reflecting the style of artist Eyvind Earle, who gave *Sleeping Beauty* its distinctive design. In this version there are animated scenes, interactive elements, and Pepper's Ghost projection effects (as also seen in Haunted Mansion).

TOURING TIPS The entrance is on the Fantasyland side of the castle near the passageway to Fantasy Faire and Frontierland. The exhibit allows for one-way traffic only. It can get a bit crowded inside, but there should rarely be a line outside the attraction. For guests unable to climb up and down two flights of stairs, a small alcove to the left of the bridge to Tomorrowland contains a collection of the animations, as well as music, allowing you to experience the attraction's elements without walking. The viewing location runs on a loop, so you might have to watch it out of order.

Snow White's Enchanted Wish ★★★½

APPEAL BY AGE	PRESCHOOL ★★★★	GRADE SCHOOL ★★★½	TEENS ★★★½
YOUNG ADULTS ★★★½		OVER 30 ★★★½	SENIORS ★★★★

What it is Track ride in the dark. **Scope and scale** Minor attraction. **When to go** Before 11 a.m. or after 5 p.m. **Duration of ride** Almost 2 minutes. **Average wait in line per 100 people ahead of you** 9 minutes; assumes 10 cars operating. **Loading speed** Slow.

DESCRIPTION AND COMMENTS Here, you ride in a mining car in the dark through a series of sets drawn from *Snow White and the Seven Dwarfs*. The attraction, which previously had a *Perils of Pauline* flavor and featured Snow White as she narrowly escapes harm at the hands of the wicked witch, was revamped in 2021 to remove the parts that made generations of preschoolers poop their pants in favor of additional friendly dwarfs and a happy ending. High-tech projection effects enhance many scenes, and the evil queen's classic magic mirror transformation is thankfully still intact.

TOURING TIPS Snow White's update defanged the ride's legendary creepiness, making it now a much more compelling pick for families with easily frightened children, and the updated effects will appeal to adults. Experience it if the lines are not too long or on a second-day visit. Ride before 11 a.m. or after 5 p.m., if possible.

Storybook Land Canal Boats ★★★

APPEAL BY AGE	PRESCHOOL ★★★★	GRADE SCHOOL ★★★½	TEENS ★★★
YOUNG ADULTS ★★★½		OVER 30 ★★★½	SENIORS ★★★½

What it is Scenic boat ride. **Scope and scale** Minor attraction. **When to go** Between an hour after opening and 10:30 a.m. or after 5:30 p.m. **Duration of ride** 6½ minutes. **Average wait in line per 100 people ahead of you** 15 minutes; assumes 7 boats operating. **Loading speed** Slow.

Thumbs Up for the Whole Family

DESCRIPTION AND COMMENTS Guide-operated boats wind along canals situated beneath the same miniature landscapes visible from the Casey Jr. Circus Train. This ride—offering stellar examples of bonsai cultivation, selective pruning, and miniaturization—is a must for landscape-gardening enthusiasts. The landscapes include scenes from more recent Disney features—such as the kingdom of Arendelle and Elsa's ice palace from *Frozen*—in addition to those from such classics as *The Wind in the Willows* and *The Three Little Pigs*. We find Storybook Land to be a serene respite from the surrounding overstimulation, but not every guest gets the attraction, as this California reader will attest:

I thought there would be beautiful flowers to see or interesting dioramas, but you just sail past small buildings meant to look like cottages, castles, and so on. There aren't even any little figurines or characters in it.

TOURING TIPS The boats are much more comfortable than the train, the view of the miniatures is better, and the pace is more leisurely. On the downside, the lines are long and slow-moving. The ride itself also takes a lot of time. Our recommendation is to ride Casey Jr. if you have children or are in a hurry. Take the boat if your party is all adults or your pace is more leisurely. Best of all, the boats' pilots deliver live narration that (depending on the driver) can be delightfully droll. If you ride the boats, try to get on before 10:30 a.m., but the ride often starts the morning with only two boats in circulation, so avoid it for the first hour of the day. If the queue isn't prohibitive, this ride is especially appealing after sunset, when the creative lighting adds a whole new dimension.

MICKEY'S TOONTOWN

MICKEY'S TOONTOWN IS SITUATED across the Disneyland Railroad tracks from Fantasyland. Its entrance is a tunnel that opens into Fantasyland just to the left of It's a Small World. Mickey's Toontown was inspired by the Disney animated feature *Who Framed Roger Rabbit?*, in which humans were able to enter the world of cartoon characters. It was reinvigorated in early 2023 with the addition of **Mickey & Minnie's Runaway Railway,** a next-generation trackless dark ride that first debuted at Walt Disney World in 2020. A green space called **CenTOONial Park** was also added, featuring figures of Mickey and Minnie in a flowering fountain, along with a "dreaming tree" inspired by Walt Disney's hometown, with shade to relax under and roots to clamber over. The attractions previously known as Gadget's Go Coaster, Goofy's House, and Donald's Boat all returned with updated themes and play features, while **Mickey's House, Minnie's House,** and **Roger Rabbit's Car Toon Spin** reopened with only minor changes.

If you want to see characters, Mickey's Toontown is the place to go. In addition to Mickey, who receives guests all day (except during parades) in his dressing room, and Minnie, who entertains in her house, you are likely to bump into such august personages as Goofy, Pete, and Pluto lurking around the streets.

Mickey's Toontown is rendered with masterful attention to artistic humor and detail. The businesses around the Fireworks Factory have interactive doorbells that elicit audible responses from their occupants. Across the street, the sidewalk is littered with crates containing strange contents addressed to exotic destinations. If you pry open the top of one of the crates (which is easy to do), the crate will emit a noise consistent with its contents. A box of "train parts," for example, broadcasts the sound of a racing locomotive when you lift the top.

Be forewarned that Mickey's Toontown is not very large, especially in comparison to neighboring Fantasyland. A tolerable crowd in most of the other lands will seem like Times Square on New Year's Eve in Mickey's Toontown. The addition of a major new attraction has made Toontown even more congested than before. Space is at such a premium that guests may be forced to park strollers outside the land.

Finally, be aware that Toontown and its attractions (including Mickey & Minnie's Runaway Railway) will close at 8 p.m. on nights when fireworks are scheduled, then reopen at 10 p.m. if the park stays open until at least 11 p.m. A "kiss goodnight" light display illuminates CenTOONial park prior to the show.

Chip 'n' Dale's GADGETcoaster ★★½

Rough   Lose Things

What it is Small roller coaster. **Scope and scale** Minor attraction. **When to go** Before 10:30 a.m., during the parades or *Fantasmic!* in the evening, or just before the park closes. **Comments** Must be 35" to ride; expectant moms shouldn't ride. **Duration of ride** About 50 seconds. **Average wait in line per 100 people ahead of you** 10 minutes. **Loading speed** Slow.

DESCRIPTION AND COMMENTS Toontown is home to a very small roller coaster themed after characters from the Rescue Rangers. The zippy ride is over so quickly that you hardly know that you've been anywhere. In fact, of the 52 seconds the ride is in motion, 32 seconds are consumed in exiting the loading area, being ratcheted up the first hill, and braking into the off-loading area. The actual time you spend careening around the track is a whopping 20 seconds.

TOURING TIPS This beginner roller coaster for young children is the perfect attraction to gauge the pluckiness of your little ones before tossing them to the coyotes on Big Thunder Mountain Railroad. The coaster cars are not very comfortable for adults, and you can expect a fair amount of whiplash, but as noted, the ride takes less than a minute. The coaster is both slow-loading and visually attractive, so you can expect long waits, except during the first 30 minutes that Toontown is open.

Disneyland Railroad

DESCRIPTION AND COMMENTS Mickey's Toontown and Fantasyland share a station on Disneyland Railroad's route around the perimeter of the park. This station becomes fairly crowded on busy days. If you are interested primarily in getting there, it may be quicker to walk. See the description beginning on page 183 for additional details regarding the sights en route.

Donald's Duck Pond ★★

What it is Creative play area. **Scope and scale** Diversion. **When to go** Anytime

DESCRIPTION AND COMMENTS Another children's play area, this time with a tugboat theme. Children can't enter the ship itself, but there are interactive "portholes" with simple underwater effects and a splash pad full of fountains around the boat to frolic in.

TOURING TIPS Usually there isn't any sort of organized line or queuing area here. Enjoy this play area at your leisure and stay as long as you like.

Goofy's How-To-Play Yard ★★½

| APPEAL BY AGE | PRESCHOOL ★★★★★ | GRADE SCHOOL ★★★★½ | TEENS ★★ |
| YOUNG ADULTS ★★★ | OVER 30 ★★★ | | SENIORS ★★★½ |

What it is A whimsical children's play area. **Scope and scale** Diversion. **When to go** Anytime.

DESCRIPTION AND COMMENTS This small but nicely themed indoor-outdoor play area for the under-6 set features fully accessible equipment for children of all abilities. Out back is Max's fort, with a short net climb and slides. Inside, Rube Golbergian candy-making appliances send colorful balls careening around Goofy's kitchen. Usually not too crowded, this play area is a pleasant place to let preschoolers ramble and parents relax while older sibs enjoy more adventurous attractions.

TOURING TIPS There's not a lot of shade, so visit early or late in the day.

Mickey & Minnie's Runaway Railway *(Lightning Lane)* ★★★★½

| APPEAL BY AGE | PRESCHOOL ★★★★ | GRADE SCHOOL ★★★★½ | TEENS ★★★★½ |
| YOUNG ADULTS ★★★★½ | OVER 30 ★★★★½ | | SENIORS ★★★★ |

What it is Indoor dark ride through the new Mickey Mouse cartoon universe. **Scope and scale** Headliner. **When to go** During the first hour after the park opens or in the last hour before park closing. **Comment** Not to be missed. **Duration of ride** 5 minutes. **Average wait in line per 100 people ahead of you** 4 minutes; assumes all trains operating. **Loading speed** Moderate.

DESCRIPTION AND COMMENTS Disney restarted regular production of Mickey Mouse cartoons from 2013 to 2023. Mostly written and directed by Paul Rudish, these 7-minute vignettes—more than 120 were made in total—are minor masterpieces of storytelling, animation, and humor. Mickey and Minnie sport a retro-1930s look, complete with "pie eyes." In settings across the world, and sometimes entirely in languages other than English, the Mouses, Goofy, Donald, and the rest of the gang embark on crazy adventures that always seem to end up just fine. If you haven't seen them, plan on binge-watching them with your kids (they're all on YouTube and Disney+).

Runaway Railway places you in the center of one of those cartoons, letting guests literally step through the movie screen during an explosive pre-show. The premise is that you're on an out-of-control railroad car, courtesy of Goofy. You careen, gently, through large cartoon show scenes, from tropical islands to cities to out-of-control factories. In each scene, Mickey and Minnie attempt to save you from disaster, with mixed results. In each scene, Disney uses a mix of traditional, three-dimensional painted sets and the latest in video projection technology to show movement and special effects. It's all done very well, and there are so many things to see on either side of the ride—with each car in the train getting a slightly different view—that it's impossible to catch everything in one or two rides. The Disneyland version of Runaway Railway has been enhanced with an expanded queue that doubles as a museum of Mickey Mouse memorabilia from across the decades, plus some expanded and enhanced show scenes not seen in the Walt Disney World version, making an excellent family-friendly adventure even more epic.

TOURING TIPS Runaway Railway was a sleeper hit at Disney's Hollywood Studios in Orlando, but average wait times for Disneyland's version rarely exceed an hour. Even so, your best bet is to get in line within an hour after the park opens or late in the evening after the fireworks. Runaway Railway initially required riders to secure a Virtual Queue boarding group (see page 107) or purchase individual Lightning Lane, but it now offers standard standby and Genie+ options.

If you ride Runaway Railway multiple times, keep your eyes peeled for "subplots" involving a chubby parakeet, a tenacious crab, and Pluto's pursuit of Mickey's lost picnic basket.

Mickey's House and Meet Mickey   ★★★

APPEAL BY AGE   **PRESCHOOL** ★★★★★   **GRADE SCHOOL** ★★★★   **TEENS** ★★★½
YOUNG ADULTS   ★★★★   **OVER 30** ★★★★   **SENIORS** ★★★★

What it is Walk-through tour of Mickey's House and Movie Barn, ending with a personal visit with Mickey. **Scope and scale** Minor attraction. **When to go** Before 10:30 a.m. or after 5:30 p.m. **Duration of tour** 15–30 minutes (depending on the crowd). **Average wait in line per 100 people ahead of you** 10 minutes.

DESCRIPTION AND COMMENTS Mickey's House is the starting point of a self-guided tour that winds through the famous mouse's house, into his backyard, past Pluto's doghouse, and then into Mickey's Movie Barn. This last stop harks back to the so-called "barn" studio where Walt Disney created a number of the earlier Mickey Mouse cartoons. Once in the Movie Barn, guests are entertained by clips from Paul Rudish's series of retro-styled Mickey Mouse shorts while awaiting admittance to Mickey's Dressing Room.

In small groups of one or two families, guests are ultimately conducted into the dressing room where Mickey awaits to pose for photos and sign autographs. The visit is not lengthy (2–4 minutes), but there is adequate time for all of the children to hug, poke, and admire the star.

TOURING TIPS The cynical observer will discern immediately that Mickey's House, backyard, Movie Barn, and so on are no more than a cleverly devised queuing area to deliver guests to Mickey's Dressing Room for the mouse encounter. For those with some vestige of child in their personalities, however, the preamble serves to heighten anticipation while providing the opportunity to get to know the corporate symbol on a more personal level. Mickey's House is well conceived and contains a lot of Disney memorabilia. You will notice that children touch everything as they proceed through the house, hoping to find some artifact that is not welded or riveted into the set (an especially tenacious child during one of our visits was actually able to rip a couple of books from a bookcase).

Meeting Mickey and touring his house are best done during the first 2 hours that Toontown is open or in the evening during *Fantasmic!*. If meeting Mickey is at the top of your child's list, consider taking the Disneyland Railroad from Main Street to the Toontown/Fantasyland Station as soon as you enter the park. Some children are so obsessed with seeing Mickey that they cannot enjoy anything else until they get Mickey in the rearview mirror. (Mickey is not available during parades.)

Minnie's House ★★½

APPEAL BY AGE	PRESCHOOL ★★★★★	GRADE SCHOOL ★★★★½	TEENS ★★
YOUNG ADULTS ★★★		OVER 30 ★★★½	SENIORS ★★★½

What it is Walk-through exhibit and character-greeting opportunity. **Scope and scale** Minor attraction. **When to go** Before 10:30 a.m. **Duration of tour** About 10 minutes. **Average wait in line per 100 people ahead of you** 12 minutes.

DESCRIPTION AND COMMENTS Minnie's House consists of a self-guided tour through the various rooms and backyard of Mickey Mouse's main squeeze. Similar to Mickey's House, only predictably more feminine, Minnie's House likewise showcases some fun Disney memorabilia. Among the highlights of the short tour are the fanciful appliances in Minnie's kitchen. Like Mickey, Minnie is usually present to receive guests.

TOURING TIPS Minnie's House can't accommodate as many guests as Mickey's House. See Minnie early and before Mickey to avoid waiting outdoors in a long queue. Minnie is not available during parades and normally knocks off for the day before Mickey; check the app for her appearance schedule.

Roger Rabbit's Car Toon Spin (*Lightning Lane*) ★★★½

APPEAL BY AGE	PRESCHOOL ★★★½	GRADE SCHOOL ★★★½	TEENS ★★★
YOUNG ADULTS ★★★		OVER 30 ★★★½	SENIORS ★★★

What it is Track ride in the dark. **Scope and scale** Major attraction. **When to go** Before 10:30 a.m. or after 6:30 p.m. **Duration of ride** A little more than 3 minutes. **Average wait in line per 100 people ahead of you** 9 minutes. **Loading speed** Slow.

Dark   Rough   Queasy

DESCRIPTION AND COMMENTS In this so-called dark ride, guests become part of a cartoon plot. The concept is that you ride in a more-or-less uncontrollably spinning cartoon taxi, following along with Roger Rabbit's glamazon gumshoe wife, Detective Jessica Rabbit, while she investigates a weasel-related crime spree in Toontown. This spinning continues as the cab passes through a variety of sets populated by cartoon and Audio-Animatronic characters and punctuated by simulated explosions. As a child of the 1960s put it, "It was like combining Mr. Toad's Wild Ride with the Mad Tea Party while tripping on LSD." The ride features an elaborate indoor queue and some of the better special effects found inside Disneyland's cartoon dark rides, climaxing in a clever "portable hole" mirror gag that remains head-scratchingly effective.

The main problem with the Car Toon Spin is that, because of the spinning, you are often pointed in the wrong direction to appreciate (or even see) many of the better visual effects. Furthermore, the story line is loose. The attraction lacks the continuity and humor of Pirates of the Caribbean or the suspense of Haunted Mansion.

The spinning, incidentally, can be controlled by the guests. If you don't want to spin, you don't have to. If you do elect to spin, you still will not be able to approach the eye-popping speed attainable on the teacups at the Mad Tea Party. Sluggish spinning aside, our advice for those who are at all susceptible to motion sickness is not to get near this ride if you are touring with anyone under 21 years of age.

A reader from Milford, Michigan, echoed our sentiments, lamenting:

The most disappointing ride to me was Roger Rabbit's Car Toon Spin. I stood in line for 45 minutes for a fun house ride, and the wheel was so difficult to operate that I spent most of my time trying to steer the bloody car and missed the point of the ride.

TOURING TIPS The ride is popular for its novelty, and it is one of the few Mickey's Toontown attractions that parents (with strong stomachs) can enjoy with their children. Because the ride stays fairly thronged with people all day long, ride in the first 90 minutes that Toontown is open, during parades or *Fantasmic!,* or in the hour before the land closes.

█ TOMORROWLAND

LOCATED DIRECTLY TO THE RIGHT of the central hub is Tomorrowland. This themed area is a futuristic mix of rides and experiences that relate to technological development and what life will be like in the years to come.

Tomorrowland's design reflects a nostalgic vision of the future as imagined by dreamers and scientists in the 1920s and 1930s. Frozen in time, Tomorrowland conjures up visions of Buck Rogers (whom nobody under age 60 remembers), fanciful mechanical rockets, and metallic cities spread beneath towering obelisks. Disney refers to Tomorrowland as the "Future That Never Was." *Newsweek* dubbed it "retro-future."

Disney Vacation Club members (and their guests) can visit the Star View Station on the second floor of **Star Wars Launch Bay**, a collection of memorabilia displays and character meet and greets that has been "temporarily" closed since the pandemic. Tomorrowland's DVC lounge offers phone-charging stations, Wi-Fi, and air-conditioning, as well as complimentary soft drinks. Its decor features murals of artwork by Mary Blair and John Hench referencing extinct attractions like Monsanto's Adventure Thru Inner Space, along with displays of Disneyland artifacts, including a 1950s-era K7 Space Suit. You must show your DVC membership card to enter.

The **Tomorrowland Theater,** located directly in front of Space Mountain, has also been defunct for several years. It previously screened earsplitting 3-D films (such as Michael Jackson's *Captain EO*) and movie previews.

Astro Orbitor ★★

**APPEAL BY AGE   PRESCHOOL ★★★★½   GRADE SCHOOL ★★★★   TEENS ★★★½
YOUNG ADULTS   ★★★   OVER 30   ★★★   SENIORS   ★★½**

What it is Very mild midway-type thrill ride. **Scope and scale** Minor attraction. **When to go** Before 10 a.m. or during the hour before the park closes. **Duration of ride** 1½ minutes. **Average wait in line per 100 people ahead of you** 12½ minutes. **Loading speed** Slow.

Thumbs Up for the Whole Family

Queasy

DESCRIPTION AND COMMENTS The Astro Orbitor is a visually appealing midway-type ride involving small rockets that rotate on arms around a central axis. Be aware that the Astro Orbitor flies higher and faster than Dumbo, and it frightens some small children.

TOURING TIPS Astro Orbitor is slow to load and expendable on any schedule. If you want to take a preschooler on this ride, place your child in the seat first and then sit down yourself.

Autopia (*Lightning Lane*) ★★½

APPEAL BY AGE PRESCHOOL ★★★★½ **GRADE SCHOOL** ★★★★ **TEENS** ★★★½
YOUNG ADULTS ★★★ **OVER 30** ★★★ **SENIORS** ★★★

What it is Drive-'em-yourself miniature cars. **Scope and scale** Minor attraction. **When to go** Before 10 a.m. or after 5 p.m. **Comments** Must be at least 54″ tall to drive unassisted; must be at least 32″ tall to ride (and one guest in car must be at least 54″ tall). **Duration of ride** Approximately 4½ minutes. **Average wait in line per 100 people ahead of you** 3½ minutes; assumes 35 cars operating on each track. **Loading speed** Moderate.

DESCRIPTION AND COMMENTS An elaborate miniature freeway with gasoline-powered cars that travel at speeds of up to 7 miles per hour. Autopia was last updated in 2016 with preshow displays (look for clips from the 1958 educational cartoon *Magic Highway USA*) and minimally moving roadside tableaus featuring Honda's humanoid robot ASIMO and his robo-bird buddy, but it still has the same basic appeal it's held for decades. The attraction design—with its sleek cars, auto noises, highway signs, and even an "off-road" section—is quite alluring. In actuality, the cars poke along on a track that leaves the driver with little to do. Pretty ho-hum for most adults and teenagers, but at least it's much more visually stimulating than the unthemed Magic Kingdom version.

TOURING TIPS This ride is appealing to the eye but definitely expendable on a schedule for adults. Preschoolers, however, love it. If your preschooler is too short to drive, place the child behind the wheel and allow him or her to steer (the car runs on a guide rail) while you work the foot pedal.

A mom from North Billerica, Massachusetts, writes:

I was amazed by the number of adults in line. Please emphasize to your readers that these cars travel on a guided path and are not a whole lot of fun. The only reason I could think of for adults to be in line was an insane desire to go on absolutely every ride. The cars tend to pile up at the end, so it takes almost as long to get off as it did to get on. Parents riding with their preschoolers should keep the car going as slow as it can without stalling. This prolongs the preschooler's joy and decreases the time you have to wait at the end.

And a Pittsburgh, Pennsylvania, couple who enjoyed the attraction wrote to warn about its intense smell of gasoline:

Both of us were gagging when we were close to the car in front of us.

Fortunately, Disney has promised to replace the Autopia fleet with zero-emission electric vehicles by fall 2026.

Buzz Lightyear Astro Blasters (*Lightning Lane*) ★★★★

APPEAL BY AGE PRESCHOOL ★★★★½ **GRADE SCHOOL** ★★★★½ **TEENS** ★★★★
YOUNG ADULTS ★★★★ **OVER 30** ★★★★ **SENIORS** ★★★★

What it is Space-travel interactive dark ride. **Scope and scale** Major attraction. **When to go** Before 10:30 a.m. or after 6 p.m. **Duration of ride** About 4½ minutes. **Average wait in line per 100 people ahead of you** 3½ minutes. **Loading speed** Fast.

DESCRIPTION AND COMMENTS Based on the space-commando character Buzz Lightyear from *Toy Story,* the marginal story line has you and Buzz trying to save the universe from the evil Emperor Zurg. The indoor ride is interactive—you can spin your car and shoot simulated laser cannons at Zurg and his minions.

A similar attraction at the Magic Kingdom at Walt Disney World is one of the most popular attractions in the park. The Disneyland version, situated across from Star Tours, is much the same, except mobile guns allow more accurate aiming. Don't forget to smile! You can email an on-ride photo to yourself for free from kiosks at the exit; these pictures are not connected to PhotoPass.

Praise for Buzz Lightyear is almost universal. This comment from a Massachusetts couple is typical:

Buzz Lightyear was the surprise hit of our trip! My husband and I enjoyed competing for the best score so much that we went on this ride several times during our stay. Definitely a must.

Each car is equipped with two laser cannons and a score-keeping display. Each score-keeping display is independent, so you can compete with your riding partner. A joystick allows you to spin the car to line up the various targets. Each time you pull the trigger, you'll release a red laser beam that you can see hitting or missing the target.

TOURING TIPS Most folks' first ride is occupied with learning how to use the equipment (fire off individual shots as opposed to keeping the trigger depressed) and figuring out how the targets work. The next ride (as with certain potato chips, one is not enough), you'll surprise yourself by how much better you do. *Unofficial Guide* readers are unanimous in their praise of Buzz Lightyear. Some guests, in fact, spend several hours on the attraction, riding again and again.

Disneyland Monorail System ★★★

APPEAL BY AGE	PRESCHOOL ★★★★	GRADE SCHOOL ★★★★	TEENS ★★★½
YOUNG ADULTS ★★★★		OVER 30 ★★★★	SENIORS ★★★★

What it is Scenic transportation. **Scope and scale** Major attraction. **When to go** During the crowded period of the day. **Duration of ride** 3 minutes one-way to Downtown Disney; 5½ minutes to return. **Average wait in line per 100 people ahead of you** 5 minutes; assumes 3 monorails operating. **Loading speed** Moderate–fast.

DESCRIPTION AND COMMENTS The monorail is a futuristic transportation ride that affords the only practical opportunity for escaping the park during the crowded lunch period and early afternoon. Boarding at the Tomorrowland monorail station, you can commute to the Disneyland Resort hotels and Downtown Disney.

Thumbs Up for the Whole Family

The monorail provides a tranquil trip with a nice view of Downtown Disney, Disney California Adventure, Fantasyland, and Tomorrowland. The Mark VII monorails have a sleek, retro look but can get quite hot inside during the summer (no air-conditioning!) and may shut down entirely between 11 a.m. and 6 p.m. on very warm days.

TOURING TIPS We recommend using the monorail to commute to Downtown Disney for a quiet, relaxing lunch away from the crowds. If you only want to experience the ride, go whenever you wish; the wait to board is usually 15–25 minutes, except in the 2 hours before closing when everyone tries to leave at once. If only one monorail train is operating, expect a minimum of a 30-minute wait. On afternoons when round-trip riders are not required to disembark and requeue at Downtown Disney, inbound guests may wait through multiple monorails for an empty seat. The monorail may suspend services from 1 hour before Disneyland Park's evening fireworks until 20–30 minutes afterward. Normally it ceases to bring guests into the park 30 minutes before closing, though you can exit the park on it as long as you've entered the queue by 5 minutes before closing.

Disneyland Railroad

DESCRIPTION AND COMMENTS The Disneyland Railroad makes a regular stop at the Tomorrowland Station. The wait to board here is usually short. See page 183 for additional details regarding the sights en route.

Finding Nemo Submarine Voyage ★★★½

APPEAL BY AGE PRESCHOOL ★★★★ GRADE SCHOOL ★★★★ TEENS ★★★½ YOUNG ADULTS ★★★½ OVER 30 ★★★ SENIORS ★★★½

What it is Simulated submarine ride. **Scope and scale** Headliner. **When to go** Before 10 a.m. or during evening parades or fireworks. **Duration of ride** 11½ minutes. **Average wait in line per 100 people ahead of you** 7 minutes; assumes 8 subs operating. **Loading speed** Slow–moderate.

DESCRIPTION AND COMMENTS The Finding Nemo Submarine Voyage ride is based on the story line of the hit Disney-Pixar animated feature. Here you board a bright-yellow electric-powered submarine. After a quick lap around the open-air lagoon, the sub passes through a waterfall and inside to follow the general *Finding Nemo* story. Special effects center on a combination of traditional Audio-Animatronics and underwater projection screens. Encased in rock and shipwrecks a few feet from the sub's windows, the screens allow the animated characters to appear three-dimensionally in the undersea world. Episodes include traveling through a minefield and a sea of jellyfish (very cool) and entering the mouth of a whale. The onboard sound system allows the story to "travel" from the front to the back of the sub, and the visual experience is different depending on what seat you're in.

Finding Nemo Submarine Voyage is not fast-paced but, rather, leisurely in the way that Pirates of the Caribbean is, although it lacks that classic's ageless atmosphere. While the attraction is well done, and you don't have to be a Nemo fan to be impressed by the scale and effort, time has taken its toll on the effects. Despite an extensive refurbishment earlier this decade, it still feels dated alongside the likes of Runaway Railway or Rise of the Resistance.

TOURING TIPS The attraction's capacity is only about 900 guests per hour, a shockingly small capacity for a headliner attraction. We've determined that, taking the day as a whole, you make much better use of your time enjoying Space Mountain, Matterhorn Bobsleds, Peter Pan's Flight, and other popular attractions during the first hour the park is open and saving the subs for later, when a parade, fireworks show, or *Fantasmic!* has siphoned a large number of guests from the line. The last 30 minutes before park closing is another good time to get in line.

Claustrophobes and galeophobes will not be comfortable with the experience, even though the sub doesn't actually submerge and the sharks keep their distance. Wheelchair-bound guests or those who can't get down the spiral staircase into the sub can view the experience from a special top-side viewing room (seats about six able-bodied persons plus two wheelchairs). The visual is nearly identical (perhaps faster), but despite a large monitor, the creatures appear smaller than when viewing them through a real porthole. The wait for the alternate viewing area is usually brief (ask a cast member how to bypass the standby line), and there are Mickeys hidden in the dive lockers inside.

A reader from Sydney, Australia, vented their dislike of Finding Nemo:

Finding Nemo was the most overrated ride. Perhaps it would rate high for those younger than 8 years old, but for our group it was one of the worst rides. It was boring, had rushing water, and moved slowly.

Space Mountain *(Lightning Lane)* ★★★★½

What it is Roller coaster in the dark. **Scope and scale** Super-headliner. **When to go** Right after the park opens, or anytime using the single-rider line. **Comments** Not to be missed. Must be 40" tall to ride; switching-off option (see page 165). **Duration of ride** 2¾ minutes. **Average wait in line per 100 people ahead of you** 3½ minutes. **Loading speed** Moderate.

Dark Scary Loss Things Queasy Rough Muss Your 'Do

DESCRIPTION AND COMMENTS Space Mountain is an indoor roller coaster with a theme of high-speed interstellar travel. It's a designer version of the Wild Mouse, a midway ride that's been around since the 1950s. There are no long drops or swooping hills as there are on a traditional roller coaster—only quick, unexpected turns and small drops. Disney's contribution essentially was to add a space theme to the Wild Mouse and put it in the dark. And this does indeed make the Mouse seem wilder.

The most surprising thing about Space Mountain is its aesthetic beauty. The vistas of the solar system and the stars, the distant galaxies, and passing comets are intoxicating and very realistic. Because you can't see the track or anticipate where your vehicle will go, your eyes are free to feast on the rich visuals, as your ears enjoy Michael Giacchino's groovy synchronized score behind your screams.

During seasonal *Star Wars* celebrations from April through early June, Disney temporarily rechristens Space Mountain into Hyperspace Mountain. This *Star Wars*–inspired version includes projections of dogfighting TIE Fighters and X-wings that swoop past your ride vehicle, blazing red and green laser blasts, and John Williams's stirring score blasting out of your in-seat speakers. Jedi junkies, who will happily jump in line over and over again for this flight, will be interested to know that it fits into official saga canon as the Battle of Jakku, which took place a year after *Return of the Jedi* and generated the crashed Star Destroyer that Rey scavenges in *The Force Awakens.* (Geek out concluded.)

TOURING TIPS Space Mountain is one of the park's most popular attractions. Experience it immediately after the park opens, or access the single-rider line, which frequently has little wait, through the ride's exit. The Lightning Lane for this attraction is one of the few that frequently backs up longer than 15–20 minutes, with the queue sometimes spilling down the entry ramp. Disabled guests may redeem their DAS return time at the Lightning Lane entrance, or they can go up the exit on the right side of the Mountain to the accessible entrance. Tell the cast member there whether you need to wait for a mobility-assistance transfer, or if you can walk up a flight of stairs after exiting (which should be much quicker).

Star Tours—The Adventures Continue
(Lightning Lane) ★★★★

APPEAL BY AGE PRESCHOOL ★★★★ **GRADE SCHOOL** ★★★★½ **TEENS** ★★★★½
YOUNG ADULTS ★★★★½ **OVER 30** ★★★★½ **SENIORS** ★★★★½

What it is Space-flight simulation ride. **Scope and scale** Headliner. **When to go** Before 11 a.m. or after 4 p.m. **Comments** Not to be missed. Frightens many small children; expectant mothers advised against riding; must be 40″ tall to ride. Switching-off option (see page 165). **Duration of ride** Approximately 7 minutes. **Average wait in line per 100 people ahead of you** 4½ minutes; assumes 4 simulators operating. **Loading speed** Moderate.

Scary Queasy Rough

DESCRIPTION AND COMMENTS Star Tours is a flight simulator that features crystal-clear digital 3-D screens and in-cabin Audio-Animatronic figures of C-3PO, your golden droid pilot. During your inevitably turbulent travels, you'll bump, twist, and dive into a Who's Who of *Star Wars* icons, with heroes Master Yoda and Admiral "It's A Trap!" Ackbar on your side, and villains Darth Vader and Boba Fett on your back. Voyages alternate between visiting planets from both the classic trilogy—such as icy Hoth and arid Tatooine—and the not-so-classic prequels, including Geonosis (home of the dreaded Death Star) and Naboo (home of the equally dreaded Jar Jar Binks); or reliving scenes from the sequels, such as taking a perilous tour of Jakku's starship graveyard and the mineral planet Crait, or braving Kef Bir and Exegol from *Episode IX*, with cameos from BB-8, Poe Dameron, and Maz Kanata. In 2024, the big twist is that the various possible cosmic destinations and multiple celebrity cameos (look for Han Solo and Chewbacca in the background) are randomly combined into hundreds of different story variations, giving the attraction unprecedented reridability. In 2024, characters and locations from the Disney+ series *Andor, The Mandalorian,* and *Ahsoka* were added to the mix, including a potential encounter with Grogu, as well as a trip to the planet Seatos (populated by space whales). With the new segments, the ride now offers more than 250 possible permutations. A wealth of references to the original Star Tours ride (along with hidden Disney characters and *Star Wars* inside jokes) can be found inside the detailed queue, and the ride is quite smooth and well synchronized.

TOURING TIPS Star Tours sees hour-plus waits on busy days, so ride as early in the day as possible. Because the Lightning Lane merge point is outside the building, Star Tours typically offers the least time savings of any headliner Genie+ attraction. The ride's long-term future seemed uncertain when Galaxy's Edge arrived, but it continues to draw both a queue and favorable comparisons to Smuggler's Run. A single-rider queue is sometimes offered here if the standby line is long enough, but it involves a confusing trek through the accessibility entrance; ask a cast member outside for instructions.

LIVE ENTERTAINMENT
and SPECIAL EVENTS

BANDS, DISNEY CHARACTER APPEARANCES, parades, singing and dancing, and ceremonies further enliven and add color to Disneyland Park on a daily basis. During the off-season, certain evening spectaculars (such as the fireworks and *Fantasmic!*) may be performed only on weekends. For specific information about what's happening on the day you visit, check the daily entertainment schedule in the app. Be forewarned, however, that if you are on a tight schedule, it is impossible to both see the park's featured attractions and take in the numerous and varied live performances offered. In our one-day touring plans, starting on page 391, we exclude most live performances in favor of seeing as much of the park as time permits. This is a tactical decision based on the fact that the parades and *Fantasmic!*, Disneyland Park's river spectacular, siphon crowds away from the more popular rides, shortening waiting lines.

The color and pageantry of live events around the park are an integral part of the Disneyland Park entertainment mix and a persuasive argument for second-day touring. Though live entertainment is varied, plentiful, and nearly continuous throughout the day, several productions are preeminent.

Fantasmic! ★★★★½

APPEAL BY AGE	PRESCHOOL ★★★★	GRADE SCHOOL ★★★★½	TEENS ★★★★½
YOUNG ADULTS ★★★★★	OVER 30 ★★★★½		SENIORS ★★★★½

What it is Multimedia water pageant with live characters. **Scope and scale** Super-headliner. **When to go** Check the app for showtimes. **Comment** Not to be missed. **Duration of show** 27 minutes. **Probable waiting time** 30-60 minutes for best view.

  DESCRIPTION AND COMMENTS *Fantasmic!* is a mixed-media show presented one or more times each evening the park is open until 10 p.m. or later. Staged at the end of Tom Sawyer Island opposite the Frontierland and New Orleans Square waterfronts, *Fantasmic!* stars Mickey Mouse in his role as the sorcerer's apprentice from *Fantasia.* The production uses lasers, images projected on a shroud of mist, fireworks, lighting effects, and music in combinations so stunning that you can scarcely believe what you have seen.

The plot is simple: good versus evil. The story gets lost in all the special effects at times, but no matter—it is the spectacle, not the story line, that is so overpowering. While *beautiful, stunning,* and *powerful* are words that immediately come to mind, they fail to convey the uniqueness of this presentation. *Fantasmic!* returned in 2024 after an extended hiatus with a restored Peter Pan stunt sequence staged aboard the Sailing Ship *Columbia,* along with a new finale showdown between Mickey and Maleficent (unfortunately no longer embodied by Murphy, the 45-foot-tall fire-breathing dragon animatronic that accidentally self-immolated). It could be argued, with some validity, that *Fantasmic!* alone is worth the price of Disneyland Park admission. Needless to say, we rate *Fantasmic!* as not to be missed.

TOURING TIPS The standby viewing areas for *Fantasmic!* are located along the far left waterfront, near the Harbour Galley restaurant; along the far right waterfront, in front of the River Belle Terrace restaurant up to the riverboat dock; in front of Tiana's Palace and Café Orléans; and on the bridge over Pirates of the Caribbean's entrance. Our favorite *Fantasmic!* standby viewing section is by Harbour Galley because you can enter later and exit easier. A section near Haunted Mansion is reserved for guests with wheelchairs, but it doesn't provide a great view. Depending on your spot, you may be looking at the side of the show rather than the front of it; make sure you can at least see the center stage on Tom Sawyer Island without obstructions. Terraced steps and other obstacles have been removed from New Orleans Square to better accommodate audiences, and planters (which are often used for stroller parking) make handy barriers for preventing others from standing directly in front of you.

Standby viewing areas begin opening 2 hours prior to the first show and can fill up within half an hour. Entry can be chaotic, and some guests get aggressively territorial over their spots, so pay careful attention to your kids, and follow the flashlight-wielding cast members' directions. To keep traffic flowing, you will be aggressively shooed away from every available vantage point outside the designated viewing sections.

Fantasmic! dining packages are available at Blue Bayou ($89 adults, $35 kids) and River Belle Terrace ($55 adults, $30 kids), both plus tax and tip. Dining packages include a three- or four-course meal and a pass for a special preferred viewing area. Most free viewing areas are standing room only, but guests in the table service dining package sections must sit on the ground (unless disabled). River Belle Terrace diners can pay $89 per adult ($45 per child) for upgraded entrée options, such as pork belly burnt ends and pot roast, and premium patio seating at 7:15 p.m. prior to the first performance, allowing them to stay and watch the show from their seat. Lunch service starts at 11 a.m., and the dinner packages begin at 4 p.m. While the meals are certainly overpriced, especially in comparison to the similar *World of Color* packages next door, the ease of entry and expansive elbow room afforded by preferred viewing passes are almost worth the expense, according to this St. Louis, Missouri, reader:

I highly recommend a Fantasmic! *dining package. It took so long to just move around the park that it was nice not to have to stake out a place for the show. We did Blue Bayou, which was expensive, but everyone enjoyed the food.*

Another reader who tried River Belle's upgraded seating agreed:

The River Belle Terrace Fantasmic! *premium dining package is a great (but expensive) way to avoid the crowds for the show. Very relaxing, with plenty of space during dinner and the show rather than standing (or hopefully sitting) on the pavement in the other dining package areas. We went on a day without the 10 p.m.* Fantasmic! *show and were allowed to stay at our table for the fireworks show.*

But one visitor from Hometown, Connecticut, wrote us about their disappointment with the River Belle patio package:

The people walking by and the cast members flashing their flashlights were so distracting. The table next to us even complained about how bad it was. Plus the food was terrible.

For a less-expensive option, there is also the *Fantasmic!* On-the-Go Dining Package at Rancho del Zocalo for $35 adults ($25 kids). This package includes an entrée (riblet, shrimp or potato tacos, or carne asada); sides and dessert; a fountain drink; and a reserved pass for the standing-room viewing section to the left of Blue Bayou's center area. We found the food quality roughly on par with Zocalo's usual fare, making this the best value of the resort's viewing upgrades.

Reservations for all *Fantasmic!* dining packages can be made online at disneyland.disney.go.com/dining/disneyland/fantasmic-dinner-packages or by calling ☎ 714-781-3463.

Fantasmic! viewing spots are first come, first served for all guests, including those in the reserved dining-experience viewing section, which is located along the waterfront from center stage to the raft landing for Tom Sawyer Island. Blue Bayou diners get the prime position, with standard River Belle and Rancho del Zocalo package-holders farther to the left along the shoreline. You can enter the dining section near the Harbour Galley restaurant beginning 90 minutes before the first showtime (or 30 minutes before the second), and the earlier you get in, the better spot you will obtain, as this Australian reader discovered:

Even with the [pass], people were lining up an hour beforehand to get prime position, and the ground is cold and very hard on your butt when you have to sit there for an hour waiting for the action to start!

If you need to sit right at the railing in the heart of the splash zone, you'll want to be the first inside the viewing pen when it opens; just be aware that you'll be watching the show through bars. You're far better off watching from farther back, taking advantage of the sloping ground's elevation to see above the crowd. You may find your reserved section filled to capacity if arriving less than 30 minutes prior to the first show; if so, you should be allowed to use your ticket for the second show.

No matter which method you use, you'll probably spend some time sitting around waiting. A mom from Lummi Island, Washington, dismantled her Disney stroller to make a nest:

We used the snap-off cover on the rental stroller to sit on during Fantasmic! since the ground was really cold.

Along similar lines, a middle-aged New York man wrote, saying:

Your excellent guidebook also served as a seat cushion while seated on the ground waiting for the show. Make future editions thicker for greater comfort.

Rain and wind conditions sometimes cause *Fantasmic!* to be canceled. Unfortunately, Disney officials usually do not make a final decision about whether to proceed or cancel until just before showtime. Note that if you purchased a *Fantasmic!* dining package earlier in the day, you will not be refunded if a show is canceled.

If you see the first *Fantasmic!* showing, stay in place afterward for the nightly fireworks (if scheduled), which should start a few minutes later; following the fireworks, you will be forced to exit Frontierland into Adventureland to make room for the next audience. To see the second showing from a standby section—which is always easier than seeing the first—watch the fireworks from Frontierland near the Golden Horseshoe, and then find a spot for *Fantasmic!* as soon as the first performance's audience has exited the viewing area. Passing through New Orleans Square during and immediately after *Fantasmic!* can be an exercise in frustration, so if you are trying to reach Haunted Mansion or Critter Country, either cut through Galaxy's Edge or try the train.

Finally, make sure to hang on to children during *Fantasmic!* and to give them explicit instructions for regrouping in the event that you become separated. Be especially vigilant when the crowd disperses after the show.

PARADES

DISNEY THEME PARKS are famous the world over for their parades. Typically, there is a parade every day, and on most days the daytime parade will run twice, at 3 p.m. and 5:30 p.m. The parades are full-blown productions with some combination of floats, huge balloons of the characters, marching bands, old-time vehicles, dancers, and costumed Disney characters. Themes for the parades vary from time to time, and a special holiday parade is always produced for the Christmas season (November through New Year's). Disneyland's latest daytime processional, titled **Magic Happens** (★★★★), features an original score co-composed by *RuPaul's Drag Race* choreographer Todrick Hall. Magic Happens combines high-energy beats, swirling dancers, and colorful twirling flags with elaborate all-new floats inspired by *Moana, Frozen II,* and *Coco*; our favorite element is the enormous puppet of Pepita, Imelda's surrealistic spirit animal. Of course, all your classic Disney friends are pulling up the rear for the grand finale, which highlights *Sleeping Beauty* and *Sword in the Stone.*

Parades always draw thousands of guests from the attraction lines. We recommend, therefore, watching from the departure point. With this strategy you can enjoy the parade and then, while the parade is continuing on its route, take advantage of the diminished lines at the attractions. Watching a parade that begins in Fantasyland from Small World Mall affords the greatest mobility in terms of accessing other areas of the park when the parade has passed. On days with two scheduled parades, the first performance will start at It's a Small World, travel past the west side of Matterhorn Bobsleds, go around the Tomorrowland side of Central Plaza, head down Main Street, and then circle Town Square counterclockwise. The second performance will begin at Town Square and run the route in the opposite direction.

The upper platform of the Main Street Station affords the best viewing perspective along the route. The best time to get a position on the platform is when the parade begins in Fantasyland. When this happens, good spots on the platform are available right up to the time the parade begins. When you are at the end of the parade route, you can assume that it will take the parade 15–18 minutes to get to you.

Most guests watch from Central Plaza or Main Street, and on busy days people begin camping out on the curbs there an hour or more before step-off time. The viewing area in front of It's a Small World will typically fill up last, so we recommend checking there if you need a spot. Any spot along the parade route will offer the same experience, so you shouldn't worry if you can't see the parade on Main Street. Once the parade has started, count on gridlock all along the route, especially on Main Street. Due to aggressive crowd-control restrictions on the sidewalks, you're best off entering or exiting the park via the backstage breezeways (if open) or Emporium shops.

The Plaza Inn offers parade-viewing packages that combine a fried chicken and short rib lunch (including a dessert and beverage) with reserved viewing for the second parade along Main Street in front of the train station. At $55 per adult ($28 kids ages 3–9; tax not included), the package is pricey, but you do get a prime seat without having to fight for elbow room. However, if you want a seat along the curb, you'll still need to line up outside the reserved section well before it opens 30 minutes prior to step-off, because those coveted spots will be claimed almost instantly. The dining package may be worthwhile if seeing the parade from Main Street is a high priority and you were already planning on eating at the Plaza Inn, but at a nearly $20 premium over the meal cost, we don't think it's as good a value as the *Fantasmic!* or *World of Color* dining options. If you want to try it, advance reservations through the app or website are recommended, but spots are sometimes available same-day.

Keep an eye on your children during parades and give them explicit instructions for regrouping in the event that you get separated. Children constantly jockey for better viewing positions. A few wiggles this way and a few wiggles the other, and presto, they are lost in the crowd. Finally, be especially vigilant when the crowd starts dispersing after the parade. Thousands of people suddenly strike out in different directions, creating a perfect situation for losing a child or two.

FIREWORKS AND PROJECTION SHOWS

STARLIT SPECTACLES featuring fireworks exploding over Sleeping Beauty Castle have been a Disneyland tradition since the park was only a television show, but the Anaheim skyflowers no longer boom on a nightly basis. Instead, Disneyland saves the pyrotechnics for select weekends, holidays, and other peak periods, while presenting pyro-free projection-mapping shows on slower evenings.

Mickey's Mix Magic (★★★★ with fireworks; ★★★½ without) is an evening spectacular created to celebrate Mickey Mouse's 90th birthday that relies on modern music and video projections more than pyrotechnics. It's currently Disneyland's go-to nighttime show when not preempted by other seasonal productions, and we think guests of most ages will enjoy this high-energy show thanks to vibrant visuals and infectious beats.

DJ Mickey spins a techno-heavy soundtrack featuring catchy dubstep remixes of classic cuts like "Everybody Wants to Be a Cat" and "Grim Grinning Ghosts," along with a pulse-pounding EDM version of "Let It Go," while dancing guests are doused with bubbles and artificial snow. And we guarantee the "It's a Good Time" theme song by The

DeeKompressors (which is also played during the morning rope drop) will have you belting "everybody get your ears on" for days to come.

Wonderous Journeys (★★★★½), which was launched for the Disney company's 100th birthday in 2023, returns to the park periodically. This production runs the full gamut of special effects—a rousing score, dynamic lighting, and lasers—not to mention spectacular fireworks effects. After an introduction evoking Walt's earliest efforts, the show manages to squeeze all 60 animated Disney feature films into under 14 minutes, paying tribute not only to the expected blockbusters like *Lion King* and *Encanto,* but even beloved bombs like *Atlantis* and *Treasure Planet.* The unspoken storyline follows the overly familiar three-act structure of the hero's journey—their call to adventure, an initial success and tragic setback, and the triumphant victory—yet finds fresh-feeling parallels between Disney's diverse protagonists. In one musical and emotional high point, Belle, Hercules, Moana, and Quasimodo all sing their "I Want" songs in a goosebump-inducing fugue.

Immersive projections are mapped onto Sleeping Beauty Castle, the Main Street buildings, the facade of It's a Small World, and mist screens on the Rivers of America, creating amazing visual effects that are a major feature of this fireworks show. Digital imagery paints landmarks around the park, transforming them into futuristic cityscapes, enchanted forests, or an animator's sketchpad. Via the projections, Main Street buildings will look like they're crumbling to ruins, then being restored by a kaleidoscope of butterflies. It's a beautiful effect that works well.

This pyrotechnic tribute to Disney's films also features flybys from *Pinocchio*'s Blue Fairy and *Big Hero 6*'s Baymax; their brief appearances are very impressive but can only be viewed from the hub immediately in front of the castle, and they're often omitted due to wind. Of course, *Wondrous Journeys* features an obligatory upbeat theme song, and "It's Wondrous," performed by Devan Garcia and Rudi, is so catchy you'll want to Spotify it at home. All these elements combine to form our favorite new Disneyland fireworks show since 2005's **Remember . . . Dreams Come True,** which is high praise indeed. *Wondrous Journeys* is a fantastic finale to your day in the park, particularly if you can see it from the proper perspective (see discussion following).

During certain times of the year, the usual fireworks shows are preempted in favor of seasonal nighttime spectaculars. During Pixar Fest (last held April 26–August 4, 2024), Disneyland presents **Together Forever—A Pixar Nighttime Spectacular** (★★★★), which features projections of characters like Luca and Mei Lee on the castle, giant inflatable skeletons from *Coco* atop Main Street's buildings, and an aerial appearance by Buzz Lightyear. The updated show has its highlights—a lyrical ballet of shooting stars based on *WALL-E* and Carl's balloon-buoyed floating house chief among them—but it isn't the most emotionally engaging fireworks show in Disney's catalog, coming across as a cut-and-paste assemblage of clips featuring plenty of familiar faces but no coherent narrative arc.

Halloween Screams (★★★★½) is the centerpiece of the park's fall celebrations (August–October). This frightfully fantastic show formerly was exclusive to attendees of the extra-cost after-hours parties, but since those have been moved to DCA, *Halloween Screams* can be enjoyed by all regular Disneyland guests every night throughout September and October (with fireworks on Friday–Sunday only). It is hosted by Jack Skellington (incarnated as an animated skull projected onto a giant balloon next to the castle) and his flying ghost-dog Zero, along with a rogue's gallery of Disney villains. Projection-mapping technology is used here to bring Sleeping Beauty Castle and the facades along Main Street, U.S.A., to life with dancing skeletons, cavorting ghouls on parade, and other animated spooks. Hair-singeing fireballs erupt alongside the castle, and the soundtrack mixes Danny Elfman's *Nightmare Before Christmas* score with wicked showstoppers like "Cruella de Vil," making this Halloween treat even tastier than the year-round fireworks show.

Believe . . . in Holiday Magic (★★★½) is a Christmas-themed fireworks show performed between mid-November and early January. No Disney characters—animated or otherwise—appear in the winter show, and the soundtrack selections focus on traditional holiday tunes, making *Believe . . . in Holiday Magic* the most dignified and least Disneyfied of the fireworks spectaculars. Fireworks are performed nightly for regular park guests during the holiday season.

Fireworks are only used in most of these shows during select weekend and peak-season performances; the presence or absence of pyro will be noted in the Disneyland app. Obviously, the music and projections lose a lot of their impact when they aren't accompanied by explosions. Be forewarned that even when scheduled, the fireworks may be canceled for safety reasons with only a few minutes' notice if there are stiff winds at upper altitudes, even if the air at ground level seems calm. On the plus side, unlike past productions, Disneyland's current shows don't have to be canceled entirely during windy weather.

We rate *Wondrous Journeys* with fireworks as not to be missed, and we think all of these nighttime shows are worth making time for, even when fireworks aren't scheduled. But seeing the show poses some challenges of which you should be aware. Without a doubt, the area around the central hub is the best vantage point for watching the show. The area immediately in front of the castle is the most popular, and it usually becomes gridlocked hours before the show, with access to the hub blocked from the surrounding lands. Stand too far down Main Street or at the train station and the castle projections will be just postage stamps. For the most immersive impression from the projection-mapping effects, you'll want to stand in the middle of Main Street, from the Carnation Café up to Coke Corner.

Unfortunately, every guest in the park won't fit in that sweet spot at the same time. Fortunately, the show can also be experienced from some other locations throughout the park.

The same projections seen on the castle and Main Street are also projected on the surface of It's a Small World. You'll be missing out on all the flying figures and effects that shoot out of Sleeping Beauty Castle, but It's a Small World will be your best option if Main Street is full. The fireworks are off-center from here, but the video looks sharper here than on the castle, and there's often space to sit on or in front of the mall stairs. Although it lacks the energy of the hub's open-air disco, we prefer the Small World mall for a more relaxing viewing experience.

Another advantage of watching from here is that you may also see a bonus limited-time projection-mapping show set to the hit song "We Don't Talk About Bruno" from *Encanto*. The 5-minute sequence, which plays intermittently from around 9 p.m. to 11:45 p.m., makes It's a Small World's facade flip and cascade like the tiles of the Madrigal family's casita, flow with flooding rain and falling sand, and bloom with colorful flowers. Catch the *Encanto* projections immediately following the fireworks, or ask a cast member in the area when the next show starts.

Your third option is viewing from the Rivers of America. Fountains and lighting fixtures come to life around Tom Sawyer Island, and video is projected onto the mist screens used in *Fantasmic!*, but they're not as detailed as the ones projected on the other two locations. You'll also miss most of the special effects immediately around the castle. The benefit of viewing from Rivers of America is that, if you have a pass for the first showing of *Fantasmic!*, you can stay in your spot through the fireworks. Though you get the least impressive view from here, it's the least stressful way to experience the show and can be very enjoyable if you haven't already seen it from a better location.

During the Season of the Force celebration (early April through early June), a symphonic soundtrack of "galactic" music from John Williams's classic film scores will play exclusively inside Star Wars Galaxy's Edge to accompany the regular fireworks; it's best viewed from the area around the *Millennium Falcon* or near the First Order's shuttle.

On nights when pyro is planned, Disneyland offers the Tomorrowland Skyline Lounge Experience, which bundles a dinner (including a selection of cold sandwiches and salads, desserts, and unlimited soft drinks) with access to the upstairs balcony of the Star Wars Launch Bay building, which affords a fine vantage for the fireworks but no view of the castle projections. Admission is $70 per person (age 3 and up), including tax, and is due in full when booking; there are no refunds if the fireworks are canceled. Visit disneyland.disney.go.com /dining/disneyland/tomorrowland-skyline-lounge or call ☎ 714-781-3463 to make reservations, and check in at Galactic Grill or near Alien Pizza Planet.

LIVE ENTERTAINMENT THROUGHOUT THE PARK

PARADES AND *FANTASMIC!* make up only a part of the daily live-entertainment offerings at Disneyland Park. The following is an incomplete list of other performances and events that are scheduled with some regularity.

DISNEY CHARACTER APPEARANCES Disney characters appear at random throughout the park but are routinely present in Mickey's Toontown, in Fantasyland, and on Main Street. Disney princesses are on call daily at the Royal Hall at Fantasy Faire (see page 209). An elaborate character-greeting area on the Tomorrowland side of the hub called Pixie Hollow offers a chance to meet Tinker Bell.

DISNEY CHARACTER MEALS Disney characters join guests for breakfast each morning until 11 a.m. at the **Plaza Inn** on Main Street and at **Storytellers Café** at the Grand Californian Hotel. Disney characters also join guests for breakfast and dinner at **Goofy's Kitchen** at the Disneyland Hotel, and the princesses host brunch at the Grand Californian Hotel's **Napa Rose** on select mornings.

FLAG RETREAT CEREMONY Every day at around sunset in Town Square, an honor guard lowers the flag as the Disneyland marching band plays patriotic tunes. Members of the armed forces are encouraged to participate in this respectful ceremony and are called up to be honored by branch.

THE GOLDEN HORSESHOE This Frontierland venue has always offered a decent show, hearty snacks, and an air-conditioned respite from the sun. Today, the stage originally headlined by Steve Martin's mentor Wally Boag, and later by Billy Hill and the Hillbillies (who currently perform at nearby Knott's Berry Farm under a slightly different name), is now commanded by occasional comedic magicians and dueling piano players. It's an amusing diversion when you want a break from big rides, but it isn't a must-see like some of its predecessors. Seating is first come, first served, so arrive 30 minutes early if you want to find a table and grab some grub. The best view is from the floor, front and center, but Walt liked the opera box seats best.

STREET ENTERTAINMENT Various bands, singers, comics, and strolling musicians entertain in spontaneous (that is, unscheduled) street performances throughout the park. Musical styles include banjo, Dixieland, steel drum, marching, and fife and drum. The Disneyland Band accompanies its repertoire of Disney tunes with more contemporary orchestrations and some drum corps–style choreography. You'll often find the Bootstrappers, a roving band of musical pirates, roaming the waterfront near New Orleans Square. For a respite from the rides, grab a snack and listen to the ragtime piano player outside the Refreshment Corner on Main Street. You don't want to miss the Dapper Dans, a slapstick barbershop quartet that has been performing on Main Street, U.S.A., in Disneyland since 1959. While the cast changes on a regular basis, the Dans really liven up the street.

TOMORROWLAND TERRACE The stage in front of Galactic Grill hosts high-energy Disney musical groups, who perform seasonally according to the entertainment schedule. It's also home to periodic character dance parties, where an interactive DJ directs guests to boogie with Pixar pals.

SEASONAL EVENTS

IF YOU'VE EVER DREAMED of getting to stay and play in the Disney theme parks at night after the daytime crowds have exited, the Disneyland Resort has a series of seasonal late-night parties that may be right up your alley.

A number of **Disneyland After Dark** themed nighttime events were held on select nights throughout 2024. The Disneyland After Dark 2024 event themes were **Sweethearts Nite,** held in late January and February; **Disney Channel Nite,** held in March; **Star Wars Nite,** held in late April and early May; and **Pride Nite** in June. Each party has a different theme with unique elements, but all feature special attractions and entertainment, rare character sightings, and the opportunity to purchase exclusive food and merchandise. Similarly, **Oogie Boogie Bash** Halloween parties are held at Disney California Adventure in the fall (see page 284).

Holiday parties and Disneyland After Dark events are "hard ticket" events, which means regular theme park admission tickets and Magic Key annual passes are not valid for admission; you must purchase a special After Hours event ticket directly from Disney, which provides access to the designated park for the party starting up to 3 hours before the event begins.

By far the most popular element of Disneyland's parties is the opportunity to spot seldom-seen characters, some of whom only appear at these special events. Event guests sometimes wait up to an hour to snap photos with a single character. Event maps point out character meet-and-greet locations but don't indicate exact set times. Be aware that characters may alternate every half hour, so the character appearing when you get in line may be gone by the time it's your turn. In addition to character encounters, a large variety of photo backdrops appear around the park, perfect for posing in front of and posting to your social media page. Some are simple background images, while others offer physical props to interact with. Each photo op is accompanied by a Disney PhotoPass photographer, whose services are included in the party ticket price; also expect to find a long, slow-moving queue for all the popular picture spots.

The second big reason to attend a Disneyland after-hours event is the chance to experience some of your favorite rides in a different way, thanks to the return of some special attraction overlays. During Oogie Boogie Bash, guests can enjoy the Monsters After Dark variation of Guardians of the Galaxy—Mission: Breakout!, a scarier heavy-metal version reserved for the Halloween season. At Star Wars Nite, guests are able to blast off to a galaxy far, far away on Hyperspace Mountain, which adds X-Wings and TIE Fighters, along with John Williams' stirring score, to the Tomorrowland classic Space Mountain. Keep in mind that both of these attraction overlays can be experienced without purchasing a special party ticket. Monsters After Dark is typically available to all DCA visitors September through October after 3 p.m., and Hyperspace Mountain was offered daily in Disneyland from April through early June.

Beyond the special attraction overlays, another highlight of the Disneyland after-hours events is the ability to experience popular E-Ticket rides with shorter-than-usual waits. Capacity for the events is capped, and many attendees are more interested in the unique characters and entertainment than re-riding old favorites. Most importantly, Genie+ and Individual Lightning Lane return times are not sold during the after-hours events, which makes the attractions' standby queues move with maximum efficiency. (DAS is still available to assist registered guests during events.) As a result, attendees can expect to encounter waits of 20 minutes or less for most attractions, especially during the final hour of the party.

Perhaps the most exclusive elements of the Disneyland after-hours events are the live shows and entertainment, some of which can't be seen anywhere else. For example, Sweethearts Nite presents a special fireworks show, as well as live jazz music aboard the *Mark Twain* Riverboat; Star Wars Nite also features a unique lightsaber instructional demonstration, along with the revival of Captain Phasma's March of the First Order character parade; and all events include themed dance parties with high-decibel DJs and dynamic lighting displays.

None of the Disneyland events' live shows require reserved seating or extensive waiting to secure a view, so in theory it should be easy to work them into your evening. But beware that special event showtimes aren't listed in the Disneyland smartphone app, so you'll need to refer to the printed Disneyland After Dark brochure to know where and when the entertainment occurs. For guests who want to be part of the live entertainment themselves, after-hours events are one of the only times that both kids and grown-ups are allowed to wear Jedi robes and other costumes inside the theme parks (although signing autographs or brandishing realistic weapons is still forbidden).

Last (and in our humble opinion least), the Disneyland hard ticket events allow guests to wait in absurdly long lines for the opportunity to purchase exclusive food, drinks, and merchandise. The locations for these sought-after items are detailed on the event maps, and some are certain to sell out within the opening hour of the evening. To be honest, the food and drinks seemed to be engineered more for their Instagram impact than actual taste (to say nothing of nutritional content), and the souvenirs for sale at the events we attended—socks and stickers—weren't especially exciting. If shopping and snacking are important to you at a Disneyland After Dark event, pick your priorities quickly and be prepared to spend a substantial portion of the party parked in queues. At least all attendees take home an event lanyard as a complimentary keepsake.

All of the Disneyland after-hours parties pack a lot into a few hours. The main difference between the annual Halloween parties and After Dark events is that no free snacks or candy are included in Disneyland After Dark admission. In addition, the Disneyland After Dark parties don't include all the entertainment and activities those familiar with similar seasonal parties might expect, and not all attractions may be offered during Disneyland After Dark events; even Rise of the Resistance is not guaranteed to operate throughout the entire Star Wars Nite.

Does it make sense to make room in your Disneyland Resort visit for an after-hours event? While it's impossible to evaluate the value of some of the unique event offerings, the Disneyland After Dark parties cost $139–$169 per person for up to 7 hours inside the park (including the preparty mix-in), which works out to $20–$24 on a strict dollar-per-hour basis; Oogie Boogie Bash tickets cost $139–$189, but those parties run an hour longer.

In comparison, a standard one-day/one-park ticket costs between $104 and $194, with the average price on dates near the Disneyland After Dark events running around $169. That's $11–$14 per hour, based on a 12–16 hour operating day, provided you can last that long in the parks without pooping out. However, if you factor in the additional cost of Genie+ and Individual Lightning Lane (which are neither offered nor needed during the special events), that daytime hourly rate increases to as much as $19 per hour, which is nearly on par with the party price. In other words, you'll pay more per hour for less time in the park with a party ticket, but if you're focusing on rides, you'll potentially accomplish more than you would during the daytime, thanks to shorter waits.

Special event admission is only good for the park where the party is taking place and does not provide park hopper access to the other park during the three-hour "mix-in" period prior to the regular park closing. On the positive side, you don't have to worry about making a park reservation when using an after-hours event ticket; evening access is automatically included in your purchase. Essential to getting full value from an after-hours event is entering the park a full 3 hours before the event officially begins. Designated turnstiles will be reserved for party guests, who will receive wristbands upon entry that allow them to remain in the park after regular hours. Long lines for event entry form outside the gates an hour or more ahead of time, but guests who are already inside the park can retrieve their credentials at an alternate location; be warned that these pick-up locations—usually Starcade at Space Mountain's exit and DCA's Golden Vine House—can get uncomfortably crowded on event evenings.

A frequent visitor from Bellingham, Washington, attended Sweethearts Nite and echoed many of our criticisms:

> I am not sure what the draw is for these after-hours events. They consist entirely of waiting in lines for photos with characters . . . and static backdrops. The lines are crazy. They need either more of these backdrops set up or multiples of the same one. The fireworks and the Royal Ball were nice, and I think the live entertainment generally is the way to go, but I'm also pretty sure that's not worth [the cost].

One final tip: We don't recommend using a regular park ticket on the same day you attend an evening event; it's more cost-effective to rest up and enjoy a nongated attraction (such as Downtown Disney or your hotel's pool) in the daytime before the party. And it's also not a bad idea to plan on sleeping in the next morning after your big night out!

UNHERALDED TREASURES *at* DISNEYLAND PARK

THESE SPECIAL FEATURES found in all of the Disney theme parks add texture, context, beauty, depth, and subtlety to your visit. Generally speaking, unheralded treasures are nice surprises that should be accorded a little time. Lani Teshima, Unofficial Guide friend and editor for mouseplanet.com, knows them all. Her list follows.

TREASURE Snow White's Grotto and Wishing Well | **LOCATION** The front right of Sleeping Beauty Castle

A SLOW STROLL around the Sleeping Beauty Castle can be romantic, but sitting quietly to its right is Snow White's Grotto and Wishing Well. If you stop for a few moments, you can hear the voice of Snow White singing "I'm Wishing" in the area. The grotto includes a trickling waterfall framing statues of Snow White and the Seven Dwarfs, placed on three tiers to make Snow White appear to be off in the distance in an optical illusion that masks the fact that her statue is the same height as those of the dwarfs. Next to the grotto is a wishing well, where you can toss a coin and make a wish. This area is a popular place for Snow White or other characters to appear for photos, so don't be surprised to see a group of people milling around.

TREASURE Disneyland Railroad | **LOCATION** Stations in Main Street, U.S.A.; New Orleans Square; Mickey's Toontown/Fantasyland; and Tomorrowland

AFTER A LONG DAY, the Disneyland Railroad offers a nice way to get from one end of the park to another. But trains held a special place in Walt Disney's heart, and the railroad offers much more than just a ride back to the park gates. Pause and turn around before you enter Main Street Station for a beautiful view of the entire length of Main Street, U.S.A. Inside the station, you can enjoy looking at model trains and other little exhibits. If you get off at the New Orleans Square Station, stop and listen—that beeping sound you hear is Walt Disney's 1955 Disneyland Park opening speech in telegraphic code. And don't forget to ride from Tomorrowland back to Main Street, so you can enjoy an unexpected treat: two large indoor dioramas inside the train tunnel, one depicting the Grand Canyon and another depicting a primeval world, complete with large-scale dinosaurs!

TREASURE Windows on Main Street | **LOCATION** Main Street, U.S.A.

THE NAMES ON THE MAIN STREET WINDOWS represent very special people who have had a profound influence on the park in some way, like guardian angels looking over park guests. The names are also often associated with "professions" related to what the person used to do when they worked for Disney. For example, the inscription for a window dedicated to the person who modeled Disneyland's waterways reads, DECORATIVE FOUNTAINS AND WATERCOLOR BY FRED JOERGER. Disneyland still occasionally bestows this window honor in official dedication ceremonies in the park; late Walt Disney Archives founder Dave Smith was memorialized with one in 2022. While you're at it, also take time to enjoy the six elaborate animated window displays on the Emporium's ground floor, each re-creating memorable scenes from a different Disney animated classic.

TREASURE Frontierland Shootin' Exposition | **LOCATION** Frontierland

SMACK IN THE MIDDLE OF FRONTIERLAND is the shooting gallery where cowpokes can close an eye and squeeze the trigger to try to get their target to ping, ting, move, or light up. Don't discount the Frontierland Shootin' Exposition as just another arcade gimmick. Everything about this well-themed attraction is dusty and rustic—except the laser-powered guns, which are both safe and cause little wear on the targets. About the only things missing are blowing tumbleweeds.

TREASURE Edible Plants | **LOCATION** Tomorrowland

THE DISNEY THEME PARKS are known for their magnificent landscaping, but did you know that many of the plants in Tomorrowland are edible, emphasizing the practicality of a future where the garden plants do double-duty as your vegetable garden? For example, the entryway to Tomorrowland is lined with orange trees, and the bushes along the walkways are planted with leafy vegetables such as lettuce, kale, and rhubarb, as well as herbs such as sage, chives, rosemary, and basil.

TREASURE Flag Retreat Ceremony | **LOCATION** Main Street Square

EVERY DAY IN THE AFTERNOON, the Disneyland Band or Dapper Dans vocal group marches to the front of Main Street to perform a number of Americana tunes. Park security guards then lower the American flag as the band plays "The Star-Spangled Banner" in this very respectful ceremony, which offers guests who are current or retired members of the U.S. armed forces an opportunity to be recognized for their service.

TREASURE *Partners* statue | **LOCATION** Central Plaza

AT THE CASTLE END of Main Street, in the center of the circular hub, is a bronze statue of Walt Disney holding the hand of Mickey Mouse. The statue, simply called *Partners,* pays homage to the two original ambassadors of Disneyland. If you stand in front of the statue, you can get a nice shot of it with Sleeping Beauty Castle in the background. The spot is encircled by a bench, and it's a great place to meet should your family decide to split up to visit different lands. Smaller statues of other popular Disney figures such as Dumbo, Goofy, and Pluto form a ring around this garden oasis in the middle of the park.

QUIET PLACES AT DISNEYLAND PARK

PEACE AND QUIET are anything but the norm at Disneyland. Yet sometimes when you're overwhelmed by it all, a place to decompress is worth a lot, as a reader from Culver City, California, points out:

> I can't tolerate the hyperstimulation as well as my husband and kids do. Sometimes when I'm on my ninth nerve, I'd give anything to put myself in time-out and just collapse for a while. Are there any nice out-of-the-way places in the park where this is possible?

Actually, there are a few. A **pier** with a canopy and benches, opposite the Matterhorn Bobsleds loading area, overlooks a quiet pool. There's still ambient noise, of course, but the pier is far enough removed from the action to afford both tranquility and a lovely setting. The **Hungry**

Bear Restaurant in Critter Country offers upper and lower covered outdoor decks overlooking the Rivers of America. In between major mealtimes, the decks are decidedly low-key. **Snow White's Grotto and Wishing Well** (see page 235) is also very pleasant, though it does have a modest-but-continuous flow of pedestrian traffic. The **Main Street Opera House's lobby** and **Golden Horseshoe's balcony** are air-conditioned and rarely crowded. There's a quiet spot in the far **back-left corner of Toontown** with shaded benches and a water bottle refilling station. Finally, the alfresco dining area of **Troubadour Tavern,** adjacent to Fantasyland Theatre, is relaxing between shows.

TRAFFIC PATTERNS
at DISNEYLAND PARK

1. WHAT ATTRACTIONS AND WHICH SECTIONS OF THE PARK DO VISITORS HEAD FOR WHEN THEY FIRST ARRIVE?   When guests are admitted, the flow of people to Star Wars: Galaxy's Edge is heaviest, followed by Tomorrowland (Space Mountain, Buzz Lightyear Astro Blasters, Star Tours, and Finding Nemo Submarine Voyage). The next most-crowded land is Fantasyland, though the crowds are distributed over a larger number of attractions. Critter Country is likewise crowded with its small area and only two attractions (Tiana's Bayou Adventure and The Many Adventures of Winnie the Pooh). Adventureland, Frontierland, and New Orleans Square fill more slowly, with Mickey's Toontown not really coming alive until later in the morning. As the park fills, visitors appear to head for specific favored attractions that they wish to ride before the lines get long. This, more than any other factor, determines traffic patterns in the mornings and accounts for the relatively equal distribution of visitors throughout Disneyland.

ATTRACTIONS HEAVILY ATTENDED IN EARLY MORNING
ADVENTURELAND Indiana Jones Adventure | Jungle Cruise
CRITTER COUNTRY Tiana's Bayou Adventure
FANTASYLAND Alice in Wonderland | Dumbo the Flying Elephant | Matterhorn Bobsleds | Peter Pan's Flight
STAR WARS: GALAXY'S EDGE *Millennium Falcon:* Smugglers Run | Star Wars: Rise of the Resistance
TOMORROWLAND Buzz Lightyear Astro Blasters | Finding Nemo Submarine Voyage | Space Mountain | Star Tours—The Adventures Continue

2. HOW LONG DOES IT TAKE FOR THE PARK TO REACH PEAK CAPACITY FOR A GIVEN DAY? HOW ARE THE VISITORS DISPERSED THROUGHOUT THE PARK?   A surge of early birds arrives before or around opening time but is quickly dispersed throughout the empty park. After the initial onslaught is absorbed, there is a bit of a lull that lasts until about an hour after opening. Following the lull, the park is inundated with arriving guests for about 2 hours, peaking 10–11 a.m. Guests continue to arrive in a steady-but-diminishing stream until around 2 p.m.

Sampled lines reached their longest length noon–3 p.m., indicating more arrivals than departures in the early afternoon. For general touring purposes, most attractions develop substantial lines 9:30–11 a.m. In the early morning, Star Wars: Galaxy's Edge, Tomorrowland, Critter Country, and Fantasyland fill up first. By late morning and into early afternoon, attendance is fairly equally distributed throughout all of the "lands." Mickey's Toontown, because it is comparatively small, stays mobbed from about 10 a.m. on. By midafternoon, however, we noted a concentration of visitors in Fantasyland, New Orleans Square, and Adventureland, and a slight decrease of visitors in Tomorrowland.

In the late afternoon and early evening, attendance continues to be more heavily distributed in Galaxy's Edge, Toontown, and Fantasyland. Though Space Mountain, Buzz Lightyear Astro Blasters, Tiana's Bayou Adventure, and Star Tours remain inundated throughout the day, most of the other attractions in Tomorrowland and Critter Country have reasonable lines. In New Orleans Square, Haunted Mansion, Pirates of the Caribbean, and the multitudes returning from nearby Critter Country keep traffic brisk. Frontierland (except Big Thunder Mountain Railroad) and Adventureland (except Indiana Jones Adventure) become less congested as the afternoon and evening progress.

3. HOW DO MOST VISITORS GO ABOUT TOURING THE PARK? IS THERE A DIFFERENCE IN THE TOURING BEHAVIOR OF FIRST-TIME VISITORS AND REPEAT VISITORS? Many first-time visitors accompany relatives or friends who are familiar with Disneyland and who guide their tour. These tours sometimes proceed in an orderly (clockwise or counterclockwise) sequence. First-time visitors without personal touring guidance tend to be more orderly in their touring. Many first-time visitors, however, are drawn to Sleeping Beauty Castle on entering the park and thus commence their rotation from Fantasyland. Repeat visitors usually proceed directly to their favorite attractions or to whatever is new. And, of course, *Star Wars* fans are sprinting en masse straight toward Galaxy's Edge.

4. WHAT EFFECT DO SPECIAL EVENTS HAVE ON TRAFFIC PATTERNS? Special events such as parades, fireworks, and *Fantasmic!* pull substantial numbers of visitors from the lines for rides. Unfortunately, however, the left hand taketh what the right hand giveth. A parade or *Fantasmic!* snarls traffic flow throughout Disneyland so much that guests find themselves captive wherever they are. Attraction lines in Tomorrowland and Adventureland diminish dramatically, making Space Mountain, Finding Nemo Submarine Voyage, Buzz Lightyear Astro Blasters, Star Tours, Jungle Cruise, and Indiana Jones Adventure particularly good choices during the evening festivities. Crowds in Mickey's Toontown and Fantasyland (behind the castle) also wane at night, but the rides there close prior to the fireworks for safety reasons. Critter Country, New Orleans Square, Frontierland, Main Street, and Small World Mall in Fantasyland are so congested with guests viewing the parade or *Fantasmic!* that it's almost impossible to move. Conversely, when *Fantasmic!* is on hiatus, the crowds that would otherwise be watching it must go elsewhere, chiefly toward the parade route and attraction queues. Because it's relatively isolated from the other lands, Galaxy's Edge crowds aren't greatly impacted by special performances.

5. WHAT ARE THE TRAFFIC PATTERNS NEAR TO AND AT CLOSING TIME?
On our sample days, which were recorded in and out of season, park departures outnumbered arrivals beginning in midafternoon, with a substantial number of guests leaving after the afternoon parade. Additional numbers of visitors departed during the late afternoon as the dinner hour approached. When the park closed early, there were steady departures during the 2 hours preceding closing, with a mass exodus of remaining visitors at closing time.

When the park closed late, departures were distributed throughout the evening hours, with waves of departures following the evening parade(s), fireworks, and *Fantasmic!* Though departures increased exponentially as closing time approached, a huge throng was still on hand when the park finally shut down. The balloon effect of this last throng at the end of the day generally overwhelmed the shops on Main Street, the parking lot, trams, and the hotel shuttles, as well as the exits onto adjoining Anaheim streets. In the hour before closing in the lands other than Main Street, touring conditions were normally uncrowded except inside Galaxy's Edge and at Indiana Jones Adventure in Adventureland, Space Mountain in Tomorrowland, and Tiana's Bayou Adventure in Critter Country.

DISNEYLAND PARK TOURING PLANS

THE GOAL OF OUR STEP-BY-STEP TOURING PLANS is to help you see as much as possible with a minimum of time wasted standing in line. They are designed to avoid crowds and bottlenecks on days of moderate-to-heavy attendance. On days of lighter attendance (see "Selecting the Time of Year for Your Visit," page 28), the plans will still save you time but will not be as critical to successful touring.

Choosing the Right Touring Plan

If you have two days to spend at Disneyland Park, the two-day touring plans are by far the most relaxed and efficient. The Two-Day Touring Plan A takes advantage of early-morning touring, when lines are short and the park has not yet filled with guests. This plan works well all year and is particularly recommended for days when Disneyland Park closes before 8 p.m. On the other hand, Two-Day Touring Plan B combines the efficiencies of early-morning touring on the first day with the splendor of Disneyland Park at night on the second day. This plan is perfect for guests who wish to sample both the attractions and the special magic of Disneyland Park after dark, including *Fantasmic!*, parades, and fireworks. The Two-Day Touring Plan for Families with Small Children spreads the experience over two more-relaxed days and incorporates more attractions that both children and parents will enjoy.

If you have only one day but wish to see as much as possible, use the One-Day Touring Plan for Adults. This plan will pack as much into a single day as is humanly possible, but it is pretty exhausting. If you prefer a more relaxed visit, read the preceding ride descriptions and drop the ones that interest you the least.

If you have small children, you may want to use the Dumbo-or-Die-in-a-Day Touring Plan for Families with Small Children. This plan includes most of the children's rides in Fantasyland and Mickey's Toontown and omits roller coasters and other attractions that small children cannot ride (because of Disney's age and height requirements), as well as rides and shows that are frightening for small children. Because this plan calls for adults to sacrifice many of the better Disney attractions, it is not recommended unless you are touring Disneyland Park primarily for the benefit of your children. In essence, you pretty much stand around, sweat, wipe noses, pay for stuff, and watch the children have fun. It's great.

An alternative to the Dumbo plan is the One-Day Touring Plan for Adults, taking advantage of switching off (see page 165). Switching off allows adults to enjoy the wilder rides while keeping the whole group together. Parents with children ages 8–12 should check out our One-DayTouring Plan for Families with Tweens, which is tailored with thrill rides and other attractions that appeal to that demographic.

For guests who really want to burn the candle at both ends (as well as a bunch of money) by buying a single-day Park Hopper, we offer a one-day/two-park touring plan that touches on the highlights of Disney California Adventure in the morning and Disneyland in the afternoon, along with a second version that starts in Disneyland before hopping to DCA. Both plans feature the top half dozen headliners in each park, but each includes different second-tier attractions in the afternoon, so guests with multiday park hopper tickets can try them both. (Note that Plan B starting in DCA contains both of the resort's water rides, which should help you pick between them if the weather is inclement.) For readers who have requested a Three-Day (or longer) Park Hopper Touring Plan, we recommend first using one or both of the One-Day/Two-Park plans, then following one of the Two-Day Disneyland Park Touring Plans mixed with the One-Day Disney California Adventure Touring Plan as you see fit. Just keep an eye on your return windows when juggling cross-park Lightning Lane reservations, as attendants enforce the expiration times.

PRELIMINARY INSTRUCTIONS FOR ALL DISNEYLAND PARK TOURING PLANS

ON DAYS OF moderate-to-heavy attendance, follow the touring plans exactly, deviating only when you do not wish to experience a listed show or ride. For instance, the touring plan may direct you to go next to Big Thunder Mountain Railroad, a roller coaster. If you do not like roller coasters, simply skip that step and proceed to the next activity.

1. Buy your admission in advance (see "Admission Options" on page 20) and link it with your park reservations inside the Disneyland smartphone app.

2. Visit disneyland.com or call ☎ 714-781-4636 the day before you go for the official opening time.

3. Become familiar with the park-opening procedures (described on page 181) and read over the touring plan of your choice, so you will have a basic understanding of what you are likely to encounter as you enter the park.

USING LIGHTNING LANE WITH A DISNEYLAND PARK TOURING PLAN

IF YOU CHOOSE TO PURCHASE Genie+, head directly to the first attraction on the touring plan upon entering the park, and make a Lightning Lane reservation for the next available participating ride in the plan while on your way there. You may also purchase an Individual Lightning Lane reservation if you wish, but wait until the return time reaches the busier midday before buying for maximum time savings. Deviate from the itinerary and work your return times into your day as necessary, reoptimizing your plan afterward (if using Lines) and always booking a new return time for the next available attraction as soon as you redeem the previous one. Visit the rides that don't offer Lightning Lane in the order of your touring plan between reservations.

On most days you should be able to utilize Lightning Lane at all or most of the park's Genie+ attractions before return times run out, but if you are attending on a very crowded day, prioritize your reservations in this order:

1. Indiana Jones Adventure	8. Big Thunder Mountain Railroad
2. Space Mountain	9. Haunted Mansion (raise priority for holiday version)
3. Matterhorn Bobsleds	10. Buzz Lightyear Astro Blasters
4. Mickey & Minnie's Runaway Railway	11. Star Tours
5. *Millennium Falcon:* Smugglers Run	12. It's a Small World
6. Tiana's Bayou Adventure (raise or lower priority with the temperature)	13. Autopia
7. Roger Rabbit's CarToon Spin	

USING EARLY ENTRY WITH A DISNEYLAND PARK TOURING PLAN

IF YOU ARE USING EARLY ADMISSION and following one of our touring plans, start your morning by following one of two routes, depending on your party's ages and interests. Families with small children should start in Fantasyland with Peter Pan's Flight (only if you are among the first few people in the queue), followed by Dumbo and Alice in Wonderland; on a slower day you may also have time for Mr. Toad or Pinocchio. For teens and thrill-seeking adults, hustle to the back of Tomorrowland for Space Mountain, then get in a couple of laps on Star Tours and Buzz Lightyear. Either way, get ready to rope-drop the first destination on your touring plan a few minutes before official opening, but don't waste your entire early admission waiting to sprint toward Star Wars. When you reach an attraction on your plan that you've already experienced during early entry, either skip that step or ride again if the wait isn't too long

THE BEST OF DISNEYLAND RESORT IN ONE DAY
(pages 391–394)

FOR Guests who really want to burn the candle at both ends (and a bunch of money) by buying a single-day Park Hopper.

ASSUMES Willingness to experience all major rides (including roller coasters) and shows in both parks and to walk a lot.

These plans are for groups who wish to visit both Disneyland and DCA in one day. Most of the major, must-see attractions are included for each park. One plan starts in DCA and switches over to Disneyland in the afternoon; the other starts in Disneyland and ends the evening at DCA. These plans are only recommended on days when the parks open early and stay open late. Try to finish up the morning portion of these plans by 1 p.m., so you have enough time to ride everything in the opposite park.

STAR WARS: GALAXY'S EDGE COMPLETE TOURING PLAN *(page 395)*

FOR Those who want to experience everything Star Wars: Galaxy's Edge has to offer to the exclusion of the rest of Disneyland.

ASSUMES Periodic stops for rest, restrooms, and refreshment.

This plan features rides on both Rise of the Resistance and *Millennium Falcon*: Smugglers Run. It also includes drinks at Oga's Cantina, the very popular lightsaber presentation at Savi's Workshop, shopping, general exploration of the land, and wraps up with viewing the evening fireworks near the *Millennium Falcon*. Also be sure to try the interactive games in the Play Disney Parks app as you wait in the attraction queues and wander around the land. At midnight PST on the 60th day before the morning of your visit, make reservations for Savi's Workshop and Oga's Cantina by using the Disneyland app or visiting disneyland.com /savisworkshop and disneyland.com/cantina. Try to schedule Savi's for late morning and Oga's for midafternoon.

DISNEYLAND PARK ONE-DAY TOURING PLAN FOR ADULTS *(page 396)*

FOR Adults without small children.

ASSUMES Willingness to experience all major rides (including roller coasters) and shows.

If you have only one day and wish to see the "classic" Disneyland plus Galaxy's Edge, use this touring plan. It packs as much into a single day as is humanly possible, but it is pretty exhausting. Be forewarned that this plan requires a lot of walking and some backtracking; this is necessary to avoid long waits in line. A little extra walking coupled with some hustle in the morning will save you 2–3 hours of standing in line. Note that you might not complete this tour. How far you get will depend on the size of your group, how quickly you move from ride to ride, how many times you pause for rest or food, how quickly the park fills, and what time the park closes.

Note: The success of this touring plan hinges on you being among the first to enter the park when it opens. Arrive at the entrance at least 45–60 minutes before official opening time.

DISNEYLAND PARK TWO-DAY TOURING PLAN FOR FAMILIES WITH SMALL CHILDREN (pages 397–398)

FOR Parents with children under age 7 who wish to spread their Disneyland Park visit over two days.

ASSUMES Frequent stops for rest, restrooms, and refreshments.

This touring plan represents a compromise between the observed tastes of adults and the observed tastes of younger children. Included in this touring plan are many of the midway-type rides that your children may have the opportunity to experience at local fairs and amusement parks. These rides at Disneyland Park often require long waits in line, and they consume valuable touring time that could be better spent experiencing the many rides and shows found only at a Disney theme park and which best demonstrate the Disney genius. This touring plan is heavily weighted toward the tastes of younger children. If you want to balance it a bit, try working out a compromise with your kids to forgo some of the carnival-type rides (such as Mad Tea Party, Dumbo, King Arthur Carrousel, and Toontown's GADGETcoaster) or such rides as Autopia. Most of the attractions have minimum height requirements of 40 inches or shorter.

Another alternative is to use one of the other two-day touring plans and take advantage of the switching-off option (see page 165). This technique allows parents of small children to take turns enjoying rides such as Indiana Jones Adventure and Matterhorn Bobsleds.

TIMING This two-day touring plan takes advantage of early-morning touring. On each day you should complete the structured part of the plan by 3 p.m. or so. We highly recommend returning to your hotel by midafternoon for a nap and an early dinner. If the park is open in the evening, come back to the park by 7:30 or 8 p.m. for the evening parade, fireworks, and Fantasmic!

Note: Because the needs of small children are so varied, we have not built specific instructions for lunch into the touring plan. Simply stop for refreshments or a meal when you feel the urge. For best results, however, try to keep moving in the morning. In the afternoon, you can eat, rest often, and adjust the pace to your liking.

DISNEYLAND PARK TWO-DAY TOURING PLAN A, FOR DAYTIME TOURING OR FOR WHEN THE PARK CLOSES EARLY *(pages 399–400)*

FOR Parties wishing to spread their Disneyland Park visit over two days and parties preferring to tour in the morning.

ASSUMES Willingness to experience all major rides (including roller coasters) and shows.

TIMING This two-day touring plan takes advantage of early-morning touring and is the most efficient of all the touring plans for comprehensive touring with the least time lost waiting in line. On each day you should complete the structured part of the plan by 3 p.m. or so. If you are visiting Disneyland Park during a period of the year when the park is open late (after 8 p.m.), you might prefer our Two-Day Touring Plan B, which offers morning touring on one day and late afternoon and evening touring on the other day. Another highly recommended option is to return to your hotel around midafternoon for a well-deserved nap and an early dinner and to come back to the park by 7:30 or 8 p.m. for the evening parade, fireworks, and live entertainment.

DISNEYLAND PARK TWO-DAY TOURING PLAN B, FOR MORNING AND EVENING TOURING OR FOR WHEN THE PARK IS OPEN LATE *(pages 401–402)*

FOR Parties who want to enjoy Disneyland Park at different times of day, including evenings and early mornings.

ASSUMES Willingness to experience all major rides (including roller coasters) and shows.

TIMING This two-day touring plan is for those visiting Disneyland Park on days when the park is open late (after 8 p.m.). The plan offers morning touring on the first day and afternoon and evening touring on the other day. If the park closes early, or if you prefer to do all of your touring during the morning and early afternoon, use the Two-Day Touring Plan A.

DUMBO-OR-DIE-IN-A-DAY TOURING PLAN FOR FAMILIES WITH SMALL CHILDREN *(page 403)*

FOR Parents with children under age 7 who feel compelled to devote every waking moment to the pleasure and entertainment of their small children.

ASSUMES Periodic stops for rest, restrooms, and refreshment.

The name of this touring plan notwithstanding, this itinerary is not a joke. Regardless of whether you are loving, masochistic, truly selfless, insane, or saintly, this touring plan will provide a small child with about as perfect a day as possible at Disneyland Park.

If this description has intimidated you somewhat or if you have concluded that your day at Disneyland Park is as important as your children's, use the One-Day Touring Plan for Adults, making use of the switching-off option (see page 165) at those attractions that impose height or age restrictions.

Because the children's attractions in Disneyland Park are the most poorly engineered in terms of handling large crowds, this touring plan is the least efficient of our options. It does represent the best way to experience most of the child-oriented attractions in one day, if that is what you hope to do. We do not make specific recommendations in this plan for lunch, but we do strongly suggest returning to your hotel around midafternoon for a well-deserved nap and an early dinner before the evening entertainment. If you can, try to hustle along as quickly as is comfortable until about noon. After noon, it won't make much difference if you stop to eat or take it a little easier.

Note: The success of this touring plan hinges on you being among the first to enter the park when it opens. Arrive at the entrance 45–60 minutes before official opening time.

DISNEYLAND PARK ONE-DAY TOURING PLAN FOR FAMILIES WITH TWEENS *(page 404)*

FOR Parents with children ages 8–12.

ASSUMES Willingness to experience all major rides (including roller coasters) and shows.

This plan is designed for families with "tweenagers" and includes every attraction that's popular with that cohort. It includes rides with minimum height requirements up to 48 inches, and it sets aside ample time for lunch and dinner.

THE DISNEYLAND NO RIDES, NO QUEUES, NO STRESS ANTI-TOURING PLAN

MOST OF OUR READERS are interested in touring plans to get them through as many attractions as possible in the most efficient manner. But, like the authors, some of you may have siblings, spouses, or other companions who are congenitally opposed to queuing for anything clanking or claustrophobic. What can Disney do to occupy your Aunt Gertie, who is dead set against standing in a line, or sitting in anything with a lap bar?

Disneyland Park is one of the few places where you can experience a full day of entertainment without getting on a ride faster than the railroad, and without waiting more than 15 minutes or so, even during the busiest season.

Yes, you can get your money's worth at Disneyland without sprinting to Space Mountain or spinning in a teacup. You just have to adjust your expectation of what constitutes an attraction. (A handful of sedate activities are available at Disney California Adventure, such as Disney Animation and the bakery tour, but not enough to justify a full-price pass.)

Because this "anti-touring" plan is designed to eliminate stress, there is no strict order to follow the steps in, nor instructions to arrive before rope drop (though it doesn't hurt). Simply tour the park as your feet take you, skipping any suggested experiences that don't interest you. If there is more than a 15- to 20-minute wait for anything you want to do, simply move along and check back later. Most important, take a break after 4 or 5 hours and leave the park for a nap, meal, or swim. The key is to take your time and (literally) stop to smell the roses.

Main Street, U.S.A.

- Ride one of the vintage vehicles up Main Street to the hub, and then take a different one back.
- Look at the memorabilia in the Main Street Station, and then ride the rails for a round-trip or two around the park.
- Explore the Disneyana shop's collectible artwork inside the old Bank of Main Street.
- Peer in the Emporium's high-tech animated window displays.
- See *Great Moments with Mr. Lincoln,* arriving early enough to see the lobby's Disney Gallery historical displays and preshow films.
- Watch the classic short films inside the Main Street Cinema.
- Snoop on the antique party line telephones inside the Market House, and then sit outside at a table on Center Street, listening to the amusing sounds emanating from the windows above.
- Check out the primitive coin-operated amusements in the Penny Arcade and use the Play Disney app for a free fortune from Esmerelda.
- Watch the chefs in the candy store whip up a batch of sweets. On select days during the holidays, the handmade supersize candy canes are a can't-miss. They are in short supply, so you'll need to arrive early and join a virtual queue to buy one, but anyone can watch them being made.
- Catch a performance or three of the Dapper Dans, Main Street Marching Band, or Coke Corner ragtime pianist. The daily flag retreat ceremony is not to be missed.
- Try to identify the names of Disney Legends and Imagineers honored on Main Street's windows.
- Stop and watch some artisans—such as the silhouette cutters and glass sculptors—work.
- Ask the prestidigitators at the Magic Shop to demonstrate some tricks for you, and stare at the creepy optical illusion in the window.
- On the right side of the street next to the silhouette shop, sit in the chairs on the porch.
- Take a picture with the *Partners* statue in the central hub, and appreciate the surrounding flora and fauna.

Adventureland

- See the *Enchanted Tiki Room,* arriving in time to buy a Dole Whip and watch the preshow. After exiting the show, visit with Rosita at the neighboring Tropical Hideaway.
- Jungle Cruise is gentle fun if the line isn't long.

- If stairs aren't an issue, climb Adventureland's Treehouse, or at least enter through the exit and see the ground-level exhibits.
- Consider walking through the Indiana Jones Adventure queue at least once, even if you aren't interested in riding. It's an impressive (if exhausting) example of scenic design; use the Play Disney app to translate the ancient pictographs inscribed along the walls. Before you climb the stairs near the loading bay, simply tell a cast member that you want to exit.

New Orleans Square

- Haunted Mansion and Pirates of the Caribbean both move guests through quickly even on busy days, and neither is likely to disturb any but the most delicate constitutions.
- Seek out the jazz and pirate bands that play in the area.
- Poke around the lovingly detailed alleyways and shops surrounding the Pirates of the Caribbean exit.
- Sit outside Café Orléans or Tiana's Palace with a snack and watch the crowds go by.
- Use the Play Disney app to get a free treasure map from Fortune Red at the Pieces of Eight gift shop.

Critter Country

- Stand on the bridge near Tiana's Bayou Adventure and watch riders take the plunge. If you dare to get damp, the single-rider wait is usually bearable.
- Observe the ducks from the porch behind the Hungry Bear Restaurant.

Star Wars: Galaxy's Edge

- Explore the environs of Black Spire Outpost, admiring the imaginative architecture and realistic rockwork and interacting with the heroes and villains who roam the area.
- Use the Play Disney Parks app on your smartphone to decode alien languages and discover other hidden features around Batuu.
- Browse for unique *Star Wars* souvenirs in Galaxy Edge's bazaar.
- Grab some galactic grub from the vendor stalls.

Frontierland

- Take a raft to Tom Sawyer Island, and explore the island.
- Ride on the Sailing Ship *Columbia, Mark Twain* Riverboat, or both. You can usually step on board just before departure time without standing in line, or board early for the best seat at the top front.
- Grab a snack and a box seat for the show in The Golden Horseshoe.
- Look for the petrified tree that was an anniversary gift from Walt to his wife; she donated it to the park. Also try to spot railroad tunnel remains from Mine Train Through Nature's Wonderland, across from Big Thunder Mountain.
- Sharpen your aim at the Frontierland Shootin' Exposition.

- Walk through the Rancho del Zocalo patio, especially when decorated for Dia de Los Muertos.

Fantasyland

- Experience the Sleeping Beauty Castle walk-through, or watch the alternative experience video.
- Make a wish at Snow White's well in front of the castle, and gaze at her grotto of handcrafted sculptures.
- Cruise Storybook Land Canal Boats or It's a Small World if lines are short.
- Try on some mouse ears in the Mad Hatter chapeau shop—and try to see the Cheshire Cat in the mirror above the counter.
- Take a break with a vendor treat on the benches at the old motorboat dock across from the Matterhorn Bobsleds.
- Stick your head in the Fantasy Faire if a show is scheduled, but don't bother with the massive queue to meet a princess.
- The elevated mall near It's a Small World is a convenient spot to stand for the parade, projections, or fireworks show.
- Enjoy the stage musical (when scheduled) inside Fantasyland Theatre.

Mickey's Toontown

- Play with the interactive doodads dotted around the building facades.
- Take a tour of Mickey's and Minnie's homes, but bail on the meet and greet if the line is out the door.
- Walk through the cleverly decorated children's playgrounds, being wary of bouncing babes, or relax on the artificial lawn.

Tomorrowland

- Take the monorail to Downtown Disney for a bite or a drink, and then return (remember your park ticket!).
- Check the schedule for upcoming entertainment on the Tomorrowland Terrace stage.
- See the alternative experience at the Finding Nemo Submarine Voyage.
- The line for Buzz Lightyear Astro Blasters moves swiftly, and almost everyone of all ages loves it.
- Browse the *Star Wars* merchandise (including build-your-own light sabers and droid action figures) in The Star Trader with a life-size X-wing overhead.
- Search for imaginatively groomed edible plants along the walkways.

PART 7

DISNEY CALIFORNIA ADVENTURE

We enjoyed DCA much more than Disneyland Park. More fun, fewer strollers and little kids, more-adventurous people. Just a different feeling all the way around.

—Mom from Bend, Oregon

▌ *A* **MOST ANTICIPATED SEQUEL**

DISNEY CALIFORNIA ADVENTURE held its grand opening on February 8, 2001. Known as DCA among Disneyphiles, the park is a bouquet of contradictions conceived in Fantasyland, starved in utero by corporate Disney, and born into a hostile environment of Disneyland loyalists who believed they'd been handed a second-rate theme park. Its parts are stunningly beautiful yet come together awkwardly, failing to compose a handsome whole. And perhaps most lamentable of all, the California theme is impotent by virtue of being all-encompassing. But after a billion-dollar metamorphosis, DCA overcame its inauspicious debut and emerged as an honorable companion to its storied older sibling across the Esplanade.

From a competitive perspective, DCA was an underwhelming shot at Disney's three Southern California competitors. The Hollywood section of DCA takes a hopeful poke at Universal Studios Hollywood, while the boardwalk-inspired area offers midway rides à la Six Flags Magic Mountain. Finally, the whole California theme has for years been the eminent domain of Knott's Berry Farm. In short, there's not much originality in DCA, only Disney's now-redundant mantra that "whatever they can do, we can do better."

Finally, after seven years of basically being in denial about DCA, the Walt Disney Company seemed willing to admit that this theme park (which pulled in only about a third of Disneyland's attendance annually) needed some help. On June 15, 2012, the Mouse held a grand reopening to celebrate the completion of a $1.1 billion effort, originally announced in 2007, to address DCA's problems.

Disney California Adventure

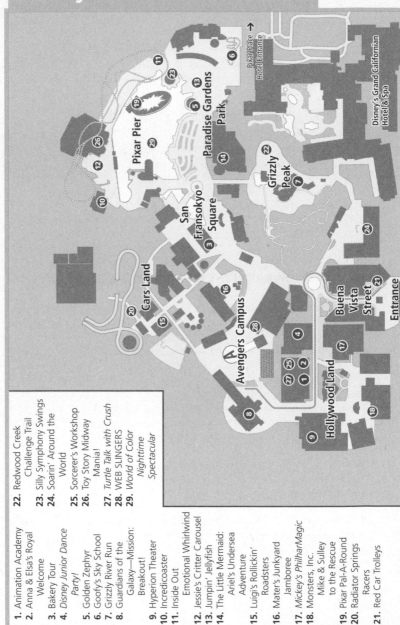

1. Animation Academy
2. Anna & Elsa's Royal Welcome
3. Bakery Tour
4. *Disney Junior Dance Party!*
5. Golden Zephyr
6. Goofy's Sky School
7. Grizzly River Run
8. Guardians of the Galaxy—Mission: Breakout!
9. Hyperion Theater
10. Incredicoaster
11. Inside Out Emotional Whirlwind
12. Jessie's Critter Carousel
13. Jumpin' Jellyfish
14. The Little Mermaid: Ariel's Undersea Adventure
15. Luigi's Rollickin' Roadsters
16. Mater's Junkyard Jamboree
17. *Mickey's PhilharMagic*
18. Monsters, Inc. Mike & Sulley to the Rescue
19. Pixar Pal-A-Round
20. Radiator Springs Racers
21. Red Car Trolleys
22. Redwood Creek Challenge Trail
23. Silly Symphony Swings
24. Soarin' Around the World
25. Sorcerer's Workshop
26. Toy Story Midway Mania!
27. *Turtle Talk with Crush*
28. WEB SLINGERS
29. *World of Color Nighttime Spectacular*

DISNEY CALIFORNIA ADVENTURE SERVICES
BABY CARE CENTER In San Fransokyo Square, near the Ghirardelli Soda Fountain
BANKING SERVICES/CURRENCY EXCHANGE At the Chamber of Commerce at Buena Vista Street, immediately to your left upon entering
DISNEYLAND AND LOCAL ATTRACTION INFORMATION Information board at Carthay Circle
FIRST AID At the Chamber of Commerce
LIVE ENTERTAINMENT AND PARADE INFORMATION At the Chamber of Commerce
LOST ADULTS AND MESSAGES At the Chamber of Commerce
LOST AND FOUND Lost and Found for the entire resort is located west of the entrance to Disneyland Park.
LOST AND FOUND In San Fransokyo Square next to the Baby Care Center
STORAGE LOCKERS Immediately to your right upon entering
GUEST RELATIONS AND DISABILITY ASSISTANCE Chamber of commerce on Buena Vista Street; Carthay Circle information board; outside Cars Land near Wine Country Trattoria; Pixar Pier near Jessie's Critter Carousel

While the park spent its first decade as a punch line, today DCA is a legitimate destination in its own right. Some Disneyholics may never forgive DCA's dire beginnings, dismissing its upgrades as expensive attempts to patch over a flawed foundation. The rest of us will have some fun enjoying the park for what it is: the theme park equivalent of a jukebox musical, featuring a greatest hits collection of attractions also found in Walt Disney World's parks, along with just enough exclusive E-tickets to give DCA a unique personality all its own.

ARRIVING *and* GETTING ORIENTED

THE ENTRANCE TO DCA faces the entrance to Disneyland Park across a brick-paved pedestrian plaza called the **Esplanade.** If you arrive by tram from one of the Disney parking lots, you'll disembark at the Esplanade. Facing east toward Harbor Boulevard, Disneyland Park will be on your left and DCA will be on your right. In the Esplanade are ticket booths, the group sales office, and resort information.

Seen from overhead, DCA is roughly arrayed in a fan shape around the park's central visual icon, Grizzly Peak. At ground level, however, the park's layout is not so obvious.

There are currently seven themed "lands" at DCA, not including **Buena Vista Street.** A left turn at the hub leads you to **Hollywood Land,** celebrating California's history as the film capital of the world. **Grizzly Peak** (which absorbed the former Condor Flats area) is reminiscent of the Pacific Northwest woods, while **San Fransokyo Square** nods to Baymax's tricultural city by the bay. You'll find Grizzly Peak by taking the first right as you approach the hub, though you must walk

NOT TO BE MISSED AT DISNEY CALIFORNIA ADVENTURE
• **AVENGERS CAMPUS** Guardians of the Galaxy—Mission: Breakout!
• **CARS LAND** Radiator Springs Racers
• **GRIZZLY PEAK** Grizzly River Run | Soarin' Around the World
• **PARADISE GARDENS PARK** *World of Color*
• **PIXAR PIER** Incredicoaster | Toy Story Midway Mania!

two-thirds of the way around the mountain to reach its namesake raft ride. The fourth land, **Pixar Pier,** recalls a seaside amusement park of the Victorian era that's been invaded by computer-generated cartoons. It is situated in the southwest corner of the park, on the far side of the large lake. **Paradise Gardens Park,** on the opposite shore of the lagoon, offers an assortment of remaining ex–Paradise Pier attractions that weren't overtaken by Pixar. **Cars Land** is the sixth land, with its primary entrance across from the Golden Vine Winery. Finally, **Avengers Campus,** the land dedicated to Marvel's Super Heroes, is sandwiched between Cars Land and Hollywood Land.

SINGLE-RIDER LINES

SOME DCA ATTRACTIONS feature time-saving single-rider lines (see page 110) that can greatly reduce your wait in exchange for being briefly separated from your friends and family (which could be considered an added bonus). Better still, none of DCA's single-rider queues bypass important preshow elements, so you aren't missing out on anything by taking advantage of them. Six attractions at DCA offer single-rider lines: Goofy's Sky School, Grizzly River Run, Incredicoaster, Radiator Springs Racers, Soarin' Around the World, and WEB SLINGERS: A Spider-Man Adventure. A similar system called Buddy Pass, which can be used by small groups of up to two adults plus one lapseated child, is occasionally available at Toy Story Midway Mania! and Monsters, Inc. Mike & Sulley to the Rescue! As always, inquire at the attraction entrance about how to access this shortcut.

PARK-OPENING PROCEDURES

IN THE MORNING, all off-site visitors and Disneyland Hotel guests must enter Disney California Adventure through the park's main entrance. Only Grand Californian guests are allowed through that hotel's private entrance into DCA's Grizzly Peak before 11 a.m., and the entrance from Disneyland Drive direct to DCA's Paradise Gardens Park is exclusively for those staying at Pixar Place (anyone can use either to exit). The hotel entrances' security checks are often overwhelmed in early mornings, and guests using them reach the rope-drop area behind those coming through the main entrance, so you may save time by walking to the front gate. All guests will be allowed through the main entrance about 30 minutes before the official opening, with those lacking early-entry benefits held on Buena Vista Street until after a brief rope-drop musical fanfare at the official opening time. Guests wishing to ride Radiator Springs Racers or WEB SLINGERS first will gather to the right of Carthay Circle, while those headed to Guardians of the Galaxy—Mission: Breakout! line up to the left outside Hollywood Land. It's also possible to walk around Grizzly Peak and wait near the Little Mermaid ride for quickest access to Pixar Pier's Incredicoaster and Toy Story Midway Mania! The crowd will be walked toward their destination at the appointed hour to avoid a stampede.

⏹️ BUENA VISTA STREET

FROM THE ESPLANADE, you pass through a Streamline Moderne entrance facade, designed after Los Angeles's fabled Pan-Pacific Auditorium. (If it looks familiar, that's because it can also be recognized as the entrance to Disney's Hollywood Studios park in Florida.)

Once past the turnstiles, you'll find yourself on **Buena Vista Street,** a re-creation of 1920s Hollywood as Walt saw it when he first arrived. Immediately upon entering, to your left you'll find **Oswald's** (a souvenir shop with a snazzy antique car parked outside) and the **Chamber of Commerce.** The street leading to the central plaza is lined on both sides with a variety of shops and eateries with backstories referring to Disney's early biography. Among the shops on the east side is **Elias & Company** (the park's largest shop, named after Walt's father). The west side of the street features an indoor shopping arcade that leads to the **Kingswell Shop** (for personalized mouse-ear hats and custom embroidery) and the **Trolley Treats** candy shop (check out the Big Rock Candy Mountain model in the window), among others.

The hub area, called Carthay Circle, is home to the *Storytellers* statue (depicting a young Walt Disney with an early version of Mickey Mouse) and a replica of the **Carthay Circle Theater,** where *Snow White and the Seven Dwarfs* premiered in 1937; in this incarnation, it encloses an upscale restaurant and bar.

Winding past the shops and facades, the **Red Car Trolley** transports guests from the park entrance to Hollywood Land's Hyperion Theater and back again.

Together, Buena Vista Street and Carthay Circle serve as a point of departure for the park's other various themed areas, as well as bring much-needed charm and warmth to DCA's opening act, forming a fantastic improvement over the flat cartoon-postcard facades that framed the former entryway.

Red Car Trolleys ★★★

APPEAL BY AGE	PRESCHOOL ★★★★	GRADE SCHOOL ★★★★½	TEENS ★★★
YOUNG ADULTS ★★★		OVER 30 ★★★	SENIORS ★★★★½

What it is Scenic in-park transportation. **Scope and scale** Minor attraction. **When to go** The first or last 2 hours the park is open. **Duration of ride** About 11 minutes round-trip. **Average wait in line per 100 people ahead of you** 12 minutes; assumes both cars in operation. **Loading speed** Very slow.

DESCRIPTION AND COMMENTS Much like the vintage vehicles that travel up and down Main Street, U.S.A., at Disneyland Park, these trolley cars add visual interest to DCA's entrance area but not much entertainment value. Modeled after the Pacific Electric Railway that served the Los Angeles area in the 1920s and 1930s (as seen in *Who Framed Roger Rabbit?*), the trolleys boast authentic details such as narrating conductors who share historical tidbits during your travels, retro-styled interior advertisements, and realistic overhead power lines—unelectrified, as the eco-friendly cars are actually battery-powered. More transportation than attraction, the Red Car Trolleys ferry guests on a one-way trip between Buena Vista Street near the park entrance and the Hyperion Theater (or back the other way), making stops in Carthay Circle and Hollywood Land along the way.

TOURING TIPS It is usually faster to walk the route than to wait for the next Red Car Trolley, but if you wish to experience this nostalgic transportation, do so in the morning. Hop on at the station near the Hyperion; it should be less crowded than the station near the park entrance.

HOLLYWOOD LAND

THE ATTRACTIONS AND SHOPPING in Hollywood Land are inspired by California's (and Disney's) contribution to television and cinema. Visually, the land is themed as a studio backlot with sets, including an urban street scene, boxy soundstages, and a central street with shops and restaurants that depict Hollywood's golden age. This area is rumored for a major makeover in the near future, possibly to make room for an *Avatar*-themed land.

DISNEY ANIMATION

THE DISNEY ANIMATION BUILDING houses a variety of shows, galleries, and activities that collectively provide a sort of crash course in animation. Because it's not a working studio, the attraction doesn't showcase artists at work on real features, and the interactive exhibits are more whimsical than educational. On entering the Animation building, you'll step into a lobby where signs mark the entrances to the various exhibits. Look up in the lobby for a moment at the ultra-high-definition oversize projections of animations in process, including Disney's and Pixar's latest hits. It takes 45–60 minutes to do all the interactive stuff and shows, not including waiting for the meet and greet. You probably won't experience much crowding here, except on weekends and holidays. Even then, the Animation building clears out considerably by late afternoon.

The four experiences located inside Disney Animation are:

Animation Academy ★★★★

APPEAL BY AGE	PRESCHOOL ★★★	GRADE SCHOOL ★★★★½	TEENS ★★★★
YOUNG ADULTS ★★★★½	OVER 30 ★★★★½		SENIORS ★★★★½

What it is Character-drawing class. **Scope and scale** Minor attraction. **When to go** See posted class schedule. **Duration of experience** 23 minutes. **Probable waiting time** 10–20 minutes.

DESCRIPTION AND COMMENTS The Animation Academy, hosted by a Disney cartoonist, teaches you how to draw a Disney character. If you have any artistic inclination, you may consider it DCA's best-kept secret and find yourself taking the class repeatedly, as a Salt Lake City reader suggests:

Thumbs Up for the Whole Family

Animation Academy turned out to be one of my absolute favorite things. I did it four times in a row and would have gone more if I wasn't starving. I plan to devote quite a bit of time to it on my next trip.

And from a Sammamish, Washington, mom:

I took three [classes], and they were the highlight of the trip. I have no drawing ability whatsoever, but following along with the instructor, I was able to make a pretty decent Donald, a passable Mickey, and a Pooh bear, though he looked like he was in a car accident. My 4-year-old loved drawing along, my husband loved it, and my 2-year-old loved scribbling on her paper and drawing board. It was fun for the whole family.

TOURING TIPS Animation Academy classes normally rotate during the day through a dozen-odd different classic and current Disney characters, but at times instruction may focus on a single theme. New characters are often added in sync with their film's release. Some popular characters (like Grogu from *The Mandalorian*) may only be taught once per day; check the daily schedule posted at the attraction each morning and arrive at least 15 minutes early.

Anna & Elsa's Royal Welcome ★★★

APPEAL BY AGE	PRESCHOOL ★★★★★	GRADE SCHOOL ★★★★★	TEENS ★★★
YOUNG ADULTS ★★★	OVER 30 ★★★½		SENIORS ★★★

What it is Character greeting with the *Frozen* sisters. **Scope and scale** Minor attraction. **When to go** Within the first 90 minutes after park opening, or an hour before closing. **Duration of experience** 3–5 minutes. **Probable waiting time** 20–30 minutes.

DESCRIPTION AND COMMENTS The popular ladies of Arendelle, Queen Elsa and Princess Anna, meet guests within the Disney Animation building. As an added bonus, Kristoff and Olaf sometimes take turns accompanying the sisters. Much like Fantasy Faire's Royal Hall, the *Frozen* character encounter is richly appointed and has multiple meeting rooms to increase capacity without ruining the magic.

TOURING TIPS *Frozen* fever has cooled off considerably, but even with the drop-off in demand, the line here isn't particularly efficient. If your party would like to meet the sisters, you should schedule it early in the day or shortly before closing.

Sorcerer's Workshop ★★

APPEAL BY AGE	PRESCHOOL ★★★★	GRADE SCHOOL ★★★★	TEENS ★★★½
YOUNG ADULTS ★★★½	OVER 30 ★★★½		SENIORS ★★★½

What it is Walk-through exhibit about animation. **Scope and scale** Diversion. **When to go** Anytime. **Duration of experience** 5–10 minutes. **Probable waiting time** None.

DESCRIPTION AND COMMENTS The Sorcerer's Workshop is a walk-through exhibit with interactive displays intended to show how animators turn still images into the illusion of motion. Originally, guests progressed through multiple rooms of exhibits that followed the Disney animation process from concept to finished film, with activities inspired by each of the steps along the way. Unfortunately, the majority of the attraction is permanently closed to guests, leaving accessible only a collection of primitive animation devices called zoetropes.

TOURING TIPS There's not much to see here, but at least there's never a wait to see it.

Turtle Talk with Crush ★★★★

APPEAL BY AGE	PRESCHOOL ★★★★½	GRADE SCHOOL ★★★★½	TEENS ★★★½
YOUNG ADULTS ★★★★	OVER 30 ★★★★		SENIORS ★★★★

What it is An interactive animated film. **Scope and scale** Minor attraction. **When to go** After you see the other attractions in the Animation Building. **Duration of show** 17 minutes. **Probable waiting time** 10–20 minutes.

DESCRIPTION AND COMMENTS *Turtle Talk with Crush* is an interactive theater show starring the 150-year-old surfer-dude turtle from *Finding Nemo*. Though it starts like a typical Disney theme park movie, *Turtle Talk* quickly turns into a surprise interactive encounter as the on-screen Crush begins to have actual conversations with guests in the audience. Real-time computer graphics are used to accurately move Crush's mouth when forming words. Crush is joined in his tank by his son, Squirt; Dory, the blue tang; Destiny, the whale shark; Bailey, the beluga whale; and Hank, the seven-legged octopus from the theatrical sequel *Finding Dory*.

A mom from Henderson, Colorado, has a crush on Crush:

Turtle Talk with Crush is a must-see. Our 4-year-old was picked out of the crowd by Crush, and we were just amazed by the technology that allowed one-on-one conversation. It was adorable and enjoyed by everyone, from Grammy and Papa to the 4-year-old!

TOURING TIPS The animation is brilliant, and guests of all ages list Crush as their favorite Animation Building feature. By late afternoon, the building has usually cleared out. Save this for your last stop there.

Disney Junior Dance Party! ★★★

APPEAL BY AGE	PRESCHOOL ★★★★½	GRADE SCHOOL ★★★★	TEENS ★½
YOUNG ADULTS ★★½	OVER 30 ★★★		SENIORS ★★★★

What it is Live show for children. **Scope and scale** Minor attraction. **When to go** Per the daily entertainment schedule. **Duration of show** 15 minutes. **Probable waiting time** 25 minutes.

DESCRIPTION AND COMMENTS Tykes can work out their wiggles as their elders develop tinnitus during this exhaustingly exuberant interactive dance party. Two iPad-wielding live hosts sing and dance their way through a structure that quickly becomes familiar: a large video screen displays a long commercial for a Disney Junior series, then a character from that show appears in the flesh (or fur) for an audience participatory dance-along song. The featured shows include *Mickey and the Roadster Racers*, *Doc McStuffins*, and *Vampirina*, with Mickey and Minnie themselves arriving in time for the grand finale.

The minimalist story line makes this production seem more like a Disney Cruise Line deck party than a coherent piece of theater, but the production values—from the slickly edited interactive video segments to squeal-inducing bubbles and streamers—are solid enough to satisfy the toddler target audience.

All the jumping, squirming, and high-stepping is facilitated by having the audience sit on the floor, so kids can spontaneously erupt into motion when the mood strikes. Even for adults without children, it's a treat to watch the tykes rev up. However, solo adults might feel creepy amid this extremely youthful exuberance, especially if they lack familiarity with any of the characters. If you have a younger child in your party, all the better: just stand back and let the video roll.

For preschoolers, *Disney Junior* will be the highlight of their day, as a Thomasville, North Carolina, mom attests:

My 3-year-old loved it. The children danced, sang, and had a great time.

TOURING TIPS The show is headquartered to the right of the entrance to Hollywood Land and has an Art Deco marquee. Because the tykes just can't get enough, it has become a hot ticket. Arrive earlier on Sundays, when all showings sometimes fill to capacity. If you arrive to find a line that extends out of the main queuing area and onto the sidewalk, you might not get into the show. Count two palm trees to the left of the theater entrance; if the line extends to the left of the second palm, you probably won't make the cut. If the line hasn't extended past the second palm tree, go ahead and get in line—chances are about 90% that you'll be admitted to the next show. Once inside, pick a spot on the floor and take a breather until the performance begins.

Mickey's PhilharMagic ★★★½

APPEAL BY AGE	PRESCHOOL ★★★★½	GRADE SCHOOL ★★★★½	TEENS ★★★½
YOUNG ADULTS ★★★★		OVER 30 ★★★★	SENIORS ★★★★½

What it is 3-D movie with in-theater effects. **Scope and scale** Major attraction. **When to go** Anytime. **Duration of show** 12 minutes. **Probable waiting time** 7 minutes.

DESCRIPTION AND COMMENTS This 3-D movie imported from Walt Disney World's Magic Kingdom features an odd collection of Disney characters, mixing Mickey and Donald with Simba and Ariel, as well as Jasmine and Aladdin. Shoehorned into the space originally occupied by Muppet-Vision 3-D, this version substitutes a single standard-size screen instead of the immersive 150-foot-wide triptych used in Florida, but the movie is still augmented by video projections on the walls and an arsenal of special effects built into the theater. The plot involves Mickey, as the conductor of the PhilharMagic, leaving the theater to solve a mystery. In his absence, Donald attempts to take charge, with disastrous results.

Brilliantly conceived, furiously paced, and laugh-out-loud funny, *Mickey's PhilharMagic* will leave you grinning. And while it is loud and in-your-face, this show is softer and cuddlier than some other 3-D films. Things pop out of the screen, but they're really not scary. It's the rare child who is frightened—but there are always exceptions.

One reader from London, England, was disappointed with our praise for the show:

Mickey's PhilharMagic was awful. It was a stitched-together series of musical numbers, done in a lifeless CGI that was vastly inferior to the original versions. Plus, it was earsplittingly loud.

TOURING TIPS There's rarely more than a single screening's wait. The theater is large, so don't be alarmed to see a gaggle of people in the lobby. A vibrant sequence featuring "Un Poco Loco" from Pixar's *Coco* was added in 2021, making this old favorite worthy of another visit, but the effects aren't nearly as impressive here as in Orlando.

Mickey's PhilharMagic is periodically preempted when the Sunset Showcase theater is used to screen movie trailers promoting Disney's hopeful cinematic blockbusters, such as the latest Marvel Cinematic Universe films.

Monsters, Inc. Mike & Sulley to the Rescue!
(Lightning Lane) ★★★½

APPEAL BY AGE	PRESCHOOL ★★★★	GRADE SCHOOL ★★★½	TEENS ★★★½
YOUNG ADULTS ★★★½		OVER 30 ★★★½	SENIORS ★★★★

What it is Dark ride. **Scope and scale** Major attraction. **When to go** Before 11 a.m. or after 6 p.m. **Duration of ride** 3¾ minutes. **Average wait in line per 100 people ahead of you** 4 minutes; assumes 23 cars in operation. **Loading speed** Moderate.

Dark

DESCRIPTION AND COMMENTS Based on characters and the story from the Disney-Pixar film *Monsters, Inc.,* the ride takes you through child-phobic Monstropolis as Mike and Sulley try to return baby Boo safely to her bedroom. If you haven't seen the film, the story line won't make much sense. In a nutshell, a human baby gets loose in a sort of parallel universe populated largely by amusing monsters. Good monsters Mike and Sulley try to return Boo to her home before the bad monsters get their hands on her.

The Imagineers did a very good job on the Monsters, Inc. ride, re-creating the humor, characters, and setting of the film in great detail. The section of the attraction where you ride through the Door Vault with all of its lifts and conveyors is truly inspired. Special effects are first-rate, and lots of subtle and not-so-subtle jokes are worked into the whole experience. You'll have to ride several times to catch them all. Before disembarking, be sure to banter with sluglike supervisor Roz, an animatronic "living character" that can see and interact with riders.

TOURING TIPS You can usually ride without too much of a wait. Because it's near several theater attractions, the ride is subject to experiencing a sudden deluge of guests when the theaters disgorge their audiences. In a unique twist on the single-rider line operated by other attractions, Monsters, Inc. sometimes offers a Moving Buddy pass. If you are a party of one or two adults, with up to two lap-sitting small children, you can ask the ride's greeter for a Moving Buddy pass, which will permit you to enter through the exit. Because Monsters, Inc.'s ride vehicles have three benches, Moving Buddy pass guests get to fill the otherwise empty back row, resulting in significantly shorter waits.

Monsters, Inc. is an iffy attraction for preschoolers: some love it and some are frightened. Increase your odds for a positive experience by exposing your little ones to the movie before leaving home.

AVENGERS CAMPUS

IN 2021, DISNEY WELCOMED Marvel Cinematic Universe fans inside a land that serves as the West Coast headquarters of Spider-Man,

Captain Marvel, Black Panther, and their fellow Super Heroes. Avengers Campus, which was built around the existing Guardians of the Galaxy attraction, encompasses the area previously occupied by the kid-centric A Bug's Land. The main gateway into the land lies just past Carthay Circle and is marked by a massive glowing Iron Man–esque Arc Reactor; secondary entrances are found near Guardians of the Galaxy—Mission: Breakout! and behind Luigi's Rollickin' Roadsters in Cars Land.

In addition to Mission: Breakout!, Avengers Campus is home to an interactive attraction that allows guests to experience what it's like to have amazing abilities like Spider-Man—or at least what it's like to flail your fingers at 3-D screens. Immersive character encounters, such as martial arts lessons from Wakanda's women warriors (see page 281); an Ant-Man–inspired eatery and bar; and a pair of snack stands round out the land's limited lineup. A third ride, announced at the 2023 D23 Expo, will allow guests to participate in a battle against a victorious variant of Thanos, fighting alongside Avengers from across the entire multiverse. Details on the attraction, including an anticipated opening year, are scarce, but concept art appears to depict an indoor ride utilizing screens.

In some ways the design of Avengers Campus feels like Disney's response to guests' complaints heard about Star Wars Galaxy's Edge. That land's adherence to a canonical timeline means fan-favorite characters like Boba Fett and Kylo Ren can never bump into each other, and a naturalistic soundscape means John Williams's iconic score is scarcely heard. In contrast, Avengers Campus exists in a unique offshoot of the Marvel multiverse where Thanos's snap never occurred, so visitors can see Natasha Romanoff and Steve Rogers team up—despite the fact that she's dead and he's 120 in the current cinematic continuity—while listening to the 8-bar Avengers theme on an incessant loop.

The entire land is layered with Easter egg details drawn from the original four-color source material, from the Gamma-irradiated "Hulk tree" to the psychedelic "Kirby Crackle" peeking through the pavement. Look for a plaque honoring Marvel Comics writer Stan "The Man" Lee at the entrance to the land. The only things you won't find in Avengers Campus are any shady spots for relaxing (apparently superheroes are immune to sunstroke) and the Marvel name; the contract with Universal Orlando's Islands of Adventure prohibits Disney from using the comic company's name in their United States parks.

Guardians of the Galaxy—Mission: Breakout!
(Lightning Lane) ★★★★½

| APPEAL BY AGE | PRESCHOOL ★★ | GRADE SCHOOL ★★★★ | TEENS ★★★★½ |
| YOUNG ADULTS ★★★★★ | | OVER 30 ★★★★½ | SENIORS ★★★★½ |

What it is Sci-fi–themed indoor thrill ride. **Scope and scale** Super-headliner. **When to go** The first hour the park is open. **Comments** Not to be missed. Must be 40″ tall to ride; switching-off option (see page 165). **Duration of ride** About 2 minutes plus pre-show. **Average wait in line per 100 people ahead of you** 4 minutes; assumes 3 elevators operating. **Loading speed** Moderate.

Dark | Rough | Scary | Lose Things | Queasy | Muss Your 'Do

DESCRIPTION AND COMMENTS
Taneleer Tivan, also known as The Collector (played here, as in the films, by Benicio del Toro), has invited park guests inside his pipe-festooned futuristic fortress to tour his museum of arcane artifacts from across the universe. Visitors can marvel at this rotating display of weapons and armor from multiple Marvel movies (plus some vintage Disney artifacts) while they wait. Tivan's greatest treasures are the Guardians of the Galaxy themselves: Peter "Star-Lord" Quill (Chris Pratt), Gamora (Zoe Saldana), Drax (Dave Bautista), and even Baby Groot have all been captured and suspended in display cases hanging over a vast abyss.

Luckily, the wily Rocket Raccoon (Bradley Cooper) has broken free and is crawling around in the ventilation system overhead. While you're waiting in The Collector's Easter egg–filled office (check out the objects on his desk), a realistic life-size Audio-Animatronic of the reckless rodent enlists you to help liberate his pals.

For the ride itself, guests board a gantry lift and are propelled up and down the tower, experiencing multiple free falls while immersed in intense visual effects and rockin' tunes ripped right from Star-Lord's *Awesome Mix* tapes. Like Walt Disney World's Twilight Zone Tower of Terror, Guardians of the Galaxy—Mission: Breakout! features multiple randomized ride profiles, with different video sequences and drop patterns synchronized to six different songs. Musical options include The Jackson 5, Pat Benatar, and even Elvis, and each soundtrack is accompanied by a different combination of comic vignettes depicting our hapless antiheroes' escape. Whichever sequence you get, you can still count on the doors opening at the top of the shaft for a bird's-eye view of the resort.

Lacking the eerie atmosphere and lateral disorientation that distinguishes the Florida attraction, DCA instead replaces suspense with nonstop acceleration as soon as the doors close, resulting in a rambunctious ride that's in keeping with the spirit of these comically chaotic characters. This reader from Calgary, Alberta, went in apprehensive but came out a fan:

I loved the original old-timey Hollywood theme and the creepy Twilight Zone *story line. But I have to say,* Guardians of the Galaxy—Mission: Breakout! *was by far our favorite ride! The ride is much faster and more thrilling than [Tower of Terror]. And the music makes it even more fun! I wasn't a huge fan of the movie, but after riding Mission: Breakout four times, I even bought a T-shirt!*

A woman from Round Rock, Texas, also wrote in to rave:

I LOVED Guardians of the Galaxy. It may be my new all-time favorite ride. It is so much fun, with great music and people dancing in their seats and laughing. It was really that fantastic!

After 3 p.m. during the Halloween season, a special Monsters After Dark overlay amps up the fear factor even further with startling special effects and original heavy metal music, as you help Rocket rescue Baby Groot from a ferocious fire dragon. During this time, the attraction will temporarily close from 2 to 3 p.m. daily to make the changeover. This scarier version is also offered during some after-hours special events.

This attraction is a whopper at 13-plus stories tall. As a result, it has great potential for terrifying young children and rattling more mature visitors. If you have teenagers in your party, use them as experimental probes—if they report back that they really, really liked it, run as fast as you can in the opposite direction. Seriously, a mom from London, England, warns:

It was terrifying! My daughter and I love a roller coaster, but that ride was gross. We were just holding on tight waiting for it to be over. My daughter watched her baseball cap floating up from under her feet and seemingly levitating midair as we dropped. I missed that as I was just trying to survive!

TOURING TIPS Because of its height, the tower is a veritable beacon, visible from outside the park and luring curious guests as soon as they enter. You can count on a footrace to get there when the park opens.

To access the attraction, bear left from the park entrance into Hollywood Land. Continue straight to the Hyperion Theater and then turn right. To save time, when you enter the preshow area, stand in the far back corner across from the door where you entered. When the doors to the loading area open, you'll be one of the first admitted.

When one (or two) of the ride's three elevator shafts stops working (which happens regularly), the queue slows to a crawl. Ask the attendant if the attraction is fully operational before jumping in line.

WEB SLINGERS: A Spider-Man Adventure
(Lightning Lane) ★★★★

APPEAL BY AGE	PRESCHOOL ★★★★	GRADE SCHOOL ★★★★½	TEENS ★★★★½
YOUNG ADULTS ★★★★½		OVER 30 ★★★★	SENIORS ★★★★

What it is Interactive 3-D dark ride. **Scope and scale** Headliner. **When to go** During the first or last hour of the day, or anytime using the single-rider line. **Duration of ride** About 4 minutes plus preshow. **Average wait in line per 100 people ahead of you** 4 minutes. **Loading speed** Moderate.

DESCRIPTION AND COMMENTS Peter Parker (played by Tom Holland) is testing out a way of allowing anyone to sling webs like his "good friend" Spider-Man can. Guests touring his Worldwide Engineering Brigade laboratory have the chance to suit up like a real superhero—or at least slap on some 3-D spectacles—and help out when Parker's adorable self-replicating Spider-Bots are accidentally unleashed on the campus. After a quick preshow briefing from Holland in holographic form, riders snake through the former Stark automotive factory before boarding cubical red-and-blue WEB SLINGER vehicles.

If you've already been on Toy Story Midway Mania!, you'll instantly recognize this attraction's format: guests sit on back-to-back benches in a slow-moving vehicle that slides past large 3-D screens showing computer-animated targets to shoot at. The twist here is that instead of aiming a physical gun and tugging on a string to launch projectiles, you simply fling your hands forward and sophisticated motion-capture cameras do the rest, transforming your flailing into flying virtual webbing. Just sit back in your seat to make sure the cameras can see you, and use small, quick movements of your wrists and forearms to flick web-goo as fast as possible.

The digital visuals in WEB SLINGERS are far sharper and more vibrant than in earlier interactive rides, and the gesture recognition technology is much more responsive than the similar system found in Legoland's Ninjago, making for a very invigorating (even exhausting) experience as you strive to out-sling your seatmates. But although the gameplay is engaging, the absence of any physical effects in between the screens, or recognizable characters other than Spidey himself, makes WEB SLINGERS seem far less ambitious and immersive than Universal Orlando's Spider-Man attraction, which is over 25 years old. Reader feedback on WEB SLINGERS has been mixed, with this Denver, Colorado, mom representing Spidey's detractors:

WEB SLINGERS is not worth the [Lightning Lane cost] for older kids. The AI is cool, but it's otherwise just the same ride as Buzz Lightyear and Toy Story Midway Mania!

While this mother from Bremerton, Washington, represents the pro–Peter Parker wing:

I did not agree with the lackluster review of WEB SLINGERS.

TOURING TIPS WEB SLINGERS is ultimately a lot of fun to play, but getting to that point can involve spending up to an hour in an unshaded outdoor queue whose theme is "ugly industrial parking lot." (Comic fans can amuse themselves here searching for characters' first appearance dates hidden in the signage.) Other options are to spring for Genie+ or opt for the single-rider queue, which can be as short as 10 minutes, and still includes the preshow. Standby wait times also drop dramatically in the last hour before closing time, after most Lightning Lane guests have redeemed their reservations.

Your first trip through will feel too chaotic to both enjoy the visuals and play competitively. To score high, aim for light blue and gold spiders; also look for gold buttons and levers in the background and corners of the screens. Teamwork counts, so focus on the quadrant in front of you instead of crossing over into your neighbors' personal space, and there's no need to make Spidey's split-finger gesture—just keep karate chopping like crazy.

Wrist-mounted WEB Power Bands that can boost your blasting power (and score) are sold for $35 in the nearby gift shop. Because the devices don't interact outside of the ride, they seem like an even bigger waste than paid upgrades in video games; if you get one, wear it on the ride until the "calibration" is complete, then remove it to reduce wrist fatigue. The customizable remote-controlled Spider-Bots ($80 and up) make much cuter and more functional souvenirs.

▐ PIXAR PIER

WRAPPED AROUND THE SOUTHERN SHORE of the kidney-shaped lake, Pixar Pier (previously known as Paradise Pier) is Disney's headquarters for the nonautomotive computer-animated heroes from Pixar's popular franchises.

The land's original tacky mid-20th-century theme was ironic, and in a perverse way it brought the story of Walt Disney and Disneyland full circle. Walt, you see, created Disneyland Park as an alternative to parks with a carnival atmosphere, simple midway rides, carny games, and amply available alcohol. Amazingly, corporate Disney had made just such a place the centerpiece of Disneyland's sister park. The 2012 refurb's clapboard buildings and retro carnival games gave the area much-needed charm, and in 2018 the area was reimagined yet again, this time as Pixar Pier, DCA's home for all Pixar characters.

Pixar Pier is subdivided into four neighborhoods. *The Incredibles* occupy the first quadrant around their Incredicoaster; *Toy Story* characters claim the block outside their Midway Mania ride; *Inside Out* has taken over the far end of the boardwalk; and the remaining area around Pixar Pal-A-Round claims a catchall of Pixar characters. Even the snack stands have Pixar landlords, like *Monsters, Inc.*'s Adorable Snowman Frosted Treats; *Inside Out*'s Angry Dogs and Bing Bong's Sweet Stuff; and Señor Buzz Churros and Poultry Palace from *Toy Story*.

Incidentally, those aforementioned carnival games, which are all themed around Pixar films like *La Luna* and *A Bug's Life,* aren't as avaricious as their unfair fair ancestors. If you and a companion play together, you can win a stuffed animal for less than you'd pay in the park's gift shops. Some games let you combine multiple wins for an impressive prize. The fishing and racehorse games seem easiest.

On your way across the bridge into Pixar Pier, look up at the Luxo Jr. desk lamp atop the archway. The animatronic incarnation of Pixar's longtime mascot nods to guests, and it even watches the nightly lagoon show with rapt attention.

Note: Pixar Pal-A-Round and Jessie's Critter Carousel close up to 1 hour before *World of Color* performances, but Incredicoaster, Toy Story Midway Mania!, and Inside Out Emotional Whirlwind remain operational.

Incredicoaster *(Lightning Lane)* ★★★★

APPEAL BY AGE	PRESCHOOL ★★	GRADE SCHOOL ★★★★½	TEENS ★★★★★
YOUNG ADULTS ★★★★★		OVER 30 ★★★★½	SENIORS ★★★★

What it is Big, bad roller coaster. **Scope and scale** Super-headliner. **When to go** Ride during the first hour in the morning or during *World of Color,* or use the single-rider line. **Comments** Not to be missed. Must be 48″ tall to ride; switching-off option (see page 165). **Duration of ride** 2½ minutes. **Average wait in line per 100 people ahead of you** 2½ minutes; assumes 24-passenger trains with 36-second dispatch interval. **Loading speed** Moderate–fast.

Scary   Lose Things   Queasy   Muss Your 'Do

DESCRIPTION AND COMMENTS California Screamin', the opening day E-ticket of Paradise Pier, has been rededicated as Pixar Pier's Incredicoaster, a high-speed adventure starring the superheroic Parr family from *The Incredibles* franchise. Guests board 24-passenger trains inside a Palm Springs–inspired mid-century modern load building, where they learn that baby Jack-Jack has broken loose from Edna Mode's care and is wreaking havoc with his explosive special powers. Dash, Elastigirl, Mr. Incredible, and Violet all appear in the form of static physical figures inside the coaster's tunnel-covered inclines, attempting to put the incendiary infant down for his nap.

This apparently old-school wooden monster is actually a modern steel coaster, and at 6,072 feet, it's the third longest steel coaster in the United States. The Incredicoaster gets off to a 0-to-55-mph start by launching you up the first hill like a jet fighter plane off the deck of a carrier (albeit with different technology). From here you will experience tight turns, followed by a second launch that sends you over the crest of a 110-foot hill with a 107-foot drop on the far side. Next, you bank and complete an elliptical loop. A diving turn followed by a series of camelbacks brings you back to the station.

We were impressed by the length of the course and the smoothness of the ride, although that lone inversion does vibrate vigorously. From beginning to end, the ride is about 2½ minutes, with 2 minutes of actual ride time. En route the coaster slows enough on curves and on transition hills to let you take in the nice view. On the scary-o-meter, the Incredicoaster is certainly worse than Space Mountain but doesn't really compare with some of the steel coasters at nearby Magic Mountain. What the Incredicoaster loses in fright potential, however, it makes up for in variety. Along its course, Disney has placed every known curve, hill, dip, and loop in roller-coaster design.

A Carlsbad, California, woman found the ride to be a smooth operator:

It was WONDERFUL, and I am a 57-year-old mom, not an adrenaline-crazed young adult! It was my first ever upside-down ride, but it was so smooth and quick that I only felt a gentle pressure pushing me into the seat. It was so fun that I went again! Don't miss this one, at any age!

A Texas woman agrees, writing:

I hate roller coasters, and I loved it. Very smooth.

TOURING TIPS The Incredicoaster is a serious coaster, one that makes Space Mountain look like Dumbo. Secure any hats, cameras, eyeglasses, or anything else that might be ripped from your person during the ride. Stay away completely if you're prone to motion sickness.

Engineered to run several trains at once, the Incredicoaster does a better job than any roller coaster we've seen at handling crowds, at least when the attraction is running at full capacity. The coaster is sometimes shut down two or more times a day for technical problems. Early in the morning, however, it's usually easy to get two or three rides under your belt in about 15 minutes. Ride in the first hour the park is open or use the single-rider line; enter up the ramp to the left of the queue, but be aware that if the singles line extends out into the boardwalk, the wait may be nearly as long as standby. Ask for an elevator if you have trouble climbing the staircases that cross over the boarding area.

If you can, try to ride after sunset; the lighting effects inside the tunnels look much better in the dark. Near the exit of Incredicoaster is Jack-Jack Cookie Num Nums, a food cart selling fresh-baked cookies. The cookies are tasty, warm, and chewy. A huge plus is that the area smells like fresh cookies. It's intoxicating.

Inside Out Emotional Whirlwind ★★½

APPEAL BY AGE	PRESCHOOL ★★★★	GRADE SCHOOL ★★★½	TEENS ★★½
YOUNG ADULTS ★★★		OVER 30 ★★★	SENIORS ★★★

What it is Kiddie spinning ride. **Scope and scale** Minor attraction. **When to go** Before 11 a.m. **Duration of ride** 90 seconds. **Average wait in line per 100 people ahead of you** 12 minutes. **Loading speed** Slow.

DESCRIPTION AND COMMENTS This is a simple spinning carnival ride that's been dressed up with an *Inside Out* theme. Surrounded by a curved wall of glowing memory balls, brightly colored gondolas gently swing as they circle the tilting central support, while riders are heckled with humorous quips from the film's emotive cast.

TOURING TIPS Though magnetically alluring to the under-8 crowd, this ride is low-capacity, slow-loading, and ridiculously brief. Our advice is to ride before 11 a.m. if you visit on a weekend or during the summer.

Jessie's Critter Carousel ★★½

APPEAL BY AGE **PRESCHOOL** ★★★★½ **GRADE SCHOOL** ★★★★ **TEENS** ★★½
YOUNG ADULTS ★★★ **OVER 30** ★★★ **SENIORS** ★★½

What it is Merry-go-round. **Scope and scale** Minor attraction. **When to go** Before noon. **Duration of ride** A little less than 2 minutes. **Average wait in line per 100 people ahead of you** 8 minutes. **Loading speed** Slow.

DESCRIPTION AND COMMENTS Guests can ride atop nine types of cute critters on this merry-go-round fronted by a large statue of Woody's cowgirl companion. The elaborately crafted dolphins and seals from the former King Triton's Carousel have been replaced with cartoonish armadillos, bunnies, buzzards, raccoons, and even adorable skunks, as depicted in "Woody's Roundup" from *Toy Story 2*.

TOURING TIPS It's worth a look even if there are no children in your party. If you have kids who want to ride, try to get them on before noon. There are two benches to sit on if you're unable or unwilling to straddle an animal. Jessie's Critter Carousel looks much better at night thanks to the lighting.

Pixar Pal-A-Round ★★½

APPEAL BY AGE **PRESCHOOL** ★★★★ **GRADE SCHOOL** ★★★½ **TEENS** ★★★★
YOUNG ADULTS ★★★½ **OVER 30** ★★★½ **SENIORS** ★★★

What it is Ferris wheel. **Scope and scale** Major attraction. **When to go** The first 90 minutes the park is open or just before the ride closes. **Duration of ride** 9 minutes. **Average wait in line per 100 people ahead of you** 6¼ minutes; assumes all 24 cabins in use. **Loading speed** Slow.

DESCRIPTION AND COMMENTS To the surprise of many, Mickey's face remains on his former Fun Wheel after the pier's transformation, though the ride is now known as Pixar Pal-A-Round and the Plutos and Goofys painted on its gondolas have been replaced with, well, Pixar pals. Higher than the Matterhorn Bobsleds at Disneyland Park, this whopper of a Ferris wheel tops out at 150 feet. Absolutely spectacular in appearance, the wheel offers stunning views in all directions. Unfortunately, however, the view is severely compromised by the steel mesh that completely encloses the passenger compartment. In essence, Disney has created the world's largest revolving chicken coop. As concerns the ride itself, some of the passenger buckets move laterally from side to side across the Ferris wheel in addition to rotating around with the wheel. Because it feels like your bucket has become unattached from the main structure, this lateral movement can be a little disconcerting if you aren't expecting it. If the movement proves too disconcerting, motion sickness bags are thoughtfully provided in each swinging car.

TOURING TIPS Ferris wheels are the slowest loading of all cycle rides, but the Pal-A-Round has a platform that allows three compartments to be loaded at once. The lateral sliding buckets are loaded from the two outside platforms, while the stationary compartments are loaded from the middle platform. Loading the entire wheel takes about 6½ minutes, following which the wheel rotates for a single revolution. And speaking of the ride, the Pal-A-Round rotates so slowly that the wonderful rising and falling sensations of the garden-variety Ferris wheel are completely absent. For our money, Pixar Pal-A-Round is beautiful to behold but terribly boring to ride. If you decide to give it a whirl, ride the first hour and a half the park is open or in the hour before the ride closes.

Toy Story Midway Mania! *(Lightning Lane)* ★★★★

APPEAL BY AGE   PRESCHOOL ★★★★½   GRADE SCHOOL ★★★★½   TEENS ★★★★½   YOUNG ADULTS ★★★★½   OVER 30 ★★★★½   SENIORS ★★★★½

What it is 3-D ride through indoor shooting gallery. **Scope and scale** Headliner. **When to go** First 60 minutes the park is open. **Comment** Not to be missed. **Duration of ride** About 6½ minutes. **Average wait in line per 100 people ahead of you** 4½ minutes; assumes both tracks operating. **Loading speed** Moderate.

DESCRIPTION AND COMMENTS Toy Story Midway Mania! ushered in a whole new generation of Disney attractions: virtual dark rides. Since Disneyland opened in 1955, ride vehicles had moved past two- and three-dimensional sets often populated by Audio-Animatronics; these detailed sets and robotic figures literally defined the Disney creative genius in attractions such as Pirates of the Caribbean, Haunted Mansion, and Peter Pan's Flight. Instead, Toy Story Midway Mania! has long corridors, totally empty, covered with reflective material. There's almost nothing there . . . until you put on your 3-D glasses. Instantly, the corridor is brimming with color, action, and activity, thanks to projected computer-graphic imagery (CGI).

Conceptually, this is an interactive shooting gallery much like Buzz Lightyear Astro Blasters (see page 218), but in Toy Story Midway Mania!, your ride vehicle passes through a totally virtual midway, with booths offering such games as ring tossing and ball throwing. You use a cannon on your ride vehicle to play as you move along from booth to booth. Unlike the laser guns in Buzz Lightyear, however, Toy Story Midway Mania's pull-string cannons take advantage of CGI technology to toss rings, shoot balls, and even throw eggs and pies. Each game booth is manned by a *Toy Story* character who is right beside you in 3-D glory, cheering you on. In addition to 3-D imagery, you experience various smells, vehicle motion, wind, and water spray. The ride begins with a training round to familiarize you with your cannon and the nature of the games and then continues through a number of "real" games in which you compete against your riding mate. The technology has the ability to self-adjust the level of difficulty so that every rider is challenged, and there are plenty of easy targets for small children to reach. *Tip:* Let the pull string retract all the way back into the cannon before pulling it again. If you don't, the cannon won't fire.

Also of note, a 6-foot-tall Mr. Potato Head interacts with and talks to guests in real time in the preshow queuing area.

TOURING TIPS Much of the queuing area for Toy Story Midway Mania! is covered, which is good, but it's not air-conditioned, which is very bad, with temperatures escalating into the 90s and higher. Not roasting in this oven is a great incentive to experience Toy Story Midway Mania! in the early morning, before it gets crowded.

As you might expect, Toy Story Midway Mania! is addictive, and though it's great fun right off the bat, it takes a couple of rides before you really get the hang of the pull-string cannon and the way the targets are presented. To rack up a high score, you must identify and shoot at high-value targets: high-value targets are small and often moving, while low-value targets are larger and easier to hit. Toward the end of the ride, the top score of the day and the top scores of the month are posted. If you're a newbie and you'd like to ride several times to gain experience and get your skill level up, consider making the attraction your first stop after the park opens.

Small parties of up to two adults and one lap-size child should ask an attendant about a Buddy Pass, which (when available) allows bearers to bypass the standby queue and fill otherwise empty rows with a much shorter wait.

▐█ PARADISE GARDENS PARK

LYING ACROSS THE LAGOON from Pixar Pier, Paradise Gardens Park is home to the leftover attractions that escaped Paradise Pier's Pixar makeover. It stretches from the western edge of the central lake, along its northern shore, to the *World of Color* viewing terraces.

Golden Zephyr ★★

| APPEAL BY AGE | PRESCHOOL ★★★★½ | GRADE SCHOOL ★★★½ | TEENS ★★★½ |
| YOUNG ADULTS ★★★ | | OVER 30 ★★★ | SENIORS ★★★½ |

What it is Zephyrs spinning around a central tower. **Scope and scale** Minor attraction. **When to go** Any time it is operating. **Duration of ride** 2 minutes. **Average wait in line per 100 people ahead of you** 8 minutes. **Loading speed** Slow.

DESCRIPTION AND COMMENTS First, a *zephyr* is a term often associated with blimps. On this attraction, the zephyrs look like open-cockpit rockets. In any event, each zephyr holds about a dozen guests and spins around a central axis with enough centrifugal force to lay the zephyr partially on its side. As it turns out, the Golden Zephyrs are very touchy, as zephyrs go: they can't fly in a wind exceeding about 10 miles per hour. Needless to say, the attraction is shut down much of the time. While the Golden Zephyr does not have a height requirement, babies must be able to sit up in order to board, and no lap sitting is allowed.

TOURING TIPS This colorful attraction is another slow-loading cycle ride. Despite its inefficiency, it rarely attracts more than a cycle or two wait to ride, assuming it's even operating (a bold assumption).

Goofy's Sky School *(Lightning Lane)* ★★★

| APPEAL BY AGE | PRESCHOOL ★★★ | GRADE SCHOOL ★★★★ | TEENS ★★★★ |
| YOUNG ADULTS ★★★★ | | OVER 30 ★★★½ | SENIORS ★★★ |

What it is Disney's version of a Wild (or Mad) Mouse ride. **Scope and scale** Major attraction. **When to go** During the first few hours the park is open or use the single-rider line. **Comments** Must be 42" tall to ride; switching-off option (see page 165). **Duration of ride** About 1½ minutes. **Average wait in line per 100 people ahead of you** 6¼ minutes; assumes 15-second dispatch interval. **Loading speed** Slow–moderate.

Scary

Lose Things

Queasy

Muss Your 'Do

DESCRIPTION AND COMMENTS Themed as Goofy teaching new pilots how to fly, Goofy's Sky School is a designer Wild Mouse (sometimes also called a Mad Mouse). If you're not familiar with the genre, it's a small, convoluted roller coaster where the track dips and turns unexpectedly, presumably reminding its inventor of a mouse tearing through a maze. To define it more in Disney terms, the ride is similar to Space Mountain, only outdoors and therefore in the light. Goofy's Sky School is an off-the-shelf midway ride in which Disney has invested next to nothing to spiff it up. In other words, it's fun but nothing special. One Denver, Colorado, woman who otherwise loves the park feels even our middling assessment is too generous, writing:

> I think Goofy's Sky School deserves a significant demotion. It doesn't deserve to be called a roller coaster. It jerked us around so much that we were aching afterward.

TOURING TIPS A fun ride but also a slow-loading one, and one that breaks down frequently. Ride during the first few hours the park is open or use the single-rider line (when open).

Jumpin' Jellyfish ★½

APPEAL BY AGE	PRESCHOOL ★★★★	GRADE SCHOOL ★★★★	TEENS ★★★
YOUNG ADULTS ★★½		OVER 30 ★★★	SENIORS ★★★

What it is Parachute ride. **Scope and scale** Minor attraction. **When to go** The first 90 minutes the park is open or just before closing. **Comments** Must be 40" tall to ride. **Duration of ride** About 45 seconds. **Average wait in line per 100 people ahead of you** 20 minutes; assumes both towers operating. **Loading speed** Slow.

DESCRIPTION AND COMMENTS On this ride, you're raised on a cable to the top of the tower and then released to gently parachute back to Earth. Mostly a children's ride, Jumpin' Jellyfish is paradoxically off-limits to those who would most enjoy it because of its 40-inch minimum-height restriction. For adults, the attraction is a real snore. Oops, make that a real bore—the paltry 45-second duration of the ride is not long enough to fall asleep.

TOURING TIPS The Jellyfish, so called because of a floating jellyfish's resemblance to an open parachute, is another slow-loading ride of very low capacity. Get on early in the morning or prepare for a long wait.

The Little Mermaid: Ariel's Undersea Adventure (Lightning Lane) ★★★½

APPEAL BY AGE	PRESCHOOL ★★★★★	GRADE SCHOOL ★★★★	TEENS ★★★½
YOUNG ADULTS ★★★½		OVER 30 ★★★½	SENIORS ★★★★

What it is Track ride in the dark. **Scope and scale** Headliner. **When to go** Anytime. **Duration of ride** 6¼ minutes. **Average wait in line per 100 people ahead of you** 3 minutes. **Loading speed** Fast.

DESCRIPTION AND COMMENTS The Palace of Fine Arts dome was incorporated into an impressive lagoon-facing facade modeled on early-20th-century aquariums. The seafoam-trimmed building, topped by a statue of King Triton, conceals Disney's 21st-century take on an old-school dark ride. The basics of The Little Mermaid: Ariel's Undersea Adventure are similar to Disneyland's Haunted Mansion: a continuously loading ride system transports you through a series of elaborately themed, darkened scenes with sophisticated special effects. In this case, The Little Mermaid attraction takes you to the bottom of the ocean in clamshell cars, where the ride recaps Ariel's journey from her father's undersea kingdom to her marriage to Prince Eric. After Scuttle the seagull recaps the backstory for you, your vehicle descends backward beneath the simulated sea surface with a spritz of cool air. You'll then meet an animatronic Ariel with "floating" hair; party down "Under the Sea" with Sebastian the crab; and be menaced by a 12-foot-wide, 7½-foot-tall undulating figure of Ursula, the evil sea witch. The adventure is all set to newly orchestrated versions of Alan Menken and Howard Ashman's classic songs, and original animator Glen Keane and actress Jodi Benson both returned to lend their talents.

Though the ride is colorful and kinetic, it suffers from shortchanged storytelling, especially in the unsatisfyingly abrupt finale. While it's a welcome addition to DCA's short roster of kid-friendly indoor rides, anyone expecting a modern-day classic to compete with Haunted Mansion and Pirates of the Caribbean may come away somewhat disappointed. But this family from Arvada, Colorado, thinks the ride serves its supporting role well:

Head for The Little Mermaid ride when you need a break. It's well done, and it's air-conditioned.

TOURING TIPS The Little Mermaid has slipped in popularity since the debut of Cars Land and Avengers Campus. The Omnimover ride system is capable of efficiently handling more than 2,000 guests per hour, keeping lines moving swiftly even on busy days, but the addition of Lightning Lane inflated standby waits. If the posted wait is more than 30 minutes, check back in the late afternoon, when you will often be able to walk on with little wait.

Silly Symphony Swings ★★★

**APPEAL BY AGE   PRESCHOOL ★★★★   GRADE SCHOOL ★★★★   TEENS ★★★★½
YOUNG ADULTS ★★★★   OVER 30 ★★★★   SENIORS ★★★★**

What it Is Swings rotating around a central tower. **Scope and scale** Minor attraction. **When to go** The first 90 minutes the park is open or just before closing. **Comments** Must be 40" tall to ride (48" tall to ride solo). **Duration of ride** Less than 1½ minutes. **Average wait in line per 100 people ahead of you** 6¼ minutes. **Loading speed** Slow.

Lose Things   Queasy   Muss Your 'Do

DESCRIPTION AND COMMENTS The theme pays tribute to the 1935 Mickey Mouse cartoon *The Band Concert,* the first color Mickey cartoon released to the public, with guests seated in swings flying around a tower. In the scary department, it's a wilder ride than Dumbo, but SSS is still just swings going in circles. A number of tandem swings are available to allow children 40–48 inches to ride with a parent; look for a separate tandem line to the left as you approach the attraction.

TOURING TIPS This is a fun and visually appealing ride, but it's also one that loads slowly and occasions long waits unless you ride during the first hour or so the park is open. Be aware that it's possible for the swing chairs to collide when the ride comes to a stop—Bob once picked up a nice bruise when an empty swing smacked him during touchdown. *Note:* Silly Symphony Swings may close early for *World of Color* performances.

▌▊ CARS LAND

THE CROWNING CAPSTONE on DCA's 2012 transformation, Cars Land was the first major "land" in an American Disney theme park devoted solely to a single film franchise. Tucked into the park's southeast corner on 12 acres of repurposed parking lot, Cars Land's main entrance is across from the Golden Vine Winery, though there is a secondary gateway in San Fransokyo Square (the vista through the stone archway is especially scenic). A massive mountainous backdrop topped with 125-foot-high peaks patterned after 1950s Cadillac tail fins, known as the Cadillac Range, cradles Ornament Valley, home to a screen-accurate re-creation of Radiator Springs. That's the sleepy single-stoplight town along Route 66 populated by Pixar's anthropomorphized automobiles. Along its main drag, in addition to three rides, you'll find eateries themed to the film's minor characters and souvenir shops selling *Cars*-themed and Route 66 merchandise.

Walking through the aesthetically astounding area is uncannily like stepping into the cinematic universe, and it's well worth the wait even if you weren't particularly enamored of the merchandise-moving movies. As striking as Cars Land is by daylight, it is even more stunning after sunset; the nightly neon-lighting ceremony set to the doo-wop classic "Life Could Be a Dream" is a magical must-see (showtimes are not publicized but occur promptly at sundown, so ask a Cars Land cast member and arrive early). Finally, a word to the wise from a Dallas, Texas, family:

Tip: *Cars Land has NO shade. Literally none. Wear a hat.*

Luigi's Rollickin' Roadsters ★★★

APPEAL BY AGE	PRESCHOOL ★★★★	GRADE SCHOOL ★★★★	TEENS ★★★½
YOUNG ADULTS ★★★½		OVER 30 ★★★½	SENIORS ★★★★

What it is Outdoor "dancing" car ride. **Scope and scale** Minor attraction. **When to go** During the first or last hours of the day. **Comment** Must be 32" to ride. **Duration of ride** About 1½ minutes. **Average wait in line per 100 people ahead of you** 10 minutes. **Loading speed** Slow.

DESCRIPTION AND COMMENTS Guests first queue inside the Casa Della Tires shop (where memorabilia from Luigi's and Guido's careers is on display), and then pass through a garden of automotive-inspired topiaries before approaching the attraction itself, which occupies an outdoor arena. Twenty small open-top faux Fiats (with the franchise's signature cartoon faces) serve as the ride vehicles. Passengers are just along for the ride, as the cars spin and "dance" autonomously around each other in unpredictable patterns, thanks to trackless technology.

With a library of Italian tunes like "Volare" and "Mambo Italiano" for the cars to dance to, each experience is a little different (you may even get a solo in the center of the floor while everyone else swirls around you), though each routine ends with a brief-but-brisk bout of spinning. But the cars' movements are surprisingly jerky, sometimes feeling like a shopping cart with a stuck wheel, and it's impossible to fully appreciate the choreographic patterns while you're in the middle of the ride. Much like the short-lived Luigi's Flying Tires hovercrafts that preceded it, Rollickin' Road-sters may actually be more fun to watch than to ride, so it's fortunate that benches are provided near the exit.

TOURING TIPS Luigi's capacity is limited. Try to ride during the first or last hours of the day.

Mater's Junkyard Jamboree ★★★

What it is Midway-type whip ride. **Scope and scale** Minor attraction. **When to go** Before noon. **Comment** Must be 32″ tall to ride. **Duration of ride** About 1½ minutes. **Average wait in line per 100 people ahead of you** 10 minutes; assumes both sides operating. **Loading speed** Slow.

Queasy

DESCRIPTION AND COMMENTS On the outskirts of town sits the junkyard home of Mater, the redneck tow truck voiced by Larry the Cable Guy. In his yard sit 22 baby tractors, each towing an open-air two-seater trailer. While Mater's voice emerges from a jury-rigged jukebox singing one of seven specially composed square-dancing tunes (plus one hilarious hidden song that plays only once per hour), the trac-tors travel in overlapping figure eight patterns along interlocking turn-tables. The vehicles are transferred from one revolving turntable to another, creating near-miss moments. In addition, Mater's trailers swing freely from side to side, creating a centripetal snapping sensation similar to vintage carnival whip rides. Mater's may look like a simple kiddie ride, but it supplies an unexpected kick that draws us back for repeated spins. This London, Ontario, dad echoed our assessment:

Mater's Junkyard Jamboree was surprisingly good. It doesn't look like much, but you have to ride it. We saw a woman lose her sunglasses because she wasn't prepared for how it swings around. The mechanically inclined adults exiting the ride were impressed with the engineering that allowed for the fig-ure eight movement.

TOURING TIPS Mater is the breakout hit character of the *Cars* franchise, and his namesake ride is visually attractive but slow loading. Still, it typically has the shortest queue of the three Cars Land attractions.

Radiator Springs Racers *(Lightning Lane)* ★★★★★

What it is Automotive dark ride with high-speed thrills. **Scope and scale** Super-headliner. **When to go** The first or last 30 minutes the park is open or use the single-rider line. **Comments** Not to be missed. Must be 40″ tall to ride; switching-off option (see page 165). **Duration of ride** About 4 minutes. **Average wait in line per 100 peo-ple ahead of you** 4 minutes. **Loading speed** Moderate–fast.

Dark   Scary   Lose Things   Miss Your 'Do

DESCRIPTION AND COMMENTS To the right of the Radiator Springs Courthouse at the end of Route 66 lies the entrance to Cars Land's ambitious headliner attraction. Dis-ney's Imagineers wedded an enhanced version of the high-speed slot cars developed for EPCOT's Test Track with immersive sets and elaborate animatronics. The ride, which covers nearly 6 of Cars Land's 12 acres, mixes slow indoor sections with thrilling open-air acceleration in a way that appeals to every demographic..

You begin your road trip by walking through Stanley's Oasis, the town's original 1909 settlement, and end up in a cavernous loading station. There you board a six-passenger convertible, each with a smiling face on its front grille, and you're off on a scenic tour of stunning Ornament Valley, on your way to compete in today's big race.

After a leisurely drive past massive rock formations and a majestic waterfall, you enter the show building for a series of indoor scenes depicting the residents of Radiator Springs. These environments don't quite match the awe-inspiring scale of scenes in Pirates of the Caribbean or Indiana Jones Adventure, but they are a big step up from the old-fashioned Fantasyland dark rides and feature movie-accurate animatronics with impressively expressive eyes and mouths (achieved through a combination of digital projections and practical effects). Along your tour, you'll be sidetracked by a tractor-tipping expedition with Mater, which leads to a run-in with an angry harvester. Before reaching the starting line, you'll need some new tires or a fresh coat of paint. Then it's time to line up alongside another carload of guests as you await Luigi's countdown. The last third of the ride is a flat-out race over camelback hills, under outcrops, and around banked curves, with a randomly chosen car crossing the finish line first. Radiator Springs Racers's top speed of 40 miles per hour falls short of Test Track's 60-plus peak, but the winding turns and airtime-inducing humps supply an exhilarating rush. After a final swing past the glowing stalactites of Tail Light Cavern and some parting praise from Lightning McQueen and Mater, you'll exit your vehicle and inspect your obligatory on-ride photo.

TOURING TIPS While Avengers Campus has diverted some demand, Radiator Springs Racers is still a massive draw from the minute the park opens every day. With a carrying capacity of about 1,500 riders per hour, the attraction sees standby waits of up to 3 hours during peak season, and even the single-rider queue can run 45 minutes or more. Your best options are to ride within the first few minutes after park opening, or step into the standby queue shortly before closing. If time permits, try to ride once by day and again after dark; evening illumination makes the outdoor portions especially enchanting.

Be warned that the ride regularly opens late due to daily maintenance, potentially wasting your valuable morning touring time. The ride also shuts down for long periods after any substantial rainstorm. Also be aware that the ride's singles queue often doesn't open until the standby line has built up a bit. You may have time for a quick spin on Luigi's or Mater's and still be among the first into Racers' single-rider entrance.

SAN FRANSOKYO SQUARE

THIS LAND TOOK THE Cannery Row–inspired eatery area adjacent to Paradise Bay, previously named Pacific Wharf, and remodeled it in 2023 after the futuristic metropolis from Marvel's *Big Hero Six*, adding a meet and greet with the robotic healthcare companion Baymax.

Across the Japanese Torii–style Golden Gate Bridge, along the **performance corridor** at the base of Grizzly Peak, you'll find a diminutive winery and **Golden Vine House** (formerly Blue Sky Cellar), an often-repurposed building that is currently a Disney Vacation Club sales center. It would be a stretch to call it an attraction, much less a themed area.

Bakery Tour ★★½

APPEAL BY AGE PRESCHOOL ★★½ GRADE SCHOOL ★★★ TEENS ★★★
YOUNG ADULTS ★★★ OVER 30 ★★★ SENIORS ★★★½

What it is Free bread! (Plus a short film and walking tour.) **Scope and scale** Diversion. **When to go** Anytime. **Duration of tour** 9 minutes. **Probable waiting time** None.

DESCRIPTION AND COMMENTS The Bakery Tour (hosted by Boudin Bakery) is a walk-through attraction featuring hosts Rosie O'Donnell and Colin Mochrie via video. It takes visitors through the history of the Boudin Bakery and also explains how the bread is baked for various restaurants across Disneyland Resort.

TOURING TIPS There's never a wait to enter this attraction, and you get a small bread sample as you walk in. The tour is a great way to kill 10 minutes. See this when you have some downtime, perhaps after a meal, on your way back to Pixar Pier, or before redeeming a Virtual Queue or Lightning Lane pass.

   If the bread sample whets your appetite, you can buy a full-size loaf (including ones shaped like Baymax) at the café adjoining the exit. Next door is the Ghirardelli Soda Fountain and Chocolate Shop, where you can indulge in ice-cream sundaes (or just inhale the free aromas) while admiring an animated diorama of San Francisco.

GRIZZLY PEAK

GRIZZLY PEAK, a huge mountain shaped like the head of a bear, is home to **Grizzly River Run,** a whitewater raft ride, and the **Redwood Creek Challenge Trail,** an outdoor playground that resembles an obstacle course. The area around **Soarin' Around the World** is known as Grizzly Peak Airfield and features woodsy theming appropriate to a national park in the High Sierras.

Grizzly River Run *(Lightning Lane)* ★★★★½

APPEAL BY AGE PRESCHOOL ★★★½ GRADE SCHOOL ★★★★½ TEENS ★★★★½
YOUNG ADULTS ★★★★½ OVER 30 ★★★★½ SENIORS ★★★★

What it is Whitewater raft ride. **Scope and scale** Headliner. **When to go** First hour the park is open, after 4:30 p.m., or use the single-rider line. **Comments** Not to be missed. Must be 42″ tall to ride. **Duration of ride** Over 6 minutes. **Average wait in line per 100 people ahead of you** 4½ minutes; assumes 32 rafts operating. **Loading speed** Moderate.

Scary Wet Lose Things Rough

DESCRIPTION AND COMMENTS Whitewater raft rides have been a hot-weather favorite of theme park patrons for decades. The ride consists of an unguided trip down a man-made river in a circular rubber raft, with a platform mounted on top seating six to eight people. The raft essentially floats free in the current and is washed downstream through rapids and waves. Because the river is fairly wide with numerous currents, eddies, and obstacles, there is no telling exactly where the raft will go. Thus, each trip is different and unpredictable. The rafts are a little smaller than those used on most rides of the genre. Because the current can buffet the smaller rafts more effectively, the ride is wilder and wetter.

What distinguishes Grizzly River Run from other theme park raft rides is Disney's trademark attention to visual detail. Where many similar rides essentially plunge down a concrete ditch, Grizzly River Run winds around and through Grizzly Peak, the park's foremost visual icon, with the great rock bear at the summit. Featuring a 50-foot climb and two drops—including a 22-footer where the raft spins as it descends—the ride flows into dark caverns and along the mountain's precipitous side before looping over itself just before the final plunge. Period-appropriate props support the mid-century national park theme.

Grizzly River Run is a heart thumper, one of the best of its genre anywhere. And at about 5½ minutes from lift hill to unload, it's also one of the longest. The visuals are outstanding, and the ride is about as good as it gets on a man-made river. While it's true that theme park raft rides have been around a long time, Grizzly River Run set a new standard that has yet to be superseded.

TOURING TIPS This attraction is hugely popular, especially on hot summer days. Ride the first hour the park is open, after 4:30 p.m., or use the single-rider line. Make no mistake—you will certainly get wet on this ride. Our recommendation is to wear shorts to the park and bring along a jumbo-size trash bag, as well as a smaller plastic bag. Before boarding the raft, take off your socks and punch a hole in your jumbo bag for your head. Though you can also cut holes for your arms, you will probably stay drier with your arms inside the bag. Use the smaller plastic bag to wrap around your shoes. If you are worried about mussing your hairdo, bring a third bag for your head.

A Shaker Heights, Ohio, family who adopted our garbage-bag attire, however, discovered that staying dry on a similar attraction at Walt Disney World is not without social consequences:

The Disney cast members and the other people in our raft looked at us like we had just beamed down from Mars. We didn't cut armholes in our trash bags because we thought we'd stay drier. The only problem was that once we sat down, we couldn't fasten our seat belts. The Disney person was quite put out and asked sarcastically whether we needed wet suits and snorkels. After a lot of wiggling and adjusting and helping each other, we finally got belted in and off we went, looking like sacks of fertilizer with little heads perched on top. It was very embarrassing, but I must admit that we stayed nice and dry.

If you forget your plastic bag, ponchos are available at the adjacent Rushin' River Outfitters. A Vancouver, Washington, reader advises availing yourself of the free short-term lockers found near Grizzly River Run:

The first time we rode Grizzly River Run, we wore ponchos per your advice. We looked ridiculous and the cast members looked at us like we were aliens. Our last two trips, we left our bags with others in our party, wore flip-flops on the ride, and had a blast! Not having to worry about our stuff getting soaked makes the ride way more enjoyable.

A bank of lockers is located across the walkway from the exit gift shop; use is complimentary for up to 2 hours.

Redwood Creek Challenge Trail   ★★★½

APPEAL BY AGE   PRESCHOOL ★★★★½   **GRADE SCHOOL** ★★★★½   **TEENS** ★★★½
YOUNG ADULTS ★★★★   **OVER 30** ★★★½   **SENIORS** ★★★

What it is Elaborate playground and obstacle course. **Scope and scale** Minor attraction. **When to go** Anytime. **Comments** Very well done; plan to spend about 20 minutes here. Must be 42" tall.

DESCRIPTION AND COMMENTS An elaborate maze of rope bridges, log towers, and a cave, the Redwood Creek Challenge Trail is a scout camp with a combination of elements from Adventureland's Treehouse and Tom Sawyer Island. Built into and around Grizzly Peak, the trail has eye-popping appeal for young adventurers. A mom from Salt Lake City writes:

Most underrated . . . If this were a city park, it would be packed every day. In Disneyland it seems to be the least popular thing. The kids, young and older, just loved it. The adults were able to change diapers, get snacks for all the kids, and sit down while the kids had a great time.

During the seasonal Lunar New Year celebrations, a corner of the wilderness explorer camp will be co-opted by lantern-lit Kumandra, where guests can meet and greet with Raya while her *Last Dragon* pal Sisu spurts jasmine-scented smoke from behind a curtain.

TOURING TIPS The largest children's play area in the park, and the only one that is dry (for the most part) and relatively shady, the Challenge Trail is the perfect place to let your kids cut loose for a while. Though the Challenge Trail will be crowded, you should not have to wait to get in. Experience it after checking out the better rides and shows. Be aware, however, that the playground is quite large; you will not be able to keep your children in sight unless you tag along with them.

Soarin' Around the World   ★★★★½

APPEAL BY AGE   PRESCHOOL ★★★★   **GRADE SCHOOL** ★★★★½   **TEENS** ★★★★½
YOUNG ADULTS ★★★★½   **OVER 30** ★★★★½   **SENIORS** ★★★★★

What it is Flight-simulation ride. **Scope and scale** Super-headliner. **When to go** The first 90 minutes the park is open or use the single-rider line. **Comments** The park's best ride for the whole family; not to be missed. Must be 40" tall to ride; switching-off option (see page 165). **Duration of ride** 4½ minutes. **Average wait in line per 100 people ahead of you** 4½ minutes; assumes 2 concourses operating. **Loading speed** Moderate.

Thumbs Up for the Whole Family

DESCRIPTION AND COMMENTS Soarin' Around the World is a thrill ride for all ages, as exhilarating as a hawk on the wing and as mellow as swinging in a hammock. If you've ever experienced flying dreams, you'll have a sense of how Soarin' feels. Once you enter the main theater, you're secured in a seat not unlike the ones used on inverted roller coasters (in which the coaster is suspended from above). Once everyone is in place, you are suspended with your legs dangling. Thus hung out to dry, you embark on a hang glider tour around the world with IMAX-quality images projected below you, and with the simulator moving your seat in sync with the movie.

The immersive images are well chosen and drop-dead beautiful, and special effects include wind, sound, and even smell.

The current ride film—which was created for the debut of Shanghai Disneyland—glides around the globe from the Matterhorn (the one in Switzerland, not Anaheim) and an arctic glacier to the Taj Mahal and Great Wall of China. Exclusive to DCA is a finale filmed over the Disneyland Resort. The visuals are stunningly sharp, thanks to laser IMAX projectors, and computer-animated animals are employed to create clever transitions, an improvement over the original's jarring location jumps. Jerry Goldsmith's memorable musical theme has returned with updated orchestrations, as has Patrick Warburton's flight attendant preshow, but there's a new trio of scents to inhale along the way; we're growing partial to Eau de Africa. While on balance we feel the updated Soarin' makes a worthy successor to what was already one of DCA's top-rated rides, some of the computer-generated imagery is distractingly artificial, and we still miss the orange-scented original's subtler emotional moments and more human scale. Fortunately, the original Soarin' Over California ride film, which many fans still consider superior to the current version, temporarily returns in the spring during DCA's Food & Wine Festival.

The ride itself is thrilling but also perfectly smooth, exciting, and relaxing. We think Soarin' is a must-experience for guests of any age who meet the height requirement. And yes, seniors we interviewed were crazy about it. But a North Carolina mom says:

Wait a minute! Soarin' was VERY cool but definitely on the scary side for people afraid of heights or who don't like that unsteady feeling. While we were "soaring" up, I was fine, but when we were going down, I had to continually say to myself, "This is only an illusion, I cannot fall out, this is only an illusion."

TOURING TIPS Aside from being a true technological innovation, Soarin' Around the World also happens to be located near the entrance of the park, thus ensuring heavy traffic all day. It should be your very first attraction in the morning after visiting Cars Land and Pixar Pier. The single-rider line can be a big time-saver, but it's not well marked; ask a cast member at the Lightning Lane entrance for a pass to access it.

The film features a number of vertical landmarks like the Eiffel Tower that look comically distorted from seats on the far ends. Once directed toward one of the two theaters, politely request to wait an extra cycle for seats in row B1 to have an ideal view.

LIVE ENTERTAINMENT *and* SPECIAL EVENTS

LIKE DISNEYLAND, DISNEY CALIFORNIA ADVENTURE offers a full slate of live entertainment, led by a nightly lagoon show that's worth the proverbial price of admission. The classic Disney characters are still in evidence here, especially around the park's entrance, but you'll also encounter heroes from the Pixar and Marvel universes, as well as original stories exclusive to DCA. And DCA is increasingly highlighting a diversity of flavors and cultures during its festive seasonal events.

Disney's World of Color—ONE Nighttime Spectacular
★★★★½

APPEAL BY AGE PRESCHOOL ★★★★ GRADE SCHOOL ★★★★½ TEENS ★★★★½
YOUNG ADULTS ★★★★½ OVER 30 ★★★★½ SENIORS ★★★★½

What it is Fountain show with special effects. **Scope and scale** Super-headliner.
When to go Check the app for showtimes and Virtual Queue availability; viewing pass
required. **Comment** Not to be missed. **Duration of show** 24 minutes. **Probable waiting time** Up to an hour for the best view.

DESCRIPTION AND COMMENTS The 1,200 high-pressure
water nozzles installed under the surface of DCA's Paradise
Bay are the infrastructure for Disney's $75 million attempt to
keep guests in the park (and spending money) until closing
time. If you've seen or heard about the spectacular fountain show at the
Bellagio in Las Vegas, *World of Color* is similar but larger, with more special effects and themed to Disney movies. The show includes a musical
score and incorporates dozens of Disney films and characters in its
24-minute performance. The show's backdrop includes Pixar Pal-A-Round,
which is fitted with special lighting effects for use in the show. Giant projection surfaces sculpted by sprayed water—even larger than those used
in *Fantasmic!*—display custom-made animations, and flamethrowers spew
almost enough heat to dry off guests standing in the splash zones. What's
most remarkable about the show is how the flashing colored lights and
pulsating fountains combine to look like low-level fireworks. The effects
are astounding, the colors are vibrant and deep, and the music includes
some beloved Disney songs.

The current incarnation of *World of Color,* introduced during 2023's
Disney100 celebration, is the first to mix in Marvel and *Star Wars* content
alongside Disney's animated franchises. Despite briefly paying lip service
to Walt in the opening and closing moments, *World of Color—ONE* mostly
features a cavalcade of characters from 1990s animated classics like *Mulan*
and *The Lion King,* along with newer films such as *Encanto, Coco, Moana,*
and *Soul,* while also making space for C-3PO and Dr. Strange. Minor tweaks
made in 2024 smoothed some jarring jumps between genres, improving
the overall pacing and making the finale feel more satisfying. The stylized
superhero silhouettes can be hard to identify, and the original theme song,
"Start a Wave," inspired by the concept of creating change through a single action, doesn't stick in your brain the way the old "Wonderful World of
Color" did. However, this is still a stunning production and a must-see finale
for your DCA day.

During the holiday season, a special "Season of Light" edition of *World
of Color* focuses on clips of Disney cartoons with wintry themes—from
Bambi to *Frozen*—synced with a soundtrack of tasteful Christmas classics.
Highlights include a *Fantasia* ballet backed by the brilliant a cappella
ensemble Pentatonix and Goofy's Trans-Siberian Orchestra–fueled lighting
display. In the interest of equal time for warmer climes, Hawaii's Stitch and
Latin America's Three Amigos even get in on the seasonal action via Bing
Crosby's "Mele Kalikimaka" and José Feliciano's "Feliz Navidad." The montage of princesses trying to evade their princes, set to Michael Bublé and
Idina Menzel's cover of "Baby, It's Cold Outside," is deliciously ironic, and a
skit with *Inside Out*'s Sadness being serenaded by Elvis's "Blue Christmas"

draws big laughs. But the stirring climax, featuring soaring hymns sung by Broadway's Heather Headley, is guaranteed to put a lump in your throat.

TOURING TIPS Entertainment value aside, *World of Color* is an operational nightmare. The effects were expressly designed to be viewed from Paradise Gardens Park, in the tiered area along the lagoon in front of The Little Mermaid attraction. Unfortunately, only about 4,500 people—less than a quarter of the park's average daily attendance—are permitted to stand there for each show. Getting a decent view for *World of Color* requires time, planning, and/or money, and therefore can almost seem to be more trouble to see than it's worth, but we still consider it not to be missed. A couple from San Jose writes:

Though the [viewing pass] line was horrible and waiting for the show was horrible, the show itself was simply amazing.

If you want anything approaching a decent view of *World of Color*, you'll need a special viewing pass, available either through the free Virtual Queue system or as part of a paid dining package.

World of Color meal packages are offered at lunch and dinner by Wine Country Trattoria and Magic Key Terrace in DCA, and for dinner at Storytellers Café at Disney's Grand Californian. The fixed-price meal runs $64 per adult ($38 for kids) at Storytellers Café, or $62 per adult ($37 for kids) at both restaurants inside DCA, which values the viewing passes at about $15 each. (The above prices do not include tax, tip, or alcohol.)

Wine Country Trattoria and Magic Key Terrace viewing-package meals include an appetizer, your choice of entrée, dessert, and nonalcoholic beverage; Storytellers Café packages include the buffet, nonalcoholic beverage, and a special dessert. After your meal, you'll receive special passes for each member of your party, permitting entry into a preferred viewing area reserved for dining-package patrons. Note that you don't actually watch the show from the restaurant, so you'll want to eat early enough to make it to the viewing area. There is also a *World of Color* dessert party for $89 per person (tax and tip included), where you snack on upscale sweets and sip sparkling wine (or nonalcoholic cider) while sitting at tall cocktail tables during the show. Dessert parties begin about an hour before the performance; check in by the Eureka water wheel (near Redwood Creek Challenge Trail) at the time on your reservation. Note that in the event *World of Color* is canceled due to technical difficulties or inclement weather, there are no refunds or rain checks for dinner packages. The viewing sections for premium dining and dessert party patrons are dead center along the waterline. Wine Country Trattoria, Magic Key Terrace, and Storytellers Café diners get the second-closest section to the water, standing immediately behind standard guests who request the splash zone along the front railing, and may catch some spray; dessert party guests get the elevated section slightly farther back, which affords a better (and drier) view. To enter the dining guests' area, look for the illuminated White (Wine Country Trattoria and Storytellers Café) or Purple (dessert party) entrance signs between the Blue and Yellow sections, directly across from The Little Mermaid ride. Though expensive, the dining and dessert packages are the only way to be guaranteed a central viewing spot with minimal crowding, and even then you should arrive up to an hour before showtime if you want to secure a prime spot for the early performance. On nights when there are multiple *World of Color* performances, early eaters receive passes to the first show (which often sells out quickly), while those eating later get less-coveted tickets to the later viewing; be sure to confirm when booking your meal which showing you'll be scheduled to attend.

Free viewing passes are distributed on a first-come, first-serve basis via the Disneyland app's Virtual Queue system starting at noon. Make sure that you get passes for your whole party at once, or you may end up in different showings. These passes are disconnected from the rest of the park's Lightning Lane system, so your *World of Color* reservation won't interfere with other attractions. On busy days, passes for the first performance may all be claimed within seconds. If seeing the earlier *World of Color* is a priority for you, we suggest getting a viewing pass the instant they become available.

Your Virtual Queue pass includes a return-time window, letting you know when you can enter either of the two color-coded viewing areas. Yellow stretches from the right side of the premium viewing section toward the Golden Zephyr, and Blue takes up the left side, including the bridge to Pixar Pier. A special section is available by request for disabled guests, and the prime areas in the middle are reserved for VIPs and dining-package purchasers. You won't be allowed into Paradise Gardens Park's viewing area until the return window starts (generally 30–45 minutes prior to the first showtime, or as late as 15 minutes before the evening's second performance), but the best viewing spots will all be claimed shortly after the area opens; don't be surprised to see lines of people stretching around the bay. Once inside the viewing area, try to move to the front of an elevated area. You're best off at the front of an elevated tier farther back, rather than at the rear of a lower section, as these readers from Langley, British Columbia, discovered:

World of Color *was great, but it was hard for me to see (wearing flat shoes and being 5'5"). My husband, who is 6'4", also found himself bobbing around trying to see. When we got there, we had good line of sight, but as people stood up and put their kids on their shoulders, it became difficult.*

And from a reader in Calgary, Alberta:

Don't trust that a [viewing pass] for World of Color *will guarantee you a good view. Get there as early as you can if seeing the show is important to you. The [pass] said to return 30 minutes prior to showtime, and I assumed that's when they would start allowing people in. Boy, was I wrong! We got there exactly 30 minutes prior, and the [viewing pass] area was already full of people! I spent most of the show staring at the backs of heads.*

If you don't mind getting drenched, ask a cast member about standing front-and-center in the splash zone. On a calm night, you'll be seriously spritzed, and if the wind blows the wrong way, you'll get completely soaked. You have been warned!

If all else fails, it's theoretically possible to view the show from various points around the park, but employees with flashlights will vigorously shoo you away from all the obvious vantage points. The best ticketless viewing spots are next to the Golden Zephyr, to the right of the Yellow section. Reservation-free viewing is also available immediately in front of The Little Mermaid attraction. You can see many of the fountain and lighting effects from the opposite side of Paradise Gardens Park and Pixar Pier, near the bases of the Pal-A-Round and Silly Symphony Swings, but the mist projections are illegible from that angle, so we can't recommend it for first-time viewers. On nights when there are multiple performances, you have much better odds of finding a good spot for the last show.

You can also watch *World of Color* from the upstairs bar of the Lamplight Lounge. The view of the projections is less than ideal, and the mobile app wait list for walk-ups can be long; but no reservations are required, and you can sit down with an adult beverage during the show, provided you can secure a perch in this popular watering hole.

The mass movement toward the exits that immediately follows each performance can be exhausting. Instead, relax and enjoy the musical encore that follows each fountain show; though not as explosive as the main performance, it's a colorful capper to the night, and it's much nicer exiting the park after the initial exodus has subsided. After the show, if you are headed to the hotels or Downtown Disney, you can bypass the crowd at the main entrance by exiting through the Grand Californian Hotel or the Pixar Place gate in Paradise Gardens Park.

PARADES

AFTER SEVERAL YEARS WITHOUT a regularly scheduled parade, DCA debuted the brand-new **Better Together: A Pixar Pals Celebration!** (★★★) parade during 2024's Pixar Fest (see page 284). This colorful processional includes floats themed to recent films like *Soul, Luca,* and *Turning Red* (featuring Red Panda Mei with 4*Town), along with a finale full of old friends from *Toy Story, Monsters Inc.,* and *The Incredibles*. With a running time under 15 minutes, and several elements (like the Luxo Jr. lamp that leads the procession) that were recycled from the old Pixar Play Parade, this isn't among Disney's most impressive entertainment efforts, but it is effective at drawing guests away from the other attractions.

The parade route runs from a gate between the Hyperion Theater and Guardians of the Galaxy—Mission: Breakout!, through Hollywood Land and around the fountain in Carthay Circle, and along the performance corridor past Cars Land to Paradise Gardens Park, where it disappears backstage through a gate to the left of Boardwalk Pizza. The second parade of the day (when scheduled) will start in Paradise Gardens Park and run the same path in the opposite direction.

Since DCA's parade route is far longer than Disneyland's, there's much less need to stake out your seat early. On busy days you may need to devote more than 30 to 60 minutes of time to make sure you secure a good viewing spot for the first showing, so we recommend riding rides during the first run, and then getting a spot shortly before the second performance. Most guests watch from Hollywood Boulevard or Carthay Circle. The viewing areas near Paradise Gardens Park usually fill up last, so we recommend checking there if you need a spot. Any place along the parade route will offer the same experience, and since the floats are exceedingly tall, you shouldn't have to be seated right up front to have an excellent view. Once the parade has started, count on gridlock all along the route. If you watch the parade near the gate where it exits, you can see a special dance finale. Dining packages with reserved parade viewing at Sonoma Terrace, and a buffet of light snacks and soft drinks, cost $69 per person (including tax and tip); parties start 45 minutes prior to each parade.

AVENGERS CAMPUS LIVE ENTERTAINMENT

ALTHOUGH AVENGERS CAMPUS sports two moving attractions, it's the abundance of character appearances that brings the land to life. In addition to the scheduled performances detailed below, you never know which heroes or villains from across the Marvel multiverse might pop up, or where. Keep your eyes open for Kate Bishop atop the Quinjet landing platform, as well as Monica Rambeau and Ms. Marvel (aka Kamala Khan) meeting fans down below.

THE AMAZING SPIDER-MAN! (★★★) A half dozen times each day, your friendly neighborhood Spider-Man will be spotted scrambling along the rooftop above his signature attraction, engaging in some unimpressive tumbling stunts while miming cringe-worthy dialogue. Sit tight because the amazing part comes at the end of this 4-minute event, when a next-generation animatronic stunt-Spidey is catapulted skyward, sailing grace-fully toward a backstage landing zone while striking a classic comic book pose. The cutting-edge robot, which was designed in part by the late Grant Imahara of *Mythbusters,* reliably brings pedestrian traffic to a halt with every flight. After this jaw-dropping moment, the web-head reappears in human form to give high-fives to his fans. Spidey sometimes returns later to pose for photos after his stunt shows are done for the day. Be aware that if you stand near the WEB SLINGERS ride entrance, you'll miss the big finale, which is best viewed near the land's main entrance.

AVENGERS ASSEMBLE (★★½) Black Widow and Black Panther (or another fellow Avenger) team up to battle Taskmasker's minions in this missable 6-minute stunt show staged atop the Quinjet landing platform overlooking Avengers Campus. The fight choreography doesn't pack much of a punch, and the ending is confusingly anticlimactic. It doesn't help that tall balcony rails block the performers' bodies unless you stand too far back to see their facial expressions. Pause and watch if it happens while you're passing by, but don't go out of your way to see it. The cast of *Avengers Assemble* rotates frequently; a special Christmas edition featuring Hawkeye is the most fun.

GUARDIANS OF THE GALAXY: AWESOME DANCE OFF! (★★★) This inter-active dance show, staged a half dozen times each day outside the Guardians of the Galaxy ride, features some of the attraction's stars. Peter Quill and Gamora (or Mantis) arrive on a mission to retrieve Star-Lord's beloved boom box and engage guests in a boogie-off to 1970s disco classics "for the sake of the universe." Stick around until the end and you might get a meet and greet with Groot, everyone's favorite anthropomorphic foliage.

WARRIORS OF WAKANDA: THE DISCIPLINES OF THE DORA MILAJE (★★★½) By far the best live show at Avengers Campus, this 10-minute interactive encounter with Wakanda's shorn-skulled women warriors combines a kinetic audience-participation movement class with a surprisingly moving tribute to fallen heroes. The presentation begins with a martial procession to the semicircular benches outside Dr. Strange's sanctuary, which serve as the training session's stage. If you're eager to pledge your allegiance to T'Challa, stand along the blue line to the right of the large "A" logo for a front-row view.

LIVE ENTERTAINMENT THROUGHOUT THE PARK

DISNEY CHARACTERS Character appearances are listed in the daily entertainment schedule. In addition to the Avengers Campus characters detailed in this section, Disney Junior characters make appearances in Hollywood Land. The "fab five" (plus a couple of obscure old-school Disney characters like Oswald the Lucky Rabbit and Clarabelle Cow) can be found around Carthay Circle in dapper roaring twenties duds. Over at the Hollywood Backlot stage, classic Disney friends cosplay as their favorite Marvel superheroes. Mater and Lightning take turns posing for photos near the Cozy Cone Motel; these life-size vehicles can deliver quips recorded by the original voice actors to grinning guests. And Baymax dispenses healing hugs with his pal Hiro in San Fransokyo Square.

HOLLYWOOD BACKLOT STAGE This open-air stage features small productions and Disney characters. During the off-season, visiting school bands, glee clubs, and dance teams frequently use this stage. Check the entertainment schedule to see what's playing.

HYPERION THEATER The 2,000-seat Hyperion Theater was DCA's premier venue for Broadway-quality live productions based on Disney animated films, like *Aladdin* and *Frozen,* before going dark during the pandemic. It temporarily reawakened in summer 2023 with *Rogers: The Musical,* a 30-minute retelling of Captain America's origin story, starring singing versions of Steve Rogers, Agent Peggy Carter, and Nick Fury. The show features the song "Save Our City," created for the Disney+ series *Hawkeye,* plus "Star Spangled Man" from the First Avenger film and five brand-new tunes. Hyperion Theater productions are very popular, and guests start filling the standby queue more than an hour before the curtain rises. If performances resume, showtimes will be listed in the app and on the marquee, and the first and last shows of the day are less crowded. Though all seats provide good sight lines, we recommend sitting upstairs for the best view of the staging or on the ground level relatively close to the entrance doors (if possible) for an easy exit after the performance. Finally, be forewarned that the sound volume for Hyperion Theater productions could give heavy metal concerts a good run for their money.

STREET ENTERTAINMENT You'll frequently find a period-appropriate klezmer, Irish, or other ethnic band playing outside Paradise Garden Grill. On Buena Vista Street, the **Five and Dime** (★★★★) musical sextet (accompanied by a zoot suit–clad Goofy) sings jazz standards of the 1920s and 1930s, such as "Million Dollar Baby," "I Got Rhythm," and

"Bye Bye Blackbird," to create one of the best street shows in Disney's repertoire. You may also bump into interactive improvisation actors portraying police officers, bicycle messengers, or other eccentric **Citizens of Buena Vista** (★★★½), a troupe similar to the popular Streetmosphere characters at Disney's Hollywood Studios. **Mariachi Divas** (★★★★) is a fabulous all-female mariachi musical group that periodically plays sets in the Paradise Gardens Park gazebo. They are probably the only multiple Grammy Award–winning recording artists with a regular theme park gig. We particularly enjoy the Divas' rendition of "It's a Small World." *Operation: Playtime!* (★★★) in Paradise Gardens Park is a Blue Man Group–esque street show of another color, featuring *Toy Story*'s Green Army Men banging up a storm on improvised drums.

SEASONAL EVENTS

FOLLOWING IN EPCOT'S FOOTSTEPS, DCA has been expanding its seasonal festival lineup, offering an ever-increasing array of events featuring temporary food kiosks and additional live entertainment. Sip and Savor Pass souvenir sampling lanyards, available during some seasonal events, are valid for a set number of selected samples from food booths. If fully used on the most expensive eligible offerings, they offer modest savings over buying à la carte, but they can't be used for alcoholic beverages. Be warned that the festival booths halt sales a full hour before DCA closes, and lines for seasonal food booths can grow excessively long, especially on weekends. Save time by paying for all your selections with any one booth's cashier, then show your receipt at the other pick-up windows around the park to enjoy all your items before the day ends.

In January and February, the **Lunar New Year** celebration brings a brief processional led by Mulan and Mushu with Raya (from *Raya and the Last Dragon*), plus a special 6-minute *World of Color* preshow with music made for Shanghai Disneyland. Look for a traditional Lucky Wishes Wall and kids' crafts at Paradise Gardens—where *Turning Red*'s Mei Lee (in partial panda form) and her mother, Ming, greet guests—and Asian culinary treats at food booths along the park's walkways.

The spring **Food & Wine Festival,** held annually in March and April, introduces a taste of the long-running, similarly named EPCOT event to Anaheim with a California twist. Vending kiosks are placed throughout the park, mostly along Paradise Gardens Park and the corridor between Carthay Circle and the bridge to Pixar Pier. The booths are comparable to those found at EPCOT's events, although far fewer in number, and likewise serve tasty-but-tiny plates and thimbles of alcohol at indigestion-inducing prices. Similar seafood and meat menu items can sometimes be found cheaper elsewhere at the resort; your best bet is to stick with the vegetarian offerings, which are filling and fairly priced. Also during the festival, Sonoma Terrace and Hollywood Land host free culinary demonstrations and hands-on kids' activities on outdoor stages, as well as extra-fee seminars with celebrity chefs. See disneyland.com/foodandwine for more details.

During **Pixar Fest** (late April though early August) Hollywood Land hosts Club Pixar interactive dance parties in the evening, with live music, games, and specialty cocktails. Pixar film–inspired food booths are found in the park, along with an installation that MagicBand+ wearers can activate.

In the fall, Cars Land's residents celebrate **Haul-O-Ween** with special decorations, custom soundtracks for the Luigi's and Mater's rides, and costumes on the car characters. To celebrate Dia de los Muertos, the Paradise Garden Grill area is rechristened from late August until November as the **Plaza de la Familia,** home to *A Musical Celebration of Coco* (★★★★). This live outdoor production, which features handcrafted folk art puppets and propulsive folklórico dancers, is not to be missed. **Oogie Boogie Bash,** the park's popular after-hours Halloween event, features a "Frightfully Fun" parade led by the Headless Horseman, a Trick-or-Treat stage show with Mickey and Minnie, themed treat trails, and rare character encounters. Parties are held on select Tuesday, Thursday, and Sunday nights in late August through October. Tickets cost $134–$189, depending on the date, and include 3 hours of admission prior to the park's regular closing time before the Oogie Boogie Bash begins. Visit disneyland.com/HalloweenParty for details, and book early if interested because the events usually sell out, and the nonrefundable tickets can't be resold or transferred.

We attended the inaugural Oogie Boogie Bash and enjoyed the special entertainment, especially the atmospheric Villains' Grove walk-through, which transforms Redwood Creek Challenge Trail into an eerie wonderland of mist and color. However, we don't think the event is a great value, especially for guests like this Daly City reader who remembers the previous event:

> *I went to the Oogie Boogie Halloween Bash at DCA. In my opinion, it is not worth the money. I was disappointed that the ticket was not a park hopper as in previous years, and [the event] just simply did not have the same quality as in the past when the Halloween party was over in Disneyland. I will not be doing it again if it remains at DCA.*

If you do attend DCA during the Halloween parties, be sure to pack some extra patience because lines at security and the turnstiles can be especially long on event nights. You'll need to receive a wristband that allows you to remain in the park after the day guests are ushered out; if there's a long line to obtain them at the park entrance, go to the Golden Vine House. Plan your evening around the exclusive entertainment and don't miss the parade, which only runs once per night; we snagged a great spot near Carthay Circle less than 20 minutes before step-off. Be sure to show up early enough to catch the Headless Horseman, who trots through the streets in a preparade 10 minutes prior to the big procession.

Finally, the **Disney Festival of Holidays** highlights a wide range of cultures from fall through New Year's, with food and entertainment honoring Christmas, Hanukkah, Diwali, Kwanzaa, and more. Cars Land gets decked out with special decor and attraction music during **Cars Land Christmas**. And **¡Viva Navidad!** honors the holidays with Hispanic flair from November through Three Kings' Day with a festive street celebration full of mouthwatering foods, live storytellers, and traditional musicians, where fans can meet Mirabel from *Encanto*. Visit disneyland.com/events-tours/disney-california-adventure to stay up-to-date on DCA's seasonal event schedule.

UNHERALDED TREASURES *at* DCA

TREASURE Lamplight Lounge bar | **LOCATION** On the bridge to Pixar Pier

LAMPLIGHT LOUNGE IS A RESTAURANT on the span connecting Pixar Pier to the performance corridor. Instead of heading downstairs to the restaurant from the entrance, though, go around the walkway. There, you'll find the outdoor bar, where you can enjoy a full-service drink menu and a small selection of food. This is also one of the best places to enjoy the view. It's a bit too sunny during the day, but as the sun sets and the evening lights come on, the Lamplight Lounge turns into a mellow hideaway where you can enjoy a beautiful view of Pixar Pier. In the background, you hear music, laughter, and the occasional sounds of a roller coaster, while watching small waves lap against the pier that houses a brightly lit carousel—enough to make you forget that you're sitting in the middle of a completely artificial environment.

TREASURE Redwood Creek Challenge Trail | **LOCATION** Opposite Grizzly Peak

MAYBE A VISIT TO A THEME PARK was your kid's idea, and you prefer a quiet walk in the woods. If you want to take a break from the hectic rush of a trip to DCA, hop over to the Redwood Creek Challenge Trail. You probably assume that this is just a playground designed for kids, but the area is actually a good representation of a wilderness park. OK, so you don't really need to bring your bird-watching book, but there are various nooks and crannies, as well as a few "ranger buildings" that are very well themed (down to the wildlife books on the shelves). You could easily spend a portion of your day just enjoying the decidedly rustic feel of Redwood Creek.

TRAFFIC PATTERNS *at* DCA

AS SOON AS THE PARK OPENS, most guests head straight for Radiator Springs Racers in Cars Land, with a smaller number heading to Avengers Campus toward WEB SLINGERS or Guardians of the Galaxy.

On days of lighter attendance, waits of more than an hour will form within a few minutes at Racers; waits of 2 hours or more appear on holidays and other days of peak attendance. Of the other attractions in Cars Land, waits for Luigi's Rollickin' Roadsters will typically be 15–30 minutes as soon as the park opens, while Mater's Junkyard Jamboree's waits will be low for the first hour or two that DCA is open.

The wait times at the attractions in Cars Land will usually peak 11 a.m.–2 p.m. Radiator Springs Racers will have consistent 75- to

120-minute waits throughout the day, possibly higher if the attraction has to shut down for unscheduled maintenance, a common occurrence. Waits for Mater's Junkyard Jamboree will start to drop by 4 p.m., and lines at Luigi's Rollickin' Roadsters will start to diminish around dinnertime.

Wait times in Avengers Campus build slightly slower than in Radiator Springs, usually peaking at WEB SLINGERS within an hour after opening and at Mission: Breakout! between 11 a.m. and noon. Lines at both rides don't drop off until close to closing time.

As crowded as Cars Land and Avengers Campus get, the good news is that traffic to the rest of DCA is relatively light for the first hour the park is open. When DCA opens before 10 a.m., lines for Soarin' Around the World, the Incredicoaster, and Toy Story Midway Mania! are usually less than 20 minutes, even during holidays.

At Grizzly Peak, Soarin's wait times start to climb about an hour after the park opens and peak 11 a.m.–2 p.m. Once the crowds are in the park, Soarin' will have waits of at least 30–35 minutes for the rest of the day during most times of year. Next door, wait times at Grizzly River Run are relatively low for the first hour the park is open. During summer and warm holidays, lines grow quickly about an hour after the park opens, peaking at around noon. Waits grow more slowly when the weather is cooler but still peak around noon. Expect waits to start dropping around 4 p.m. regardless of the time of year.

Waits at Monsters, Inc. in Hollywood Land usually peak 11 a.m.–noon, then typically drop off at 6 p.m. most days and 8 p.m. on holidays. *Disney Junior Dance Party!* draws good-size crowds throughout the late morning and afternoon.

Toward the back of the park, long waits develop fastest at Toy Story Midway Mania! and the Incredicoaster—still about an hour after the park opens—and peak by 11 a.m. Like Soarin' Around the World, Toy Story will remain popular for the rest of the day, regardless of season. Secondary attractions, including Goofy's Sky School and Pixar Pal-A-Round, won't usually be too crowded until about 2 hours after the park opens. Like the attractions at Hollywood Land, most lines at B-list Paradise Gardens Park/Pixar Pier attractions start to drop after 4 p.m. Lines at The Little Mermaid seem to be low throughout the day and on any day of the year.

Park departures begin around 3 p.m., when families with small children start heading home. However, park hoppers and local Magic Key passholders start coming into the park in the afternoon and generally stay for the evening. It's common to see waits hold steady or even rise from early evening until the park closes, undoubtedly because of Cars Land, Avengers Campus, and *World of Color*.

World of Color viewing passes are generally available until 11 a.m. or noon most days. Guests with *World of Color* passes will begin queuing in the Grizzly Peak and Paradise Gardens Park walkways an hour or more before showtime. The largest wave of departing guests occurs at the end of *World of Color*. Just before closing, crowd levels are thin, except, of course, at Cars Land, Soarin' Around the World, and Avengers Campus.

DCA TOURING PLANS

PRELIMINARY INSTRUCTIONS FOR ALL DISNEY CALIFORNIA ADVENTURE TOURING PLANS

ON DAYS OF MODERATE-TO-HEAVY ATTENDANCE, follow the touring plans exactly, deviating only when you do not wish to experience a listed show or ride.

1. Buy your admission in advance (see "Admission Options" on page 20) and link it with your park reservations inside the Disneyland smartphone app.

2. Visit disneyland.com or call ☎ 714-781-4636 the day before you go for the official opening time.

3. Become familiar with the park-opening procedures (described on pages 252–253) and read over the touring plan of your choice, so you will have a basic understanding of what you are likely to encounter as you enter the park.

USING LIGHTNING LANE WITH A DCA TOURING PLAN

IF YOU CHOOSE TO PURCHASE Genie+, head directly to the first attraction on the touring plan upon entering the park, and make a Lightning Lane reservation for the next available participating ride in the plan while on your way there. You may also purchase an Individual Lightning Lane reservation if you wish, but wait until the return time reaches the busier midday before buying for maximum time savings. Deviate from the itinerary and work your return times into your day as necessary, reoptimizing your plan afterward (if using Lines) and always booking a new return time for the next available attraction as soon as you redeem the previous one. Visit the rides that don't offer Lightning Lane in the order of your touring plan between reservations.

On most days you should be able to utilize Lightning Lane at all or most of the park's Genie+ attractions before return times run out, but if you are attending on a very crowded day, prioritize your reservations in this order:

1. WEB SLINGERS: A Spider-Man Adventure	5. Grizzly River Run *(raise or lower priority with the temperature)*
2. Guardians of the Galaxy—Mission: Breakout!	6. Incredicoaster
3. Toy Story Midway Mania!	7. Monsters, Inc. Mike & Sulley to the Rescue!
4. Soarin' Around the World	8. Goofy's Sky School

USING EARLY ENTRY WITH A DCA TOURING PLAN

IF YOU ARE USING EARLY ADMISSION and following one of our touring plans, your first stop will be influenced by which gate you enter. Everyone coming through the front turnstiles should swing to WEB SLINGERS first, followed by Guardians of the Galaxy (for grownups) or Mater's (for little kids). Grand Californian guests will reach Soarin' first, while the Pixar Place gate is closest to Little Mermaid and Incredi-coaster. Note that the two hotel entrances start their security screenings only minutes prior to early entry, which is the time that the front gate opens. No matter where you enter, get into the standby (or single-rider) line for Radiator Springs Racers before the off-site hordes arrive, unless you're purchasing a Lightning Lane for later. When you reach an attraction on your plan that you've already experienced during early entry, either skip that step or ride again if the wait isn't too long.

DCA ONE-DAY TOURING PLAN FOR ADULTS
(page 405)

FOR Adults without small children. **ASSUMES** Willingness to experience all rides and shows.

Height and age requirements apply to many attractions. If you have kids who aren't eligible to ride, try switching off (see page 165) or use the One-Day Touring Plan for Families with Small Children.

DCA ONE-DAY TOURING PLAN FOR FAMILIES WITH SMALL CHILDREN *(page 406)*

FOR Adults with small children. **ASSUMES** Willingness to experience all rides and shows.

All of the attractions on this plan have minimum height requirements of 40 inches or shorter. If you have kids who aren't eligible to ride, try switching off (see page 165). This touring plan includes most of the amusement park rides in Paradise Gardens Park and Pixar Pier.

DCA ONE-DAY TOURING PLAN FOR FAMILIES WITH TWEENS *(page 407)*

FOR Adults with children ages 8–12. **ASSUMES** Willingness to experience all rides and shows.

The attractions in this plan have minimum height requirements up to 48 inches. If you have kids who aren't eligible to ride, try switching off (see page 165). It includes every attraction popular with this age group and sets aside ample time for lunch and dinner.

THE BEST OF DISNEYLAND RESORT IN ONE DAY
(pages 391–394)

See page 242 for a description of these plans.

PART 8

DINING *and* SHOPPING *in and around* DISNEYLAND

▌▌ DINING *in* DISNEYLAND RESORT

IN THIS SECTION, we aim to help you find good food without going broke or tripping over one of Disneyland Resort's many culinary land mines. More than 50 restaurants operate in Disneyland Resort, including about 20 full-service restaurants, several of which are inside the theme parks. Collectively, Disney restaurants offer reasonable variety, serving everything from Louisiana Creole to California fusion, and a broader array of international cuisines—including Korean and Caribbean—are now represented.

On the downside, while Disneyland Resort restaurant quality is much better now than it was in the early aughts, we've seen repeated portion reductions and price increases at some of our former favorite eateries in recent years. These downgrades have been especially apparent in the wake of postpandemic inflation, although "shrinkflation" has been less severe at Disneyland than at our local supermarket. Unlike other attractions and shops inside the resort, the food and beverage operation remains in constant flux. Venues open and close, add and delete menu items, and change decor throughout the year. We strive to provide you with the most accurate information possible; however, we do eventually have to go to press with the most current information we have at the time. Keep this in mind when using the guide. You can find up-to-date Disneyland Resort menu information in the Lines app and the official Disneyland app.

You can expect to pay hefty prices for food within Disneyland Resort. Nearly every entrée, snack, and drink purchased inside the theme parks and resort hotels will cost anywhere from 50% to 300% more than similar items at your hometown eateries. On the concession markup scale, Disneyland falls just behind airports and sports stadiums. As a Vancouver, Washington, reader observed:

After visiting the park several times in the last couple of years, I've finally come to accept that the price charged for food, souvenirs, and lodging is probably double what they are actually worth. Sort of like getting charged $10 for a Bud Light at an NBA game.

However, its food is a bargain compared to some regional theme parks, and you can find munchies at more moderate (or at least mall-like) prices in Downtown Disney. To prepare your belly and budget, Disneyland's official app lets you browse the menu (including prices) for every eatery in the resort, from fine dining to the churro carts.

DISNEY DINING 101

DISNEYLAND RESORT RESTAURANT RESERVATIONS: WHAT'S IN A NAME

DISNEY TINKERS CEASELESSLY with its restaurant-reservations policy. Disney Dining issues reservations that aren't exactly reservations. Your name and essential information are taken, well, as if you were making a reservation, but a table isn't actually being held for you; rather, you will be seated ahead of walk-ins—that is, those guests without reservations. Disneyland's online dining reservations system allows you to book a table without any pesky human interaction. On your computer or smartphone, visit disneyland.disney .go.com/dining, or tap "Check Dining Availability" in the Disneyland app's main menu, to see restaurant availability; most tables may be

unofficial **TIP**
Dining reservations are available to all Disneyland visitors—not just guests of the resort hotels. In the theme parks, you can make reservations for the next 60 days using the free Disneyland app.

reserved through either method, but some dining packages for shows and parades may need to be booked via a web browser rather than the mobile app. You will need to create a Disney login account (if you don't already have one) and supply a credit card and phone number to secure a booking (see the discussion below). You can also try calling Disney Dining at ☎ 714-781-3463, but plan on spending hours on hold before reaching a human being. Reservations can be booked 60 days in advance for Disneyland Resort hotel guests and off-site visitors alike, starting at midnight PST online or 7 a.m. PST over the phone.

Disneyland's dining reservations scheme is somewhat less stress-inducing than Walt Disney World's. However, while some in-park restaurants still offer same-week (or sometimes same-day) availability, demand for table-service reservations at popular venues has skyrocketed since the resort's 2021 reopening, making it more important than ever to book your mealtimes as soon as eligible. If your preferred seatings are unavailable at first, keep checking back because cancellations are common. And if you still can't get the table you want online, inquire at the restaurant in person; glitches in the reservation system sometimes leave open tables even when the computer says they are fully booked.

BEHIND THE SCENES AT
DISNEYLAND RESORT DINING

DISNEY RESTAURANTS OPERATE on what they call a template system. Instead of scheduling reservations for actual tables, reservationists fill time slots. The number of slots available is based on the average observed length of time that guests occupy a table at a particular restaurant. Disneyland Resort Dining (DRD) tries to fill every time slot for every seat in the restaurant, or come as close to filling every slot as possible. No seats—repeat, none—are *reserved* for walk-ins, though all restaurants accommodate such customers on a space-available basis.

With dining reservations, your waiting time will almost always be less than 20 minutes during peak hours, and often less than 10 minutes. If you just walk in, especially during busier seasons, expect to wait 40–75 minutes.

Note: Disneyland dining reservations are the Disney-restaurant equivalent of Lightning Lane. This feature, available where noted, gives you the option of picking a time and cutting to the head of the line. You may still have to wait, but it's from the front of the line instead of the back.

GETTING YOUR ACT TOGETHER

DRD HANDLES reservations for both Disney-owned and independent restaurants at the theme parks, Disney hotels, and Downtown Disney.

If you fail to make dining reservations before you leave home, or if you want to make your dining decisions spontaneously, your chances of getting a table at the restaurant of your choice are dependent on the travel season. Blue Bayou at Disneyland Park, Carthay Circle at DCA, Napa Rose at the Grand Californian Hotel, and the various character-meal venues are the most likely to sell out. If you visit Disneyland during a busy time of year, it's to your advantage to make dining reservations.

Disneyland collects a credit card number with every dining reservation. If you poop out in the park and are a no-show for your meal, you will be charged $10 per person. Your reservation will be voided 15 minutes after the scheduled time, and the penalty will apply unless you cancel or modify your booking using the app at least 2 hours before your seating (some restaurants or events require more notice). A 24-hour cancellation policy applies to appointments at Bibbidi Bobbidi Boutique, as well as cabanas at the hotel pools. If you've lined up many seatings, it's a good idea to log in a few days before you arrive to make sure that everything is in order. If you stay at a Disney resort, Guest Services can print out a summary of all your dining reservations. If you have a seating for a theme park restaurant at a time before park opening, as is sometimes the case for a character breakfast, simply proceed to the turnstiles and inform a cast member, who will admit you to the park.

You can still sit down to eat at select restaurants without a reservation. Simply search for the restaurant of your choice in the Disneyland app and look for a "walk-up list" button with estimated wait times. You'll only be able to join the wait list if you are standing close to the restaurant. Disneyland app has an unfortunate habit of saying that no walk-ups are available even when there are plenty of empty tables. This is especially common at locations frequented by locals, such as DCA's Magic Key Terrace and Trader Sam's at the Disneyland Hotel. Ask in person at the restaurant if you can join the waiting list, even if the app insists it's full.

DRESS

DRESS IS INFORMAL at all theme park restaurants, but dressy casual is appropriate for resort restaurants such as Napa Rose. That means dress slacks (or dress shorts) with a collared shirt for men and slacks, skirts, or dress shorts with a blouse or sweater (or a dress) for women.

FOOD ALLERGIES AND SPECIAL REQUESTS

WITH MILLIONS OF AMERICANS now reporting sensitivity to certain foods or following specific diets, the restaurants at Disneyland Resort are receiving a record number of special dietary requests. Happily, Disney has responded to this trend and is now able to accommodate most guests' gustatory needs. If you have dietary concerns, call ☎ 714-781-3463 to discuss any special requests when making dining reservations, and ask to speak with a chef or manager before your meal when you arrive at a restaurant to confirm that your needs can be met.

Disneyland provides allergy-friendly menus upon request at many of its table- and quick-service restaurants, both inside and outside the theme parks. These menus explicitly call out dishes without ingredients such as gluten, dairy, peanuts, tree nuts, eggs, soy, or shellfish. If you have one of these common allergies or are vegetarian, you can be confident of finding something to eat almost anywhere without needing to make special arrangements ahead of time. However, if you have an uncommon or complicated allergy or a metabolic disorder, email special.diets@disneyland.com with your needs at least two weeks before your visit.

Kosher meals are available on request at Plaza Inn, Rancho del Zocalo, and Galactic Grill at Disneyland Park, and at Smokejumpers Grill, Mortimer's Market, and Carthay Circle at DCA. Kosher meals can also be delivered to table-service locations with 24 hours' notice (call the above number). All locations also have vegan or vegetarian dishes, and meat substitutes like Impossible Burger are now available across the property. Alert your server if you're on a strictly plant-based diet; otherwise, they often don't alert you to incidental animal products in things such as cooking oil.

The Disney folks do their best to meet guests' needs, but they don't have separate allergen-free kitchen facilities or dining areas, so inadvertent cross contamination is always a possibility. Large coolers are prohibited unless your dietary issue is a matter of life or death.

However, you are allowed to bring your own food and medication into the parks in small soft-sided coolers; loose ice cubes and dry ice are prohibited, but you can bring reusable ice packs or a frozen bottled water. Medication can be refrigerated at First Aid. Glass containers are still prohibited, but snacks and EpiPens are OK; just know that Disney employees aren't allowed to hold or heat up your personal food.

Do Disney's attempts at dietary accommodation work? Well, a Phillipsburg, New Jersey, mom reports her family's experience:

> My 6-year-old has many food allergies, and we often have to bring food with us to restaurants when we go out to eat. I was able to make reservations at the Disney restaurants in advance and indicate these allergies to the reservation clerk. When we arrived at the restaurants, the staff was already aware of my child's allergies and assigned our table a chef who double-checked the list of allergies with us. Each member of the waitstaff was also informed of the allergies. The chefs were very nice and made my son feel very special (to the point where my other family members felt a little jealous).

However, a reader from Centennial, Colorado, warns:

> If you have more than four food allergies, it would be an excellent idea to take shelf-stable foods and use lockers while in Disneyland and DCA, as Disney does not deal well with multiple food allergies. I had to talk to about five people before I could talk to a chef. Due to my numerous food allergies, he cooked my meal himself. I have to admit, what I ate was excellent. Unfortunately, the rest of my family ate and left before I was finished.

In particular, employees at outdoor food carts, as well as at the temporary kitchen kiosks used during special events, may not be as well educated about allergies, as a reader from Salt Spring Island, British Columbia, discovered:

> We were there for the start of Festival of Holidays, and it was impossible to get anything gluten-free. Cast members did not have answers to dietary restrictions.

A FEW CAVEATS

BEFORE YOU BEGIN EATING YOUR WAY through Disneyland, take our advice:

1. However creative and enticing the menu descriptions, avoid fancy food at full-service restaurants in the theme parks. Order dishes that the kitchen is unlikely to botch. Stick with what's familiar in most cases and you won't be disappointed.

2. Don't order baked, broiled, poached, or grilled seafood unless the restaurant specializes in seafood or rates at least ★★★½ in our dining profiles.

3. Theme park restaurants rush their customers to make room for the next group of diners. Eating at high speed may appeal to a family with young, restless children, but for people wanting to relax, it's more like dining in a pressure chamber. The exceptions to this rule may be Wine Country Trattoria and Carthay Circle Restaurant inside DCA, upscale venues that encourage a respite over a glass or bottle of premium wine. But, sadly, you may feel pressure even there in peak season.

If you want to linger over your expensive meal, don't order your entire dinner at once. Order drinks, study the menu while you sip, and then order appetizers. Tell the waiter you need more time to decide among entrées. Order your main course only after appetizers have been served. Dawdle over coffee and dessert.

DISNEYLAND RESORT RESTAURANT CATEGORIES

IN GENERAL, food and beverage offerings at Disneyland Resort are defined by service, price, and convenience:

FULL-SERVICE RESTAURANTS Full-service restaurants are in Disneyland Resort hotels, both parks, and Downtown Disney. Disney operates most of the restaurants in the theme parks and its hotels; contractors or franchisees operate those at Downtown Disney. The restaurants accept Visa, MasterCard, American Express, Discover, JCB, and Diners Club.

BUFFETS AND FIXED-PRICE MEALS With set-price character meals, you can choose one item each from a limited selection of appetizers, salads, main courses, and desserts. Character buffets, such as the one at Goofy's Kitchen in the Disneyland Hotel, have a separate children's menu featuring kid favorites such as hot dogs, burgers, chicken tenders, pizza, macaroni and cheese, and spaghetti and meatballs, as well as healthier options such as sliced fruit, yogurt, and whole-grain baked goods. Dining reservations are highly recommended for all character meals. For an extensive discussion of character dining, see pages 175–176.

COUNTER SERVICE Counter-service fast food is available at both theme parks and Downtown Disney. The food compares in quality with McDonald's, Long John Silver's, Pizza Hut, or Taco Bell but is more expensive, though it's often served in larger portions.

INTEGRATING MEALS INTO THE UNOFFICIAL GUIDE TOURING PLANS

ARRIVE BEFORE the park of your choice opens. Tour expeditiously, using your chosen plan (taking as few breaks as possible) until about 11–11:30 a.m. Once the park becomes crowded around midday, meals and other breaks won't affect the plan's efficiency. If you're short on time and you want to see the theme parks, avoid full service. Ditto if you're short on funds. If you want to try a Disney full-service restaurant, arrange dining reservations to minimize your wait. If you intend to stay in the park for evening parades, fireworks, or other events, eat dinner early enough to be finished in time for the festivities. Note that table-service restaurants inside the parks often stop seating 2 hours before the park closes, and many counter-service locations close 1 hour or more before the park.

unofficial **TIP**
Bottom line: Young children are the rule, not the exception, at Disney restaurants.

FULL-SERVICE DINING FOR FAMILIES WITH YOUNG CHILDREN

NO MATTER HOW FORMAL A RESTAURANT appears, the staff is accustomed to impatient and often boisterous children. In Disneyland Resort's finest dining rooms, it's not unusual to find at least two dozen young diners attired in basic black . . . mouse ears.

Almost all Disney restaurants offer children's menus, and all have booster seats and high chairs. Waiters will supply little ones with crackers and rolls and serve your dinner much faster than in comparable restaurants elsewhere. In fact, letters from readers suggest that being served too quickly is much more common than having a long wait.

QUIET, ROMANTIC PLACES TO EAT

RESTAURANTS WITH GOOD FOOD *and* a couple-friendly ambience are rare in the theme parks. **Blue Bayou** at Disneyland Park satisfies both requirements. In DCA, **Wine Country Trattoria** offers one of the quietest and more relaxed environments, along with a California wine country–inspired menu, while the elegant **Carthay Circle Restaurant** ranks as one of the best restaurants in any theme park. Among the hotels at the resort, **Napa Rose** at the Grand Californian Hotel is the leading candidate for a romantic adult dining experience. At Downtown Disney, try **Jazz Kitchen Coastal Grill & Patio**; ask for a quiet table, though, if you're not interested in the jazz music.

Eating later in the evening and choosing a restaurant we've mentioned will improve your chances for intimate dining; nevertheless, know that children, well behaved or otherwise, are everywhere at Disneyland, and you can't escape them.

FAST FOOD IN THE THEME PARKS

BECAUSE MOST MEALS during a Disneyland vacation are consumed on the run while touring, we'll tackle counter-service and vendor foods first. Plentiful at all theme parks are hot dogs, hamburgers, chicken sandwiches, salads, and pizza. They're augmented by special items that relate to the park's theme or the part of the park you're touring. In the alpine village setting of Fantasyland, for example, counter-service bratwurst is sold; in New Orleans Square, Cajun and Creole dishes are available. Counter-service prices are fairly consistent from park to park. Expect to pay the same amount for your coffee or hot dog at DCA that you would at Disneyland Park.

If you are used to counter-service food at Walt Disney World, the quality and variety in Anaheim may catch you off guard, as it did a Cottleville, Missouri, reader:

I was surprised that the counter-service food was so excellent. Selection and quality were clearly better than even table service at WDW.

Getting your act together in regard to counter service is more a matter of courtesy than necessity. Rude guests rank fifth among reader complaints. A mother from Fort Wayne, Indiana, points out that indecision can be as maddening as outright discourtesy, especially when you're hungry:

Every fast-food restaurant has menus the size of billboards, but do you think anybody reads them? People waiting in line spend enough time in front of these menus to memorize them and still don't have a clue what they want when they finally get to the order taker. Tell your readers to PULEEEZ get their orders together ahead of time!

Another reader offers a tip about counter-service food lines:

Many counter-service registers serve two queues each, one to the left and one to the right of each register. People are not used to this and will instinctively line up in one queue per register. We had register operators wave us up to the front several times to start a left queue instead of waiting behind others on the right.

unofficial **TIP**
Restaurants with a **Disney Check** logo on their menus (Mickey's head with a check mark) offer special meals for kids ages 3–9. Menu items (including turkey meatballs, chicken skewers, and PB&J sandwiches) are designed to meet balanced nutritional guidelines with zero saturated and trans fats, less sugar, and reduced sodium.

Healthful Food at Disneyland Resort

One of the most commendable developments in food service at Disneyland has been the introduction of healthier foods and snacks. Diabetics, vegetarians, those watching their weight, those requiring kosher meals, and guests on restricted diets should be able to find something to eat. The same goes for anyone seeking wholesome, nutritious food. Health-conscious choices (including gluten-free bread) are available at most fast-food counters and even from select vendors. A simple request is likely to get you what you need even if it doesn't always appear on the menu.

Cutting Your Dining Time at the Theme Parks

Even if you confine your meals to vendor and counter-service fast food, you lose a lot of time getting sustenance in the theme parks. When it comes to fast food, *fast* may apply to the time you spend eating it, not the time invested in obtaining it.

Here are suggestions for minimizing the time you spend hunting and gathering food:

1. Don't waste touring time on breakfast at the parks. Restaurants outside Disneyland offer some outstanding breakfast specials. Many hotels furnish small refrigerators in guest rooms, or you can rent one. If you can get by on cold cereal, rolls, fruit, and juice, having a fridge in your room will save a ton of time. If you can't get a fridge, bring a cooler.

2. After a good breakfast, buy snacks from vendors in the parks as you tour, or stuff some snacks in a hip pack. This is very important if you're on a tight schedule and can't spend a lot of time waiting in line for food.

3. All theme park restaurants are busiest 11:30 a.m.–2:15 p.m. for lunch and 6–9 p.m. for dinner. For shorter lines and faster service, don't eat during these hours, especially 12:30–1:30 p.m.

4. Many counter-service restaurants sell cold sandwiches. Buy a cold lunch (except for drinks) before 11:30 a.m., and carry it until you're ready to eat. Ditto for dinner. Bring small plastic bags in which to pack the food; purchase drinks at the appropriate time from any convenient vendor.

5. Most fast-food eateries have more than one service window. Regardless of the time of day, check the lines at all windows before queuing. Sometimes a window that's staffed but out of the way will have a much shorter line or none at all. Note, however, that some windows may offer only certain items.

6. If you're short on time and the park closes early, stay until closing and eat dinner outside Disneyland before returning to your hotel. If the park stays open late, eat dinner about 4 or 4:30 p.m. at the restaurant of your choice. You should miss the last wave of lunchers and sneak in just ahead of the dinner crowd. Be warned, however, that most eateries at Downtown Disney and the Disneyland Resort hotels stop serving at 10 p.m., even when the parks are open until midnight.

7. Crowds pack nearby eateries before, during, and immediately after special events, parades, and shows such as Disneyland's *Fantasmic!* and *World of Color* in DCA. Conversely, dining venues far from the action are almost empty during their run times, and you can typically walk right up to the counter without any wait at all.

Mobile Ordering

Disneyland Resort has rolled out Mobile Ordering to the majority of counter-service restaurants and snack windows inside both parks—and sometimes makes its use mandatory at certain locations. If you have a Disney online account (with an associated credit card), you can use the mobile app to make your family's meal selections before arriving at the restaurant. The Disneyland app's Mobile Order page will display a list of participating restaurants and the wait until their soonest available pick-up time. Tap on a restaurant to see the full list of possible time slots. After making your order, you can modify your pick-up time to be later (if you're running behind schedule) or earlier (if a sooner slot becomes available). Once you're ready to dine, alert the app to your presence, and your food will soon be ready to pick up from a designated window, without ever needing to engage with a human cashier. Mobile Ordering even automatically applies Magic Key pass discounts and allows limited customization of entrées and side dishes, along with options for specific allergy requirements. We are huge fans of using Mobile Ordering, which has saved us up to 30 minutes of standing in line for a register, though you'll still wait a few minutes for your order to be assembled. Search available time slots and submit your order ahead of time while waiting in line for an attraction. Then ask the app to prepare your meal as you walk toward the restaurant, and your food should be ready as you arrive.

Beyond Counter Service: Tips for Saving Money on Food

Though buying food from counter-service restaurants and vendors will save you time and money compared with full-service dining, additional strategies can bolster your budget and maintain your waistline. Over the years, our readers have offered the following suggestions:

1. Go to Disneyland during a period of fasting and abstinence. You can save a fortune *and* save your soul!

2. Wear clothes that are slightly too small and make you feel like dieting. (No spandex!)

3. Whenever you're feeling hungry, ride the Mad Tea Party, the Incredicoaster, or other attractions that can induce motion sickness.

4. Leave your cash and credit cards at your hotel. Buy food only with money your children fish out of fountains and wishing wells.

5. There's no official limit on sourdough bread slices from Boudin Bakery at DCA. Test that theory until you're sufficiently carb-loaded, or security leads you away.

BEST SNACKS AT DISNEYLAND RESORT

We share our snacking insights on keeping your tummy happy at The Happiest Place on Earth.

DISNEYLAND PARK

- Frozen lemonade *(vending cart)*   • Ronto Wrap *(Star Wars: Galaxy's Edge)*
- Turkey legs *(vending cart)*   • Churro toffee *(Candy Palace, Trolley Treats, Pooh Corner)*
- Stuffed baked potatoes *(Troubadour Tavern)*   • Tigger tails *(Pooh Corner)*
- Pommes frites *(Café Orléans)*   • Taffy, English toffee, and peanut brittle *(Candy Palace)*
- Pickles *(Critter Country Fruit Cart, Adventureland Tropical Imports)*
- Fresh-baked chocolate chip cookies *(Harbour Galley)*   • Apple pie apple *(Pooh Corner)*
- Mickey-shaped beignets, nonalcoholic mint juleps *(Mint Julep Bar)*
- Mickey-shaped crispy rice treat *(Candy Palace)*
- Pork belly skewer *(Bengal Barbecue)*   • Berbere-spiced popcorn *(Troubadour Tavern)*
- Walt's chili with cheese *(Carnation Cafe)*   • Bacon-wrapped asparagus *(Bengal Barbecue)*
- Corn dog *(Stage Door Cafe)*   • Bratwurst with sauerkraut *(Edelweiss Snacks)*
- Mickey-shaped waffles *(breakfast at Carnation Café)*
- Chili-lime corn on the cob *(central hub vendor cart)*
- Mango Dole Whip, bao *(Tropical Hideaway)*
- Coconut macaroons shaped like the Matterhorn *(Jolly Holiday Bakery Café)*
- Ice cream in a freshly made, chocolate-dipped waffle cone *(Gibson Girl Ice Cream Parlor)*
- Pretzels stuffed with jalapeño cheese *(Refreshment Corner)*
- Pineapple Dole Whip soft serve and floats, pineapple juice *(Tiki Juice Bar)*

Cost-conscious readers also have volunteered ideas for stretching food dollars. A Missouri mom writes:

> We stocked our cooler with milk and sandwich fixings. I froze water in a milk jug, and we replenished it daily from the resort ice machine. I also froze small packages of deli meats for later in the week. We ate cereal, milk, and fruit each morning, with boxed juices. I also had a hot pot to boil water for instant coffee, oatmeal, and soup.
>
> Each child had a hip pack, which he filled from a box of goodies each day. The box included actual food, such as packages of crackers and cheese or peanuts and raisins, and worthless junk, such as candy. They grazed from their packs throughout the day, with no interference from Mom and Dad. Each also had a small water bottle that could hang on the belt. We filled these at water fountains before getting into lines and were the envy of many.
>
> We left the park before noon; ate sandwiches, chips, and soda in the room; and napped. We purchased our evening meal in the park at a counter-service eatery. We budgeted for morning and evening snacks from a vendor but often did not need them. It made the occasional treat all the more special.

Our top budget-trimming tip is to skip the soft drinks and instead order free ice water with every meal. It's far healthier and more hydrating than soda (sugared or artificially sweetened), and at over $5 per large fountain drink, you'll be shocked how swiftly the savings add up. The park's drinking fountains are potable in a pinch, but the filtered

BEST SNACKS *(continued)*

DISNEY CALIFORNIA ADVENTURE

- Charcuterie board *(Magic Key Terrace)* • Hot-link corn dog *(Corn Dog Castle)*
- Hand-dipped ice-cream bars *(Clarabelle's)* • Street tacos *(Studio Catering Co.)*
- Character-inspired candy apples *(Trolley Treats)* • Mickey shake *(Schmoozies)*
- Funky flavored popcorn *(Cozy Cone Motel)* • Saltwater taffy *(Bing Bong's Sweet Stuff)*
- Milkshakes with cookie "road gravel" *(Flo's V8 Cafe)* • Asada fries *(Award Wieners)*
- Cosmic Cream Orb *(Terran Treats)* • Breakfast shawarma *(Shawarma Palace)*
- Quantum Pretzel; Choco-Smash cake *(Pym Test Kitchen)*
- Chocolate chip cookie *(Jack-Jack Cookie Num Num)*
- Freshly made caramel popcorn *(cart near Carthay Circle)* • Onion rings *(Smokejumpers)*

DOWNTOWN DISNEY

- Candy unique to Disneyland *(Marceline's Confectionery)*
- Churro ice-cream sandwich *(vending cart)*
- Beignets and coffee *(Beignets Expressed)*
- Milkshakes *(Black Tap Craft Burgers & Shakes)*

RESORT RESTAURANTS

- Tuna or salmon poke *(GCH Craftsman Grill at Grand Californian Hotel)*
- Tempura-fried green beans *(Tangaroa Terrace and Trader Sam's Enchanted Tiki Bar at Disneyland Hotel)*

water that all counter-service restaurants (excluding vending carts) give away tastes as good as the bottled Dasani they sell for about $4.

A mom from Whiteland, Indiana, who purchases drinks in the parks, offers this suggestion:

> One must-take item if you're traveling with younger kids is a supply of small cups to split drinks, which are both huge and expensive.

We interviewed one woman who brought a huge picnic for her family of five packed in a large diaper–baby paraphernalia bag. She stowed the bag in a locker on Main Street and retrieved it when the family was hungry.

Note: Disney prohibits loose or dry ice, glass containers, and alcoholic beverages, as well as coolers larger than a six-pack and backpacks larger than 18x25x37 inches (the maximum dimensions that will fit inside the parks' lockers).

THEME PARK COUNTER-SERVICE RESTAURANT
Mini-Profiles

TO HELP YOU FIND PALATABLE fast-service foods that suit your taste, we have developed mini-profiles of Disneyland Park and DCA counter-service restaurants. The restaurants are listed alphabetically by park. We have noted locations that usually offer Mobile Ordering, but the participating lineup is subject to change. Detailed profiles of all Disneyland full-service restaurants follow this section, beginning on page 311. Be aware that menu items may change or be unavailable.

The restaurants profiled in the following pages are rated for quality and portion size as well as value. The value rating ranges from A to F as follows:

A = Exceptional value, a real bargain	D = Somewhat overpriced
B = Good value	F = Significantly overpriced
C = Fair value, you get exactly what you pay for	

DISNEYLAND PARK

Alien Pizza Planet *(Mobile Ordering)*

QUALITY Fair-Good   **VALUE** C   **PORTION** Medium-Large   **LOCATION** Tomorrowland
READER-SURVEY RESPONSES 76% 👍

SELECTIONS Large slices of pizza, pasta with shrimp or chicken, Caesar or Asian salads.

COMMENTS Alien Pizza Planet is loosely themed after the arcade eatery from the *Toy Story* movies. The restaurant is set up cafeteria-style, so all hot items sit under heat lamps until someone grabs them, but servers will be happy to mix up a fresh bowl of pasta or a pizza on request (a better choice). The Little Green Men–shaped macarons are almost too cute to eat (almost). Free drink refills are available. You must order and pay before picking up your food; use Mobile Ordering to avoid the chaotic cashier queues. The AC system is on steroids, making it a really cool place on a hot day. Even on the busiest days, there's ample room to sit on the outdoor patio.

Bengal Barbecue *(Mobile Ordering)*

QUALITY Good-Excellent   **VALUE** B–   **PORTION** Small   **LOCATION** Adventureland
READER-SURVEY RESPONSES 97% 👍

SELECTIONS Beef, chicken, pork, or veggie skewers; pineapple spears; dill pickles; hummus trio, garlic-herb breadsticks.

COMMENTS Skewers are small, but most items cost less than $7, and you can get a combo plate with two skewers served over rice and citrus slaw. The bacon-wrapped asparagus, hot-and-spicy Banyan beef, and pork belly skewers are best, proving the old adage that everything tastes better on a stick. Portions have shrunk over the years, but this is still a good and relatively healthy fast-food alternative to the dine-in options inside the park. A couple dozen tables are inside the covered bazaar behind the food stand.

Cafe Daisy *(Mobile Ordering)*

QUALITY Fair-Good   **VALUE** C–   **PORTION** Medium   **LOCATION** Mickey's Toontown
READER-SURVEY RESPONSES 86% 👍

SELECTIONS Pepperoni and cheese pizzas, hot dogs, vegetarian wraps, mini-doughnuts.

COMMENTS Toontown's main eatery specializes in pizza "flop-overs" (a personal-size flatbread folded in half) and foot-long hot dogs (with or without chili mac and cheese). The house-made potato chips might be the best thing on the kid-friendly menu. A grocery stand around the corner sells picnic baskets of fruit and other healthy snacks.

Docking Bay 7 *(Mobile Ordering)*

QUALITY Good-Excellent   **VALUE** B+   **PORTION** Large   **LOCATION** Galaxy's Edge
READER-SURVEY RESPONSES 93% 👍

SELECTIONS Beef, chicken, and vegan entrées featuring Mediterranean and Asian flavors with a sci-fi flair. Nonalcoholic drinks and desserts.

COMMENTS Chef Strono "Cookie" Tuggs (a blink-and-you-missed-him background character from Episode VII) moved his "Tugg's Grub" mobile kitchen atop Black Spire's ramshackle shipping station, converting a cluttered cargo depot into a futuristic food hall with booths made from abandoned shipping crates. Look for the seafood vendor's stall and a tiny carbonite freezing chamber. All dishes are named after unpronounceable alien species, but rest assured they're really made of earthbound ingredients. Endorian Tip-Yip (actually chicken) is served roasted on a quinoa salad, or (our favorite) compressed into cubes and deep-fried with herbaceous gravy. Vegans will rejoice at meatless Garden Spread, featuring Impossible Foods; the kefta and hummus will even win over hardened carnivores. The food here is a cut above typical theme park fare, and approaches the resort's sit-down restaurants in quality and price. No alcohol is served here, but you can sip a cold brew black caf (coffee with sweet cream) while eating your chocolate dessert.

Galactic Grill *(Mobile Ordering)*

QUALITY Fair   **VALUE** C+   **PORTION** Large   **LOCATION** Tomorrowland
READER-SURVEY RESPONSES 81% 👍

SELECTIONS Breakfast burritos and funnel cake fries in the morning. Cheeseburger, chicken tenders, chopped salad with chicken, fish-and-chips, or veggie wrap; kids' meals of mac and cheese, burger, or smoothie with fruit and crackers.

COMMENTS The food isn't anything special, despite some of the dishes' *Star Wars*–related names. The Bantha Burger's patty is half beef, half plant-based. Seating is available outdoors overlooking the Tomorrowland Terrace stage, which hosts live music.

The Golden Horseshoe *(Mobile Ordering)*

QUALITY Fair   **VALUE** C   **PORTION** Medium   **LOCATION** Frontierland
READER-SURVEY RESPONSES 85% 👍

SELECTIONS Chicken tenders, fish-and-chips, grilled chicken salad, mozzarella sticks, ice-cream sundaes, and floats.

COMMENTS The Golden Horseshoe hosts live interactive entertainment and serves fair fried food. The meaty chili that was a tribute to Walt has been removed from the menu (look for it at Carnation Cafe instead), but you can get your chicken tenders topped with lemon pepper or buffalo sauce. Service can be slow. Opera box–style seating next to the stage is best.

Harbour Galley *(Mobile Ordering)*

QUALITY Good-Excellent   **VALUE** B+   **PORTION** Medium   **LOCATION** Critter Country
READER-SURVEY RESPONSES 91% 👍

SELECTIONS Clam chowder, vegetable stew, or seasonal soup, all served in a sourdough bread bowl; tuna salad; lobster roll with house-made potato chips; fresh-baked cookies.

COMMENTS The overstuffed bread bowls are always a reliable choice, especially with lobster bisque (when in season) or mushroom-farrow stew. The lobster roll is an excellent pick, with minimal filler and well-balanced seasoning on a buttery roll, and the warm chocolate chip cookies (sold in freshly baked 6-packs and baker's dozens) are a big hit. Pelican's Landing provides two sections of seating with scenic views over the river.

Hungry Bear Restaurant *(Mobile Ordering)*

QUALITY Fair–Good **VALUE** B- **PORTION** Medium–Large **LOCATION** Critter Country
READER-SURVEY RESPONSES 81% 👍

SELECTIONS Cheeseburger, chicken tenders, and a fried chicken sandwich with honey mustard; healthier entrées include barbecue chicken salad and an Impossible vegan burger; Mickey-shaped beignets.

COMMENTS Popular and crowded during busier times of the year. During slower times, grab a snack and sit on the deck overlooking the Rivers of America. The honey-spiced chicken is dry and doesn't have much of its advertised flavor; the burgers are by the numbers but can be ordered with onion rings. The barbecue salad is a good lighter choice.

Jolly Holiday Bakery Café *(Mobile Ordering)*

QUALITY Good–Excellent **VALUE** B+ **PORTION** Medium **LOCATION** Main Street, U.S.A.
READER-SURVEY RESPONSES 93% 👍

SELECTIONS Egg-and-bacon croissants for breakfast; mixed greens with pecans and feta, toasted cheese sandwich with tomato soup, turkey or roast beef sandwich, assorted pastries and coffees.

COMMENTS Themed to *Mary Poppins,* with stained glass windows featuring penguin waiters, this is a good spot for a light breakfast or lunch, though lines can grow long at peak mealtimes. Seating is outdoors only, and soup portions are small, but the salads and sandwiches are substantial and savory. Don't miss the massive Matterhorn coconut macaroons, and be sure to ask about the tasty-yet-affordable seasonal items. The Jolly Holiday Combo is especially good on chilly nights.

Kat Saka's Kettle

QUALITY Good **VALUE** B- **PORTION** Medium **LOCATION** Galaxy's Edge
READER-SURVEY RESPONSES 76% 👍

SELECTIONS Kettle-cooked popcorn.

COMMENTS This small stand serves colorful kernels coated in exotic spices collected from across the galaxy. Seasonal flavors can be sweet or savory, such as sea salt to Cajun-citrus spice; we really liked the banana-and-chocolate combo. Soda is sold in collectible spherical bottles that make affordable souvenirs.

Market House

QUALITY Good **VALUE** B- **PORTION** Medium **LOCATION** Main Street, U.S.A.
READER-SURVEY RESPONSES 94% 👍

SELECTIONS Starbucks coffee, cocoa, tea, pastries, and breakfast sandwiches.

COMMENTS Starbucks's usual vast array of blended beverages is available (including seasonal flavors), accompanied by its trademark long lines. You can also get a selection of hot breakfast sandwiches in the morning and sweets all day. Starbucks loyalty cards are valid for payment at in-park locations, but you can only earn and redeem rewards or use Mobile Ordering at the Downtown Disney location. The coffee shop features a seating area themed after a vintage bookshop. Look for the potbellied stove, checkerboard, and antique party line phones, all holdovers from the former decor.

Milk Stand *(Mobile Ordering)*

QUALITY Poor-Fair   VALUE C-   PORTION Small   LOCATION Galaxy's Edge
READER-SURVEY RESPONSES   87% 👍

SELECTIONS Frozen nondairy "milk" drinks.

COMMENTS Direct from the Bubo Wamba Family Farms comes Disney's ill-fated attempt at a Butterbeer-style must-try beverage. Luckily, guests don't have to drink this vegan coconut-and-rice-milk frozen slushie straight from a sea cow. Green (as seen in *The Last Jedi*) has tropical flavors like orange blossom and tangerine; the blue beverage from *A New Hope* tastes of berry and melon. Both have the cloying mouth-feel of fruit-scented shampoo, and it's debatable which is more undrinkable; we advise splitting one with a group or skipping it altogether.

Oga's Cantina

QUALITY Good   VALUE B-   PORTION Medium   LOCATION Galaxy's Edge
READER-SURVEY RESPONSES   76% 👍

SELECTIONS Alcoholic and nonalcoholic cocktails, exclusive wines and beer, chips and salsa, edamame, pretzels, charcuterie platter.

COMMENTS This cantina will instantly remind fans of the Mos Eisley watering hole seen in *A New Hope*. DJ R-3X (better known as Captain Rex, the former Star Tours droid pilot voiced by Paul "Pee Wee Herman" Rubens), spins an original 80s-style synth-pop soundtrack. Bartenders dispense drinks from a tangle of tubes and bubbling tubs behind the bar; all beverages here are premixed and *Star Wars* themed, so you can't order a gin and tonic or other terrestrial tipple. Our favorite signature alcoholic cocktails are the Outer Rim margarita with black salt, the Coruscant Cooler, and the bourbon-based Jet Juice shooter. Draft craft beers and private-label wines are also served, as are nonalcoholic drinks (such as the frozen cookie-crowned Blue Bantha) and a selection of bar snacks, including a yummy soft pretzel with cheese dip.

Use the Disneyland app or visit disneyland.com/cantina at 12 a.m. PST 60 days before the morning of your visit to book your bar time; beware of a $10-per-person penalty for no-shows. A wait list is sporadically available via the app, and walk-ups are usually accepted until around 10 a.m., if you want an out-of-this-world eye-opener. There are only a few booths, so most patrons (including children) must stand along the bar. Service can be brusque at best, and if you linger too long over your libation, you may be asked to exit after two drinks or 45 minutes. Don't wander around admiring the decor until you've finished drinking because your seat will probably be taken before you return.

A longtime reader from Petaluma, California, sums up the Oga's experience aptly:

The drinks and snacks were good, and there were some fun things to see, but it really wasn't a top experience. Not sure how this place works—were we supposed to bribe the doorman in Galactic credits?

A reader from Seattle, Washington, was even rougher in her review:

As a Star Wars *fan, Oga's Cantina wasn't magical. The menu and styling were great, but it was unpleasantly crowded and had the worst service I've ever had in the parks. Not worth getting up early to make the reservations.*

Plaza Inn

QUALITY Good **VALUE** B **PORTION** Medium–Large **LOCATION** Main Street U.S.A.
READER-SURVEY RESPONSES 90% 👍

SELECTIONS Daily character breakfast features Mickey waffles. Fried chicken, pot roast, salmon with rice, Cobb salad, pasta. Nonalcoholic drinks and desserts.

COMMENTS Plaza Inn is a hit-or-miss bufeteria with gorgeous Victorian B&B ambience. The spacious dining room has lots of brocade and brass, and the large patio commands a great view of Main Street. Kids love the daily character breakfast (see page 176), but the only real reason to visit for lunch and dinner is the fried chicken, which some claim is better than Knott's famous birds. The pot roast is too inconsistent to recommend, ricocheting from flavorful and moist to bone-dry and bland, but the salmon is a tasty alternative. Parade dining packages (see page 227) include fried chicken and a slab of tender-but-salty short ribs, topped with chimichurri sauce.

Rancho del Zocalo

QUALITY Fair–Good **VALUE** B- **PORTION** Medium–Large **LOCATION** Frontierland
READER-SURVEY RESPONSES 87% 👍

SELECTIONS Chips and salsa; cheese fries with carne asada; burritos, bowls, and street tacos with beef, chicken, or plant-based chorizo; achiote-marinated half chicken; chicken Caesar salads. For kids, bean burritos and chicken tacos. Agua fresca, cinnamon crisps, and seasonal desserts.

COMMENTS Three words sum up the Zocalo: Mexican, cafeteria style. You grab a tray and head to the serving stations for your food and drinks, then wait in a separate line to pay. Faux adobe, wooden beams, and Mexican tile ring a dark interior, while all seating is outdoors on a (mostly) covered patio. Headliners here are the burritos with chicken or beef, served Sonoran-style with chips and salsa; sides of rice and beans cost extra. The flavorful fire-grilled chicken is marinated in chile and citrus, and it comes with tortillas to make your own tacos. This can be a nice, quiet place for a meal when you can't possibly choke down another burger. Anyone not intimately familiar with really good Mexican cuisine may rate this place higher. It's nowhere near the quality (or price) of your favorite local hole-in-the-wall Mexican food spot, but it does the job. *Fantasmic!* dining packages (see page 225) are available here for $35 ($25 ages 3–9) on show nights; they represent your best value for reserved show viewing, but reservations are required.

Red Rose Taverne *(Mobile Ordering)*

QUALITY Good **VALUE** B- **PORTION** Medium **LOCATION** Fantasyland
READER-SURVEY RESPONSES 87% 👍

SELECTIONS Scrambled eggs and pancakes for breakfast. Cheese, sausage, or pepperoni flatbreads; chicken tenders and sandwiches; bacon cheeseburgers; plant-based burgers; kale salads. Kids can pick a hamburger, chicken tenders, or power pack with carrots and crackers.

COMMENTS Red Rose Taverne is inspired by the 2017 live-action *Beauty and the Beast* remake. This is a good spot for a quick-service breakfast in Disneyland Park, with a hearty bacon-and-egg sandwich and healthy quinoa hash on offer. Later in the day, the flatbreads are flavorful and full-size, but the crusts are never crispy; it's still a better pick than Alien Pizza Planet. Vegetarians can get a black bean burger, and the sandwiches are served with tater tots instead of basic fries. For dessert, the movie-themed Grey Stuff Gateau (made of cookies-and-cream mousse atop red velvet cake) tastes better than it looks.

Refreshment Corner *(Mobile Ordering)*

QUALITY Fair–Good   **VALUE** C   **PORTION** Medium   **LOCATION** Main Street, U.S.A.
READER-SURVEY RESPONSES 91% 👍

SELECTIONS Hot dogs, chili-cheese dogs, cheese-filled pretzels, and chili.

COMMENTS Some of the topping selections may give you heartburn (mac and cheese with bacon?), but the dogs are good. Limited seating; time it right to catch the ragtime pianist or Dapper Dans performing on the patio.

Ronto Roasters *(Mobile Ordering)*

QUALITY Good–Excellent   **VALUE** B+   **PORTION** Medium–Large   **LOCATION** Galaxy's Edge
READER-SURVEY RESPONSES 96% 👍

SELECTIONS Flatbread sandwich filled with roast pork and grilled Portuguese sausage, vegan sandwich, nonalcoholic fruit punch.

COMMENTS A disgruntled smelting droid named 8D-J8 does the cooking here, turning alien meats on a rotating spit as they roast underneath a recycled podracing engine. The pita sandwiches, dressed with tangy slaw and spicy szechuan peppercorn "clutch sauce," are our favorite snack in Batuu, and the plant-based version is perhaps even better than the original; the breakfast version with scrambled eggs and cheese is also very good.

Royal Street Veranda *(Mobile Ordering)*

QUALITY Good   **VALUE** B   **PORTION** Medium   **LOCATION** New Orleans Square
READER-SURVEY RESPONSES 94% 👍

SELECTIONS Waffle Cristo breakfast sandwiches. Seasonal soup served in a sourdough bread bowl, fritters with dipping sauce.

COMMENTS It can get quite crowded, especially around *Fantasmic!* showings, but it's usually worth the wait. The ham, turkey, and Swiss sandwich on sugar-dusted waffles makes for a filling breakfast; split one or ask for a half-order. Clam chowder is the best of the rotating soups, though all are seasoned well. Don't miss the sweet and savory fritters, served with an ever-changing variety of dipping sauces. The seating area is microscopic, so take your food to Pelican Landing or Rancho Del Zocalo.

Stage Door Café *(Mobile Ordering)*

QUALITY Fair–Good   **VALUE** C   **PORTION** Medium   **LOCATION** Frontierland
READER-SURVEY RESPONSES 97% 👍

SELECTIONS Chicken tenders, fish-and-chips, corn dogs, and funnel cakes.

COMMENTS The corn dogs are better here than those from Main Street's Little Red Wagon (which no longer cooks them fresh), with a shorter line. The sugar-topped funnel cakes are tasty, and the fried fish is edible (albeit previously frozen), but the fries and chicken tenders are bland.

Tiana's Palace *(Mobile Ordering)*

QUALITY Good-Excellent   **VALUE** B+   **PORTION** Medium-Large
LOCATION New Orleans Square   **READER-SURVEY RESPONSES**   90% 👍

SELECTIONS Beef po'boy and muffuletta sandwiches, traditional and vegan gumbo, shrimp and grits, and cornbread. Kids can choose roasted drumsticks, toasted ham and cheese, or baked mac and cheese. For dessert, glazed beignets with lemon icebox filling and cold-brew chicory coffee.

COMMENTS The restaurant formerly known as French Market was remodeled into Tiana's dream restaurant from *Princess and the Frog,* whose on-screen design was inspired by the Disneyland original. It suggests a laid-back Southern vibe with riverboat-style smokestacks and wrought iron, and props referencing the film adorn the walls. Seating is outdoors on a large tree-shaded patio where you might catch roving jazz musicians performing, or Tiana herself passing through.

Tiana's Palace features comfort food with a Cajun-Creole flair. The heavenly gumbos are the best things on the menu, whether you choose the chicken-and-sausage style or the seven-greens vegetarian version. Shrimp are perfectly seasoned and cooked, although the grits are a bit cheesy for some, and the savory slow-cooked beef po'boys are let down by lackluster bread (unlike the olive-forward muffuletta). Get an individual tin of tasty cornbread as a side, but skip the signature house-filled beignet, which is cold and deflated. We prefer the hot Mickey-shaped beignets served from the building's popular **Mint Julep Bar** walk-up window. The cafeteria-style service line often looks long, but it moves swiftly; Mobile Ordering may be faster, but meals come served in plastic instead of on china.

Tropical Hideaway

QUALITY Good-Excellent   **VALUE** C   **PORTION** Small   **LOCATION** Adventureland
READER-SURVEY RESPONSES   99% 👍

SELECTIONS Pineapple, mango, and strawberry Dole whip soft serve in cups, floats, or sundaes; bao steamed buns stuffed with meat or veggies.

COMMENTS Formerly Aladdin's Oasis, and before that the Tahitian Terrace, this outdoor eating area alongside the Jungle Cruise shoreline is a thematic extension of both that ride and the neighboring *Enchanted Tiki Room;* look for Rosita, an animatronic bird mentioned in the show who cracks corny jokes at passing boats. The small bao are savory (especially the roasted pork) but insanely overpriced, and the loaded Dole whip with chamoy (pickled fruit) and chile-lime spices is definitely an acquired taste.

Troubadour Tavern *(Mobile Ordering)*

QUALITY Good   **VALUE** B-   **PORTION** Medium   **LOCATION** Fantasyland
READER-SURVEY RESPONSES   88% 👍

SELECTIONS Stuffed baked potatoes, candy-coated popcorn, mac-and-cheese bites, ice-cream bars, cold brew coffee.

COMMENTS Built as a concession stand for Fantasyland Theatre, Troubadour Tavern is overwhelmed during shows but often overlooked the rest of the day. Its ever-changing menu celebrates seasonal events with a variety of themed snacks, but loaded baked potatoes, flavored popcorn, and fruit punch are staples.

Vendor Treats

LOCATIONS Throughout the park   **READER-SURVEY RESPONSES** 90% 👍

SELECTIONS Popcorn, pickles, smoked turkey legs, ice cream, churros, corn on the cob, and more.

COMMENTS There's something undeniably primal about tucking into a huge, meaty smoked turkey leg. For a quick snack, try Maurice's Treats, close to Fantasy Faire; it serves sweet (if overpriced) pastries, as well as a boysenberry apple freeze. Its cheddar-garlic bagel twist is tough and tasteless, so get the danish or croissant.

DISNEY CALIFORNIA ADVENTURE

Aunt Cass Cafe *(Mobile Ordering)*

QUALITY Good-Excellent   **VALUE** A   **PORTION** Medium
LOCATION San Fransokyo Square   **READER-SURVEY RESPONSES** 86% 👍

SELECTIONS Asian noodle salads; shrimp katsu or turkey pesto sandwiches; beef curry, mac and cheese, or clam chowder served in hollowed-out sourdough loaves from San Francisco's famous Boudin bakery. Turkey sandwiches and macaroni and cheese for the kids. Honey lemonade with popping boba, peach soju cocktail.

COMMENTS The eatery originally known as Pacific Wharf Cafe, a longtime favorite of ours, is now adorned with an abundance of lucky cat symbols. Our favorite items are the clam chowder—which has heaps of clams with bacon and white miso—and the flavorful vegan soba noodle salad with edamame. For dessert, try the Japanese-style cheesecake (if it isn't sold out), or step across the street to **Ghirardelli Soda Fountain & Chocolate Shop** for candy, hot cocoa, ice-cream sundaes, or milkshakes.

Award Wieners *(Mobile Ordering)*

QUALITY Fair-Good   **VALUE** B-   **PORTION** Medium   **LOCATION** Hollywood Land
READER-SURVEY RESPONSES 92% 👍

SELECTIONS Chili-cheese dogs and hot dogs; vegan sausage, grilled mushroom, onion, and pepper sandwich; asada fries.

COMMENTS Guy recommends the Bacon Street Dog, which is dipped in red pepper ketchup; topped with crispy bacon crumbles, grilled onions, and bell peppers; and served on a toasted bun. Check out the rotating seasonal specialty sausages for some seriously strange condiments. The film strip fries are great topped with carne asada beef, cheese, and cilantro. The plant-based Philly Dog has so much flavor you'll never guess they left out the meat.

Boardwalk Pizza & Pasta

QUALITY Good   **VALUE** B   **PORTION** Medium-Large   **LOCATION** Paradise Gardens Park
READER-SURVEY RESPONSES 87% 👍

SELECTIONS Pizzas come with cheese, pepperoni, or barbecue chicken. Pasta offerings include spaghetti and meatballs, chicken pasta in a garlic cream sauce, or vegan rigatoni primavera. Freshly tossed salads include a wedge with blue cheese and an Italian chef salad with salami, fresh mozzarella, roasted peppers, and olives in a red-wine vinaigrette.

COMMENTS Part of Paradise Garden, this Victorian-era outdoor courtyard has freestanding beer and corn dog stands outside the plaza. Salads are large enough to split three ways; say "hold the olives" (or another ingredient) for a fresh-mixed serving. The uncompelling pizza pies come with steep prices. This location gets extra points for its wonderful ambience; it's a great place to relax and unwind for a bit even if you aren't eating, especially when live musicians are performing in the gazebo.

Cocina Cucamonga Mexican Grill *(Mobile Ordering)*

QUALITY Good–Excellent **VALUE** A– **PORTION** Large
LOCATION San Fransokyo Square **READER-SURVEY RESPONSES** 89% 👍

SELECTIONS Street tacos with beef or chicken; vegan potato tacos; street corn with togarashi mayo; chorizo-stewed pinto beans and lime-cilantro rice; horchata, margaritas, and micheladas (beer with tomato juice mix). Kids' choices include steak or chicken tacos.

COMMENTS This wharf-side walk-up window features flavorful street tacos, served in pairs on soft corn tortillas with lime wedges and raw radishes for added authenticity. The street corn and crispy *papas* are perfect if you're eating plant-forward, and Guy especially recommends the QuesaBirria braised beef-and-cheese tacos served with a side of tomatillo salsa and consomé. Located adjacent to Cocina Cucamonga, the **Port of San Fransokyo Cerveceria** pours a full range of draft Karl Strauss brews.

Corn Dog Castle *(Mobile Ordering)*

QUALITY Good **VALUE** B **PORTION** Medium **LOCATION** Paradise Gardens Park
READER-SURVEY RESPONSES 95% 👍

SELECTIONS Corn dogs (regular or hot link), cheddar cheese sticks.

COMMENTS The corn dogs served here have gained a cult following, and deservedly so: they're the freshest, lightest version of the deep-fried fair favorite you'll ever find, especially the hot link kind. This location can draw long lines but is capable of serving swiftly. The deep-fried cheese sticks also have their vocal fans, but ours always come out hollow and quickly turn cold. All the dogs are priced to include a mandarin orange or a small bag of chips.

Cozy Cone Motel *(Mobile Ordering)*

QUALITY Fair–Good **VALUE** B– **PORTION** Small–Medium **LOCATION** Cars Land
READER-SURVEY RESPONSES 89% 👍

SELECTIONS Bread cones stuffed with chili or bacon mac and cheese, ice cream, and churros. Cone #5 coats popcorn in unusual flavors such as dill pickle and sriracha, with multiple rotating varieties offered daily. Signature beverages include a syrupy pomegranate limeade (available with or without vodka) and a peach-chamoy lemonade served with tequila or cerveza.

COMMENTS Each conical commissary in this food court, based on Sally's construction-cone motel from the film, serves different snacks and drinks with punny names such as "chili cone queso" and "route beer floats." A limited number of picnic tables are behind the motel office, whose interior features a number of hidden Pixar references.

Fiddler, Fifer & Practical Café

QUALITY Good   **VALUE** B-   **PORTION** Medium   **LOCATION** Buena Vista Street
READER-SURVEY RESPONSES 85% 👍

SELECTIONS Starbucks coffee, hot breakfast sandwiches, cinnamon rolls with cream cheese icing, premade cold sandwiches, and salads.

COMMENTS This quick-service eatery, named after both the Three Little Pigs and an imaginary songstress trio whose manufactured mementos hang inside, boasts a large open dining area in the Arts and Crafts style. You can get your morning jolt of Starbucks-brand joe and grab-and-go breakfast pastries here, but expect long waits around opening. Starbucks loyalty cards can be used for payment but not for free refills or other rewards.

Flo's V8 Cafe *(Mobile Ordering)*

QUALITY Fair–Good   **VALUE** C   **PORTION** Medium–Large   **LOCATION** Cars Land
READER-SURVEY RESPONSES 90% 👍

SELECTIONS Lunch and dinner offer fried chicken, cheeseburgers, turkey club, Cobb salad, Impossible burgers, and milkshakes.

COMMENTS Cars Land's largest eatery serves standard roadside diner fare. The burgers are utterly generic, although they're served with steak fries, and the fried chicken isn't nearly as good as the Plaza Inn's. Your best bets are the turkey club and the milkshakes. Memorabilia from proprietor Flo's past as a famous Motown singer is featured in the decor. Sit on the back patio for a spectacular view of Radiator Springs Racers' high-speed finale.

Lucky Fortune Cookery *(Mobile Ordering)*

QUALITY Fair–Good   **VALUE** B-   **PORTION** Medium   **LOCATION** San Fransokyo Square
READER-SURVEY RESPONSES 90% 👍

SELECTIONS Teriyaki chicken with steamed rice and vegetables, beef bulgogi burrito, beef birria ramen soup, karaage-style chicken on a sandwich or yaki udon, pot stickers. Thai tea, strawberry lychee cocktail, and Japanese rice lager. Teriyaki chicken and rice for kids.

COMMENTS Lucky Fortune serves a pan-Asian selection of Chinese stir-fry and Japanese noodles, but inconsistent quality here makes it our last pick when eating in San Fransokyo Square. Guy thinks the Korean-style beef wrap is fantastic, and Seth likes the ramen; but the fried noodles are greasy, the chicken isn't crispy, and the potstickers taste previously frozen. Skip the cloying cocktails in favor of a margarita from **Rita's Turbine Blenders,** the neighboring frozen beverage stand.

Paradise Garden Grill *(Mobile Ordering)*

QUALITY Good   **VALUE** C+   **PORTION** Medium   **LOCATION** Paradise Gardens Park
READER-SURVEY RESPONSES 96% 👍

SELECTIONS When no events are happening, the barbecue-focused menu includes St. Louis–style chicken, North Carolina–style pulled pork, and Kansas City–style ribs. During ¡Viva Navidad! and Lunar New Year, the menu offers some excellent international entrées. During the Festival of Holidays, the fare runs to fried fish and meatless meatballs. And for spring's Food & Wine Festival, Paradise Garden Grill serves a variety of creative Californian cuisines, with meat- and plant-based options.

COMMENTS This open-air venue, with a Victorian beer garden theme, shares seating with Boardwalk Pizza. It usually changes its offerings with the season to tie in with whatever event is currently being promoted.

Pixar Pier Snack Vendors

QUALITY Fair–Good   **VALUE** C-   **PORTION** Small–Medium   **LOCATION** Pixar Pier
READER-SURVEY RESPONSES   89% 👍

SELECTIONS Soft-serve ice cream, cookies, churros, fried chicken, hot dogs.

COMMENTS When transforming Paradise Pier into Pixar Pier, Disney handed the reins of several snack stands around the area to second-string CGI characters. The hit menu item at **Adorable Snowman Frosted Treats** is "It's Snow-Capped Lemon," a nondairy lemon dessert topped with white chocolate, but the line here moves very slowly. **Jack-Jack Cookie Num Nums** also attracts crowds in front of the Incredicoaster with its ginormous chocolate chip cookies. **Señor Buzz Churro** is the spot to get the popular pastry in special seasonal flavors. **Poultry Palace,** which looks like an oversize happy meal box, and **Angry Dogs,** featuring a statue of the hot-tempered *Inside Out* character, both make more memorable photo ops than eateries, but Angry Dogs is the park's only hot dog vendor offering spicy brown mustard.

Pym Test Kitchen and Tasting Lab *(Mobile Ordering)*

QUALITY Good   **VALUE** B-   **PORTION** Medium–Large   **LOCATION** Avengers Campus
READER-SURVEY RESPONSES   88% 👍

SELECTIONS At breakfast, cinnamon French toast, eggs and bacon, vegan egg-and-sausage sandwich. For lunch and dinner, oversize pretzels, sandwiches, buffalo chicken wings, shrimp salad, plant-based meatballs and pasta, chocolate cake for dessert. At the outdoor Tasting Lab bar, alcoholic and nonalcoholic cocktails, craft beers, bagged sweet-and-salty bar snacks.

COMMENTS The colorful bread pudding–like Cinna-Pym French toast is one of Guy's favorite breakfast items in the park, but vegetarians should skip the dry Quantum Garden Breakfast in favor of an Impossible-based wrap with spicy maple syrup from the neighboring **Shawarma Palace** cart. Later in the day, launch your meal by sharing a ginormous pretzel, served with beer-cheese dipping sauce or stuffed with buffalo chicken. The signature sandwiches—an Italian cold-cut pressed Pym-ini available in an eye-popping eight-person portion, and the eye-catching Not So Little Chicken sandwich—taste just OK. At the outdoor Tasting Lab bar, you can grab beer served in cups that "magically" fill from the bottom (like Thor's stein), or in a flight of miniature mugs on a souvenir oversize ruler.

Mobile Ordering is highly recommended here. The Freestyle dispensers offer free refills in 100-plus flavors, including an exclusive Pingo Doce citrus soda. The Shawarma Palace cart outside often draws a long queue; look for a satellite stand with shorter lines outside the Hyperion Theater, near the **Terran Treats** cart serving cosmic cream puffs.

Smokejumpers Grill *(Mobile Ordering)*

QUALITY Fair–Good   **VALUE** B-   **PORTION** Medium–Large   **LOCATION** Grizzly Peak
READER-SURVEY RESPONSES   89% 👍

SELECTIONS Sausage, egg, and cheese sandwiches or burritos for breakfast. Bacon cheeseburger, Impossible burger, or chicken sandwich with onion rings or crinkle-cut fries; chicken tenders; grilled chicken salad; seasonal milkshakes.

COMMENTS The burgers come with a variety of toppings and sauces, including one with chipotle barbecue sauce. The onion rings and crinkle-cut fries are decent, and this is the only place in DCA that serves them. The handsome location, inspired by "brave men and women who fight wildfires in our California forests," features ample seating surrounded by lush pine trees.

DISNEYLAND RESORT RESTAURANTS:
Rated and Ranked

TO HELP YOU make your dining choices, we've developed profiles of full-service restaurants at Disneyland Resort. Each profile lets you quickly check the restaurant's cuisine, location, star rating, cost range, quality rating, and value rating. Profiles are listed alphabetically by restaurant. In addition to all full-service restaurants, we also list and profile a couple of counter-service restaurants in the theme parks that transcend basic burgers, hot dogs, and pizza. All restaurants listed here have disabled access.

PAYMENT All Disney restaurants accept American Express, MasterCard, Visa, Diners Club, Discover, and Japanese Credit Bureau.

STAR RATING The star rating represents the entire dining experience: style, service, and ambience, in addition to taste, presentation, and food quality. Five stars, the highest rating, indicates that the restaurant offers the best of everything. Four-star restaurants are above average, and three-star restaurants offer good, though not necessarily memorable, meals. Two-star restaurants serve mediocre fare, and one-star restaurants are below average. Our star ratings don't correspond to ratings awarded by AAA, Forbes, Zagat, or other restaurant reviewers.

COST RANGE The next rating tells how much an entrée (or, depending on the restaurant, an entrée and side dish) will cost. Appetizers, desserts, drinks, and tips aren't included. We've rated the cost as inexpensive, moderate, or expensive.

INEXPENSIVE	$15 or less per person
MODERATE	$15–$35 per person
EXPENSIVE	More than $35 per person

QUALITY RATING The food quality is rated on a scale of one to five stars, five being the best. The quality rating is based on the taste, freshness of ingredients, preparation, presentation, and creativity of food. There is no consideration of price. If you want the best food available and cost is no issue, look no further than the quality ratings.

VALUE RATING If, on the other hand, you are looking for both quality and value, check the value rating, also expressed as stars.

★★★★★	Exceptional value; a real bargain
★★★★	Good value
★★★	Fair value; you get exactly what you pay for
★★	Somewhat overpriced
★	Significantly overpriced

Ballast Point ★★½

CALIFORNIAN MODERATE QUALITY ★★½ VALUE ★★½
READER-SURVEY RESPONSES 86% 👍

Downtown Disney; ☎ 714-781-DINE (3463)

Reservations Not accepted. **When to go** Lunch or dinner. **Entrée range** $20–$26.
Service ★★. **Friendliness ★★**. **Bar** Beer. **Dress** Casual. **Hours** Daily, 11 a.m.–10 p.m.

SETTING AND ATMOSPHERE Ballast Point, a popular San Diego–based brewer, has brought the Disneyland Resort its first-ever on-site brewery, just as Walt would have wanted. The boatwright-inspired restaurant boasts 4,000 square feet of interior space, including a tasting room and an open kitchen, plus a 3,000-square-foot outdoor beer garden in which to imbibe.

HOUSE SPECIALTIES Southern California–style sandwiches, burgers, salads, and small plates, focusing on sustainable seasonal ingredients. A brunch menu with breakfast sandwiches and flatbreads is available until 2 p.m. on weekends.

OTHER RECOMMENDATIONS Beer, beer, and more beer.

SUMMARY AND COMMENTS We had great expectations for the menu here, but despite the impressive ingredient lists, the food turned out like the old ESPN Zone's sports bar fare, only at a higher price point. Stick with the award-winning craft brews (available in flight-friendly sampling sizes), perhaps paired with a Bavarian pretzel, and enjoy the second-story view over Downtown Disney, but save your appetite for dinner elsewhere.

Black Tap Craft Burgers & Shakes ★★★

AMERICAN MODERATE QUALITY ★★★ VALUE ★★★
READER-SURVEY RESPONSES 95% 👍

Downtown Disney; ☎ 714-781-DINE (3463)

Reservations Not accepted. **When to go** Lunch or dinner. **Entrée range** $19–$24. **Service ★★★**. **Friendliness ★★★**. **Bar** Beer, wine, and cocktails. **Dress** Casual. **Hours** Daily, 10 a.m.– midnight.

SETTING AND ATMOSPHERE A classic New York–style luncheonette, done on a Disney scale with indoor and outdoor seating. Think subway tile, street art, and neon signage.

HOUSE SPECIALTIES Burgers, both beef-based and vegan, and chicken wings in a range of sauces. For dessert, signature CrazyShakes with over-the-top toppings like cotton candy.

OTHER RECOMMENDATIONS Craft beers from around the country, on draft and in bottles. Burger-topped salads for those avoiding carbs, Korean barbecue chicken sandwiches, and sweet potato fries.

SUMMARY AND COMMENTS Stick to the burgers and you won't be disappointed. The menu offers about a dozen different topping combinations, from the basic All-American (lettuce, tomato, pickles, American cheese, and "special sauce") to the fancy-pants Greg Norman (Wagyu beef topped with blue cheese and arugula). Prime beef is the primary offering, but chicken sandwiches and Impossible burgers are available. Shakes are pricey but big enough to share.

Blue Bayou ★★★½

CAJUN/CREOLE   EXPENSIVE   QUALITY ★★★½   VALUE ★★½
READER-SURVEY RESPONSES   84% 👍

Disneyland Park; ☎ 714-781-DINE (3463)

Reservations Required. **When to go** Early or late lunch, early evening. **Entrée range** $28–$58. **Service ★★★**. **Friendliness ★★★**. **Bar** Wine, beer, and cocktails. **Dress** Casual. **Hours** Daily, 11 a.m.–10 p.m.

SETTING AND ATMOSPHERE Blue Bayou overlooks Pirates of the Caribbean and maintains an appropriately dark, damp ambience. The best tables ring the perimeter and afford a view of the faux bayou, replete with fireflies flickering among the weeping willows and mangroves, dilapidated houseboats, and soft lantern lights. If you're not lucky enough to get a table bayou-side, there's still enough wrought iron, uneven lighting, and twilight allure to soften the most hardened soul.

HOUSE SPECIALTIES Filet mignon or rib eye with crab cake at dinner; the Monte Cristo sandwich at lunch.

OTHER RECOMMENDATIONS Sustainable fish or plant-based pesto pasta. For starters, try the mildly spiced chicken gumbo or Brussels sprout salad with tasso ham.

SUMMARY AND COMMENTS Easily the fanciest restaurant in Disneyland Park, Blue Bayou is as close to fine dining as you'll get here. The restaurant fills quickly and stays busy, so make reservations before you leave home (up to 60 days in advance) or try joining the mobile app's walk-up list as soon as you get to the park. Though there's a children's menu, this isn't the place to bring wound-up or tired kids for a leisurely meal; they'll be bored. Tables are tightly packed, and nothing disrupts the busy servers more than wild kids up and out of their seats. Blue Bayou is more of a place where adults can escape the noise and happy chaos in the rest of the park without having to exit the gates. For lunch, we love the Monte Cristo sandwich, a deep-fried turkey, ham, and cheese creation that you don't find on many menus outside Disneyland these days. Side dishes—including the buttery mashed potatoes and fresh vegetables—are quite good as well. Servers are Disney-pleasant, if a tad harried, but they're more than happy to accommodate the random request. And the dinner rolls are great! If seated at an unromantically overlit table near the kitchen, don't be shy about requesting a relocation. On days when *Fantasmic!* is shown, Blue Bayou offers a dining package for $89 per adult ($35 for kids 3–9), plus tax. Packages include a starter, selected entrée, specialty nonalcoholic beverage, and dessert, as well as a pass to *Fantasmic!*'s center viewing section. Unless you order the most expensive items on the prix-fixe menu, you'll be paying a lot for that patch of cement.

DISNEYLAND RESORT RESTAURANTS BY CUISINE

CUISINE	LOCATION	OVERALL RATING	COST	QUALITY RATING	VALUE RATING
AMERICAN					
GREAT MAPLE MODERN AMERICAN EATERY*	Pixar Place Hotel	★★★½	Mod/ Exp	★★★★	★★★
GCH CRAFTSMAN BAR & GRILL*	Grand Californian	★★★½	Mod	★★★½	★★★½
LAMPLIGHT LOUNGE	DCA	★★★½	Mod	★★★½	★★★
TANGAROA TERRACE*	Disneyland Hotel	★★★½	Inexp	★★★½	★★★½
BLACK TAP CRAFT BURGERS & SHAKES	Downtown Disney	★★★	Mod	★★★	★★★
CARNATION CAFÉ*	Disneyland Park	★★★	Mod	★★★	★★★
SPLITSVILLE LUXURY LANES	Downtown Disney	★★★	Mod/ Exp	★★★	★★★
THE RIVER BELLE TERRACE*	Disneyland Park	★★★	Mod	★★★	★★★
GOOFY'S KITCHEN*	Disneyland Hotel	★★	Exp	★★	★★½
ASIAN/PACIFIC ISLANDER					
DIN TAI FUNG	Downtown Disney	TBD	Mod	TBD	TBD
TANGAROA TERRACE*	Disneyland Hotel	★★★½	Mod	★★★½	★★★½
CALIFORNIAN/FUSION					
NAPA ROSE	Grand Californian	★★★★★	V. Exp	★★★★★	★★★½
CARTHAY CIRCLE RESTAURANT	DCA	★★★★½	Exp	★★★★½	★★★½
STORYTELLERS CAFÉ*	Grand Californian	★★★★	Exp	★★★★	★★★

Café Orléans ★★★½

CAJUN/CREOLE   MODERATE   QUALITY ★★★½   VALUE ★★★
READER-SURVEY RESPONSES 89% 👍

Disneyland Park; ☎ 714-781-DINE (3463)

Reservations Recommended. **When to go** Early or late lunch, early evening. **Entrée range** $22–$29. **Service** ★★★★. **Friendliness** ★★★★. **Bar** Wine, beer, and cocktails. **Dress** Casual. **Hours** Daily, 11 a.m.–9 p.m.

SETTING AND ATMOSPHERE Across the alley from Blue Bayou, Café Orléans overlooks the Rivers of America. There's a small patio and limited inside seating, but the table-side service offers a nice break from the serve-yourself and buffet options in the same price range. It's nice to kick back amid the wrought iron and scrolled-wood accents.

HOUSE SPECIALTIES The *pommes frites* (included with the Monte Cristo sandwich) have to be among the best sides in the park: traditional thick-cut fries tossed with Parmesan and garlic and served with a mildly spicy Cajun rémoulade sauce. If they aren't served piping hot, send them back.

DISNEYLAND RESORT RESTAURANTS BY CUISINE
(continued)

CUISINE	LOCATION	OVERALL RATING	COST	QUALITY RATING	VALUE RATING
CALIFORNIAN/FUSION (CONTINUED)					
WINE COUNTRY TRATTORIA	DCA	★★★★	Mod/Exp	★★★★	★★★
BALLAST POINT	Downtown Disney	★★½	Mod	★★½	★★½
CAJUN/CREOLE					
CAFÉ ORLÉANS	Disneyland Park	★★★½	Mod	★★★½	★★★
BLUE BAYOU	Disneyland Park	★★★½	Exp	★★★½	★★½
JAZZ KITCHEN COASTAL GRILL & PATIO*	Downtown Disney	★★★½	Mod/Exp	★★★½	★★½
CUBAN					
PORTO'S BAKERY & CAFE	Downtown Disney	**TBD**	Mod/Exp	**TBD**	**TBD**
CHARACTER DINING					
NAPA ROSE	Grand Californian	★★★★★	V. Exp	★★★★★	★★★½
STORYTELLERS CAFÉ*	Grand Californian	★★★★	Exp	★★★★	★★★
GOOFY'S KITCHEN*	Disneyland Hotel	★★	Exp	★★	★★½
ITALIAN					
NAPOLINI*	Downtown Disney	★★★½	Inexp	★★★½	★★★★
NAPLES RISTORANTE E BAR	Downtown Disney	★★★	Mod	★★★	★★★½
MEXICAN					
PASEO AND CENTRICO	Downtown Disney	**TBD**	Mod/Exp	**TBD**	**TBD**

* Serves breakfast

OTHER RECOMMENDATIONS Chicken pasta with Creole sauce, beef bourguignon, and plant-based risotto.

SUMMARY AND COMMENTS Café Orléans's menu has shrunk significantly, but the *pommes frites* (currently only served with an entrée) are still worth the price of admission. The Monte Cristo sandwiches they accompany are as good as Blue Bayou's but several bucks cheaper, and they're easily large enough to share. Kids love the three-cheese version: Swiss, mozzarella, and double-cream Brie between thick slices of deep-fried, egg-battered bread. We like to hit Café Orléans for a midafternoon break, kick our feet up with a soda or sweet tea, and people-watch. The small menu (only six entrées) makes ordering easy, provided you bring a big appetite and aren't afraid of a little cholesterol.

Carnation Café ★★★

AMERICAN   MODERATE   QUALITY ★★★   VALUE ★★★
READER-SURVEY RESPONSES 89% 👍

Disneyland Park; ☎ 714-781-DINE (3463)

Reservations Recommended. **When to go** Breakfast or late lunch. **Entrée range** $16–$24. **Service** ★★★★. **Friendliness** ★★★★. **Bar** Wine, beer, and cocktails. **Dress** Casual. **Hours** Daily, 8 a.m.–9 p.m.

SETTING AND ATMOSPHERE A Main Street staple since the park opened in 1955, Carnation Café serves up an American menu heavy with traditional favorites in a parlor circa 1890.

HOUSE SPECIALTIES The loaded baked potato soup (a hot, creamy concoction with cheddar cheese, chives, and large chunks of baked potato) is a favorite, as is Walt's hearty chili. Other specialties include buttermilk pancakes at breakfast and a sourdough patty melt (with pepper Jack cheese, grilled onions, and spicy sauce) for lunch. Sadly, the superb meatloaf is no longer served.

OTHER RECOMMENDATIONS For starters, try the deep-fried dill pickle spears, dipped in a rémoulade-style sauce. The menu also features a braised short rib with mac and cheese, smoked turkey sandwich, and classic wedge salad with iceberg lettuce and blue cheese.

SUMMARY AND COMMENTS Here, adults can find a decent plate, the kids can choose from their favorites, and it's easy on the wallet. Because of its location on Main Street, close to restrooms and across from the lockers, it gets busy—expect to see lines stretching down the street. Service is friendly and unusually patient; someone's briefed these cast members on how an hour's wait and low blood sugar can quickly erode a diner's mood. Once you're seated, the order comes quickly and with a smile.

Carthay Circle Restaurant and Lounge ★★★★½

CALIFORNIA   EXPENSIVE   QUALITY ★★★★½   VALUE ★★★½
READER-SURVEY RESPONSES 90% 👍

Disney California Adventure; ☎ 714-781-DINE (3463)

Reservations Recommended. **When to go** Lunch or dinner. **Entrée range** $46–$70. **Service** ★★★. **Friendliness** ★★★★. **Bar** Full bar. **Dress** Dressy casual. **Hours** Daily, 4–8 p.m. (lounge opens at 11 a.m.; hours can vary with park closing).

SETTING AND ATMOSPHERE Intimate booths, wood paneling, and candle sconces evoke the setting of the opening night in 1937 of *Snow White and the Seven Dwarfs.* Alfresco dining is also available.

HOUSE SPECIALTIES Warm cheddar rolls, sustainable fish with seasonal vegetables, duck breast, pork chop.

OTHER RECOMMENDATIONS The menu here is revamped too frequently to recommend any particular item, but the fish poke appetizers and fresh pasta entrées are reliably delicious. Skuna Bay salmon, Wagyu beef, and truffles are among the upscale ingredients that make frequent appearances on the menu. The kids' menu offers chicken skewers, quesadillas, or pasta.

SUMMARY AND COMMENTS The chefs of Napa Rose developed the Southern Californian menu. A downstairs lounge with alfresco patio seating serves craft cocktails and small plates, while the larger upstairs restaurant requires reservations. Terrace seating is available, providing picture-perfect views of Hollywood Land and Buena Vista Street. Though service is sometimes unexpectedly inattentive, this is among the finest restaurants found inside the gates of any American theme park (including the vaunted Club 33) and one of the best dining experiences at Disneyland Resort outside of its sibling at the Grand Californian, at a slightly less astronomical price point.

Din Tai Fung *(not yet rated)*

CHINESE   MODERATE   QUALITY TBD   VALUE TBD
READER-SURVEY RESPONSES   TOO NEW TO RATE

Downtown Disney; dintaifungusa.com

Reservations Recommended (via Yelp). **When to go** Lunch or dinner. **Entrée range** $14–$30. **Service** TBD. **Friendliness** TBD. **Bar** Full service. **Dress** Casual. **Hours** Daily, 10 a.m.–9:30 p.m.

SETTING AND ATMOSPHERE The opulent Asian-influenced building design features a striking pagoda-like roofline and a circular bar inside.

HOUSE SPECIALTIES Xiao Long Bao dumpling filled with hot soup, beef or chicken noodle soup.

OTHER RECOMMENDATIONS Steamed buns and wontons, stir-fried bok choy, fried rice or noodles.

SUMMARY AND COMMENTS This family-run chain from Taiwan has earned a Michelin star for its Shanghai-style soup dumplings. Limited reservations are booked one month out, but critics claim the walk-up wait is worth it. *Pro tip:* poke a hole in your dumpling with a chopstick and suck out the soup, so it doesn't dribble when you bite it.

GCH Craftsman Bar & Grill ★★★½

AMERICAN   MODERATE   QUALITY ★★★½   VALUE ★★★½
READER-SURVEY RESPONSES   88% 👍

Grand Californian Hotel; ☎ 714-781-DINE (3463)

Reservations Available. **When to go** When you need a break from DCA. **Entrée range** $14–$28. **Service** ★★★. **Friendliness** ★★★. **Bar** Full service. **Dress** Casual. **Hours** Daily, 6 a.m.–10 p.m.

SETTING AND ATMOSPHERE Polished hardwood, rustic bricks, and rough-hewn stone serve as the foundation for this outdoor restaurant with wrap-around views of the hotel's High Sierras-inspired swimming complex.

HOUSE SPECIALTIES At breakfast, egg-and-potato burritos, bagels with lox, and avocado toast. For a light lunch or dinner, poke bowls with fresh tuna or salmon and spinach salad with salmon and grilled pine nuts. .

OTHER RECOMMENDATIONS Double-baked nachos with beef or chicken are big enough to feed an army.

SUMMARY AND COMMENTS Mere steps from the Grand Californian's side entrance into DCA, this poolside oasis often has reservations available on short notice even when other venues are booked, making it an ideal escape from the theme park for hotel guests and day visitors alike. In the mornings, this is a convenient spot for grab-and-go snacks before rope drop.

Goofy's Kitchen ★★

CHARACTER DINING/AMERICAN   EXPENSIVE   QUALITY ★★   VALUE ★★½
READER-SURVEY RESPONSES   80% 👍

Disneyland Hotel; ☎ 714-781-DINE (3463)

Reservations Recommended. **When to go** Breakfast. **Entrée range** $52–$59 ($31–$34 kids ages 3–9). **Service** ★★★★. **Friendliness** ★★★★. **Bar** Wine, beer, and cocktails. **Dress** Casual. **Hours** Daily, 7 a.m.–1 p.m. and 4–9 p.m.

SETTING AND ATMOSPHERE Bright, fun, and modern, but also very loud. Goofy, Pluto, and other characters always put a smile on kids' faces.

HOUSE SPECIALTIES It's a buffet and your chef is Goofy, which should tell you everything you need to know. Breakfast features Mickey-shaped waffles, sausages, pancakes, bacon, scrambled eggs, and other traditional breakfast items. Dinner offers everything from prime rib to salads.

OTHER RECOMMENDATIONS Kids love Goofy's peanut butter pizza.

SUMMARY AND COMMENTS You come for two reasons: 1) It's convenient, especially if you're staying at the resort, and 2) the youngsters haven't yet had their fill of dining with a rotating cast of Disney characters. Breakfast is your best option for both food and wait times. Goofy's Kitchen has many fans, including this Alpine, Utah, grandmother:

Goofy's Kitchen, even at the staggering price, was well worth it. The food was really good, a lot of the menu is designed for children, and the character visits are worth the price. What a thrill to see my grandchildren's delight at being visited by Minnie, Pluto, Chip, and Snow White (with whom my 2-year-old grandson flirted brazenly!).

Great Maple Modern American Eatery ★★★½

AMERICAN **MODERATE–EXPENSIVE** **QUALITY ★★★★** **VALUE ★★★**
READER-SURVEY RESPONSES 67% 👍

Pixar Place Hotel; ☎ 714-239-5655

Reservations Available. **When to go** Brunch or dinner. **Entrée range** $17–$45. **Service** ★★★. **Friendliness** ★★★½. **Bar** Full service. **Dress** Casual. **Hours** Daily, 8 a.m.–2 p.m. and 5–9 p.m.

SETTING AND ATMOSPHERE This bright, airy upgrade of the hotel's bland restaurant now boasts big, comfy booth seats and an expansive white-topped bar, as well as a patio with a fire pit. Look for the subtle photographs of Pixar characters in the corner.

HOUSE SPECIALTIES Buttermilk fried chicken, served in a sandwich or on maple-bacon doughnuts. Portabella mushroom fries with pesto aioli. Baby-back ribs in soda pop barbecue sauce.

OTHER RECOMMENDATIONS Ribeye hash, burgers, seasonal salads. Maple-infused craft cocktails.

SUMMARY AND COMMENTS The first franchised restaurant inside a Disneyland Resort hotel marks a big improvement over the forgettable character meal that formerly filled this space. Prices are borderline extortionate, but the ingredients are high-quality, and the huge portions are easily sharable. Diabetics be warned: although the candied ingredients in many recipes are surprisingly well-balanced, you may leave feeling like you have syrup running through your veins.

Jazz Kitchen Coastal Grill & Patio ★★★

CAJUN/CREOLE **MODERATE–EXPENSIVE** **QUALITY ★★★** **VALUE ★★**
READER-SURVEY RESPONSES 85% 👍

Downtown Disney; ☎ 714-776-5200; jazzkitchencoastalgrill.com

Reservations Recommended (via OpenTable). **When to go** Lunch or dinner. **Entrée range** $20–$48. **Service** ★★★. **Friendliness** ★★½. **Bar** Full bar. **Dress** Casual. **Hours** Sunday–Thursday, 11 a.m.–10 p.m.; Friday–Saturday, 11 a.m.–10:30 p.m. (*Beignets Expressed:* Daily, 9 a.m.–10:30 p.m.)

SETTING AND ATMOSPHERE This restaurant originally transported diners a step back in time and space to the 19th-century French Quarter of New

Orleans, but a 2023 rebranding stripped it of both chef Ralph Brennan's name and its distinctive Bourbon Street aesthetic, in favor of a much less architecturally distinctive SoCal-modern motif. Regardless of the redecoration, you can still people-watch from a balcony dining area, or enjoy the daily live jazz music from anywhere.

HOUSE SPECIALTIES Gumbo Ya-Ya and pasta jambalaya are favorite holdovers from the previous menu. Newer items include blackened chicken mac and cheese and crawfish lettuce wraps.

OTHER RECOMMENDATIONS Barbecue shrimp and grits. Sliders, flatbreads, and discounted drinks are offered during happy hour Monday–Friday, 2–4 p.m.

SUMMARY AND COMMENTS This used to be one of our favorite restaurants in or immediately around the resort, but a major remodeling, steering it away from its Creole roots, has made for a much blander experience. The Brennan family's involvement has been deemphasized, and a "vibrant California energy" has been incorporated into the Louisiana-inspired menu and ambience. For a quick breakfast or afternoon break, the creative beignets and coffee from the adjoining quick-service counter can't be beat.

Lamplight Lounge ★★★½

AMERICAN   MODERATE   QUALITY ★★★½   VALUE ★★★
READER-SURVEY RESPONSES 83% 👍

Disney California Adventure; ☎ 714-781-DINE (3463)

Reservations Recommended. **When to go** Anytime. **Entrée range** $22–$29. **Service** ★★★★. **Friendliness** ★★★★. **Bar** Wine, beer, and cocktails. **Dress** Casual. **Hours** Daily, 11:30 a.m.–8:30 p.m.; brunch Friday–Sunday, park opening–noon.

SETTING AND ATMOSPHERE This seaside hangout has a backstory as a wharf warehouse, with exposed steel and reclaimed wood attesting to its faux history. Look for a hanging sculpture of concept sketches and knickknacks left behind by the Pixar artists who allegedly loiter here.

HOUSE SPECIALTIES Gastropub appetizers and sandwiches with signature cocktails. Lobster nachos, salmon PLT (pancetta, romaine, and plum tomato), doughnuts with dipping sauces.

OTHER RECOMMENDATIONS Salmon poke and roasted chicken salad. Cinnamon-sugar French toast and spiced ham benedict for brunch.

SUMMARY AND COMMENTS Adults (with or without their children) can escape upstairs to the alfresco Boardwalk Dining bar for a glass of wine, a cocktail, or a bottle of beer. The bar also serves a selection of appetizers, including the overrated lobster nachos that are a cult favorite. We prefer the creative poke and the decadent doughnuts. Bigger Bites and selected kids' meals are only available in the downstairs dining room, where some open-air tables sport built-in fire pits. This is a good spot to catch *World of Color* without a Virtual Queue reservation; views of the fountains from here are great, but the oblique angle to the projection screens isn't ideal.

Napa Rose ★★★★★

CALIFORNIAN/FUSION   VERY EXPENSIVE   QUALITY ★★★★★   VALUE ★★★½
READER-SURVEY RESPONSES 93% 👍

Grand Californian Hotel; ☎ 714-781-DINE (3463)

Reservations Required. **When to go** Dinner. **Entrée range** $62–$72; $150 for four courses. **Service** ★★★★★. **Friendliness** ★★★★. **Bar** Impressive wine list. **Dress** Dressy casual. **Hours** Daily, 5:30–9 p.m.

SETTING AND ATMOSPHERE Napa Rose is Disneyland Resort's flagship fine-dining experience. The Grand Californian's Craftsman theme is carried into this premier room with sweeping views of DCA from virtually every table. A large, open demonstration kitchen lets you watch the magic happen, and wine, in all its glory, is displayed at every turn. Fine linens and china are the norm. This is an absolutely gorgeous room, with food and service to match.

HOUSE SPECIALTIES The menu, rotated seasonally, focuses on the cuisine of California's wine region, ranchlands, farm belts, and coastline. Wine finds its way onto most of the menu in sauces, reductions, infusions, and dressings. Dishes may include asparagus with meyer lemon, portabello mushroom "cappuccino," seared beef filet mignon, and sustainably caught seasonal fish, as well as a chocolate tart or homemade ice cream for dessert.

OTHER RECOMMENDATIONS Game meat, ranch and free-range beef and poultry, and the chef's prix fixe Vintner's Table are constantly changing and always exciting. On select mornings, the restaurant hosts a brunch with the Disney princesses (see page 176).

SUMMARY AND COMMENTS Napa Rose may be the best restaurant in Orange County and has been at the top of most critics' lists since its debut. Top talent in the kitchen (award-winning chef Andrew Sutton leads the charge) and in the dining room make this an incomparable gustatory experience. Every server has earned sommelier status, a designation that takes years of study and practical experience with wine and winemaking, easing the chore of choosing a wine from its cellar of more than 16,000 bottles. The waitstaff brings the whole experience, from wine rookies to experts, to match your level of knowledge and tastes. Look for unusual ingredients (Tahitian vanilla, smoked sturgeon, truffled quail eggs, lemongrass, almond oil) married to top-notch staples (Colorado lamb, Berkshire pork, pheasant breast, sustainable fresh fish), all deftly handled by a world-class kitchen crew. And though staff are very accommodating in the usual Disney manner, this is definitely not an adventure for the kids. Napa Rose should be on every adult's Disney bucket list, a must-do at least once. If the full menu is too rich for your blood, sit in the cozy lounge and order appetizers; ask in person about lounge walk-in availability at 5:15 p.m. if you can't snag a reservation. An Albuquerque, New Mexico, woman wrote in to recommend the restaurant:

Prices were quite high, but we had a very good time. Napa Rose was the highlight of the trip, and our waiter was very good.

But a couple from Armonk, New York, took issue with our "fawning" review, reporting:

The food is still fine, but in no way is this a special restaurant for a grown-up night out. So many people had small (loud) children with them that we felt uncomfortable there as two adults without kids. People don't dress up; it's not a special experience.

Finally, a Suffern, New York, reader with good taste advises:

If you're doing the Napa Rose Chef's Counter, get the tasting menu.

Naples Ristorante e Bar ★★★

ITALIAN   MODERATE   QUALITY ★★★   VALUE ★★★½
READER-SURVEY RESPONSES 88% 👍

Downtown Disney; ☎ 714-776-6200 or 714-781-DINE (3463);
patinagroup.com/naples-ristorante-e-bar

Reservations Recommended (via OpenTable). **When to go** Late lunch or early dinner.
Entrée range $18–$31. **Service** ★★. **Friendliness** ★★★. **Bar** Extensive wine list and
full bar. **Dress** Casual. **Hours** Daily, 11 a.m.–10 p.m.

SETTING AND ATMOSPHERE Food aside, this is a really fun restaurant:
modern, colorful, and spacious, with tile floors, an open demonstration
kitchen, and whimsical design touches that mirror nearby Disneyland. It's
also noisy and crowded, typically filled with families. During peak hours,
it's difficult to hear yourself think, let alone carry on a meaningful conversation. Nonetheless, it's a great gathering place, and there's something to
appeal to everyone from small children to adults.

HOUSE SPECIALTIES Wood-fired Neapolitan-style pizzas: thin, crispy crusts
with a hearty, almost-spicy red sauce; handmade mozzarella cheese; and
fresh toppings of choice.

OTHER RECOMMENDATIONS Some of the non-pasta entrées, such as pan-
seared salmon with roasted tomatoes and lemon, are the real highlights.

SUMMARY AND COMMENTS This Patina–Joachim Splichal venture boasts
one of Downtown Disney's best outdoor dining and bar areas, along with
an extensive-but-accessible menu. The kids will enjoy the colorful decor
and activities, while adults can get a good glass of wine or a cocktail and
feed the entire crew for less than $100.

Napolini ★★★½

ITALIAN/DELI   INEXPENSIVE   QUALITY ★★★½   VALUE ★★★★
READER-SURVEY RESPONSES 91% 👍

Downtown Disney; ☎ 714-781-DINE (3463);
patinagroup.com/napolini-pizzeria

Reservations Not accepted. **When to go** Lunch or a quick dinner. **Entrée range** $12–
$14. **Service** ★★. **Friendliness** ★★★. **Bar** Wine and beer only. **Dress** Casual. **Hours**
Sunday–Thursday, 10 a.m.–11 p.m.; Friday–Saturday, 11 a.m.–midnight.

SETTING AND ATMOSPHERE This is next-door Naples's cousin—a quick-in,
quick-out deli with grab-and-go salads and sandwiches, plus made-to-
order pizzas at remarkably reasonable prices.

HOUSE SPECIALTIES Wood-fired Neapolitan-style pizzas and Filo's Italian
gelato for dessert.

OTHER RECOMMENDATIONS Choose a pie with your pick of toppings from
the menu of signature combos, like California barbecue chicken or Salsic-
cia spicy sausage.

SUMMARY AND COMMENTS Napolini represents one of the best dining
deals in all of Downtown Disney. If you like Blaze Pizza or Pizza Press, you
should be very satisfied with a pie from here.

Paseo and Céntrico *(not yet rated)*

MEXICAN   MODERATE–EXPENSIVE   QUALITY TBD   VALUE TBD
READER-SURVEY RESPONSES TOO NEW TO RATE

Downtown Disney; paseoanaheim.com

Reservations Recommended. **When to go** Lunch or dinner. **Entrée range** $35–$60. **Service** TBD. **Friendliness** TBD. **Bar** Full service. **Dress** Casual. **Hours** TBD.

SETTING AND ATMOSPHERE A spiraling wooden staircase leads to Paseo's main dining room on the second floor, which opens to a balcony overlooking the Céntrico bar in the middle of the plaza below. Natural materials and hanging greenery give the space a fresh, airy feeling.

HOUSE SPECIALTIES At Paseo, lamb barbacoa, roasted pork, and tetelas (stuffed corn triangles). At Céntrico, quesabirria, chicken enchiladas, and tlayuda (Oaxacan "pizza").

OTHER RECOMMENDATIONS Ceviche and mejillones (mussels) at Paseo; tequila-based cocktails at Céntrico.

SUMMARY AND COMMENTS This trio of eateries was created by Chef Carlos Gaytán, Mexico's first Michelin-starred chef, and is operated by the Patina Restaurant Group. Paseo is the spot for a special sit-down dinner, while Céntrico is the place for sipping a cocktail while people-watching. They are joined by Tiendita, a self-order, quick-service kiosk offering Mexican street food such as breakfast burritos, esquites (off-the-cob elote), chocolate tacos stuffed with ice cream, and arroz con leche (a nostalgic treat from Chef Gaytán's childhood).

Porto's Bakery & Cafe *(opening TBA)*

CUBAN   INEXPENSIVE–MODERATE   QUALITY TBD   VALUE TBD
READER-SURVEY RESPONSES   TOO NEW TO RATE

Downtown Disney; portosbakery.com

Reservations Not accepted. **When to go** Anytime. **Entrée range** $TBD. **Service** TBD. **Friendliness** TBD. **Dress** Casual. **Hours** TBD.

SETTING AND ATMOSPHERE The former La Brea Bakery, which was temporarily taken over by Earl of Sandwich, is scheduled for demolition to make way for a brand-new outpost of Porto's, whose other locations are known for their airy, white bakeries with bold block-letter signage. However, plans for Porto's appeared to be paused at press time.

HOUSE SPECIALTIES The bakery's signature items are sweet and savory pastry rolls, stuffed with cheese and guava, and papa rellena potato balls. The cafe features slow-cooked meat platters with rice and beans, pressed Cuban sandwiches, and salads.

OTHER RECOMMENDATIONS Tamales, empanadas, ham or chicken croquettes. Breakfast croissant sandwiches and wraps. Hot and cold coffees and teas.

SUMMARY AND COMMENTS A California staple since 1976, this table-service restaurant and takeaway bakery preserve the classic Galician and Cuban comfort food recipes passed down by founder Rosa Porto. You can take whole loaves of fresh bread from the bakery back to your hotel.

The River Belle Terrace ★★★

AMERICAN   MODERATE   QUALITY ★★★   VALUE ★★★
READER-SURVEY RESPONSES   79% 👍

Disneyland Park; ☎ 714-781-DINE (3463)

Reservations Available. **When to go** Brunch, lunch, or dinner. **Entrée range** $19–$27. **Service** ★★★. **Friendliness** ★★★. **Bar** Wine, beer, and cocktails. **Dress** Casual. **Hours** Daily, 11 a.m.–8 p.m.

SETTING AND ATMOSPHERE Situated between New Orleans Square and Frontierland, The River Belle Terrace has an Old South–style exterior replete with wrought iron and wood siding. Large shuttered windows belie a small indoor-dining area; most of the seating is outdoors on a large patio covered with colorful umbrellas.

HOUSE SPECIALTIES Apple pie pancakes, loaded house fries, and biscuits with gravy for brunch. Pork chop, fried chicken sandwich, and pappardelle pasta with beef brisket burnt ends for dinner.

OTHER RECOMMENDATIONS Plant-based meatballs and roasted squash.

SUMMARY AND COMMENTS This 1955 Disneyland original offers homey Southern dishes at lunch and dinner. This used to be our least-favorite table-service restaurant in Disneyland, but menu improvements have made it into an underrated gem. The outdoor seating area is good for people-watching or just taking in the view of Rivers of America from the patio, and this is often the only table-service restaurant inside Disneyland with available reservations. On days when *Fantasmic!* is shown, River Belle Terrace offers a 3-course package for $55 per adult ($30 for kids 3–9) that includes a pass to the show's second-best viewing section; for an extra $34 per adult ($15 per kid), you can stay seated on the patio through the first performance (see page 224 for details).

Splitsville Luxury Lanes ★★★

AMERICAN   MODERATE-EXPENSIVE   QUALITY ★★★   VALUE ★★★
READER-SURVEY RESPONSES 96% 👍

Downtown Disney; ☎ 714-781-DINE (3463);
splitsvillelanes.com/location/anaheim

Reservations Available. **When to go** Lunch or dinner. **Entrée range** $15–$42. **Service** ★★★½. **Friendliness** ★★★½. **Bar** Full service. **Dress** Casual. **Hours** Sunday–Thursday, 11 a.m.–11 p.m.; Friday–Saturday, 11 a.m.–midnight.

SETTING AND ATMOSPHERE Splitsville is part of a multistate chain of hybrid bowling alleys–restaurants. The two-story Anaheim branch looks like a mid-century movie star's mansion, with rich hardwood surfaces, space-age lighting fixtures, and faux-vintage billboards referencing the region's history. It isn't nearly as loud as the Orlando location, and the 20 bowling lanes are split up and secluded among the various dining rooms, making eating here feel like less of an afterthought.

HOUSE SPECIALTIES The sushi—salmon, shrimp, tuna, crab, and various combinations thereof—is the best thing on the menu.

OTHER RECOMMENDATIONS Cheeseburger sliders, fish-and-chips, and chicken fingers. Ghiradelli chocolate brownie for dessert.

SUMMARY AND COMMENTS The menu is more spread out than a 7/10 split: burgers, sushi, pizza, seafood, barbecue, Mexican, and Italian are represented, plus nachos and other bar food. It would be a stretch for any kitchen to make half of these things well, let alone a kitchen in a bowling alley, but this California venue makes a better effort at it than its Floridian cousin. Ingredients taste fresh and are of consistent quality, but the flavor profiles are unbalanced, often overwhelming savory dishes with sweet sauces. Stick with the potent cocktails and appetizers. Bowling costs $25 per person ($20 before 4 p.m., Monday–Friday) for shoe rental and 60–105 minutes of lane time, depending on party size; to reserve a private lane for an additional $10 per bowler, visit bowl.splitsvillelanes.com.

Storytellers Café ★★★★

CHARACTER DINING/CALIFORNIAN EXPENSIVE QUALITY ★★★★ VALUE ★★★
READER-SURVEY RESPONSES 86% 👍

Grand Californian Hotel; ☎ 714-781-DINE (3463)

Reservations Recommended. **When to go** Breakfast or dinner. **Entrée range** $47–$52 ($26–$31 kids ages 3–9). **Service** ★★★★★. **Friendliness** ★★★★. **Bar** Extensive wine list and full bar. **Dress** Casual. **Hours** Daily, 7 a.m.–1:15 p.m. and 4:30–9:30 p.m.

SETTING AND ATMOSPHERE Storytellers Café carries the Grand Californian Hotel's Arts and Crafts theme throughout with large, open beams; natural wood and wood carvings; milled stone; and stained glass. The walls are adorned with impressive murals depicting the state's rich literary history, from Mark Twain's "The Celebrated Jumping Frog of Calaveras County" to Scott O'Dell's *Island of the Blue Dolphins.*

HOUSE SPECIALTIES Children under age 10 will love the character breakfast buffet. Hosted by Mickey and Minnie Mouse, the meal features a complement of cartoon friends who visit the tables; sing songs; and pose for photos between bites of omelets and Mickey-shaped waffles. The dinner buffet features flatbreads, a meat-carving station with prime rib, rotating selections of seafood and pasta, and a variety of salads and vegan options.

OTHER RECOMMENDATIONS The *chilaquiles* with fresh eggs and tomatillo salsa is the best item on the breakfast buffet. The charred corn chowder with rotisserie chicken is almost worth the price of dinner. Kids can have cheeseburger sliders and chicken fingers.

SUMMARY AND COMMENTS You may experience a little sticker shock at first, but there's real value here. It's not quite on par with Napa Rose across the way, but the same dedication to quality and originality is evident from the menu to the service. Kids will find lots to like about the food, while adults will enjoy the California wine country–inspired menu options and a leisurely cocktail or glass of wine. You'll want to save some room for dessert too— who could pass up mini s'mores tarts or warm bread pudding with vanilla sauce? The *World of Color* dining package only costs $17 more per adult ($12 more per child) than the regular dinner buffet, and it also includes 3 hours of valet parking at the hotel, making this the best bargain for reserved viewing of a nighttime spectacular. A Manitowoc, Wisconsin, reader recommends the café as an alternative to dining inside DCA, writing:

We ended up eating at Storytellers Café on a spur-of-the-moment decision, and it was one of the best places at which we ate at the park, as far as food, price, and atmosphere.

Tangaroa Terrace Tropical Bar and Grill ★★★½

AMERICAN/PACIFIC ISLANDER MODERATE QUALITY ★★★½
VALUE ★★★ READER-SURVEY RESPONSES 86% 👍

Disneyland Hotel; ☎ 714-781-DINE (3463)

Reservations Not accepted at Tangaroa (Mobile Ordering); recommended at Trader Sam's. **When to go** Anytime. **Entrée range** $15–$24. **Service** ★★★★. **Friendliness** ★★★★. **Bar** Beer, wine, and tropical cocktails. **Dress** Casual. **Hours** Daily, 7 a.m.– 10 p.m. Trader Sam's open daily, 11:30 a.m.–midnight.

SETTING AND ATMOSPHERE This is Disneyland Hotel's poolside tropical retreat. Tiki torches and South Seas music are a dead giveaway that they want to evoke that island feeling.

HOUSE SPECIALTIES Breakfast has French toast with guava syrup and avocado toast topped by a scrambled egg. Lunch and dinner feature a one-half-pound Hawaiian cheeseburger with teriyaki sauce, bacon, and caramelized pineapple on a brioche bun.

OTHER RECOMMENDATIONS Pacific Rim–style specialties get a little more exotic with short rib or teriyaki chicken on jasmine rice and delicious macaroni salad, but the tonkotsu ramen broth isn't quite unctuous enough. Tangaroa Terrace serves the same drinks and bar snacks as Trader Sam's next door, and you can be served outside in a matter of minutes using Mobile Order, as opposed to the typical 2–3-hour wait to be seated inside.

SUMMARY AND COMMENTS This eatery has something for everyone, as long as everyone enjoys food with an Asian-Polynesian flair. Tangaroa Terrace's breakfast menu blows away any other quick-service breakfast inside the theme parks. Adults can enjoy a cocktail (maybe something a little exotic with a fruit garnish and little pink umbrellas) while kids frolic in the nearby pool in between bites. The adjoining Trader Sam's Enchanted Tiki Bar (restricted to adults 21+ after 8 p.m.) serves exotic cocktails and Asian-inspired appetizers in an intimate and elaborately decorated environment reminiscent of Walt Disney World's extinct Adventurers Club. Order an Uh Oa, Krakatoa Punch, or Shipwreck on the Rocks to see some explosive special effects, or a potent Sea Monster's Embrace to see the underside of your barstool. The best bet for late-night snacks are Sam's tempura-fried green beans or sweet-and-spicy Asian wings. If the interior is at capacity (a frequent occurrence), try the patio, which has live music and a cozy fireplace.

Wine Country Trattoria ★★★★

CALIFORNIA NOUVELLE   MODERATE-EXPENSIVE   QUALITY ★★★★
VALUE ★★★   READER-SURVEY RESPONSES 84% 👍

Disney California Adventure; ☎ 714-781-DINE (3463)

Reservations Recommended. **When to go** Lunch or dinner. **Entrée range** $20–$38. **Service** ★★★. **Friendliness** ★★. **Bar** Wine, beer, and cocktails. **Dress** Casual. **Hours** Daily, 11 a.m.–8 p.m. Magic Key Terrace (passholders and guests only): Daily, 11 a.m.–8 p.m.

SETTING AND ATMOSPHERE Arguably one of the better dining options at either park, the trattoria is a leisurely place to park yourself and family away from the frenetic crowds. Whether you choose one of three themed patios outside or the "patio" inside, this spacious bistro captures the California-casual mood with plenty of tile, wood, and trellised greenery, whisking you away from downtown Anaheim and positing you in the middle of California wine country.

HOUSE SPECIALTIES Try the pasta: spaghetti Bolognese, spaghetti with seasonal vegetables, or fettuccine shrimp Alfredo.

OTHER RECOMMENDATIONS Salmon with dill-butter sauce, rib eye steak, or vegetable lasagna. And to finish: traditional tiramisu.

SUMMARY AND COMMENTS Wine Country Trattoria is a popular spot for a Mediterranean-style or California-inspired meal, paired with a glass of wine from its extensive cellar. The trattoria appeals more to adults without children, though an improved kids' menu and *World of Color* fixed-price dining packages ($62 adults, $37 kids ages 3–9; all plus tax and gratuity) have made this a more attractive option for families. Note that patrons with a viewing package for lunch or dinner each receive a ticket for a reserved viewing area but do not watch the show from the restaurant itself. The soup or salad and desserts included in the viewing package are all acceptable (if a bit over-seasoned), and the entrées are equal to the à la carte selections; the thin rib eye isn't worth the $10 upcharge if you like your meat medium-rare. From a Richfield, Ohio, mom:

One place we all agreed on was the Wine Country Trattoria at DCA. The service was a bit on the slow side, but the food was delicious and fresh.

For a refreshing afternoon break, Magic Key passholders and their guests can order a Heimlich Chew-Chew juice cocktail and Bountiful Valley charcuterie plate (or other appetizers named after extinct DCA attractions) at the alfresco patio on the upstairs terrace. This pleasant private lounge was expanded to encompass the restaurant's entire upper floor, due to popular demand, and is adorned with tributes to the adorable feral housecats who call this area home. Reservations can be scarce, but walkups are usually accommodated; if allowed upstairs, share a flatbread or the sliders. Otherwise, get takeaway snacks at the Sonoma Terrace around the corner. The terrace offers its own *World of Color* package for the same price that's even better than the one downstairs; we really like the pepita-sprinkled Caesar salad and the earthy tomato soup starters, as well as the delicious (if indelicate) whole fried hen and roasted cauliflower entrées.

DINING *Outside* DISNEYLAND RESORT

UNOFFICIAL GUIDE RESEARCHERS LOVE GOOD FOOD and invest a fair amount of time scouting new places to eat. And because food at Disneyland Resort (all of the Disney complex, including the theme parks, hotels, and Downtown Disney) is so expensive, we (like you) have an economic incentive for finding palatable meals off campus. Redevelopment of the surrounding real estate has attracted a whole new glut of fine-dining and fast-casual options. Choices range from the familiar **(Tony Roma's, Denny's, Ruth's Chris Steak House)** to local favorites **(Roscoe's).** Unique dining experiences are also prevalent. While the average Disneyland visitor stays for only two to four nights, there are more than enough fine-dining and fast-casual venues outside Disneyland Resort to keep you happy for that amount of time. Good ethnic dining, however, is woefully underrepresented. Especially hard to find are high-quality Thai, Chinese, Japanese, Korean, and Greek restaurants. We've confined our coverage to restaurants that you can reach by car in 15 minutes or less. If you're willing to range farther afield, your choices increase exponentially.

Among restaurants in and out of Disneyland Resort, location and price will determine your choice. For example, a decent Italian restaurant is in Downtown Disney, and several independent Italian eateries are within 5 miles of the Disney complex. Which one you select depends on how much you want to spend and how convenient the restaurant is.

Better restaurants outside Disneyland Resort cater primarily to adults and aren't as well equipped to deal with children. This is a plus, however, if you're looking to escape children and eat in peace and quiet.

The Anaheim GardenWalk retail and entertainment complex is east of the park. Popular chains such as **The Cheesecake Factory, Roy's Restaurant, California Pizza Kitchen,** and **Bubba Gump Shrimp Co.** are still serving diners, despite the decline of the surrounding shops. The best of the lot is probably **McCormick & Schmick's Grille,** which serves well-prepared fresh seafood at outrageous prices.

The **Anaheim Packing House** (440 S. Anaheim Blvd., ☎ 714-533-7225, anaheimpackingdistrict.com; open daily, 11 a.m.–9 p.m., but individual merchants' hours vary) is a century-old Sunkist citrus warehouse that has been reborn as a trendy urban food hall, not unlike New York's Chelsea Market, filled with more than two dozen independent eateries and bars. We like the kebabs and naan at **Adya Fresh Indian Flavors,** ramen noodles at **Zabon,** and the baguette sandwiches and crepes from **Le Parfait Paris.** If you're thirsty for a Prohibition-inspired cocktail, check out the reservations-only **Blind Rabbit** speakeasy. On weekends, locals pack the house, as well as the neighboring Packing District's farmers' park and breweries, jockeying for scarce parking spots. Instead, park for free at the City Hall garage and use the A-Way WeGo app to hail a FRAN (rideart.org/fran) electric micro-van for a free ride around the block.

ANAHEIM-AREA FULL-SERVICE RESTAURANTS

SOUTHERN CALIFORNIA offers a mother lode of wonderful dining, and if we directed you to Newport Beach, La Jolla, or LA, we could guarantee you a fantastic eating experience every night. In that you've chosen Disneyland as your destination, however, we've elected to profile only solid restaurants that you can reach by car or cab in 15 minutes or less. That said, here are our picks; all of them offer disabled access.

Bierstube German Pub at the Phoenix Club ★★★½

GERMAN	INEXPENSIVE–MODERATE	QUALITY ★★★½	VALUE ★★★★

375 W. Central Ave., Brea; ☎ 714-563-4166; thephoenixclub.com

Reservations Recommended. **When to go** Lunch or dinner. **Entrée range** $12.75–$22.75. **Service** ★★★. **Friendliness** ★★★★. **Bar** Wine list, extensive draft beer offerings, and full bar. **Dress** Casual. **Hours** Wednesday–Friday, 11 a.m.–9 p.m.; Saturday, 10:30 a.m.–9 p.m.; Sunday, 10 a.m.–9 p.m. Kitchen closes at 8 p.m. daily.

SETTING AND ATMOSPHERE Once a private club reserved for family members of the original German settlers of Anaheim and more recent émigrés,

GREAT EATS IN AND AROUND ANAHEIM

BEST ASIAN BUFFET

Teppanyaki Grill Supreme Buffet 1630 W. Katella Ave., Anaheim; ☎ 714-530-9699; teppanyaki-grill-supreme-buffet.cafes-guide.com. Dinner: $19 adults, Monday–Thursday; $20 adults, Friday–Sunday; $15 for children ages 7–10, $9 for children ages 3–6, free for children under age 2. Features made-to-order Japanese hibachi and sushi, in addition to Chinese dishes, including excellent soup and dim sum.

BEST BOBA

Pink Pig Boba & Pizza 1650 S. Harbor Blvd. Ste. B, Anaheim; ☎ 909-316-9777; pinkpigbobapizza.com. The closest place to the Disneyland Resort to get fresh fruit tea, milk tea, or cloud tea with popping boba, red beans, lychee jelly, and other tasty toppings. Skip the pizza, which tastes previously frozen, and stick with the superb Asian tea selection.

BEST INDIAN

Punjabi Tandoor 327 S. Anaheim Blvd., Ste. A, Anaheim; ☎ 714-635-3155; punjabi tandoor.com. The fresh tandoori in the evening is exceptional. Offers original dishes and excellent naan.

BEST INDIAN BUFFETS

Gateway to India 1188 W. Katella Ave., Anaheim; ☎ 714-808-6777; gatewaytoindia anaheim.com. Lunch buffet served Tuesday–Sunday for $20 on weekdays ($16 for children) or $23 on weekends ($19 for children).

Masala Craft 575 W. Chapman Ave., Anaheim; ☎ 714-406-4314; masalacraft.us. Lunch buffet served Friday–Sunday, 11:30 a.m.–2:30 p.m. for $26.

BEST JAPANESE

Sushi Pop 1105 S. Euclid St., Fullerton; ☎ 714-278-1062; sushipopus.com. An unpretentious strip mall eatery offering nigiri and unusual maki rolls at reasonable prices.

BEST MEDITERRANEAN

Zankou Chicken 2424 W. Ball Road, Anaheim; ☎ 714-229-2060; zankouchicken.com /anaheim. Forget that this place is a chain, disregard the cheesy ambience, and go for the spit-roasted chicken, hummus, and shawarma beef. Inexpensive and delicious.

BEST MEXICAN

La Casa Garcia 531 W. Chapman Ave., Anaheim; ☎ 714-740-1108; lacasagarcia.com. Carnitas, *barbacoa* (beef slow-cooked in a red-chile sauce), and three-flavor chimichangas, all with a Tex-Mex twist, are not to be missed.

Los Sanchez 11906 Garden Grove Blvd., Garden Grove; ☎ 714-590-9300. This locals-only gem serves authentic Sonoran cuisine at reasonable prices. Fish ceviche, *lengua* (tongue) tacos, seafood soup, and the best chicken mole you've ever had.

BEST PIZZA

The Pizza Press 1700 S. Harbor Blvd., Anaheim; ☎ 714-833-5868; thepizzapress.com. Excellent artisanal thin-crust pies with upscale toppings for a very reasonable price—plus tossed-to-order salads, craft beers, and an 11 p.m. closing time—make this Anaheim-based chain pizzeria across from Disneyland a perfect post-park pit stop.

this Anaheim landmark was relocated after 62 years to nearby Brea. It has more than a half dozen German beers on tap. Its menu is somewhat limited, trending toward less-fancy preparations, but it's these basic dishes that keep folks coming back. The pub is conducive to raucous eating, drinking, and carousing. Live music seems omnipresent, from local and guest polka bands to renowned accordion artists.

HOUSE SPECIALTIES Wursts, kraut, pork roast, mixed platters, and sauerbraten are the best in a 100-mile radius.

OTHER RECOMMENDATIONS Pork in a creamy mushroom sauce.

SUMMARY AND COMMENTS The bastion of Anaheim's founding families and subsequent waves of German immigrants, The Phoenix Club offers a little taste of the *Mutterland* far from home. The food is good, occasionally great; the beer is always cold; and the help is always ready to show you a good time, German or not. During Oktoberfest, the place rocks. Kids will love the oompah bands, Mom and Dad will love the German beers, and everyone will love the sweet-and-sour flavors of German cuisine.

Carolina's Italian Restaurant ★★★

SOUTHERN ITALIAN	MODERATE	QUALITY ★★★	VALUE ★★★½

12045 Chapman Ave., Garden Grove; ☎ 714-971-5551; carolinasitalianrestaurant.com

Reservations Recommended. **When to go** Dinner. **Entrée range** $15–$35. **Service** ★★½. **Friendliness** ★★★½. **Bar** Extensive beer and wine lists. **Dress** Casual. **Hours** Daily, 11 a.m.–midnight; dine-in service until 10 p.m.

SETTING AND ATMOSPHERE A classic Italian family restaurant replete with wall murals of the motherland, comfortable seating, and the overwhelming aroma of garlic and olive oil. It's like walking through a time warp.

HOUSE SPECIALTIES You can't go wrong with any of the many hearty pasta dishes, from a traditional meat sauce to an outstanding lasagna.

OTHER RECOMMENDATIONS The house-made tiramisu, if you can manage more food after the large plates, is a treat.

SUMMARY AND COMMENTS Family owned and operated for three generations, Carolina's also features more than 200 beers from around the globe and a rather well-selected wine list for such a place. Portions tend toward the gigantic, so bring your appetite.

Gabbi's Mexican Kitchen ★★★

GOURMET MEXICAN	MODERATE	QUALITY ★★★★	VALUE ★★★½

141 S. Glassell St., Orange; ☎ 714-633-3038; gabbipatrick.com

Reservations Recommended. **When to go** Lunch or dinner. **Entrée range** $18–$34. **Service** ★★★. **Friendliness** ★★★. **Bar** Full bar. **Dress** Casual. **Hours** Sunday–Thursday, 11 a.m.–9:30 p.m.; Friday–Saturday, 11 a.m.–10 p.m.

SETTING AND ATMOSPHERE Locals flock to Gabbi's vintage storefront that has no sign (look for the *poquito* patio next door to the Army surplus store). Just steps south of Orange's beloved plaza in charming Old Town, Gabbi's adds style to the narrow space with tall ceilings, exposed brick, and giant, colorful Mexican urns.

HOUSE SPECIALTIES Braised Berkshire pork or carne asada tacos.

OTHER RECOMMENDATIONS Chicken enchiladas and signature margaritas made from a tequila collection that would make a desperado blush.

SUMMARY AND COMMENTS In this county teeming with taco stands and burrito counters, chef-owner Gabbi Patrick stands apart with her more refined, regional takes on Mexican food that reflect both her Napa training and her Latino family's roots in the restaurant business.

Haven Craft Kitchen + Bar ★★★

GASTROPUB	MODERATE-EXPENSIVE	QUALITY ★★★★	VALUE ★★★½

190 S. Glassell St., Orange; ☎ 714-221-0680; havencraftkitchen.com

ANAHEIM-AREA RESTAURANTS BY CUISINE

CUISINE/LOCATION	OVERALL RATING	COST	QUALITY RATING	VALUE RATING
AMERICAN				
ROSCOE'S HOUSE OF CHICKEN & WAFFLES S. Harbor Blvd.	★★★★	Inexp/Mod	★★★★	★★★½
CAJUN/CREOLE				
HOUSE OF BLUES RESTAURANT & BAR Disney Way	★★★	Mod	★★★½	★★½
CALIFORNIAN				
TANGERINE ROOM W. Katella Ave.	★★★★½	Mod/Exp	★★★★½	★★★★
CHINESE				
MA'S HOUSE CHINESE HALAL E. Orangethorpe Ave.	★★★½	Mod	★★★	★★★½
GASTROPUB				
HAVEN CRAFT KITCHEN + BAR S. Glassell St.	★★★	Mod/Exp	★★★★	★★★½
GERMAN				
BIERSTUBE GERMAN PUB AT THE PHOENIX CLUB W. Central Ave.	★★★½	Inexp/Mod	★★★½	★★★★
ITALIAN				
CAROLINA'S ITALIAN RESTAURANT Chapman Ave.	★★★	Mod	★★★	★★★½
MEXICAN				
GABBI'S MEXICAN KITCHEN S. Glassell St.	★★★	Mod	★★★★	★★★½
SEAFOOD				
MCCORMICK & SCHMICK'S GRILLE W. Katella Ave.	★★★	Mod/Exp	★★★	★★★
SPANISH				
TOP OF THE V S. Anaheim Blvd.	★★★★½	Exp	★★★★½	★★★½
STEAK				
MORTON'S S. Harbor Blvd.	★★★★	Exp	★★★½	★★★½
PRIME CUT CAFÉ & WINE BAR W. Katella Ave.	★★★	Mod/Exp	★★★	★★★½

Reservations Recommended. **When to go** Lunch or dinner. **Entrée range** $14–$67. **Service** ★★★. **Friendliness** ★★★½. **Bar** Full bar. **Dress** Casual. **Hours** Monday–Friday, 11 a.m.–11 p.m.; Saturday–Sunday, 10 a.m.–11 p.m.

SETTING AND ATMOSPHERE The restaurant is in Old Town Orange, a historic area of preserved homes and businesses, including this little gem. Like its neighbor, Gabbi's, Haven is housed in a restored brick building. Inside, you'll find a large open dining room packed with tables and booths, framed by a massive bar on one side and an open kitchen on the other.

HOUSE SPECIALTIES Definitely try the burger with aged white cheddar and umami aioli.

OTHER RECOMMENDATIONS Locally raised roasted chicken.

SUMMARY AND COMMENTS Think beer, anything made with beer, and all the food that goes with beer, and you have a grasp of what executive chef

Craig Brady has put together here. Combine more than 200 craft beers on tap and in a bottle—and a service crew who knows every one of them intimately—with an adventurous menu of faux familiar and exotic foods, and you have Haven. The place is a favorite for the local college students and fills quickly on weekends.

House of Blues Restaurant & Bar ★★★

CAJUN/CREOLE	MODERATE	QUALITY ★★★½	VALUE ★★½

400 Disney Way, Anaheim GardenWalk; ☎ 714-520-2334; houseofblues.com/anaheim

Reservations Recommended. **When to go** Dinner. **Entrée range** $15–$29. **Service** ★★★. **Friendliness** ★★★. **Bar** Wine list and full bar. **Dress** Casual. **Hours** Thursday-Saturday, 5–10 p.m. (plus show nights).

SETTING AND ATMOSPHERE Located at the Anaheim GardenWalk, House of Blues has a rustic-but-trendy blues club vibe; think somewhere along the Mississippi River, maybe St. Louis. The restaurant has a more open feel than its previous location at Downtown Disney, as well as a built-in stage with live music almost every night. The walls feature a fantastic collection of American folk artists, including artworks created especially for the venue.

HOUSE SPECIALTIES Jambalaya, baby back ribs, pulled pork sandwich, and barbecue bacon burgers.

OTHER RECOMMENDATIONS Shrimp po'boys and brisket sandwiches.

SUMMARY AND COMMENTS House of Blues is first and foremost a major concert site, with marquee names, up-and-comers, and strong local talent taking the stage every night. Unless stated otherwise, the separately ticketed concert hall is strictly an adult venue (18 and older), but children are always welcome in the restaurant.

Ma's House Chinese Halal ★★★½

NORTHERN CHINESE	MODERATE	QUALITY ★★★	VALUE ★★★½

601 E. Orangethorpe Ave., Anaheim; ☎ 714-446-9553; mashouserestaurants.com

Reservations Recommended. **When to go** Lunch or dinner. **Entrée range** $13–$37. **Service** ★★★. **Friendliness** ★★★½. **Dress** Casual but modest (no shorts). **Hours** Daily, 11 a.m.–3 p.m. and 5–8:30 p.m.

SETTING AND ATMOSPHERE One of a small chain of Islamic Chinese restaurants, this is the real deal. Ma's dining room is spacious, with comfortable booths and large tables. The decor blends Middle Eastern and Chinese motifs with lots of tile, repetitive patterned mosaics, and lofty arches.

HOUSE SPECIALTIES Get the thick sesame bread with green onions as a starter. Any mutton dish is a sure bet.

OTHER RECOMMENDATIONS The warm pots—northern-Chinese stews—are great, as is the beef with green onions.

SUMMARY AND COMMENTS This is a veritable institution among local Muslims (Arabs and East and Southeast Asians), so expect to see women in veils and burkas and men dressed very conservatively; also, note that no alcohol is served. Service is gracious, if a bit English-challenged. Stick to the northern-Chinese specialties—the more familiar Chinese side of the menu is less exciting.

McCormick & Schmick's Grille ★★★

SEAFOOD	MODERATE-EXPENSIVE	QUALITY ★★★	VALUE ★★★

321 W. Katella Ave., Anaheim GardenWalk; ☎ 714-535-9000; mccormickandschmicks.com

Reservations Recommended. **When to go** Lunch or dinner. **Entrée range** $21–$99. **Service** ★★★. **Friendliness** ★★★★. **Bar** Full bar and extensive wine list. **Dress** Business casual. **Hours** Sunday–Thursday, 11:30 a.m.–9 p.m.; Friday–Saturday, 11:30 a.m.–10 p.m.

SETTING AND ATMOSPHERE This large chain of seafood eateries designs each of its units differently to match its local surroundings. In addition to lots of dark hardwoods and spacious booths, the decor here takes its cues from the rich agricultural history of the area.

HOUSE SPECIALTIES Fish is fresh and infinitely variable. The menu changes daily; each chef is free to choose from among 80 different preparations. You can't miss with king crab, lobster, salmon, or killer fresh swordfish.

SUMMARY AND COMMENTS This is a very popular spot with local business types, and waits without reservations can be long. The menu can be overwhelming; on the other hand, there's something for everyone, even folks who don't eat fish. Happy hour specials (Monday–Friday, 3:30–6:30 p.m.) somewhat soften the sting of expensive entrées, but you must sit at the bar or patio and order a drink.

Morton's ★★★★

STEAK HOUSE	EXPENSIVE	QUALITY ★★★½	VALUE ★★★½

1895 S. Harbor Blvd., Anaheim; ☎ 714-621-0101; mortons.com/anaheim

Reservations Recommended. **When to go** Dinner. **Entrée range** $34–$139. **Service** ★★★★. **Friendliness** ★★★★. **Bar** Extensive wine list and full bar. **Dress** Dressy casual. **Hours** Sunday–Saturday, 4–10 p.m.

SETTING AND ATMOSPHERE Classic steak house with overstuffed booths, soft lighting, and dark hardwoods.

HOUSE SPECIALTIES Try the center-cut filet mignon Oscar-style (with lump crab, asparagus, and béarnaise sauce).

OTHER RECOMMENDATIONS The bone-in rib eye is a Chicago staple and beef-eater's dream: 22 ounces of prime steak, grilled to order.

SUMMARY AND COMMENTS Morton's is a carnivore's delight—beef, beef, and more beef dominate the menu. Of course, there's a smattering of chicken and seafood options, including shrimp and lobster in several different iterations, but this place is really about the beef.

Prime Cut Café & Wine Bar ★★★

STEAK HOUSE	MODERATE-EXPENSIVE	QUALITY ★★★	VALUE ★★★½

1547 W. Katella Ave., Ste. 101, Stadium Promenade, Orange; ☎ 714-532-4300; primecutcafe.com

Reservations Recommended. **When to go** Lunch or dinner. **Entrée range** $19–$56. **Service** ★★★. **Friendliness** ★★★. **Bar** Full bar. **Dress** Casual. **Hours** Sunday–Thursday, 11 a.m.–9:30 p.m.; Friday–Saturday, 11 a.m.–10:30 p.m.

SETTING AND ATMOSPHERE Polished but laid-back, this dapper café is a welcome independent in a sea of chain operations. A massive granite bar anchors the attractive space that also offers a roomy patio overlooking the shopping center's water fountain.

HOUSE SPECIALTIES Slow-roasted prime rib is offered in two sizes, both partnered with good Yorkshire pudding. A huge pork chop is another winner, paired with butter-braised bacon and apple cider reduction.

OTHER RECOMMENDATIONS Prime rib may hog the spotlight, but steaks, burgers, and entrée salads often outshine the showy star of the menu. Sides such as potato gratin are scene-stealers, as are from-scratch desserts.

SUMMARY AND COMMENTS Prime Cut Café does a good job of making first-rate dining affordable and approachable. Sixty-plus wines sold by the glass or bottle are an attraction for wine lovers, though wine snobs might find the list a bit lowbrow. The menu offers lots of appetizers and snacks that pair well with wine, making this a great option for a quick bite or grown-up get-together. The central location means that crowds swell or recede according to events at nearby Anaheim Stadium and Honda Center.

Roscoe's House of Chicken & Waffles ★★★★

AMERICAN   INEXPENSIVE-MODERATE   QUALITY ★★★★   VALUE ★★★½

2110 S. Harbor Blvd., Anaheim; ☎ 714-823-4130; roscoeschickenandwaffles.com

Reservations Not accepted. **When to go** Anytime. **Entrée range** $12–$30. **Service** ★★★. **Friendliness** ★★★. **Dress** Casual. **Hours** Sunday–Thursday, 8 a.m.–10 p.m.; Friday–Saturday, 8 a.m.–midnight.

SETTING AND ATMOSPHERE The plain, almost featureless, exterior is surrounded by palm trees. The interior decor is also sparse, save for the occasional cheap painting or neon sign. Going on only looks, you'll wonder why there's a huge line to get in, especially on nights and weekends.

HOUSE SPECIALTIES It's right there in the name: chicken and waffles.

OTHER RECOMMENDATIONS We love the Jeanne Jones Omelette and the macaroni and cheese side dish.

SUMMARY AND COMMENTS Roscoe's is a longtime Los Angeles institution that finally made its way to Orange County in 2014. Like all the other locations, locals flock to Roscoe's for its delicious Southern-style comfort food, including the signature chicken and waffles. While the fried chicken is good, it may not be the best you'll ever have. But the waffles are excellent, and the macaroni and cheese is a must-try.

Tangerine Room ★★★★½

CALIFORNIAN   MODERATE-EXPENSIVE   QUALITY ★★★★½   VALUE ★★★★

1030 W. Katella Ave., Anaheim; ☎ 657-279-9786; tangerineroom.com

Reservations Recommended. **When to go** Anytime. **Entrée range** $26–$52. **Service** ★★★★. **Friendliness** ★★★. **Bar** Full bar with extensive Californian wine list. **Dress** Business casual. **Hours** Daily, 6:30 a.m.–3 p.m. and 5–10 p.m.

SETTING AND ATMOSPHERE Located inside the Westin's luxurious lobby, Tangerine Room shares the hotel's generically upscale decor, with high ceilings and hard surfaces. An open show kitchen is complemented by wooden artwork, purple accents, and glowing geometric chandeliers hanging overhead.

HOUSE SPECIALTIES Full American and Continental breakfasts in the morning. At dinner and lunch, slow-braised short ribs, seared seasonal fish, and organic green salads.

OTHER RECOMMENDATIONS The old-fashioned butter cake topped with fruit and house-made sorbet is a perfect meal-ender.

SUMMARY AND COMMENTS Although aimed at convention-goers and hotel guests, Tangerine Room makes food that rivals Disneyland's fanciest tables at a slightly more palatable price. The short ribs, which are cooked for 10 hours, fall apart when you look at them, and the salmon is served medium-rare with its crispy skin still attached. In the mornings, you can order a fancy avocado toast with soft-boiled eggs à la carte, but the expansive breakfast buffet is a better bargain.

Top of the V ★★★★½

SPANISH   EXPENSIVE   QUALITY ★★★★½ VALUE ★★★½

1601 S. Anaheim Blvd., at The Viv, Anaheim; ☎ 657-439-3289; topoftheviv.com

Reservations Recommended. **When to go** Dinner. **Entrée range** $10–$55. **Service** ★★★★. **Friendliness** ★★★. **Bar** Extensive wine list, local beers, sangrias, and full bar. **Dress** Casual. **Hours** Wednesday–Thursday, 4–9:30 p.m.; Friday–Saturday, 5–10 p.m. (Last call for food is 15 minutes before closing.)

SETTING AND ATMOSPHERE Gorgeous indoor-outdoor rooftop restaurant furnished with an artfully eclectic mix of modern and vintage textures, where you're more likely to lounge on a sofa than be seated at a formal table. The main room is dominated by an open kitchen (proudly displaying whole legs of Iberian ham) at one end and a U-shaped marble bar illuminated by dangling globes at the other. Motorized shades slide down to save guests in west-facing window seats from being blinded by the setting sun, then rise to reveal postcard-perfect views of Disneyland's landmarks.

HOUSE SPECIALTIES Fine hams, sausages, and cheeses imported from Spain; arroz bomba rice platters with pork or shellfish; Galician-style steaks.

OTHER RECOMMENDATIONS Pan cristal con tomate (toasted bread with tomatoes) and gambas al ajillo (garlic shrimp).

SUMMARY AND COMMENTS Named the area's best new restaurant in its debut year by the *Orange County Register,* this crowning jewel atop the upscale Viv hotel is the place to see and be seen over Spanish small plates, at least among the business convention crowds. Be sure to leave the T-shirts and mouse ears back at the hotel room. The food lives up to the hype, with prices to match; consider passing on the entrées and making a meal of the tapas-style appetizers. If you want to go whole hog, the 5-course Basque Country Experience will set you back $125, plus $50 for wine pairings.

◗ SHOPPING *at* DISNEYLAND

SHOPS ADD REALISM and atmosphere to the various theme settings and offer souvenirs, clothing, novelties, jewelry, decorator items, and more. Much of the merchandise displayed (with the exception of Disney trademark souvenir items), though, is available back home and elsewhere, so we recommend bypassing the shops on a one-day visit. If you have two or more days to spend at Disneyland Resort, browse in the early afternoon, when many attractions are crowded.

Our recommendations notwithstanding, we realize that for many guests, Disney souvenirs and memorabilia are irresistible. One of our readers writes:

> People have a compelling need to buy Disney stuff at Disneyland. When you get home, you wonder why you ever got a cashmere sweater with Mickey Mouse embroidered on the breast, or a tie with tiny Goofys all over it. Maybe they put something in the food?

To bypass long lines at the cash registers, most larger stores in the resort offer mobile checkout through the smartphone app. Scanning barcodes with your own camera is fast and easy, and after showing your phone to the designated cast member, you'll be out the door in a fraction of the time; passholder discounts are even automatically applied.

If you don't want to lug your packages around, you can leave them at the shop where you made your purchase and pick them up before you exit the park, or have them delivered to your hotel if staying onsite. If you have a problem with your purchases or need to make a return, call Disneyland Exclusive Merchandise at ☎ 877-560-6477. If you return home and realize that you forgot to buy mouse ears or some similarly essential tchotchke, a large selection of park-exclusive merchandise is available at shopdisney.com/parks. To reduce the resort's use of single-use plastic, Disneyland Resort now offers reusable themed bags with your purchases for $2–$3; free disposable bags are still available upon request for now.

DOWNTOWN DISNEY

VERDANT AND LANDSCAPED BY DAY, Downtown Disney pops alive with neon and glitter at night. The complex offers more than 300,000 square feet of specialty shopping, restaurants, and entertainment. The AMC Movieplex, Earl of Sandwich, and other existing structures on the western end of Downtown Disney were demolished in 2022, making way for new shops and open-air gathering spaces. The refreshed Downtown Disney features a new mid-century Palm Springs–inspired entry portal on the west side, along with artificial green space for relaxing. Busking musicians enliven the area, and free live concerts are held nightly on a Googie-inspired stage near the western end of the complex.

Din Tai Fung, a popular West Coast Taiwanese restaurant chain that attracts long waits for its authentic dim sum, has been added to the complex; and Catal Restaurant & Uva Bar gave way to **Paseo, Centrico,** and **Tiendita,** serving Mexican fare from Michelin-starred chef Carlos Gaytán. The **Parkside Market** food hall (which was built atop the former AMC movie theater) includes **Seoul Sister** Korean bibimbap rice bowls; **Sip & Sonder** Caribbean food and frozen drinks; and **GG's Chicken Shop,** as well as a second-story alfresco bar with views of the district. The popular **Earl of Sandwich** is receiving a new two-story location at Downtown Disney, with quick-service sandwiches on the ground floor and full-service dining upstairs; until it opens, a temporary takeaway is located near Star Wars Trading Post. Tortilla Joe's will be taken over by a steakhouse and a barbecue restaurant. The former La Brea Bakery is slated to be removed for the Cuban **Porto's Bakery & Cafe,** and **Jazz Kitchen Coastal Grill & Patio** has been reimagined, with a Californian vibe replacing its French Quarter flair.

Many of the restaurants offer entertainment in addition to dining, including **Splitsville Luxury Lanes,** an improbably but surprisingly successful mash-up of bowling alley and sushi bar. Other restaurant options include **Naples Ristorante e Bar, Ballast Point,** and **Black Tap Craft Burgers & Shakes.** An elegant **Starbucks,** across from the parking tram stop, serves all the chain's beverages and sandwiches (including beer and wine in the evenings) and offers free Wi-Fi, phone-charging stations, and full loyalty card benefits (though it doesn't accept Disney gift cards or Magic Key pass discounts). If you have a sweet tooth, **Marceline's Confectionery** makes the same character candy apples found inside the parks, and **Salt & Straw** offers one-of-a-kind ice-cream flavors like honey lavender, roasted strawberry coconut, and (for real) black olive brittle and Humboldt fog goat cheese.

If you're not hungry, a 40,000-square-foot **World of Disney** store anchors the shopping scene; watch for Tinker Bell in the paint jars behind the main checkout area and animated artwork on the walls. Other retailers include **Disney Dress Shop,** a boutique of vintage-style apparel inspired by old-school Disney icons like the Orange Bird; **Sephora,** featuring cosmetics; **Pandora,** which carries jewelry; **Disney Home,** where you can stock up on Mickey towels and utensils for your bath and kitchen; **Curl Surf,** with everything you need to hit the beach; **Lovepop,** with 3D pop-up cards; and **Pelé Soccer,** with soccer gear galore. If expensive designer sunglasses are your thing, head to **Sunglass Icon** for a large variety of shades. For an artistic memento, **WonderGround Gallery** showcases edgy (and expensive)

FREE DISNEYLAND SOUVENIRS

Although there's no such thing as a free lunch, there are such things as free souvenirs at Disneyland. Here's a sampling of the gratis gifts that frugal visitors can bring home as giveaways for family and friends.

- Celebration buttons *(guest services, see page 123)*
- Fortunes from Esmerelda and Fortune Red *(via the Play Disney app, see pages 246–247)*
- Park maps in a variety of languages *(park entrances)*
- Disney character stickers *(guest services)*
- Animation Academy drawings *(Hollywood Land, see page 254)*
- Mardi Gras beads *(New Orleans Square, seasonally)*
- Batuu creature guide *(Star Wars Galaxy's Edge, see page 195)*
- Sourdough bread sample *(Bakery Tour, see page 273)*

Downtown Disney

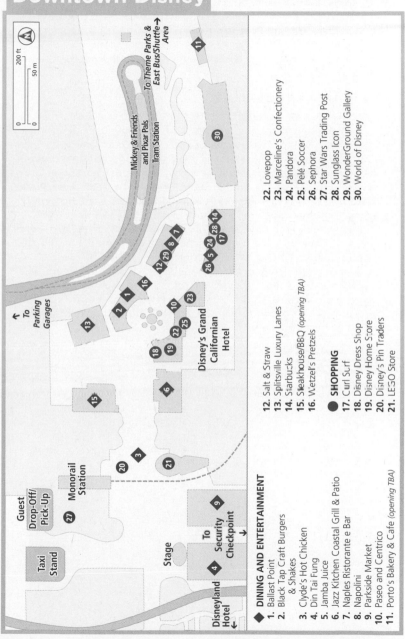

♦ DINING AND ENTERTAINMENT
1. Ballast Point
2. Black Tap Craft Burgers & Shakes
3. Clyde's Hot Chicken
4. Din Tai Fung
5. Jamba Juice
6. Jazz Kitchen Coastal Grill & Patio
7. Naples Ristorante e Bar
8. Napolini
9. Parkside Market
10. Paseo and Centrico
11. Porto's Bakery & Cafe *(opening TBA)*
12. Salt & Straw
13. Splitsville Luxury Lanes
14. Starbucks
15. Steakhouse/BBQ *(opening TBA)*
16. Wetzel's Pretzels

● SHOPPING
17. Curl Surf
18. Disney Dress Shop
19. Disney Home Store
20. Disney's Pin Traders
21. LEGO Store
22. Lovepop
23. Marceline's Confectionery
24. Pandora
25. Pelé Soccer
26. Sephora
27. Star Wars Trading Post
28. Sunglass Icon
29. WonderGround Gallery
30. World of Disney

reinterpretations of classic Disney images, often signed by their creators. **LEGO Store** features interactive play tables with LEGO bricks and life-size statues of Disney characters made entirely of LEGOs, and **Star Wars Trading Post** is a Resistance base supplying anything you forgot to buy on Batuu.

Our map of Downtown Disney, listing storefronts and restaurants, appears on page 337.

ANAHEIM GARDENWALK

BUILT ON THREE LEVELS AND NICELY LANDSCAPED, Anaheim GardenWalk is a shopping, dining, and entertainment venue that stretches from West Katella Avenue to Disney Way. It effectively doubles the restaurant, lounge, and shopping choices for Disneyland Resort visitors and attendees of conventions at nearby Anaheim Convention Center. Restaurants include **Bubba Gump Shrimp Co., California Pizza Kitchen, The Cheesecake Factory, House of Blues, Fire + Ice, McCormick & Schmick's Grille, P.F. Chang's Chinese Bistro,** and **Roy's Restaurant.**

For entertainment, there's an AMC movie theater, an escape-room game, a 41-lane bowling complex and nightspot combo, a UFC fitness center, a Ridemakerz remote-controlled car-building store, and a tiny cabaret hosting magic shows (kipbarryscabaret.com). The GardenWalk has long struggled to retain tenants; there are more shuttered storefronts than open ones, giving the entire venue a depressing *Dawn of the Dead* vibe. For additional information, see anaheimgardenwalk.com.

PART 9

UNIVERSAL STUDIOS HOLLYWOOD

UNIVERSAL STUDIOS HOLLYWOOD (USH) was the first film and TV studio to turn part of its facility into a modern theme park. By integrating shows and rides with behind-the-scenes presentations on moviemaking, USH created a new genre of theme park, stimulating a number of clone and competitor parks. First came Disney-MGM Studios (now Disney's Hollywood Studios) at Walt Disney World, followed shortly by Universal Studios Florida, also near Orlando. Where USH, however, evolved from an established film and TV venue, its cross-country imitators were launched primarily as theme parks, albeit with some production capability on the side. Disney is also challenging Universal in California with Disney California Adventure (DCA). While DCA does not have production facilities, one of its themed areas focuses on Hollywood and the movies.

Located just off US 101 north of Hollywood, USH operates on a scale and with a quality standard rivaled only by Disney, SeaWorld, and Busch Gardens parks. Unique among American theme parks for its topography, USH is tucked on top of, below, and around a tall hill. The studios consist of an open-access area and a controlled-access area. The latter contains the working soundstages, backlot, wardrobe, scenery, prop shops, postproduction facility, and administration offices. Guests can visit the controlled-access area by taking the Studio Tour. The open-access area, which contains the park's rides, shows, restaurants, and services, is divided into two sections. The main entrance provides access to the upper section, the Upper Lot, on top of the hill. Two theater shows and six rides (soon to be seven), as well as two walk-through attractions and the loading area for the Studio Tour, are located in the Upper Lot. The Lower Lot, at the northeastern base of the hill, is accessible from the Upper Lot via escalators. There are four rides and a couple of meet and greets in the Lower Lot.

On April 7, 2016, USH capped a half-decade of redevelopment with the grand opening of The Wizarding World of Harry Potter, a West Coast annex of the wildly popular Hogsmeade area originally

Universal Studios Hollywood

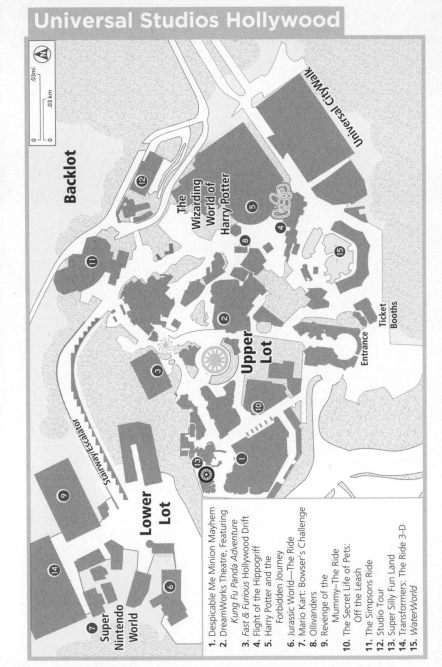

Backlot

The Wizarding World of Harry Potter

Universal CityWalk

Upper Lot

Lower Lot

Super Nintendo World

Stairway/Escalator

Ticket Booths

Entrance

1. Despicable Me Minion Mayhem
2. DreamWorks Theatre, Featuring
   Kung Fu Panda Adventure
3. Fast & Furious Hollywood Drift
4. Flight of the Hippogriff
5. Harry Potter and the
   Forbidden Journey
6. Jurassic World—The Ride
7. Mario Kart: Bowser's Challenge
8. Ollivanders
9. Revenge of the
   Mummy—The Ride
10. The Secret Life of Pets:
    Off the Leash
11. The Simpsons Ride
12. Studio Tour
13. Super Silly Fun Land
14. Transformers: The Ride 3-D
15. *WaterWorld*

found at Universal Orlando's Islands of Adventure. The parapets of Hogwarts Castle that now tower over the Upper Lot, forming a beacon visible for miles around, are merely the most visible effect of Universal's ambitious Evolution expansion plan, which completely overhauled three-quarters of the park in under five years. Casualties of the expansions included the old Wild West arena, *Terminator 2: 3-D*, the tram tour's Mummy tunnel, the Curious George playground, and Gibson Amphitheater. But the extreme makeover has brought USH a beautiful new Art Deco entry corridor and central plaza, upgraded points of interest along the tram tour, and the global attention that comes with The Wizarding World.

Universal didn't stop there in its bid to attract Disneyland guests: America's first Super Nintendo World opened on the Lower Lot in 2023. Permits have been filed to construct new on-site hotels, with opening dates and themes yet to be announced. A high-speed "drifting" roller coaster themed to the *Fast & Furious* films is well underway, replacing the demolished *Special Effects* and *Animal Actors* stages, and additional attractions are rumored to be in the works.

The park offers all standard services and amenities, including stroller and wheelchair rental, lockers, diaper-changing and nursing facilities, a quiet room (for guests with sensory issues), car assistance, and foreign-language assistance. Almost all services are in the Upper Lot, just inside the main entrance.

Most of the park is accessible to disabled guests, and TDDs are available for the hearing impaired. Guests needing special accommodations should preregister for Universal's **Attractions Assistance Pass,** which is similar to Disney's DAS (discussed on pages 126–128). It allows up to four guests to wait outside the standard queue if an attraction's wait exceeds 45 minutes. Universal has partnered with the International Board of Credentialing and Continuing Education Standards (IBCCES) on an online Accessibility Card registration process, which guests requesting accommodations (or their guardians) should complete at least 48 hours prior to visiting the park. Go to accessibilitycard.com and fill out the registration form, which requires providing the contact information for a healthcare or education professional, who will verify your needs, and uploading supporting documentation, such as a doctor's statement or Individualized Education Plan. Once your application is approved, you can download your digital IBCCES Accessibility Card (IAC), and a Universal employee will contact you regarding your needs. They'll give you a case number that you can take to Guest Services upon arrival and pick up your accommodation pass. Unlike Disney's app-based accommodation services, Universal's uses a paper pass that the registered guest with special needs must present at the attraction every time a return time is received or redeemed. If an attraction wait time is 45 minutes or less, USH's attractions assistance pass offers users immediate access to the Express entrance.

GATHERING INFORMATION

THE MAIN UNIVERSAL STUDIOS information number is ☎ 800-864-8377. Universal Studios' website, universalstudioshollywood.com, is easy to navigate. Once inside the park, use the USH official iPhone or Android app on your smartphone to see current wait times and show schedules and to secure Virtual Line reservations for attractions. The app also has a digital wallet, which can scan your physical tickets to store your party's park admission. Incidentally, USH offers free public Wi-Fi (look for SSID "Universal"), but it quickly gets overloaded on busy days, and cell reception can be spotty depending on which side of the hill you're on.

WHAT MAKES UNIVERSAL STUDIOS HOLLYWOOD DIFFERENT

WHAT MAKES USH DIFFERENT IS THAT THE ATTRACTIONS, with a couple of exceptions, are designed to minimize long waits in line. The centerpiece of the Universal experience is the Studio Tour. While on the tram, you experience a high-speed car chase and come face-to-face with King Kong, among other things. In other parks, including Universal's sister park in Florida, each of these is presented as an individual attraction with its own long queue. At USH, by contrast, you suffer only one wait to board the tram and then experience all of these events as part of the tour.

Another difference from Disney is that Universal's thrill rides use more restrictive restraints, which larger guests may have difficulty fitting into. Always test the sample seat outside the attraction entrance before joining the queue.

One more distinguishing feature of Universal is that it's *loud*. Unlike Disney's background music, which is carefully curated to create a relaxing ambience, Universal insists on blasting high-energy soundtracks at full volume through every available speaker. (Thankfully, the atmosphere audio isn't as aggressive in Hollywood as at their Orlando resort.) And we haven't even addressed the rides themselves, which typically feature frequent explosions and other earsplitting sound effects played at decibel levels that would make Spinal Tap shudder. As a father from Petaluma, California, put it:

> *Universal Studios loves its soundtracks. Every ride had blaring sound effects, and even as we just walked around the park, the music was blaring from various attractions so loud that you had trouble talking to the person next to you. Crowd noise was so loud that you couldn't hear the magical effects in the windows at Hogsmeade! We were frazzled by the end of the day. I highly recommend putting in earplugs when you arrive and keeping them in for the whole day.*

A Vancouver, Canada, visitor was even blunter:

> *Universal is an assault on the senses. Where Disney is so often quaint and genteel, Universal is brash, loud, and in your face.*

◼ TIMING *Your* VISIT

CROWDS ARE LARGEST around spring break, Easter, and specific holiday periods during the rest of the year. December 25–January 1 is extremely busy, as are Thanksgiving weekend and the week of Presidents' Day. Summers used to be peak season, but crowds in June and July have moderated. The least busy time is from after Thanksgiving weekend until the week before Christmas. The next slowest times are late August and September through the weekend preceding Thanksgiving (except for during the popular Halloween Horror Nights event), the week after New Year's through the first week of March, and the week following Easter to Memorial Day weekend. We don't currently maintain a crowd calendar for USH, but you'll find a useful free one at isitpacked.com/crowd-calendars/universal-studios-hollywood.

SELECTING THE DAY OF THE WEEK FOR YOUR VISIT

WEEKENDS ARE MORE CROWDED than weekdays year-round. Saturday is the busiest day. Sunday, particularly Sunday morning, is the best bet if you have to go on a weekend, but it is still extremely busy. During the summer, Friday is very busy; Monday, Wednesday, and Thursday are usually less so; Tuesday is normally the slowest of all. During the off-season (September–May, holidays excepted), Tuesday is usually the least-crowded day, followed by Thursday.

HOW MUCH TIME TO ALLOCATE

THOUGH THERE'S A LOT TO SEE and do at USH, you can (unlike at Disneyland) complete a comprehensive tour in one day. If you follow our touring plan, which calls for being on hand at park opening, you should be able to check out everything before the park closes, even on a crowded day.

Never mind that USH claims to cover 400 acres; the area you will have to traverse on foot is considerably smaller. In fact, you will do much less walking and, miracle of miracles, much less standing in line at Universal Studios than at Disneyland.

Increased attendance since the opening of the Harry Potter attractions has helped transform USH from a half-day attraction to one that merits a full day's visit. And the arrival of Mario and his video game friends has propelled USH's attendance to new peaks; on some peak days the park may have to close its ticket windows and hang SOLD OUT signs.

UNIVERSAL STUDIOS HOLLYWOOD FOR YOUNG CHILDREN

WE DO NOT RECOMMEND USH for preschoolers. Of 13 (soon 14) major attractions, all but 2 (Ollivanders and Secret Life of Pets) have the potential for flipping out sensitive little ones. See the Small-Child Fright-Potential Table on page 344.

UNIVERSAL STUDIOS HOLLYWOOD SMALL-CHILD FRIGHT-POTENTIAL TABLE

DESPICABLE ME MINION MAYHEM Loud with some intense visual effects.

DREAMWORKS THEATRE Special effects may frighten preschoolers.

***FAST & FURIOUS* HOLLYWOOD DRIFT** *(opening 2026)* Intense spinning coaster is frightening for all ages.

FLIGHT OF THE HIPPOGRIFF Frightens a small percentage of preschoolers.

HARRY POTTER AND THE FORBIDDEN JOURNEY Extremely intense special effects and macabre visuals with wild simulated movement that may frighten and discombobulate guests of any age.

JURASSIC WORLD—THE RIDE Intense water-flume ride. Potentially terrifying for people of any age.

MARIO KART: BOWSER'S CHALLENGE Slow-moving dark ride with augmented-reality effects simulating high speed and video-game baddies may be too intense for preschoolers.

OLLIVANDERS Loud bells and lightning may bother sensitive kids.

REVENGE OF THE MUMMY—THE RIDE Scares guests of all ages.

SECRET LIFE OF PETS: OFF THE LEASH A slow-moving ride with nothing too frightening, but you may expire from an overload of adorableness.

SILLY SWIRLY Simple carnival-style spinner, perfect for preschoolers.

THE SIMPSONS RIDE Motion simulator too intense for many children age 7 and younger tall enough to ride.

STUDIO TOUR Parts of the tour are too frightening or intense for many preschoolers.

TRANSFORMERS: THE RIDE 3-D Too intense for children younger than age 7, and potentially terrifying for visitors of any age.

WATERWORLD Fighting, gunplay, and explosions frighten children age 4 and younger.

All Universal rides with a height requirement offer child switch, which is superior to Disney's rider swap; most attractions allow everyone to wait in line together and have a quiet room where the nonriding parent can wait with the kids while their partner rides. Ask the greeter at each attraction's entrance how to take advantage of child switch.

COST

JUST LIKE DISNEYLAND, USH uses a demand-based tiered ticket pricing system that strongly encourages guests to select the date of their visit in advance; however, no park reservations are required to visit. One-day adult tickets are $164 at the gate but can be purchased online for as low as $109 if you select your visit date in advance. Tickets for kids ages 3–9 cost $6 less than adult tickets; children 2 and under are free. A two-day admission ticket to USH is available online for $159–$204, depending on the date selected for first use during purchase; the second day must be used within 7 days, but no reservation is needed. Save money and time by avoiding the ticket booths and purchasing your admission online.

A pass that allows you to skip the regular line once at each participating attraction (including Harry Potter and the Forbidden Journey) using the Universal Express entrance runs $219–$319 (depending on season) for adults or children, including admission. Express Passes are now accepted at Mario Kart, and they also provide expedited entry into Super Nintendo World if Virtual Line is being used to restrict access to the land. Save $10 by buying online in advance.

The Silver Annual Pass is $249 ($239 if purchased online) and is good for 12 months after your first visit, with more than 275 valid days, including more than 50 weekend days. The Gold Annual Pass offers 325-plus valid days (including more than 75 weekend days) and costs $339 ($329 online). Finally, the Platinum Annual Pass ($639, $629 online) is the only pass valid 365 days a year with no blackouts. Silver, Gold, and Platinum Passes can be purchased on interest-free monthly installments with FlexPay. The Gold and Platinum Passes include free self-parking before 6 p.m. and also provide 15% discounts on most in-park food and merchandise. The Platinum Pass also throws in a Halloween Horror Nights ticket (valid select nights only) and priority access to all rides and shows that offer Universal Express after 3 p.m. Locals can buy a California Neighbor Pass for only $189 ($179 online) per year, but it's blacked out more often than it's valid and isn't eligible for FlexPay.

For Hollywood-happy high rollers, USH offers a VIP Experience ($379–$519), depending on season; $10 off if ordered online) that includes admission, valet parking, escorted queue-cutting at all attractions, off-tram walking tours of sets and soundstages, light breakfast and buffet lunch, and amenities such as ponchos and bottled water. The quality of service provided by the VIP touring guides is exceptional, and you'll get to explore places—like Universal's gargantuan prop warehouse or the *War of the Worlds* airliner crash site—that are usu-ally inaccessible to ordinary guests. Best of all, you travel in style, in a luxury air-conditioned bus that beats the heck out of the standard Studio Tour trams. If you have the spare dough, it's undoubtedly a bet-ter deal than Disney's pay-per-hour VIP guides, and since it also pro-vides Express access to Mario Kart (both during and after your tour), this service is worth its weight in spinning gold coins. Reservations are required; call ☎ 818-622-8477 to book or visit universalstudios hollywood.com/tickets/vip-experience for more information.

In addition to the website discounts, admission discounts are some-times offered in area freebie publications available in hotels. Admis-sion discounts are also periodically offered to AAA members.

While Universal's team members don't have a reputation for the exceptionally sunny service for which their pixie-dusted counterparts at Disneyland are famous, they do excel at guest recovery when things go wrong. For example, when rides at USH break down (as they inevi-tably seem to do), guests who get stuck on the attraction usually receive a free single-use Express Pass.

STAYING ON-SITE AT UNIVERSAL STUDIOS HOLLYWOOD

HILTON AND SHERATON both operate hotels on USH's property, but if you've experienced the exceptional perks offered to guests at

Universal Orlando's Loews hotels, lower your expectations before booking an on-site room at USH. Both on-property hotels are pricey for the room size and service quality, the parks are a poorly marked 5–10–minute hike away, and no theme park bonuses—such as front-of-the-line passes or even early entry—are included. You can also walk into Universal from a handful of off-site hotels along Cahuenga Boulevard, though it's a 15-minute hike up an extremely steep slope.

THE SHUTTLE

UNIVERSAL CITY is on the Red Line of **Los Angeles Metro Rail,** which makes it relatively easy to commute by light-rail from downtown LA and many other places, though not from Anaheim. Across the street from the subway station and the bus stop, at Lankershim Boulevard and Universal Hollywood Drive, is a free Universal Studios shuttle bus that will conveniently take you to the main entrances of USH and CityWalk. The bus runs daily, beginning at 7 a.m., with pickups about every 10–15 minutes; service continues until about 2 hours after the theme park closes. Refer to the posted times at each shuttle stop for information on the last departing shuttle. For rail and bus schedules and additional public transportation information, call the Los Angeles Metropolitan Transportation Authority at ☎ 323-466-3876, or visit metro.net.

Alternatively, you can reach USH by taxi, Uber, or bus tours like **Anaheim Tour Co.** (anaheimtourcompany.com), which combine round-trip transportation from Disneyland-area hotels with park admission. Just beware that shuttle services must pick up at multiple hotels and might not get you to the park before rope drop. A reader from Calgary, Alberta, strongly suggests the shuttle option:

> I checked Uber prices a couple of times, and they showed about $45 USD one-way. What I didn't factor in was the effect rush hour would have on prices. At the last minute we booked a shuttle and were so glad we did. When I checked Uber prices that morning from the shuttle bus, prices had doubled! It's also much more comfortable to sit through Los Angeles rush hour for 2 hours in a big tour bus than the back seat of someone's car.

ARRIVING *and* GETTING ORIENTED

MOST FOLKS ACCESS Universal Studios by taking US 101, also called the Hollywood Freeway, and following the signs to the park. If the freeway is gridlocked, you can also get to the Studios by taking Cahuenga Boulevard and then turning north toward Lankershim Boulevard. If you are coming from Burbank, take Barham Boulevard toward US 101, and then follow the signs.

Universal Studios has a number of big, multilevel parking garages at the top of the hill, including a massive *E.T.*-inspired facility. Signs directing you to the garages have improved but can still be a bit confusing, so pay attention as you come up the hill. Even after you have made it to the pay booth and shelled out $35 to park, it is still not exactly clear where you go next. (Preferred parking costs $50 before 5 p.m., or $70 for even closer front-gate parking; parking costs extra if your RV is more than 15 feet long. All parking rates except valet are discounted by $25–$30 after 5 p.m. Rates may temporarily increase during peak season.) Drive slowly, follow other cars proceeding from the pay booths, and avoid turns onto ramps marked EXIT. You may become a bit disoriented, but ultimately you will blunder into the garage. Once parked, make a note of your parking level and the location of your space by snapping a photo or using USH's smartphone app. Valet parking ($25 for the first 2 hours, $60 for more than 2 hours, $15 for up to 3.5 hours with restaurant validation) is located on the ground floor of the Jurassic Park garage, steps from the center of CityWalk. Drop-off/pick-up areas for rideshare services can be found inside the Frankenstein garage outside the park gates or between the Jurassic Park and E.T. garages in CityWalk. Take the Lankershim exit off US 101 for easier access to drop-off and the on-site hotels.

Walk toward the opposite end of the garage from where you entered and exit into Universal CityWalk, a shopping, dining, and entertainment complex (no admission required) situated between the parking structure and the main entrance of the park. As an aside, CityWalk is much like Downtown Disney at Disneyland. Some of Universal's better restaurants and more interesting shops are at CityWalk, and it's so close to the theme park entrance that you can conveniently pop out of the park to grab a bite. If "riding the movies" at the theme park inspires you to watch one, the 19-screen AMC IMAX Cineplex boasts plush reclining seats, Dolby Atmos surround sound, and razor-sharp Christie RGB laser projectors; plus, your parking is only $5 with purchase of a movie ticket.

Universal Studios' ticket booths and turnstiles are about 100 yards from the main parking garage. Before approaching the ticket booths and turnstiles, you'll have to pass through an expansive TSA-style security checkpoint; fortunately, Universal's X-ray baggage screening is fairly efficient. If you need cash, an ATM is outside and to the right of the main entrance. There are also ATMs inside the park at the Kwik-E-Mart outside *WaterWorld,* near the Jurassic Cafe on the Lower Lot, and even a Gringotts money machine in Hogsmeade. Nearby is a guest-services window. As you enter the park, be sure to check an information board or smartphone app for the daily entertainment schedule.

EARLY ENTRY AND OPENING PROCEDURES AT UNIVERSAL STUDIOS HOLLYWOOD

ONE HOUR OF EARLY ADMISSION to Super Nintendo World is available in advance online for an additional $20–$30 per person; quantities are limited and busy days will sell out. Express access to the Studio Tour before 11 a.m. is also included. Early-entry guests use designated turnstiles to the left of the entrance archway; guests with regular park admission only enter through the turnstiles on the right side. When early entry is offered, Universal's gates open up to 90 minutes before the official opening time, and eligible guests are allowed down the escalator and into Super Nintendo World 15 minutes before the bonus hour begins. Everyone else is held near the Upper Lot's central plaza until shortly before regular operating hours begin, with the Wizarding World of Harry Potter typically opening 30 minutes early for all guests. Mario Kart is not guaranteed to operate during early entry, but it may still be worthwhile even without the ride if you're playing with the interactive Power-Up bands. If you prepurchase early access, then accidentally oversleep, they'll allow you inside Super Nintendo World without a Virtual Line reservation (if needed) once you arrive but won't offer refunds.

UNIVERSAL STUDIOS HOLLYWOOD ATTRACTIONS

UPPER LOT

THE UPPER LOT is essentially a large, amorphous pedestrian plaza. The website references "10 themed lands," such as Production Plaza, Hollywood, and Minion Land, but on foot these theme distinctions are largely lost, and placement of buildings appears almost random. The park's Mission Revival entry corridor features facades recalling the Golden Age of Hollywood (look for tributes to the studio's past talents, like makeup artist Jack Pierce), and an Art Deco tower serves as a central landmark to navigate by, but outside of The Wizarding World of Harry Potter, don't expect Disneyland's dedication to thematic integrity.

Inside the main entrance, stroller and wheelchair rentals are on the right, as are rental lockers. Straight ahead is the park's largest gift store, and beyond that is the Universal Box Office, where Express passes and ticket upgrades can be purchased.

Attractions in the Upper Lot are situated around the perimeter of the plaza. Near The Simpsons Ride (straight ahead) are the escalators and stairs that lead to the Lower Lot.

Despicable Me Minion Mayhem ★★★½

**APPEAL BY AGE   PRESCHOOL ★★★★   GRADE SCHOOL ★★★★★   TEENS ★★★★★
YOUNG ADULTS ★★★★   OVER 30 ★★★★   SENIORS ★★★**

What it is Motion simulator ride. **Scope and scale** Major attraction. **When to go** As soon as the ride opens or after 4 p.m. **Comment** Must be 40″ tall to ride. **Duration of ride** 5 minutes, plus 10-minute preshow. **Average wait time per 100 people ahead of you** 3½ minutes. **Loading speed** Moderate–slow.

DESCRIPTION AND COMMENTS Despicable Me Minion Mayhem is a motion simulator ride similar to The Simpsons Ride and Disneyland's Star Tours. You're seated in a ride vehicle that faces a large video screen, on which the attraction's

NOT TO BE MISSED AT UNIVERSAL STUDIOS HOLLYWOOD

- **UPPER LOT** Harry Potter and the Forbidden Journey | The Secret Life of Pets: Off the Leash | Studio Tour | *WaterWorld*
- **LOWER LOT** Jurassic World—The Ride | Transformers: The Ride 3-D | Mario Kart: Bowser's Challenge

story is projected. When the story calls for you to drop down the side of a mountain, your ride vehicle tilts forward as if you were falling; when you need to swerve left or right, your ride vehicle tilts the same way. The main difference between Minion Mayhem and other simulators is that most other simulators usually provide one video screen per ride vehicle, while Minion Mayhem arranges all of its eight-person vehicles in front of one large IMAX-size video screen. The ride vehicles are set on raised platforms, which get slightly higher toward the back of the theater, affording good views for all guests.

The preshow area is inside the home of adorably evil Gru (voiced by Steve Carell), where you see his unique family tree and other artifacts. The premise of the ride is that you've been turned into one of Gru's yellow Minions. Once converted, you must navigate the Minion training grounds, where your "speed, strength, and ability not to die" are tested. Something soon goes amiss, though, and your training turns into a frenetic rescue operation.

The ride is a fast-paced series of dives, climbs, and tight turns through Gru's Rube Goldberg–esque machines. Like The Simpsons Ride, there are more sight gags and interesting things to see here than anyone possibly could in a single ride. Guests exit the ride into a colorful disco dance party and carnival-themed gift shop.

TOURING TIPS Minion Mayhem, a hit import from Universal Studios Florida, features a much more elaborate facade (try ringing doorbells on the homes neighboring the attraction entrance) than the Orlando ride; this version is also blessed with a second theater and preshow, effectively doubling the attraction's capacity. Two stationary seats in each theater make the attraction accessible to those who don't meet the height requirement or can't handle the shaking simulators. Minion Mayhem may open 60 minutes later than the rest of the park. If you have kids, hit this one early after riding Secret Life of Pets; try it in late afternoon or in the hour before park closing if the wait exceeds 30 minutes. Adjacent to the ride's exit, the Super Silly Fun Land area should help small tykes burn off some steam, with wet and dry playgrounds, carnival midway games, and **Silly Swirly** (★★½), a simple Dumbo-style spinning ride sporting wacky bug-shaped vehicles and Minion-ized disco music.

DreamWorks Theatre, Featuring *Kung Fu Panda Adventure* ★★★★

APPEAL BY AGE   PRESCHOOL ★★★★   **GRADE SCHOOL** ★★★★½   **TEENS** ★★★★½
YOUNG ADULTS ★★★★   **OVER 30** ★★★★   **SENIORS** ★★★★

What it is Multisensory theater show. **Scope and scale** Headliner. **When to go** The first 2 hours the attraction is open or after 4 p.m. **Duration of show** About 10 minutes, including 3-minute preshow. **Probable waiting time** About 20 minutes.

DESCRIPTION AND COMMENTS The Art Deco Dream-Works Theatre screens short films, featuring franchises from the Universal-owned computer-animation studio; namely, an all-new adventure starring Master Po, the portly protagonist of the *Kung Fu Panda* series, and his Furious Five friends. After a scene-setting preshow featuring cameos by Shrek (the building's former occupant) and the Trolls, the audience enters what appears to be an ornate theater outfitted with opera boxes and curtains; keep a close eye on those seemingly solid ornamentations. The show incorporates the usual slate of multisensory 4-D effects—water, wind, moving seats, 360-degree surround sound, LED lighting, fog—but instead of 3-D glasses, it uses advanced projection-mapping effects to extend the action beyond the edges of the screen. The plot is inconsequential; this experience is all about kinetic eye candy, interspersed with Jack Black wisecracks, and on that level it certainly succeeds. The venue hosts all-day screenings of *Kung Fu Panda Adventure* but is equipped to rotate programming, and has been used for immersive horror movie previews during Halloween events.

TOURING TIPS DreamWorks Theatre holds 224 seats for an hourly capacity of about 1,300 guests. Pop in early, or check back in the late afternoon when wait times should drop below 30 minutes. During the preshow, jockey for a view of both the main door and the trophy case (watch the hammer at the end). In the main show, sit toward the back of the room for the best view of the immersive sidewall imagery. The motion simulation can be quite vigorous, so ask an employee for a stationary seat if you have a sensitive back.

Fast & Furious Hollywood Drift *(opening 2026)*

APPEAL BY AGE   NOT YET RATED

What it is High-speed spinning roller coaster. **Scope and scale** Super-headliner. **When to go** The first or last hour of the day (if open). **Duration of ride** About 90 seconds. **Average wait time per 100 people ahead of you** TBD. **Loading speed** TBD.

DESCRIPTION AND COMMENTS At press time, Universal is constructing a brand new roller coaster themed to the *Fast & Furious* franchise, which will start in a garage-styled queue building on the Upper Lot, across from the entrance to Hogsmeade. The 4,600 feet of steel track run downhill, around the escalators to the Lower Lot, and then back again. This Intamin launch coaster will feature 16-passenger trains with rotating ride cars that can "drift" around curves, turning riders to face scream-deadening barriers built alongside the track. With four inversions, multiple launches, and a top speed over 70 miles per hour, this looks to be the West Coast's rotating response to Orlando's acclaimed VelociCoaster.

TOURING TIPS As Universal Hollywood's first big outdoor coaster, this ride is certain to attract big crowds all day. All loose items (including cell phones and keys) will need to be stored in a free double-sided locker located just before the loading station, and you'll pass through a metal detector before boarding.

The Secret Life of Pets: Off the Leash ★★★★

**APPEAL BY AGE   PRESCHOOL ★★★★   GRADE SCHOOL ★★★★   TEENS ★★★★
YOUNG ADULTS ★★★★   OVER 30 ★★★★   SENIORS ★★★★**

What it is Family-friendly dark ride. **Scope and scale** Headliner. **When to go** During the first hour the ride is open or use Virtual Line. **Comment** Must be 34" tall to ride.

Duration of ride 5 minutes. **Average wait time per 100 people ahead of you** 4 minutes. **Loading speed** Moderate–slow.

DESCRIPTION AND COMMENTS Anchoring a block of Manhattan-inspired facades leading to the Despicable Me area, Secret Life of Pets: Off the Leash provides Universal Studios Hollywood with welcome placemaking, along with a much-needed attraction that the entire family can enjoy together. This animatronic-filled dark ride, featuring Max the Jack Russell (Patton Oswalt), Snowball the bunny rabbit (Kevin Hart), and all their furry friends from the animated Illumination films, casts guests as stray puppies on the streets of New York City, searching for their forever homes.

An innovative switchback-free queue takes visitors on a tour through the pets' detailed brownstone apartments—filled with multiple aw-inspiring critters—before embarking on a gentle journey to their own "adoption." The 5-minute ride crawls through sight-gag-stuffed sets, enhanced with explosive projection-mapping effects and populated by dozens of huggable hairy animated figures. It put a big silly smile on our faces from start to finish and rewards repeat rides.

Though not quite on the same scope and scale as Haunted Mansion or Pirates of the Caribbean, Secret Life of Pets has almost as much charm and imaginative detail as those all-time Disney classics, and it's easily the best family-friendly dark ride Universal has built since the E.T. Adventure.

TOURING TIPS If the wait exceeds 60 minutes, Secret Life of Pets may use a Virtual Line system to control access to its queue. You can get a spot in the Virtual Line after entering the park by using Universal's app or by visiting the kiosks to the left of the ride's entrance. Additional time slots are released periodically throughout the day. Once your return window arrives, you should wait no more than 20–30 minutes before boarding; Universal Express guests can enter the queue at any time without a Virtual Line reservation and skip about half the wait.

Our only knocks against this exceptional attraction are that the unnecessarily restrictive seat restraints and too-short moving walkways at boarding and unloading make the ride needlessly unfriendly for infants, larger folks, and the disabled. Be sure to test the sample seat outside the entrance, and let an employee know if you have mobility issues.

The Simpsons Ride ★★★½

What it is Simulator ride. **Scope and scale** Headliner. **When to go** In the first hour of the morning. **Comment** Must be 40" tall to ride; not recommended for pregnant women or people prone to motion sickness; switching-off option (see page 165). **Duration of ride** 4⅓ minutes, plus preshow. **Average wait time per 100 people ahead of you** 3 minutes. **Loading speed** Moderate.

DESCRIPTION AND COMMENTS This ride is based on the Fox animated series that is TV's longest-running sitcom. Featuring the voices of Dan Castellaneta (Homer), Julie Kavner (Marge), Nancy Cartwright (Bart), Yeardley Smith (Lisa), and other cast members, the attraction takes a wild and humorous poke at thrill rides, dark rides, and live shows "that make up a fantasy amusement park dreamed up by the show's cantankerous Krusty the Clown."

Two preshows involve *Simpsons* characters speaking sequentially on different video screens around the line area. Their comments help define the characters for guests who are unfamiliar with the TV show.

The storyline has the conniving Sideshow Bob secretly arriving at Krustyland, the aforementioned amusement park, and plotting his revenge on Krusty and Bart, who, in a past *Simpsons* episode, revealed that Sideshow Bob had committed a crime for which he'd framed Krusty. Sideshow Bob gets even by making things go wrong with the attractions that the Simpsons (and you) are riding.

The attraction is a simulator ride similar to Star Tours at Disneyland Park, but with a larger domed Omnimax-type screen more like that of Soarin' at Disney California Adventure. The computer-animated 4K video is showing its age, and the movement can be quite jerky. Like the show on which it's based, The Simpsons Ride definitely has an edge, and more than a few wild hairs. There will be jokes and visuals that you'll get but will fly over your children's heads—and most assuredly vice versa. A mom from Huntington, New York, had this to say:

The ride is lots of fun and suitable for all guests. I'm not a fan of wild motion simulators, but I was fine on this ride.

TOURING TIPS Expect large crowds all day. We recommend arriving at the park before opening and making the ride your first stop after Mario Kart or the *Fast & Furious* coaster. For the best view, ask to wait for the level A and room 6. Several families we interviewed found the humor a little too adult for their younger children. Don't miss the neighboring Simpson-ized carnival games and Kwik-E-Mart gift shop for more snarky *Simpsons* sight gags, as well as an expansive strip of Springfield-inspired shops and eateries. Featured destinations include Krusty Burger, Luigi's Pizza, Phineas Q. Butterfat's Ice Cream, Moe's Tavern, and Duff Brewery Beer Garden. You'll also find funny facades of iconic cartoon locations such as Springfield's police station, elementary school, and nuclear power plant; try pressing the button outside Homer's workstation for an explosive surprise.

Studio Tour ★★★★★

**APPEAL BY AGE PRESCHOOL ★★★ GRADE SCHOOL ★★★★ TEENS ★★★★
YOUNG ADULTS ★★★★ OVER 30 ★★★★ SENIORS ★★★★**

What it is Indoor-outdoor tram tour of soundstages and backlot. **Scope and scale** Super-headliner. **When to go** Before 11 a.m or after 6 p.m.; closes 105 minutes before park closing. **Duration of tour** 45–60 minutes, depending on studio productions. **Average wait time per 100 people ahead of you** 2½ minutes. **Loading speed** Fast.

Loud Scary

DESCRIPTION AND COMMENTS The Studio Tour is the centerpiece of USH and is one of the longest attractions in American theme parks. The tour departs from the tram boarding facility to the *right* of The Simpsons Ride and down the escalator. (Note that there's also an escalator to the left of The Simpsons Ride, so don't get confused.)

The tour is hosted by a live guide, whose narration is supplemented with prerecorded segments starring celebrities like Jimmy Fallon, George Lopez, and Chris Pratt. All trams are equipped with high-definition monitors showing clips from actual movies that demonstrate how the sets and soundstages were used in creating the films; the newest models are powered by quiet electric motors and feature an eco-minded video introduction from the *Today Show*'s Al Roker.

The Studio Tour circulates through the various street scenes, lagoons, special-effects venues, and storage areas of Universal's backlot. The tram passes several soundstages where current films and TV shows such as *The Voice* are in production, and it actually enters three soundstages where action inspired by *Earthquake, King Kong,* and *The Fast and the Furious* is presented. Other famous sets visited include those from *Psycho, Jaws,* and *War of the Worlds.* Universal has reconstructed the Jupiter's Claim sets seen in Jordan Peele's film *NOPE* near the end of the tour, where spooky sound effects assault trams as they pass by Wild West storefronts. Live actors may invade the sets for the Terror Tram during Halloween Horror Nights.

To celebrate the Studio Tour's 60th anniversary in 2024, Universal refurbished the classic *Earthquake* disaster simulation, modernizing the subway set's decor but retaining the exploding truck and derailing train effects. They also temporarily redressed a handful of trams as the vintage red-and-white-striped "Glamor Trams," erected additional photo ops along the tram route, and even allowed regular guests to disembark and walk around the Bates Motel and past a 10-foot-tall replica of the iconic Hollywood sign.

The tour's two centerpieces are a pair of 3-D simulation segments: the award-winning *King Kong 360/3-D* virtual experience, inspired by Peter Jackson's 2005 remake, and *Fast & Furious: Supercharged,* starring Vin Diesel and "family" from the long-running action franchise. In both, guests enter a darkened tunnel where tram-length curved projection screens transform into the jungles of Skull Island, where Kong himself swings to save you from a family of hungry *V. rexes,* or a virtual high-speed highway chase filled with CGI car crashes. Hydraulic lifts under the cars rattle your seat in sync with the 4K 3-D images, making it appear as if your tram is sliding off a cliff into a chasm or speeding at 100-plus miles per hour through the streets of Los Angeles. The experiences are visceral and immersive, especially when seen from the middle of a row (sitting on the outside exposes the top of the screen, spoiling the illusion). At only about 90 seconds each, they are too short to be satisfying as stand-alone attractions (both were substantially expanded for their Orlando incarnations, with mixed results), and *Supercharged* is frankly disappointing, with shockingly cheesy dialogue and visual effects that fail to advance the once-stunning *Kong 360* technology in a meaningful way.

The great thing about the Studio Tour is that you see everything without leaving the tram—essentially experiencing four or five major attractions with only one wait.

TOURING TIPS Though the wait to board might appear long, do not be discouraged. Each tram carries several hundred people and departures are frequent, so the line moves quickly. We recommend taking the tram tour after experiencing the other headliners on the Upper Lot. The attraction entrance typically closes 105 minutes prior to the park's closing time, so we recommend getting in line at least 2 hours before the park closes.

Tour trams are four cars long. The front car allows you to see your guide in the flesh; aim for the elevated back row. The third car is the sweet spot for experiencing the 3-D 360 visuals, and the back car bounces around the most from the motion simulation.

Including your wait to board and the duration of the tour, you will easily invest an hour or more at this attraction. Remember to take a restroom break before queuing up. This is one of the few attractions that allows food and beverages to be brought on board. Though the ride as a whole is gentle, some segments may induce vertigo or motion sickness—especially the *Kong* encounter and *Fast & Furious* finale. Finally, be aware that several of the scenes may frighten small children.

WaterWorld ★★★★

What it is Arena show featuring simulated stunt-scene filming.
Scope and scale Headliner. **When to go** After experiencing all
the Upper Lot rides and the tram tour. **Duration of show** 20
minutes. **Probable waiting time** 15–30 minutes.

Thumbs Up for the Whole Family

Loud

DESCRIPTION AND COMMENTS Drawn from the film *WaterWorld,* this outdoor theater presentation features stunts and special effects performed on and around a small artificial lagoon. The action involves various watercraft and, of course, a lot of explosions and falling from high places into the water. Fast-paced and well adapted to the theater, the production is in many ways more compelling than the film that inspired it. The show's climax features stunts and pyrotechnics, making for a rousing finale.

TOURING TIPS Wait until you have experienced all the rides and the tram tour before checking out *WaterWorld*. Because the show is located near the main entrance, most performances are filled to capacity. Arrive at the theater about 30 minutes before the showtime listed on directory boards and in the app. Be careful if you sit in on a green bench; when this show says "splash zone," it means it. *WaterWorld* cast members usually hang out at the exit greeting guests after a show.

The Wizarding World of Harry Potter

The main entrance into Universal Studios Hollywood's Wizarding World of Harry Potter is an imposing gate adjacent to the DreamWorks Theatre that leads to **Hogsmeade,** a village depicted in winter and covered in snow. (A secondary entryway is found between The Simpsons Ride and the Studio Tour escalator.) The towering castle houses **Hogwarts School of Witchcraft and Wizardry,** flanked by the **Flight of the Hippogriff** kiddie coaster and **Hagrid's Hut.** The grounds and interior of the castle contain part of the queue for the super-headliner **Harry Potter and the Forbidden Journey.** Universal went all out on the castle, with the intention of creating an icon even more beloved and powerful than Sleeping Beauty Castle at Disneyland.

In front of the gate, the **Hogwarts Express** locomotive sits belching steam, and a small station houses a train-themed gift shop. The village is rendered in exquisite detail: stone cottages and shops have steeply pitched slate roofs, bowed multipaned windows, gables, and tall, crooked chimneys. Your first taste—literally—of the Harry Potter universe comes courtesy of **Honeydukes.** Specializing in Potter-themed candy such as Acid Pops (no flashbacks, guaranteed), Tooth Splintering Strong Mints, and Fizzing Whizbees, the sweet shop offers no shortage of snacks that administer an immediate sugar high. The big draw is the elaborately boxed Chocolate Frogs; the packaging looks as if it came straight from a *Harry Potter* film, complete with a wizard trading card. Taking up a small corner of Honeydukes is **Fortean Fortescue's,** selling cones of vanilla soft-serve ice cream with flavored ribbons like butterbeer, toffee apple, and chocolate.

Next door to Honeydukes and set back from the main street is **Three Broomsticks,** a rustic tavern serving English staples such as fish-and-chips, shepherd's pie, bangers and mash, and Guinness stew. To the rear of the tavern is the **Hog's Head** pub, which serves a nice selection of beer and is the quickest place to get The Wizarding World's signature nonalcoholic brew, **Butterbeer** (vanilla soda with butterscotch-marshmallow foam, available cold, frozen, or hot, with vegan topping on request). There's even Butterbeer fudge (tooth-shatteringly sweet), Butterbeer potted cream (like butterscotch pudding in a jar), and Butterbeer ice cream, sold hard-packed in prepackaged cups. For adults, exclusive beers are available; we like the Wizard's Brew, a rich chocolate stout. If all that imbibing inspires you to heed nature's call, be warned that Moaning Myrtle haunts both the men's and ladies' sides of the land's only facilities; hearing her cries while you're trying to go can be distracting to say the least.

On the far side of the pub is **Ollivanders,** where young wizards are matched with magic wands (see the full description on pages 358–359) in a brief but charming show. Adjoining the wand shop (where you can browse without queuing for the show) is **Wiseacre's Wizarding Equipment,** where you can buy binoculars or telescopes.

Roughly across the street from the pub, you'll find benches in the shade at the **Owlery,** where animatronic owls (complete with lifelike poop) ruffle and hoot from the rafters. Next to the Owlery is the **Owl Post,** where you can purchase stationary and have mail stamped with a Hogsmeade postmark before dropping it off for delivery. The Owl Post is attached to **Dervish and Banges,** a magic supplies shop selling brooms and Quidditch equipment, and **Gladrags Wizardwear,** ground zero for getting outfitted in fashionable school robes.

Finally, at the exit of Hogwarts Castle is **Filch's Emporium of Confiscated Goods,** which offers all manner of Potter-themed gear. In keeping with the stores depicted in the Potter films, the shopping venues in The Wizarding World of Harry Potter–Hogsmeade are small and intimate—so intimate, in fact, that they feel congested when they're serving only 12–20 shoppers. USH also sells most of its Potter merchandise, including wands, at two easily accessible stores near the park entrance.

Super Nintendo World has diverted attention away from Hollywood's Potter attractions, but you should still prepare for the land to be packed to the gills if you visit during a peak period. The land and its attractions usually open for all guests 30 minutes prior to park opening, so your best bet for experiencing Harry Potter is to visit in the opening hours, when everyone is headed to the Lower Lot, or wait until afternoon. Crowds flood in after sundown to see the seasonal light show on Hogwarts Castle, but ride wait times are often minimal in the hour before closing.

Flight of the Hippogriff ★★★

APPEAL BY AGE   PRESCHOOL ★★★½   GRADE SCHOOL ★★★★   TEENS ★★★
YOUNG ADULTS ★★½   OVER 30 ★★★½   SENIORS ★★★

What it is Kiddie roller coaster. **Scope and scale** Minor attraction. **When to go** Before 10 a.m. or after 2 p.m. **Comment** Must be 39″ tall to ride. **Duration of ride** 1 minute. **Average wait time per 100 people ahead of you** 6¼ minutes. **Loading speed** Slow.

Lose Things

DESCRIPTION AND COMMENTS Below and to the right of Hogwarts Castle, next to Hagrid's Hut, the Hippogriff is short and sweet but not worth much of a wait. This outdoor, elevated coaster is designed for children old enough to know about Harry Potter but not yet tall enough to ride Forbidden Journey. The ride affords excellent views of the area within Wizarding World and of Hogwarts, and the theming is also very good, considering that this isn't a major attraction. As a children's coaster only slightly taller and longer than the coaster in Disneyland's Toontown, there are no loops, inversions, or rolls: it's just one big hill and some mild turns, and almost half of the 1-minute ride time is spent going up the lift hill. Hollywood's coaster has a layout similar to the Orlando original, but this one is a brand-new model manufactured by Mack (rather than an aging Vekoma) and gives a much smoother and somewhat snappier ride.

For fans of Harry Potter, there are two gorgeous items in this attraction that you will want to see. The first is a faithful re-creation of Hagrid's Hut in the queue (complete with the sound of Fang howling) while the second is an incredible animatronic of Buckbeak that you pass by while on the ride. Remember that when Muggles (also known as humans) encounter hippogriffs like Buckbeak, proper etiquette must always be maintained to avoid any danger. Hippogriffs are extremely proud creatures and must be shown the proper respect by bowing to them and waiting for them to bow in return.

TOURING TIPS Have your kids ride in the morning while older siblings enjoy Forbidden Journey, or save it for late in the day.

Harry Potter and the Forbidden Journey ★★★★★

APPEAL BY AGE   PRESCHOOL ★   GRADE SCHOOL ★★★★½   TEENS ★★★★★
YOUNG ADULTS ★★★★★   OVER 30 ★★★★★   SENIORS ★★★★★

What it is Motion-simulator dark ride. **Scope and scale** Super-headliner. **When to go** Before 10 a.m. or after 3 p.m. **Comments** Must be 48″ tall to ride; switching-off option (see page 165). Single-rider line. All bags must be placed in a free locker. **Duration of ride** 4¼ minutes. **Average wait time per 100 people ahead of you** 3 minutes. **Loading speed** Fast.

Dark

Loud

Scary

Lose Things

Queasy

DESCRIPTION AND COMMENTS This ride provides the only opportunity at Universal to come close to Harry, Ron, Hermione, and Dumbledore as portrayed by the original actors. From Hogsmeade you reach the attraction through the imposing Winged Boar gates and progress along a winding path past the Weasleys' crashed Ford Anglia from *The Chamber of Secrets.* Entering the castle on a lower level, you walk through a sort of dungeon festooned with various icons and prop replicas from the Potter flicks, including the Mirror of Erised from *Harry Potter and the Sorcerer's Stone.* You later emerge back outside and in the Hogwarts greenhouses. The greenhouses compose the larger part of the Forbidden Journey's queuing area, and despite some strategically placed mandrakes, there isn't much here to amuse beyond the majestic view of the mountains.

Having finally escaped horticulture purgatory, you enter the castle's passageways, passing towering statues and tapestries. Inside a multistory gallery of moving portraits, you'll meet the four founders of Hogwarts, who argue about Quidditch and Dumbledore's controversial decision to host an open house at Hogwarts for Muggles (garden-variety mortals). Next, after you've navigated more passages, you'll enter Dumbledore's office, where the wizard headmaster himself appears on a balcony and welcomes you to Hogwarts. The headmaster's appearance is your intro-duction to Musion Eyeliner technology—a high-definition video-projection system that produces breathtakingly realistic, three-dimensional, life-size moving holograms.

After his remarks, Dumbledore dispatches you to the Defence Against the Dark Arts classroom to hear a presentation on the history of Hogwarts. Here, Harry, Ron, and Hermione pop out from beneath an invisibility cloak, inviting you to ditch the dull lecture in favor of joining them for a proper tour of Hogwarts, including a Quidditch match. The briefing and instruc-tions are presented inside the Gryffindor common room by animated por-traits and an animatronic Sorting Hat. All this leads to the Room of Requirement, where hun-dreds of candles float overhead as you board the ride vehicle: a four-seat flying bench mounted on the end of a Kuka robotic arm similar to the kind used in heavy manufacturing.

Your mind-blowing 4¼-minute adventure is a headlong sprint through the most thrilling moments from the first few Potter books: you'll soar over Hogwarts Castle, narrowly evade an attacking dragon, spar with the Whomping Willow, get tossed into a Quidditch match, and fight off

unofficial **TIP**
Even if your child meets the height requirement, consider carefully whether Forbidden Journey is an experience he or she can handle. Because the seats on the benches are com-partmentalized, kids can't see or touch Mom or Dad if they get frightened.

Dementors inside the Chamber of Secrets. Scenes alternate between enor-mous physical sets and high-definition video-projection domes that sur-round your field of view, similar to Soarin' Around the World or The Simpsons Ride. Those Kuka-powered benches really do "levitate" in a man-ner that feels remarkably like free flight, and while you don't go upside down, the sensation of floating on your back or being slung from side to side is certainly unique. Hollywood's version is amped up compared to the Orlando original, with enhanced lighting effects and scarier animatronics. The greatest-hits montage plotline may be a bit muddled, but the ride is enormously effective at leaving you feeling as though you just survived the scariest scrapes from the early educational career of The Boy Who Lived.

TOURING TIPS Free lockers, which are required for bags and wands, are located outside the castle. Alternatively, have a nonriding member of your party hold your bags for you in the child swap area. This ride makes a couple of moves that will empty your trousers faster than a master pickpocket—ditto and worse for shirt pockets.

The singles line, located to the left inside the castle, can be as little as one-tenth of the wait in standby. Because the individual seating separates you from the other riders whether your party stays together or not, the singles line is a great option, as this wife from Edinburgh, Scotland, discovered:

Trust me—sitting next to hubby on Forbidden Journey, romantic though it may be, is not as awesome as having to wait only 15 minutes as a single rider.

To understand the storyline and get the most out of the attraction, watch a full run-through of each preshow, which takes 20–25 minutes. Try to find a place to stop where you can let those behind you pass; as long as you're not creating a logjam, the team members should leave you alone. Universal Express users get to see all the important preshow elements, only bypassing the greenhouses and some minor scenery. Nonriders should ask the greeter if they can tour the secondary queue without waiting in line.

Larger guests should try out the sample seats stationed outside the castle entrance before standing in line. For you to be cleared to ride, the overhead restraint has to click three times; it's body shape rather than weight (unless you're over 300 pounds) that's key. Passing the test by inhaling sharply is not recommended.

Ollivanders ★★★★

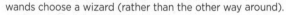

What it is Combination wizarding demonstration and shopping op. **Scope and scale** Minor attraction. **When to go** Before 9 a.m. or after 2 p.m. **Comments** No seating provided. **Duration of presentation** 6 minutes. **Average wait time per 100 people ahead of you** 18 minutes.

DESCRIPTION AND COMMENTS Inside this musty store stacked high with dusty boxes, 24 guests at a time can experience the little drama where

Thumbs Up for the Whole Family

wands choose a wizard (rather than the other way around). Every few minutes, following a script from the Potter books, a wand-selection show takes place in which a random customer (often a child dressed in Potter regalia) is selected to take part in a wand-choosing ceremony. Usually just one person in each group gets to be chosen by a wand,

though occasionally siblings are selected together. This is one of the most truly imaginative elements of The Wizarding World: a Wandkeeper sizes you up and presents a wand, inviting you to try it out; your attempted spells produce unintended, unwanted, and highly amusing consequences. Ultimately, a wand chooses its wizard, with all the attendant special effects. The wands ($65) presented in the ceremony interact with shop windows throughout The Wizarding World (see the facing page).

After the presentation, guests exit into a gift shop, where interactive wands are also available for purchase for a vast variety of characters, along with toy "learner" wands ($30) for li'l wizards.

TOURING TIPS To increase your odds of being picked, be a cute kid, stand up front, and make eye contact. If your young 'un is selected to test-drive a wand, be forewarned that you'll have to buy it if you want to take it home. You do not need to see the wand-selection show to purchase a wand at Ollivanders— just enter the store directly rather than wait in the long outdoor queue.

INTERACTIVE WANDS AND SPELL-CASTING LOCATIONS Interactive wands ($65) are available in 13 Ollivanders Original styles (including one exclusive to Universal Studios Hollywood) and include an explanation of the wand's lore. Interactive wands modeled after those wielded by a variety of characters (including Harry, Hermione, Dumbledore, Sirius Black, and Luna Lovegood) are also available. The widest selection of wands is found in the Ollivanders shop, but stores outside of The Wizarding World at the entrance of the park, as well as at CityWalk's Universal Studios Store, carry a limited variety of interactive wands. Wands can also be ordered from Universal Orlando's merchandise website; wands from Florida or Japan are fully compatible with Hollywood's effects (and vice versa).

Medallions embedded in the ground designate more than a dozen locations around The Wizarding World where hidden cameras in storefront windows can detect the waving of these special wands and respond to the correct motions with special effects both projected and practical. You might use the swish and flick of Wingardium Leviosa to levitate one object or the figure four Locomotor spell to animate another. It can take some practice to get the hang of spell casting, but you'll feel a sense of accomplishment when you unlock a door or make flames erupt from a chimney. Wizards wander around the area to assist novices and demonstrate spells (though they may not loan their wands), but queues to trigger certain effects can grow to a dozen deep at peak times. A map provided with each wand details the location and movement for the effects.

Note that the price of the interactive wands includes unlimited activations of the hidden effects; you don't have to pay to recharge your wand on subsequent visits or even replace a battery. If you encounter a spell-casting location with a sign saying it currently has an anti-jinx in place, just move along to the next one; that's Potter-speak for "it's broken." Damaged wands are cheerfully "repaired" for free at Ollivanders, even without a receipt.

We've received positive feedback on the interactive wands, like this praise from a New York, New York, family:

> We took our interactive wand and map and explored all the many surprises for well over an hour and had a fantastic time. An interactive wand is highly recommended. Our girls (12 and 14) had a blast making the wand motions and watching the windows come to life.

On the other hand, some guests have found the wands maddeningly difficult to master, as a father from Petaluma, California, warns:

> After getting their wands, my boys were soon frustrated to tears that the wands didn't work and that they had wasted their allowance on "a piece of plastic junk," in my oldest son's words. We searched desperately

for one of the robed employees to assist us, but it seemed they were all on break somewhere. After a long while we finally located one. He gave a quick tutorial on where to point the wand, how much to move it, where to stand, and so on, and my boys were able to get their wands to work. My best advice is that, after buying the wand, keep it in the box until you find someone helping at one of the magic windows, and get a lesson on how to use it. Many of the magic spells worked the opposite of how you would think, or were so subtle that you weren't sure if the spell had worked or not. The best windows for beginners are (in order) #11 Dominic Maestro's, #2 Three Broomsticks, and #1 Honeydukes.

LOWER LOT

THE LOWER LOT is accessible only via the escalators and stairs descending from the back left section of the Upper Lot. The trip takes at least 7 minutes in each direction, and a bypass shuttle runs every 10–15 minutes for disabled guests, acrophobics, or anyone requesting it. Configured roughly in the shape of the letter *T*, the Lower Lot is home to Transformers, Jurassic World, and Revenge of the Mummy, all headliner attractions at USH. The newest addition to the Lower Lot is Super Nintendo World, featuring a Mario Kart ride, which opened its green warp pipe to guests in early 2023. Be aware that the Lower Lot stops admitting new arrivals 15 minutes before the park closes, though its attractions remain operating until closing time.

Jurassic World—The Ride ★★★★½

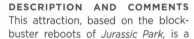

APPEAL BY AGE PRESCHOOL ★★★ GRADE SCHOOL ★★★★½ TEENS ★★★★½ YOUNG ADULTS ★★★★ OVER 30 ★★★★ SENIORS ★★★★

What it is Indoor-outdoor adventure ride based on the movie *Jurassic World.* **Scope and scale** Super-headliner. **When to go** The first hour the park is open or after 4 p.m. **Comments** Must be 42″ tall to ride; switching-off option (see page 165). Single-rider line. **Duration of ride** 6 minutes. **Average wait time per 100 people ahead of you** 2¼ minutes. **Loading speed** Fast.

Scary Wet Lose Things Queasy Rough

DESCRIPTION AND COMMENTS This attraction, based on the blockbuster reboots of *Jurassic Park,* is a boat tour of the dinosaur-filled theme park, which begins tranquilly before turning traumatic. Along the way, a massive Mosasaurus snaps at you from inside its titanic tank, before you float into a face-off with an angry *Indominus rex.* Instead of the ubiquitous *T. rex* being the bad guy, this time she stomps in to save your bacon at the climactic moment, allowing the boat and its passengers to escape over an 84-foot waterfall.

The Jurassic World ride still follows the same river path as the original Jurassic Park version it replaced in 2018, but everything from the scenery and props to sound and lighting were overhauled, with new animatronics that more accurately resemble the newer films' dino designs. The finale's enormous *I-Rex* is among the most fluid and frightening animatronics we've ever encountered, and she earns the ride an additional half star all on her own. The final drop to safety is still a doozy, though it's a foot shorter (and slightly less intense) than its Orlando sibling.

TOURING TIPS You can get very wet on this ride. Once the ride is underway, there's a little splashing but nothing major until the big drop at the end. When you hit the bottom, enough water will cascade into the boat to extinguish a three-alarm fire. Bring along an extra-large garbage bag and (cutting holes for your head and arms) wear it like a sack dress. If you forget to bring a garbage bag, you can purchase a poncho at the park for about $10, or rent a locker to stow your stuff for a few bucks less.

Young kids must endure a double whammy. First, they are stalked by giant, salivating reptiles, then they are catapulted over the falls. Wait until your kids are fairly stalwart before you spring Jurassic World on them, or let them sit out the ride inside the fossil-themed playground near the entrance.

Jurassic World is one of the park's top draws, and the ride will always be jammed on warm days. Ride early in the morning, in late afternoon, or immediately before closing, if you don't mind being wet on your way back to the hotel, since it looks best after dark. The single-rider entrance can be tricky to access but saves significant time (when available).

Revenge of the Mummy—The Ride ★★★½

APPEAL BY AGE   PRESCHOOL —   GRADE SCHOOL ★★★½   TEENS ★★★★½
YOUNG ADULTS ★★★★½   OVER 30 ★★★★   SENIORS ★★★½

What it is High-tech dark ride. **Scope and scale** Super-headliner. **When to go** Before 10 a.m. or late afternoon. **Comments** Must be 48" tall to ride; switching-off option (see page 165). Single-rider line. All bags must be placed in a free locker. **Duration of ride** About 2 minutes. **Average wait time per 100 people ahead of you** 7 minutes. **Loading speed** Slow.

Dark   Scary   Lose Things   Queasy   Rough

DESCRIPTION AND COMMENTS This is an indoor dark ride based on *The Mummy* flicks, where guests fight off "deadly curses and vengeful creatures" while flying through Egyptian tombs and other spooky places on a high-tech roller coaster.

The queuing area serves to establish the storyline: you're in a group touring a 1944 archaeological dig of an Egyptian tomb when evil Imhotep decides to make another comeback. The theming includes authentic hieroglyphics as the queue makes its way to the loading area, where you board a somewhat clunky, jeep-looking vehicle. The ride begins as a slow, elaborate dark ride passing through various chambers, including one where golden treasures are offered in exchange for your soul. Suddenly you're shot at high speed straight into a minute's worth of pitch-black hills and tight curves, dead-ending in an encounter with leg-tickling scarab beetles. We don't want to divulge too much, but the roller-coaster part of the ride has no barrel rolls or any upside-down stuff.

After an all-too-brief backward section, the attraction anticlimaxes in a darkened dome, where the mummy moans and then blinds you with a strobe. Compared to Universal Studios Florida's ride of the same name, this abbreviated attraction severely disappoints with shorter drops, simpler Audio-Animatronics, and no pyrotechnics.

TOURING TIPS Revenge of the Mummy has a very low riders-per-hour capacity for one of the park's top draws. Ride the Mummy immediately after riding Jurassic World and Transformers. If you can ride Space Mountain without getting sick, you should be fine on this.

Transformers: The Ride 3-D ★★★★

What it is Multisensory 3-D dark ride. **Scope and scale** Super-headliner. **When to go** Before 10 a.m. or late afternoon. **Comments** Must be 40" tall to ride; single-rider line. **Duration of ride** 4½ minutes. **Average wait time per 100 people ahead of you** 3 minutes. **Loading speed** Moderate–fast.

Dark   Loud   Scary   Rough

DESCRIPTION AND COMMENTS Transformers—Hasbro's toy robots from the 1980s that you turned and twisted into trucks and planes—have been around long enough to go from commercial to kitsch to cool and back again. Thanks to director Michael Bay's movies, "Robots in Disguise" are again a blockbuster global franchise. Recruits to this cybertronic war enlist by entering the N.E.S.T. Base (headquarters of the heroic Autobots and their human allies) beneath a massive dimensional mural depicting Optimus Prime and his nemesis, Megatron, locked in mortal metal combat. Inside an extensive, elaborately detailed queue, video monitors catch you up on the backstory. Basically, the Decepticon baddies are after the All-Spark, source of cybernetic sentience. We're supposed to safeguard the shard by hitching a ride aboard our friendly Autobot ride vehicle Evac, presumably without getting smooshed like a Lincoln in a souvenir penny press when he shifts into android form. For the ride's 4½ minutes, you play human Ping-Pong ball in an epic battle between these Made-in-Japan behemoths. To do justice to this Bay-splosion–packed war of good versus evil, Universal has harnessed the same ride system behind Islands of Adventure's Amazing Adventures of Spider-Man ride, blending motion simulation and live effects with impressive photo-realistic high-definition 3-D imagery.

The plot amounts to little more than a giant game of keep-away, and the uninitiated will likely be unable to tell one meteoric mass of metal from another, but you'll be too dazzled by the debris whizzing by to notice. Fanboys will squeal with delight at hearing original cartoon actors Peter Cullen and Frank Welker voicing the pugilistic protagonists, while the rest of us might need a breather afterward. We'll admit slight disappointment at not getting to see an actual four-story-tall animatronic transform, but the ride's mix of detailed (though largely static) set pieces and video projections makes for one of Universal's more intense, immersive thrill rides.

TOURING TIPS Though the openings of The Wizarding and Super Nintendo Worlds have taken some of the heat off, Transformers still draws heavy crowds, so ride immediately after Jurassic World upon arriving on the Lower Lot. The single-rider entrance will often let you walk on the attraction, even when the standby wait is an hour, but its queue lacks any theming, so fans may want to take at least one trip through the regular line. It can be difficult for your eyes to focus on the fast-moving imagery from the front row; center seats in the second and third rows provide the best perspective. Be sure to say hello to the towering robots posing for photos outside the entrance; they can talk back to you!

SUPER NINTENDO WORLD

FOLLOWING THE 2021 DEBUT of the original Super Nintendo World at Universal Studios Japan, the first North American theme park land dedicated to Nintendo's world-famous video game characters opened at Universal Studios Hollywood in early 2023, ahead of its arrival as an anchor property in Universal Orlando's Epic Universe expansion. Guests enter Super Nintendo World through an iconic green warp pipe in the back corner of the Lower Lot and emerge through a swirl of colored lights and 8-bit sound effects into the courtyard of **Princess Peach's castle.** Flag-topped Mount Beanpole and a range of terraced hills screen out the surrounding studio, and everywhere you turn there's another moving animatronic—marching Koopas, waddling Goombas, and spinning coins—enlivening the area with infectious kinetic energy. Hollywood's version may lack the Donkey Kong roller coaster and family-friendly Yoshi ride found in the other locations, but it still features the anchor **Mario Kart attraction,** and it has been an even bigger hit for Hollywood than Harry Potter.

To keep track of your Mario Kart score, as well as fully participate in the interactive elements around the land, we strongly suggest that you install the smartphone app and purchase a colorful character-themed Power-Up Band ($42), which allows you to "punch" blocks and participate in activities throughout the multilevel complex. Even though the bands (which also double as Amibos for the Switch) don't need batteries or charging, their level of interactivity is far more sophisticated than Hogsmeade's magic windows, reacting readily to the scores of sensors secreted around the land.

Beyond simply discovering all the sound and light effects you can activate—thereby adding digital badges to your app's bragging board—you can participate in four physical challenges, each with multiple difficulty levels to keep veterans on their toes. The wacky tasks have you slapping alarm clocks so a monstrous Piranha Plant stays snoozing, slapping a touchscreen wall of sliding blocks, as well as other tests of timing and coordination. Once you've conquered at least three of the key activities, you (and one companion) are allowed inside **Bowser Jr.'s lair** for an arm-waving interactive "boss battle" that's a fantastic full-body workout. After you've beaten Bowser Jr., head upstairs to the **Frosted Glacier** overlook and use the augmented reality binoculars to find the final hidden key on the hovering airship. To save time in the morning, purchase your Power-Up Band in City-Walk and link it to your phone before entering the park; ask inside the 1UP gift shop for a free security sleeve to prevent your snap bracelet–style wristband from flying off when you fling your fists.

Super Nintendo World is going to be USH's top draw for some time to come. On rare days of peak attendance, Universal may require Virtual Line reservations simply to enter the area. If that's the case, grab a free return time through the app as soon as you arrive, or pick up one from the ATM-style kiosks next to the exit of

Transformers. Those who purchase early-entry privileges or Express passes won't need Virtual Line reservations but will still have to wait in lines once inside the land.

Mario Kart: Bowser's Challenge ★★★★★

APPEAL BY AGE NOT YET RATED

What it is Augmented-reality dark ride. **Scope and scale** Super-headliner. **When to go** As soon as the park opens during early entry, just before closing, or whenever possible using single rider. **Comments** Must be 40″ tall to ride; switching-off option (see page 165). Single-rider line. **Duration of ride** About 5 minutes. **Average wait time per 100 people ahead of you** 4 minutes. **Loading speed** Moderate.

Dark Loud Queasy

DESCRIPTION AND COMMENTS Based on the long-running series of racing games, Mario Kart combines traditional dark-ride elements with cutting-edge augmented reality technology that blurs the line between the real and virtual worlds. The storyline sees Bowser, the villainous King of the Koopas, challenging Mario and his pals to a kart race through flaming lava fields, floating clouds, and other iconic tracks from the best-selling Mario Kart games. Prospective competitors enter Bowser's castle, touring its bowels where his anthropomorphic bomb minions are built, before being handed special visors styled after Mario's distinctive red cap. Once riders strap into the four-seater vehicles, a video display with angled transparent lenses snaps onto the visor, creating Pepper's Ghost–style digital holograms that appear to float among the physical sets.

During the ride, racers cooperate to claim the coveted Universal Cup by aiming at their virtual opponents with their heads, then pressing buttons on their steering wheels to shoot shells, as well as by turning the wheels in response to flashing arrows. Everyone on your team will need to collect at least 100 coins in order to beat Bowser to the finish line, and ammunition is limited, so look down along the track for crystal blocks to reload. *TIP:* Press both buttons during the starting countdown on "2" for a bonus, and look behind you for hidden coin blocks. The ride spins quite a bit but doesn't actually move particularly fast; however, the combination of game-play elements and projection effects creates a chaotic sense of speed, especially during the climactic Rainbow Road sequence.

TOURING TIPS Mario Kart develops a multihour wait by the time the general public enters the land in the morning, and lines don't drop until closing time. Although the best time to ride Mario Kart is during early entry or shortly before closing, be warned that the ride may open late or close early due to maintenance. An Express option is offered, and the easily overlooked singe-rider entrance (on the right immediately inside the queue) can be a lifesaver, although it bypasses the Easter egg–filled queue and the cartoon preshows instructing players on how to score. Universal advises guests with waist sizes over 40 inches to test the vehicle restraints outside the attraction before entering the queue, but the lap bars are actually less restrictive than those on some other rides in the park, such as Revenge of the Mummy or Secret Life of Pets.

LIVE ENTERTAINMENT *and* SPECIAL EVENTS *at* USH

THE THEATER ATTRACTIONS operate according to the entertainment schedule available in the official park app and on information boards around the park. The number of daily performances of each show varies from as few as 3 a day during less-busy times of year to as many as 10 a day during the summer and holiday periods. Characters like Gru's Minions, The Simpsons, and the Transformers can be spotted hanging out near their respective rides. Characters from DreamWorks films—including the *Shrek, Kung Fu Panda,* and *Madagascar* series, as well as *Trolls*—greet guests at designated photo ops around the central Universal Plaza, while Hello Kitty holds court at the Animation Studio Store, and others (Beetlejuice, Dracula, Frankenstein's Monster and his Bride, and Scooby-Doo) frequently wander the Upper Lot. Don't miss bantering with the New York apartment dwellers leaning out of the second-story windows or being heckled by the interactive animatronic Snowball, who periodically appears on a balcony across from the Secret Life of Pets ride. Near the Jurassic World ride, you can take a selfie with a real-life velociraptor (actually an actor inside an impressive full-body puppet) and her wry wrangler. Mario, Luigi, Toad, and Princess Peach can be found inside Super Nintendo World.

Two brief street entertainments are staged in a raised outdoor alcove at the Forbidden Journey end of Hogsmeade. Showtimes are listed in the park's app.

THE TRIWIZARD SPIRIT RALLY (★★★) showcases a group of three men performing martial arts–type moves, including jumps, kicks, and simulated battle with sticks, as well as a group of women performing rhythmic gymnastics. The entire performance lasts about 6 minutes. After each show, the students of Beauxbatons Academy of Magic and the Durmstrang Institute are available for group photos. Hollywood's version of this show is marginally more exciting than Orlando's but is still only a must-do for major Potter fans.

THE FROG CHOIR (★★★), which only performs during the holiday season, is composed of four singers, two of whom are holding large amphibian puppets sitting on pillows. Inspired by a brief scene in *Harry Potter and the Prisoner of Azkaban,* the group sings three or four a cappella wizarding-related Christmas songs, including "The Most Magical Yule Ball of All" and "I Cast a Spell on Father Christmas." The 13-minute show concludes with a photo op. Though cute, *The Frog Choir* isn't much more than filler for USH's attraction list and probably not worth going out of your way for.

HOGWARTS ALWAYS (★★★½) brings the Forbidden Journey facade to life on select evenings throughout the year with colorful spells and magical creatures, all thanks to the Muggle miracle of digital projection mapping. The images evoke iconic milestones from a year in the life of a Hogwarts student, from shopping for school supplies in Diagon Alley to celebrating the winner of the House Cup; with four different rotating endings, each house gets its chance to shine. The 7-minute show, which also features vocal cameos from Dumbledore and Hagrid, is capped with a quick burst of pyrotechnics. The holiday season's special *MAGIC OF CHRISTMAS AT HOGWARTS* version of the show is also about 7 minutes long and features additional fan-favorite characters like the Weasley twins, who transform the castle's turret into a big Boggart Banger. John Williams' stirring music and the spectacular lighting effects make all the Hogwarts projection shows worth staying late for. Performances repeat every 20 minutes after sunset on select evenings; check the park's app for showtimes. People tend to camp out for views of the first two showings of the evening, making it a perfect time to ride the Potter attractions; you should have plenty of elbow room if you stick around for the final runs of the night.

HALLOWEEN HORROR NIGHTS

(Select nights September–early November)

HALLOWEEN HORROR NIGHTS—or HHN, as it's known to its legions of bloodthirsty fans—is one of the nation's most popular haunted theme park events, behind its bigger brother in Orlando. This hard-ticket after-hours event ain't no Oogie Boogie Bash: HHN is a gory, gruesome bacchanalia of simulated violence and tasteless satire, marinated with a liberal dose of alcohol and rock 'n' roll. Needless to say, it's not appropriate for young children, though you will likely see many there.

The basic elements of each year's event are haunted houses (or mazes), outdoor scare zones, and theater shows. The haunted houses—often based on films and TV shows such as *The Last of Us, Stranger Things,* and *A Quiet Place*—are the signature attractions at HHN and quickly develop wait times, ranging from moderate to absolutely ridiculous. Scare zones are open-air mazes (minus the conga line queues) haunted by roving "scareactors," and afford great people-watching and selfie-taking opportunities. Some years, the Terror Tram drops guests off on the backlot for a walk past the Psycho House and War of the Worlds crash set, which serve as supersize scare zones. DreamWorks Theater and the WaterWorld stadium both present seasonal live shows based on hyper-violent films like Blumhouse's *M3GAN* and *The Purge;* also watch out for a pack of Death Eaters stalking Hogsmeade Village. Universal also makes many of its regular rides available during HHN, including Harry Potter and the Forbidden Journey in The Wizarding World of Harry Potter (but not Super Nintendo World).

Even more so than daytime touring, a successful HHN visit requires careful planning; visit hollywood.halloweenhorrornights.com for the event calendar and tickets. All Saturdays (especially the final three Saturdays leading up to Halloween) and Fridays in October are very busy. Wednesdays are usually the least crowded, followed by Thursdays (especially the first two) and Sundays (especially the first, but excluding the last). Opening weekend brings out all the local fans, so your best bets are the last three weeks of September or the first week of October. Halloween night itself and any nights after it are often extremely quiet. Tickets start at $77, and admission including Express Passes starts at $209; the higher the cost, the larger the crowds will be. VIP tours ($389 and up) and Frequent Fear season passes ($209 and up) are also offered.

Guests with an "After 2 p.m." combo ticket ($117 and up) or daytime admission and an Early Event Access add-on ($10 and up) get exclusive access to select haunted houses 90 minutes before the event begins at 7 p.m. Queues for participating mazes on the Lower Lot begin filling by 4:45 p.m., and attractions on the Upper Lot open between 6:30 and 6:45 p.m., just before the front gates open. With early access, you can complete more than half the houses before 8 p.m., when things become crowded. Ride the Terror Tram, then see the shows and scare zones during the busiest time of the night, and save the remaining haunts for the final hours.

GRINCHMAS (mid-November–early January)

YOU'LL FIND CHRISTMAS DECOR throughout the park and City-Walk (which hosts a giant tree), and Hogsmeade celebrates Christmas in The Wizarding World with festive ornamentation, holiday treats, and a spectacular light show on Hogwarts Castle (see previous page). But the star of Universal's holiday celebrations is Dr. Seuss's Grinch, the iconic icky-green grump who famously stole Christmas from the Whos, only to return it when his undersized heart finally grew. You can meet an actor wearing professional prosthetic makeup, who impersonates Jim Carrey's live-action film incarnation; he takes time to interact before each photograph, usually to hilarious effect, which results in a very slow-moving line. Storytime meet and greets with Cindy-Lou Who are also scheduled, along with a nightly lighting ceremony of the Seussian tree. All of the above activities are included in regular park admission.

∎ DINING *at* USH

THE COUNTER-SERVICE FOOD at Universal Studios runs the gamut from burgers and hot dogs to pizza, fried chicken, crepes, and Mexican specialties. We rank most selections marginally better than fast food, though the resort has made great strides in creativity and ingredient quality recently. Prices are comparable to those at Disneyland, and Universal's app offers a useful Mobile Food & Drink Ordering option like Disney's. **The Three Broomsticks** is the best restaurant at USH by far and ranks with the finest quick-service food found in any theme park. The wait at **Toadstool Cafe** inside Super Nintendo World isn't worth the hassle, although the food is tasty and super *kawaii*. The mushroom soup, short rib, and Luigi chicken sandwich are all excellent, but the tart lemon drink with chewy boba is an acquired taste. (Same-day reservations are available via a QR code posted outside the land, but tables fill up within 2 hours after opening; count on waiting at least 30 minutes to order and receive your food once allowed inside.) For Mario-themed snacks without the long wait, try the filling mushroom-shaped calzone from Toadstool Cafe in the Upper Lot.

Our other favorites in the park are the tacos and margaritas at **Cocina Mexicana** and the soups and salads at **French Street Bistro. Mel's Diner** has upgraded its burgers and decor, and **Jurassic Cafe** on the Lower Lot serves barbecued ribs, burgers, smoked brisket, and "raptor" legs, with tropical cocktails mixed at **Isla Nu-Bar** next door. **Minion Café** (near Despicable Me Minion Mayhem) serves grilled cheese sandwiches with pulled pork, chicken tinga–topped nachos, bacon mac and cheese, and banana-flavored desserts to mollify your Minions' munchies. **Hollywood and Dine** rotates menus seasonally, ranging from Asian fare for Lunar New Year to special Halloween and holiday selections. The Simpsons **Fast Food Boulevard** eateries are a great bet; give Cletus's chicken and waffles, Bumblebee Man's tacos, or a Krusty burger a try, with a Duff beer to wash it down.

For $19 (reactivate for $12 per day) you get a large Coca-Cola Freestyle souvenir soda sipper cup and one day of unlimited refills from the park's Freestyle fountains, each of which can mix 100-plus varieties of soft drinks; try the Orange Coke!

If you're looking for full-service dining, try **VIVO Italian Kitchen, Antojitos Cocina Mexicana, Buca di Beppo, Dongpo Kitchen,** or the **NBC Sports Grill & Brew** in Universal CityWalk just outside the park entrance. Also in CityWalk, **Jimmy Buffett's Margaritaville** serves his signature laid-back libations and Floribbean bar food, and **Toothsome Chocolate Emporium & Savory Feast Kitchen,** also imported from Florida, features decadent milkshakes and cocoa-infused entrées. Reservations for most table-service restaurants are available through Universal's website or app and are recommended on weekends and during holiday periods. If you prefer counter service, an upstairs food court is full of well-known franchises, plus some more-adventuresome eateries like **Voodoo Doughnut** and **Uncle Sharkii Poke Bar.** If you leave the park for lunch, be sure to have your hand stamped for reentry and hold onto your ticket. To service your caffeine addiction, there are **Starbucks** outlets in the park on both the Upper and Lower Lots, plus one in CityWalk.

❚ USH ONE-DAY TOURING PLAN

THIS PLAN (see page 408) is for groups of all sizes and ages and includes thrill rides that may induce motion sickness or get you wet. If the plan calls for you to experience an attraction that does not interest you, proceed to the next step.

Before You Go

1. Call ☎ 800-864-8377 the day before your visit for the official opening time and install the official smartphone app.
2. If you have young children in your party, consult the Small-Child Fright-Potential Table on page 344.

ADDITIONAL AREA ATTRACTIONS

FOR THEME PARK ENTHUSIASTS who have exhausted the activities on Universal's and Disney's properties, here are a few other related attractions in the area for you to explore:

THE ACADEMY MUSEUM OF MOTION PICTURES (6067 Wilshire Blvd., Los Angeles; ☎ 323-930-3000; academymuseum.org) is a must-see for serious cinephiles and houses artifacts—including original props and costumes from *Star Wars, Avatar,* and Marvel movies—that will appeal to even casual fans. The permanent "Stories of Cinema" galleries begin with an immersive montage of iconic clips, then progress through three floors of multimedia-filled exhibits honoring the diverse arts that combine in filmmaking. Of particular note are the golden gallery, displaying 20 important Oscar statuettes; the restored *Jaws* shark, once displayed inside Universal Studios Hollywood; and a room dedicated to animation with Disney Legend Frank Thomas's original animation desk, along with a frank discussion of the company's complicated legacy. If you just want to see R2-D2 and David Bowie's *Labyrinth* getup, you could blow through the galleries in about an hour, but those who like to linger reading labels will want at least 3 hours here. The museum has a marvelous bookstore and two state-of-the-art theaters screening award-winning classics, but eat before arriving, because the trendy bar/restaurant downstairs is noisy and expensive. Timed entry tickets cost $25 ($19 for seniors 62+, $15 for students, free for children under 18) and must be purchased online in advance; a $15 add-on gets you the "Oscars Experience," a brief "simulation" where you're videoed on a podium holding an unengraved Oscar, delivering your acceptance speech. There's no free on-site parking, and street parking is scarce, but you can valet for $15 (with validation) or pay at the Pritzker garage or Petersen Automotive museum nearby for about $20.

Make a day of it and explore the rest of the **LACMA complex,** including the sprawling **Los Angeles County Museum of Art** (5905 Wilshire Blvd.; ☎ 323-857-6000; lacma.org), which is currently completing a massive reconstruction. Across the street is the far-more-manageable **Los Angeles Craft Contemporary Museum** (5814 Wilshire Blvd.; ☎ 323-937-4230; craftcontemporary.org), whose ever-rotating exhibits highlight handicrafts and folk arts—such as embroidery, woodworking, and collage—especially by self-taught or traditionally underrepresented artists. Admission is just $9 ($7 for students and seniors), and Sundays are "pay what you can"; closed on Mondays. When you get hungry, head less than a mile north to the world-famous **Farmers Market** (6333 W. 3rd St.; ☎ 323-933-9211; farmersmarketla.com), a haven for chowhounds and chefs since 1934, with gourmet groceries and upscale street food. Parking is free for 90–120 minutes with validation, but up to $47 if you don't make a purchase. Spend the night nearby at the **Beverly Laurel Motor Hotel**

(8018 Beverly Blvd; ☎ 800-947-7666; beverlylaurelhotel.info), a mid-century mod time capsule with a charming courtyard pool and funky late-night diner (swingersdiner.com).

BEETLE HOUSE (7080 Hollywood Blvd., Los Angeles; ☎ 929-291-0337; beetlehousela.com) is a nightmare before Christmas come true for fans of director Tim Burton. At this unofficial Burton-inspired bar, drinks fizz and foam, Jack Skellington puppets and Johnny Depp look-alikes roam, and retro music and freak shows fill the evenings. Skip the pricey prix fixe dinner and stick to drinks. A mile farther down Hollywood Boulevard is the equally unauthorized **Scum & Villainy Cantina** (6377 Hollywood Blvd.; ☎ 424-501-4229; scumandvillainycantina.com), which looks remarkably like Mos Eisley's notorious watering hole and even serves alcoholic blue milk. Unfortunately, there are no interactive actors or alien musicians, only awful 1980s karaoke. Just be careful; both venues are on the sketchier end of the street, 0.75 mile east of the more tourist-friendly home of Disney's El Capitan Theatre.

THE J. PAUL GETTY MUSEUM AT THE GETTY CENTER (1200 Getty Center Dr., Los Angeles; ☎ 310-440-7300; getty.edu) is like the Disneyland of art museums. An entry plaza welcomes guests with historical multi-media presentations, and easily digestible exhibits and exquisite themed landscaping surround a central hub. There's even a monorail-like tram to ride up the mountain! The Getty's stunning ultramodern architecture actually outshines its second-rate artworks, but the million-dollar views alone are worth the short drive from Hollywood. Best of all, admission is free, and parking is only $25 ($15 after 3 p.m.); however, you may need to claim a free timed entry ticket in advance on the website. The museum is closed on Mondays.

KNOTT'S BERRY FARM (8039 Beach Blvd., Buena Park; ☎ 714-220-5200; knotts.com) can credibly lay claim to being America's first true theme park, predating nearby Disneyland by decades. Thrill seekers will love the roller coasters, like GhostRider, Silver Bullet, and HangTime; dark ride enthusiasts can enjoy Ghost Town's Calico Mine Ride and Timber Mountain Log Ride, which inspired iconic Disney E-tickets, plus the Bear-y Tales 3-D shooter; and little kids get to party with Snoopy and the *Peanuts* gang. Old-fashioned live entertainment is Knott's forte, especially Krazy Kirk and the Hillbillies (formerly of Disneyland) and Bob Baker's Marionettes, who perform seasonal shows. Single tickets ($99 at the gate, $60–$85 online) and season passes ($130–$399) are significantly cheaper than Disneyland, so Knott's attracts lots of locals. Seasonal events like Knott's Scary Farm during Halloween and the springtime Boysenberry food festival draw big crowds. Queues for the top rides can often exceed 2 hours; even with a Fast Lane pass ($75–$120 for unlimited use on all participating rides, or $8 and up à la carte), you can expect to wait a half hour or more for each roller coaster. Food inside the park is pricier than Disneyland, but Mrs. Knott's famous chicken dinner just outside the gates should be on your bucket list; order it from the takeaway window if the wait for a table is too long.

PALM SPRINGS (visitpalmsprings.com) is the perfect overnight side trip for Disney fans seeking a 24-hour respite from the resort. The scenic 100-mile drive past vast wind farms takes about 2 hours, or double that during weekend traffic. On your way there, stop for a selfie at the **Cabazon Dinosaurs** (50770 Seminole Dr., Cabazon; ☎ 909-272-8164; cabazondinosaurs.com), founded by Knott's Berry Farm sculptor Claude Bell and made famous by *Pee Wee's Big Adventure*. You can climb inside Dinney the brontosaurus for the free museum and gift shop, but the rest of the dino displays require paid admission.

As you approach downtown, pull over at the **Palm Springs Aerial Tramway** (1 Tram Way, Palm Springs; ☎ 888-515-8726; pstramway. com) for a thrilling 2½-mile ascent into the pristine peaks of Mt. San Jacinto State Park aboard the world's largest rotating tram car (built by Doppelmayr, makers of Disney World's Skyliner). The 360-degree views are stunning, but the swinging motion can be scary, especially during the descent; stand in the cabin's center behind a railing for extra stability. At the top, there's a small nature museum and theater showing documentaries, along with a cafe, but the real attraction is access to over 50 miles of hiking trails within the 14,000-acre preserve. You'll want to to bring a warm jacket (the temperature is typically 30–40 degrees cooler at the top) and sturdy shoes; free day permits are also required if you want to walk into the wilderness beyond the ranger's station, but none are needed to enjoy the paved pathways and well-maintained ¾- to 1½-mile trails around Long Valley, making it ideal for families. Tram tickets cost $31 for adults, $19 for children ages 3–10, $29 for seniors 65+; parking is an additional $15. Cell service is poor in the mountains, so download the tramway's free app and any maps before driving up to the parking area.

Once you arrive in Palm Springs proper, explore downtown's charming boutique stores and art galleries along Palm Canyon Drive, as well as the surrounding residential neighborhoods, which are a showcase of the city's mid-century modern architectural heritage. Street parking is at a premium, so use the free public garage at 275 S. Indian Canyon Drive. Artist Josh Agle's **SHAG Store** (745 N. Palm Canyon Dr.; ☎ 760-322-3400; shagstore.com) is a must-see for his whimsical modernist interpretations of Disney and *Star Wars* characters. You can see Walt Disney's personal Grumman G-159 Gulfstream I airplane (aka *Mickey Mouse One*), which has been restored and placed on exhibit at the **Palm Springs Air Museum** (745 N. Gene Autry Trail; ☎ 760-778-6262; palmspringsairmuseum.org). When you get hungry, try **French Miso Cafe** (19 La Plaza; ☎ 760-699-7730; frenchmisocafe.com) for innovative fusion bento boxes in a magical gardenlike atmosphere, or devour a throwback Pu-Pu platter on the junglelike patio of **The Tropicale** (330 E. Amado Rd.; ☎ 760-866-1952; thetropicale.com) if you can get a seat during the hopping happy hour (daily, 4–7 p.m.). End the evening with a beverage at one of Palm Springs' tiki bars, such as **The Reef** (411 E. Palm Canyon Rd.; ☎ 760-656-3839; thereefpalm springs.com), where it's far easier to get a seat than at Trader Sam's.

When it's time to call it a night, Disney superfans may be tempted to book a cottage at nearby **Smoke Tree Ranch** (1850 Smoke Tree Ln.; ☎ 800-787-3922; smoketreeranch.com), where Walt himself had a vacation home. Rates there start at $510 per night, and rooms are equally expensive in the heart of Palm Springs. Instead, look a few minutes south of downtown for a cheap yet cheerful motel like the **Vagabond Motor Hotel** (1699 South Palm Canyon Dr.; ☎ 760-325-7211; vagabondmotorhotel.com). It's conveniently located right next door to another attraction you must see in the morning before leaving town: the **Moorten Botanical Gardens** (1701 S. Palm Canyon Dr.; ☎ 760-327-6555; moortenbotanicalgarden.com), a nearly 90-year-old wonderland of cacti and other desert flora that supplied the towering succulents found in Disneyland's Frontierland.

THE RMS *QUEEN MARY* (1126 Queens Hwy., Long Beach; ☎ 877-342-0738; queenmary.com) has been moored in California for more than 50 years, longer than it sailed the Atlantic, but history buffs and ghost hunters alike should enjoy a visit to the vintage vessel, which is larger than the legendary *Titanic*. The ship was off-limits to visits for several years but reopened to the public in spring 2023. Three different one-hour guided tours are offered for $40 each ($10 on Tuesdays), including access to the ship's exhibits: a **Glory Days** historical tour of the opulent public areas, a **Steam & Steel** visit to the engine room, and a **Haunted Encounters** ghost walk. In the evenings, immersive paranormal experiences are offered for $65–$100 per adult. Despite ambitious ongoing restoration efforts, the old girl has seen better days—as a night in one of the dingy cabins will demonstrate—but you can still appreciate its once-peerless glory beneath the rust and duct tape.

APPENDIX

READERS' QUESTIONS to the AUTHORS

QUESTION: *When you do your research, are you admitted to the park for free? Do the Disney people know you are there?*

ANSWER: We pay the regular admission, and usually the Disney people do not know we are on-site. Both in and out of Disneyland, we pay for our own meals and lodging.

QUESTION: *How often is* The Unofficial Guide to Disneyland *revised?*

ANSWER: We publish a new edition once a year but make corrections every time we go to press.

QUESTION: *I have an older edition of* The Unofficial Guide to Disneyland. *How much of the information in it is still correct?*

ANSWER: Veteran travel writers will acknowledge that 5%–8% of the information in a guidebook is out-of-date by the time it comes off the press! Disneyland is always changing. If you are using an old edition of *The Unofficial Guide to Disneyland,* the descriptions of attractions existing when the guide was published should still be generally accurate. Many other things, however—particularly the touring plans and the hotel and restaurant reviews—change with every edition. Finally, and obviously, older editions of *The Unofficial Guide to Disneyland* do not include new attractions or developments.

QUESTION: *Do you write each new edition from scratch?*

ANSWER: We do not. With a destination the size of Disneyland, it's hard enough to keep up with what's new. Moreover, we put great effort into communicating the most salient and useful information in the clearest possible language. If an attraction or hotel hasn't changed, we are reluctant to tinker with its coverage for the sake of freshening up the writing.

QUESTION: *Do you stay at Disneyland hotels? If not, where do you stay?*

ANSWER: We do stay at Disneyland-area hotels from time to time, usually after a renovation or management change. Since we began writing about Disneyland in 1984, we have stayed in more than 100 different properties in various locations around Anaheim.

QUESTION: *How are your age-group ratings determined? I am 42 years old. During Star Tours, I was quite worried about hurting my back. If the senior citizens rating is determined only by those brave enough to ride, it will skew the results.*

ANSWER: The reader makes a good point. Unfortunately, it's impossible to develop a rating unless the guest (of any age group) has actually experienced the attraction. So yes, all age-group ratings are derived exclusively from members of that age group who have experienced the attraction. Health problems, such as a bad back, however, can affect guests of any age, and Disney provides more-than-ample warnings on attractions that warrant such admonitions. But if you are in good health, our ratings will give you a sense of how much others your age enjoyed the attraction.

QUESTION: *I have heard that when there are two lines to an attraction, the left line is faster. Is this true?*

ANSWER: In general, no. We have tested this theory many times and usually have not gained an advantage of even 90 seconds by getting in one line versus another. The few rare exceptions are noted in the ride descriptions. What *does* occasionally occur, however, is that after a second line has *just been opened,* guests ignore the new line and persist in standing in the established line. Generally, if you encounter a two-line waiting configuration with no barrier to entry for either and one of the lines is conspicuously less populated than the other, get in it.

AND FINALLY . . .

To end on a high note, consider this compliment from a Redding, California, reader:

> *Thanks to your book, this trip turned out much better than our last, so much, in fact, that I required only half as much Valium.*

And so it goes . . .

LODGING INDEX

RESTAURANT INDEX

SUBJECT INDEX

The Best of Disneyland Resort in One Day Plan A

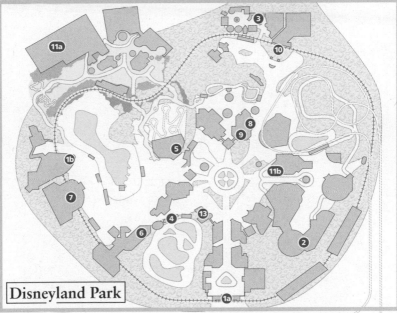

Disneyland Park

1. Arrive at the a) park entrance at least 45 minutes before the official opening time. Check Disneyland's app for b) Tiana's Bayou Adventure virtual boarding passes, and set an alarm for 11:55 a.m. to remind yourself to secure Virtual Queue viewing passes for *World of Color* exactly at noon.
2. As soon as the park opens, ride Space Mountain in Tomorrowland.
3. Enjoy Mickey & Minnie's Runaway Railway in Toontown.
4. Ride Indiana Jones Adventure in Adventureland.
5. Ride Big Thunder Mountain Railroad in Frontierland.
6. Ride Pirates of the Caribbean in New Orleans Square.

7. See Haunted Mansion.
8. Ride Alice in Wonderland in Fantasyland.
9. Ride Peter Pan's Flight.
10. Ride It's a Small World.
11. Go to Galaxy's Edge and ride a) Rise of the Resistance only if the posted wait time is under 60 minutes. Otherwise, head to Tomorrowland and ride b) Buzz Lightyear Astro Blasters now, and try Rise of the Resistance later in the day.
12. Use the Disneyland app to obtain a Virtual Queue spot for *World of Color* at 12 p.m. sharp.
13. Eat lunch at Jolly Holiday Bakery Café before hopping to DCA.

(continued on next page)

The Best of Disneyland Resort in One Day Plan A

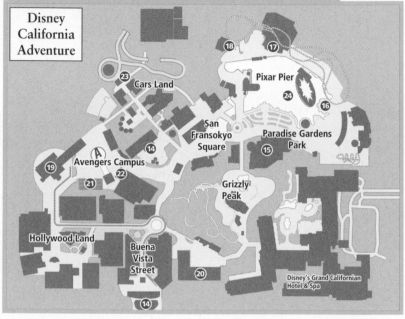

Disney California Adventure

Cars Land

Pixar Pier

San Fransokyo Square

Paradise Gardens Park

Avengers Campus

Grizzly Peak

Hollywood Land

Buena Vista Street

Disney's Grand Californian Hotel & Spa

(continued from previous page)

14. Enter DCA and experience Mater's Junkyard Jamboree in Cars Land.

15. Ride The Little Mermaid: Ariel's Undersea Adventure in Paradise Gardens Park.

16. Enjoy the Silly Symphony Swings if the line is short.

17. Try Toy Story Midway Mania! in Pixar Pier.

18. Ride the Incredicoaster in Pixar Pier.

19. Ride Guardians of the Galaxy—Mission: Breakout! in Avengers Campus.

20. Experience Soarin' Around the World in Grizzly Peak.

21. Eat dinner. Use mobile ordering if you want to try Pym Test Kitchen in Avengers Campus.

22. Ride WEB SLINGERS: A Spider-Man Adventure in Avengers Campus.

23. Ride Radiator Springs Racers if there's enough time before *World of Color,* or save it for immediately after the show.

24. Use the Virtual Queue spot you obtained earlier to watch *World of Color.*

25. If Disneyland is open later than DCA, hop back over to revisit your favorite ride or any you missed.

The Best of Disneyland Resort in One Day Plan B

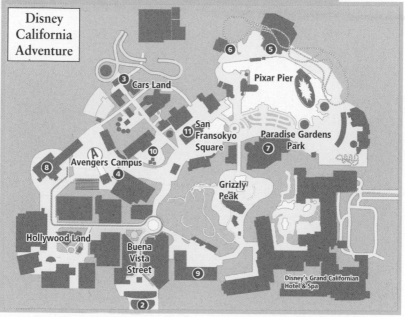

Disney California Adventure

Cars Land

Pixar Pier

San Fransokyo Square

Paradise Gardens Park

Avengers Campus

Grizzly Peak

Hollywood Land

Buena Vista Street

Disney's Grand Californian Hotel & Spa

1. Check the performance schedule prior to your visit, and consider booking a *Fantasmic!* dining package (if available).
2. Arrive at the park entrance at least 45 minutes before the official opening time, and check Disneyland's app for Tiana's Bayou Adventure virtual boarding passes.
3. As soon as the park opens, ride Radiator Springs Racers in Cars Land.
4. Ride WEB SLINGERS: A Spider-Man Adventure in Avengers Campus.
5. Try Toy Story Midway Mania! in Pixar Pier.

6. Ride the Incredicoaster.
7. Ride The Little Mermaid: Ariel's Undersea Adventure in Paradise Gardens Park.
8. Ride Guardians of the Galaxy Mission: Breakout! in Avengers Campus.
9. Experience Soarin' Around the World.
10. If you have time, ride Mater's Junkyard Jamboree in Cars Land.
11. Eat lunch in San Fransokyo Square before hopping to Disneyland.

(continued on next page)

The Best of Disneyland Resort in One Day Plan B

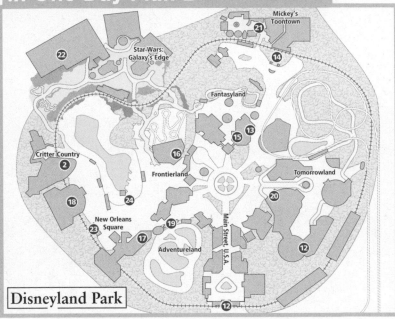

Disneyland Park

(continued from previous page)

12. Enter Disneyland and ride Space Mountain in Tomorrowland.
13. Ride Alice in Wonderland in Fantasyland.
14. Ride It's a Small World.
15. Ride Peter Pan's Flight.
16. Ride Big Thunder Mountain Railroad in Frontierland.
17. Ride Pirates of the Caribbean in New Orleans Square.
18. See Haunted Mansion.
19. Enjoy Indiana Jones Adventure in Adventureland.

20. Ride Star Tours—The Adventures Continue in Tomorrowland.
21. Ride Mickey & Minnie's Runaway Railway in Toontown.
22. Get in line for Star Wars: Rise of the Resistance before the standby queue closes (see app for exact time).
23. If you have time before the evening entertainment, eat dinner in New Orleans Square or take a round-trip on the Disneyland Railroad.
24. Watch *Fantasmic!* and/or the evening fireworks (when scheduled) or revisit any attractions.

Star Wars: Galaxy's Edge Complete Plan

Star Wars: Galaxy's Edge

1. Visit disneyland.com at midnight PST 60 days before the morning of your visit to make reservations for Savi's Workshop in late morning and Oga's Cantina in midafternoon. Attempt to purchase a Lightning Lane return time for Star Wars: Rise of the Resistance upon entering the park. Depart from this plan when your boarding time arrives and return to it after riding.

2. Arrive at the park entrance at least 45 minutes before official opening time. If you were unable to get a reservation for Oga's, walk-ups are usually accommodated during the opening hour.

3. Ride *Millennium Falcon: Smugglers Run.*

4. Shop for droids at Mubo's Droid Depot.

5. Arrive at Savi's Workshop 20–30 minutes before your scheduled appointment.

6. Eat lunch inside a working hangar bay at Docking Bay 7 Food and Cargo.

7. When your reservation time comes, grab a drink and listen to DJ R-3X spin some music at Oga's Cantina.

8. Browse Jedi and Sith artifacts at Dok-Ondar's Den of Antiquities.

9. See all the galactic creatures at Creature Stall; look for the snoozing Loth Cat and other animatronic critters.

10. If you have little ones, head over to Toydarian Toyshop and take a look at the goods. Keep an eye out for Zabaka the Toydarian.

11. Try some Outpost Mix at a) Kat Saka's Kettle, or grab a sausage that's been grilled by a podracer engine at b) Ronto Roasters.

12. Use any remaining time to explore Star Wars: Galaxy's Edge, interact with the local inhabitants, and complete missions in the Play Disney Parks app's Datapad.

13. Get in the standby line for Rise of the Resistance shortly before it closes (see app for exact time) if you were unable to ride earlier using Lightning Lane.

14. Watch the evening fireworks (when scheduled) from near the *Millennium Falcon.* Special music is piped in during the springtime Season of the Force celebration.

One-Day Plan for Adults

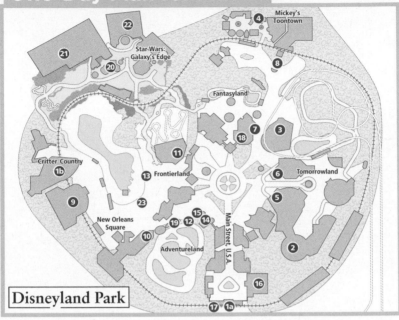

Disneyland Park

1. Arrive at the a) park entrance at least 45 minutes before the official opening time, and check Disneyland's app for b) Tiana's Bayou Adventure virtual boarding passes.
2. As soon as the park opens, ride Space Mountain in Tomorrowland.
3. Ride the Matterhorn Bobsleds in Fantasyland.
4. Enter Toontown and ride Mickey & Minnie's Runaway Railway.
5. Return to Tomorrowland and ride Star Tours—The Adventures Continue.
6. Try Buzz Lightyear Astro Blasters.
7. Ride Alice in Wonderland in Fantasyland.
8. Ride It's a Small World.
9. Visit Haunted Mansion in New Orleans Square.
10. Experience Pirates of the Caribbean.
11. Ride Big Thunder Mountain Railroad in Frontierland.
12. Take the Jungle Cruise.
13. Ride the Sailing Ship *Columbia* or the *Mark Twain* Riverboat, whichever is boarding first.
14. Eat lunch at Jolly Holiday Bakery Café.
15. See *Enchanted Tiki Room* in Adventureland.
16. See *The Disneyland Story,* presenting *Great Moments with Mr. Lincoln.*
17. Board the Disneyland Railroad at Main Street, take a round-trip, then get off at Toontown.
18. Ride Peter Pan's Flight in Fantasyland.
19. Go to Adventureland and ride Indiana Jones Adventure.
20. Eat dinner at Docking Bay 7 in Galaxy's Edge.
21. Ride Star Wars: Rise of the Resistance.
22. Ride *Millennium Falcon:* Smugglers Run.
23. Watch *Fantasmic!* and/or the fireworks spectacular (when scheduled).
24. Revisit any favorite attractions or visit any you may have missed earlier.

Two-Day Plan for Families with Small Children: Day One

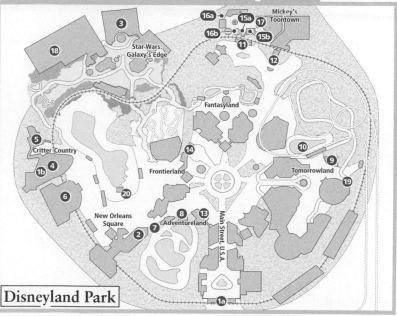

Disneyland Park

1. Arrive at the a) park entrance at least 45 minutes before the official opening time, and check Disneyland's app for b) Tiana's Bayou Adventure virtual boarding passes.
2. As soon as the park opens, ride Pirates of the Caribbean in New Orleans Square.
3. Ride *Millennium Falcon:* Smugglers Run.
4. Ride Tiana's Bayou Adventure in Critter Country (if Virtual Queue isn't required).
5. Ride The Many Adventures of Winnie the Pooh.
6. See Haunted Mansion in New Orleans Square.
7. Explore the Adventureland Treehouse.
8. Take the Jungle Cruise in Adventureland.
9. Ride Autopia in Tomorrowland.
10. Ride Finding Nemo Submarine Voyage in Tomorrowland.
11. Take a round-trip on the Disneyland Railroad from Toontown, then get off in Tomorrowland. If the line for the train is too long, skip it and walk.
12. Ride It's a Small World in Fantasyland.

13. Eat lunch at Jolly Holiday Bakery Café on Main Street, U.S.A.
14. Meet Disney Princesses at Royal Hall in Fantasy Faire.
15. Visit Toontown and explore a) Donald's Duck Pond and b) Goofy's How-to-Play Yard.
16. Visit a) Minnie Mouse's house and ride b) Chip 'n' Dale's GADGETcoaster if the lines aren't too long.
17. Try Roger Rabbit's Car Toon Spin.
18. Go to Star Wars: Galaxy's Edge and ride Star Wars: Rise of the Resistance.
19. Take a round-trip ride on the Disneyland Monorail; or use it to exit the park for a nap and dinner.
20. Visit any attractions you may have missed earlier and then get a spot for *Fantasmic!* and/or the fireworks (if scheduled) at least 30 minutes before showtime.

Two-Day Plan for Families with Small Children: Day Two

Disneyland Park

1. Arrive at the a) park entrance at least 45 minutes before the official opening time, and check Disneyland's app for b) Tiana's Bayou Adventure virtual boarding passes.
2. As soon as the park opens, ride Space Mountain in Tomorrowland.
3. Ride Star Tours—The Adventures Continue.
4. Ride the Matterhorn Bobsleds if your kids meet the 42-inch height requirement.
5. Ride a) Mickey & Minnie's Runaway Railway in Toontown, then b) Meet Mickey inside his house if the line is still short.
6. Ride Alice in Wonderland in Fantasyland.
7. Ride Peter Pan's Flight.
8. Ride Snow White's Enchanted Wish.
9. Go on Mr. Toad's Wild Ride.
10. Ride a) Storybook Land Canal Boats or b) Casey Jr Circus Train.
11. Experience Dumbo the Flying Elephant.

12. Ride Pinocchio's Daring Journey.
13. Take a spin on the Mad Tea Party.
14. Eat lunch. Try Red Rose Taverne in Fantasyland.
15. Take a raft to Tom Sawyer Island, and let the kids run around the island's Pirates Lair.
16. Ride Big Thunder Mountain Railroad in Frontierland.
17. Try Buzz Lightyear Astro Blasters in Tomorrowland.
18. Watch the afternoon parade from near It's a Small World.
19. Take a turn on the King Arthur Carrousel.
20. See the *Enchanted Tiki Room* in Adventureland.
21. Revisit any favorite attractions or visit any you may have missed earlier.
22. Watch the evening fireworks and/or projections (when scheduled) from Main Street or near Small World.

Two-Day Plan A: Day One

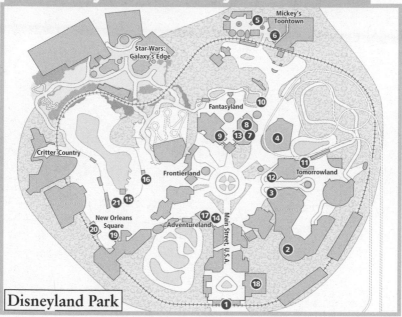

Disneyland Park

1. Arrive at the park entrance at least 45 minutes before the official opening time.
2. As soon as the park opens, ride Space Mountain in Tomorrowland.
3. Ride Star Tours—The Adventures Continue.
4. Ride Matterhorn Bobsleds.
5. Ride Mickey & Minnie's Runaway Railway in Toontown.
6. Try Roger Rabbit's Car Toon Spin.
7. Experience Alice in Wonderland in Fantasyland.
8. Take Mr. Toad's Wild Ride.
9. Ride Snow White's Enchanted Wish.
10. Take a cruise on the Storybook Land Canal Boats.
11. Take the Finding Nemo Submarine Voyage in Tomorrowland.
12. Ride Buzz Lightyear Astro Blasters.
13. Ride Peter Pan's Flight in Fantasyland.
14. Eat lunch at Jolly Holiday Bakery Café.
15. Take a raft to the Pirate's Lair on Tom Sawyer Island.
16. Ride the Sailing Ship *Columbia* or the *Mark Twain* Riverboat, whichever is boarding first.
17. See the *Enchanted Tiki Room* in Adventureland.
18. See *The Disneyland Story,* presenting *Great Moments with Mr. Lincoln* on Main Street, U.S.A.
19. Eat dinner in New Orleans Square or take a late-afternoon break and eat outside the park.
20. Take a round-trip on the Disneyland Railroad.
21. Watch *Fantasmic!* and/or the fireworks (when scheduled).

Two-Day Plan A: Day Two

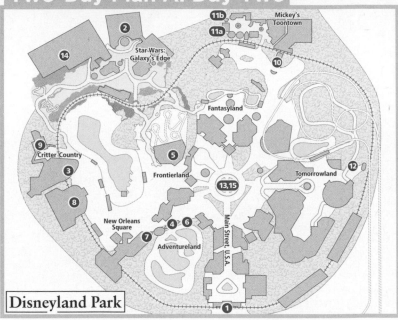

Disneyland Park

1. Arrive at the park entrance at least 45 minutes before the official opening time, and check Disneyland's app for Tiana's Bayou Adventure virtual boarding passes.

2. As soon as the park opens, go to Star Wars: Galaxy's Edge and ride *Millennium Falcon: Smugglers Run.*

3. Exit Galaxy's Edge and ride Tiana's Bayou Adventure in Critter Country (if Virtual Queue is not required).

4. Experience the Indiana Jones Adventure in Adventureland.

5. Ride Big Thunder Mountain Railroad in Frontierland.

6. Ride the Jungle Cruise in Adventureland.

7. Ride Pirates of the Caribbean in New Orleans Square.

8. See Haunted Mansion.

9. Ride The Many Adventures of Winnie the Pooh in Critter Country.

10. Ride It's a Small World in Fantasyland.

11. Enter Mickey's Toontown and visit a) Mickey's House. See b) Minnie's House, too, if the line is short.

12. Take the monorail from Tomorrowland to Downtown Disney for a long lunch break.

13. Return to the park in time to catch the afternoon parade from Main Street.

14. Ride Star Wars: Rise of the Resistance in Galaxy's Edge (check app for closing time).

15. Watch the evening fireworks or projections (when scheduled).

16. Revisit any favorite attractions or visit any you may have missed earlier.

Two-Day Plan B: Day One

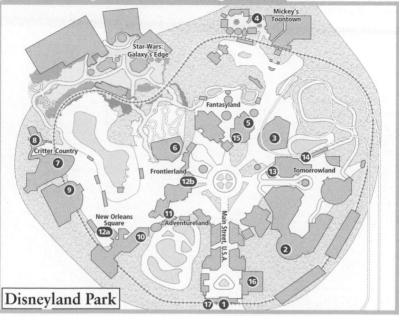

Disneyland Park

1. Arrive at the park entrance at least 45 minutes before the official opening time, and check Disneyland's app for Tiana's Bayou Adventure virtual boarding passes.
2. As soon as the park opens, ride Space Mountain in Tomorrowland.
3. Ride Matterhorn Bobsleds in Fantasyland.
4. Ride Mickey & Minnie's Runaway Railway in Toontown.
5. Experience Alice in Wonderland in Fantasyland.
6. Ride Big Thunder Mountain Railroad in Frontierland.
7. Ride Tiana's Bayou Adventure in Critter Country (if Virtual Queue isn't required).
8. Ride The Many Adventures of Winnie the Pooh.
9. Experience Haunted Mansion in New Orleans Square.
10. Ride Pirates of the Caribbean.
11. Ride Indiana Jones Adventure in Adventureland.
12. Eat lunch in a) New Orleans Square or at b) Rancho del Zocalo.
13. Experience Buzz Lightyear Astro Blasters in Tomorrowland.
14. Take the Finding Nemo Submarine Voyage.
15. Ride Peter Pan's Flight in Fantasyland if the wait time is 30 minutes or less.
16. See *The Disneyland Story*, presenting *Great Moments with Mr. Lincoln*.
17. Take a round-trip on the Disneyland Railroad from the Main Street station before exiting the park.

Two-Day Plan B: Day Two

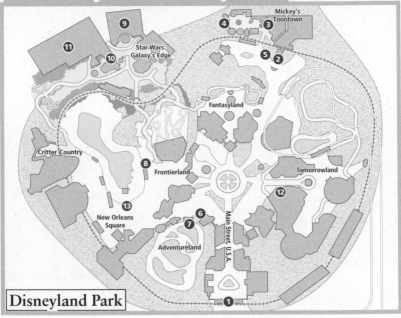

Disneyland Park

1. Arrive at Disneyland Park around 1 p.m.
2. Ride It's a Small World in Fantasyland.
3. Enter Toontown and ride Roger Rabbit's Car Toon Spin.
4. Meet Mickey Mouse inside his house, or explore the streets of Toontown.
5. Watch the afternoon parade from the mall near It's a Small World.
6. Go to Adventureland and see the *Enchanted Tiki Room.*
7. Take the Jungle Cruise.
8. Ride the Sailing Ship *Columbia* or the *Mark Twain* Riverboat, whichever is boarding first.
9. Enter Star Wars: Galaxy's Edge and ride *Millennium Falcon: Smugglers Run.*
10. Explore the shops in Black Spire Outpost and eat dinner at Docking Bay 7.
11. Ride Star Wars: Rise of the Resistance.
12. Ride Star Tours—The Adventures Continue in Tomorrowland.
13. Watch *Fantasmic!* and/or the evening fireworks (when scheduled).
14. Revisit any favorite attractions or visit any you may have missed earlier.

Dumbo-or-Die-in-a-Day Plan

Disneyland Park

1. Arrive at the park entrance at least 45 minutes before the official opening time.
2. As soon as the park opens, ride Pirates of the Caribbean In New Orleans Square.
3. See Haunted Mansion.
4. Take the Jungle Cruise in Adventureland.
5. Take Mr. Toad's Wild Ride in Fantasyland.
6. Ride Alice in Wonderland.
7. Ride Dumbo the Flying Elephant.
8. Ride Snow White's Enchanted Wish.
9. Try Buzz Lightyear Astro Blasters in Tomorrowland.
10. Ride Autopia.
11. Ride Finding Nemo Submarine Voyage.
12. Take a spin on the Mad Tea Party in Fantasyland.
13. Ride King Arthur Carrousel.
14. Ride the Casey Jr. Circus Train.
15. Ride the Storybook Land Canal Boats.
16. Ride Peter Pan's Flight.
17. Experience the a) Royal Hall princess meet and greet. If your party isn't interested in princesses, meet b) Tinker Bell and her pixie friends at Pixie Hollow or c) Mickey and friends, who can usually be found in Town Square.
18. See the *Enchanted Tiki Room* in Adventureland.
19. Take a round-trip on the Disneyland Railroad and get off at the Toontown Station.
20. Let the kids run around a) Goofy's How-To-Play Yard and b) Donald's Duck Pond, if they're up to it.
21. Ride It's a Small World in Fantasyland.
22. Ride Big Thunder Mountain Railroad in Frontierland.
23. Take a raft to explore the Pirate's Lair on Tom Sawyer Island.
24. Experience The Many Adventures of Winnie the Pooh in Critter Country.
25. Ride Star Wars: Rise of the Resistance in Galaxy's Edge, and explore Black Spire Outpost.
26. Return to Toontown and ride a) Mickey & Minnie's Runaway Railway, then visit b) Mickey's House if the line isn't too long.
27. Try Roger Rabbit's Car Toon Spin.
28. Watch *Fantasmic!* and/or the evening fireworks (when scheduled).
29. Visit any attractions you may have missed earlier.

One-Day Plan for Tweens and Their Parents

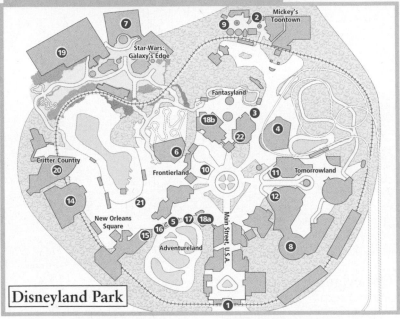

Disneyland Park

1. Arrive at the park entrance at least 45 minutes before the official opening time, and check Disneyland's app for Tiana's Bayou Adventure virtual boarding passes.
2. As soon as the park opens, ride Mickey & Minnie's Runaway Railway in Toontown.
3. Take a spin on the Mad Tea Party in Fantasyland.
4. Ride the Matterhorn Bobsleds.
5. Ride Indiana Jones Adventure in Adventureland.
6. Ride Big Thunder Mountain Railroad in Frontierland.
7. Enter Galaxy's Edge and experience *Millennium Falcon:* Smugglers Run.
8. Go to Tomorrowland and ride Space Mountain.
9. Meet Mickey Mouse at his house in Toontown.
10. Eat lunch, then try to see the storytelling show at Royal Theatre near the castle.
11. Try Buzz Lightyear Astro Blasters in Tomorrowland.
12. Ride Star Tours—The Adventures Continue.
13. Watch the afternoon parade.
14. Head to New Orleans Square and experience Haunted Mansion.
15. Ride Pirates of the Caribbean.
16. Explore the Adventureland Treehouse.
17. Take a trip on the Jungle Cruise.
18. Have dinner at a) Jolly Holiday Bakery Café or b) Red Rose Taverne.
19. Return to Galaxy's Edge and ride Star Wars: Rise of the Resistance (see app for closing time).
20. Ride Tiana's Bayou Adventure in Critter Country (if Virtual Queue isn't required).
21. Watch *Fantasmic!* and/or the fireworks spectacular (when scheduled).
22. Try to ride Peter Pan's Flight near park closing.

One-Day Plan for Adults

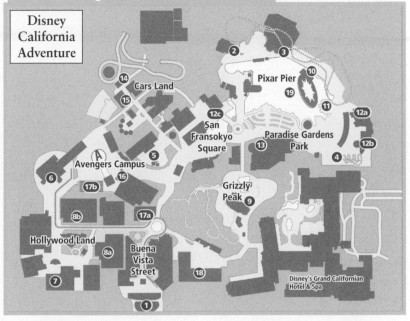

Disney California Adventure

Labels on map: 14, Cars Land, 15, 12c, San Fransokyo Square, A, Avengers Campus, 5, 6, 17b, 16, 8b, 17a, Hollywood Land, 8a, Buena Vista Street, 7, 18, 1, 2, 3, Pixar Pier, 10, 19, 11, 12a, 13, Paradise Gardens Park, 12b, 4, Grizzly Peak, 9, Disney's Grand Californian Hotel & Spa

1. Arrive at the park entrance at least 45 minutes before the official opening time. Set an alarm for 11:55 a.m. to remind yourself to secure Virtual Queue viewing passes for *World of Color* exactly at noon.

2. As soon as the park opens, go to Pixar Pier and ride the Incredicoaster.

3. Try Toy Story Midway Mania!

4. Ride Goofy's Sky School in Paradise Gardens Park.

5. Go to Cars Land and take a spin on Mater's Junkyard Jamboree.

6. Enter Avengers Campus and ride Guardians of the Galaxy—Mission: Breakout!

7. Ride Monsters, Inc. Mike & Sulley to the Rescue in Hollywood Land.

8. Watch a) *Mickey's PhilharMagic* or participate in b) an Animation Academy drawing class.

9. Ride Grizzly River Run in Grizzly Peak.

10. Continue around the lagoon to the Pixar Pal-A-Round. Ride the swinging side, unless the wait is

long or you are susceptible to motion sickness.

11. Try the Silly Symphony Swings in Paradise Gardens Park if the line is short.

12. Eat lunch at a) Boardwalk Pizza, b) Paradise Garden Grill, or c) San Fransokyo Square.

13. Ride The Little Mermaid: Ariel's Undersea Adventure.

14. Ride Radiator Springs Racers. Consider using the single-rider line to save time.

15. Ride Luigi's Rollickin' Roadsters.

16. Ride WEB SLINGERS: A Spider-Man Adventure.

17. Eat dinner. Splurge on a) Carthay Circle (reservations recommended) or use mobile ordering at b) Pym Test Kitchen in Avengers Campus.

18. Ride Soarin' Around the World in Grizzly Peak if there's enough time before *World of Color*, or save it for immediately after the show.

19. Watch *World of Color* using the Virtual Queue spot you obtained earlier.

20. Revisit any favorite attractions or visit any you may have missed earlier.

One-Day Plan for Families with Small Children

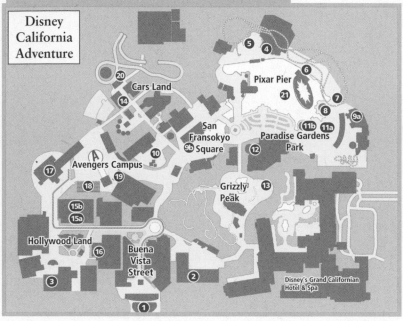

Disney California Adventure

Cars Land

Pixar Pier

San Fransokyo Square

Paradise Gardens Park

Avengers Campus

Grizzly Peak

Hollywood Land

Buena Vista Street

Disney's Grand Californian Hotel & Spa

1. Arrive at the park entrance at least 45 minutes before the official opening time. Set an alarm for 11:55 a.m. to remind yourself to secure Virtual Queue viewing passes for *World of Color* exactly at noon.

2. As soon as the park opens, go to Grizzly Peak and ride Soarin' Around the World.

3. Go to Hollywood Land and ride Monsters, Inc. Mike & Sulley to the Rescue.

4. Ride Toy Story Midway Mania! in Pixar Pier.

5. Ride Jessie's Critter Carousel.

6. Ride the Pixar Pal-A-Round, using the nonswinging cars.

7. Ride Inside Out Emotional Whirlwind.

8. Try the Silly Symphony Swings in Paradise Gardens Park.

9. Eat lunch at a) Boardwalk Pizza & Pasta or b) San Fransokyo Square.

10. Try Mater's Junkyard Jamboree.

11. Ride a) Jumpin' Jellyfsh and/or b) Golden Zephyr, only if their lines are short.

12. Ride The Little Mermaid: Ariel's Undersea Adventure.

13. Explore the Redwood Creek Challenge Trail in Grizzly Peak.

14. Go to Cars Land and ride Luigi's Rollickin' Roadsters.

15. Participate in a) an Animation Academy drawing class and b) Turtle Talk with Crush.

16. Watch *Mickey's PhilharMagic*.

17. Go to Avengers Campus and ride Guardians of the Galaxy—Mission: Breakout!

18. Use mobile ordering to eat dinner at Pym Test Kitchen in Avengers Campus.

19. Ride WEB SLINGERS: A Spider-Man Adventure.

20. Ride Radiator Springs Racers if there's enough time before *World of Color*, or save it for immediately after the show.

21. Watch *World of Color* using the Virtual Queue spot you obtained earlier.

22. Revisit any favorite attractions or visit any you may have missed earlier.

One-Day Plan for Tweens and Their Parents

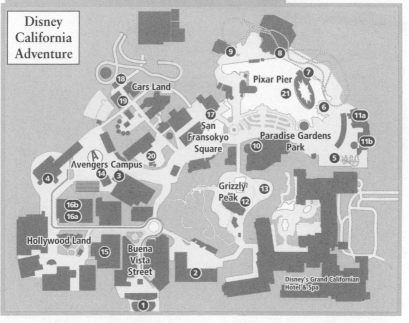

Disney California Adventure

1. Arrive at the park entrance at least 45 minutes before the official opening time. Set an alarm for 11:55 a.m. to remind yourself to secure Virtual Queue viewing passes for *World of Color* exactly at noon.
2. As soon as the park opens, go to Grizzly Peak and ride Soarin' Around the World.
3. Go to Avengers Campus and ride WEB SLINGERS: A Spider-Man Adventure.
4. Ride Guardians of the Galaxy—Mission: Breakout!
5. Ride Goofy's Sky School in Paradise Gardens Park.
6. Try the Silly Symphony Swings if the line is short.
7. Continue around the lagoon to the Pixar Pal-A-Round. Ride the swinging side, unless the wait is long or you are susceptible to motion sickness.
8. Try Toy Story Midway Mania!
9. Take a ride on the Incredicoaster.
10. Ride The Little Mermaid: Ariel's Undersea Adventure.
11. Eat lunch at a) Boardwalk Pizza & Pasta or b) Paradise Garden Grill.
12. Ride Grizzly River Run in Grizzly Peak.
13. Explore the Redwood Creek Challenge Trail.
14. Catch the *Amazing Spider-Man!* stunt show and other scheduled character encounters in Avengers Campus.
15. Watch *Mickey's PhilharMagic*.
16. Participate in a) an Animation Academy drawing class and b) Turtle Talk with Crush.
17. Have dinner in San Fransokyo Square.
18. Ride Radiator Springs Racers in Cars Land.
19. Ride Luigi's Rollickin' Roadsters.
20. Take a spin on Mater's Junkyard Jamboree.
21. Watch *World of Color* using the Virtual Queue spot you obtained earlier.
22. Revisit any favorite attractions or visit any you may have missed earlier.

Universal Studios One-Day Touring Plan

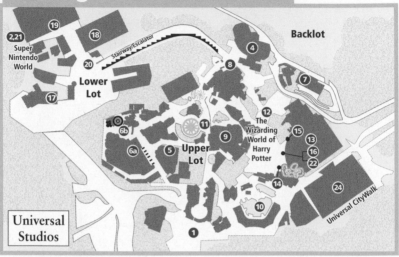

1. Arrive 90–120 minutes before official park opening time; the park gates typically open 30 minutes before early entry hour starts.

2. Early-park-admission guests should immediately visit Super Nintendo World and ride Mario Kart: Bowser's Challenge.

3. If at least 30 minutes remain before official opening, early-entry guests can enjoy the Power-Up band activities. Guests without early admission can enjoy the Wizarding World up to 30 minutes before official opening.

4. Return to the Upper Lot before official park opening and experience The Simpsons Ride. Guests without early entry can start here.

5. Ride The Secret Life of Pets: Off the Leash. Check the park app for Virtual Line reservation availability or standby line access.

6. Ride a) Despicable Me Minion Mayhem as soon as it opens, and explore b) Super Silly Fun Land.

7. Take the Studio Tour. Allocate 80 minutes for the attraction.

8. Use the mobile app to order lunch at Springfield in the Upper Lot.

9. See *Kung Fu Panda Adventure* at the DreamWorks Theatre.

10. Check the park app or digital directory boards for showtimes in the Upper Lot for *WaterWorld* and arrive 20 minutes prior.

11. Visit with the classic movie and cartoon characters in the Upper Lot. Ask a character attendant for specific characters and set times.

12. Enter The Wizarding World of Harry Potter. Check the app for showtimes for *Triwizard Spirit Rally* and *Frog Choir* (holiday season only).

13. Ride Harry Potter and the Forbidden Journey.

14. Enjoy Flight of the Hippogriff.

15. See the show inside Ollivanders Wand Shop.

16. If hungry, eat dinner at Three Broomsticks.

17. Descend to the Lower Lot and experience Jurassic World: The Ride.

18. Ride Revenge of the Mummy: The Ride.

19. Enjoy Transformers: The Ride 3-D.

20. Interact with the talking Transformers or dinosaur keepers.

21. Enter Super Nintendo World to enjoy the Power-Up activities, meet characters, and ride (or re-ride) Mario Kart using the single-rider line.

22. Watch the light show at Hogwarts Castle (when scheduled). The last two shows of the night are the least busy. Check the park app or digital directory boards for showtimes.

23. Repeat any favorite attractions or see any you missed earlier. *Note:* the entrance to the Lower Lot closes 15 minutes before the park closes.

24. End your day with a bite or beverage at Universal CityWalk (opens 11 a.m. daily; closing time varies).